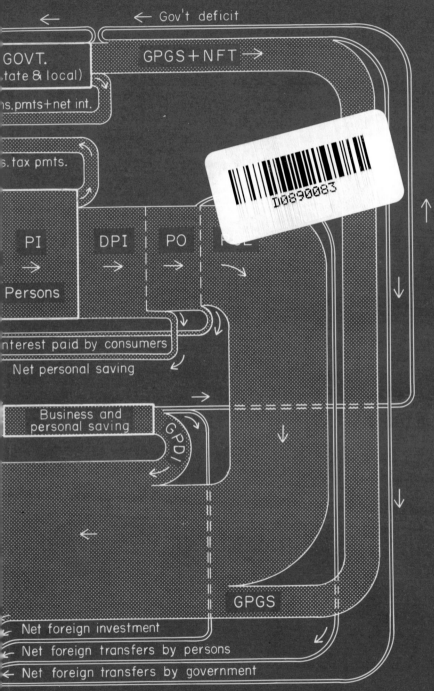

← Gov't deficit

GOVT.
tate & local)

GPGS+NFT →

ns.pmts+net int.

s. tax pmts.

PI →   DPI →   PO ↗   PCE

Persons

nterest paid by consumers

Net personal saving

Business and
personal saving

GPDI

GPGS

Net foreign investment

Net foreign transfers by persons

Net foreign transfers by government

come accounts; the more precise term is "Charges against GNP."
trated.

Ex Libris

Ryan

Iona College

Library

BUSINESS CONDITIONS
ANALYSIS

DISCARDED

DISCARDED

BUSINESS CONDITIONS ANALYSIS

ANALYSIS

second edition

John P. Lewis
graduate school of business, indiana university

Robert C. Turner
graduate school of business, indiana university

McGraw-Hill Book Company
new york st. louis san francisco toronto london sydney

118011
338.54
L 67-1

Business Conditions Analysis

Copyright © 1959, 1967 by McGraw-Hill, Inc. All
Rights Reserved. Printed in the United States of America. This book, or parts thereof, may not be reproduced
in any form without permission of the publishers.

Library of Congress Catalog Card Number 66–21396

37600

3 4 5 6 7 8 9 0   MP   7 3 2 1 0 6 9 8

To our loyal and indulgent wives
June and Lenora

PREFACE

The eight years since Professor Lewis wrote the first edition of this book have been highly significant for the business conditions analyst. Much has been added to our knowledge of methods of economic analysis, including contributions both to the body of macroeconomic theory and to the practical forecaster's kit of statistical and analytical tools. The national income accounts have undergone two definitional revisions and numerous statistical revisions. A major objective in preparing this second edition has therefore been to incorporate these recent developments into the book.

An important pedagogical objective of the revision has been to make the book more useful for teaching purposes. The present edition, like the first, is addressed to advanced undergraduate and graduate students who have a knowledge of economics about equivalent to that obtained in the conventional one- or two-semester course in principles of economics. It has been our experience with the first edition, however, that many students found certain passages of the book rather heavy going. We have therefore revised or deleted many passages, as well as one entire chapter, replacing them with less difficult but, we hope, equally informative material. In several instances, new material has been added to round out the argument and clarify the reasoning where the first edition has assumed too much knowledge on the part of the where the first edition has assumed too much knowledge on the part of the reader. In addition, we have attempted to simplify the style throughout the book.

It would be hard to find two practicing economists whose experience, predilections, and methods of economic reasoning more closely coincide than do those of the present authors. Thus, no basic changes in the organization and argument of the book have been necessary. But an obvious objective of the second author is to reflect some of the color of his own thinking in the book. The reader who is familiar with the first edition will easily identify these changes.

It is difficult to identify, let alone thank adequately, the many persons who have contributed directly or indirectly to this book. In addition to those mentioned in this preface, others are named in the footnotes and bibliography. Among our colleagues at Indiana University who suggested ideas, read drafts, made critical comments, and simply helped to clarify thinking by lively argument are Howard G. Schaller, Ross M. Robertson, David D. Martin, Irvin M. Grossack, Edward E. Edwards, Jerome W. Milliman, George W. Wilson, Henry M. Oliver, Franz Gehrels, and George J. Stolnitz. Robert F. Wallace of the University of Montana, a visiting professor at Indiana during the summer of 1966, read the galleys and made a number of helpful suggestions; Richard W. Graves, before he left Indiana University for the University of Southern California, gave us many ideas. Colleagues in other universities, including Professors S. M. Frizol of Loyola University of Chicago, Paul W. McCracken of the University of Michigan, John Lintner of Harvard University, and others unidentified to us, also offered valuable written and oral comment.

The authors have taken advantage of many friends in the Federal government to obtain advice and assistance. Charles L. Schultze, formerly of Indiana University, now Director of the Bureau of the Budget, assisted the authors in many ways; Samuel M. Cohn of the Bureau reviewed the chapter on forecasting government expenditures with the knowledge that only he could provide; and Bureau members William B. Ross, Naomi R. Sweeney, Karl D. Gregory, and Manuel Helzner also provided helpful information. George Jaszi, Director of the Office of Business Economics of the Department of Commerce, together with some of his colleagues in the National Income Division, contributed helpful suggestions and corrections to the chapters on national income accounting; and L. Jay Atkinson, also of the Office of Business Economics, read the section on forecasting residential construction expenditures. Susan Lepper of the Council of Economic Advisers assisted extensively in drafting the chapter on the economic history of the 1950s and 1960s; Locke Anderson of the Council read critically the early drafts of some of the chapters on business forecasting; and David W. Lusher and Frances James also provided helpful information. Several members of the staff of the National Income Division of the Department of Commerce, notably Morris R. Goldman, Robert C. Wasson, and Edward O. Bassett permitted themselves to be pestered repeatedly for data which would not otherwise have been available. Julius Shiskin, Chief Economic Statistician of the Bureau of the Census, provided invaluable help and data on the leading indicators; and Ewan Clague, Commissioner, Leon Greenberg, Assistant Commissioner, and Jerome A. Mark, Deputy Assistant Commissioner, all of the Bureau of Labor Statistics, also made statistical information available and checked paragraphs for accuracy. Another source of valuable information was John A. Schnittker, Under Secretary of Agriculture.

Thanks is given to Andrew T. Court, General Motors Corp., for supplying materials on the forecasting of automobile expenditures.

An especially heavy debt of gratitude is due to our graduate assistants at Indiana University, several of whom not only worked on the book while they were graduate assistants, but continued to aid us after leaving the university. These include Kenneth D. Babka, for his help in revising and drafting several chapters, notably the chapter on forecasting net exports; William J. Hocter, now with the Federal Reserve Bank of Chicago, for his assistance in drafting the section on flow-of-funds accounting; Jay R. Becklin, particularly for his imaginative and untiring help on the forecasting chapters; John A. F. Nicholls, for his assistance in running innumerable correlations through the computer, and for undertaking the tedious job of compiling the bibliography and checking the footnotes; David A. Patterson, now at the University of Tennessee; Richard M. Bailey, now at the University of California; and Ronald S. Bond, Ronald J. Ammerman, Arthur R. Preiss, Dodd Harvey, and Karl L. Gunterman.

Thanks is given to Dean W. George Pinnell, and at an earlier date, Dean Arthur M. Weimer, for releasing time and providing graduate assistance so that the revision could be worked into a very busy schedule.

A word of special thanks is due to Mrs. Marion Karas, who not only typed all the drafts of the manuscript but also brought to the job a lively interest and intelligence that saved us from many an error.

Needless to say, extensive as has been the assistance of these and other persons too numerous to name, responsibility for errors which no doubt remain despite our efforts, rests solely with the authors.

The authors have long been jointly engaged in teaching and practicing business conditions analysis. The first, now again working for the United States government, records here his gratitude to the second author, who has himself lately returned from his most recent government assignment, for undertaking the work and responsibility of bringing out this extensive revision. And the second author wishes to record here his thanks to the first, not only for providing a first edition that was so eminently worth revising, but also for not complaining even once at the occasional excising of a scholar's most prized possession, his own creative words.

John P. Lewis
Robert C. Turner

CONTENTS

BUSINESS CONDITIONS ANALYSIS

THE SUBJECT AND
THE BOOK

Young American naval officers traditionally are told to keep three topics—politics, religion, and women—out of their wardroom conversation, but there is no similar injunction about business. Whether they are at sea, abroad, or at home, Americans talk about the general condition of American business almost as much as they do about the weather, and worry about it a good deal more. The state of business is a technical subject about which an exceptionally large number of us feel that we have some expert knowledge. It is controversial. And yet, as the Navy in its inscrutable wisdom rightly judges, business conditions is a relatively safe topic. We usually manage to keep our tempers while discussing it.

Of course, this last is not always true; arguments over whether a new year will bring boom or bust, or even over which of these currently prevails, sometimes get heated. And frequently the dispassionate coolness of business conditions debating is only a matter of appearances; it may be thinly disguised special pleading for a course of policy over which the disputants differ rancorously.

All the same, when compared with most of the other controversial topics in the social studies realm, business conditions *is* a relatively unemotional subject. Set a business executive and a union leader, a Democrat and a Republican, a conservative and a liberal to talking about the current composition of the nation's income and product, about next year's economic prospects under existing public policies, or about the economy's long-run growth potentials. Then listen to the same pairs debate wage rates, tax rates, or the manner in which government should promote economic growth. They may argue about the first set of issues, but they have a much better chance of discussing them civilly than they do the second set. There are good reasons for the difference.

In the first place, there is no longer much real disagreement among Americans over basic objectives in the business conditions area. None but a few ideological extremists now think either significant unemployment or substantial inflation desirable for the country generally. Almost everybody favors vigorous economic growth. As a result, there is a large measure of agreement about what good business conditions are. In the second place, dispute is tempered by this circumstance: the sovereignty of demonstrable, and particularly of measurable, facts is more widely and readily accepted in the business conditions area than in most other fields of social discourse. These are both very inviting circumstances from the viewpoint of the social scientist. Together with the patent importance of the subject, they make the economic state of the union a prime candidate for the laying on of analytical hands.

ONE SUBJECT AND SEVERAL PERSPECTIVES

The invitation to analytical exploration that the business conditions field presents has not gone unattended. As a matter of fact, it is hard to think of any area of knowledge into which more busy analysts have crowded in recent years. A fraction of the economics profession traditionally has devoted itself to the study of the overall performance of the American economy, and that fraction has increased markedly during the past quarter century. Hundreds of books, scores of them recent, having to do with the analysis of business conditions have been published in the United States. Our college and university curricula are now studded with courses concerning business cycles, fluctuations, and conditions. The volume of general economic statistics regularly reported in the United States, particularly by the Federal government, has increased rapidly during the last twenty years; and the number of people who make a living interpreting, evaluating, and writing about such data has risen even faster. The job of reporting and commenting upon general business conditions now occupies a considerable segment of the journalistic fraternity; it is an inevitable assignment of every trade association staff; it engages many full-time corporate staffs; and it accounts for a significant fraction of the manpower employed in our Federal and state governments.

Business conditions literature, in short, is voluminous, and professional and semiprofessional practice of business conditions analysis has become very widespread. However, there still is distressingly little interchange among groups who enter the field from different directions and with different interests. The largest of these groups are, first, businessmen, business staff advisers, and business journalists; second, the academic economists; and third, politicians, public administrators, government economists, and others primarily interested in public-policy questions. There is some tendency in each of these groups to stick to its own crowd, talk its own language, and confine itself to a particular approach to business conditions analysis, and some of the same compartmentalization infects the curricula of the colleges and universities. This is an unfortunate situation. It raises unnecessary impediments to discussion and deliberation in a common problem area. And, characteristically, a confinement to any one of these specialized perspectives robs the student of skills, knowledges, or insights that other approaches to the field offer.

FACTS, THEORIES, AND SOCIAL OBJECTIVES

From the business point of view, the study of business conditions is essentially a study of markets—but not of marketing. The marketing discipline, like most subjects in a business administration curriculum, is primarily concerned with the analysis of certain variables that the individual business firm can advantageously control or at least influence. Important elements in every firm's market situation, however, lie beyond reach of its own policies and controls. These are the elements, determined by the general conditions of the overall economy, with which we shall be concerned here.

The fact that he cannot manipulate them, of course, does not dampen the interest a sensible businessman has in general market forces and factors. On the contrary, he is doubly concerned to understand and, if possible, foretell them so that he can adjust his own policies accordingly. If he fails in this, neither the most brilliant internal management nor the most inspired marketing is likely to protect him from grievous business errors.

The business approach to business conditions analysis is characteristically practical. Analysts of this school like to get down to facts and figures without much delay, and they assemble and consume great quantities of them. They are impatient with theorizing; they would rather work with actual data than with hypothetical models; their preference is for current applied analysis with a minimum of academic preliminaries.

To a considerable extent, the present volume inclines toward this factual, practical bias of the business student. This bias, incidentally, has much to offer those would-be pure economists and students of public affairs who find themselves concerned with business conditions problems. Budding economists sometimes get so wrapped up in their abstract constructs that they develop a curious aversion to actual data. Their tendency is to shun the greatest of all laboratories for testing their analytical hypotheses—the complex reality of the contemporary economy.

In a less esoteric but more impetuous fashion, students of government, public administration, and public economic policy frequently become so fascinated with policy devices calculated to revise the current or prospective economic environment that they scarcely pause to consider precisely what the condition of the environment actually is. Such people are a little like a medical doctor who is so enthusiastic about the art of prescription that he has no time for diagnosis.

When it is carried to undisciplined extremes, however, the most fruitless one-sidedness of all is the factual bias of our budding businessman. There is nothing sillier than a man who runs around grubbing for facts without knowing what to do with them. The world is crawling with facts; any collection of them must be highly selective. Without a thorough, preconceived (although revisable) theoretical framework on which to hang them, an analyst cannot know which facts are pertinent to his problem. And he cannot evaluate facts adequately without some reasonable social perspective in which to view them.

Such a perspective is something businessmen nowadays need, and not simply for the good of their souls. There is still some argument over whether Mr. Charles E. Wilson, when he appeared before a Senate committee as nominee for Secretary of Defense in early 1953, implied that what was good for General Motors was good for the country. But everybody agrees that he definitely did say that "what was good for the country was good for General Motors. . . ." There is an increasing consensus among business leaders that they have a lively vocational interest in the economic welfare of the nation as a whole.

A factual emphasis, analytical rigor, and an eye to the public interest—all these, then, are aspects of fruitful business conditions study. But we have not established yet in any very precise way what the subject matter of such study is.

THE GROUND TO BE COVERED

There are three questions any thoughtful student of business conditions must ask. Logically, the first is: How do you define and measure business conditions? Second, if a student has any intellectual curiosity, he cannot inspect general economic data for long without starting to wonder what causes changes in business conditions. This is the obvious question to an economic scientist, and it is an essential one for both the business and the public-policy practitioner. Finally, we all are pushed to a third query. Generally stated, it takes this form: Can we predict business conditions and, if so, how?

This last question raises the problem of forecasting. In some parts of the economics profession it is still apparently a little risky to admit that economic scientists have any legitimate concern with the art of forecasting. Certainly it is true that no completely scientific method of probing the future of the economy has yet been invented. Thus, if the effort to define the economic outlook were only an incidental or esoteric undertaking, economists' diffidence about forecasting would be justified. However, the fact is that, in one form or another, the forecast is the payoff for all general analyses of business conditions.

The ultimate test of any science is the power to predict. The ultimate test of the economic analyst's science is his power to predict either the extent and character of economic activity in general or the consequences of particular alternative courses of action. For the policy maker, whether private or public, the whole point of economic analysis is to anticipate economic behavior so that policies may either respond to or alter that behavior intelligently and purposefully. Every economic decision maker in business or in government is doomed to be a forecaster regardless of whether his forecasts are implicit or explicit, subconscious or conscious. The only real question for the economist, therefore, is whether he is going to contribute whatever scientific aids he can to the forecasting job, or whether he is going to leave the unavoidable task entirely to laymen, pundits, and charlatans.

The primary focus of this volume, therefore, will be on the problem of analyzing the nation's economic outlook. We shall find that, if such analysis is to produce any real prognosis of the country's economic health, it must consider not only the outlook for the actual, achieved volume of business but also the outlook for changes in the economy's productive capacity—in its business potential. We shall also need to distinguish rather sharply between analysis of the short-run economic outlook (confining that term to the next twelve to fifteen months) and the long-run outlook. The reasons for this distinction will become plainer as we proceed, but, in general, they come down to this: the economist's ability to read the prospects for actual business activity —not necessarily the prospects for the economy's productive potential— deteriorates very rapidly for periods beyond one year hence.

Thus it is only for the near term that one can make a more or less literal forecast of general business conditions that is reasonably comprehensive. Such forecasting has great practical significance to the businessman worrying about next year's sales and profits, the consumer worrying about prices, the worker concerned with wage and employment prospects, and the government official trying to anticipate tax collections or the impact of a changed spending program. Moreover, there is no better way than the study and practice of short-run outlook analysis to develop one's knowledge of the whole economy and its interrelationships. The subject will occupy one of the larger parts of the book.

At the same time, decision makers' interest in the economy's future is not confined to the near term. The long-run outlook has much significance for public policy. It is of particular interest to businesses trying to plan what investments should be made now in plant and equipment so that they will be tooled up to serve potential markets several years hence. Accordingly, we shall want also to consider the extent to which long-term projections of the economy's physical growth can be safely extended five, ten, and fifteen years or longer into the future.

While outlook analysis, then, is our major objective, there are some indispensable preliminaries. In the first place—working backward from the target—one should be able to analyze adequately the economy's performance in the recent past and present before he tackles the future. Before we can undertake either analysis of the recent past or outlook analysis, there is the matter of a needed analytical framework. Thus we shall have to consider— in relatively brief but intensive fashion—the theory of aggregative economic behavior offered by modern economics. Finally—still working backward—in order to permit facts and figures to be married to theories throughout the book, we shall need to inspect social accounting systems even before we look at aggregative economic theory.

Recapitulating—now from front to rear—Part One will treat social accounting, especially the structure and character of national income account- ing in the United States; Part Two, the subject matter of modern macro- economic theory; Part Three, the recent history of the United States business conditions; Part Four, the problem of short-run outlook analysis; and Part Five, the limited contributions that economic analysis can make to diagnoses of a nation's long-term prospects.

TWO MISSING WORDS

The title of this volume requires several footnotes. In the first place, it really should begin with the word "general." Our concern will be with the behavior of the overall economy, not with that of particular industries or segments viewed in isolation. This does not mean that we shall avoid particular-industry considerations. Any general business conditions analysis, for example, would be exceedingly thin if it did not give a lot of explicit atten- tion to the demand for housing and automobiles. We shall be concerned with such particular-industry discussion for the light that it can shed upon eco- nomic activity in general. Industries and other sectors of the economy will be considered as components and not as entities in themselves.

Such a restriction of the subject is a matter of arbitrary choice. For example, much intrinsically good material on forecasting from a local or regional or a firm-by-firm or industry-by-industry perspective might have been included. If you are using the book in an organized course, you may be directed to readings which supplement the present volume in these respects.

In the second place, if the book had a fully accurate title, the word "introduction" or "introductory" should appear in it somewhere. Neither the book nor the courses with which it is likely to be associated can pretend to turn out professional business conditions analysts—although many who are thus exposed may go on, via further study and the route of apprenticeship and experience, to become full-fledged professionals. Our more immediate and modest objective is to train people to become intelligent *users* of professional business conditions analysis.

Today, and even more tomorrow, the average executive of a larger corporation is likely to have the services of a full-time economic analysis staff available within his own organization. So is the average public administrator within the Federal government. In somewhat similar fashion, line people in smaller organizations, whether business or governmental, are apt to use the services of consultants or, at least, of the specialized press that devotes itself to business conditions comment. None of these services, however, completely absolves the decision maker from responsibility for business conditions analysis.

The decision maker in business or government must be able to evaluate the work of the professional analyst. He must know how the analyst's forecast was derived in order to know its limitations and usefulness. He cannot rely simply on an ex post facto testing of the accuracy of the analyst's forecast; for if his advisers have been right for the wrong reasons, their record is a poor guide to their future reliability. Moreover, reliance upon past batting averages may be a very expensive way of weeding out bad advisers if meanwhile the decision maker has been following their advice during the times they struck out. As the decision maker scans the range of professional business conditions intelligence flowing to him, he himself must possess criteria for appraising analytical techniques and for sifting the good from the bad. Our purpose here will be to provide some help along these lines.

IS THIS A BOOK ON CYCLES?

The present work is intended as a contribution to what in the past usually has been called business cycles literature. And yet the authors would be less than candid if they did not admit, at the outset, to a certain prejudice against the business cycles label.

There is little evidence that there is presently at work in the American economy anything that can be correctly called a general business "cycle," if that word is meant to suggest a fairly rhythmical, periodic pattern of ups and downs. Even historically it seems possible that some of the apparent rhythms in American business fluctuations are the result of statistical averaging. In certain industries and in certain phases of general activity—for example, inventory investment—it is true that fairly rhythmical patterns are quite evident. We shall note some of these with considerable care. Nevertheless, we shall mostly avoid the word "cycle," not only because of its objectionable rhythmical connotation but because of the flavor of inevitability and uncontrollability that it carries. The latter view, which would enervate stabilization policy if it were taken seriously, has now been superseded in most business as well as in government thinking. It seems rather archaic to perpetuate it in academic nomenclature.

The same objections, it should be noted, do not apply to the term "business fluctuations." The only reason for avoiding it as a book title is that it emphasizes one important aspect of American business conditions at the expense of others equally important. Notable among the latter are the economy's growth characteristics and needs.

There is one specific respect in which this clearly is not a conventional business cycles book. It provides no catalog of dozens of old business cycle theories, which past generations of economists contrived to explain the uncertainly established phenomenon of cyclical fluctuations. Such theories are of intrinsic interest to the historian of economic ideas, and certainly they contain the seeds of many ideas that are highly relevant for present-day analysis. Our own view, however, is that students whose lives are short and who do not seek a knowledge of theoretical history per se can spend their time more fruitfully studying contemporary analytical techniques.

IS THIS A BOOK ON PUBLIC POLICY?

In a sense, the answer to this question is No. The purpose here is not to discuss, as such, public economic policies in general or even the stabilization and growth varieties of policy, which are the analogues of business conditions analysis. Public economic policy is an immensely intricate topic. An adequate discussion of it would need, among other things, to examine in considerable detail the political and constitutional environment in which public policies are made and to emphasize that it is rarely possible to develop Federal policies in single-minded pursuit of a particular clear-cut objective, such as stabilization or economic growth. Always, it is necessary to evolve a working compromise among a variety of major and partly conflicting objectives. Such a discussion cannot be satisfactorily compressed into a portion of a book of this kind. So far as any intensive, critical debate over stabilization and growth policies is concerned, it should be apparent that the most we can do here is to develop the factual and analytical bases from which such debate might sensibly proceed—once the other political and institutional ingredients were added.

This does not quite dispose of the problem, however. For with the government playing its present central role in the economy, it is obvious that existing policies can be, indeed usually are, important ingredients of the economic situation. Moreover, in evaluating the outlook, a thoughtful forecaster must consider not only the prospects under existing policies but also the "feedback effect," that is, the reactions decision makers—including strategically positioned government decision makers—are likely to have toward such prospective developments as they unfold. Thus the contemporary business conditions analyst never can wholly divorce himself from a consideration of public policies—past, present, or future. But he *can* view them as ingredients of the business situation, not as objects for study in their own right; and he can focus on what they are, or are most likely to be, rather than upon what they ought to be. Such will be our practice here.

THE STUDY OF BUSINESS CONDITIONS

Neither a book of this kind nor the series of classroom lectures that may accompany it can begin to exhaust a subject about which the current literature and opinion are so rich and varied. The book or the lectures can plot a track and offer you the opportunity to become an informed student of business conditions. But whether you do or not will depend largely upon how much thinking you do yourself, upon how widely and deeply you dip into the literature, and upon how wisely you choose from among the mass of available material. Reasonably extensive bibliographies for each major part of the volume are provided at the end of Part Five. In addition, a word about sources of current comment and data may be in order.

The most generally useful periodicals that carry current statistics on the overall United States economy are those published by the Federal government. Particularly helpful, because of its succinctness and the relative speed with which it is released, is the monthly publication *Economic Indicators*, prepared by the President's Council of Economic Advisers and published by Congress's Joint Economic Committee. Older, fuller, and somewhat slower monthly sources of current data, including a good deal of interesting textual material, are the Department of Commerce's *Survey of Current Business*, the Federal Reserve Board's *Federal Reserve Bulletin*, the Department of Labor's *Employment and Earnings and Monthly Labor Review*, and the Department of Commerce's *Business Cycle Developments*. Other, more specialized, sources will be noted as we proceed.

The *Economic Report of the President*, transmitted to the Congress each January, presumably is the most authoritative analysis of recent economic developments and future prospects as far as the Federal administration is concerned. A perusal of it is virtually essential for any serious student of business conditions, as is attention to (1) the hearings on the President's Report which the congressional Joint Economic Committee holds each February, (2) the Joint Committee's own report, published after those hearings are concluded, and (3) various studies intermittently prepared by the Joint Committee's staff.

A welter of private weeklies, monthlies, and quarterlies are devoted either partially or wholly to business conditions discussion—magazines like *Business Week* and *Fortune*, the various newsletters, and publications by trade associations, general business organizations, banks, labor unions and federations, private research organizations, state bureaus of business research, etc. Some of the best of this literature can be obtained free if one is on the mailing lists for monthlies and quarterlies published by the various (district) Federal Reserve banks and by some of the larger city banks.

A student of business conditions will want to follow the daily press coverage of economic developments rather closely—and critically. For it is a fact that most working journalists on the general dailies are not specialists in business or economic analysis. As a result, if you begin to feel like something of a specialist yourself, you may find it interesting to try evaluating the comparative quality of the commentary in the financial sections of several large daily papers. You may also wish to consider the usefulness, for your own purposes, of the more specialized reporting provided by such daily business journals as the *Wall Street Journal* and the *Journal of Commerce.*

One has to evolve one's own habits in seeking a balanced and informative reading diet in the business conditions field. All that can be urged here, really, is the importance of embarking upon such a venture and of not confining oneself to any particular analyst or any particular book, including this one.

PART ONE

SOCIAL ACCOUNTING

2

THE GENERAL ARCHITECTURE OF NATIONAL INCOME ACCOUNTING

Statisticians commonly are regarded as even duller people than economists, and sometimes they deserve the reputation. Any discipline, however, occasionally is capable of dramatic and far-reaching innovations; so it has been with economic statistics during the past generation. In the United States and most other countries since the 1920s, there have not only been substantial improvements in the quantity, quality, coverage, and timeliness of regularly reported economic series in general, but also the period has witnessed, in the development of the theory and practice of national income accounting, one of the great social inventions of our time.

At the start of World War II, the beginnings of national accounting were about as well advanced in Germany and Italy as they were in the United States and the United Kingdom. But the Allied powers were much quicker than the Axis governments to adopt the new aggregative statistics as an operative framework for wartime anti-inflationary policy and overall resource programing. This more aggressive use of national accounting techniques was one of our important technical advantages in that conflict. It helped us to achieve a much better calculated and bolder use of our total resources than any of the Axis nations attained.

National income accounting has been an equally valuable technique in the planning and administration of United States foreign aid programs in Europe and in the design of economic development efforts in underdeveloped countries. In the United States it has vastly improved our knowledge of the structure and current behavior of the domestic economy. It provides what now is generally regarded as the most useful frame of reference for economic forecasting, and it supplies the quantitative framework within which our debates over public economic policies increasingly are conducted.

The statistical half of the so-called Keynesian revolution in economics, which has so largely colored modern applied economic analysis, has been at least as important as the other (theoretical) half. It is a subject about which competent students of business conditions must have a reasonably precise knowledge.

It helps if, from the beginning, one can view national income statistics as an invention—a piece of craftsmanship. National income statistics are not, by any means, literal or automatic mirror images of the economic world around us. As a matter of fact, no economic series is. All economic statistics deal with the real world only in a selective and simplified way, cramming some of the myriad variety and detail into relatively few boxes or categories. In this process they tend to change differences of degree into differences of kind.

The man-made aspect, the element of craftsmanship, is particularly pronounced in national income statistics simply because they are the most complicated and sophisticated economic statistics now in general usage. Any national income system is a structure of carefully and deliberately designed concepts. The objectives of the system must be decided. A whole network of precise definitions must be developed, and many puzzling matters of classification determined. There must be detailed decisions on valuation procedures. Nor is it enough for determinations of this kind to be theoretically sound and internally consistent. They must also serve the needs of those who will use the statistics for policy and other practical purposes, and they must meet the limitations set by the availability of primary data. Finally, if a national accounting system is to have any lasting significance, a permanent fact-gathering and -processing organization must be established which fits the system's conceptual requirements.[1]

---

[1] The man who deserves the greatest credit for the initiation of modern national accounting is Simon Kuznets, who did his pioneer work mostly in the 1930s under the auspices of the National Bureau of Economic Research. (See Simon Kuznets, *National Income and Capital Formation, 1919–1935*, National Bureau of Economic Research, Inc., New York, 1937; *Commodity Flow and Capital Formation*, 1938; and a number of subsequent publications of the National Bureau of Economic Research, Inc.) Since the early 1930s in this country, continuing official development and reporting of the national income series has been carried forward by the National Income Division of the U.S. Department of Commerce under the leadership, successively, of Robert R. Nathan, Milton Gilbert, Edward F. Denison, Charles F. Schwartz, and George Jaszi. In Britain, people

THE TARGET: TOTAL ECONOMIC ACTIVITY

The formal purposes of modern national income accounting are two-fold. The first purpose is to provide a regular and continuing measure of total economic activity, comparable over time. For at least a half century before the 1930s, and particularly during the 1910s and 1920s, various German, British, Italian, and American economists had intermittently formulated estimates of their nations' output or income. However, although these efforts did yield occasional, global measures of economic activity, they were discontinuous; they were not backed up by organizations and procedures designed to produce continuing *series* of such estimates.

To this first purpose the inventors of modern national income accounting have added a second major purpose: to subdivide such total activity estimates into enough segments or sectors to reveal the structural character and pattern of total national economic activity as well as its magnitude. It is this emphasis upon interrelationships of parts and whole, together with the practice of maintaining continuous series, that has so vastly increased the importance and usefulness of national accounting. Yet total economic activity remains the formal target toward which any national income estimate is aimed. It is the whole to which all the parts are supposed to add up.

That we are dealing with activity, with flows of value through time and not with the stocks of wealth or assets that the economy has accumulated at any particular moment in time, is a fact that deserves an immediate word of emphasis. If, in our official national accounting in this and other countries, we had well-developed sets of balance sheet concepts to match the income statement concepts we do have, our national income series would be matched by a set of national wealth series. As yet, unfortunately, no generally accepted or periodic national wealth data have been produced. A number of research organizations have worked on the problem, but such data have not yet been added to the tool kit of the average business conditions analyst.[2]

It is worth noting, too, that other measures of general economic activity were available to American business conditions analysts before the advent of modern national accounting. Although these measures are still important, none of them was very satisfactory as a comprehensive indicator of overall economic performance. For example, the Federal Reserve Board's industrial production index (instituted in the 1920s) supplied a very good indication of relative changes in the physical output of the manufacturing and mining in-

---

like Richard Stone have played similar roles. During national accounting's formative years, many other economists and statisticians outside the official national income agencies—for instance, in Britain, J. R. Hicks, and in this country, Gerhard Colm—contributed greatly, as constructive critics, to the improvement of the system.

[2] The present status of national wealth accounting in the United States is discussed briefly in Chap. 4.

dustries; but it did not cover agriculture, distribution, services, government, or the other productive sectors of the economy. Another indicator of general business activity favored by many analysts a few decades ago—the figures showing total bank debits and clearings—was comprehensive enough. But it did not necessarily reflect changes in production, employment, and other physical aspects of the economy. While most American business is done by check, changes in the activity of checking accounts may simply register changes in the rate at which money is circulating in our financial markets, that is, the rate at which people are swapping one kind of already-produced assets for another kind. Similarly, employment and unemployment data—available at least in crude form in the early 1930s and, then as now, indicative of one vital dimension of total economic activity—did not necessarily reflect the economy's output or accomplishment. They measured the country's busyness better than they did its business.

THREE CONCEPTS OF TOTAL ACTIVITY

There was no more mystery before the national income innovators did their work than afterward about the usefulness of measures of total economic activity. The problem was to put the measures into effect and to reconcile them. In the abstract, three such measures were available.

Production or Output

One thing you could do was to count up the production or output, not just of mining and manufacturing, but of the entire economy during an accounting period. To say "count up production" is immediately, of course, to imply the old apples-and-oranges problem. Here, as in the two other approaches which follow, a common denominator is necessary; and the only one available is value. What can be totaled is the *value* of production, whether that is expressed, finally, in terms of an index number or of monetary units.

Consumption or End Use

The second thing that one looking for a good measure of total activity might do is to value the total consumption of goods and services by members of the economy during the period in question; or, since consumption usually is given a more restricted meaning than this implies, we can say, simply, total end uses. That this is a different concept from production or output is plain to anyone who has been involved in a foreign aid program. Whenever the United States, for instance, undertakes to supply aid to a country that, temporarily at least, lacks the ability to support itself at what is judged to be a minimum standard of living, two distinct calculations are necessary: (1) What will the minimum needs (minimum end uses) of the aided country be during a coming period?   (2) How much can the country contribute to those needs by its own production?

Incomes

Finally, one can measure total economic activity by tabulating incomes in the conventional meaning of that term.   What are the receipts, the rewards, the claims against goods and services that have accrued during the period in question to everybody in the economy, that is, to all individuals and any other income-receiving entities?[3]

THE PRINCIPLE OF EQUALITY

The genius of national income accounting is that it adopts all three of these basic measures of economic activity and combines them in such fashion that they become, in principle, interchangeable.   This result depends first on the decision to value all three of the activity concepts in the money of the realm.   This is a well-nigh inevitable way to proceed, but it does introduce a basic ambiguity into national income series: their period-to-period changes may reflect changes in physical activity, changes in prices, i.e., in per-unit valuations, or changes in both.   This gives users of national income statistics a problem—that of distinguishing real change from price changes, to which we shall have to return in Chapters 5 and 6.

The second decision that underlies the interchangeability of national income accounting's three activity concepts is not at all inevitable.   It is to establish definitions that make the economy's total product, its total use of its product, and its total income conceptually equal.

This definitional practice is a matter of craft, not of inexorable logic. For instance, it is a commonplace of current business commentary to speak of production as running ahead of sales (or buyers' purchases), thereby causing an accumulation of inventories.   This sounds very much like a case of use lagging behind production or output.   Or, again, most people would say that consumer use of refrigerators is much greater during a hot summer than during a cold one, even if the purchase—and the production—of refrigerators is the same in the two cases.   Similarly, the existence of an exact parallel

---

[3] Although to the average American aggregate income may seem the most obvious of the three total activity concepts just listed, it should be noted that it is conceptually distinguishable from aggregate output and aggregate end use only in a monetized economy, i.e., one in which most transactions are monetary.   In a situation where end users either supply themselves out of their own production or rely upon barter transactions, incomes accrue only in a real form that is synonymous with one of the other concepts. But in a monetary economy where income transactions are typically distinguishable from output transactions, the total current accrual of financial claims against production is a matter of interest in its own right.

kinds of analysis. For example, one cannot, by studying the detail of income by type of income and of production by expenditure on final products, make a direct comparison of receipts and expenditures by the same groups. In the United States, as we shall see in Chapter 4, this circumstance has prompted some rearrangements of the basic national income data that do provide such a cross classification.

CRUCIAL DEFINITIONS

The pivotal axiom in national income accounting can be put this way: *the controlling measure of total economic activity shall be production of valued goods and services for end users.* This is a short sentence, and it may not sound like much; but actually it contains three subpropositions, each of which is essential to the national income scheme. By the time we have explored the implications of each of these, we shall have the whole scheme pretty well spelled out.

POSTULATE 1: OUTPUT CALLS THE TUNE

The first step in national accounting's definitional scheme is the adoption of output, rather than either consumption or income, as the key concept of economic activity. When, in order to maintain the principle of equality, reconciliations among the approaches are necessary, the other two are defined to conform with the output concept of activity, not vice versa. This rule has four major consequences for the architecture of the system, and it will be well to detail them in sequence.

The Definition of Income

The dominance of the production concept means that national income is defined as rewards resulting from current production—and nothing else. In the next chapter, when we inspect the actual series published by the National Income Division of the U.S. Department of Commerce, we shall find that all uses of the term "income" are not bound by this rule. The series on *personal* income (PI) and *disposable personal* income (DPI), which are part of the family of national income series in this country, include receipts that do not represent payments for current production by the recipients. Nevertheless, whenever the Department of Commerce attaches the adjective "national" to "income," it confines the concept to payments for current output and calls all other incomelike receipts something else.

Consistent with this production-oriented definition of national income, various pensions, unemployment compensation, and other individual receipts that are not payments for currently produced goods or services are classed as transfer payments rather than earned income. Similarly, receipts from sales of old goods, such as old houses, or of any existing assets, such as land or securities, are excluded from the tabulation of gross national product (GNP) and national income.[4] So are the capital gains resulting from exchanges of existing assets, which are profitable to specific individuals but which, from the community's viewpoint, represent no new creation of value, i.e., production.

The Adoption of Expenditures as a Measure of Use

Because it is at the time of transactions—not when output actually is used, but when it is purchased—that use and production most nearly match, use is measured for national income purposes by purchases or expenditures. Thus it is decided, for instance, to measure the "use" of refrigerators by expenditures for refrigerators and to disregard the fact that they yield up their utility (i.e., are consumed) gradually over a period of years. Moreover, as a practical statistical matter, it is much more feasible to secure reasonably reliable data on purchases than on the actual use or consumption of goods.

Treatment of Inventory Change

If a producer makes more or less than he sells, i.e., if production runs ahead of or behind sales, as that term usually is construed, his commodity stocks either pile up or decline. His inventories change. In national income accounting, in order to make the purchase's measure of total economic activity conform to the production measure, such inventory increases or decreases are treated as positive or negative purchases by the seller. In the economy as a whole, net increases or decreases in total business inventories are treated as positive or negative components of total business investment spending. Actually, this language is not out of line with normal business terminology. For an expansion of inventories does constitute an increase in working capital. Table 2–1 illustrates how an increase in inventories, in period 1, and a decrease, in period 2, would show up in the national income accounts.

Treatment of Exports and Imports

If a national economy is not isolated from the rest of the world, it is unlikely that, in any particular accounting period, total end-user purchases by its inhabitants will exactly match domestic production. For some of the

---

[4] As we shall describe later, purchases or sales of existing fixed assets among the several sectors of the economy (persons, business, government, and foreign) are netted within each of these sectors. Only the net amounts (plus or minus) for each sector are reflected in the national income accounts. These sector entries are therefore offsetting and do not affect total GNP. Thus, the sale of a ship by government to business would reduce government expenditures and increase business investment by a like amount.

Table 2-1.   Hypothetical Production and Sales Data, National Income Nomenclature

	Period 1	Period 2
Production	100	100
Sales:		
To consumers or others not buying for resale	90	110
Inventory investment	10	−10
Total sales	100	100

things bought will be supplied by foreigners, and some of the things produced will be sold abroad. Of course, if the nation's foreign trade on current account were exactly balanced, i.e., if imports and exports of goods and services were exactly equal, there would be no problem. The purchases and production measures of total activity would be identical. But this is not apt to happen very often. In most accounting periods, the country will buy abroad more than it sells, or vice versa. If the principle of equality is to be maintained, a reconciliation is required.

Here again, as in the case of inventories, the adjustment is made on the purchases, not on the production, side of the ledger. If the domestic economy buys more than it produces, with the difference coming from abroad, the balance is treated as a negative purchase by the rest of the world from the economy; the balance is deducted from domestic purchases in order to pull the total purchases figure into line with domestic production. An opposite adjustment is made in the event of net sales to the rest of the world. The general character of these adjustments (they are entered under the heading of "net exports" in the United States national income series) is described more fully a few pages hence.

As indicated earlier, the treatments of inventory investment and exports and imports have the combined effect of converting the expenditure tabulation from an estimate of domestic end use as such to an estimate of production *measured by* end-user expenditures. It is for this reason that tables in official statistical sources (e.g., *Economic Indicators*) showing GNP data are usually titled "Gross National Product *or Expenditure*," which is somewhat ambiguous shorthand for "Gross National Product Measured by Expenditure."

POSTULATE 2: CONCERNING COVERAGE

The second of the three subpropositions contained in the national accounting axiom is that only "valued" goods and services shall be counted in the output estimates. As it stands, this conveys very little. But it is shorthand notation for the fact that all national income estimators must work out a detailed solution to the questions of what goods and services they shall include in their tabulations and what price tags they shall put on them. Estimators are pulled in two directions on these issues. On the one hand, they want their figures to have as comprehensive a coverage as possible; but, on the other hand, they are reluctant to inject their own subjective judgments into their estimating procedures.

The general solution is to follow the rule of the market. If a particular output has been exchanged in the market, it will be counted, and at the price at which it was exchanged; if it has not been traded for a monetary consideration, it is apt to be excluded. This practice disposes of most of national income accounting's coverage difficulties in a highly monetized economy such as the United States. It means, for example, that the services university students deliver in their course work and the products of do-it-yourself home workshops are not reflected in the national product—unless someone buys them. Reliance upon the market also absolves estimators from any attempt to weight the essentiality or social desirability of different kinds of production. A dollar's worth of whisky counts as much as a dollar's worth of milk.

At the same time, as we shall see when we consider the United States accounts, every national income system makes a few exceptions to the rule of the market. For example, in the United States accounts we do impute value to the rent earned by owner-occupied houses and to the food that farmers supply themselves, although neither involves market transactions. Such imputations are made only when the estimators decide that adherence to the market rule would clearly produce a more distorted or erroneous report of productive activity than would the departure. And, typically, such a judgment is reached only where goods or services that are closely analogous to the nonexchanged items *are* being traded in nearby markets. In such cases, an oversight of the nonmarketed output would be particularly glaring; and there are some actual market prices handy that can be readily imputed to the nonmarketed items. It is because these conditions are not met that in the United States we do not include the services of housewives, for instance, in our estimates of national output, although, intrinsically, these certainly are far more important than the self-supplied output of farmers.

POSTULATE 3: DEFINING END USE

The final element in the national income axiom is the restriction of the (controlling) total output measure to production for end users. It requires the national income accountant to have a working definition of what economic end use is. Production and distribution characteristically are multistage processes. They are particularly so in advanced economies. Most producers produce for sale—not to ultimate buyers but to other producers or distributors who buy commodities for resale. These buyers process, assemble, distribute, or otherwise add value to the goods in question and then pass them along, either to still other processors or distributors who add more value or to final

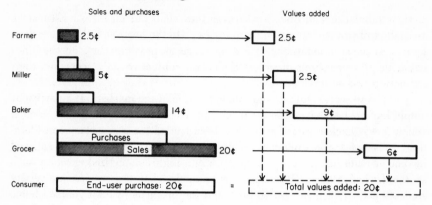

Figure **2–2.**   The value of a loaf of bread by end-user purchase and by industrial origin.   Total sales transactions: 2.5¢ + 5¢ + 14¢ + 20¢ = 41.5¢; – 20¢ = 21.5¢.

buyers. Thus, as indicated in Figure 2–2, a flour miller, a wholesale baker, and a retail grocer may all add value to the farmer's wheat before it finally reaches a consumer as a loaf of bread.

The point here is a familiar one. Every introductory economics text nowadays makes it. To total the sales at the successive stages of the productive-distributive process and to call the sum "total value of output" would involve double counting. In the example, over half of such a cumulative total sales figure would be duplicative.

For the economy as a whole, a cumulative tabulation of sales would have a certain significance as a measure of total goods and services transactions; changes in it, for instance, would indicate changes in the production-distribution process' demand for money. (As a matter of fact, we shall see that the flow-of-funds social accounting system, which will be discussed in Chapter 4, strives for just such a tabulation of all monetary goods and services transactions.) But changes in a total transactions figure would not necessarily reflect changes in the economy's productive activity. Suppose vertical integration occurs—say between the miller and the baker in our example—thereby eliminating one level of market transactions. This could lower the cumulative sales figure by 5 cents; but there is no reason to think it would reduce the production or value of bread.

Clearly, one of two things must be done if we want a measure of output that nets out duplicative transactions: (1) We can count only transactions that occur at the last stage of the production-distribution process. (2) We can sum up the values added at each stage, determining the latter by subtracting from the sales of each productive enterprise the cost items that it purchases from other businesses.[5] As the figure indicates, however, the non-

[5] This sentence points up an oversimplification in Fig. 2–2. The latter implies that the only production expense that the miller incurs outside his own firm is the purchase

duplicative concept of output, whichever way it is calculated, equals production for end users.

This is a familiar point; and we usually are inclined to dismiss it with a rather glib definition of what we mean by end user: someone who buys a commodity or service not for resale. We remember as an afterthought that we mean not *quite* that; we also mean any businessmen who raise or lower their inventories during the period, and the rest of the world insofar as it makes net purchases of any kind from our economy.

The definition of end users, however, is not really as obvious as it seems. For as we ponder it, such questions as these arise: How exactly do you tell when a businessman is purchasing for resale? Take an automobile manufacturer. Are his purchases of car radios from a radio manufacturer purchases for resale? Certainly. How about the steel sheet he buys for making bodies? This too is a pretty clear case. But what about purchases of paper clips to be used in the office? These are not going to be resold in any literal or physical sense. Yet we may be inclined to say that they will be incorporated into the product in the same way in which the services of office workers and factory labor are. But what then of the purchases of a drilling machine or a new factory? Will not these also be gradually converted into, and finally resold in the form of, automobiles?

Or, to take a different tack, if we have been assuming that all consumer purchases are clearly purchases not for resale, is this necessarily so? Who is to say that an automobile worker—or a banker—does not buy his working clothes or even his food to be resold in the form of personal services?

Actually, the definition of who the end users are in an economy is not self-evident at all. Such a definition is a product of the national income estimator's craft. The definition of end use that a particular country adopts is apt to depend partly on its characteristic philosophies and value judgments, partly on practical considerations drawn from economic and business analysis, and partly on statistical feasibility.

The definition that has evolved in the United States and in a number of other countries is that end use consists essentially of three things: consumption, real-capital formation or the accumulation of physical assets, and net purchases from the domestic economy by foreigners—providing that all end use by government can be classified into one or the other of these three categories. Some national income experts have theoretical objections to such a treatment of government spending. They argue that government, as in its national defense activities, for example, is not simply "all of us" consuming or forming capital collectively, but a separate entity. In any event, it is not

---

of wheat; that the baker's only such expense is for flour; and so on. Actually, many other materials and services must also be purchased from other businesses. Hence the breakdown of the values added in a loaf of bread, in fact, is much more complex than the figure indicates; and the values added by the four businesses shown actually are smaller than the figure suggests.

easy to allocate end use by government to the private consumption and investment sectors. Thus, in practice, end use acquires a four-way breakdown:
personal consumption expenditures, domestic capital formation or investment,
net exports, and government purchases of final products.

Consumption

The national accounting principle at this point is wholly consistent
with the orthodox view of traditional, individualistic, Western economics.
Adam Smith, John Maynard Keynes, and generations of British and American
economists in between have laid down the postulate that the ultimate purpose
of economic activity is the satisfaction of consumer wants. This, of course, is
not the only possible way of looking at things. Other societies may regard
their basic economic objective as the aggrandizement of national power or
wealth. But if so, they should not measure their economic progress by a
national accounting system which, like ours, treats consumer goods and
services as the principal component of final products.

In most national account systems, personal consumption expenditures and purchases by households are regarded as interchangeable concepts.[6]
This means, for one thing, that consumer goods and services are identified
as those items which are bought for household purposes; businesses, insofar
as they can be distinguished from households, by definition do not "consume."
For another thing, the identification of personal consumption and household
purchases means that *all* the latter are assumed to be end-use expenditures.
That is to say, the work-clothes problem raised above is disregarded; the
acquisition of a pair of overalls is treated not as a means to some other end
but as just as much of an end accomplishment of economic activity as the
acquisition of a bathing suit.

This identification of personal consumption and household purchases
involves one rather curious adjustment in the United States accounting system that it may be well to identify at this point. Statistically speaking, any
consumer good is consumed at the moment of retail purchase. There is no
further trace of it in national income statistics. The more durable the good
purchased by a household, the less realistic this fiction of instantaneous consumption becomes. It is rather unrealistic, for example, in the case of a man's
suit; and it approaches the ridiculous in the case of an electric refrigerator or
an automobile. However, partly because of the statistical infeasibility of estimating the rates at which such goods continue to deliver services to consumers
after their purchase, our national income accountants have swallowed their
common sense in these cases and have classified everything up to and including household appliances and automobiles as consumer goods.

But they have balked in the case of houses. It would be downright
silly to regard a house as being consumed at the moment of purchase, when

---

[6] Households are defined to include private nonprofit institutions such as colleges,
hospitals, and churches.

the occupant not only may continue to receive services from it for the next twenty years but may be paying for it that long. So, quite realistically, we treat the purchase of a new house as capital formation, not consumption. However, since most new houses are purchased by households, this classification threatens the household purchase-consumption identity. We evade the difficulty in this country with a harmless fiction: we say that when a household buys a house it is not acting as a household but rather as a business. As a business, it invests in a house; then it sells housing services to itself as a household (or consumer). As a consumer it then proceeds, during subsequent years, to pay imputed (or make-believe) rent to the business side of its split personality; and this imputed rent is regularly included in the personal consumption component of end-user purchases.

This imputation procedure may look rather strange. However, it constitutes an appropriate departure from the rule of the market under the principles outlined above: if rent were not imputed to owner-occupied houses, the national accounts in effect would say that such houses produce no valuable services during their lifetimes, although identical houses, owned by a landlord (an *investor* in houses) and occupied by tenants, do. Moreover, because a substantial proportion of houses is in fact owned by one party and rented to another, data are readily available for imputing rents to the analogous owner-occupied houses.

The imputed-rent case illustrates the general proposition that national income estimators sometimes have to engage in rather elaborate gymnastics to keep their definitions reasonably realistic and, at the same time, internally consistent. The particular effect of these imputations is to preserve the identity between the purchasing group and type of purchases in our United States end-use classification. Thanks to the fiction about house purchases, which, to repeat, classifies households as "business" in their capacity as house buyers and owners, we can say that the only expenditures consumers (or households) make are personal consumption expenditures and that private domestic capital formation (or domestic investment) is exclusively a business function.

Domestic Capital Formation

One who really takes the Smith-Keynes consumption thesis seriously might well argue that consumption is the *only* end use that national income accounting should recognize. On this theory, as suggested above, General Motors's purchase of a new factory would be accounted as an end use of products only gradually over time, as the factory is consumed bit by bit in the form of Chevrolets or some other consumer goods. The judgment of virtually all national income experts, however, is that such an end-use concept would be too restrictive. It would show a decline in national income and product whenever resources were shifted from the production of consumer goods to the production of capital goods, and few of us would regard this as a fair representation of the economy's current accomplishment. Moreover, by leaving current investment out of the national accounts, a consumption-only concept of end use would disguise a volatile area of demand that most economists regard as especially instrumental in causing business fluctuations.

Thus the case for making capital formation an end-use category is overwhelming. But once again, there are some difficult issues of specific definition. In particular, there is the paper-clip problem of a few pages back. In principle, the difference between an automobile manufacturer's purchase of paper clips and its purchase of machinery or buildings seems to be only one of degree. But business accounting normally makes a distinction between them, treating one as a current-expense item and the other as a capital-expense item. Moreover, economists traditionally have regarded the durability of most investment goods as a partial explanation of the wide variability in investment spending. So, here again, national income accounting converts a difference in degree into one of kind: purchases of capital goods are defined as those nonhousehold purchases of goods which are not bought for physical resale *and* are of a minimum specified durability. In United States national income accounting, a commodity must be expected to have a useful life of at least one year to qualify as a capital good. Purchases of less durable items are classified as business expenses.

So defined, capital goods purchases, of course, include residential construction expenditures as well as the plant and equipment expenditures that actual business enterprises make. The bulk of domestic capital formation, or domestic investment, takes the form of such capital goods spending. To complete the category, any net change in inventories must be (algebraically) added.

Net Exports

National income accountants include this item in their definition of end use for the reason already explained—namely, to make the end-use tabulation a valid measure of domestic production. If their purpose were simply to round out a meaningful concept of domestic *end use* itself, then domestic consumption plus domestic capital formation would fill the bill (assuming, for the moment, that both of these include public as well as private expenditures). Given this definition, the accounts for the kingdom of Swat for the year 19XX might look like this:

(In millions of corona)

Resources		Use of resources	
Total national production	225	Domestic consumption	170
Less: Total exports	−50	*Plus:* Domestic capital	
Plus: Total imports	25	formation	30
Equals: Total resources available for use	200	*Equals:* Total use of resources	200

Or, consolidating the import-export items, the figures would be:

(In millions of corona)

Resources		Use of resources	
Total national production	225	Domestic consumption	170
Net exports	−25	Domestic capital formation	30
Total resources available for use	200	Total use of resources	200

This is not, however, the way the national income accountants show the figures, because the totals do not represent total *output*. To provide a production-oriented accounting system, the data are shown as follows:

(In millions of corona)

National product measured by value of production		National product measured by end-user expenditures	
		Domestic consumption	170
		Domestic capital formation	30
		Net exports	25
Total national production	225	Total end-user purchases	225

The figures on the right-hand side of this table show domestic consumption of domestically produced *and imported* goods and services, and the same for capital expenditures and for foreign purchases of domestic output *less imported* goods and services (which have already been counted in the first two categories). Thus we have, on the left-hand side of the table, gross national product (the value of total output) and on the right-hand side, gross national expenditure (total expenditures for that output).

END USE BY GOVERNMENTS

Governments, at least according to democratic philosophies, are simply agents of the people; and one of their important roles is that of purchasing agent. Through them we buy all manner of things—military services, police protection, roads, public schools, flood control, national parks and monuments, labor-relations regulation, etc.—which, via our political processes, we have decided we want but which we feel it would be impossible, infeasible, inefficient, or undesirable to buy for ourselves individually or privately. Since, in almost all countries, the volume of such collective or communal wants is large and their urgency high relative to other wants, the national government usually is the biggest single purchaser in the economy. In principle, it might be argued that this need not disturb the consumption-plus-investment definition of end use. All that is theoretically necessary for the validity of the definition is to make consumption include the things we consume collectively through government purchase, as well as what we consume individually through private purchase, and to make domestic capital formation include public as well as private additions to the economy's stock of productive assets.

In practice, however, such an effort to consolidate government purchases into the consumption and investment categories would run into many difficulties. In the case of many government purchases it is very hard to say whether they should be classified as consumptionlike or investmentlike expenditures. (Note that the criterion that usually decides the issue in the private sector of the economy—Is the buyer a household or a business?—cannot be used here.) Should expenditures for highways, for example, be classified as an investment expenditure, as are the trucks bought by business, or a consumption expenditure, as are automobiles bought by consumers? Actually, because the decision-making process in government is so different from that of business or consumers, it is useful for analytical purposes to segregate the whole government-financed portion of end-user purchases, or "final demand," a synonym we shall be using increasingly in the pages that follow. Accordingly, this is the usual practice of national accounting systems. Two further issues remain:

1. Are *all* government expenditures to be regarded as final demand? Here we need to differentiate between government, in general, and business enterprises owned and operated by government. With regard to the first, there are three parts to the answer. First, we should clearly apply the same rule to government expenditures that we apply to private consumption and capital expenditures, namely, to preserve the identity of expenditures and output by including only purchases of currently produced goods and services. Government purchases of existing fixed assets (excluding land) from the other sectors (business, persons, etc.) are included in the total of government purchases, but they are offset by negative entries in the accounts of the selling sectors, so that total expenditures (GNE) will not be affected.[7] Also excluded are government transfer payments, such as pensions and unemployment compensation, which are not paid for current production but for some other reason. In the United States, we also exclude government interest payments, which, as discussed in the next chapter, are treated as analogous to transfer payments.

Second, should we rule out certain public expenditures on the ground that they are wasteful or that they are an unproductive "necessary evil," as in case of war expenditures? Here, the sensible estimator, just as he accepts the rule of the market in the matter of most private spending, does not try to appraise the usefulness or value of expenditures made through the political process.

In practice, the same judgment is reached concerning a third category of possible exclusions. It can be contended that some things that governments buy contribute to end use only indirectly, when the value they add is incorporated into final products marketed by private business. For example, what

[7] Similarly, government sales of fixed assets (excluding land) are a negative entry in government purchases of goods and services, and are offset by positive entries in the accounts of the buying sectors. This treatment of transfers of existing assets among sectors was introduced in the 1965 revision of the national income accounts.

about government spending for making highways thick enough to carry heavy trucks, paid for by somebody's taxes? Is it not double counting to include such expenditures under "government," and then include the full value of the final consumer products, the price of which presumably is enough to cover the tax costs of providing the government services (heavier highways in our example)? Should not such government purchases be classified as intermediate, not final, products, and be excluded from the end-use tabulation? Theoretically, the better answer may be Yes. But in practice the answer is No, since the errors introduced in trying to single out such items and in calculating their value contributions to private products would exceed the error involved when they are treated as end use by government.

2. Government enterprises present a special problem. Some government agencies operate very much like private businesses in that most or all of their costs are met out of revenues from the sale of wares, e.g., electric power or local transport, which they market. Most or all of the current expenses of such government enterprises, obviously, are for intermediate products—for goods or services incorporated into the products the agencies market, just as in the case of private enterprise. And, like current expenses of private business, these purchases should be excluded from a tabulation of final demand. If such government enterprises are to be merged (statistically) with the rest of the government sector, their current expenses therefore must be deducted from total government purchases of goods and services if a measure of government final demand is sought. Alternatively, government enterprises might be wholly consolidated into the private business sector. In this case, it should be noted, their current expenses would automatically be eliminated from final demand, but their capital expenditures would be included in private domestic investment. A third possibility, if the importance of government enterprises warrants it, is to break them out as an independent sector, distinct from both general government enterprises and private enterprises, eliminating their current expenses from final demand but including as a separate component of final demand the "investment by government enterprises."

This is one of the many issues each national accounting system must thresh out to its own satisfaction. In the United States, partly because of the relatively small size of government enterprise in this country and partly because of the difficulties we have in unraveling revenue sources, business and nonbusiness objectives, and profits and subsidies in those public enterprises we do have, the National Income Division has adopted a kind of mongrel practice. Government enterprises are treated as private business in most respects; thus their current expenses are excluded from government purchases of goods and services. But their *capital* expenditures are included in government purchases, not in private domestic investment; and their profits, or "current surpluses," are treated as government revenue, not as business income. This is a kind of eat-your-cake-and-have-it-too proposition. It preserves the validity of government purchases of goods and services as a final demand component; and, at the same time, it facilitates an evaluation of total government financial operations within a national income framework. But the logic of the practice is a bit tortured.

THE DEFINITIONAL FRAMEWORK: A SUMMARY

The basic conceptual framework of national income accounting has now been set forth. It can be summarized in the following propositions or conventions:

1. The total flow of economic activity in a country during an accounting period can be calculated in three ways: by valuing output, by summing up incomes received, and by totaling use of goods and services as measured by expenditures on final products (or end-user purchases).

2. These three measures are defined in such fashion that they are conceptually equal.

3. Of the three, the controlling measure is the value of domestic production. Accordingly, the national income concept is restricted to payments for current output; and the tabulation of end-user expenditures is adjusted (notably in the cases of inventory change and net exports) to become an alternative measure of domestic production.

4. In order to eliminate double counting, however, the controlling production concept is restricted to the output of end-use items (or final products). This is the result whether the production total actually is reached by tabulating the full value only of the final products produced or by tabulating the values added by all producers.

5. End uses of domestic production are defined as domestic consumption, domestic investment (including inventory change), and net purchases of goods and services by foreigners—if end use by government can be classified as either consumption or investment. In practice, the breakdown is likely to be personal consumption expenditures, private domestic investment, net exports, and government purchases of goods and services.

6. Since the purpose is to measure economic activity, only marketed output, generally speaking, is counted; and usually it is valued at market prices. But all national accounting systems make a number of specific, commonsensical exceptions to this rule when the available standards for imputing values to nonmarketed output are not excessively arbitrary.

THREE STATISTICAL ROUTES TO THE SAME TARGET

The propositions just recited summarize adequately the topic of this chapter, "The General Architecture of National Income Accounting." The discussion to this point, however, has been too exclusively architectural to be left where it stands. For it may have created the impression that national accounting is a largely abstract, structural affair in which the only real problems are those of definition. Actually, a national income system is, above all, a procedure or activity in which facts are assembled and marshaled. A system's logical structure and definitions have meaning only as they are adaptable to a program of current and continuing statistical reporting. Thus it will be well to conclude this survey of national methodology on an operational note.

So far, the global measures of economic activity around which our discussion has revolved—production, income, and expenditure—have been treated simply as conceptual alternatives. But they are much more than that. Drawing upon quite different factual sources, they mark out distinct statistical routes which national income estimators may follow to reach their assigned objective. The variety of approaches open to the estimator has a number of (mostly helpful) consequences. It offers a country that is starting a national accounting system a choice of models to fit its (usually weak) budget of primary economic data. This choice facilitates an earlier development of reasonably respectable national income estimates than would be possible if a complete array of production, income, and expenditure data had to be built up before any global estimate could be made. In countries with more advanced national accounting, the variety of approaches permits the making of two or more independent estimates that can be used to cross-check each other. Finally, the alternative approaches automatically produce very different classifications or breakdowns of economic activity, which, if sometimes confusing in juxtaposition, nevertheless greatly enrich the detailed picture of the economy that national income series provide.

FACT-GATHERING ALTERNATIVES

One of the most gallant national accounting attempts ever made, considering its timing and circumstances, was that which the government of South Korea initiated during the depths of the Korean War in December, 1951. In the short run, the effort was unsuccessful—the odds against it were too great. But the estimating program the Korean authorities instituted at that time, largely untutored as they were in national income matters and without benefit of much foreign kibitzing, nicely illustrates how naturally national accounting subdivides into different statistical enterprises.

As soon as the Korean Minister of Finance had secured the establishment of an interagency National Income Committee, he divided it into three agency teams. The Office of Planning was told to build up an estimate of 1951 national income out of production data; the Tax Bureau of the Ministry of Finance was to make an independent estimate by income payments; and the Bank of Korea's research staff was to make a third estimate by what they called the "consumption" (or expenditures-on-final-products) approach.[8]

Thereupon, each of the teams steered off into its own factual province.

[8] The subsequent Korean experience suggests that to carry the division of labor, as they did, to the point of actual interagency competition may inject excessive rivalry and even political manipulations into the estimating effort. But the story still aptly illustrates the alternative-routes principle.

The production group dug into crop estimates, data on manufacturing output, and other production figures collected by the government's agricultural and commerce ministries, by trade associations, and by government enterprises. The group tried to determine the value of output in the various industrial sectors of the economy and then to screen out the purchases from other sectors in order to sum up values added. The income group, meanwhile, tried to build up estimates of wage payments, farm incomes, business profits, and other incomes from the base of the government's tax records. The bank group struggled with the relatively thankless job (in Korea) of making a direct esti-mate of end-user purchases from available data on retail and capital goods sales, from newly instituted consumer budget surveys, and from the govern-ment's budgetary documents.

The same division of labor would be appropriate in any other country, although the promise of the alternative approaches would depend heavily upon the nature of local statistical resources. In Korea, for example, and in other countries whose economies and economic statistics both are underdeveloped, the value-of-production route usually has the best chance of early success. This is because physical output data for agriculture, fisheries, forestry, mining, and manufacturing are apt to be among the first economic series to become reasonably extensive and trustworthy. The direct estimation of consumption, on the other hand, is likely to be extremely difficult because of the scantiness of retail sales reporting, the large number of extremely small retailers who have no fixed place of business, and the large amount of consumption that occurs outside the monetized market. Moreover, in such countries as well as in many considerably more advanced economies in which tax enforcement is lax, an income payments type of national income estimation may be completely infeasible, either because of an uncertainly large volume of nonmonetary-in-kind incomes or because of the unreliability of tax data.

In the United States, by way of contrast, relatively accurate income tax reporting plus the existence of highly accurate payroll data collected under the social security system make income payments a quite reliable avenue to a global estimate. The availability of these data, together with extensive sales information for estimating final demand, has reduced the value-of-output approach to an almost subsidiary position in the national accounts. Thus, to repeat a point already made, the route options allow national accounting both to make a beginning with very meager primary data and to take advantage of all additional information that comes to hand. Moreover, to add a point, the existence of alternative routes sometimes permits a detour from one approach to another, and then back again, around statistical blank spots that otherwise would block completion of an estimate.

THE OPPORTUNITY FOR CROSS-CHECKING

A country that is able, as a regular matter, to make at least two of the independent calculations of national income that the alternative approaches permit, automatically acquires an invaluable insight into the reliability of its estimating procedures. Since even the best source materials are imperfect and even the most scientific estimating procedures include some arbitrary judgments, no isolated national income estimate can be completely accurate. But when two or more independent calculations arrive at approximately the same figure, one can be much more confident of the result. It is always possible, of course, that the errors in one estimate could be of just the same magnitude and sign as in the other; but this is unlikely.

Somewhat paradoxically, therefore, an entry labeled "statistical discrepancy"—reporting the amount by which two separate calculations of national income miss each other—is one of the most reassuring things that can be found in any system of national accounts. Of course, it is more reassuring to find a small reported discrepancy than a large one. But even a sizable one is better than none, for the latter simply evidences a lack of any cross-checking calculation at all.[9]

It is surprising how often these very simple points escape analysts. In the United States, for example, it is not uncommon to hear the significance of our national income series ridiculed because they frequently show a statistical discrepancy of, say, $3 billion. The fact is that a statistical discrepancy averaging less than 1 percent of gross national product is one of the United States system's hallmarks of comparative reliability.[10]

[9] By referring to a single statistical discrepancy, this paragraph implies that only two of the national income calculations are made independently of each other. This is the practice in the United States where, as will be discussed in the next chapter, two of the three possible approaches are merged. A system in which all three were pursued independently would, of course, have to show two statistical discrepancies, i.e., between the result of approach A and approach B and between A and C (the discrepancy between B and C being determined by the other two).

[10] The foregoing comments assume that the statistical discrepancy has not been calculated by a method which one of the authors once encountered in South Korea. On this occasion, at a time when national income accounting there was virtually nonexistent, a bright, enterprising young civil servant in one of the ministries produced a handwritten sheet of paper which showed a whole array of precise figures for the latest year's gross national product, net national product, national income, and a great many intermediate magnitudes. One of the latter was a figure for "statistical discrepancy," which was detailed down to the last *won* (the *won* then being worth about one twenty-thousandth of a dollar). When asked how in the world he had determined that, he replied, "Oh—same per cent of GNP as in the United States."

Subfootnote: That is a joke. If you did not laugh, reread the chapter.

3

THE UNITED STATES
NATIONAL INCOME
SYSTEM

Of all the official national accounting enterprises in the world, the American is one of the more accurate, the oldest, and probably the most elaborate. It takes thirty full-time professionals in the National Income Division of the U.S. Department of Commerce Office of Business Economics to man the system; and they, in turn, draw upon thousands of other people from the other divisions in the Office of Business Economics, in the Department of Commerce generally, and in the scores of public and private agencies that gather the source data from which our national income series are derived.

The Division's handiwork may strike you as a little overwhelming when you start digging into the official statements describing and defining the system.[1] The United States national accounting scheme, however, is no more

---

[1] The official bible of national income accounting has been the 1954 *National Income Supplement to the Survey of Current Business,* and the 1958 *U.S. Income and Output* which supplements the 1954 publication. The August, 1965, *Survey of Current Business* describes most, but not all, of the changes made in the 1965 revision of the national income accounts. The National Income Division plans to publish a document that will replace all three of these publications, but at this writing, no publication date has been set.

than a variant of the basic, skeletal system described in Chapter 2. Much of the similarity—and the difference—is apparent when you compare Figure 3–1, which outlines the United States system, with Figure 2–1 in the previous chapter.

MAJOR CHARACTERISTICS OF THE UNITED STATES SYSTEM

Like any specific accounting system, the Commerce Department's mode of national accounting has many peculiarities. But the chief distinguishing characteristics of the United States system can be grouped under just four headings: (1) its modification of the route relationships among the three converging concepts of total economic activity, (2) its treatment of gross and net measures of total activity, (3) the way it defines what might be called national income proper (this involves, among other things, the difference between the "factor-cost" and "market-price" concepts of aggregate income), and (4) its appendage of two related personal income series to its national income and national product measures. We shall take up these matters in sequence.

ROUTE RELATIONSHIPS

In Chapter 2, we examined three alternative routes to a measure of a nation's total output: production, income, and expenditures. In the United States, our supply of primary production, income, and expenditure data may eventually permit the operation of this kind of national accounting system— one, that is, which produces three statistically independent measures of the same national income and product aggregate. Our Department of Commerce estimators, however, do not do things quite that way.

Instead, as Figure 3–1 indicates, for calculation purposes, they merge route 1 (production) and route 2 (income). The Department of Commerce recognizes the conceptual difference between income or product by industry (i.e., by industrial origin) and income by type of income (i.e., by distributive shares) and publishes both of these breakdowns of United States national income. But the totals they add up to are a statistical identity. The total net national income at factor costs (usually called simply national income) emerges from a *single calculation process* employing both value-of-output and income payments data. There is no statistical discrepancy at this point, because, although two routes are used, they are used simultaneously to reach a single total.

This practice, of not preparing a separate, independent estimate of total output per se (i.e., by industrial origin) is often a source of confusion to students of national income accounting. "Output calls the tune," we have said. And where conceptual reconciliations are required, they shall be made

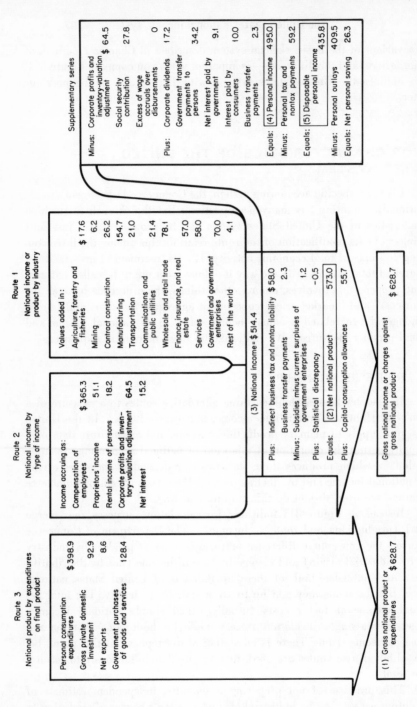

Figure **3-1.** The United States national income system showing illustrative data for 1964. (In billions of dollars. Details will not necessarily add to totals because of rounding.) Read "plus" and "minus" in the direction of the arrows. Note: Personal outlays = PCE (route 3) plus interest paid by consumers plus net foreign transfers by persons. Source: *Survey of Current Business,* U.S. Department of Commerce, August, 1965.

in such a fashion as to preserve the identity between total output (which is controlling), total income, and total expenditures. Yet there is no complete series on GNP built up from production (value-added) data. Furthermore, as Figure 3–1 shows, the statistical discrepancy is introduced in the combined route 1–2 calculation to bring the total into line with the total of route 3 (expenditures). This looks very much as though expenditures were controlling, and the output figures are adjusted to bring them into line with total expenditures.

The answer to this seeming paradox is that output *is* controlling conceptually. The accounts are so designed that the total, whichever route is used, conceptually should add up to total output. Theoretically, there should be no discrepancy between the totals. But in the world of statistical reality, the figures are imperfect and of varying quality. Probably the best and most accurate *measure* of total output that we have is the sum of expenditures defined to fit this conceptual framework. Further, the expenditures figures are the ones most widely used, often without reference to the other two series, and it would be an inconvenience to users to have to worry about the statistical discrepancy every time they worked with the figures. For these reasons, the statistical discrepancy is added (algebraically) in calculating the total derived from the combined route 1–2 calculation to make it equal to the total of route 3.

In 1962, the Department of Commerce initiated publication[2] of a series of *gross* national income by industrial origin. This new breakdown was developed by adding to the figures on national income by industrial origin a proration of the items that are added (algebraically) in going from national income to gross national income (see the lower half of the arrow for routes 1 and 2 in Figure 3–1). Because this new series is calculated in this way, it is *not* a new route 1 measure of GNP, independent of route 2. But it does reveal, or permit computation of, much useful information about the nation's productive process.

THE GROSS-NET DISTINCTION

The terms "gross" and "net" have a good many particular meanings in economic and business usage, and at least two of them might be adopted by national accountants. For one thing, gross output, or gross product, could mean the summation of the total values of industry-by-industry output before duplicative interindustry purchases had been netted out. This, as we have seen, is not the case; the United States national income accounts are not *that* gross.

---

[2] See Martin L. Marimont, "GNP by Major Industries," *Survey of Current Business*, U.S. Department of Commerce, vol. 42, no. 10, pp. 6–18, October, 1962, and "GNP by Major Industries, 1958–62 Revised and Updated," *Survey of Current Business*, U.S. Department of Commerce, vol. 43, no. 9, pp. 9–10, September, 1963.

Instead, in United States national accounting, the gross-net distinction refers to whether or not a series, in measuring the economy's accomplishment during a period, nets out the wear and tear on the country's existing stock of private capital goods. If this consumption of existing capital is deducted from income and product, the series is net; if not, it is gross.

The United States gross national product is gross because it includes *gross* private domestic investment. The latter is an estimate of all private capital formation outlays (as defined in Chapter 2) without any deduction for that portion of the stock of capital used up in the course of producing the current period's output. United States national accounting affords no direct estimate of the volume of capital consumption and, hence, no estimate of the portion of the gross investment total that should be counted as replacement.[3] By the same token, we have no direct measure of *net* private domestic investment. The reasons are practical ones. Although American economists and statisticians are devoting a good deal of energy to the problem, they have yet to agree on a satisfactory technique for making a comprehensive estimate of the actual wear and tear, obsolescence, destruction, and accidental losses of physical capital that occur throughout the economy during any given accounting period.[4]

In theory, our lack of trustworthy techniques for estimating net private domestic investment is a significant deficiency. If our interest in capital formation concerns the impact of capital formation upon productive capacity, expansion investment is, by definition, the thing that concerns us. A net-investment series obviously would provide a much cleaner statistical tool for such analytical purposes than a gross-investment series does. If, however, the rate of capital exhaustion and hence the (unidentified) replacement part of gross investment maintains a fairly steady proportionate relationship to

---

[3] The difficulty of measuring replacement investment often is described as that of sorting out, in the particular investment programs of particular firms, those projects or portions of projects which should be counted as expansion investment from those which should be designated as replacement. It is pointed out that business purchase records ordinarily do not make the distinction and that, in fact, many projects are mixtures in this respect. While this is perfectly true, it is not the real issue so far as the measurement of aggregate replacement investment is concerned. Considering the economy's capital stock as a whole, the amount of gross investment to be counted as replacement is the amount needed to offset current deterioration in the total stock of capital, whether or not capital is replaced in the particular locales where it is consumed. Aggregate replacement investment can differ from actual capital consumption only in instances where consumption exceeds replacement—in periods, that is, when there is a net decline in the stock capital.

[4] For a discussion of and limited attack on this problem, see Donald G. Wooden and Robert C. Wasson, "Manufacturing Investment since 1929 in Relation to Employment, Output and Income," *Survey of Current Business*, U.S. Department of Commerce, vol. 36, no. 11 pp. 8–20, November 1956; and George Jaszi, Robert C. Wasson, and Lawrence Grose, "Expansion of Fixed Business Capital in the United States," *Survey of Current Business*, U.S. Department of Commerce, vol. 42, no. 11, pp. 9–18 and 28, November, 1962.

total output, the error involved in relating changes in gross investment to changes in output would be uniform and therefore not very significant.

In any case, the aspect of investment that often interests us in business conditions analysis is not investment's future capacity-creating effect but rather its current demand effect, i.e., its impact as a component of current total spending. From this point of view, replacement expenditures are just as consequential as expansion expenditures. On balance, therefore, our lack in this country of a net private domestic investment series (and hence, strictly speaking, of a net national product series) need not be mourned excessively.

But how is it, in view of what has just been said, that series 2 in Figure 3–1 is labeled *"net* national product . . ."? The answer is that American business, in distributing the revenues it receives from sales, characteristically does make an accounting provision for the capital replacement problem. It allocates a portion of gross revenues to depreciation reserves; and on the receipts, or income payments, side of the United States national income system, the sum of these business depreciation charges is accepted as indicative of the gross-net difference.

Business' charges to depreciation reserves constitute the great bulk of the item called "capital-consumption allowances," which the Department of Commerce deducts from GNP to get what it terms, when it is using words carefully, *"charges against* net national product," rather than simply "net national product."

It must be emphasized that capital-consumption allowances for a given period bear no necessary relationship to actual capital consumption in the same period. The allowances, i.e., depreciation charges, are based upon arbitrary formulas that often have little relationship to the actual length of life of particular assets and ordinarily pay no attention to the exent of their use in a given year. Also, after periods of significant price change, business' depreciation accounting often is bound, partly by tax laws, to outmoded valuations of existing assets which cause serious understatements or overstatements of the present replacement cost of current capital consumption.

All the same, our United States national accountants feel that, as a representation of the gross-net difference, business' capital-consumption allowances are better than nothing. They do, at least, have a very real impact upon the distribution of total income payments. For if they were not withheld from net income as a reserve for future capital replacement, they would accrue to other private and (via taxes) public accounts in a way that might cause a considerable change in the pattern of total spending.

CALCULATION OF NATIONAL INCOME PROPER

It already has been established that *the* national income (NI), in the specialized sense in which the Department of Commerce uses the term, is net of capital-consumption allowances. But it is also net of certain other charges.

These other adjustments are all necessitated by the concept of national income the Commerce Department employs: "National income is the aggregate earnings of labor and property which arise from the current production of goods and services by the Nation's economy. Thus, it measures the total factor costs of the goods and services produced by the economy."[5] On the surface, there is nothing surprising about this official Commerce definition; it limits national income to income actually earned by the factors of production by current production of goods and services. What gives it a somewhat specialized quality, however, is the restriction of the factors of production—"labor and property"—to *private* persons or agencies. Conceptually, government *could* be defined as a factor of production, which produces certain services and earns income (tax revenues). In the national income accounts, however, government per se is not defined as a productive factor and hence cannot be treated as a direct recipient of the national income.[6]

The focus upon the earnings of private productive factors has two consequences. It means, first, that Commerce's basic breakdown of the distributive shares into which the national income is divided is on a before-tax, before-transfer basis. It is not a breakdown of disposable receipts after taxes and transfers. Government is the biggest single spender of the national income, but it is not shown as a receiver; similarly, government transfer payments are a major source of the receipts out of which private individuals make their expenditures, but these cannot be shown as part of the income shares received by these individuals since the latter did not earn them with current output. As a record of the legally entitled earned accruals to private accounts, United States national income by type of income consequently is of only limited economic significance or analytical interest. For most purposes, it needs to be recast on an after-tax, after-transfer basis. We shall return to this point in the next chapter.

Second, the restriction of national income to the earnings of private productive factors necessitates the so-called market-price versus factor-cost adjustments, which are adjustments appearing between national income and charges against net national product in the route 1–2 column of Figure 3–1. In the simplified economy discussed in the previous chapter, the receipts from production, i.e., income payments to productive factors, must equal the sales of production, i.e., product by expenditures on final product. If so, the market-price and factor-cost valuations of total income and product would be identical. In an actual economy such as the United States, however, some

---

[5] *National Income, 1954 Edition: A Supplement to the Survey of Current Business,* U.S. Department of Commerce, 1954, p. 58. The definition was not changed in the 1965 revision of the national income accounts, although definitions of some of the items going into national income were changed.

[6] Qualification: As a consequence of the way in which interest is treated in the national income accounts, interest and dividends *received* by government, because they are paid by business, are reflected in national income. See the Appendix to this chapter.

elements of market prices never accrue to the accounts of private producers, and some earnings of private producers do not originate in any markets. The Department of Commerce recognizes four such discrepancies.

Indirect Taxes

Whether a tax is direct or indirect depends on its incidence. It is direct if the burden of the tax actually falls on the person or business from whom the tax is collected. On the other hand, if a business can successfully shift a tax to its customers by adding it to the selling prices of its products, the tax is indirect. There is an ancient debate among economists about how different taxes should be classified in this regard, and the National Income Division has wrestled with the issue. In 1947, for example, it altered its practice with respect to corporate income taxes, switching them from the indirect to the direct category. The point for our purposes, however, is that the Division does have a list of taxes that it regards as indirect—notably sales taxes, excises, and the real property taxes paid by business. These are assumed to be—and presumably are—included in the market prices paid by end users and are therefore included in the tabulations of GNP measured by expenditures. However, Commerce feels that they should be excluded from the national income at factor costs. The rationale for the latter practice is that indirect taxes are not factor costs; the businesses from whom they are collected simply serve as collection agencies for Federal, state, and local governments. They therefore have no place in a national income total composed solely of private earnings.

Current Surpluses of Government Enterprises

The profits of government marketing activities, such as local transit authorities, electric power authorities, and the Post Office, pose exactly the same kind of adjustment problem as do indirect taxes. On the one hand, since these profits arise from sales revenues, they obviously are included in a total-expenditures-at-market-price measure of total activity. On the other hand, since they are governmental rather than private accruals, they cannot be included in a national income figure that (with the exception footnoted earlier) is restricted, by definition, to private earnings. So, in the United States accounts, they must be added in going from national income to gross national product.

Government Subsidies to Private Business

American governments, particularly the Federal government, extend a number of monetary subsidies to business firms that, for one reason or another, the law says do not earn so much as they should from ordinary market transactions. Such payments are made, for example, to the merchant marine, air carriers, and farmers who do not redeem crop loans made under the farm price support program.[7]

These monetary subsidies to business bear a close resemblance to government transfer payments to individuals. The latter appear neither in GNP nor in national income. They are screened out of government purchases of goods and services because they are not payments for any current output purchased by government, and they are excluded from national income because they are not income earned by the recipients. On the expenditures side of the GNP tabulation, the same thing applies to subsidies to business; they are not purchases of goods and services, and therefore are excluded from government expenditures. On the national income side, however, the Commerce Department treats subsidies differently from transfer payments. It reasons, in effect, that the market is wrong and that our political authorities are right in their allotment of income to subsidized firms, and hence to the factors of production. Thus subsidies are treated as *earned* private incomes, just like the rest of national income. Because they are included in national income, but not in GNP, it is necessary to deduct the total of such subsidies in going from NI to GNP.

Subsidies sometimes are distributed to private businesses in the form of intentional (or sometimes unintentional) losses in the operations of government enterprises. Because of the difficulty of sorting out private subsidies from public surpluses in such cases, the National Income Division combines national income's exclusion of the current surpluses of government enterprises and its inclusion of government subsidies to private business into a single adjustment entry. This is called "subsidies minus the current surpluses of government enterprises" and is subtracted when one is moving from national income to GNP and added when the adjustments are being made in the opposite direction. The typically small size of the item does not mean that either subsidies or government enterprise surpluses are insignificant; it means only that the two usually just about stand each other off.

[7] The subsidies which appear in United States national accounting as an adjustment item between GNP and national income, i.e., those subsidies under discussion here, cover only a minority of all the government-engineered subsidies in the American economy, if "subsidies" is to be understood in the broad sense which economists often give it—namely, a shift of income from other groups to a particular favored industry or group, the shift being caused by government interference with the market's allocation of incomes. This definition of subsidies is a troublesome one because some of the markets that government conditions are also conditioned by other arbitrary institutional forces, and it is hard to see why government should be singled out as the interloper. But if we accept this definition, then probably the two largest subsidies in the United States are those created by the protective tariff and by the impact of the farm price support program upon the market prices of farm commodities. But neither of these involves direct government payments to producers. Only the latter variety of subsidies appears as such in the national accounts.

Business Transfer Payments

In 1965, $2.3 billion of the difference between United States net national product and national income fell under this heading. The two major types of such transfers from businesses to persons are corporate gifts to non-profit institutions and consumer bad debts. In addition, the category covers personal injury payments by business to others than employees, unrecovered thefts of cash and other assets from business, and the cash prizes that firms give away in such promotional activities as television and radio contests. All these things are gifts by business (some intentional, others, like bad debts, quite unintentional) to persons (nonprofit institutions being regarded as such in the United States system) for which no reciprocal value is received. Since all are paid out of business sales revenues, they represent charges against gross and net national product. But since their recipients do not earn them, they are excluded from national income. They must therefore be added in going from NI to GNP.

The Related Personal Income Series

As Figure 3–1 is drawn to suggest, the personal income portion of the United States national income system is an addendum to the basic national accounting structure outlined in the previous chapter. But the calculation of the personal and disposable personal income series is an integral part of the work of the National Income Division; and, for purposes of business conditions analysis, they are two of its most useful products.

"Persons," as Commerce uses the word, includes everybody and everything that receive claims against the economy's output, except governments and corporations. In the latter respect, you will note, the usage differs from legal terminology in which corporations are treated as persons. When the national accountant says "persons," he is thinking of human individuals and probably even of individual consumers or households; but the category (in this country) spreads somewhat wider than this. It includes individuals in their roles not only as consumers or householders but also as unincorporated businessmen, since, for national income purposes, we have not succeeded in disentangling the household and business accounts of the great mass of retailers, self-employed professional people, farmers, and other individual entrepreneurs. Moreover, besides individuals, the term "persons" also includes nonprofit institutions, such as private colleges and hospitals, private trust funds, and private pension, health, and welfare funds.

Personal income is a somewhat curious concept. Of all the national income series, it is closest to the man in the street's idea of income. And yet, when closely examined, its definition seems rather tortured. Roughly speaking, the purpose of the definition is to encompass all before-tax income and incomelike payments actually received by the catchall class of persons, as just defined. But in the pursuit of this purpose some odd contradictions arise.

Personal income, as one would expect, includes government and business transfer payments, and, among them, the benefits paid by government pension, health, and welfare programs. But, surprisingly enough, the very similar benefits paid by private pension, health, and welfare programs are excluded on the ground that both employer and employee contributions to such private programs are counted as personal income at the time the income is earned, and the same income cannot be counted twice. Conversely, employer and employee contributions to government-operated social security funds are excluded from personal income because, as just noted, benefits are counted instead. And this last practice—although probably preferable to the opposite treatment of private pension, health, and welfare fund operations—entails a further anomaly: personal income is supposed to be a before-tax concept. But, from a practical viewpoint, the social security taxes (or "contributions") an employee pays are just as much personal taxes as are the employee's personal income, property, and other taxes included in personal income. His title to the part of his nominal pay that is withheld for social security certainly is no more tenuous than that which is withheld for the Federal income tax. Yet the latter finds its way into this before-tax income concept, while the former does not.

The treatment of corporate profits is uncomplicated. All corporate profits are included in national income, because they were "earned" by the stockholders. But corporations pay out only a portion of their profits to stockholders (persons) ; about half of the total is paid to governments as corporate profit taxes, and another portion is retained by corporations as undistributed profits. Only the remaining portion, actually paid to persons, is included in personal income.

The relationship between national income and personal income is indicated in Figure 3-1. In summary, the additions to national income are (1) government transfer payments, (2) interest payments on government debt, (3) interest payments by consumers (these two types of interest payments, as we have noted, are treated by the National Income Division as transfers rather than as earned income), and (4) business transfer payments. The deductions necessary when one is deriving personal income from national income are (1) social security contributions, (2) all the corporate profit component of national income except the part (dividends) distributed to individuals, and (3) an adjustment item, excess of wage accruals over wage disbursements. This last little technicality stems from the fact that all of Commerce's national income and product accounts are on an accrual basis, following the predominant business practice. The wage and salary component of personal income, on the other hand—following the usual thinking and practice of households— is estimated on a cash receipts basis.

The present discussion has yet to mention the greatest virtue of the personal income series. Personal income, of all of the United States national income series, is the only one calculated and reported monthly. The others are estimated, at best, only quarterly. The greater frequency in the reporting of personal income is extremely helpful in short-run business conditions analysis, since intraquarter changes in personal income frequently anticipate interquarter changes, not only in disposable personal income but also in GNP and national income. Whereas personal income is a logical derivative from national income, as Figure 3–1 indicates, the statistical sequence is the other way around; it takes less processing to get the raw income payments data that Commerce receives into personal income form than into national income form.

Disposable personal income is, analytically, one of the most valuable of all economic series; and we shall be harking back to it again and again. But with the personal income series explained, there is, at this point, no need to linger over DPI, which is simply personal income less personal taxes, fees, and so-called personal nontax payments to governments (e.g., traffic fines).

The great value of the disposable personal income series is as a measure of the spendable purchasing power individuals and other persons derive from current income. One very important consequence of the basic definition of persons should be underscored, however: DPI is not a clean-cut, exclusive measure of the purchasing power of households, for it also includes that part of unincorporated entrepreneurial income actually retained in businesses and unavailable for household disposition. But it is the best aggregative measure of spendable household income we have; and, in practice, we often treat it as such.

Persons can do four things, by Commerce's definitions, with their disposable income: (1) spend it on consumption goods and services, (2) make personal interest payments (treated by Commerce as a transfer payment), (3) give it to foreigners, such as relatives abroad (also classified as a transfer payment), and (4) save it. The sum of the first three is called "personal outlays."[8] As Figure 3–1 shows, personal saving is defined as simply the difference between disposable personal income and personal outlays. This means that a portion of personal saving, which we shall consider in the next chapter, is composed of the capital purchases of unincorporated business.

THE DETAIL OF THE COMMERCE SERIES

The principal end products of the National Income Division's handiwork are the five series that are numbered and boxed in Figure 3–1 at the beginning of the chapter, namely, gross national product (GNP), net national income (or charges against net national product) (NNI), national income (NI), personal income (PI), and disposable personal income (DPI).[9]

---

[8] A term incorporated in the national income accounts in the 1965 revision. Prior to this revision, (2) and (3) were included in (1), personal consumption expenditures.

[9] In addition to these series, the Division also produces a number of other highly valuable supporting series and special analyses.

The aggregate concepts measured by these series have already been discussed at some length, as have the relationships among them. The latter are conveniently summarized in the figure on the inside covers of this book.

Figure 3–2 supplies a timetable showing how frequently and quickly each of the series is published. On this last score, two further bits of information are noteworthy: (1) all monthly and quarterly national accounting estimates ordinarily are expressed in seasonally adjusted annual rates; and (2) each July the *National Income* issue of the *Survey of Current Business* carries a full and fairly firm array of figures for the preceding calendar year. The early estimates undergo successive revisions as more complete primary data become available. Usually, these revisions are relatively minor, especially those for the major aggregates. (This was not the case, however, in the 1965 revision.)

There is no occasion to reproduce or discuss here all the breakdowns in these five official Commerce series. Instead, this is the point at which you should, if you have not done so already, carefully examine the composition of each of them in a recent July issue of the *Survey of Current Business*.[10]

[10] In 1965, the August issue.

Where and When National Income Series Data Reported

National income series	Time period employed	Frequency of data publication✶	Publisher†	Publication‡	Time of publication
GNP	Quarter	Quarterly	CEA	*EI*	Month following quarter
			Commerce	*SCB*	Month following quarter
NNP	Quarter	Quarterly	Commerce	*SCB*	Month following quarter
NI:					
By type of income	Quarter	Quarterly	CEA	*EI*	2d month following quarter
			Commerce	*SCB*	3d or 4th month following quarter
By industrial origin	Quarter	Annually	Commerce	*SCB*	July issue of following year
PI	Month and quarter	Monthly and quarterly	Commerce	*SCB* Press release	Month following month or quarter
DPI	Quarter	Quarterly	CEA	*EI*	Month following quarter
			Commerce	*SCB*	Month following quarter

✶ All data published yearly in July issue of Department of Commerce's *Survey of Current Business*, and as indicated in column. In addition, preliminary estimates of the major series are published in the January or February issue of the *Survey of Current Business* and in the annual *Economic Report of the President*, issued in January.

† CEA=Council of Economic Advisers; Commerce = Department of Commerce.

‡ *EI = Economic Indicators; SCB = Survey of Current Business.*

Figure **3–2.** The United States national income series.

Nevertheless, for our purposes, it is desirable to examine fairly closely certain components of the United States series that are not self-explanatory, including, among the components of GNP, the exclusion of government interest payments from government purchases of goods and services and consumer interest payments from personal consumption expenditures and, among the national income components, the inventory valuation adjustments, rental income of persons, and net interest, as well as three aspects of the industrial-origin breakdown.

These are all matters that a business conditions analyst must understand if he is not to have a disturbingly fuzzy view of the United States national accounting system.   At the same time, they are matters of detail.   Pursuing them adequately at this point might so interrupt the exposition as to obscure the overview of the system we are principally interested in establishing.   Thus the items listed have been relegated to the Appendix to this chapter.   Careful readers, however, should not avoid them for that reason.

SPECIAL FEATURES OF THE UNITED STATES ACCOUNTS

This discussion of national accounting is addressed to prospective consumers, not producers, of national income data.   Any reader who seeks a career as a national income estimator eventually will need to spend a great deal of time studying the whole question of where the National Income Division gets, and how it processes, its primary data.   This is an extremely complex subject.   The official accounts of the estimating procedures and sources involve such things as the particular uses made of census, tax, social security, wage-and-hour, sales, and inventory data and the nature of such estimating techniques as the "commodity-flow" method for gauging most consumer goods expenditures.   The subject, moreover, does not invite generalizations if one wants a professional knowledge of it.

Fortunately for our present purposes, the subject of national income sources and estimating methods is not one about which a user of the series needs to have a professional knowledge.   About all he needs—beyond the kind of general appreciation of the national accounting job that the last chapter tried to convey—is some sense of the statistical quality of the major components of the series and a working understanding of two special features of the United States technique.   One of the latter is the Commerce Department's use of a "national accounts" format in assembling its data.   The other concerns the imputations which its estimating process entails.

THE NATIONAL INCOME AND PRODUCT ACCOUNTS

No member of the United States National Income Division would have gotten this far in an exposition of national income accounting without mentioning the "national income and product accounts," published under the heading "Summary Data" in the annual (July) national income number of the *Survey of Current Business*. These five accounts, which should not be confused with the five-member family of national income *series* that we have been studying, condense and summarize the data found in the detailed tables that follow.

Each account has a debit and a credit side, reflecting the two sides to any transaction. The first account, the national income and product account itself, is nothing new to us; it summarizes the GNP tabulation by route 2 (national income by distributive shares and the adjustment items between national income and GNP), and route 3 (GNP by expenditure categories).

The other four accounts are *sector* accounts covering persons, governments, foreign transactions, and saving-investment.[11] The first sector account summarizes the income and outlay of persons, personal income by form (wages, proprietors' income, etc.) on the credit side and the uses of that income (personal outlays, personal taxes, and personal saving) on the debit side. The second sector account summarizes government receipts, on the credit side, and the uses of those receipts (including the government surplus or deficit) on the debit side. The third sector account shows exports on the debit side, with imports, government transfer payments to foreign countries, personal transfer payments to foreigners, and "net foreign investment" as the balancing item on the credit side. The final account, the gross saving and investment account, shows the various forms of saving in the economy (personal saving, undistributed profits, capital-consumption allowances, the government surplus $(+)$ or deficit $(-)$, etc.), on the credit side, and the uses of that saving for gross private domestic investment and net foreign investment on the debit side. The statistical discrepancy is arbitrarily entered in the last account.

The national income and product accounts serve the legitimate accounting purpose of summarizing the debits and credits in the national income accounts. As such, however, they are not very useful for economic analysis purposes. For such purposes, we need a credit and debit (receipts and expenditures) arrangement of the national accounting data that meets two specifications: (1) it breaks down into the same sectors on both the receipts and the expenditures sides, and (2) it adds up into meaningful aggregates. The analyst's complaint is that the national accounts do not pass both these tests. The first (summary) national income and product account itself, which is simply a presentation of the national income series, meets the second requirement but not the first; the sector accounts are fine on the first score but

---

[11] The last account is not a sector account in the literal sense of the term. It includes the business sectors (all of which is saving-investment), but it also includes the saving and investment activities of the other sectors.

no good on the second. We shall have to wait for "The Nation's Economic Budget," a section of the next chapter, to find something that will fill the bill.

IMPUTATIONS

As Chapter 2 noted, all national accounting systems occasionally abandon the so-called rule of the market and conjure up income and product transactions that have no monetary reality. Several of the imputations practiced by the United States estimators already have been mentioned, but it will be well to set down a full list of them. A user of national income data does not need a technician's knowledge of how all the imputed estimates are made, but it is useful to him to know what they are and to have a rough notion of how much difference they make in the income and product totals. Those which the National Income Division inserts into the United States accounts fall into four groups. Each has an output and income aspect.

Payments of Wages and Salaries in Kind

Some business firms, governmental units, and private institutions furnish food, clothing, or other in-kind compensation to their employees. To reflect the full volume of a period's income and output, such compensation needs to be translated into its monetary equivalent and added, on the one hand, to the wages and salaries component of national and personal income, and, on the other, to personal consumption expenditures. In the United States series such imputations are made for food furnished to employees by government (including military) and commercial employers, meals furnished to domestic servants and nurses, employees' lodging, and standard clothing issued to military personnel.

Food and Fuel Produced and Consumed on Farms

This item has been mentioned already. It is added to business income and to personal consumption expenditures.

Rental Value of Owner-occupied Housing

Already discussed at considerable length, this imputation is by far the largest of the lot. The $39 billion that it (farm plus nonfarm) added to personal consumption expenditures in 1964 was well over half the total rental payments included in that series.[12]

---

[12] The difference between "space rental value of owner-occupied houses" in the GNP series and the imputed component of the national income series "rental income of persons" is noted in the Appendix to this chapter.

Interest Payments and Service Charges by Financial Intermediaries

A large part of the net interest component of United States national income (see the Appendix to this chapter) is imputed. The same is true of the personal business component, which you will find in a detailed breakdown of personal consumption expenditures. The reason is that the monetary transactions that persons and businesses carry on with financial intermediaries—institutions like commercial banks, investment trusts, life insurance companies, and savings and loan associations, which serve as go-betweens for conveying funds from savers to investors and for conveying back the interest paid for the use of the funds—do not, on close inspection, provide a reasonable measure of the services of those institutions.

The National Income Division treats financial intermediaries as organizations in the business of supplying *services* to their depositors, shareholders (in the case of saving and loan associations), or policyholders (in the case of life insurance companies). They lend or (in a financial sense) invest their depositors' money for them, and supply them with various other services including checking, in the case of commercial banks, and life insurance protection, in the case of life underwriters. However, instead of working as straight financial agents, who would pass along to their depositors all the interest and other income they earned on the depositors' funds and, in turn, make an explicit charge on depositors for all services rendered to them, the intermediaries typically short-circuit the process. They do not charge depositors the full costs of their service; on the other hand, they do not distribute to depositors the full earnings on the latter's funds. This is particularly true of demand deposits, for which no interest is paid. If the product of the intermediaries is to be regarded as their service to depositors (or policyholders or shareholders), this practice causes the intermediaries' monetary transactions with depositors to understate the value of the service added by the financial institutions. Accordingly, in the case of commercial banks and other financial intermediaries, the National Income Division imputes as additional interest income to persons an amount equal to the estimated value of the services rendered.[13] An exactly offsetting amount is imputed as additional service charges that the intermediaries levy on their depositors (a personal consumption expenditure).[14]

---

[13] In the case of business depositors, the imputation cancels out as far as the income and product totals are concerned. It adds to gross revenue but likewise increases the purchases from banks, which must be deducted in figuring value added.

[14] Another change involving financial intermediaries was introduced in the 1965 revision of the national income accounts. Mutual institutions (mutual life insurance companies, savings and loan associations, savings banks, credit unions, etc.) technically do not make "profits"; they simply have retained earnings which are owned by the policyholders, shareholders, etc. Prior to 1965, these earnings had been credited, in the form of imputed interest, to persons. In the revised version of the accounts, the National

SUMMARY

The great danger, in one's first encounter with the highly elaborate United States national income accounting system, is losing sight of the woods for all the trees. A fresh look at Figure 3–1 may bring the overall United States system back into sharper focus, and it will recall the route we have followed. First, we identified the major differences between the United States accounting system and the basic scheme developed in Chapter 2. These were (1) the peculiarities of the route relationships in the United States scheme, (2) the nature of the gross-net distinction the scheme employs, (3) its special definition of what we have called national income proper, which in turn led us to examine the difference between market-price and factor-cost measurements in the United States system, and (4) the appendage of personal and disposable personal income series to the national income and product structure.

Next, we reviewed the interrelationships among, and noted the publication schedule of, the five official aggregative series of the National Income Division. We left for examination in the Appendix that follows this chapter those components of the series which a novice should not be expected to figure out for himself. Last, we have considered briefly certain special features of the United States national income accounting system: (1) the national income and product accounts, which summarize the detailed accounts, and (2) the particular collection of imputations employed in the United States.

Income Division, in order to give a more accurate picture of the profitability of business enterprise, credits these institutions with profits of their own. For life insurance companies, this profit is the "net gain from operations." Additions to policy reserves are credited to policyholders as interest income. For other mutual institutions, the "profits" are equal to net operating earnings that they retain.

APPENDIX: Some Troublesome Components of the United States Series

GNP COMPONENTS

The breakdown of the United States gross national product was rather fully anticipated in Chapter 2. These notes will be confined to one aspect of the GNP series, the exclusion of government interest payments from government purchases of goods and services and of personal interest payments from personal consumption expenditures.

Interest Payments by Government and by Persons

The National Income Division's treatment of interest payments by government and by persons is controversial. Government interest payments are counted as a transferlike payment to persons, not a purchase of goods and services. Hence they are not included in GNP (GNE) or in national income. Personal interest payments similarly are not included in personal consumption expenditures but are treated as a transferlike payment from persons. Interest payments by business, on the other hand, are counted as a factor cost and are reflected in the national income accounts the same as any other factor cost.

This treatment seems to imply that interest paid by business is a reward for a service rendered, but that interest paid by government or by consumers is not. If you lend money to General Motors so that it can acquire capital equipment to produce automobiles, the interest you receive is tabulated as income earned, and therefore a part of national income. But if you lend the same money to the government to build highways, the interest income is *not* tabulated as income earned; it is not included in national income. Or if you lend the money to another person (via, say, a consumer finance company) so that he can enjoy the use of an automobile a year sooner than he could without the loan, the interest you receive is again not counted as income earned.

The National Income Division explains this anomalous treatment by looking at the effects of interest on the *payer* of interest, rather than the receiver. In the case of business, the Division says, interest should be included in GNP because it is a cost of production of current output. If interest payments should go up (e.g., owing to a rise in interest rates) with no increase in the value of the output of business, the increase would be offset by a decrease in profits. In the case of consumers and government, however, there is no profits item to provide the offset. An increase in interest paid by consumers or government, e.g., again owing to a rise in interest rates, if interest were treated as it is in the case of business, would result in an increase in GNP. Further, the Division says, in the case of business, interest can be regarded as the contribution of business capital to production. But in the case of government and consumers, debt (and hence interest payments) may be incurred without the acquisition of corresponding capital assets. There can be no presumption, therefore, of a "correspondence between government and consumer interest payments, on the one hand, and the services of government and consumer capital, on the other."

The National Income Division would agree that an increase in business interest payments resulting from a rise in interest rates should be reflected in an increase in GNP if the market value of the output of business were increased correspondingly. That is, if business passes the higher interest rates on to consumers in the form of higher prices, it is appropriate that current-dollar GNP should rise. What they object to is having interest costs *themselves*, i.e., other than those incorporated in the value of business output, reflected in GNP.

The issue raised by this treatment can be adequately answered only by a discussion of the reasons for the payment of interest. Why is interest paid? What is it a payment for? And why are interest rates higher at some times than at others? These are questions which we shall explore in some depth in Chapter 10. Suffice it for the present to say that it is the general view of economists that interest is paid for the sacrifice of liquidity and that the level of interest rates is determined (the supply of liquidity being given) by the importance attached to liquidity, i.e., by the demand for liquidity. According to this view, the person who gives up liquidity (e.g., by exchanging his bank deposit for a bond or a share of stock or a mortgage) "earns" the interest he receives. He is performing a service by giving up liquidity, and the interest paid is payment for a service rendered. It follows that a loan to a government to enable it to build highways, or to use for some other purpose *not* involving a capital asset (e.g., to finance general government), is productive, and its productivity is measured by the interest paid. Similarly, a loan to a person to buy an automobile, or simply to go on a vacation, is productive in that it enables the borrower (who *gains* liquidity) to enjoy a time utility, and again the productivity of the loan is measured by the interest paid.

Another reason provided by the National Income Division for excluding consumer and government interest payments from GNP and national income is that "the procedure is the one recommended by the United Nations and used by most countries." It clearly is desirable to have a uniform system of national income accounts, and the United States should probably not object to making minor procedural concessions in its national income accounting in the interest of international comparability.

The National Income Division recognizes, as do we, that the treatment-of-interest issue is a controversial one, but concludes that, "on balance the considerations seem to favor the change that has been made" (in the treatment of consumer interest, which, before August, 1964, was included in GNP). It should be obvious that, to the present authors, the considerations seem to lead to the opposite conclusion.[1]

NATIONAL INCOME

As already noted, the Commerce Department subdivides United States national income proper into both type-of-income and industrial-origin components. In addition, in its annual July compilation of national accounting data, it offers a third breakdown—national income by legal form of organization—which is a recasting of the type-of-income figures. Three items in both the type-of-income and industrial-origin breakdowns deserve specific comment.

The Inventory-valuation Adjustment

Strictly speaking, there are two such adjustments in the distributive shares series, one associated with the income of unincorporated enterprises and the other with corporate profits. But since the principles are the same in both cases, they can be discussed as a single item.

The inventory-valuation adjustment (IVA) is occasioned by a discrepancy between national and business accounting practices. A cardinal rule of

---

[1] See *Survey of Current Business*, U.S. Department of Commerce, August, 1965, p. 10, for a statement of the National Income Division's position on this point. The quotations above are from that source.

national income accounting is that a final-demand tabulation, like United States GNP, counts only expenditures for current production; similarly, income is limited to payments for current production. Capital gains (or losses) resulting, not from current production but from changes in prices, are not included. An implicit corollary of this rule is that current production is *valued at current prices*. The GNP item, net change in business inventories, conforms strictly with these principles. It measures the physical change in business' commodity stocks from the end of the previous period to the end of the current period, both valued in current prices.

Business firms, however, typically do not keep their books this way. Inventories are evaluated, not at current prices (i.e., replacement costs), but at some book value, usually original cost. Similarly, withdrawals from inventory are charged, not at current prices, but at the same book method of evaluation. As a consequence of this method of accounting, when businesses sell the previously inventoried item (or a product in which it is incorporated) after a period of rising prices, they make a capital gain, which shows up in their reported profits. The inventory-valuation adjustment is simply an operation that screens out this capital gain. The adjustment is necessary to prevent what is, from a national income viewpoint, business accounting's overstatement or understatement of earned profits in periods of changing prices.

A numerical example will make this clearer. Suppose a business had 1,000 physical units of inventory at the beginning of 1966, valued on its books at \$2 apiece. On January 1, 1966, the cost-price of these items became \$3. The firm used up 900 units in the course of the year's production and bought 800 more. In national income terms, the inventory change during 1966 was −100 units × \$3, or −\$300. But the change in book value, if the firm's accountants figured that the old stock was being used first and valued it at \$2 per unit, would be calculated as follows:

$$(800 \times \$3) - (900 \times \$2) = + \$600$$

On the firm's books, its end-of-year assets and consequently its book profit include \$900 [i.e., \$600 − (−\$300)], which was not the result of current production but rather was a capital gain. An inventory-valuation adjustment of *minus* \$900 is necessary. We can generalize from this, incidentally: IVA always is negative when prices have been rising and positive when they have been falling. This is because the replacement cost of withdrawals exceeds their book value in the first case and falls short of it in the second.

Now, one final point. So far, we have made no effort to identify business' book methods of inventory valuation, except to say that, in general, they tend not to value withdrawals from inventory at current prices. Actually, as you probably know, such business accounting procedures break down into a number of fairly distinct types of which fifo (first in first out) and lifo (last in first out) are the best known. The nature of the inventory-valuation adjustment sometimes is explained very roughly as "converting all inventory accounting to a lifo basis." It is true that the need for adjustment is much greater in the case of the fifo method and its variants in which, as in our numerical example, stocks used up are valued at their original cost and are assumed to be the oldest items on hand. But there is some need for adjustment even in the lifo case, because even though the newest items of stock are assumed to be those withdrawn, they too are valued at their (recent) original costs, not their (current) reproduction costs—and sometimes there is a difference.

Rental Income of Persons

This component of national income—which in 1965 accounted for 3.4 percent of the total—does not, by any means, include all the rent earned in the economy, whether "rent" is used in its practical business sense or in the specialized sense of economic theory. In brief, the rental income of *persons* (the term, you will remember, excludes corporations and governments) covers only the net rent and royalty income of persons who are *not* primarily engaged in the renting business. The rents received by individual entrepreneurs whose main business is property ownership and management are shown, after deduction for depreciation (which enters capital-consumption allowances) and mortgage interest (which enters the net interest component of national income), as profits of unincorporated enterprises. All rents received by corporations, whether or not their main business is real estate and whether or not the rents are actual or imputed, are reflected, net of costs, in corporate profits.

As a result, about half of the rental incomes of persons are the rents that are imputed to the owners of owner-occupied nonfarm houses in the manner described in Chapter 2.[2] The remainder of the category is composed of receipts from actually rented nonfarm property and from farm realty.

Net interest

The National Income Division counts only part of Americans' total receipts of interest during an accounting period as income earned in current production, and only part of the latter shows up as the net interest component of national income by distributive shares. The following figures, which are the actual data for 1964, adapted from the August, 1965, *Survey of Current Business*, will make this clearer.

---

[2] It might be noted that, because of the gross-net distinction in the United States series, the imputed rent included in personal consumption expenditures is not identical with the imputed-rent portion of the rental income of persons. The former is a gross or "space-rent" concept, which includes depreciation and other deductions excluded from the latter.

The total flow of interest payments and receipts within the American economy in 1964 can be summed up this way:

	Interest payments*	Interest receipts*
U.S. business†	(1) $60,890	(5) $46,658
U.S. persons (other than business)†	(2) 9,986	(6) 34,265
Foreigners to and from the U.S.	(3) 1,265	(7) 344
U.S. governments, net‡	(4) 9,126	(8)
Total	$81,267	$81,267

* In millions of dollars.

† While, as we already have seen, the National Income Division usually treats "business" and "persons" as overlapping concepts (as in the inclusion of unincorporated business profits as personal income, for example), here, in the interest calculations, the categories are meant to be mutually exclusive. Thus, interest payments by business include those of proprietorships, partnerships, mutual financial institutions, non-profit organizations servicing business, and personal (including own) landlords, as well as corporations. This leaves virtually only the interest on consumer debt for the payments-by-persons category. On the receipts side, business includes corporations and mutual financial institutions but excludes (and includes in the persons category) the interest receipts of all proprietorships and partnerships except those which are primarily in the moneylending business.

‡ Only a net government interest paid figure is shown in the *Survey of Current Business* since the 1965 revision.

Two deletions must be made from the total flow of interest receipts and payments to derive a measure of interest earned in current production. First, foreigners' interest receipts from the United States must be subtracted since they are not a part of current United States production.[3] Second, interest payments by governments and persons, for reasons given in the previous section, are not included. (They are included, however, in the computation of *personal* income.)

All earned interest is included in the national income but not all of it is classified as net interest. This is because, in the classifications of business income, profits take precedence over interest just as they do over rent. Thus business receipts of interest are reflected in the profits share of national income and must be deducted from the total flow of interest payments and receipts.

---

[3] Foreigners' interest receipts from the United States are a payment for services rendered by foreign capital. These receipts are, therefore, a part of current foreign production.

The preceding argument can be summed up as follows:

U.S. business:		
Interest payments	$ 60,890	
Interest receipts	−46,658	
Net interest originating in U.S. business		$14,232
Foreigners:		
Interest received from abroad	$ 1,265	
Interest paid to abroad	−344	
Net interest originating in rest of world		921
Net interest component of national income		$15,153
Plus: Interest paid by government (net)		9,126
Interest paid by consumers		9,986
Equals: Personal interest income (component of personal income)		$34,265

Note: All figures in millions of dollars.

As implied by the table, net interest may be defined either as the interest receipts of United States persons (personal interest income) less interest paid by government and consumers (net), or as the net interest paid to Americans by United States business and by the rest of the world. The Department of Commerce actually calculates the figures on the latter (payments) basis.

The Industrial-origin Breakdown

Three very brief notes will suffice here. They concern the portions of national income by "industrial" origin that do not originate in activities or places normally thought of as industries.

First, as just indicated in our reference to interest receipts by nonbusiness persons, some production and income is counted as originating in the households and nonprofit institutions of the economy, despite the United States system's exclusion of the services of housewives. This private domestic nonbusiness output, which is reflected at several points in the breakdown of national income by industrial origin but shows up clearly in the breakdown of national income by legal form of organization, consists mainly of the services of hired household and institutional employees.

Second, despite the already-noted fact that the National Income Division does not view government per se as a factor of production, it does not slander itself and others in government employ by treating government workers as nonproductive. Rather, it assumes that product and earned income originate in government to the extent of employee compensation. Looking back at Figure 3–1, you will note that this figure amounted to $70 billion in 1964. The difference between it and the $128 billion that American governments spent on goods and services that year represents their purchases from business. Note too that, for purposes of the industrial-origin classification, government enterprises fall under the government heading rather than under the various private industrial sectors to which they correspond. One reason for this is that, as with other government activities, their value added is restricted to employee compensation. You will remember that their payments of interest and earnings of profit (surplus) are screened out of the national income.

Finally, there is a tiny fraction of the earned income of Americans each year—in 1964, $4.1 billion—that does not originate in any United States business, government, or household but rather takes the form of compensation for United States factor services delivered directly to foreigners. These include wage and salary receipts from employment by foreigners and international receipts of property income: interest and corporate dividends and branch profits.

4

MORE ON SOCIAL ACCOUNTING

More than any other body of economic data, the national income series supply the quantitative vocabulary for description and analysis of modern business conditions. The fact that we have just completed a reasonably close inspection of the United States national income system, however, does not mean that we now are ready to leave the problem of business conditions measurement.

In the first place, there is a great variety of economic series which do not belong to any social accounting system but which, nonetheless, a competent analyst of the current economic situation must understand and use. He needs price data, for instance, if for no other reason than to sort out the real changes and the price changes that are blended together in all the (current price) national income figures we have considered so far. In addition, labor force, employment, unemployment, working hours, and wage rate series; monetary and credit statistics; and various sales, inventory, and production series lying outside the social accounting framework all bear close watching. All these will require some explanatory comment when occasions for referring to them arise in later chapters.

In the second place, with respect to the national income data themselves, there is still a matter of format to be discussed. When Commerce's

official national income series are rearranged into a form that often goes by
the name "The Nation's Economic Budget," they become far more illuminating for some analytical purposes. At least that is the view of many economists
and the one adopted here. It is essential for our purposes, therefore, to discuss this rearrangement and its derivation from the five official series that
the National Income Division puts on the statistical market. An examination
of the nation's economic-budget format also can yield a useful by-product:
it can clarify the statistical relationship between saving and investment, two
concepts that play critical roles in the aggregative economic theory we shall
be exploring in Part Two.

In the third place, the working business conditions analyst needs at
least a general familiarity with other forms of social accounting. At present,
only two of these other forms—balance-of-payments accounting and flow-of-
funds accounting—have been developed into as readily available and usable
a current statistical source as the national income system. Within a few years,
however, American analysts should have routine access to official published
series of national wealth estimates and national input-output tables. The need
to get acquainted with these complementary forms of social accounting and
with their relationships to national income accounting already is well upon us.

THE NATION'S ECONOMIC BUDGET

WANTED: A CROSS CLASSIFICATION OF DISPOSABLE RECEIPTS AND EXPENDITURES

The income-by-type-of-income breakdown in the national income accounts, while appropriate for many economic analysis purposes, is not quite
the breakdown needed for business conditions analysis purposes. We need
a breakdown on the income side that matches, and therefore can be compared
with, the breakdown on the expenditures (GNE) side of the accounts. Moreover, we would like the breakdown to be after taxes and after transfers, to
indicate the actual accrual of purchasing power of the several spending
groups. And we should like a breakdown of *total* receipts (GNI), not just
national income, by spending groups.

THE NATION'S ECONOMIC-BUDGET FORMAT

The Nation's Economic Budget (NEB) is a rearrangement of the
national income data to achieve these purposes.[1] The format is as follows:

[1] The format of the Nation's Economic Budget was devised in the early 1940s by
Gerhard Colm and his then associate Grover Ensley. Colm, later chief economist of the
National Planning Association, was at the time a leading government economist; Ensley
subsequently served for many years as staff director of the congressional Joint Economic
Committee.

	Receipts	Expenditures	Balancing item
Persons	Disposable personal income less transfers by persons	Personal consumption expenditures	Net personal saving (+)
Business	Gross retained earnings	Gross private domestic investment	Excess of investment (−)
Foreign	Net foreign transfers by government and persons	Net exports	Excess of transfers (+) or net exports (−)*
Government	Tax and nontax receipts less transfers, interest, and subsidies	Government purchases of goods and services	Surplus (+) or deficit (−)
Total	GNI	GNE (GNP)	0

* Net foreign investment with sign changed.

Most of the terms in this arrangement are familiar, and we shall define the new ones in a moment.

Basically, all that the rearrangement involves is a reshuffling of the income data into an array of consumer, business, foreign, and government receipts, after taxes and after transfers. The format adopts the conventional GNP breakdown without change. The juxtaposition of receipts and expenditures for the same purchasing groups permits the showing of a balance between receipts and expenditures (an excess of receipts showing as a plus and an excess of expenditures as a minus) for each of the four sectors. These sector balances are items that, in view of the equality of gross national income and gross national product, necessarily add (algebraically) to zero if allowance is made for the statistical discrepancy.

The "budget" label may be an unfortunate one, for it has a planning or programing connotation. American users of the NEB format usually have no such purpose. Certainly they do not when they cast their historical data in this mold; and even when the figures are speculative and reach into the future, the analyst's purpose generally is to predict prospects rather than to alter or control them. Thus either the label of "the nation's income, expenditure, and saving," used in *Economic Indicators,* or "receipts and expenditures by major economic groups," used by the *Survey of Current Business,* would be a more appropriate one. However, we shall adhere to the more familiar "budget" terminology because it avoids the confusion that otherwise arises between this national accounting formulation and the very different "nation's income and product accounts" of the Department of Commerce.

It should be noted that some highly competent social accountants are not particularly enamored of the nation's economic-budget concept. Their complaint is that the NEB does not live up to its billing; it does not really achieve a clean-cut separation between household and business receipts that matches up properly with the household-business classification on the expenditure side of the budget. This is correct. The first difficulty is the one we encountered in our discussion of disposable personal income in the previous chapter. In the case of noncorporate business, Commerce does not attempt to distinguish between income that unincorporated proprietors receive and retain in their role as businessmen and that which they allocate to themselves as householders. Thus, the National Income Division classifies all such income as disposable personal income, the consumer receipts item in the Nation's Economic Budget. But actually all of it is not available for consumer expenditure; some of it is retained for direct investment in the proprietor's business. By the same token, the gross retained earnings of business are understated in the Nation's Economic Budget. The undistributed profits component of gross retained earnings includes only the profits of corporations; the corresponding item on the expenditure side, however, gross private domestic investment, includes investment expenditures of unincorporated enterprises.[2]

An analogous problem arises with respect to consumer purchases of houses. You will recall that expenditures by owner-occupants for new houses are tabulated, not as a personal consumption expenditure, but as a capital expenditure. The income that persons use for this purpose is included in disposable personal income, but the capital expenditure on the other side of the budget is included, not in personal consumption expenditures, but in gross private domestic investment along with investment expenditures by incorporated (and unincorporated) businesses in housing (presumably, rental units).

Both these problems become manageable, however, if we take care to remember that a part of personal saving is direct investment by unincorporated enterprises in their businesses and by persons in homes, and that a portion of gross private domestic investment is offset by such saving.

Both the *Survey of Current Business* and *Economic Indicators* carry quarterly NEB figures, and it is well to understand the content of those components of the NEB disposable receipts breakdown. Actually there are only two that are not already familiar national income accounting concepts— the gross retained earnings of business and the net receipts of government. The consumer receipts entry is disposable personal income, the derivation of which we have already studied, less the two transfer payments by persons: net interest paid by persons and net foreign transfers by persons. The receipts

---

[2] The same problem, it should be noted, does not arise with respect to depreciation. The income of unincorporated enterprises is calculated net of depreciation, and the capital-consumption allowances component of gross retained earnings includes depreciation (and other allowances) of both incorporated and unincorporated enterprises.

side of the foreign sector is net foreign transfer payments by government and by persons, since the net export component already represents the plus or minus excess of foreigners' purchases from the United States over their sales to the United States. The balancing item, net foreign investment, represents the excess of foreigners' purchases from the United States over their receipts through sales to the United States plus government and personal transfer payments. The derivation of the two new concepts, the gross retained earnings of business and the net receipts of government, is detailed in Table 4–1.

Table 4–1. Calculation of Selected Receipts Components of the Nation's Economic Budget for 1965* (In billions of dollars)

	Reported by the Commerce Dept.	NEB components	NEB entries
Capital-consumption allowances	58.7	58.7	
Corporate profits and IVA	73.1		
Less: Corporate-profits-tax liability	30.1		
Dividends	18.9		
Equals: Undistributed corporate profits and IVA		24.0	
Excess of wage accruals over disbursements	0	0	
Gross retained earnings of business			82.8
Personal tax and nontax payments	65.4		
Corporate-profits tax liability	30.1		
Indirect business taxes and nontax liability	62.0		
Contributions for social insurance	29.5		
Gross receipts of government		187.0	
Less: Government transfer payments to persons	36.8		
Government transfers to foreigners	2.2		
Net interest paid by government	9.5		
Subsidies less current surplus of government enterprises	1.2		
Total deductions		49.7	
Net receipts of government			137.3

* Details will not necessarily add to totals because of rounding.
Source: U.S. Department of Commerce.

SAVING AND INVESTMENT IN THE NATIONAL INCOME ACCOUNTS

The idea that our national economic well-being somehow depends very importantly on the relationship of saving and investment has become imbedded in American thinking during the past twenty years. Many who credit the assertion, however, are not even clear about the definitions of these presumably critical concepts. Some popularizers of modern economics report that investment is good and saving antisocial. Others leap to the defense of the Franklin virtues with the arguments, on the contrary, that thrift is the very thing on which our whole economic progress has depended; that increased saving never can hurt business because saving automatically flows into investment; and that, anyhow, it is an axiom of the "new economics" that saving and investment always are equal.

For the most part, these are issues which we shall not be able to sort out until we have gone some distance into the theoretical portion of our discussion. But this much is clear already: if the theoretical concepts we develop are to have realistic applications, the treatment of saving and investment in the abstract is going to have to correspond rather closely to their statistical treatment in United States national income accounting. If we can get the latter straight at this point, it will give us a running start on saving-investment theory. This statistical saving-investment relationship can best be understood as a part of the whole pattern of relationships among the receipts and expenditures items of the Nation's Economic Budget.

The national income accounting definitions of saving and of investment warrant close attention. While they are very simple, they depart widely from various business and financial usages.

Investment, in the national income accountant's sense, has already been defined. It is the purchase of new capital goods or of additions to business real assets, plus net foreign investment. The one exception is transfers of existing capital assets (excluding land) *among sectors,* e.g., sales of buildings by government to business. (As we noted earlier, the positive entry in gross private domestic investment is offset by a negative entry in government purchases of goods and services.)

Saving, in the national income accounting sense, is essentially a negative concept. Like investment, it is actually used in our United States national accounts only with respect to private activity. Private personal saving is the allocation of private disposable income to other than personal outlays (personal consumption plus net interest paid by persons and net foreign transfers by persons). Since saving is a synonym for "not spending," to say that so much disposable private income is being saved is not in itself to say anything about what nonconsumption use has been made of it. Saving may take the form of direct investment, as in the purchase of a house or in an unincorporated entrepreneur's purchase of inventory. It may take various financial forms, such as the making of deposits in banks, the hoarding of cash, and the purchase of corporate or government securities. As a matter of fact, if you used your next paycheck for lighting a cigar, a good national accountant would have to decide that you saved it. Later we shall have occasion to look into these alternative forms of saving with some care and to consider the structure of past savings.[3] For the moment, however, the definition of saving as "not spending" will suffice.

Note, incidentally, that when the word is used carefully, saving refers only to a flow or activity, not to stocks of assets accumulated in the past. The word "savings" with an "s" on the end of it often is applied to such past accumulations when they take a liquid form, but these as such do not show up in the national income accounts. Economists are not always meticulous about this narrow but deep difference between saving and savings, but it is a good one to adopt.

With the definitions just established, one can locate the saving and investment items in the Nation's Economic Budget.

The balance item in the consumer sector—the difference between disposable personal income and personal outlays—is what the Department of Commerce calls "net personal saving." Business, by definition, does not consume. Thus gross retained earnings are nothing more than gross business saving. Taken together, net personal saving and gross business saving constitute gross private saving.

Now ignoring the statistical discrepancy, the equality of the receipts and expenditures totals in the Nation's Economic Budget can be used to establish the relationship between statistical saving and statistical investment. For this purpose let us assign the following symbols:

Consumer sector:

Y_p = Disposable personal income less transfer payments by persons*

C = Personal consumption expenditures

S_p = Net personal saving $(Y_p - C)$

* Transfers by persons equals interest paid by consumers and personal transfer payments to foreigners.

Business sector:

S_b = Gross business saving (i.e., gross retained earnings)

I_d = Gross private domestic investment

Foreign sector:

F_t = Foreign net transfers by government and by persons

E_n = Net exports

Government sector:

T = Net receipts of government

G = Government purchases of goods and services

And:

S = $S_p + S_b$ (Gross private saving)

---

[3] In this connection, a particularly valuable article is that of Edward F. Denison, "Saving in the National Economy," *Survey of Current Business*, U.S. Department of Commerce, vol. 35, no. 1, pp. 8ff., January, 1955.

What the Nation's Economic Budget says is that total receipts equal total expenditures. In symbols;

$$Y_p + S_b + F_t + T = C + I_d + E_n + G$$

But disposable personal income, after personal transfer payments, is used either for personal consumption expenditures or for saving. Thus,

$$Y_p = C + S_p$$

Substituting in the first equation,

$$C + S_p + S_b + F_t + T = C + I_d + E_n + G$$

Subtracting the item (C) common to both sides of the equation, and combining net personal saving and business saving,

$$S + F_t + T = I_d + E_n + G$$

Rearranging,

$$S = I_d + (E_n - F_t) + (G - T)$$

Putting the matter into words, in any accounting period actual gross private saving exactly equals gross private investment plus the excess of net exports over net foreign transfers[4] (or minus the excess of transfers over net exports) plus the government deficit (or minus the government surplus). Defining $I_d + (E_n - F_t)$ as gross private investment, or in an economy in which $E_n - F_t = 0$,[5] gross private saving is always equal to gross private investment plus the government deficit: $S = I + (G - T)$. Or the statement can be rephrased: gross saving plus taxes (net receipts of government) equals gross private domestic investment plus government purchases of goods and services: $S + T = I + G$. This is an invariable rule that follows from the nature of the national income accounting definitions. It will be a useful rule to have in hand when we get to saving and investment theory.

OTHER SOCIAL ACCOUNTING SYSTEMS

THE FLOW-OF-FUNDS ACCOUNTS

The year 1955 saw the unveiling by the Board of Governors of the Federal Reserve System of a second system of social accounts. The new

---

[4] Net foreign investment.

[5] For example, in a completely self-contained economy with neither exports nor imports and no foreign transfers (i.e., both E_n and $F_t = O$), or in an economy in which exports and imports exactly balance and there are no foreign transfers (again both E_n and $F_t = O$), or in one in which net exports are exactly balanced by foreign transfers (i.e., $E_n = F_t$).

system had originally been dubbed an accounting of "moneyflows" by its originator, Morris Copeland of Cornell University.[6] It was relabeled the "flow-of-funds accounts" by the Division of Research and Statistics of the Board of Governors, which converted Copeland's brainchild into a statistical going concern.[7]

The thought that immediately occurs to anyone viewing this system of social accounts is, How does it compare with the national income accounts? Is it a more elaborate, more complicated but superior, system of national income accounting?   Or is it an entirely different system, unrelated to the national income accounts?

The answer is that the two systems are related, complementary not rival, constructs.   The national income accounts attempt to measure the current income and output of the nation's economy.   They net out purely financial transactions such as loans and the purchase and sale of existing assets.[8]   The flow-of-funds accounts, on the other hand, include these financial transactions.

It might be said that the implied logic of the national income accounts is that income and output are primary; developments and decisions in financial markets are largely passive reactions to developments and decisions related to production, income, and expenditures for goods and services.   To the extent that financial events play an active, causative, rather than a passive, role, it is necessary to evaluate their effect separately, outside the national income accounting framework.   An increase in commercial bank loans, for example, would no doubt have an indirect effect on income and output, but it would not be directly reflected in the national income accounts. The logic of the flow-of-funds accounts, on the other hand, is that because events in the financial markets are sometimes independent causes of events in product markets, and in any event are related to them, an accounting system should be available that encompasses both.   This the flow-of-funds system does, at the expense, admittedly, of a rather considerable increase in complexity and difficulty of interpretation.

The two systems of accounts reflect two different sets of purposes that

---

[6] M. A. Copeland, *A Study of Moneyflows in the United States*, National Bureau of Economic Research, Inc., New York, 1952.

[7] The first public presentation appeared in "A Flow of Funds System of National Accounts Annual Estimates, 1939–54," *Federal Reserve Bulletin*, vol. XLI, pp. 1085–1124, October, 1955. The document bearing the same relationship to the flow-of-funds accounts as the *National Income Supplement* does to the national income accounts is *Flow of Funds in the United States, 1939–53*, published by the Federal Reserve System. The current accounts are described in the August, 1959, *Federal Reserve Bulletin* article, "A Quarterly Presentation of the Flow of Funds, Saving and Investment," p. 828, and in the November, 1965, *Federal Reserve Bulletin* article, "Revision of Flow of Funds Accounts," p. 1533.

[8] It will be recalled that the national income accounts record transactions in secondhand fixed assets (excluding land) among sectors of the economy. These are offsetting entries, however, and do not affect the total (GNP).

the analyst may have in mind. Whereas the purpose of national income accounting is to provide reliable estimates of the scope and structure of the economy's productive achievement and of the income this generates, the purpose of flow-of-funds accounting is to supply a comprehensive, revealing picture of the economy's uses of money and credit and of the sources from which these funds arise. The two social accounting systems both measure flows through time; they both tabulate transactions; and because (1) most United States income and product transactions involve a transfer of money and (2) such income and product transactions constitute a sizable minority of all monetary transactions, the two systems cover many of the same transactions. The two systems use the same statistical sources in this overlapping area so that, although the classifications differ somewhat, the data are consistent. But outside this overlapping area, the coverage of the two systems is quite different, conforming in each system to the purposes for which the accounts are intended to be used.

The Flow-of-funds Format

The arrangement of the flow-of-funds data has a certain kinship to the Nation's Economic Budget; the purpose of each is to show, for each sector of the economy, receipts and uses made of those receipts. However, there are a number of differences between the NEB and flow-of-funds arrays:

1. The basic juxtaposition in the flow-of-funds accounts is not of receipts and expenditures but of sources of funds and uses of funds, essentially on the model of the familiar sources and uses statements of corporate accounting. Because the system's purpose is to encompass all moneyflows, not just monetized income and product flows, sources are not restricted to income sources; they also include sales of existing assets and a sector's net borrowing. And uses are not limited to expenditures for current output; they also include purchases of land, used commodities and structures, and securities, as well as additions to a sector's cash balances. Since all sources of funds are by definition used in some way, there is an exact sources-uses balance for each sector; the third column (balances) of the NEB format is therefore not needed in the flow-of-funds statement.

In practice, though not in principle, the flow-of-funds statement differs from the NEB format in another respect. Since the 1959 revision of the accounts, the Federal Reserve has not published on a current basis a detailed breakdown of current receipts and current expenditures. The only figure given, for example, for consumer purchases of soft goods and services is the total. And because the Federal Reserve defines a current expenditure somewhat differently (to be discussed below), the national income accounts breakdown cannot be used. For those who want to use the accounts for an analysis of consumer behavior, therefore, this is a gap in the reported accounting system.

2. The sectoring of the flow-of-funds system differs from, and is con-

siderably more elaborate than, that of the Nation's Economic Budget. In the first place, the consumer sector is defined differently. On the sources side, the flow-of-funds accountants, attempting what the national income accountants doubted the feasibility of doing, have deleted from household income sources of funds that portion of unincorporated business profit that is retained in the businesses. Thus not all monetized personal income enters the flow-of-funds consumer account. Moreover, on the uses side of the same account, flow of funds abandons the national income accounting fiction that household purchases of homes are *business* investment. Instead, such purchases together with household purchases of other durable goods are classified as consumer investment.

In the second place, the flow-of-funds sectoring of business and government purchase groups is more detailed than that in the NEB. In place of a single account for business, there are three separate accounts: farm business, nonfarm unincorporated business, corporate business. Government transactions are shown separately for the Federal government and state and local governments.

In the third place, the flow-of-funds format adds three major sectors for financial intermediaries—one for the monetary authority, one for commercial banks, and a third for nonbank financial institutions. The nonbank group is further subdivided into sections recording selected financial transactions for savings and loan associations, mutual savings banks, life insurance companies, other insurance companies, noninsured pension plans, finance companies, security brokers and dealers, and open-end investment companies.

Thus, including the "rest of the world" account, there are ten sectors in the flow-of-funds accounts: one for households, three for business, two for government, three for financial institutions (with eight subsectors) and one for "foreign."

3. Whereas the Nation's Economic Budget is only a single statement, analogous to the income account of a business firm, the flow-of-funds system yields two statements, analogous to the income account *and the balance sheet* of the business firm. In the "income account," called "sector statements of sources and uses of funds in _____" (quarter or year), transactions are divided into three broad categories: current, nonfinancial investment, and financial investment. Current transactions include all current flows to the sector in the current accounting period and expenditures on nondurable goods and services. With some exceptions, the Commerce Department definitions are followed. The two most notable exceptions are, as we noted earlier, consumer expeditures on durable goods and residential structures, which are classified as consumer nonfinancial investment. The imputed rental value of owner-occupied housing, which is included in residential housing expenditures in the national income accounts, is excluded from the flow-of-funds accounts because no actual flow of funds takes place. Nonfinancial investment records investment in real assets, i.e., expenditures for tangible goods with a useful service-providing life in excess of the current accounting period including

purchases of consumer durable goods, residential structures expenditures, plant and equipment spending, and net change in inventories.

Financial investment, the third section of the source and use statement, includes investment in financial assets and net increments to sector indebtedness. A financial receipt of one sector is offset somewhere in the accounts by a financial expenditure. Financial flows are recorded on a net basis for each sector. The asset entry represents the total investment by the sector in a particular asset less total funds received from the disposition of that same type of asset during the accounting period. Credit entries also are on a net basis: net credit extension less repayments. Financial transaction categories cover changes in: (1) gold, official United States foreign currency holdings, and Treasury currency, (2) demand deposits and currency, (3) fixed-value redeemable claims (time deposits and savings and loan shares), (4) saving through life insurance, (5) saving through pension funds, (6) credit and equity market instruments (Federal obligations, state and local obligations, corporate and foreign bonds, corporate stock, mortgages on one- to four-family properties, other mortgages, consumer credit, bank loans not classified elsewhere, and other loans), (7) trade credit, (8) proprietors' net investment in noncorporate business, (9) miscellaneous financial transactions.

The balance sheet, in principle, should record assets and liabilities, as of a point in time, by the same classification. In practice, it does not. Real assets are not included (even though transactions in real assets are included in the income account), because of the inadequacy of wealth data. Consequently, net worth totals for the sectors cannot be computed, as they can in the balance sheet of the private business firm.[9]

One of the major contributions of the revised system of the flow-of-funds accounts is the direct focus on the flow of funds into saving and into investment, for each sector and in the aggregate. Total sector saving is defined in a manner similar to that of the Nation's Economic Budget. Saving is defined in terms of current transactions and is shown on both a net and a gross basis. Net saving is the difference between receipts and expenditures in the current account. Gross saving is net saving plus capital-consumption allowances from the sector's tangible asset holdings.

Investment, defined in terms of capital transactions, is the sum of net

---

[9] The flow estimates, in the source and use of funds statement, are reported on a quarterly basis in the statistical section of the *Federal Reserve Bulletin* with a four-month lag between the end of the quarter and the publication of the estimates. The balance sheet estimates are usually reported on an annual basis in the October issue of the *Bulletin*. Quarterly flow estimates are valued at the time of the transactions. The annual balance sheet estimates are recorded at the current market value of the assets and liabilities at the year's end. Since some financial assets, especially corporate stock and others that are actively traded in organized financial markets, are subject to price fluctuations, the sum of the four quarterly investment flows may not equal the annual change in the balance sheet account for some assets. The net change in the balance sheet entry of an asset represents the sum of the four quarterly investment flows and any change in capital value.

tangible asset investment plus net financial investment flows. Net investment in tangible assets is the total expenditure on both newly produced and existing assets minus funds realized from the disposition of tangible assets during the period. Net financial investment is the sum of the net investment in financial assets less the net increment in sector indebtedness during the period.

Aggregate saving and investment are equal to the sum of the several sectors' saving and investment expenditures. Because of the interlocking accounting framework—a financial expenditure of one sector is a financial receipt of another sector—financial flows cancel out when the sectors are added together. Financial claims, which are important determinants of sector activity, are thus eliminated from the national summary. The net increments of tangible stock and financial transactions with the rest of the world sector represent the net national investment. Similarly, when the sector balance sheets are combined, financial assets and liabilities also cancel out, since each sector asset is another sector's liability.

Conceptually, saving and investment totals are equal for each sector and for the national economy. That is, gross saving from the current account represents the funds used by a sector or the economy for investment in financial and tangible assets. In practice, the two entries are not always equal. The difference, on both the sector and the aggregate level, is accounted for by a statistical discrepancy entry—similar to the practice in the national income accounts.

The two basic accounts of the flow-of-funds framework, the source and use statement and the partial balance sheet, for the consumer sector are shown in Tables 4–2 and 4–3 (see pages 76–78). Table 4–2 is the "income account"; Table 4–3 is the partial "balance sheet." Table 4–4 is a summary table for all sectors for 1964.

In summary, while the flow of funds is the second domestic system of social accounts, it is not a competitor of the national income accounts. The two accounting systems are different in purpose, sector classifications, and transactions classifications. The flow of funds is concerned with measuring total moneyflows, on a net basis, associated with a given level of output with particular emphasis on saving and investment flows and national totals. The national income accounts are concerned only with recording the moneyflows and imputed moneyflows associated with newly produced output. The flow of funds is divided into eleven sectors with a source and use statement and a partial balance sheet for each sector. The national income accounts are divided into four final demand sectors and, in NEB format, present the income, consumption, and saving of each sector. The flow of funds, allowing for different coverage, defines saving in the same fashion—but also records the disposition of savings as investment in financial and tangible assets.

The flow-of-funds accounts were designed with significant flexibility to provide maximum usefulness in economic analysis.[10]   The major use appears to be in testing hypotheses that relate to the interdependence between financial markets and product markets.   However, the accounts are quite compatible with analysis of a single sector of the capital markets.   The saving and investment totals are easily modified to suit a variety of hypotheses.   The accounts are structured to provide convenient summaries of current and capital flows that are important in the analysis of aggregate and sector consumption and investment patterns.

Lawrence Ritter,[11] in the article footnoted above, concludes as follows:

> "The potential usefulness of the flow-of-funds accounts as a theoretical tool is still largely unrealized.   In the flow of funds we now have a complete and internally consistent body of data on financial flows, interlocked with national income data.   Data on the financial markets are meshed with data on the goods and services markets.   However, these still consist of logical ex post identities.   Upon this foundation, we need to proceed to the even more important job of testing alternative hypotheses regarding the interaction between the financial and non-financial variables, with the ultimate objective of moving from the logical identities to the construction of a set of behavior relationships possessing explanatory value."

THE REST OF THE SOCIAL ACCOUNTING FAMILY

It will be sufficient for our purposes simply to note the remaining three varieties of social accounting customarily identified as distinct species.

National Wealth Statistics

These bear precisely the same conceptual relationship to national income and product data as does a corporation's balance sheet to its income statement.   The object is to measure the size and composition of the economy's quantifiable wealth or, to the extent that natural resources either are ignored or can be treated as capital, of its stock of capital at specified moments in time.   This may be the next form of United States social accounting to achieve official published series status.   For many years the National Bureau of Economic Research (NBER), the principal sponsor of American social accounting research, has regarded income and wealth accounting as

---

[10] See: Conference on Research in Income and Wealth: *The Flow of Funds Approach to Social Accounting: Appraisal, Analysis, and Applications*, National Bureau of Economic Research, Inc., Studies in Income and Wealth, vol. 26, Princeton University Press, Princeton, N. J., 1962; and Lawrence S. Ritter et al., "The Flow of Funds Accounts: A New Approach to Financial Market Analysis," *Journal of Finance*, vol. XVIII, pp. 219–263, May, 1963.

[11] *Ibid.*, p. 230.

Table **4-2.**   Sector Statement of Sources and Uses of Funds, 1960–IIQ 1965 (In billions of dollars)

(A) Households [1]

Category	1960	1961	1962	1963	1964	1963 II	1963 III	1963 IV	1964 I	1964 II	1964 III	1964 IV	1965 I	1965 II	
1 Personal income	400.9	416.8	442.6	464.7	495.0	460.1	467.1	475.6	483.0	490.6	499.1	507.2	516.6	525.0	1
2 Less: Personal taxes & nontaxes	50.9	52.4	57.4	60.9	59.2	60.6	61.0	61.6	60.4	56.9	58.8	60.7	64.8	66.0	2
3 Personal outlays	333.0	343.2	363.7	383.4	409.5	380.5	386.3	389.5	399.3	406.3	415.3	416.9	428.1	436.0	3
4 Equals: Personal saving	17.0	21.2	21.6	20.4	26.3	18.9	19.8	24.4	23.4	27.3	25.0	29.5	23.8	23.0	4
5 Plus: Credits from govt. insur.[2]	3.1	3.4	3.5	4.0	4.8	4.2	3.9	4.2	4.5	4.6	5.1	4.9	5.2	6.2	5
6 Other adjustments[3]	0.5	0.6	0.6	0.6	0.7	0.6	0.6	0.6	0.5	0.6	0.7	0.9	0.8	0.7	6
7 Net durables in consumpt.	5.1	2.9	6.7	8.5	10.8	8.1	8.9	8.9	10.6	11.6	12.2	8.9	14.1	13.1	7
8 Purchases	45.3	44.2	49.5	53.4	58.7	52.6	54.1	54.9	57.4	59.1	60.5	57.9	63.9	63.7	8
9 Less: Cap. consumpt.	40.2	41.3	42.8	45.0	47.9	44.5	45.2	46.0	46.8	47.5	48.3	49.0	49.8	50.5	9
10 Equals: Net saving	25.7	28.0	32.4	33.5	42.6	31.7	33.2	38.2	38.9	44.1	43.0	44.2	43.9	43.0	10
11 Plus: Capital consumpt.[4]	46.3	47.8	49.7	52.4	55.8	51.9	52.7	53.6	54.5	55.4	56.2	57.1	58.0	58.9	11
12 Equals: Gross saving	72.0	75.8	82.1	85.9	98.4	83.6	85.9	91.8	93.4	99.5	99.3	101.3	101.9	101.9	12
13 Gross investment (14+18)	72.8	78.0	87.8	91.5	102.1	86.8	94.3	97.6	98.2	103.0	100.8	106.4	106.0	106.8	13
14 Capital expend. (net of sales)	68.3	65.0	71.7	76.0	82.3	74.8	76.8	78.1	81.2	82.8	84.1	81.0	86.7	86.8	14
15 Residential construction	19.8	17.5	18.7	18.9	19.5	18.6	19.0	19.5	19.9	19.7	19.5	18.9	18.7	19.0	15
16 Consumer durable goods	45.3	44.2	49.5	53.4	58.7	52.6	54.1	54.9	57.4	59.1	60.5	57.9	63.9	63.7	16
17 Plant and equip. (nonprofit)	3.2	3.3	3.5	3.7	4.0	3.6	3.7	3.8	3.9	4.0	4.1	4.1	4.1	4.2	17
18 Net finan. investment (19+37)	4.4	12.9	16.1	15.5	19.8	12.0	17.5	19.5	17.0	20.2	16.7	25.4	19.3	20.0	18
19 Net acquis. of finan. assets[5]	22.6	29.9	36.6	44.9	47.2	39.1	45.5	46.1	44.7	49.9	41.5	52.8	47.3	48.9	19
20 Demand dep. and currency	−0.9	0.8	4.1	5.3	7.4	3.0	6.7	6.8	10.6	3.4	2.8	13.1	7.7	8.6	20
21 Savings accounts	12.4	17.4	23.4	23.0	23.9	22.6	22.5	23.0	19.6	23.8	25.4	27.0	24.6	20.1	21
22 At commercial banks	2.8	6.2	10.3	7.9	8.2	7.7	8.5	8.0	4.9	8.1	8.5	11.4	11.6	7.8	22
23 At savings institutions	9.6	11.2	13.0	15.1	15.7	14.9	14.0	15.0	14.7	15.7	16.8	15.6	13.1	12.3	23

		3.2 / 8.1	3.5 / 8.6	3.7 / 8.8	4.3 / 9.9	4.4 / 11.6	4.2 / 9.9	4.4 / 10.7	4.6 / 9.3	4.6 / 10.9	4.4 / 12.3	4.3 / 11.0	4.2 / 12.4	4.2 / 10.6	4.3 / 14.7		
21	Life insurance reserves															24	
25	Pension fund reserves															25	
26	Cr. and equity mkt. instr.	1.1	0.7	-1.7	1.3	3.5	0.1	2.4	5.8	2.7	9.2	1.2	0.9	4.6	4.4	26	
27	U.S. govt. securities	-0.5	-0.5	0.4	3.7	2.1	1.9	5.2	7.6	2.3	4.0	0.8	1.1	4.2	6.8	27	
28	Savings bonds	-0.3	0.8	0.4	1.2	0.9	1.1	1.1	1.2	0.8	0.9	0.8	1.0	0.8	0.4	28	
29	Short-term mkt.	-2.6	-0.1	0.5	2.9	-1.8	0.6	5.0	2.9	-0.7	-4.3	-1.9	-0.5	4.3	0.4	29	
30	Other direct	2.7	-1.2	-0.9	-0.9	2.0	-1.1	-2.1	1.6	2.4	5.1	0.3	0.3	1.1	3.6	30	
31	Nonguaranteed	-0.2	*	0.3	0.5	1.0	1.4	1.2	1.9	-0.2	2.2	1.6	0.3	-2.0	2.4	31	
32	State and local oblig.	1.8	1.1	0.4	1.6	2.6	1.3	1.7	3.3	2.3	4.9	0.3	2.9	4.1	1.2	32	
33	Corporate and fgn. bonds	-0.1	-0.2	-0.9	-0.5	-0.7	-0.6	-2.1	0.4	-1.7	-2.4	0.8	0.6	0.6	-0.4	33	
34	Corporate stock	-0.3	0.4	-1.6	-2.9	-0.6	-2.8	-1.3	-4.4	*	2.5	-0.9	-3.9	-3.3	-2.1	34	
35	Mortgages	0.2	-0.2	*	-0.6	0.1	0.3	-1.0	-1.1	-0.2	0.3	0.2	0.2	-1.0	-1.0	35	
36	Net invest. in noncorp. bus.	-2.1	-1.8	-2.3	-2.6	-4.2	-2.6	-2.6	-2.7	-3.8	-4.7	-4.5	-3.8	-4.7	-4.4	36	
37	Net increase in liabilities	18.2	16.9	20.6	26.3	27.4	27.1	28.0	26.6	27.7	29.7	24.8	27.4	28.1	29.0	37	
38	Credit mkt. instruments	16.5	13.4	18.9	22.1	23.6	22.0	23.2	21.8	24.3	23.9	23.9	22.2	25.9	24.2	38	
39	1- to 4-family mtgs.	11.3	11.2	12.9	14.9	16.0	15.2	15.5	14.8	16.3	16.0	16.2	15.6	15.7	14.7	39	
40	Other mortgages	0.9	0.9	0.9	1.0	1.0	0.9	1.0	1.0	1.0	1.0	1.0	1.0	1.0	1.0	40	
41	Consumer credit	4.5	1.7	5.5	6.7	6.9	6.5	6.9	6.6	7.4	7.2	7.1	6.0	9.6	8.7	41	
42	Bank loans n.e.c.	0.6	0.9	0.5	0.9	2.6	1.3	0.7	2.1	2.2	3.8	0.1	4.3	0.7	2.9	42	
43	Other loans [6]	0.7	0.6	0.6	0.5	0.6	0.2	0.9	0.5	0.6	0.7	0.6	0.6	0.6	0.7	43	
44	Security credit	-0.1	1.3	-0.1	2.0	-0.2	2.7	2.6	1.3	-0.4	0.7	-0.8	-0.3	-0.1	0.8	44	
45	Discrepancy (12–13)	-0.7	-2.2	-5.7	-5.7	-3.7	-3.1	-8.4	-5.8	-4.8	-3.5	-1.5	-5.0	-4.1	-4.9	45	

Source: *Federal Reserve Bulletin*, vol. LI, p. 1611, November, 1965. See that source (p. 1617) for definitional footnotes.

Table 4-3. Sector Statements of Financial Assets and Liabilities, 1951–1964 (In billions of dollars)

(A) Households

Category	1951	1952	1953	1954	1955	1956	1957	1958	1959	1960	1961	1962	1963	1964	
Total financial assets	**468.5**	**501.1**	**513.0**	**604.6**	**684.0**	**727.7**	**714.8**	**849.1**	**911.4**	**930.9**	**1072.7**	**1048.0**	**1176.0**	**1305.2**	1
Demand deposits and currency	59.2	61.2	61.9	63.3	63.8	64.8	63.6	65.3	66.8	65.9	66.7	70.8	76.1	83.8	2
Savings accounts	71.6	79.3	87.6	96.7	105.5	115.0	127.0	141.1	152.8	165.3	182.7	206.0	229.1	253.0	3
At commercial banks	33.7	36.4	38.9	41.4	43.1	45.3	50.5	55.8	59.4	62.2	68.4	78.7	86.6	94.8	4
At savings institutions	37.9	42.9	48.7	55.3	62.4	69.7	76.6	85.3	93.5	103.1	114.3	127.3	142.5	158.2	5
Life insurance reserves	57.8	60.7	63.7	66.3	69.3	72.7	75.5	78.5	82.0	85.2	88.6	92.4	96.7	101.0	6
Pension fund reserves	27.4	32.1	37.0	41.9	49.7	55.7	61.7	71.7	81.2	89.5	102.2	107.8	121.4	136.6	7
Credit market instruments	243.5	258.1	252.6	325.4	384.4	408.0	375.0	479.8	515.3	511.1	617.8	555.7	636.8	714.4	8
U.S. government securities	66.2	66.0	66.2	64.9	67.3	68.4	68.3	66.0	70.8	70.3	69.9	70.3	63.9	76.0	9
Savings bonds	49.1	49.2	49.4	50.0	50.2	50.1	48.2	47.7	45.9	45.6	46.4	46.9	48.0	49.0	10
Short-term marketable	n.a.	5.8	7.8	5.4	5.8	7.3	9.5	7.3	10.8	8.2	8.0	8.5	11.4	9.6	11
Other direct	n.a.	10.6	8.6	9.1	10.3	9.7	8.8	9.2	11.0	13.6	12.5	11.6	10.7	12.8	12
Nonguaranteed	0.5	0.4	0.5	0.4	0.9	1.3	1.9	1.9	3.1	2.9	2.9	3.3	3.7	4.7	13
State and local obligations	10.2	11.2	13.0	14.4	18.1	20.6	23.6	23.3	25.4	28.0	30.1	32.4	34.5	36.6	14
Corporate and foreign bonds	3.6	3.6	3.7	3.7	4.8	5.5	6.2	6.6	6.7	6.6	6.4	5.5	4.8	4.1	15
Corporate stock, mkt. value	155.4	169.0	161.0	233.3	284.9	303.6	266.0	372.3	400.8	394.3	499.7	435.9	512.5	586.5	16
Mortgages	8.0	8.3	8.8	9.1	9.3	9.9	10.8	11.5	11.6	11.8	11.6	11.6	11.1	11.2	17
Security credit	0.8	0.7	0.7	1.0	0.9	0.9	0.9	1.2	1.0	1.1	1.2	1.2	1.2	1.2	18
Miscellaneous	8.3	9.0	9.6	9.9	10.4	10.7	11.2	11.6	12.2	12.8	13.5	14.1	14.7	15.3	19
Total liabilities	**80.8**	**93.7**	**106.9**	**119.1**	**139.9**	**156.3**	**169.2**	**182.0**	**204.0**	**222.2**	**239.1**	**259.6**	**286.0**	**313.4**	20
Credit market instruments	70.4	82.0	93.8	103.8	122.6	137.6	149.6	159.4	179.2	195.6	209.1	228.0	250.1	273.7	21
1- to 4-family mortgages	44.5	51.3	58.9	67.5	79.7	90.9	99.8	109.1	121.9	133.2	144.4	157.3	172.1	188.1	22
Other mortgages	2.8	3.3	3.8	4.5	5.1	5.8	6.6	7.4	8.3	9.2	10.2	11.1	12.1	13.1	23
Consumer credit	22.7	27.5	31.4	32.5	38.8	42.3	45.0	45.1	51.5	56.0	57.7	63.2	69.9	76.8	24
Bank loans n.e.c.	3.2	3.5	3.7	4.1	4.4	4.8	5.0	5.7	6.7	7.2	8.1	8.6	9.6	12.2	25
Other loans	3.2	3.3	3.5	3.8	4.0	4.3	4.8	5.2	5.7	6.4	7.0	7.6	8.1	8.7	26
Security credit	2.4	2.6	3.0	4.1	4.8	4.8	4.4	5.5	5.5	5.4	6.7	6.6	8.6	8.4	27
Trade credit	0.9	1.1	1.2	1.3	1.4	1.6	1.7	1.8	1.9	2.0	2.1	2.1	2.2	2.3	28

Source: *Federal Reserve Bulletin*, vol. LI, p. 1622, November, 1965.

intimately related undertakings, and in 1955, under NBER auspices, Raymond Goldsmith completed the prodigious task of making some initial comprehensive national wealth estimates.[12]   In 1962, these estimates were revised for the 1945–1949 period and continued through the year 1958.[13]   In 1963, Goldsmith supplemented the wealth estimates with companion estimates of intangible assets, of liabilities, and of net worth of the main sectors of the economy.[14]   These wealth estimates are of necessity rough and approximate, largely because of inadequate bench-mark data.   The Office of Business Economics of the Department of Commerce has undertaken several projects aimed at measurement and analysis of the nation's capital stock and its characteristics.   The results of the first of these projects were reported in the *Survey of Current Business* in 1962;[15] other reports are scheduled to follow. Data on the liabilities and financial assets of the flow-of-funds sectors by the Federal Reserve System have added, in a fragmentary way, to our knowledge of national wealth.   More recently, a "Wealth Inventory Planning Study" was launched by The George Washington University under the direction of John W. Kendrick; the purpose of the study was to analyze the problems connected with, and to prepare proposals for, a possible comprehensive bench-mark inventory or census of national wealth.[16]

All these efforts indicate the importance that many economists attach to wealth statistics.   It is probable, however, that comprehensive, official wealth data will not be available until the 1970s.   And until they are available on a reasonably current basis, their usefulness to business conditions analysis cannot be tested.

Input-Output Tables

These inventions of Wassily Leontief of Harvard may eventually be the most illuminating of all the social accounting systems.[17]   At least they constitute the system best designed to show the resources used in production

---

[12] R. W. Goldsmith, *A Study of Saving in the United States*, Princeton University Press, Princeton, N.J., 1955, 3 vols.

[13] R. W. Goldsmith, *The National Wealth of the United States in the Postwar Period*, Princeton University Press, Princeton, N.J., 1962.

[14] Raymond Goldsmith, *Studies in the National Balance Sheet of the United States*, Princeton University Press, Princeton, N.J., 1963, 2 vols.

[15] George Jaszi, Robert C. Wasson, and Lawrence Grace, "Expansion of Fixed Business Capital in the United States," *Survey of Current Business*, vol. 42, no. 11, pp. 9–18, U.S. Department of Commerce, November, 1962.

[16] For a summary of the results of this study, see John W. Kendrick's statement in *Measuring the Nation's Wealth, Hearings before the Subcommittee on Economic Statistics of the Joint Economic Committee*, 89th Cong., 1st Sess. June 1, 2, and 3, 1965.

[17] W. Leontief, *The Structure of the American Economy, 1919–1939*, 2d ed., Oxford University Press, Fair Lawn, N.J., 1953; and Leontief et al., *Studies in the Structure of the American Economy*, Oxford University Press, Fair Lawn, N.J., 1953.

Table 4-4. Summary of Flow-of-funds Accounts for 1964 (In billions of dollars)

		Private domestic nonfinancial sectors								U.S. govt.	
Sector Transaction category		House-holds		Busi-ness		State and local govts.		Total			
		U	S	U	S	U	S	U	S	U	S
1	**Gross saving**		98.4		61.8		-2.1		158.1		-5.0
2	Capital consumption		55.8		47.0				102.8		
3	Net saving (1-2)		42.6		14.9		-2.1		55.3		-5.0
4	**Gross investment (5+10)**	102.1		58.3		-3.6		156.8		-2.9	
5	**Private cap. expend., net**	82.3		68.5				150.7			
6	Consumer durables	58.7						58.7			
7	Residential constr.	19.5		7.5				27.0			
8	Plant and equipment	4.0		56.2				60.2			
9	Inventory change			4.8				4.8			
10	**Net financial invest. (11-12)**	19.9		-10.2		-3.6		6.1		-2.9	
11	**Financial uses, net**	47.3		15.4		6.2		68.8		4.7	
12	**Financial sources**		27.4		25.6		9.8		62.7		7.7
13	Gold & off. U.S. fgn. exch.									-0.2	
14	Treasury currency										*
15	Dem. dep. and currency										
16	Private domestic	7.4		-2.6		0.7		5.6			
17	U.S. govt.									0.6	
18	Foreign										
19	Time and svgs. accounts	23.9						28.8			
20	At coml. banks	8.2		3.2		1.7		13.1			*
21	At svgs. instit.	15.7						15.7			
22	Life insur. reserves	4.4						4.4			*
23	Pension fund reserves	11.6					3.5	11.6	3.5		1.3
24	Consol. bank items										
25	Credit mkt. instr.	3.5	27.3	1.3	22.3	3.7	6.2	8.6	55.8	3.8	6.7
26	U.S. govt. securities	2.1		-1.5		0.4		0.9			6.2
27	State and local oblig.	2.6				-0.6	5.9	2.0	5.9		
28	Corp. and foreign bonds	-0.7			4.0	3.5		2.8	4.0		
29	Corp. stocks	-0.6			1.4			-0.6	1.4		
30	1- to 4-family mortgages	0.1	16.0		-0.2	0.4		0.5	15.8	-0.2	
31	Other mortgages		1.0		9.1				10.1	0.4	
32	Consumer credit		6.9	1.4				1.4	6.9		
33	Bank loans n.e.c.		2.6		5.0				7.6		
34	Other loans		0.8	1.4	3.0		0.4	1.4	4.1	3.6	0.5
35	Open market paper			1.4	n.a.			1.4	n.a.		
36	Federal loans		0.1		0.9		0.4		1.3	3.5	
37	Security credit	-0.1	-0.2					-0.1	-0.2		
38	To brkrs. and dealers	-0.1						-0.1			
39	To others		-0.2						-0.2		
40	Taxes payable				0.2	*		*	0.2	0.2	
41	Trade credit		0.1	8.9	4.8		0.1	8.9	5.0	0.2	-0.2
42	Equity in noncorp. business	-4.1			-4.1			-4.1	-4.1		
43	Misc. financial trans.	0.6	0.2	4.6	2.5			5.2	2.6	0.1	-0.2
44	Sector discrepancies (1-4)	-3.8		3.6		1.5		1.3		-2.1	

Source: *Federal Reserve Bulletin*, vol. LI, p. 1608, November, 1965.

Total		Monetary auth.		Coml. banks		Nonbank finance		Rest of the world		All sectors		Discrepancy	Natl. saving and investment	
U	S	U	S	U	S	U	S	U	S	U	S	U		
	3.4		0.1		1.9		1.4	−5.8			150.6	−1.0	156.5	1
	0.8				0.4		0.4				103.6		103.6	2
	2.6		0.1		1.5		1.0	−5.8			47.0		52.9	3
4.3		0.1		2.0		2.3		−4.7		153.5		−1.9	156.3	4
0.9				0.4		0.5				151.6			151.6	5
										58.7			58.7	6
										27.0			27.0	7
0.9				0.4		0.5				61.1			61.1	8
										4.8			4.8	9
3.4		0.1		1.6		1.8		−4.7		1.9		−1.9	4.7	10
63.5		3.4		23.2		36.9		3.5		140.5			8.1	11
	60.1		3.3		21.7		35.1		8.1		138.6		3.5	12
*		*						0.1	*	*	*			13
−0.2		−0.2								−0.2	*	0.2		14
	7.4		2.6		4.8					6.9	7.4			15
0.2	6.8		2.4		4.4	0.2				5.8	6.8	1.0		16
	0.2		0.2		*					0.6	0.2	−0.5		17
	0.5		0.1		0.4			0.5			0.5			18
0.2	30.4					0.2					30.4			19
0.1	14.6				14.6	0.1		1.4			14.6			20
0.1	15.8					0.1	15.8				15.8			21
	4.3						4.3				4.4			22
	6.9						6.9				11.6			23
0.5	0.5	0.1	0.4	0.4	0.1					0.5	0.5			24
60.9	6.5	3.4		21.8	0.6	35.8	5.9	0.4	4.6	73.8	73.6			25
4.8		3.5		−0.5		1.8		0.4			6.2			26
3.8				3.6		0.2					5.9			27
4.6	2.6			0.1	0.5	4.5	2.1	0.2	0.9		7.6			28
3.8	1.7				*	3.8	1.6	−0.3	−0.2		2.9			29
15.1	−0.3			2.3		12.9	−0.3				15.5			30
9.7				2.2		7.4					10.1			31
5.5				2.8		2.8					6.9			32
10.0	0.5			10.0			0.5		1.9	10.0				33
3.7	2.0	−0.1		1.4		2.4	2.0	0.2	2.0	8.9	8.7	−0.2		34
0.5	1.5	−0.1		0.7		−0.1	1.5	0.2	0.4		2.1			35
	0.5						0.5		1.7		3.5			36
*	0.1			0.5		−0.5	0.1	*	*		−0.1			37
0.2	0.1			0.2		*	0.1	*			0.1			38
−0.2				0.3		−0.5			*		−0.2			39
	0.4				0.3		0.1			0.2	0.6	0.5		40
0.2						0.2				9.3	4.8	−4.5		41
											−4.1			42
1.7	3.5		0.3	0.6	1.2	1.1	2.0	1.0	3.6	8.0	9.6	1.6		43
−0.9			*			−0.9		−1.2		−2.9		−2.9	0.2	44

*Less than $0.05 billion.

and thus to provide guidance for those attacking problems of resource allocation and investment programing. The purpose of input-output accounting is
to provide a detailed view of the industrial interrelations in the productive
process that produces the gross national product. To this end the economy
is subdivided into a large number of industries (the final-demand sectors
being included as industries), and the various inputs of goods and services
they get from each other and the outputs they supply to each other are
arranged in the form of a matrix, i.e., a cellular table, like the intercity
mileage chart on a road map, which has the same industries listed down the
side that it lists across the top.

From such an input-output table it is possible to calculate for each
industry the amounts of inputs from other industries required to produce one
unit of the given industry's output during the year the table represents. With
the help of some mathematics and an electronic computer this information
can become a very powerful weapon for attacking a number of important business and public-policy problems in succeeding periods—as long as the technological relationships imbedded in the table do not change. Unfortunately,
however, the enormous body of information required for producing a reliable
input-output matrix is extremely difficult, expensive, and time-consuming to
gather, and ideally the matrix ought to be revised fairly frequently because
technology does not stay put. Thus far the Federal government has attempted the calculation of only two input-output tables, one, published in
1952, for the year 1947,[18] and a second, published in 1964, for the year
1958.[19] These years were selected, incidentally, because they were Census
of Manufacturers years; the necessary detailed data were therefore available.
Both of these studies took a sizable staff several years to prepare. The fact
that the data in these tables pertain to a year some five or six years prior to
publication date does not detract from their value as much as might be
assumed; the *relationships* among industrial sectors presumably do not
change drastically over relatively short intervals of time. Nevertheless, more
current tables would be more valuable for business conditions analysis purposes, and there seems to be no immediate prospect of a series of official
input-output tables on a regular and reasonably current basis.

Balance-of-payments Accounting

This last listed of the social accounting systems actually was the
earliest to be developed in something like its modern form in the United
States and to be incorporated into standard government statistics. The

[18] W. D. Evans and M. Hoffenberg, "The Interindustry Relations Study for 1947,"
Review of Economics and Statistics, vol. 34, no. 2, pp. 97ff., May, 1952.
[19] Morris R. Goldman, Martin L. Marimont, and Beatrice N. Vaccara, "The Interindustry Structure of the United States: A Report on the 1958 Input-Output Study,"
Survey of Current Business, U.S. Department of Commerce, November, 1964.

balance-of-payments series, compiled by the Department of Commerce Balance of Payments Division, measures the magnitude and composition of United States international transactions, both on current and capital accounts. The current account portion of the series contains an itemized statement of exports and imports of goods and services, while the capital account contains a list of financial transactions that arise either independently or in conjunction with current account transactions. Since the 1965 revision of the national income accounts, the definitions employed are consistent with those used in balance-of-payments accounting. We shall have more to say about the details of balance-of-payments accounting in the chapter on forecasting net exports.

PART TWO

AGGREGATIVE ECONOMIC THEORY

Mr. Lippmann may well blanch at even the narrower issue of what constitutes the good economy. Such questions are inescapably complex. The things that count in an economy's performance—the basic dimensions of performance—are numerous; and people differ, not only over what they include in their personal scales of values, but also over how to rank the performance criteria for the economy as a whole.

Moreover, the problem of rating the economy's performance has perplexing interdisciplinary ramifications; the more the economist tries to solve it, the more he finds himself venturing into the precincts of social philosophy and social psychology. Even within the usual boundaries of economics, there are basic dimensions of economic performance that lie outside the conventional limits of aggregative analysis. Notable in this regard are questions concerning efficiency of resource allocation and equity of income distribution among individuals.

Nevertheless, granting that the following list is somewhat arbitrary and that it bypasses a number of difficult and important issues, there are four distinct performance criteria upon which most debate about the general health of the American economy explicitly or implicitly converges. These are (1) the fullness of production, (2) the fullness of employment, (3) the stability of prices, and (4) the rate of capacity growth. Together they will provide a serviceable framework for this discussion.

THE FULLNESS OF PRODUCTION

One measure of how well an economy is doing is the volume of its physical output.[2] The gross national product series is the best comprehensive measure of national output, but not until it has been adjusted for price changes—not, that is, until it has been "deflated" by a price index that represents average changes in all the prices paid by end users. In the next chapter, where we consider the whole subject of price indexes and price behavior, we shall discuss the subject of adjustment for price variation. At the moment it is sufficient to know that the Department of Commerce does calculate and publish such a deflated or "real" GNP series.

In a growing economy, however, an evaluation of productive performance cannot safely be based upon a knowledge of real output alone. The United States economy's productive performance in 1929 was excellent. But in 1965 the same level of actual output—in 1965 prices, some $226 billion worth—would have been catastrophic. In 1965 even the 1962 level of production would have been far less satisfactory than it was in 1962. As time

---

[2] The composition of output also is important, but this is a function of resource allocation, and generally we shall be assuming that, via the market mechanism and other devices, the economy has techniques for solving the resource-allocation problem well enough so that it is safe for us to focus our attention on the total volume of activity.

passes, the size of the economy—its productive capacity—grows. Thus the quality of productive performance is essentially a relative thing; it must be gauged by the relationship between current output and current capacity, not by output alone.

This last is a view on its way to becoming a commonplace among students of business conditions. However, you still will find commentators who seem to challenge the whole concept of capacity when it is applied to the overall economy. There are good, but far from sufficient, reasons for such skepticism.

One of these reasons is that we have no statistical series that directly measures the changing productive capacity of the economy as a whole. As we shall have occasion to see in Part Four, it is not particularly difficult, from data we do have, to make some rough estimates of what the general course of United States capacity growth has been in the past and what it will be a short distance into the future. But such figures have nothing like the solidity or refinement of our output series. Consequently, the whole capacity idea remains shrouded in a statistical mist.

On top of this, capacity is not a clean-cut idea in any case. The economy, at any given moment of time, never has a literally unique capacity to produce just so much and no more. In unusual periods, such as national defense emergencies, the work force may be augmented by people who normally would choose to be at school, or keeping house, or in retirement. Under pressure, the productive plant may be used more intensively than usual, as when an industry goes from two to three shifts or from a five- to a six-day week, or when normal maintenance operations are postponed. World War II provides the classic case of a sudden, dramatic stretching of capacity to meet emergency needs and suggests the wisdom of refining our capacity concept to "normal peacetime capacity." Even in normal peacetime, however, there is no doubt that capacity is somewhat responsive to the ebb and flow of demand. In slack times, people teetering on the edge of retirement tip over into it; others stay in school longer; machines are removed from operation for repair and maintenance a little more freely; and so on.

This is a case, however, where it is fallacious to confuse imprecision with unimportance or unreality. Capacity is an imprecise concept in most individual firms, but no sane management can safely dispense with it. Statistically and conceptually fuzzy as it is, the normal productive capacity of the economy is just as real a phenomenon as output. The employed and unemployed factories, transport facilities, stores, workers, managements, and productive processes that make up normal productive capacity are just as concrete things as marketed goods and services. Because capacity and output differ and because capacity—in the short run, at least—moves persistently, almost irresistibly, upward, the basic question to be answered about the economy's productive performance is not simply, What are we doing? but, How nearly are we doing what we are tooled up to do and are disposed to do? Assuming away the statistical difficulties, we can say that an economy performs well, as far as production is concerned, when it minimizes the shortfall of actual from potential output. This shortfall, which we might call the "underproduction gap," can be shown either in (constant) dollar figures (e.g., $30 billion) or as a percentage of capacity (e.g., 5 percent).

THE FULLNESS OF EMPLOYMENT

Full employment is a far more familiar idea than full production. When the economy is producing at less than its currently normal capacity, it has various unemployed resources, including some unemployed labor. When a machine or a factory is out of work, an economic loss to the owners of the capital and to society results: the output that the machine or factory could be producing and is not. But when a man who is able to work and wants work has none, this is an evil in its own right, distinguishable from the loss of output to which his unemployment contributes. It is an evil, not simply because unemployment probably denies him access to income that he and his family need, but because it denies him the psychologically precious privilege of participating in what the society counts as productive activity. It is on this principle, basically, that full employment of labor becomes an ultimate criterion of economic welfare, separable from that of full production.

The best index of the economy's employment performance is the amount of involuntary unemployment. This is the difference between actual civilian employment and the civilian labor force. As we shall see shortly when we consider the character of data on the United States labor force, employment, unemployment, and working hours, it is not easy to get a measurement of the labor force that includes all the involuntarily unemployed and, at the same time, excludes those who are idle by choice. Moreover, some questions concerning units of measurement arise. Both the labor force and employment can be measured in terms either of workers or of man-hours. The former is the customary practice. However, this means that to obtain an accurate representation of total labor supply, one needs to multiply the number of persons in the labor force by the number of hours that, under normal circumstances, the average worker is willing to work. In addition, the expression of employment and unemployment in numbers of persons rather than in man-hours leaves the treatment of part-time involuntary unemployment in doubt. Is the latter hidden within the employment figure or added to unemployment in the form of whole-worker equivalents?

But these are matters of detail that we can consider later. In principle, the economy performs well in the employment dimension to the extent that it minimizes involuntary unemployment. Again, unemployment can be expressed either in numbers of persons (e.g., 4,300,000) or as a percentage of the civilian labor force (e.g., 5.8 percent).

THE STABILITY OF PRICES

Our economy rarely gets a high score on all four of the performance criteria under discussion; indeed, the circumstances that yield a high score by one criterion may compel a low score by another. This becomes evident when we consider the third basic criterion of economic welfare on our list, that of price stability. For the very boom-period circumstances that are likely to squeeze underproduction and underemployment down to their barest minima are also apt to cause upward pressure on prices.

The "good economy" has little room in it for a rising price level. Because prices and incomes never rise uniformly, inflation treats people unfairly.[3] It discriminates against creditors and against those with relatively fixed incomes. It can dangerously upset a nation's international trade balance and, in rampant form, can thoroughly disrupt the producing and distributing mechanism.

It is true that inflation, rather like intoxication, doesn't always feel bad, and some economists hold that a little of it is positively healthy. However, experience suggests that policies deliberately designed to produce a little inflation might well produce more than we want. At the very least, anyone diagnosing the current economic health of a nation must regard a rising price level as something to be watched closely and suspiciously.

What about price *de*flation? This also would seem to be an essential part of the stability issue. American fears of price-level misbehavior since the 1930s have focused upon rising rather than falling prices only because rising prices have appeared to be the more proximate danger. Violent price deflation would be at least as inequitable as violent inflation, and probably more demoralizing. On this side of the question, too, there is a minority of moderation advocates. They would like to see a slow downsettling of average prices over the long run. However, for the time being we shall be safe in assuming that avoidance of general deflation as well as inflation is ordinarily the best course.

Before leaving this subject, we should note that the system of prices in our or any other economy is a very complex thing, and the abstraction of *the* price level represents a tremendous oversimplification that we shall have to face in the next chapter.

THE RATE OF CAPACITY GROWTH

If you were convinced that the world was going to be blown up a year from next Thursday, the three norms already mentioned might be all you

---

[3] Some economists, who mean by inflation an expansion in total demand or in the money supply, insist that rising prices are only an effect of inflation, not the thing itself. For our purposes, however, inflation *is* a rise in average prices. This is the more pragmatic and familiar usage, and, in addition, avoids the misleading implications of the other.

would need for evaluating general economic performance. As it is, we have a much more enduring interest in the future. We want not only to use the productive capacity we have and to maintain full employment without inflation; we want continuing expansion in productive capacity. It would be hard to find any public figure in the United States who would contest the proposition that we need at least enough economic growth (1) to match our continuing increases in population and (2) to maintain the average growth in per capita real incomes that Americans have enjoyed during the past half century. In the past decade, perhaps more than ever before, economic expansion has seemed almost an end in itself. The actual rate of economic growth has become, in the United States, but also in a number of other countries, a major political campaign issue; both parties are firmly committed to the proposition that vigorous economic growth is a requisite of the good society.

While any reasonably conventional business conditions analyst must therefore count the rate of capacity growth as a principal dimension of economic performance, it is not so easy to say what our ideal rate really is. *Maximum* growth is not necessarily what we want, since increments in our productive potential usually require the sacrifice of some current consumption and of leisure time. We shall have to fall back on the question-begging word "optimum." The ideal is optimum growth, which implies the particular compromise between consumption and capital formation in the present and between capacity and leisure time in the future that is most congenial to the community as a whole. Whatever that optimum is, its value for any given year (or other unit of time) could be expressed either in dollars (e.g., $30 billion at 1957–1959 prices) or as a percentage increase (e.g., 4 percent).

AGGREGATE DEMAND AND ECONOMIC WELFARE: THE LINKAGES

We have identified four dimensions of economic performance: the fullness of production (or conversely the degree of underproduction), the fullness of employment (or the degree of underemployment), general price stability, and growth in productive capacity. As we have noted, economic performance seldom if ever gets a perfect score by all four of these criteria and not often, for any sustained period of time, by any one of them. Aggregative economic theory is an attempt to explain why economic performance meets, or fails to meet, these criteria, and why it meets them, individually and in combination, only to the degree that it does. In effect, aggregative economic theory is a set of hypotheses about *causation*[4]—

[4] We are using the term "causation" in its empirical sense; i.e., as a matter of observation one can determine that a given combination of circumstances generally produces a certain result, and if the identification of circumstances is complete enough, and

hypotheses that are sufficiently tenable to be useful in explaining past economic performance and, it is to be hoped, in predicting future economic performance.

The theorist approaches the problem of identifying tenable hypotheses by two devices. First, he breaks his problem into pieces. For example, we have already started to theorize by breaking the problem of total economic performance into four pieces: fullness of production, fullness of employment, stability of prices, and rate of economic growth. Further, we have said that fullness of production, in the most immediate sense, is the relationship between actual output and productive capacity. Similarly, we have said that fullness of employment is the relationship between actual employment and the labor force. We have thus broken our problem down into more manageable components.

Second, the theorist tries to identify lines of causation. What determines capacity? What determines output? And then he tries to build a family tree of determinants. What are the determinants of the determinants of capacity? Of the determinants of output? And so on.

It is the nature of systematic analysis that unanswered questions about the determinants of determinants always remain. The curtain of ignorance never is entirely rolled back. But, in practice, particular pieces of analytical work pause or stop because the investigator finds he is no longer able to identify the immediately underlying causal factors, or feels that, given his limited purpose, such identification is not worth the time it will take.

Furthermore, analysis of the economic process, which takes place over time, is complicated by the fact that causation is often not simple, one-way causation, but two-way or circular. For example, we observe that employment is determined, in part, by the level of aggregate demand, but also that as more people are employed over time, their incomes augment aggregate demand. That is, aggregate demand is a determinant of employment but, over time, employment is a determinant of aggregate demand. This problem of circularity is one of the most difficult ones to handle in economic theorizing, but failure to do so is sure to result in unsound hypotheses.

Economic theorists have long recognized that the most conspicuous determinant of overall economic performance is aggregate demand, and the biggest part of macroeconomic theory—and most of the remainder of this book—has to do with the determination of aggregate demand. Before delving into the determinants of aggregate demand, however, we need to specify more clearly the linkage between aggregate demand and the economy's ultimate performance, and in addition, the linkages between other major determinants and economic performance. This we shall do, first in broad, swift strokes, and then in the rest of this chapter and the next, in more detail.

---

if the observation is precise enough, it can be said that the probability of that result ensuing is very high. An absolute or physical cause-effect relationship may or may not be involved.

THE DETERMINANTS OF UNDERPRODUCTION AND CAPACITY GROWTH

We have already noted that the fullness of production, or the degree of underproduction, is the relationship between actual output and capacity. The next step is to identify, if we can, the determinants of each of these.

Capacity

In order to push back our line of causation another step, it is convenient and useful to break capacity into two components: the labor supply (in man-hours) and the ability to produce per man-hour, or labor productivity. Thus, by definition;

$$\frac{\text{Capacity}}{\text{Labor supply (in man-hours)}} = \text{capacity per man-hour}$$

Therefore,

$$\text{Capacity} = \text{labor supply (in man-hours)} \times \text{capacity per man-hour}$$

The labor supply is obviously determined, fundamentally, by the size of the population, or more particularly, given existing customs and laws regarding child labor, by the size of the portion of the population of working age. A discussion of the determinants of the size of the population had better be left to others than economists, except for one point. Birthrates, in the United States and abroad, do seem to be somewhat responsive, after a certain lag, to changes in the level of economic activity, or more specifically, personal incomes.[5] The low United States birthrates of the mid-1930s are a case in point.[6] However, the effect of fluctuations in the birthrate on the *labor force* follows after a lag of fourteen years or more. And death rates, in the United States at least, show no clear, short-run responsiveness to changes in the level of economic activity. Thus, although we have here an example of circularity of causation—the size of the population being a determinant of productive capacity and hence the level of economic activity, but the level of economic activity being a determinant of population growth—the circularity is irrelevant for short-run analysis.

Not all those who are of working age want to work. The ratio of the number of persons "at work or seeking work" to the age-eligible population is called the labor-force "participation rate," and the number of persons at

[5] See Irma Adelman, "An Econometric Analysis of Population Growth," *American Economic Review*, vol. LIII, no. 3, pp. 314–339, June, 1963.

[6] It should be noted, however, that the birthrate in the United States had been declining quite steadily for decades prior to the 1930s and the steep decline began in the late 1920s, before the onset of the Great Depression. Influences other than purely economic were apparently at work.

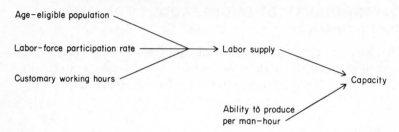

Figure **5–1.** Determinants of the labor supply.

work or seeking work is called the "labor force."[7]   We shall have more to say about the determinants of the participation rate later in this chapter.   A third determinant of the economy's supply of available man-hours of work, also to be discussed later in the chapter, consists of customary working hours—the average workweek, or more accurately (because of the increasing importance of vacations and holidays), the average work year.

Together, the three factors just identified—the size of the age-eligible population, the participation rate, and customary working hours—wholly determine the labor supply, which is the first determinant of capacity.   Expressed diagrammatically, with the arrows representing lines of causation, what we have said would appear somewhat as illustrated in Figure 5–1.

Next, what are the determinants of ability to produce per man-hour—labor productivity?   This is a very difficult question, and we shall give considerable attention to it later in the chapter.   Suffice it to say at this point that the determinants are numerous and complex; they include *all* the factors that influence total output except, by definition, the number of man-hours available for productive activity.   They include, for example, the availability and real cost of material resources.   One of the reasons (but by no means the only or chief reason) that certain of the underdeveloped countries of the world have such low levels of output per man-hour is that the raw material resources needed for production are so scarce; America, on the other hand, is richly endowed.   A second is the supply of capital, the result of past

---

[7] The reader who is experienced in these matters will note that we have identified, as a determinant of capacity, the labor force rather than the number of persons employed, thus subsuming away the problem of unemployment. It is true that, under the best of circumstances, there will no doubt always be *some* unemployment. With a given labor force, there is some practical maximum—less than 100 percent—which employment could reach. Thus most practicing economic analysts define "normal" capacity as a level of output that would still leave some specified percentage (e.g., 4 percent or 3 percent) of the labor force unemployed. Determination of the inevitable minimum, however, is so difficult—and controversial—that we have chosen here to define capacity in terms of its theoretical maximum. So defined, of course, capacity is not a completely attainable goal. Moreover, because the minimum feasible percentage of unemployment may change over time, an increase in the labor force may increase capacity more at one time than would the same proportionate increase at another time.

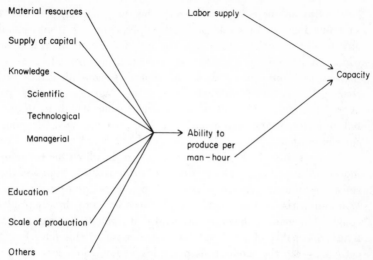

Figure 5–2.   Determinants of ability to produce per man-hour.

saving and capital formation.   It is well known that the use of machines and other equipment multiplies the productivity of the human hand.   Another is the level of knowledge, both scientific and technological, and managerial. Another is the level of manual skill, and more importantly, the level of education of the labor force, including both general education and professional education.   Still another is the scale of production, which is influenced, in turn, by the size of markets.   One of the important reasons for the rapid rise in recent years in output per man-hour in Western Europe may be the expansion, via the Common Market, of markets (and hence of the scale of production) to sizes more comparable to those prevailing in the United States.

There are many other determinants of output per man-hour, some of which we shall discuss later.   But those just identified are enough to suggest the pattern.   Expressed diagrammatically, again using arrows to indicate lines of causation, this "branch of our family tree" appears somewhat as illustrated in Figure 5–2.

Output

Because identification of the determinants of actual output is the main concern of the remainder of this book, we shall not try to pursue the determinants-of-determinants route very far at this point.   Clearly, aggregate demand—the total spending for final goods and services, gross national expenditure—is one of the proximate determinants.   This in turn is determined by personal consumption spending, business spending for new plant and equipment and inventory accumulation, net exports, and spending by Federal, state, and local governments.

But an increase in total spending may or may not lead to a corresponding increase in actual physical output. Instead, it may simply result in an increase in prices, with little or no increase in output. The extent to which an increase in aggregate demand will have its effect on prices rather than on real output depends on a complex of economic relationships that we shall call by the formidable name, the "aggregate-supply path." The aggregate-supply path will be discussed at some length in the next chapter, but it is important at this point to know what, shorn of refinements, the concept means.

Let's take, first, an extreme situation, in which the economy is operating at full capacity. The economy is "drum-tight." Suppose, then, that for some reason aggregate demand—total spending—increases by, say, 5 percent. Will output rise? Presumably not, because we were already producing all we could. (Remember, however, we said that capacity was not a clean, absolute figure, incapable of any stretching—but more of this later.) At the other extreme, when the economy is operating at far below capacity, so that there are unemployed resources of all sorts, an increase in aggregate demand bumps into no capacity barrier. Actual output can easily be increased, perhaps even at decreasing costs. In this case, the 5 percent increase in aggregate demand should result in an increase in output rather than in prices.

In between these extremes, the answer is not so easy. The relative impact of an increase in aggregate demand on prices and output will depend on the interaction of a variety of influences, including labor union policies, the price and wage policies of business firms, the effect on production costs of changes in the level of output, the character of markets and the influence of such government policies as antitrust, utility rate regulation, and the Kennedy and Johnson administrations' "wage-price guideposts," as well as the level of output in relation to capacity. It is this bundle of influences, and the way they seem to work out in practice, that we call the aggregate-supply path.

Now we are prepared to diagram two more limbs of our family tree of determinants—although the branches are pretty big branches with plenty of boughs and twigs to come. (See Figure 5–3.)

If the lines of causation were neatly one-way, we could ignore further determinants of determinants, consolidate our diagrams, and have a useful illustration of the process by which the level of underproduction is determined. Unfortunately, however, such is not the case. Economic forces do circle back on each other. To illustrate these back-circling effects, we have to abandon, in part, the analogy with the family tree—grandparents do not often marry their grandchildren. So our consolidated tree, showing a few of these back-circling effects, would look something like Figure 5–4.

There are innumerable back-circling lines that we could draw. But the five in Figure 5–4 illustrate the point. Line 1 says that changes in the labor supply influence production costs because, when labor is scarce, em-

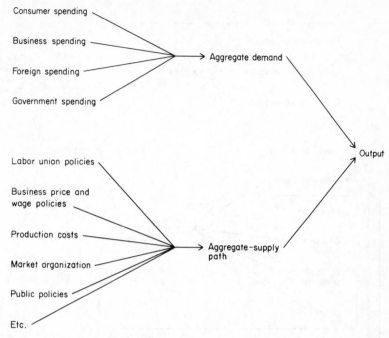

Figure **5–3.**   The determinants of output and the determinants of the determinants of output.

ployers may have to pay more to get workers and may have to hire less efficient persons. By affecting production costs, changes in the labor supply indirectly affect the aggregate-supply path.   Line 2 makes the obvious point that changes in labor productivity affect production costs, and hence the aggregate-supply path.   Line 3 says that changes in scientific and tech-nological knowledge are an important influence in business spending on new plant and equipment, which in turn is a determinant of aggregate demand. Line 4 reminds us that business investment, over time, affects the supply of capital, and therefore indirectly influences labor productivity.   Line 5 says that changes in aggregate demand are an important determinant of the scale of production, which in turn is a determinant of labor productivity.   And so on.   It would be helpful if, at this point, you stopped and drew some more back-circling lines on this diagram, explaining to yourself what they mean.

Aside from the particular back-circling relationships, however, this diagrammatic presentation illustrates a more general point.   We have alluded to this point already, but it warrants special emphasis.   This is that the factors determining underproduction do not arrange themselves into a simple hierarchy in which banks of determinants are neatly insulated from one another and causation all flows in a single direction.   Instead, particular variables can exert more than one significant determinative effect and, in so

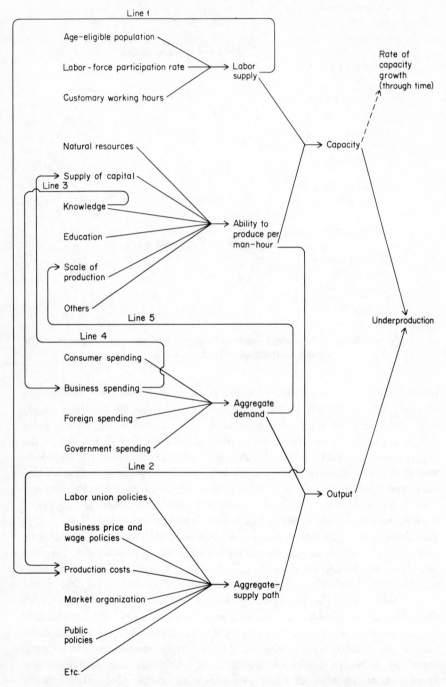

Figure 5-4. Determinants of underproduction and capacity growth.

doing, can be a more proximate cause of the economy's productive performance in one chain of determination than in the other.   Thus, for example, the labor supply and labor productivity jointly determine capacity and hence, in one sense, belong to the same level of abstraction as do the aggregate-supply path and aggregate demand, which jointly determine output; but since the labor supply and labor productivity also affect enterprises' costs of production, they also are what might be called "once-removed" determinants of the aggregate-supply path.

Finally, the figure rather clearly establishes the linkage between aggregate demand and the underproduction dimension of aggregate economic behavior.   The degree of underproduction is not uniquely determined by demand.   Rather, three other major variables—labor supply, output per man-hour, and the aggregate-supply path—combine with aggregate demand exhaustively to determine underproduction.   Changes in aggregate demand will cause changes in the underproduction gap to the extent that the labor supply, labor productivity, and the aggregate-supply path do not change. Thus the apparent linkage between demand and productive performance— the extent to which aggregate demand in practice seems to determine performance—will depend on the stability of the other three factors.

The importance of considering the nature and variability of these other major determinants of productive performance will become doubly apparent in a moment.   For these same factors also combine with demand to determine the degree of price stability and the fullness of employment that the economy achieves.

THE DETERMINANTS OF PRICE STABILITY AND UNEMPLOYMENT

In the previous section, we concluded that the extent to which changes in aggregate money demand cause changes in real output depends upon the shape of the aggregate-supply path.   This concept is of sufficient complexity and importance to supply the focus for the whole of the next chapter.   But even before we know much about the aggregate-supply path, it is evident that the same factors that determine how much of a change in money demand translates into an output change also determine how much of it translates into a price change.   Thus, diagrammatically:

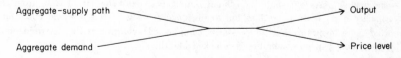

All this simple diagram says is that the same combination of influences that determine output also determine the general level of prices, and that any changes in the determinants of prices and output, and in the determinants of those determinants, are likely to affect *both* prices and output; just how

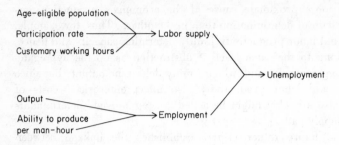

Figure **5–5.**   Determinants of unemployment.

much and in what degree depends on the shape of the aggregate-supply path. This may seem to be an obvious conclusion, but it is one that many politicians could not get through their heads in the years during and immediately following World War II.

We have defined unemployment as the difference between the labor supply and actual employment (all expressed in man-hours rather than men). Actual employment (in man-hours), in turn, is determined by actual output and average output per man-hour. That is, by definition,

$$\frac{\text{Output}}{\text{Output per man-hour}} = \text{employment (in man-hours)}$$

In other words, a rise in production must cause a rise in employment unless there is an offsetting rise in production per unit of labor.[8]   Consolidating this information with some drawn from our previous charts, we can diagram the determinants of unemployment (in man-hours) as in Figure 5–5.

Although this should be familiar material by now, it would pay you to stop and think out the linkages shown in Figure 5–5, putting plus and minus signs on each variable.   If the participation rate goes up $(+)$, other things remaining unchanged, what would be the effect $(+ \text{ or } -)$ on unemployment? And so forth.

[8] At this point the text glosses over a distinction that will be made later but should be mentioned now: as a determinant of capacity, "ability to produce per man-hour" represents output per man-hour under normal full-capacity operations.   However, it is the actual, not potential, output per man-hour that combines with actual output to determine employment.   As we shall see, actual output per man-hour can deviate from its full-capacity norm when operations fall to subcapacity levels.   Thus it would make for somewhat more accurate (but unnecessarily complicated) charting if the determinants of the employment portion of our Fig. 5–5 looked like this:

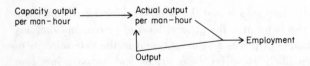

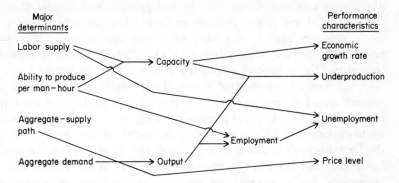

Figure **5–6.** The major determinants of the economy's aggregative
performance.

THE DETERMINATIVE PATTERN SUMMARIZED

Consolidating even more, Figure 5–6 puts together in one picture some
of the major relationships that have been encountered in this preview discussion of the linkages between the major determinants of economic performance. This is a deliberately selective picture, even in terms of our
analysis thus far. It shows none of the antecedent determinants of the labor
supply, labor productivity, the aggregate-supply path, or aggregate demand;
and the lines of causation that it indicates are exclusively ones that can be
deduced by definitional logic. Further, it leaves out of account all the causal
effects, back-circling and otherwise, that these four major determinants—and
their determinants—work on each other. This would be a dangerous oversimplification had not some of the less obvious interrelationships already been
anticipated in previous diagrams and were not others to be identified in subsequent chapters. As it is, the present chart has the virtue of spotlighting
those linkages between aggregate demand and economic welfare which are
incontrovertible, given the definitions that have been adopted. Again, it
would be worth your time to spend a few moments tracing through these
linkages.

PRODUCTIVITY AND ITS MEASUREMENT

PRODUCTIVITY CONCEPTS

All productive activity is like the baking of a cake in the sense that it
is a transformation process; it involves the conversion of a collection of
ingredients (inputs) into a product (output). This is as true of distributing
or marketing activities as it is of farming or manufacturing; even though

distributors may not change the physical products they handle, they attach
new locational and other attributes to them. The productive activity of the
whole economy may be regarded as a vast and complex transformation
process that converts various inputs into a variety of products. It is in this
context that the concept of productivity can best be understood.

It should be emphasized at once that productivity is not a synonym for
production. The term refers not to the outcome of the productive process
but to a characteristic of the process—namely, its productiveness as measured
by the relation of its output to the volume of one or more of its inputs.
Productivity is the *ratio* between output and input. Using the symbol O
for output, and borrowing temporarily I for any or all inputs (later it will
be reserved for investment), we can say that any productivity concept concerns one version or another of the fraction O/I.

This last statement, however, may leave you dissatisfied. As we
learned in the chapters on social accounting, in a given time period the total
value of inputs (measured by income payments generated in the course of
production) must, by definition, be exactly equal to the total value of output,
i.e., GNP = GNI. The ratio of *total* output to *total* inputs is therefore
obviously and invariably 1—a not very illuminating statistic. Further, this
inevitable equality between total inputs and output also holds in a technical
or engineering sense. Production never involves the making of something
out of nothing. It follows that the interesting and significant productivity
concepts are those which relate total output to *some* but not all of the inputs.
Such productivity concepts, when they are followed over time, are the ones
that give us quantitative approximations of the idea of productive efficiency.

The identification and classification of all the relevant inputs in a
single production process, let alone in the immensely complex multiple
processes of the entire economy, is a slippery job. Traditionally economists
have tried to do it by lumping all the possible inputs into the three crude
factor-of-production categories—the services of land, labor, and capital. The
problem, however, is that each of these three traditional factors actually
represents a mixture of some things that are essentially quantitative—the
amounts of labor, capital, and natural resources employed in or available
for the production process—with other things that are nonquantitative, or at
least not directly measureable.[9] These other things concern generally the
qualities of the physical factors and the processes, including the proportions,
in which they are combined. We might list some of these qualitative inputs
as the character of the tools (not just their weight or constant-dollar cost)

---

[9] See, however, Edward Denison's heroic effort to estimate the quantitative contribution to productivity increase of such "nonmeasurable" factors as increased scientific
and technological knowledge, increased efficiency resulting from economics of scale, increase in the quality of the labor force through general education, etc., in his *The
Sources of Economic Growth in the United States*, Committee for Economic Development,
Supplementary Paper no. 13, New York, 1962.

with which the economy works; the nature of its productive processes, e.g., types of plant layouts and of chemical processes; the organization of its production—including its transportation, communications, and marketing—operations; and the intelligence, skills, education, and personal attitudes of workers and managers.

For present purposes, it is less important to itemize these qualitative inputs, however, than to distinguish between them and the quantitative inputs. For what we mean by a rise in productive efficiency is a rise in output relative to the quantitative inputs. If total input may be said to equal $I_L + I_K + I_N + I_a + I_b + \cdots + I_n$, where the subscripts L, K, and N designate the quantities of labor, capital, and natural resources available or employed, and all the other subscripts refer to qualitative inputs, then the best measure of productive efficiency is the concept $O/(I_L + I_K + I_N)$, i.e., the ratio of output to the sum of the quantitative inputs only. And the best measure of change in efficiency is the change in the value of this fraction over time, for all such change must be explained by changes in other variables than the quantities of labor, capital, and natural resources employed.

We said a moment ago that the quantitative inputs of labor, capital, and natural resource services are directly measurable. This is true conceptually. But statistically it is very hard to make good estimates of capital and natural resource inputs, partly because of the lack of reliable national wealth data and partly because of the very difficult price deflation problems encountered when we try to add labor, capital, and natural resource inputs together.

Partly for these statistical reasons, the most popular and familiar productivity concept has become that which relates output simply to the labor input, i.e., O/I_L. It is relatively easy to estimate the quantity of labor services available or supplied in a particular period, and, because in this concept there is no need for adding labor, capital, and other inputs together, the labor input can be expressed simply in terms of its own physical units—i.e., units of labor time. Thus it is that, when most analysts say "productivity," they mean, unless they explain otherwise, "output per man-hour." This is the productivity concept ordinarily used in this book.

LABOR, CAPITAL, AND "TOTAL FACTOR" PRODUCTIVITY

The contemporary focus upon the output-per-man-hour variety of productivity is not entirely a matter of statistical expediency. In terms of human values, labor is our most precious resource, and, insofar as the labor force is representative of the total population, changes in output per man-hour signal changes in real income per capita, which is about as good a single indicator of economic welfare as there is. However, since we shall use it extensively, we should be sure we understand what output per man-hour means. Changes in this variable represent changes in output that cannot be attributed to changes in the physical quantity of labor but may be attributable to anything else, including changes in the physical quantities of capital and natural resources.[10]

The usual term for output per man-hour, "labor productivity," is technically correct in that it identifies the physical quantity of labor as the denominator of the productivity fraction.   But it can easily be misunderstood because increases in labor productivity do not necessarily evince improved skill, resourcefulness, or morale on the part of labor. They may, but they also may not. Increases in output per man-hour may, for example, be the result solely of increased use of capital or of technological innovation. Properly construed, labor productivity measures not the efficiency of labor but the efficiency with which labor time is used in the production process, whether that efficiency is the result of labor's own efforts or of other influences.

It is common knowledge that output per man-hour has risen historically in the United States, and so has the ratio of capital inputs to labor inputs.   But what has been happening to capital productivity—to O/I_K? This is by no means self-evident. Theoretically it would be possible for the efficiency with which capital is used in the productive process to fall while, at the same time, the increasing provision of plant, tools, and inventories per unit of labor raised output per man-hour—although it would also seem probable, in this event, that declining real rewards to capital would sooner or later discourage investment.

The evidence is that capital productivity also has risen secularly. John Kendrick, formerly of the U.S. Department of Commerce, has completed for the National Bureau of Economic Research one of the first attempts to develop a sustained series of annual capital productivity estimates for the United States.[11] In a trail-breaking assault on the statistical difficulties noted above, Kendrick has grouped the physical quantities of capital and natural resources into a single "property" category. He finds that capital productivity O/I_{KN} has risen, but not so rapidly as labor productivity. Any other finding would have been strange, in view of the rise in the capital-labor

[10] If we assume that the geographic boundaries of an economy are fixed, it may sound strange to suggest an increase in the physical quantity of its natural resources. One answer, of course, is that changes in technology may, in effect, create natural assets out of what have been useless possessions. If, however, such advances are to be treated as occurring exclusively in qualitative inputs, upward variability of natural resources is still possible through the acquisition of increased raw material imports, presumably in exchange for increased exports of finished goods or services. Since some natural resources can be depleted, it is evident that they are capable of downward variation.

[11] John Kendrick, *Productivity Trends in the United States*, National Bureau of Economic Research, Inc., New York, published by Princeton University Press, Princeton, N.J., 1961, and his earlier *Productivity Trends: Capital and Labor*, National Bureau of Economic Research, Inc., New York, Occasional Paper no. 53, 1956; reprinted from *Review of Economics and Statistics*, vol. 38, no. 3, pp. 248–257, August, 1956.

ratio. He estimates that from 1889 to 1957, in the United States private economy, real gross product per unit of capital input increased by 1 percent (by $\frac{1}{2}$ percent from 1889 to 1919 and by $1\frac{1}{3}$ percent from 1919 to 1957).[12]

In the same work, grouping all the physical inputs together, Kendrick developed the first major series of estimates of total factor productivity for the United States. As one would expect, he finds that this concept, $O/(I_L + I_{KN})$, has grown faster than capital productivity alone but slower than labor productivity alone. Kendrick's work may presage increasing attention by analysts to total factor productivity.[13] For the time being, however, labor productivity will continue to occupy center stage.

VARIATIONS AMONG LABOR PRODUCTIVITY CONCEPTS

A point footnoted earlier now deserves emphasis. To maintain the familiar input-output terminology, we have been talking only about output per man-hour, without any modifying adjective. Yet labor productivity found its place in the conceptual framework adopted earlier in the chapter as a determinant not of actual output but of potential, capacity output.

The difficulty can be resolved by recognizing that, depending upon the purpose at hand, output per man-hour may refer either to actual labor productivity or to full-capacity labor productivity. The two are distinct, yet closely related. And quantitatively they are not apt to differ too widely.

---

[12] John Kendrick, *Productivity Trends in the United States, op. cit.*, p. 60.

[13] Note that the term "total factor productivity" is a misnomer if total factors is a synonym for total inputs but is proper if total factors can be equated to total physical inputs.

The following is an extreme arithmetical example of the relationships among the three productivity concepts:

	Period 1	Period 2	Period 2 as a percent of period 1
(A) Total output	100	480	480
(B) Man-hours	10	20	200
(C) Constant labor cost per man-hour	5	5	100
(D) Total labor cost at constant factor prices (B × C)	50	100	200
(E) Units of capital	10	40	400
(F) Constant capital cost per unit of capital	5	5	100
(G) Total capital cost at constant factor prices (E × F)	50	200	400
(H) Total factor inputs (D + G)	100	300	300
(I) Output per man-hour (A/B)	10	24	240
(J) Output per unit of capital (A/E)	10	12	120
(K) Output per total factor input (A/H)	1	1.6	160

Strictly speaking, "ability to produce per man-hour" in our earlier diagrams represents potential labor productivity; it is this which helps determine capacity. However, actual output per man-hour is also in the scheme, for it is this, rather than capacity per man-hour, which is among the direct determinants of employment and of production costs (and, hence, of price-output relationships). But actual productivity is not independent of full-capacity productivity. Instead it is largely governed by the factors that determine capacity per man-hour, and deviates from the latter only when subnormal or supernormal operations cause a less efficient use or more efficient use of productive facilities, a change in worker morale, or the subtraction of less efficient employees. These fluctuations of actual productivity around the normal, it should be noted, are much less extreme than the differences between total output and total capacity, since the latter reflect, not only variations in labor productivity, but also differences between actual and full employment.

Schematically, therefore, it can be assumed that capacity per man-hour is the more representative norm, and more stable than actual output per man-hour. Statistically the dependence is the other way around. Normal capacity per man-hour, like capacity itself, cannot be directly measured. Its course can be estimated only from observations of actual output per man-hour in periods judged to be ones of normal full employment.

Measures of output per man-hour may be calculated for productive units of all sizes—for firms, subdivisions of firms, industries, groups of industries, or the whole economy. Aside from the matter of their scope, measures of labor productivity differ most significantly in their measurement of output—particularly as to whether they adopt the value-added or the total-transactions concept of production. Virtually all aggregative productivity measurements concern national product per man-hour; they exclude duplicative transactions. Thus in the United States the usual measure is GNP/man-hour.[14] However, in the past most *industry-by-industry* productivity measurements have reflected the gross value of products delivered. Since the changes in such estimates may reflect variations in an industry's acquisitions (in agriculture, for example, increased purchases of farm equipment, fuels, and fertilizers from other industries) rather than in its own productive contributions, they are not strictly comparable with aggregative productivity figures.

One other possible source of difference among the trends of industry-by-industry and of national productivity estimates should be noted. It is quite possible for *national* productivity to rise without any increase in produc-

---

[14] Technically, because our method for estimating in GNP the relatively small volume of government product, i.e., government wage and salary payments, does not permit the calculation of productivity changes in that sector, the more exact aggregate measure is gross *private* product divided by private man-hours—GPP being GNP minus government product.

tivity on an industry-by-industry basis, if there is a shift in the economy's product mix.   For example, if workers shift from agriculture (a low-productivity industry) to manufacturing (a high-productivity industry), average output per man-hour for the nation as a whole would rise even though there were no change in output per man-hour in either agriculture or manufacturing.

AMERICAN PRODUCTIVITY EXPERIENCE

The Department of Labor has published annual indexes of output per man-hour in the United States private economy since 1947, and estimates going back to 1909 are available.   Two series are offered, one based on man-hour data developed by the Bureau of Labor Statistics (BLS), the other on labor force and man-hour statistics compiled by the Bureau of the Census for the BLS. The former series uses in the denominator of the O/I_L fraction total man-hours *paid*; the latter series uses total man-hours *worked*. Theoretically, the differences between the two series represent the change in the proportion of hours for paid vacations and paid sick leave to total paid hours. Actually, the two series also reflect differences in statistical methods in collecting the basic data.   The Census data, for example, are from sample surveys of households, whereas the Bureau of Labor Statistics data are obtained from reports of establishments.[15]   Both series use as the numerator of the O/I_L fraction, for the period since 1929, the Commerce constant-dollar GNP series (GPP, actually, for reasons explained in an earlier footnote).

For historical productivity estimates in the United States prior to 1909, we must rely on the findings of private researchers.   Several have done very substantial pieces of work in this area; perhaps the most extensive is that of a Twentieth Century Fund group under the leadership of J. Frederic Dewhurst.[16]   The more recent studies of Kendrick have the advantage of using pre-1929 output data that are explicitly linked to the official (post-1929) Commerce GNP series.[17]   For our purposes, however, we shall use the Department of Labor series, which has the advantage of being annually updated.

Before we examine these productivity figures, several caveats should be noted.   First, data on both output and man-hours are incomplete in many

[15] See *Trends in Output per Man-Hour in the Private Economy, 1909–1958*, U.S. Department of Labor, Bulletin 1249, 1959, and current issues of the *Annual Report of the Labor Force*, U.S. Department of Labor.   See also *Manpower Report of the President and a Report on Manpower Requirements, Resources, Utilization, and Training*, U.S. Department of Labor, March, 1966. The same productivity data are also published in the Statistical Appendix to the annual *Economic Report of the President*.

[16] J. Frederic Dewhurst and Associates, *America's Needs and Resources*, The Twentieth Century Fund, Inc., New York, 1947; and Dewhurst and Associates, *America's Needs and Resources: A New Survey*, The Twentieth Century Fund, Inc., New York, 1955.

[17] Kendrick, *Productivity Trends in the United States, op, cit.*, pp. 332ff.

industries or categories, and various imputations are therefore necessary. Second, existing techniques for converting current to constant dollars do not adequately correct for changes in quality of product.[18] The estimates therefore probably significantly understate actual productivity increase over the past half century or so. (This source of error is usually not significant for short-run comparisons.) Third, maintaining consistency between output and man-hour input data is difficult, especially for periods of time when there are major shifts in the composition of output (e.g., during World War II). For this reason, great significance should not be attached to small, year-to-year changes. Nevertheless, with these qualifications, the data do give us a reasonably reliable picture of productivity experience in the United States.

The data, in index form, are shown in Figure 5–7. The outstanding fact revealed by these figures is the substantial and sustained growth in aggregate output per man-hour in the United States. The average annual gain in output per man-hour during the entire period, 1909 to 1965, was about $2\frac{1}{3}$ percent. Substantial variations from this long-run average, however, have occurred. There was almost no net gain in productivity from 1909 to 1918, but then productivity surged upward during the 1920s. A major setback occurred, output per man-hour actually declining, in the early years of the Great Depression. Another upward surge came, however, in the pre-World War II years. During and immediately following World War II, as workers shifted first into then out of war-related industries, productivity experience was uneven; the periods of conversion to and reconversion from war production were years of rather poor productivity performance. After reconversion, however, another vigorous rise occurred; output per man-hour increased by an average of nearly $4\frac{1}{4}$ percent a year from 1947 to 1955. The year 1956 saw virtually no gain. Since then, productivity performance, though less spectacular than during the pre-1956 years, has been substantial; the average rate of increase from 1956 to 1965 amounted to about 3 percent.

Offhand, figures like $2\frac{1}{3}$, 3, or even 4 percent may not sound particularly momentous. However, when it is recognized that this has been our average experience *per year;* that a constant rate of increase means increasing absolute increments in output; that a $2\frac{1}{2}$ percent growth in productivity alone—without any increase in the labor supply—would mean a doubling in the size of the economy every generation, reckoned at twenty-eight years; that productivity gains alone accounted for more than two-thirds of the expansion in total real output from 1909 to 1965; and that at present a 3 percent a year advance in productivity means about $20 billion of additional capacity in the United States, it can be appreciated that here we have hold of the most arresting statistical characteristic of the American economy.

A second important fact that emerges from United States productivity

---

[18] See the next chapter for further discussion of this point.

experience is the wide dispersion of productivity levels and rates of change among the various productive subdivisions of the economy.   Figure 5–7 refers to gross productivity experience only.   In his later work Kendrick managed to develop respectable value-added-per-man-hour estimates for a large number of particular industries.   And more recently the Bureau of Labor Statistics has carried his pioneering work forward with a series of studies of the relationship between output in physical units and man-hours of production workers in selected industries.   These studies indicate higher productivity levels in manufacturing than in the distribution and service areas; a very considerable dispersion among the productivity experiences of particular manufacturing industries; and, finally, wide variations in the rate of productivity growth in individual industries over time.   They show, as one

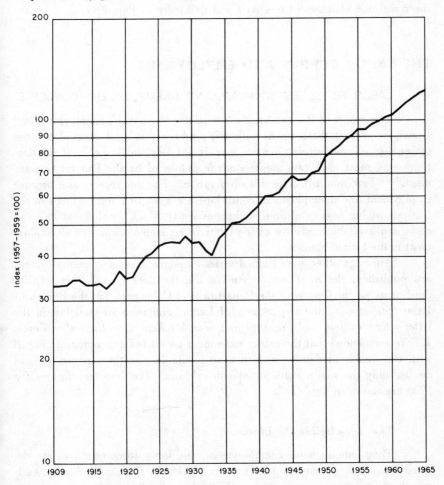

Figure 5–7. Gross private product per man-hour (labor force series) in the United States, 1909–1965 (Index, 1957–1959 = 100). Source: U.S. Department of Labor.

would expect, that the extent and timing of increases in productivity in individual industries have been closely associated with the introduction of machinery and equipment that permits substitution of mechanical energy for human (or animal) energy. Agriculture, for example, displayed relatively low productivity performance (measured both absolutely and by rate of increase) until the widespread adoption in the late 1930s of the tractor and associated equipment. Probably, at any given moment, only a few sectors of the economy are doing most of the job of carrying forward our economic progress. If so, however, the gains made by these (for the time being) highly progressive industries tend to be generalized to the rest of us through adjustments in costs, prices, and income payments. This last matter, that of productivity-gains distribution, we shall encounter tangentially in some of the remaining chapters of this part and pointedly in Part Five.

THE LABOR SUPPLY AND EMPLOYMENT

LABOR FORCE, EMPLOYMENT, AND UNEMPLOYMENT CONCEPTS

The report of the President's Committee to Appraise Employment and Unemployment Statistics opens with this sentence: "It has been said that the seasonally adjusted unemployment rate is—at least in its political implications—the most important single statistic published by the Federal Government."[19] Few would dispute this observation. For this reason, and because employment and unemployment conditions are a major point of focus in the analysis of business conditions, it behooves us to look carefully at the concepts and available measures of the labor force, employment, and unemployment in the United States.

Although other more limited series on employment and unemployment are published, the most comprehensive are the data compiled jointly by the Bureau of the Census of the Department of Commerce and the Bureau of Labor Statistics of the Department of Labor, and released in detail in the latter's *Employment and Earnings and Monthly Report on the Labor Force*. It is recommended that the reader examine a recent issue to acquaint himself with the wealth of detailed information available. In these pages, we can discuss only the major concepts and definitions. The summary figures for 1965 are shown in Table 5–1.

The Age-eligible Population

These employment, unemployment, and labor force estimates are derived from a single sampling exercise conducted by the Census Bureau each month. The survey covers some 35,000 households in 357 labor market

---

[19] *Measuring Employment and Unemployment*, prepared by the President's Committee to Appraise Employment and Unemployment Statistics, 1962, p. 9.

Table 5-1. Population, Labor Force, Employment, and Unemployment in the United States, 1965

	Millions of per- sons *
(A) Total population	194.6
(B) Noninstitutional population 14 years of age and older	136.2
(C) Total labor force	78.4
(D) Labor-force participation rate (C as a percent of B)	57.5%
(E) Armed forces	2.7
(F) Civilian labor force (C − E)	75.6
(G) Civilian employment	72.2
(H) Nonagricultural employment	67.6
(I) Agricultural employment	4.6
(J) Unemployment (F − G)	3.5
(K) Unemployment as a percent of the civilian labor force	4.6%

* Except as indicated.

Source: *Survey of Current Business*, U.S. Department of Commerce, April,
1966, p. S-12.

areas, selected to be representative of all types of areas in the nation's cities,
small towns, rural districts, and farms. The results (inflated into national
totals) are published in *Employment and Earnings and Monthly Report on
the Labor Force*.[20] The survey technique would not be essential for compiling employment figures; data gathered from employers might suffice for this
purpose.[21] But the survey is necessary for getting a good estimate of unemployment. The Census surveyors question a scientifically selected sample of
all persons in each labor market area who are eligible for employment by
reason of age and by reason of not being locked up in an institution. Those
surveyed (or other members of their family on their behalf) elect themselves,
by their answers to prescribed questions, into or out of the labor force, and
thereby, if they are not employed, into or out of the ranks of the unemployed.

Under Census procedures the eligible portion of the population from
which survey samples are drawn is defined as the noninstitutional population
fourteen years of age and older. In 1965 this amounted to 136.2 million
persons, or some 70 percent of the total United States population.

The Labor-force Participation Rate

As Figure 5-8 attests, the percentage of the age-eligible population that
joins the total labor force appears to be one of the least volatile variables in
the American economy. The participation rate, however, reflects a complex

[20] Summary data are published regularly in the *Survey of Current Business* and
in *Economic Indicators*.

[21] However, this technique, used by the Bureau of Labor Statistics in compiling a
series on nonagricultural employment by industry, results in one person who holds two
jobs being counted as two employed persons.

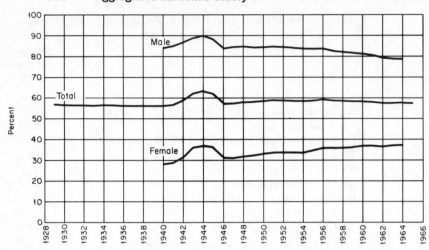

Figure 5–8.   Labor-force participation rates in the United States: Total, male
and female, 1929–1965.   (Total labor force as a percentage
of the noninstitutional population fourteen years of age and
older.   Data on noninstitutional population prior to 1940 estimated at 99 percent of total population.) Source: U.S. Department of Labor.

of social influences, which are subject to gradual change and do not all move
in the same direction.   For example, for many years, and especially since
World War II, the average age at which individuals leave school has been
rising, and the average retirement age has been falling.   But these negative
effects upon the total participation rate have been more than offset by the
increasing numbers of women seeking remunerative work.   These offsetting
tendencies are indicated on the chart by the gradual convergence of the
participation rate lines for males and females.   Moreover, the participation
rate is not entirely impervious to the character of current business conditions;
when jobs are easy to get, some of them are taken by people, particularly
married women, who are on the margin of the labor force and at other times
might not regard themselves as job seekers.

Nevertheless, the only time in recent decades in the United States that
the labor-force participation rate has undergone rapid change was during
and immediately after World War II.   At that time, under intensive social
and economic pressure, the rate rose some 7 percentage points, from 56 percent in 1940 to 63 percent in 1944.   It is interesting to note that after the
war, as these marginal participants left the labor force, the participation rate
did not quite get back to the prewar level; the low point was 57.2 percent
in 1946.   Since 1956, the effect on the participation rate of the tendency for
young folks to remain in school longer has been amplified by the increase in
the proportion of our population composed of persons in the age range of
fourteen to twenty-two years.

The Civilian Labor Force, Employment and Unemployment

The age-eligible civilians canvassed in the Census Bureau's monthly survey of the labor force are asked whether, in the survey week, they are working at least one hour for pay, or at least fifteen hours without pay in a family farm or business. If they say they are, or that they are not because they are on vacation, are ill, or are striking, they are classified as employed.[22] Of the remaining respondents, those are classified as unemployed who say they are actively seeking work, or have been laid off with instructions to return to work, or have stopped looking for work only because they are convinced there is none to be had in their localities. Together the unemployed and the civilian employed constitute the civilian labor force. And the latter plus the Armed Forces (the size of which is ascertained from government sources) constitute the total labor force.

The Census Bureau breaks down total United States civilian employment into only two components, agricultural and nonagricultural. Much more detailed employment figures by industries are available in the Bureau of Labor Statistics series on nonagricultural employment. However, the BLS series on nonagricultural employment is not entirely comparable with the Census series of the same name, partly for the reason indicated in an earlier footnote.

The Variety of Unemployment Concepts

Economists and labor supply statisticians use the term "unemployment"—either with or without modifying adjectives—in a number of different ways.

What the Census Bureau calls, simply, unemployment is exclusively involuntary unemployment in the economic sense. Those, such as retired persons, who are voluntarily unemployed are, insofar as the Census Bureau is concerned, not members of the labor force.

Economists classify some, but not necessarily all, involuntary unemployment as "frictional." This term refers to that minimum number of persons who, in a dynamic economy where products and tastes change and firms and industries rise and fall, are looking for their first jobs or are in transit between jobs. Analysts differ in their estimates of how much frictional unemployment is really necessary if the economy is to run smoothly and is not to encounter serious labor bottlenecks. The answer depends heavily upon the mobility of labor. Moreover, it is difficult to distinguish between purely frictional unemployment and what has been called "structural" unemployment. Although the term frictional unemployment is sometimes used

---

[22] Prior to January, 1957, persons who had been temporarily laid off with instructions to return to work in not more than thirty days were also classified as employed, i.e., as "with a job but not at work." Now, however, they are classified as unemployed.

to include structural unemployment, a more useful definition is to limit the term "frictional" to quite temporary unemployment, regardless of cause, and to refer to unemployment that is "the result of deep-seated and relatively permanent changes in the quality and location of the demand for a supply of labor"[23] as structural. It is also probably desirable to separate out of frictional unemployment that which is the result of annually repetitive seasonal influences related to the weather, holidays, or customs, and identify it as "seasonal unemployment." The Bureau of Labor Statistics does not attempt to measure the amount of seasonal unemployment per se, but it does adjust the employment and unemployment data for "normal seasonal variation"—a statistical process that has aroused a certain amount of rather technical controversy in recent years. Any unemployment over and above purely seasonal, frictional, and structural unemployment might be called "cyclical" or "aggregate-demand" unemployment.

It is obviously a very difficult statistical job to draw a clean line between these various types of unemployment, and the Bureau of Labor Statistics makes no such attempt. The Bureau does classify unemployment by duration, age, sex, color, occupational group, and reason for not working, and it provides data on part-time employment that are helpful in determining to what extent the short hours are voluntary or a form of partial unemployment.

Aside from the statistical difficulties of distinguishing among these types of unemployment, it should be recognized that the concepts are not clearly separate and distinct. Although seasonal, frictional, and even structural unemployment are likely always to be present, unemployment attributable to these influences tends to be reduced under conditions of strong aggregate demand. It is not clear, therefore, whether such unemployment should be classified as aggregate-demand unemployment or one of the other categories. The conceptual distinctions are nevertheless useful.

Full employment can be understood, if you prefer, as a literal absence of involuntary unemployment. In this case, in view of the frictional factor, it is neither a healthy nor entirely attainable objective. The more conventional practice, which is being followed here, is to define full employment as an absence of all but frictional (including seasonal) unemployment. And because the labor force itself is, to some extent, a function of the level of demand, "normal full employment" also implies a normal labor-force participation rate.

Another significant distinction is that between partial and complete (involuntary) unemployment. Some people working only part time do not want to work more and should not be counted as partially unemployed. But, particularly in times of slack business, much partial idleness plainly is in-

[23] Suggested by the Subcommittee on Economic Statistics of the Joint Economic Committee in *Unemployment: Terminology, Measurement, and Analysis*, 1961, p. 8.

voluntary and should figure in a total unemployment estimate. Since the Census Bureau's unemployment series covers only full-time idleness, it understates the full extent of involuntary unemployment. In recognition of this fact, the Bureau of Labor Statistics publishes a series on labor force time lost through unemployment *and part-time work*. This series is calculated on the assumption that unemployed persons lost 37.5 hours a week, and that those on part time for economic reasons lost the difference between 37.5 hours and the actual number of hours worked. This series, of course, yields a somewhat higher figure than the more commonly quoted series on unemployment as a percentage of the labor force. In 1965, for example, when 4.6 percent of the labor force was unemployed, 5 percent of labor force time was lost through unemployment or involuntary part-time work.

Finally, mention should be made of the weekly and monthly series on insured unemployment that emerges from the social security system as a by-product of unemployment compensation operations. This is valuable information because of the speed and great geographic detail in which it is reported. But it is only a very rough indicator of total unemployment because (1) it concerns only industries and occupations covered by the unemployment compensation laws, and (2) it reports persons only while they are drawing benefits. It misses unemployed persons who have never worked, or have lost their jobs but have not yet passed the waiting period before benefits start, or have exhausted their benefits without finding new employment.

WORKING HOURS

Historically, Americans have chosen to take a sizable part of their labor productivity gains in the form of greater leisure. Thus, the average workweek in the United States is not much more than half of what it was a century ago. In any five-year period the secular decline in the workweek may be scarcely visible, but there is no reason to believe it has stopped. In addition to this long-term trend, working hours are highly susceptible to short-run or cyclical changes in business conditions. Firms whose business is falling off are apt to put employees on short workweeks before they resort to complete, even though temporary, layoffs, let alone to outright discharges. Similarly, expansions in production often occasion longer working hours before firms start to add to their work forces.

Working hours usually are expressed on an average-hours-per-week basis. The most readily available and widely cited such series is the monthly tabulation by the Bureau of Labor Statistics. This, however, covers only production workers in manufacturing (and subdivisions thereof), mining, contract construction, and certain portions of the retail and wholesale trade. For purposes of making total labor-supply estimates, it is safest to use the more comprehensive indexes of total man-hours in the private economy, on both an establishment and a labor force basis, published in the annual *Manpower Report of the President* (and in the Statistical Appendix to the *Economic Report of the President*).

In working hours, as in productivity, the agricultural sector of the economy is sharply differentiated from the remainder. Farmers work substantially longer hours than nonfarm workers, on the average, although the disparity has been narrowing over time. The secular shift of labor out of agriculture contributes to the downward secular trend of total working hours.

SUMMARY

It is the business of aggregative economic theory to build a conceptual model of the economic system that provides a generalized but illuminating explanation of some important aspects of the economy's behavior. The construction of such a model has been started in this chapter.

An essential first step in any such theorizing is to choose the aspects or dimensions of economic behavior that are to be explained. We have suggested four: the fullness of production, the fullness of employment, the behavior of average prices, and the rate of capacity growth.

The first half of the chapter identified the more immediate determinants of these basic performance characteristics and, in particular, spelled out the logical linkages between them and aggregate demand. Most modern aggregative economic theorists have spent most of their time pondering the problem of demand determination. We have started with the question of whether they have spent their time wisely. To what extent is it safe to focus upon demand as *the* active determinant of the economy's production, employment, price, and real growth performances?

Deductive analysis points to three other variables, along with aggregate demand, that jointly determine the aspects of general economic behavior that interest us: labor productivity, the labor supply, and the prevailing pattern of price-output relationships. The latter half of the chapter has been devoted to exploratory discussions of the first two.

Labor productivity is the variable in the present model that represents all the various inputs into the productive process other than the quantity of labor itself. Plainly, its determination is exceedingly complex, and we scarcely have begun to unravel it in this chapter; the subject is one to which we shall return more than once. However, we have examined the concept of labor productivity rather closely; noted its relationship to other productivity concepts; touched upon productivity measurement problems; and reviewed aggregate labor productivity behavior in the United States during the past half century. Despite significant short-run fluctuations, actual output per man-hour has recorded a remarkably sustained upward trend, and normal capacity per man-hour, although not directly observable, must have been even steadier in its progress.

Our discussion of the determination of the labor supply has been largely definitional, establishing the manner in which the size of the age-eligible population, the labor-force participation rate, and normal working hours govern the availability of man-hours of work. We also have taken the opportunity to pin down the labor force, employment, and unemployment terminology used in American business conditions discussion and, particularly, in the statistics compiled by the U.S. Bureau of the Census and the Bureau of Labor Statistics.

This initial reconnoitering of the labor productivity and labor supply topics does not suggest that either of them is a wholly motionless or phlegmatic variable, which the general business conditions analyst can safely overlook. But yet each of them does appear to be reasonably predictable some distance into the future. Conventional theory's implicit contention that aggregate demand is a much more volatile determination of the economy's performance than is either labor productivity or the labor supply looks reasonable enough. It remains to be seen whether we form the same impression about the third of the major determinants that conventional theory slights: the aggregate-supply path.

6

PRICES AND
PRICE-OUTPUT
RELATIONSHIPS

Can we expect to achieve full production and full employment without inflation? If there is one domestic economic issue that has stood out in bolder relief than any other during the years since World War II in the United States and other advanced Western economies, certainly this is it. It will recur again and again in the chapters that follow. But it cannot be brought into clear focus without an explicit theory of price-output relationships.

We have seen that aggregate demand (total end-user spending) equals total real output times the average price of that output. Thus, changes in demand will bring about proportionate changes in output *if* average prices remain constant. Furthermore, if both prices and productivity stand pat, changes in demand will cause proportionate changes in man-hour employment. But will average prices stay fixed? What are likely to be the comparative price and output reactions to changes in aggregate demand?

Figure 6–1 puts the issue graphically. Suppose that initially, in response to a volume of spending represented by the area D_1, the economy produces O_1 units of output which sell at an average price of P_1 ($D_1 = O_1 P_1$). Then, suppose that, for some reason, demand rises. If prices remain unchanged, output will rise to O_3, the increment demand would be $O_1AB'O_3$,

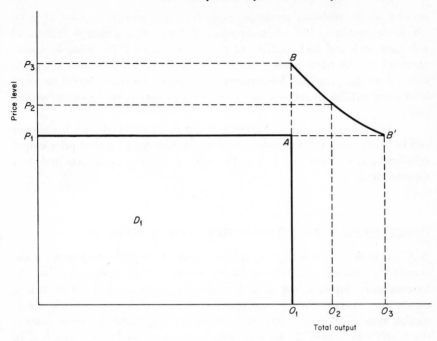

Figure **6–1.** Alternative price and output responses to a given change in demand.

and the total volume of demand will take on the dimensions O_3 times P_1. At the other extreme, the full force of increased demand could be vented in price increases with no rise in real output. In this case the increment in demand would be the area P_1ABP_3, and total demand would be O_1 times P_3. Alternatively, any price-output combination falling in between these extremes —falling anywhere on the curve BB'—might result. For example, total demand might be O_2 times P_2.[1]

Similarly, a *decline* in demand from the initial D_1 amount would result in some new price-output combination (not illustrated on the chart). It is this price-output track, in our diagram upward and to the right in the case of an increase in demand, downward and to the left in the case of a decrease in demand, that we shall call the "aggregate-supply path."[2] We never can be

---

[1] BB' is a portion of a rectangular hyperbola, that is, a curve under which all inscribed rectangles that are bounded by the axes have equal areas.

[2] In the first edition of this book, the same concept was called "the aggregate-supply function," partly because Lord Keynes's use of that phrase for a closely related concept had firmly established it in the literature. Strictly speaking, however, the term "supply function," which suggests the alternative quantities that suppliers would offer at alternative prices *at any one moment of time*, is a misleading designation for the present concept, which refers to the succession of actual, irreversible price-output responses that changing aggregate demand would trace out *through time*. The aggregate-supply path

sure of its whereabouts or shape, aside from the particular point of it on which we now are. But whenever an analyst says that a change in demand will have such and such output—or price—results, he is assuming he knows about where the track leads. Anyone, in fact, who focuses upon aggregate demand as the principal determinant of changing business conditions must have some implicit hypothesis about the shape of the current aggregate-supply path.

Our business in this chapter is to see to what extent such hypotheses can be made explicit. But before we can consider the matter of price-output relationships, we must first look at the subject of prices themselves and their measurement.

PRICE SERIES AND THE PRICE STRUCTURE

It is usual in the United States to speak of the price mechanism as the economy's fundamental self-regulating device. This term refers to the tremendously intricate network of commodity, service, and factor prices, mostly free of centralized government control, which characteristically are in motion relative to each other—in response to competitive pressures, innovations, shifts in buyers' tastes, and changes in supply and cost conditions. In the United States we have never left the allocation of economic resources entirely up to the price mechanism; such things as our tax laws and the size and character of government spending also have major impacts. Considerable portions of the price fabric have been brought under full or partial public control. Nevertheless, relative price changes still constitute the principal communication channels by which end users' preferences with respect to resource allocation are translated into commands to producers; in a market economy relative price movements are at the heart of the allocative mechanism.

But such relative price changes are not our principal concern here. The student of general business conditions is more interested in those mass movements of price, or changes in average prices or in the price level, which occur violently from time to time and in some degree all the time. No careful analyst, however, can literally confine his attention to *the* price level; the latter is simply too much of an abstraction.

As a matter of fact, among professional economists the last man to talk freely and easily about the price level is the specialist in price behavior. He knows too much of the complexity and variety of pricing in the American economy to be able to generalize easily about all commodity and service

---

is still a *supply* concept, since any particular point on it does represent a composite *supplier* response in a given time and demand context. But, as will be explained in the text, the path as a whole abstracts neither from the timing nor from the direction of demand changes.

prices at once. He will prefer, instead, to speak of the price structure—the general pattern of individual prices in relation to one another—and to generalize only about groups of prices that have something like comparable markets or comparable commodities in common. Then he may wish to emphasize the different behavior of these differing elements in the price structure. And finally, he may identify the price indexes that isolate these differing types of price behavior.

MEASURING THE SHAPE OF THE PRICE STRUCTURE

Figure 6–2 is an attempt to picture something of the nature of the structure of commodity and service prices in the United States and of the different ways certain major price series impinge upon it.

The concept of price structure implies some classification of commodity and service prices. As a minimum, a two-dimensional classification suggests itself: (1) by the types of commodities or services involved and (2) by the closeness of transactions to end users. Prices, of course, also can be classified in other ways, e.g., according to the geographic locations at which they occur. But the two just mentioned are the most basic, and they constitute the dimensions of the simplified price structure pictured in Figure 6–2.

Proceeding from bottom to top in the chart, the succession of horizontal bars represents the sequence of processing and distributing levels through which commodities pass from raw material producer to end user. The subdivisions within the bars are meant to suggest the variety of products offered for sale at each stage. The gaps between the bars represent markets in which transactions between basic producers, processors, distributors, and end users occur.[3] Some commodities pass through a long succession of such transactions in making the transit from primary producer to end user; raw cotton that finally is sold to consumers in the form of dresses is a good example. On the other hand, many commodities bypass some of the stages. Some housewives, for instance, buy their eggs directly from farmers. Here the primary market is also the retail market. Many manufactured commodities are sold directly to business purchasers of capital goods and to government buyers. Some lines of business typically employ wholesalers in moving finished goods from processors to retailers; others do not. And the seller of consumer services has no direct wholesale or manufacture antecedent at all.

The next question is how the available general price series reflect this price structure.

[3] One of the many respects in which the chart oversimplifies the actual situation is that it implies that the different processing and distributing levels are always occupied by different firms. Actually there is a great deal of vertical integration in the American economy. In the case of many particular firms this forecloses the possibility of market transactions as commodities move from one stage to another. In most industries where such vertical integration exists, however, there are also enough nonintegrated firms that a significant number of market transactions does occur between the processing stages.

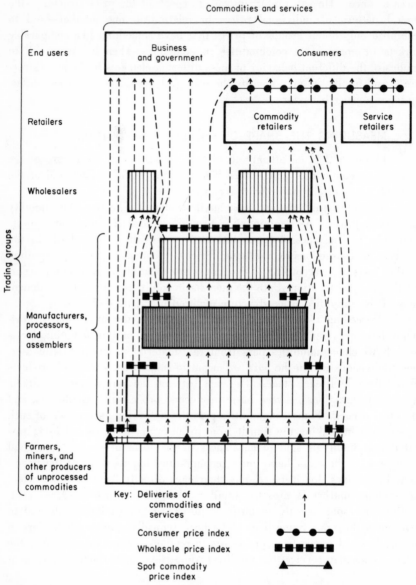

Figure **6–2.** The product price structure and its coverage by three U.S. Bureau of Labor Statistics price indexes.

General Price Indexes as Indicators of the Price Structure

The business conditions analyst usually can content himself with three frequently published indicators of general United States price behavior, all of which are prepared by the Bureau of Labor Statistics in the U.S. Department of Labor, plus a fourth, the "GNP deflator," to be described later. One of these three is the well-known monthly consumer price index; a second is the wholesale price index, calculated both weekly and monthly; and the third is the daily index of spot market prices, which measures price changes for selected raw materials and other basic commodities. There are other price series of which the average analyst makes occasional use. Among Federal government statistics, the Department of Agriculture's indexes of the prices received and the prices paid by farmers are widely used, and certain privately prepared indexes are frequently helpful. But the three BLS indexes provide a fairly revealing picture of major changes within the price structure.

This is not the place to go into the statistical procedures involved in index making. In general the idea of most price indexes is to identify a fixed collection of goods and services and then to record, through time, the varying prices that are charged for this collection in the same or similar markets, expressing the composite prices as percentages of the composite price in a chosen base period. All compilers of price indexes thus face the problem of "weighting," i.e., of determining the composition of the collection of goods and services to be priced. The weights presumably should reflect the composition of unit sales in the relevant market. But this raises the question of what to do about changes in the composition of sales. In a dynamic economy there are always some new products rising and some old products declining in the buyers' favor. How, then, can the weights in an index be allowed to reflect this without damaging the integrity of the price measure?

Another common problem is that of how frequently prices should be canvassed and the index calculated. Another is the basic problem of coverage. In part, this is a question of sampling; seldom being able to canvass every price charged in the universe that the index embraces, the index maker must adopt a satisfactory technique for choosing a representative selection of prices. More fundamentally, the question of coverage concerns the commodity range of an index and the market levels from which the price sample should be drawn.

All three of the BLS indexes represent carefully worked-out answers to these and other basic issues of index making. The distinct differences among the coverage decisions underlying the construction of the BLS series are particularly pertinent from our point of view.[4]

The consumer price index (CPI), reported monthly, is a relatively elaborate price series that measures the average retail prices paid for the whole range of consumer goods and services bought by moderate-income groups within the United States urban population. The index's weighting is based upon detailed studies of consumer budgets that the Bureau makes

---

[4] See *1966 Supplement to Economic Indicators*, U.S. Government Printing Office, Washington, D.C., 1966, for a fuller but still concise description of the major price indexes.

from time to time, the present weights being derived from studies made during 1960–1961 and revised in 1964. The Bureau also makes minor interim changes in weights as the composition of average consumer purchases alters. For purposes of constructing the index, approximately four hundred commodity and service items are price regularly in some fifty cities throughout the United States. The results are compiled into local consumers' price indexes which, on the basis of geographic weights, are combined into a national index.

Because the calculation of the CPI is an elaborate process, it also is slow. The index is not reported until five or six weeks after the midmonth date it represents. The comprehensiveness of the CPI and the care with which it is prepared are particularly appropriate in view of the index's wide adoption, in recent years, as the arbiter of cost-of-living adjustments in labor contracts. This development has given the index a greater direct, operational impact upon the economy than any other statistical series.

The coverage of the CPI is extremely broad in the commodity-service dimension, embracing virtually the whole range of items purchased by consumers (although not the purchases of other end users). It is extremely narrow in the other dimension of the price structure, since it covers only retail markets.

The wholesale price index (WPI) is also intricate and comprehensive. In addition to the overall index, a variety of subindexes are published. One family of subindexes breaks the total into commodity groups under three main headings: farm products, processed foods, and industrial commodities. Another provides price indexes by stage of processing: crude materials; intermediate materials, supplies, and components; and finished goods. Another gives a durable-nondurable breakdown for all commodities, total manufactures, and total raw or slightly processed goods. The monthly WPI reflects the prices of a sample of some 2,200 items. The weekly index, intended to give a tentative indication of the same price movements, is based upon a much more limited sample. Beginning with a major revision of the index introduced in January, 1952, the weights reflect the net selling value of commodities distributed through all the relevant markets (see the next paragraph) in this country. The weights are revised periodically, as data from successive Censuses of Manufactures become available. Weights derived from the 1958 industrial censuses were introduced in 1961; the next weight revision will use data from the 1963 censuses.

In terms of coverage, the wholesale index represents a broader range of commodities than the CPI, since these include items moving to business and government end users as well as consumers. Unlike the CPI, it includes no service prices. The contrast with respect to production-distribution levels is even more pronounced, for the wholesale index actually reflects a multiplicity of market levels. The index prices commodities at their last processing stage as they pass into purely distributive channels. Thus some of the prices

reported are those charged in primary markets, some occur after one processing stage, and others after several processing stages. Instead of bringing any
single market level into sharp focus, the index is more or less representative
of all market levels short of retail. The monthly index actually refers to
prices prevailing on a single day in the month, normally the Tuesday of the
week containing the fifteenth.

The daily spot market price index, as the Bureau's primary markets index sometimes is called, is an extremely simple construct that relies
for its significance upon the speed with which it is reported, the representativeness of its very small commodity sample, and the sharpness of its focus
on the raw materials market level. With the help of a very simple weighting
system, the index in its present form reports combined price changes in just
22 unprocessed commodities sold in certain geographically specified American
markets. These commodities, all of which are traded on organized exchanges
or through markets of sufficient interest to cause trade or government publications to record the results of the day's activity, fall into two main
categories—foodstuffs and raw industrial materials. The former includes
butter, cocoa beans, corn, cottonseed oil, hogs, lard, steers, sugar, and wheat;
and the latter, burlap, copper scrap, cotton, hides, lead scrap, print cloth,
rosin, rubber, steel scrap, tallow, tin, wool tops, and zinc. The same items
are rearranged under such headings as livestock and products, metals, textiles
and fibers, and fats and oils, and for each of these subgroups, as well as for
foodstuffs and raw industrials, a separate index is computed.

Although the index's sample is altogether too small to be fully representative of all primary-market transactions, it does supply a very quick
reflection of the direction and pace of the movement of overall raw materials
prices.

STRATIFIED PRICE BEHAVIOR

It cannot necessarily be concluded that variant movements in the three
BLS price indexes mean variant price behavior at different market levels.
There is some vertical overlap, mainly in the case of farm prices, between
the daily index and the wholesale index. And, more important, the commodity and service coverages of the consumer and wholesale indexes are
by no means identical. If the latter two diverge, it may be only because of
differences between the behavior of consumer services prices, on the one
hand, and of capital goods prices on the other. However, there is a sufficient
commodity overlap and a sufficient distinctiveness among the market-level
coverages so that, collectively, the three indexes provide a fairly good rough
picture of differing price behavior at differing market levels.

Figure 6–3 makes it plain that the differences in such behavior frequently are dramatic. The study of such comparative price records prompts
certain observations on the character of the United States price structure.

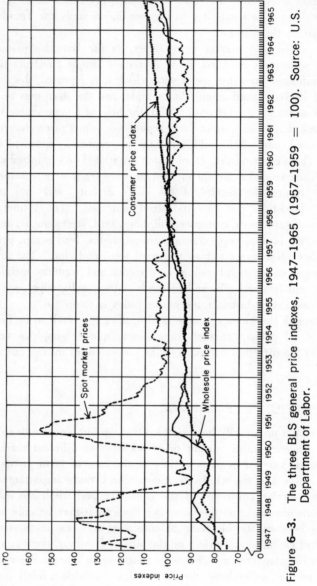

Figure 6–3.   The three BLS general price indexes, 1947–1965 (1957–1959 = 100).   Source: U.S. Department of Labor.

Variability of Price Behavior

It is evident that price fluctuations are most volatile in primary markets, less so at the intermediate levels, and least so at the retail market. Perhaps the most important reason for this well-known phenomenon is that market conditions in organized primary markets most nearly approximate the conditions of pure competition. Such markets characteristically include many sellers, and there is little differentiation of commodities among sellers. Prices generally are set by the free bidding of competing buyers and sellers; they respond almost instantaneously to shifts in supplies and in demand; and, of all commodity prices, they are the most fully exposed to speculative forces.

In the middle ranges of the price structure many markets more closely approximate the oligopolistic models of microeconomics. Prices typically are administered; that is to say, they are the result of conscious, deliberative group-thinking processes, processes that in the larger corporate organizations often are rather ponderous; decisions are neither lightly arrived at nor lightly changed. Although this type of market is more characteristic of manufacturing than of retailing, most retail markets are relatively remote from the conditions of pure competition. In addition, all the way up the price structure more and more labor, which, partly because of union organization, is characteristically less volatile than commodities in its pricing, is mixed together with the material ingredients of products. This is particularly true of services included in the CPI but not included in either the WPI or the primary-markets index. Furthermore, at the retail level products are more thoroughly differentiated than at any point short of it, and there is a larger element of custom in many prices. There are more cases at the retail level than at any other level in which buyer acceptance of products attaches to particular familiar price quotations. A further reason for the relatively dampened character of price fluctuations in finished goods and distributive markets is suggested by the factors next listed.

Price Lags

Price changes in the higher levels of the price structure are frequently instigated by changes in the lower levels and therefore are apt to register their impacts at somewhat later dates. The fact of lag itself would not explain the comparative moderateness of retail price fluctuations if all raw material price increases and decreases had to be fully passed through, first in the processing stages, and then at retail. The fact is, however, that they do not. Often by the time manufacturers or retailers get around to reacting to sharp changes in raw material prices, they find that some of the changes have been reversed. Because of the frictions involved in moving processors' and distributors' prices, cost pressures can build up considerably underneath them before causing finished prices to rise, and, similarly, the cost underpinnings of such prices can recede for considerable periods before causing the prices to sag very much. And by the time the bulge or sag in the more advanced markets is about to occur, its original cause often has been wholly or partially removed.

Resiliency of the Price Structure

The United States price structure is highly compressible and stretchable. But after being squeezed or stretched, it has a strong tendency to return to its original shape, or to what is its normal shape in any short-run period.

Finished goods prices are, in effect, tissues composed of successive layers of gross margins. When the margins at a particular processing or distributing level get abnormally distended, pressures arise to reduce them, both from the competition of sellers and from the countervailing efforts of firms on the opposite sides of the favored industry's selling and/or buying markets. In similar fashion, when margins get abnormally compressed, the producer has a strong incentive to recoup them. And in this effort he follows the line of least resistance, whether that involves pushing prices up in markets closer to final purchasers or pushing them down in markets farther away from final purchasers.[5]

Long-term Alterations in the Price Structure

To emphasize the short-run resiliency of the price structure is not to assert that any particular pattern of gross margins tends to be fixed for all time. With the introduction of new processing stages and new types of marketing, the normal pattern of differentials between raw materials and finished goods prices gradually changes. For the most part, the long-run tendency in the United States has been for the spread between the bottom and top of our price structure to widen. Increased efficiencies in retailing have tended to narrow the spread, but these seem to have been more than offset by expanded marketing services, including more expensive forms of packaging, more variety in design and style, credit sales, advertising, etc.[6]

MEASURING THE PRICE LEVEL

With something of the complexity and behavioral variety of the price

[5] Perhaps the best modern example of the resiliency of the United States price structure is the record of commodity-price changes during the Korean War. This is discussed at some length in Chap. 14.

[6] To the extent that these expanded marketing services are in fact an improvement in the *quality* of the final product, the increased spread may reflect the failure of the CPI to measure fully prices of products *constantly defined* over time—a point that we shall come back to later.

structure now in view, it is easy to understand why price statisticians wince
when they are asked for a single, unique measure of the price level. Whether
such a measure is presently available for the United States depends on
which of two distinct price-level concepts one has in mind.

If by the price level is meant the average prices charged in all goods
and service transactions in the economy, we need an index that weights
together in some meaningful way the prices charged at all market levels.
In the United States, until very recently, we have not had any satisfactory
basis for assigning weights to such a total-transactions price-level index,
for we have had no comprehensive tabulation and breakdown of all, *including*
duplicative, commodity and service transactions themselves. The new flow-
of-funds data largely fill this gap, and if one of these days some Federal
agency works up a composite price deflator for all the nonfinancial transactions covered by those series, we shall have a pretty good transactions price-
level index. Meanwhile, if an analyst desperately needs such a total-
transactions version of the price level, probably the BLS wholesale index is
as good a makeshift as any. It is roughly representative of the middle ranges
of the price structure and thus of price behavior that usually falls somewhere
between the extremes at the opposite ends of the structure.

By the price level, however, an analyst may also mean the average
price that end users pay for the economy's total output, *excluding* duplicative
transactions at the lower marketing levels. What is needed, in this case, is a
price index for the gross national product. In response to the demands of
analysts for a constant-price GNP series, the Commerce Department undertook some years ago to calculate an annual price index specifically designed
for use as a GNP deflator, and it is a very satisfactory indicator of what
might be called the output and income price level.[7]

The Commerce deflator is a composite of price indexes that has been
developed for each of the principal components of the gross national product.
More precisely, the deflator for GNP as a whole is GNP in current prices
divided by GNP in base-year prices after each of the components of GNP
has been converted to base-year prices by an appropriate price index. Com-

---

[7] The difference between the total-transactions and income-and-product versions of
the price level has an interesting relevance to monetary theory. The familiar truism
embodied in the so-called quantity theory of money is usually expressed in the equation
$MV = PT$, where M indicates the quantity of money, V the velocity of circulation, P
the price level, and T total commodity and service transactions (as well as asset transactions, which for present purposes we shall ignore). The income-and-product version of
the same equation ordinarily is expressed as $MV' = PO$, where O represents total output
in a national income accounting sense, and V' the so-called income velocity of money,
which is less than the transactions velocity because O is less than T. However, the implication of the text is that the income equation actually should be written $MV' = P'O$,
since not only velocity but also the price level may change when nonduplicative transactions are excluded.

merce has used 1958 as the base year, which means, of course, that its constant-dollar GNP series is expressed in terms of 1958 prices.[8]

Figure 6–4 compares the 1929–1965 record of the changes in the price level, in real GNP, i.e., output, and in current-price GNP, i.e., aggregate money demand.

The question to which we now return is, What is a sensible hypothesis about the nature of price-output responses to changes in aggregate demand? Or, more concretely, What price-output relationships are changes in total spending likely to trace out in the contemporary United States?

THE AGGREGATE-SUPPLY PATH

The first thing we should note about the concept of the aggregate-supply path is that it has an implicit time dimension. It attempts to describe the course that price-output relationships would take in a particular economy, beginning where we now are and traced out through time, if aggregate demand were to increase (or, alternatively, decrease) from its present level. The implicit time dimension becomes particularly noteworthy when we see, as we shall, that any realistic description of price-output relationships in the United States is in fact not reversible; that is, the price-output track that demand traces out when it increases is ordinarily a very different track from that which it subsequently follows as demand shrinks. It is for this reason that, in diagraming possible aggregate-supply paths, we shall use arrows to indicate the direction of change through time.

Such a time-dimensioned relationship cannot, however, be simply or directly derived from historical price-output statistics, such as those shown in Figure 6–5. This figure shows the record of the annual price level and total output combinations that actually occurred in the United States during the years 1947 to 1965. Certainly something about price-output relationships can be learned from the study of such data. It is noteworthy, for example, that the price level rose in every year of this period—even in the four years during which output declined or failed to rise: 1947, 1949, 1954, and 1958. It is also significant that from 1951 to 1955, in years of almost uniformly

---

[8] The method of calculating the GNP deflator injects a slight upward bias into the index. This is because, in the GNP tabulation, the services of government workers are valued simply in terms of the wage rates per hour, week, month, or year paid for them. This means that for this component of GNP the method of estimation prevents the identification of increased labor productivity; increased output per man-hour cannot be measured when output itself is measured in man-hours. Thus all increases in government wage rates are treated as increases in end-user prices; statistically, there is no off-setting rise in government workers' productivity. This is a false price rise (and hence represents an upward bias) if there has in fact been a real (although unmeasured) rise in the government workers' output per man-hour. There is clear evidence that, at least in certain government activities where it is possible to measure physical output (e.g., the Post Office), the productivity of government workers has in fact increased substantially over time.

high employment in which output, for the most part, rose rapidly, the price level increased relatively little—about 1 percent a year. On the other hand, from 1957 to 1964, when unemployment was fairly high, prices rose by over 1½ percent a year.

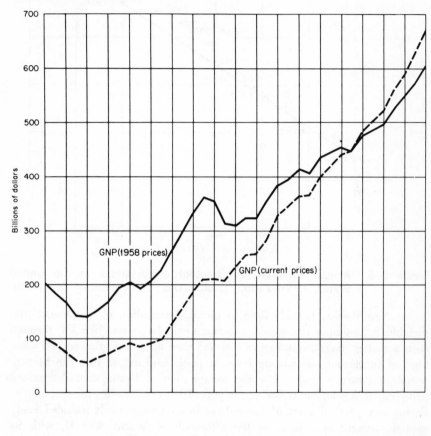

Figure **6–4.** Total final demand, real output, and the price level in the United States, 1929–1965. Source: U.S. Department of Commerce.

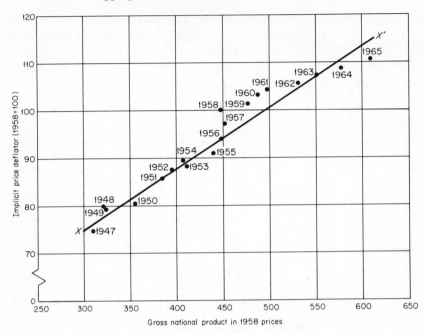

Figure 6–5. Annual aggregate price-output combinations in the United States, 1947–1965. Source: U.S. Department of Commerce.

Nevertheless, it adds little to our understanding of systematic, predictable, price-output relationships to run a correlation line like XX' through such a scatter diagram as Figure 6–5 and then argue that this reveals some kind of functional relationship between prices and output that can be projected to future periods. For the combination of factors that determined price-output developments during the years 1946 to 1962—or, for that matter, during any particular set of years—was in part unique. It included many special circumstances such as the aftermath of World War II, with its temporary shortages of civilian capacity and enormous overhang of liquid assets, as well as the violent, unexpected impact of the Korean outbreak during the latter part of 1950. Data like those in Figure 6–5 reflect too many changing conditions and influences to be directly interpreted.

As in most economic theorizing, it is necessary to approach the problem of the aggregate-supply path by steps, using the technique of abstraction. By making certain assumptions, we hypothesize a simpler situation than those which our real-world data reflect. Then we deduce what the relationships in question might be under such circumstances. And then—the present discussion will make a particular effort in this respect—we shall progressively drop the simplifying assumptions, thereby moving the hypothesized relationships closer and closer to real-world conditions.

In the present discussion, moving closer to real-world conditions in-

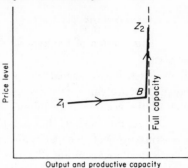

Figure **6–6.** The early Keynesian aggregate-supply hypothesis.

volves several things.   First, we shall need to allow for market conditions that more accurately reflect the real world than those assumed in the initial, simplified hypothesis.   And we shall need to note the different effects that relaxing these market assumptions has on price-output responses in the case of increasing demand and in the case of decreasing demand.   Then we shall try to generalize as to how the shape of the aggregate-supply path is affected by stretching out our initial short period to one with a longer time dimension. And finally, we shall speculate as to what would be likely to happen to the aggregate-supply path in alternating periods of rising and falling demand.

A SIMPLIFIED, SHORT-RUN PRICE-OUTPUT HYPOTHESIS

The simplified version of the aggregate-supply path with which we start is one that gained a good deal of currency some two or three decades ago, labeled, somewhat inaccurately, as "Keynesian."[9]   It is pictured in Figure 6–6.

[9] If we can date the great modern upsurge of European and American interest in aggregative economic theory from the publication of John Maynard Keynes's *The General Theory of Employment, Interest, and Money*, Harcourt, Brace and World, Inc., New York, 1936, there was much less attention within the economics profession to the shape of price-output relationships in the first of the two succeeding decades than in the second.

In the late 1930s and early 1940s, analysts typically seized upon a tidy, simplified hypothesis about price-output relationships that allowed them to move on quickly to the more exciting issues of aggregate-demand management.   It was a hypothesis that distinguished sharply between the problems of unemployment and inflation and thus seemed to fit nicely the sudden, radical shift from the first to the second of those problems which all Western economies negotiated during the first decade of Keynesian economics.   Somewhat ironically, most of these analysts would have described this price-output hypothesis as Keynesian and would have asserted that it stemmed from *The General Theory*.   While it is true that the heavy emphasis upon demand analysis certainly stemmed from there and that Keynes did present the hypothesis, he did so only to point out its oversimplification.   In fact, his chap. 21 on "The Theory of Prices" in *The General Theory* is a classic job of debunking the price-output hypothesis.   During the second decade of Keynesian economics, the profession, in effect, returned to chap. 21 with renewed interest. As is so often the case in the social sciences, more mature reflection and further evidence have tended to make the original hypothesis less tidy, but more realistic.

Assumptions

This version of the hypothesis is based upon the following two crucial premises:

First, it is assumed that we are talking about a period of time short enough that we can safely disregard any changes in the structure and character of the economy, including particularly any changes in its productive capacity, yet not so short that output could not be expanded, within the limits of existing productive capacity, in response to an increase in demand. (This is equivalent to assuming that the short run, so defined, is long enough to merit serious consideration and to have some policy significance.) Under this assumption the economy's total capacity is so firmly fixed that, when output already is at, or very near, capacity, further expansion in demand cannot serve to raise output appreciably.

Second, the hypothesis assumes perfectly competitive factor and product markets in which there are very high degrees of both price competition and resource mobility.

The Logic of the Kinked Aggregate-supply Curve

Given these assumptions, and starting from the lower end of the curve Z_1BZ_2, in Figure 6–6, it is easy to infer why an expansion in demand would tend to trace out the track indicated.

As the chart is drawn, the Z_1B phase of the curve does suggest some rise in the price level in response to an increase in demand, on the ground that increasing variable costs in some industries would outweigh the declines in unit fixed costs. But more noteworthy is the suggestion that, with competitive factor and product markets, the curve would be highly elastic almost up to the point of full employment. At increasing levels of demand, price increases would be minimized, and output expansion would be maximized by the competition of still-unemployed labor and other resources for the new employment afforded by the expansion in demand. Competition, by keeping the lid on prices, would concentrate the impact of increased spending upon output.

Under the fixed-capacity assumption, however, this process would reach a limit at some point just short of literal full capacity. Here the only remaining unemployment of labor and other resources would be frictional. Further increases in demand would run into the stone wall of fixed capacity, and the only way left for the price-output curve to go would be up. What had been buyers' markets would suddenly turn into sellers' markets, and the same competitive forces that had minimized price increases when actual output was appreciably short of capacity now would maximize them. The aggregate price-output curve would encounter a sharp kink and suddenly would become highly inelastic.

The Policy Appeal of the Kinked Curve

The concept of a kinked relationship, it is worth noting, sets a sharp, clear target for public stabilization policy which seeks to maintain full employment without inflation. Given such a pattern of price-output relationships, public fiscal and monetary policies designed to regulate the total volume of aggregate demand are all that are needed for running a highly successful stabilization program. If public policy is capable of varying demand significantly and sensibly, then it should be possible, say in the case of a recession situation, to push the volume of demand exactly up to point *B* in Figure 6–6 without incurring significant inflationary penalties. If the recovery were a trifle excessive, an upward spurt in prices would sound a clear warning signal, and demand could be throttled back to the stability target.

All the practical problems of regulating aggregate demand, of course, would remain in such a situation. The scope of the government's ability to vary taxes, spending, and monetary policies might not be sufficient to provide the needed change in demand. There would be the further problem of reducing the lag between policy decisions and their economic impacts. And there would be the fundamental question of whether the regulatory hands on the aggregate-demand throttles were nimble enough and guided by wise enough brains.

The point, however, is that, given the simple aggregate-supply hypothesis, the achievement of high scores in both the employment-production and the price-stability dimensions of economic welfare becomes almost exclusively an aggregate-demand problem. Here was a way, it appeared, by which governments could carry out their newly accepted responsibilities for maintaining economic stability simply by employing certain indirect kinds of control they had always traditionally exercised anyway. Governments always had collected taxes, made public expenditures, and regulated the money supply. Now all that was necessary was to do these same, traditional things in a fashion more closely and vigorously attuned to economic needs. There was no need for any detailed, meddling interventions into such customary zones of private decision making as price and wage making or the planning of plant and equipment expenditures.

It is in this sense that Keynesian fiscal policy often has been characterized as a highly conservative solution to the enormous problems of mass unemployment and violent inflation, which the thirties and forties thrust upon national governments throughout the Western world. By putting the previous paragraph in the past tense, we do not mean to suggest that the optimistic view that fiscal and monetary measures ordinarily can constitute a sufficient stabilization program is wholly outmoded. But the supply hypothesis upon which the view originally rested requires a good deal of modification.

RECONCILING THE HYPOTHESIS WITH MARKET REALITIES

In the American economy as we know it, a number of factors undermine the tidy simplicity of the kinked aggregate price-output curve. These
can be summarized under two headings: (1) those realities of the American
marketplace which tend to smooth out the kink in the short run—thereby
making the achievement of full employment without inflation a more difficult
and ambiguous task than aggregative economists generally assumed two
decades or so ago, and (2) those realities of the economic growth process
which make the assumption of fixed capacity risky even for very short-run
periods.   While all the factors in the first group do not involve departures
from competition, they may all be thought of as conditions that crop up
when we drop the simplifying assumption about market conditions.   And,
as we shall see, one of the significant consequences of dropping the simplifying assumptions—of recognizing market realities—is that we must differentiate between increases and decreases in demand in analyzing price-output
responses.   That is, the effects of a rise in demand are not the exact reverse
of the effects of a fall in demand.   Our approach, therefore, is first to trace
the effects (still in the very short run) of a rise in demand, and then to trace
the effects of a decline in demand.   As we have implied earlier, because of
this lack of symmetry, the shape of the aggregate-supply path at any point
in time depends on where we are, as far as output is concerned, in relation to
capacity, to start with.   To simplify the argument, we shall assume for the
moment that we are starting from a point in time when output is significantly,
but not drastically, below capacity levels.   This gives us room for analytical
maneuver in either direction.

Prices during Rising Demand

When demand rises from a point where output and employment are
significantly below capacity to one close to capacity, a number of the actual
characteristics of American markets modify the price-output relationships
thus far pictured.

Bottlenecks.   The simple price-output hypothesis, as well as much of our own
previous talk about capacity, seems to imply that the capacities of all individual industries are nicely coordinated with the capacity of the economy as
a whole—that is, that when we have full employment of labor, every industry
is operating at exactly its capacity level. This is an oversimplification.   At
any given time some industries always are laggards in capacity.   In established industries new investment may have failed to keep up with the pace
of investment generally.   And new industries may not yet have had time to
grow up to the new levels of demand facing them.   As a result, in any
period of rising demand, some commodities and facilities turn up in short
supply well before the economy as a whole reaches full employment.   If such

a scarce material is being priced in a competitive market, the same thing happens to its price that the simple hypothesis suggests will happen to the whole price level at full employment. As demand expands, prices in the bottleneck areas tend to move upward well short of full employment in the economy as a whole. Particularly in the case of key raw materials, such price increases can spread to other markets. In any event, demand increases short of full employment tend to cause a steeper upward pitch in the whole aggregate-supply path than the simplified version would imply.

Farm Prices. In the predominant nonagricultural part of the American economy, the characteristic result of a slump in demand is reduced output and employment. But this is not true of agriculture, where characteristically prices, not output, fall when demand falls off. Indeed, when there is a decline in demand (and prices), some farmers may try to produce even greater output, in order to maintain their incomes. The price-output curve in agriculture is not kinked; the whole curve is inelastic. Thus, during a general upswing the tendency of farm prices is to rise. This is not an unexceptional rule, of course, as the experience of 1957–1959 attests. Special factors may raise agricultural prices when aggregate demand is falling off (as in 1958), and depress them when total spending is on the increase (as in 1964). But if agriculture does partake of an upswing in demand, it almost invariably partakes in the form of rising farm prices. And this tends to place upward pressure on the general price level in the early as well as in the later stages of an upswing.

Collective Wage Bargaining. Collective bargaining by organized labor, plus the imitative reaction of nonunion labor markets, makes for a very different labor market than the simple price-output hypothesis assumes. The experience of the last decade or so suggests that unions are not only disposed but also able to push up wages or other labor benefits considerably earlier and faster in periods of rising demand than would be possible in a thoroughly unorganized labor market. This may be especially true after a slump severe enough to cause a general interruption in annual wage demands.

Administered Pricing. The price policies of those American firms, particularly the large industrial manufacturing and processing corporations, which exercise substantial discretionary control over their selling prices, are apt to violate the simple price-output hypothesis in several ways. In the first place, if the increase in demand occurs immediately after a slump so severe as to reduce the firms to charging prices that cover only their out-of-pocket or marginal costs, as competitive theory would suggest, they will be much quicker than the competitive theory would suggest to return to full-cost pricing when demand conditions permit.

Second, with almost any increase in demand, administered price makers are inclined to pass through (with some lags, to be sure) increases in raw material or labor costs. In part, this is explained by the close attention that many corporate price policies pay to the maintenance of satisfactory gross unit margins, or of profit as a percentage of sales.

In the third place, however, once they have their prices set in accordance with their established policies and aside from passing through cost increases, many administered price makers are slow to raise prices in response to further increases in demand. Prices in such markets usually do not skyrocket after demand reaches the full-employment point. The reasons for this widely observed aspect of administered price behavior in boom periods have been widely debated, and we can no more than allude to some of them here. In certain cases, undoubtedly, self-restraint in pricing reflects a sense of social responsibility or, at least, an effort to avoid the bad publicity attached to price increases by major manufacturers when everyone is worrying about inflation. Such considerations, however, did not deter the steel industry in 1962 and again in 1963. Where such self-restraint by administered price makers does exist, there are also more mundane explanations. Many firms are fearful of creating ill will among their buyers that will come home to roost when demand slackens. As has just been suggested, some corporate price policies seek to maintain satisfactory *rates* of profit on sales rather than, literally, to maximize profits. And the simple bureaucratic inertia of the price-making process in many a large corporation is not without its effect.

The two characteristics of administered price making last named—on the one hand, the relative quickness to pass through increases in unit costs, and on the other hand, the slowness to take the market for all it will bear in boom periods—may seem inconsistent. What reconciles them is the fact that administered price making typically is much more cost-oriented than demand-oriented. To pass through a cost increase usually is simply to adhere to an established price policy. However, to respond to increased demand by raising gross margins requires the making of new policy.

In combination, the factors just reviewed make for a much less angular price-output path under conditions of rising demand than the simple hypothesis suggests. As long as we retain the assumption of fixed capacity (which we shall abandon shortly), the aggregate price-output hypothesis pictured in Figure 6–7 is a much more reasonable one for the American economy under conditions of rising demand than the sharply kinked curve with which we started. As important as the changed shape of the curve itself is our knowledge now that any such picture of average price-output relationships cloaks a much greater diversity of price behavior in particular industries and markets than the original hypothesis seemed to imply.

Prices during a Decline in Demand

While some of the factors just outlined would reverse themselves if confronted with a slump in total spending, both American wages and ad-

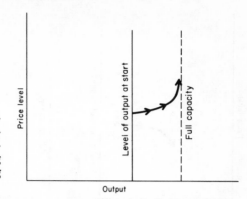

Figure **6–7.** The path of price-output relationships under conditions of rising demand, assuming fixed capacity.

ministered prices are powerfully resistant to declines in demand. Corporate price makers and labor leaders alike are deeply afraid of deflationary spirals in which prices and wages start chasing each other down, and many officials in the Federal government share the same fear. The downward stickiness of United States wages and prices is dramatically attested by the fact that in the 1949, 1954, 1958, and 1961 recessions, the price level, as measured by the GNP deflator, not only failed to fall but actually rose a little. These, of course, were cases of only moderate declines in total spending; sharper declines in demand would no doubt have met less resistance to price decreases. Thus perhaps Figure 6–8 is a fair picture of the shape of the short-run aggregate-supply path under conditions of declining demand.

RECONCILING THE HYPOTHESIS WITH FLEXIBLE CAPACITY

One further step is necessary if our concept of the short-run aggregate-supply path is to be reasonably consistent with economic realities in the United States. This is to abandon the assumption of fixed capacity.

Even in the very short run for which it is reasonable to regard the normal productive capacity of the economy as fixed, the actual capacity is not completely inflexible. Under the pressure of heavy demand, people are apt to work overtime; others either postpone their exodus from, or hasten their entry into, the labor force; and some employers put on additional shifts. The gains in output resulting from such intensified efforts usually cost more and have higher prices. But they are perfectly possible. Thus the vertical full-employment line in our charts of the aggregate-supply path, instead of being a stone wall, is, even in the very short run, a kind of hinged spring barrier. Sufficient demand can rotate it to the right, yielding higher than normal full-employment output—along with higher prices. This tends to make the upper leg of the short-run curve somewhat more elastic than the initial hypothesis suggested. (See Figure 6–9.)

ADDING A TIME DIMENSION

So far, we have been considering the shape of the aggregate-supply

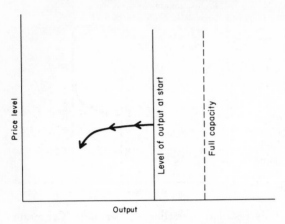

Figure **6–8.** The path of price-output relationships under conditions of declining
demand, assuming fixed capacity.

path over a period of time short enough that the *ceteris paribus* assumption
is a reasonable one. Our final step is to attempt to trace the path of actual
price-output relationships *over time*. This we can do only in part, because
abandonment of the *ceteris paribus* assumption opens a Pandora's box of
possible changes that would affect price-output relationships. However, we
can identify two time-dimensioned effects.

The first of these is that over time the capacity of the American
economy seems to expand inexorably. As we emphasized in the previous
chapter, the labor force grows almost every year, and so does productivity.
In the last half of the decade of the 1960s, from any one year to the next,
it is a fairly safe bet that the United States economy's productive capacity
will increase by at least $25 billion in 1965 prices. Even for periods as
short as six months, some allowances for capacity growth usually must be
allowed for in a realistic analysis of American business developments.

The effect of such growth is to stretch out the aggregate-supply path
in its output dimension. Capacity growth reduces the likelihood that, even
in a relatively short-run period, we shall encounter the inelastic range of the
curve that the early Keynesians hypothesized. It provides a greater scope
in which competitive forces can exercise a restraining effect upon prices. We
have argued that actual market conditions in the United States make such
competitive forces intrinsically weaker than the simple price-output hypothesis
assumed. But capacity expansion over time magnifies the effectiveness of
those forces which do remain.

Essentially these same remarks about the effects of expanding capacity
upon the aggregate-supply path can be put in terms of the effects of rising
output per man-hour. Rising labor productivity, which is the principal
source of rising capacity, tends to reduce unit labor costs and thereby
partially offset the impact of advancing wage rates on unit costs. Thus

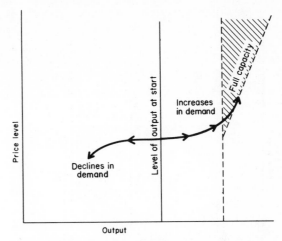

Figure **6–9.** The path of price-output relationships under conditions of increas-
ing and decreasing demand, assuming flexible capacity.

productivity gains neutralize some of the upward cost pressures on the
aggregate-supply path and, over time, by raising capacity, shift the curve
to the right.

The second time-dimensioned effect arises from our conclusion that
the price-output response to a decline in demand is not the mirror image
of the response to a rise in demand. Because, over time, demand will presumably go through alternating periods of increase and decrease, we need
to trace out the effect over time of this lack of symmetry.

Again, let us start from a point in time when actual output is appreciably, but not drastically, below capacity. And let us suppose that, for
some reason, demand rises at a rate faster than would be absorbed by the
normal, long-run growth in productive capacity. The tendency would be, as
we have seen, for both output and the price level to rise. And the more
closely output approached the (flexible) capacity barrier, the more the
increase in demand would be vented in price increases rather than output
increases. Some two years later, say, the rise in demand comes to an end.
We are now at a new point in time, a new starting point in our diagrams.
We must construct a new picture of the shape of the aggregate price-output
response.

Presumably the left-hand portion of our diagram of the aggregate
price-output response will be approximately the same as before, *except* that
it will start at the price-output combination actually prevailing at this new
point in time. Thus, our diagram might look like Figure 6–10.

What the diagram tells us is that, when demand declines, the price-
output combination is not likely to retrace the path it took during the period
of rising demand. On the contrary, prices are likely to fall very little and the

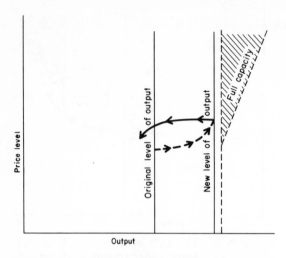

Figure **6–10.**   The path of price-output relationships under conditions of declin-
ing demand, assuming flexible
capacity, at a new point in time
after a period of rising demand.

brunt of the decline in demand will fall on output. Thus, output may fall
to the level it was originally, but the price level will be higher.

At some point in time, the decline in demand comes to an end, and
we have a second new starting point. But this time, we start with a higher
level of prices, relative to ouptut, than we had originally. So we construct
another new diagram of the aggregate-supply path, the right-hand portion of
which may be similar in shape to what it was before, *but at a higher level.*
Figure 6–11 illustrates this new development.

And so on, as demand alternatively rises and falls. This is what has
been called the "ratchet effect." Because of the nonreversible character of
the aggregate-supply path in contemporary America, alternative short-run
periods of rising and falling demand tend to raise prices in periods of demand increase more than they decrease them during periods of demand
decrease.

A somewhat similar thesis, without the assumption of alternating
periods of rising and falling *aggregate* demand, has been advanced by
Charles L. Schultze.[10] He argues that, even though total demand may not
change, a *shift* in demand from one sector of the economy to another will
tend to have the same ratchet effect. In those sectors where demand is rising
(even though the level of demand in the economy as a whole is unchanged at

[10] Charles L. Schultze, "Recent Inflation in the United States," Study Paper no. 1,
materials prepared in connection with the *Study of Employment, Growth, and Price
Levels*, Joint Economic Committee, Congress of the United States, September, 1959.

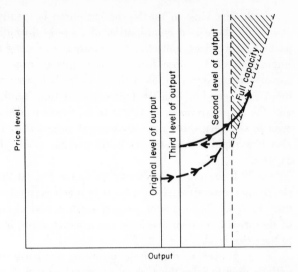

Figure **6–11.** The path of price-output relationships under conditions of rising demand, assuming flexible capacity, at a new point in time after alternating periods of rising and falling demand.

levels appreciably below full capacity), prices will tend to rise. In those sectors where demand is declining, however, prices are not likely to fall very much. The *average* of prices, including those which rise appreciably and those which do not decline appreciably, will go up.

We hasten to add that the ratchet effect, as we have described it, is a highly stylized description of the sequence of events in the American economy. We have, implicitly or explicitly, assumed away important possible changes in character of the American economy—significant changes in labor union powers or attitudes, in business pricing practices, in government policies. But in an approximate way, it may be a reasonable explanation of price-output behavior in the United States in recent years.

CONCLUSIONS

We now are in a position to draw some conclusions from the present discussion.

1. The practice of implicitly taking price-output relationships as a given, and of focusing analysis largely upon demand developments, is riskier than the original Keynesian hypothesis suggests. The wise business conditions analyst today keeps all the issues that are packaged together in any aggregate-supply hypothesis within the scope of his active attention. At no time can he afford to forget about price considerations for very long.

2. The kink in the Keynesian curve is greatly exaggerated. On the one hand, there is a combination of factors—including bottlenecks, the impact of farm prices, collective wage bargaining, administered pricing, and the interaction of all those forces—that tends to cause the elastic part of the Keynesian curve to rise faster than was initially assumed. On the other hand, there is a combination of factors—including administered price behavior and the responsiveness of output to increases in demand at full employment even in the very short run—that causes prices at or near full employment to rise less rapidly than the inelastic portion of the Keynesian curve would suggest.

3. Price-output developments in the United States on the average are clearly not reversible. Typically, it is much easier for the price level to rise than to fall. Thus, under present institutional circumstances, an upsliding of the price level over the long run is much more likely than a downsliding of the price level.

4. However, the whole upsliding tendency in the aggregate-supply path is modified by the fact of persistent growth in productivity and in the labor force, which together give us a persistently growing productive capacity. This is true even in the relatively short run, and it leads to a very important conclusion:

Because of the fact of persisting capacity expansion, the shape of the aggregate-supply path in the United States is not only a function of time in the sense that successive upswings and downswings of demand do not move along the same tracks; price-output relationships during an expansion depend importantly on the *rate* at which demand grows.

The spring-hinged full-employment barrier in our charts actually is moving to the right on a slow but relatively imperturbable schedule. Price-output relationships depend largely on whether demand grows at a significantly faster rate than this. In essence, the aggregate-supply problem is one of relative motion. An unexpected, explosive increase in demand—the most dramatic instance of which in recent years was touched off by the Korean outbreak in mid-1950—is likely to cause a sudden rise in the price level, almost without regard to whether such an explosive increase in demand occurs when output is well short of, or at, its capacity levels. In either case, shortages, bottlenecks, and inflationary psychology quickly take over. But if the same volume of increased demand is spread over enough time so that the rate of increase does not greatly exceed the rate of capacity growth, it may exert little disturbing effect upon the price level.

7

DEMAND AND INCOME DETERMINATION: The Consumption-function Hypothesis

In Chapter 5, the labor supply, labor productivity, the aggregate-supply path, and aggregate demand were identified as four coordinate determinants of the economy's overall performance. We now have inspected the first three of these enough to know that no comprehensive analysis of the economic situation or outlook can safely overlook them. We have also learned, however, that, although the labor supply and labor productivity both are changing almost constantly, the rates of change typically are fairly steady and the direction of change is nearly always upward. Considerable stability also attaches to most of the factors that determine the shape of the aggregate-supply path in the short run. Indeed, to the extent that any of these three determinants are unstable, the instability can be attributed largely to variations in aggregate demand.

Aggregate demand, on the other hand, can at times be quite unstable, not only in rate of change, but also in direction. It is plain why most modern analysts of business conditions give such emphasis to the role of demand.

THE STRUCTURE OF DEMAND THEORY

THE SIMPLEST THEORY

Anyone familiar with national income accounting already knows one wholly valid, indisputable theory of aggregate-demand determination. It is that an economy's gross national income and total final demand are identities; that the latter is the sum of, and hence is determined by, personal consumption spending, domestic investment spending, net exports, and government purchases of goods and services; and that changes in final demand are the composite of changes in these components.

Admittedly, this is not a very sophisticated theory. It is no more than a truism. But before we hurry on to something more challenging, it is worth noting that much highly respected business conditions analysis today employs no more complex a general economic model than this. Its practitioners simply go down the list of the GNP components, revise last year's figures, one by one, into estimates for the upcoming year on the basis of any and all specific items of intelligence about market trends that come to hand, and add up the sector estimates into a GNP forecast.

Such analysts who equip themselves with no more elaborate a theory of demand determination than $D = C + I + E + G$ are forgoing some powerful tools. On the other hand, the working analyst who becomes so completely the captive of a more elaborate economic model that he sternly ignores any and all insights into the outlook that cannot be cranked into one or another of his equations is even more foolish.

THE KEYNESIAN DEMAND MODEL

John Maynard Keynes did not carve out his place in history with the assertion that total final demand equals consumption plus investment plus net exports plus government spending. His explanation of demand determination—the outlines of which still provide the framework for most contemporary demand theory—is more ambitious in two respects.

In the first place, in *The General Theory*, Keynes tried to identify the determinants of each of the components of final demand.

In the second place, he asserted certain vital interrelationships among the components of demand. Consequently, the structure of demand no longer appeared to be a random matter; if private investment or government spending fell, for example, it was not a matter of chance whether consumption would also fall, or rise to fill the vacated capacity. The behavior of the consumption and of the nonconsumption components of demand were, in Keynes's view, linked together. The analysis of aggregate demand became more rigorous. The effects on total demand of an assumed or predicted change in a particular component became more predictable.

The branches into which demand theory divides coincide more or less automatically with the conventional breakdown of GNP into consumption, investment, and government spending. (Assuming a self-contained economy, as demand theory often does in the interest of relative simplicity, net exports are not involved.) However, to the economist who sets out to find a relatively exhaustive explanation for demand determination within the subject matter of his own discipline, the government sector presents an immediate problem. For the determinants of government spending are not primarily economic.[1] Instead they are usually the events of international relations or domestic politics. Thus if the economic theorist's business is to explain *why* changes in total spending occur, he immediately reaches the end of his rope in one major sector of the GNP.

As a model builder, Keynes disposed of this difficulty by assuming away government spending and hypothesizing a simple economy that had only two purchasing sectors, consumption and private investment.[2] For our purposes, a somewhat different course will be more realistic. We shall keep government in the picture but shall distinguish sharply between the questions, What determines government spending? and What are the relationships between government spending and the other demand components? Aggregate-demand theory has a good deal of light to shed on the second of these questions, but it cannot greatly illuminate the first.

This chapter and the next concern the determination of private consumption. Because of the nature of the argument, the topic to be discussed necessarily includes the relationships between the consumption and the nonconsumption components of demand as well as the determination of consumption itself.

THE CONSUMPTION-FUNCTION HYPOTHESIS

The most crucial proposition of the Keynesian demand theory is that consumption is a function of income. Empirically this contention is supposed to be a generalization of observable facts; the habits and mores of people are said to be such that changes in income typically cause changes in consumption. Conceptually the proposition follows, in a sense, from the familiar assumption of Western economics that consumption is an end

[1] See Chap. 12 for a possible modification of this statement, discussed there as the "feedback" concept of government stabilization policy.

[2] At some points Keynes seems to have been thinking not, as the text states, of an economy in which there literally were no government operations but rather of one in which government expenditures simply were not separately classified, being instead included in the consumption and investment categories. Such an interpretation of his model conforms nicely to the basic definition of end use (or final demand) discussed in Chap. 2. However, it does not fit the subsequent logic of his argument, wherein the determination of consumption and investment is explained in terms of circumstances and motivations exclusively applicable to private, not public, spending decisions.

purpose of economic activity.   If this is so, then it never is necessary to explain the existence of people's desire for consumer goods.   The volume of consumer wants is always large enough that, in general, the only limiting and hence determining factor, so far as consumption is concerned, is people's ability to finance their wants.   And, the proposition assumes, in the economy as a whole the ability to finance consumption is basically conditioned by the level of income.

Keynes hypothesized a particular type of income-consumption relationship.   But before we specify what that was (or is), two immediate comments are in order.

In the first place, you may already be worrying about the circularity of the reasoning that seems to be developing.   For first we have said that total money income is determined by the sum of consumption, investment, and government spending.   And now we say that the very first of these demand components, consumption, is determined by income.

In a sense, the reasoning *is* circular.   Very often, the kind of causation involved in the interrelationship of economic variables is not the simple type of push-pull causation that, following the model of seventeenth-century Newtonian physics, twentieth-century thinking still so largely employs.   In push-pull causation, for example, one pool ball hits another and "causes" it to drop in the pocket; one variable is clearly cause, the other, effect.   But in most economic relationships the *interdependency* of the variables is important.   All are partly the causes of all the others; each is partly the effect of the others.   Usually in economics the most precise and exhaustive statement of causation that can be made takes the form of a functional equation that accurately and adequately describes the interrelationship among the variables in question.   The reasoning involved in any functional equation can, if you wish, be called circular.   The point, simply, is that the complaint is inappropriate; two-way causation is in fact involved.

However, in the case of the Keynesian hypothesis about the relationship between income and consumption, it is possible to break out of this circle of reasoning.   The hypothesis goes beyond the assertion that consumption and income are each functions of the other.   It assigns a *passive* role to consumption.   Changes in consumption are to be explained as responses to changes in income—this despite the fact that changes in income are to be explained by the collective changes in the components of total final demand, one of which is consumption.

The real protection against circularity in this reasoning is the implied *activeness* of the other (nonconsumption) components of demand.   Given the proposition that consumption is exclusively responsive to income, the nonconsumption components of demand become by default the active or autonomous determinants of changes in total spending.   Thus, to a degree, the so-called consumption-function hypothesis does involve a push-pull sequence of reasoning: when nonconsumption demand changes (for whatever reason), it causes or induces income to begin changing, which induces consumption to change, which causes income to change further, which causes consumption to change further, and so on. The reasoning is sequential, but it does not circle pointlessly upon itself; there is a prime mover. The circular process is more analogous to a turning wheel that continues to rotate, partly because of its own momentum, partly because an external force adds energy to the rotation.

The proposition that consumption is a function of income may have aroused a second kind of uneasiness in your mind. Surely there are factors in the economy other than income that have casual impacts on consumption; the consumption-function hypothesis must be an oversimplification. This is perfectly correct. Keynes himself took pains to emphasize this, but he felt that the relationship between income and consumption was so predominantly important that it should be singled out in a function that treated consumption as though it were exclusively determined by current income. This procedure requires that all other influences on consumption be treated as causing *shifts* in this function. (This last will become clearer in a moment, when we reach the graphical portion of our analysis.)

Such a hypothesis, treating consumption as an exclusive function of current income, is what we mean when we speak of "the simple" or "the basic" or sometimes just "the" consumption-function hypothesis. This nomenclature conforms to the present vocabularies of most general economists and business conditions analysts. Actually, however, it somewhat misrepresents the present state of consumption theory, for the theorists have been busy, particularly since World War II, recognizing that the simple hypothesis does leave too many things out of account; and, accordingly, many of them have developed much more complicated consumption functions that include a number of variables besides current income.

For our purposes, however, it will make for better exposition to devote this chapter simply to spelling out the mechanics and the implications of the basic consumption-function hypothesis. Then, in the next chapter, we shall consider what additional factors must be included to make the hypothesis serviceably realistic, and we shall try to reach conclusions as to how the consumption function behaves over time.

THE PROPENSITY TO CONSUME: THE CONCEPT

The consumption-income relationship that Keynes hypothesized was the tendency of consumption to rise as income rises, but not by the same amount. In Keynes's two-sector model, in which final demand equaled consumption plus investment, and total income equaled consumption plus saving, this was equivalent to saying that a part of every increment in total income is saved. Furthermore, Keynes believed that the relationship was reversible: when income falls, consumption likewise falls, but not so much.

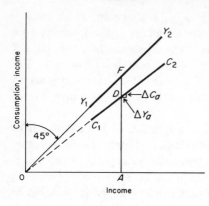

Figure 7–1. A consumption-income diagram.

The Mechanics of the Concept

One possible variant of the consumption function is shown in Figure 7–1. In this chart, the scales for consumption on the vertical axis and income on the horizontal axis are the same. We first erect a 45-degree diagonal line from the origin. All the points on such a line, of course, are equidistant from the two axes. Thus, we are able, by reference to this line, to measure income as the vertical distance to the diagonal line, as well as along the horizontal axis. Thus $OA = AF$.

Next, we draw a line C_1C_2 representing the assumed relationship between income and consumption. This line says that if income is AF (which equals OA), consumption will be AD, income not consumed will be DF, and the ratio of consumption to income at income A is the fraction AD/AF. The line of relationship between income and consumption can be expressed as an equation, if it is a straight line, in the form of $C = a + bY$, where C and Y are consumption and income, b is the slope of the line, and a is a constant (the value of C where $Y = O$).

Keynes called the kind of ratio just noted, i.e., that of consumption to income at any given level of income, the "average propensity to consume." He contrasted this concept with the responsiveness of consumption to a small change in income. The latter, which he called the "marginal propensity to consume," can be expressed symbolically as the fraction $\triangle C/\triangle Y$, in which $\triangle Y$ is a small increment in income and $\triangle C$ is the corresponding increment in consumption. Graphically, the marginal propensity to consume is represented by the slope of the consumption curve at any particular income level; for example, in Figure 7–1 the marginal propensity to consume is $\triangle C_a/\triangle Y_a$ in the near vicinity of income A.[3]

In the particular type of consumption function pictured in Figure 7–1, where C_1C_2 is a straight line, the marginal propensity to consume is constant

---

[3] Keynes labeled the whole consumption-income relationship pictured by a curve like C_1C_2 in Fig. 7–1 as "the propensity to consume," a term for which the leading American Keynesian, Alvin Hansen, has supplied the more concrete synonym "the consumption function."

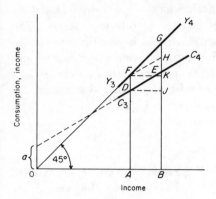

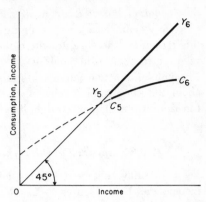

Figure **7–2**. The conventional consumption-function hypothesis.

Figure **7–3**. A declining marginal propensity to consume.

throughout the range of $C_1 C_2$; further, because the $C_1 C_2$ line extended backward passes through the origin, the average propensity to consume is also a constant, and the average propensity to consume and the marginal propensity to consume are identical, i.e., changes in income and consumption are proportionate. The equation for the consumption function is simply $C = bY$. The marginal propensity, as we noted a moment ago, is the slope of the line (b in the $C = a + bY$ equation), and the average propensity to consume is C/Y which, in this case, obviously is equal to b.

Such a proportionate relationship of consumption to income was not actually the one that Keynes thought was most descriptive of consumption behavior in advanced Western economies. Rather, he thought that the consumption function probably takes the form depicted in Figure 7–2, at least during periods of limited duration (how enduring the relationship is supposed to be is something we have yet to consider). In Figure 7–2 the extension of the consumption curve $C_3 C_4$ crosses the 45-degree line and intercepts the vertical axis a distance a above the origin in the chart. Under this hypothesis, the responses of consumption are not only absolutely less but also relatively less than the changes in income that induce them. This means that, as income *declines*, the average propensity to consume rises. It may reach a value of 1 (zero saving), or even more than 1 (negative saving, involving the liquidation of existing assets), if income falls far enough. This is the consumption hypothesis around which much modern demand theory has revolved.

In both Figures 7–1 and 7–2 consumption is a straight-line function of income. Its slope is the same throughout; the marginal propensity to consume is constant. There has been a good deal of speculation among economists that the marginal as well as the average propensity to consume actually may decline as income rises. If this should be so, the consumption function would have some such shape as that indicated in Figure 7–3. In this country, however, no real statistical evidence has been adduced to corroborate the idea of a declining marginal propensity to consume. For this reason and because, for the moderate changes in income that are usually relevant to real-world analysis (i.e., for relatively small segments of the consumption-function curve), a straight line and a slightly bent curve yield about the same results, conventional demand theory usually has assumed a function of the simpler, straight-line type shown in Figure 7–2.

The Significance of the Hypothesis

We have not yet taken up the vital question of exactly what kind of income the Y in Figures 7–1, 7–2, and 7–3 represents. However, if we assume for the moment that it stands for gross national income, then, since total spending equals total income, it follows that the vertical distance between the consumption curves and the 45-degree lines in Figures 7–1, 7–2, and 7–3 represent the sum of all kinds of spending other than consumption spending.[4] In the Keynesian two-sector model, this would be business investment spending. It does not follow that such nonconsumption spending is a function of income in the same sense that consumption is; nonconsumption spending is presumably *not* passive. But it does mean that at any given level of nonconsumption spending, there is only one level of consumption spending (and therefore of total spending) at which the economy is in equilibrium.[5]

Consequently, if the hypothesis is correct, consumption tends to magnify fluctuations in total spending that are instigated by changes in nonconsumption spending. If in Figure 7–2, for example, nonconsumption spending rises from FD to GE, the total increase in spending will not be simply the difference GH. In addition, gains in consumption to the extent of EJ will be induced, making the total increase in spending GH plus EJ,

---

[4] For present purposes, consumption is defined, in United States national income accounts terms, as personal outlays (PO), i.e., personal consumption expenditures (PCE) plus interest payments by consumers and net transfers by persons to foreigners.

[5] An economy is defined as being "in equilibrium" when, not only does total spending equal total income and total saving equal total investment (by definition), but also savers (business and persons) are saving the exact portion of incomes that they want to save, and investors (businesses and persons in the case of direct peronal investment) are investing exactly the amounts, relative to the level of consumer expenditures, that they want to invest.

In a three-sector model, the difference between the consumption-function line and the 45-degree line would include, in addition to investment spending, government spending. In this case, equilibrium might be defined as a condition such that savers are saving and investors are investing exactly as much as they want to save and invest, *and* the deficit or surplus in the consolidated budgets of governments is exactly the amount currently intended. See the last section of this chapter for a further discussion of the meaning of "equilibrium."

thus increasing total income by AB. [The dashed lines on the chart are intended to show that GH plus EJ equals AB. Because FH is parallel to DE and DJ is parallel to FK, $HK = EJ$; therefore, $GH + EJ = GH + HK$ (or GK). Inasmuch as Y_3Y_4 is a 45-degree line, $GK = FK = AB$.] Similarly, a reduction in nonconsumption spending will cause a drop in total demand that magnifies the original decline to the extent of consumption's responsiveness to declining income.

Constant-price versus Current-price Diagrams

There is no consensus among economists about whether one should expect to find a stronger relationship between consumption and income in current-price or constant-price terms.

Keynes himself was a strong partisan of the view that the relationship he hypothesized was between real consumption and real income. This makes good sense if the relationship involved is the one usually assumed, and diagramed in Figure 7–2. For in this case the fraction of income allocated to consumption falls as income rises. And ordinarily one would not expect consumers to behave this way if the increase in their money income were purely nominal, i.e., were fully offset by advances in consumer prices. Rather, in this event, unless they are highly subject to a "money illusion," one would expect them to maintain their real consumption by raising nominal (i.e., current-dollar) consumption in proportion to the rises in their nominal incomes.[6]

---

[6] One important exception to the generalization in the text should be noted. The proposition that consumers normally raise nominal consumption proportionately to purely nominal increases in incomes, thereby maintaining their real consumption and average propensity to consume, fortunately does not usually hold good for very long in the United States when we encounter major inflationary experiences. If it did, we would come out of those experiences less successfully.

When, with the economy already at full employment, there is a sizable increase in nonconsumption, e.g., defense, spending, prices and nominal incomes begin rising, and for a time nominal consumption usually keeps pace as consumers pay the higher prices and try to defend their level of real consumption. But as long as they persist in this effort, the nonconsumption purchasers are frustrated in their demand for a larger share of output and tend to bid prices up still further. If consumers do not give ground, settling for lower real consumption and higher real saving, the inflationary spiral could become prolonged and violent. Actually, consumers do tend to give ground for various reasons—the failure of the incomes of some to keep pace with the average rise, dissatisfaction with the height of prices judged by previous standards, and commodity shortages.

It is possible that, in a current-price consumption-function diagram, all this would be reflected simply by enough rightward movement along the function to reduce the average propensity to consume the required amount. But under such hectic circumstances it would be happenstance for the observed regularities in the economy to hold so neatly. The constant-price consumption function, at any rate, would be forced into a downward shift.

THE THEORY'S DPI/GNI GAP

The original versions of Keynesian consumption theory slurred over one question that should suggest itself insistently to any student of national income accounting. That is whether consumption is supposed to be a function of gross national income or disposable personal income.

The consensus of contemporary economists is that the consumption-function hypothesis has practical significance only as an explanation of consumer behavior. If so, then the logic of the hypothesis argues a relationship between consumption and disposable personal income. To reason directly from changes in gross national income to changes in consumption is to bypass the whole question of how GNP (GNI) is distributed between consumers on the one hand and business and government on the other. This would be a safe procedure only if the relationship between GNP and DPI were highly stable and systematic. Actually, in the United States, it is not. It depends upon a wide variety of influences, such as the tax structure and changes in tax laws, the nature and extensiveness of government transfer payments, the relationships among wages, commodity prices, and profits, and changes in the proportion of corporate earnings paid out in dividends. Moreover, there are significant but variable lags in the DPI/GNI relationship. Such things as the pace of wage negotiation, the extensiveness of overtime pay, and the mode of tax collections affect the speed at which changes in total demand register their effects upon disposable personal income.

As Figure 7–4 indicates, the joint result of all these influences has

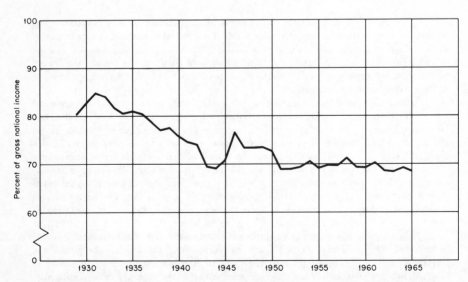

Figure 7–4. Disposable personal income as a percent of gross national income in the United States, 1929–1965. Source: U.S. Department of Commerce.

been a quite variable, although not highly volatile, DPI/GNI ratio in the United States during the past several decades. When we get to the problem of forecasting in Part Four, we shall need to evolve some workable rules of thumb for guiding assumptions about the course of this ratio during the near-term future. And in Chapter 12, when we analyze the impact of government on the economy, we shall have to consider government's effects upon the distribution of income among the major purchasing groups. This will force us to probe some distance into the nature of the relationship between GNI and DPI. At the moment, since there is no crisp, succinct theory that generalizes that relationship, we shall simply earmark it as a gap that remains to be filled in the demand model we are building.

The simplest interpretation of consumption-function diagrams such as Figures 7–1 and 7–2 is that their income dimension represents disposable personal income. However, as we shall see below, there are occasions when it is useful to diagram consumption as though it were functionally related to gross national income. But whenever this is done it should be understood either (1) that a constant DPI/GNP ratio is being arbitrarily assumed or (2) that, because of the instability of the DPI/GNP ratio, the whole consumption curve can shift bodily without signifiying any change in the functional relationship between consumption and DPI.

One final point remains—a point that should be obvious from what has been said already. To assert that consumption is a function of income is also to assert that saving is a function of income, because, by definition, saving is income not consumed. Thus, we can derive a saving function that expresses the relationship between income and saving. Figure 7–5 illustrates the saving function S_3S_4 that is the residual of the consumption function C_3C_4 in Figure 7–2; the distances between the base line and S_3S_4 equal the corresponding distances between C_3C_4 and Y_3Y_4. For any particular consumption function, the average propensity to save equals 1 minus the average propensity to consume, and the marginal propensity to save equals 1 minus the marginal propensity to consume.

If income is defined as DPI and consumption as PO, then "saving" is net personal saving, and the latter clearly is a function of DPI in the same sense that consumption is. The same combination of causal relationships

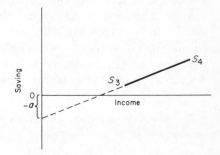

Figure **7–5.**   The conventional saving-function hypothesis.

that determines what proportion of DPI is consumed also determines automatically the proportion that is not consumed—i.e., saved.

If however, income is defined as GNP, then the difference between consumption and GNP, as you will recall from the discussion of the Nation's Economic Budget in Chapter 4, includes, besides net personal saving, gross business saving plus (algebraically) the government surplus (+) or deficit (−).[7] And the relationship between this gross national saving total and GNP is complex, just as is the relationship between consumption and GNP. It depends not only on the propensity to consume (and save) DPI, and on the strength of the nonconsumption components of total spending, but on the distribution of the gross national income between DPI and spendable receipts accruing to businesses and governments.

THE PROCESS OF INCOME CHANGE: THE MULTIPLIER

What remains to be done, so far as the mechanics of basic consumption theory are concerned, is to explain more fully the process by which changes in aggregate demand and total income come about. This is a matter usually discussed in terms (1) of the operation of the so-called multiplier and (2) of the relationship between saving and investment as income changes.

The multiplier concept has the strengths and the weaknesses of an intellectual gadget. Its catchy name, which Keynes borrowed from his fellow English economist, Kahn, and the rather neat mechanical precision of the concept fool many students into thinking it is a more indispensable element in demand theory than it actually is. As a matter of fact, it adds nothing intrinsically new to the concepts that already have been set forth. Once it is properly understood, however, the multiplier does provide a better step-by-step explanation of what happens over time as the magnitude of total spending increases or decreases than do other expositions of consumption theory.

First, let it be established that the multiplier is a facet of consumption theory—not of investment theory. It is easy to get confused on this point since expositions of the multiplier process almost invariably start with the assumption of an autonomous increase or decrease in investment spending. Thus the multiplier, which is the ratio of this initial, instigating increase to the rise in total spending that it occasions, seems to concern the effects of investment. However, the size of the multiplier depends entirely upon the responsiveness of consumption to increments of income; in fact, it is nothing more than an alternative expression of the marginal propensity to consume.

[7] Also (algebraically) plus—if we are dealing with actual figures rather than concepts—the statistical discrepancy.

Like the rest of Keynesian consumption theory, the multiplier focuses the analytical spotlight on investment simply because, in a two-sector model in which consumption is a passive function of income, investment is the *only* nonconsumption sector of demand. It is, therefore, the only sector in which an autonomous increase in spending can be posited without contradicting the consumption-function hypothesis itself. This is not true, however, of the rather more elaborate demand model being developed here, in which government spending is segregated as a distinct spending sector and in which disposable personal income is interposed between gross national income and consumption. In such a model—even with the most rigorous consumption function—an autonomous rise may occur in government purchases, or in consumption as the result of a shift in DPI relative to GNI, quite as readily as in private investment.

THE CONVENTIONAL MULTIPLIER CONCEPT

As Figure 7–6 indicates, the multiplier concept requires the assumption of a series of time periods. These are very abstractly defined lengths of time, that is, the length of time it takes typical consumers to respond to changes in income. This is an extraordinarily difficult thing to measure statistically. Economists sometimes have speculated that the typical multiplier period in the United States may be two, or three, or four months, but such estimates should be regarded as highly tenuous.

At any rate, the story that Figure 7–6 tells is that in period 1 there is

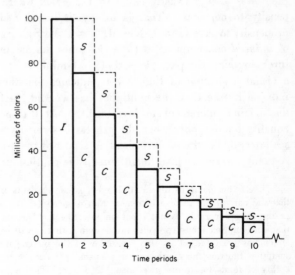

Figure **7–6.**   The conventional multiplier concept (with a marginal propensity to consume of 0.75).

an autonomous increase of $100 million in spending—let's say, to be conventional, that it is a rise in investment. This accrues immediately as income to those in the economy who are on the other side of the counter over which the investor purchases his newly produced real asset. If the consumption behavior of these income recipients conforms to the average consumption behavior described by the consumption function, then, in period 2, they allocate to consumption spending whatever fraction of this increment in income is indicated by the marginal propensity to consume, and save the rest. In Figure 7–6 the marginal propensity to consume is assumed to be 0.75. In period 2, therefore, $75 million of new consumption spending is induced.[8] But this also, of course, accrues as an increment of income to still other recipients; and if they too are typical consumers, in period 3 they spend three-fourths of $75 million, or $56.3 million, on consumption.

And so the story continues. Theoretically the process goes on forever, but it rather quickly approaches a limit. In the example in Figure 7–6, by the end of the tenth period, the cumulated total of new spending, including the original $100 million, amounts to about $377 million. In this case, because the marginal propensity to consume is three-fourths (i.e., the marginal propensity to save is one-fourth), the limit that the process approaches is $400 million, or four times the original increment. The multiplier is 4.

If the marginal propensity to consume had been two-thirds, the multiplier would have been 3; if it had been one-half, the multiplier would have been 2. This can be generalized. In the usual exposition (which implicitly assumes that all income accrues as disposable personal income) the multiplier k is always exactly equal to $1/1 - b$, where b is the marginal propensity to consume. That is to say, it is the reciprocal of the marginal propensity to save ($k = 1/1 - \text{MPC} = 1/\text{MPS}$). Similarly, the total amount of *induced* consumption is ($k - 1$) times the original autonomous expenditure; in our example, ($4 - 1$)($100 million) = $300 million. Further, a visual inspection of Figure 7–6 indicates that the total amount of saving induced by the time the multiplier has worked itself out is exactly equal to the original increment in investment. (At this point it appears that the equality obtains *only* when the process has run its course. But, as we shall see later, this is the most misleading aspect of the usual multiplier exposition. Actually the saving-investment equality is continuous.)

[8] At this point in the multiplier exposition students frequently ask how we know that the part of the income increment that is saved (in the present instance, $25 million in the second period) is not spent on investment. The answer is that it may be, but that consumption theory provides no assurance that it will be. The increment in saving, which has been caused by the interaction of the increment of investment and the consumption function, may or may not (depending on the form it takes) add to the availability of funds for future investment. Moreover, whether a second increment of investment occurs will depend on many other things beside the availability of investable funds. Certainly the generation of saving to match the initial round of investment does not guarantee further investment.

Finally, to complete the conventional exposition of the multiplier, if the original increment in spending is sustained—that is, if investment, for example, moves from a lower to a higher level and then stays there for successive periods—what will eventually result, in the manner indicated by Figure 7–7, is an expansion of total current spending that is k times the autonomous increase in spending.

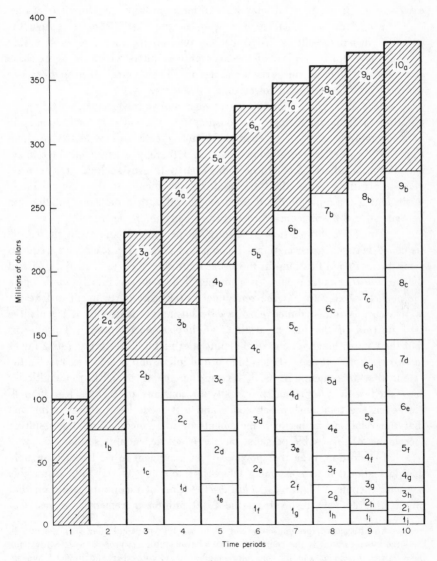

Figure 7–7. The multiplier effect of a sustained autonomous increase in spending.

A MODIFIED MULTIPLIER

The account of the multiplier process just recited has some obvious weak spots. For one thing, it may be unrealistic to generalize so sweepingly about the reactions to differing kinds of autonomous increases in spending. At any given time a rise in residential construction, a gain in purchases of producer's equipment, an advance in defense spending, and the rise in consumption resulting from an increase in personal income tax exemptions, for example, all may have different multipliers—for two reasons.

First, the particular groups who, in the first instance, receive the gains in income resulting from specific autonomous increases in spending actually may not be typical of the average consumers whom an aggregative consumption function purports to represent. Their marginal propensities to consume may be higher or lower than the average.

Second, a given autonomous change, say in government spending, in addition to inducing changes in consumption, may also induce changes in nonconsumption areas. For example, it may create a more favorable situation or prospect for certain businesses and thereby cause some investment spending that otherwise would not have occurred. Any such effect, of course, alters the ratio between the total resulting increment and the original increment, and if the multiplier is defined as this ratio, then the exact relationship between it and the marginal propensity to consume is destroyed.[9]

The explicit insertion of disposable personal income into the causal sequence between gross national income and personal consumption requires some further modifications in the usual multiplier theory. For only part of the income that autonomous rises in spending create ordinarily winds up in the pockets of consumers; the remainder is taken by government in taxes or is retained as undistributed earnings by business. However, it is only the DPI portion of the increment that can induce consumption. This means that the conventional version of the multiplier pictured in Figure 7–6 is faulty in two respects. It suggests too high a multiplier, and it is too exact. To the extent that increments in GNI exceed increments in DPI, the multiplier associated with a marginal propensity to consume of 0.75 is less than 4. Moreover, the relationship between k and b is made less precise by the fact that the relationship between increments of total income and the resulting increments of disposable personal income is not dependably stable.

In addition, even that portion of an increment in GNI that ultimately does get allocated to consumers takes time to filter its way into disposable personal income. Figure 7–8 outlines the kind of income distribution that might progressively result from the $100 million increment in investment

[9] An alternative formulation would be to say that the total change in demand in the situation indicated is the combined effect of two multiplier processes—one, involving the original increment and its consumption effects, and the other, the induced nonconsumption change and its consumption effects. Such a formulation preserves the definition of k as $1/1 - b$, but it employs a multiplier concept that is even less susceptible to empirical investigation than is that in the text.

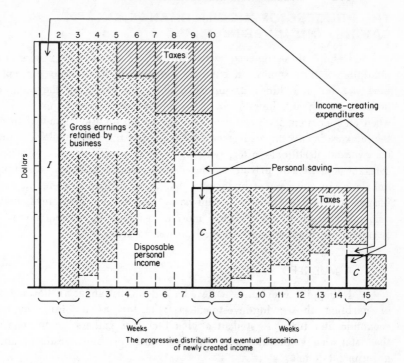

The progressive distribution and eventual disposition
of newly created income

Figure **7–8.** A modified multiplier diagram showing the gradual
redistribution and eventual disposition of newly generated income.

we hypothesized in Figure 7–6. The time periods shown are weeks, not
abstract multiplier periods. In the first instance all the increased income
may flow into the gross retained earnings of business. Then, increasingly,
DPI responds via increased employment, wage rate changes, overtime payments, dividend increases, and the like, and government begins to take its tax
bite of the increment. Most of each multiplier period in the conventional
multiplier exposition is occupied with such a reshuffling of income, so that
the pictures of completed consumer responses to income changes that Figure
7–6 shows for its periods 2, 3, 4, etc., actually are only intermittent snap-
shots taken at weeks 8, 15, etc., in Figure 7–8.[10]

---

[10] No importance should be attached to the selection of eight weeks as the apparent length of a multiplier period.

It should be added that, while more realistic than Fig. 7–6, Fig. 7–8 still is not
completely realistic, for it implies that all the consumers who receive their shares of
the original income increment at various times during weeks 3, 4, 5, 6, and 7 delay their
spending response to week 8, when they make it in unison. Actually, the consumption
response would come in bits and pieces, each piece supplying a new increment of GNI,
some of which would, in turn, begin to filter in DPI. Although it can only be charted
in terms of a series of discrete periods, actually the process is a continuous one in which
the consumption responses overlap. See Fig. 7–9.

THE PROCESS OF INCOME CHANGE: SAVING AND INVESTMENT

Despite these defects, even the simple, unmodified version of the multiplier would remain, on balance, a distinctly illuminating concept if it were not for one thing: its unforgivable sin is confusing the relationship between saving and investment. It seems to imply (see Figure 7–6) that, when an increment in investment occurs, enough additional saving to match the increase in investment is generated only after the whole multiplier process has worked itself out—after, perhaps, several years. If this were so, the constant equality of private saving and private investment (assuming no imbalance in government budgets[11]) that we have found inheres in national income accounting statistics would carry over to our theoretical model of demand determination only on a most occasional, intermittent basis. This is emphatically not so, and we shall do well to prove it.

A MUDDLED PICTURE

Unhappily, economics writers have done just about as thorough a job of garbling the saving-investment relationship as anything in macro-economic literature. A student of that literature gathers, on the one hand, that, statistically, private saving always equals private investment plus the government deficit.

But he also knows that, institutionally, saving and investment are different things, done for different motives, for the most part by different people. How is it that investors always choose to use just the quantity of saving that savers choose to supply? Doesn't saving sometimes fail to find an investment outlet—for instance, when you salt away part of your paycheck in a safe deposit box, or when you deposit it in a bank account but the bank fails to loan an equivalent amount to a business investor? And conversely, don't investors sometimes spend more than the current supply of saving, the difference being made up by an expansion of bank credit or by a liquidation of existing assets? It sounds as though our national accountants, who make saving and investment always come out equal, were pulling some kind of statistical sleight of hand.

There is also the alleged clash between the Keynesian and so-called Robertsonian models of changing demand and income. Keynes, it is said, used a model in which saving and investment always are equal, while D. H. Robertson, his eminent colleague at Cambridge, is credited with a model in which the inequality between saving and investment provides the very motive power that drives total spending and income up or down.

And then there are the Swedish economists who have tried to come to

---

[11] Including government, as we noted in Chap. 4, the equality is $S + T = I + G$ or, rearranged, $S = I + (G - T)$, in which G is government expenditures and T is government (largely tax) revenues. If there is no imbalance in the consolidated government budgets, i.e., if $T = G$, S obviously equals I.

the rescue with their distinction between *ex ante* (before-the-fact) saving
and investment, on the one hand, and *ex post* (after-the-fact) saving and
investment, on the other. Translated into a contrast between planned or
expected S and I and actual or realized S and I, this distinction has been
spotlighted by many American authors. Undoubtedly it helps. It is asserted
that the saving and investment that are planned for a period before it starts
normally do not equal each other, but that, when the results are added up at
the end of the period, realized S and I always match up as a result of
unintended saving or investment (chiefly inventory change). The first of
these propositions seems to be institutionally sound, and the second is statistically sound.

But there are some difficulties. It is not always clear how the unequal
plans get converted into equal realities. What of the relationship of actual
S and I during the course of a period? If investors embark on increased
spending, does saving only come into line gradually, as the period unfolds
—as the conventional multiplier exposition seems to suggest? If so, why is
it that the process always manages to get finished tidily by just those times
when the national income estimators close their accounts?

Moreover, the concept of planned saving does not ring very true in a
theoretical framework where consumption is treated as a wholly passive
function of income. It sounds somewhat incongruous to speak of consumers, whom the theory credits with about as much initiative as Pavlov's
dogs, as planning the negative aspect of their spending activity.

THE SAVING-INVESTMENT RELATIONSHIP CLARIFIED

How can all this confusion be straightened out? By establishing just
three propositions:

1. A sharp distinction must be drawn between the saving process and
the process of financing investment.

Saving, strictly construed, is the nonconsumption (technically, the
"nonpersonal outlay") of current private spendable income—nothing more.
The concept has nothing necessarily to do with the *forms* that saving takes.
It is true that the source of many of the funds with which investment expenditures are financed are liquid assets accumulated out of past saving and
conveyed by our financial institutions from those who save them to investors
who spend them. But, on the one hand, accumulated liquid savings are not
the only source of investable funds—an expansion of bank credit is another
—and, on the other hand, there is no assurance that any particular stock of
liquid assets accumulated by savers will be spent by investors.

This is not to say that the availability of funds, including those which
are the fruits of past saving, is not an important determinant of investment.
Nor is it to say that a change in investors' demand for funds may not
induce savers to increase their total saving somewhat at the expense of consumption. (In our demand model, where consumption and saving are treated

as being predominantly functions of income, such an increase in saving in response to an intensified demand for investable funds would take the form of an upward shift of the saving function and a downward shift in the consumption function.)

But there is no direct, necessary, and precise relationship between the volume of current saving and the mode of financing current investment. Moreover, it is misleading to imagine that there is any causal sequence that runs even from past saving to current investment. There may be something of a chronological sequence that can be traced out from part of past saving to part of current investment, but this is another matter. The real causal sequence, as we shall emphasize in a moment, is that which runs in the opposite direction from current investment to income and hence (via the consumption function) to current saving.[12]

2. Every change in total spending causes an instantaneous matching change in private saving or in tax receipts.

Much of our difficulty with the role of saving in the income process stems from our habit of thinking of saving as necessarily taking some particular form, such as a savings account deposit or a down payment on a house. Moreover, we are apt to associate saving only with personal saving, forgetting that business firms save, too, whenever they take income from consumers without incurring an equivalent liability to pay income to other persons. With these preconceptions, it is natural to view saving as something that takes time to catch up with changes in investment, and can do so only after some conscious decision making by consumers.

The fact is that whenever an autonomous change in total spending occurs, nothing requires less forethought than for the economy to execute an immediate, identical change in saving (assuming no change in tax collections). It cannot help doing so, for the simple reason that there are two sides to every business counter. Every transaction that marks an increase or decrease in total spending occasions a simultaneous and equal increase or

---

[12] It evidently was an effort to treat saving as a source of investment funds that caused D. H. Robertson to develop the income model that has contributed so materially to saving-investment confusion. Despite the fact that it pivots around a nominal inequality between S and I, Robertson's model actually did not clash with Keynes's. He simply adopted a different definition of saving than the one used by Keynes and about everybody else since. Robertson defined current saving not as the difference between current (today's) income and current consumption but as the difference between yesterday's income and today's consumption ($S_1 = Y_0 - C_1$). Apparently he was thinking of saving as flowing through financial channels to investment outlets, a process that takes time. Given this definition, of course it is true that today's investment, equal to $Y_1 - C_1$, may exceed today's saving, with the excess being financed, say, by credit expansion; and it is true that such an excess will cause an expansion in total spending and income. But virtually the same point can be made by stating in more conventional terms that if today's investment exceeds yesterday's saving, which is also to say, if today's investment exceeds yesterday's investment, today's spending and income will rise. There is nothing wrong with Robertson's definition of saving, except that almost no one, including the national income estimators, presently uses it.

decrease in private income (again assuming no change in tax collections). This change in income does not immediately occasion a change in consumption—either because none of the gain or loss in income has yet been passed on to consumers or because it takes consumers a while to adjust their spending to a new rate of income. Initially, therefore, all of any increment in private income is, by definition, additional saving—in most instances, additional business saving. In the case of the consumers who first receive some or all of the additional income, some or all of this willy-nilly increase in saving probably will be short-lived; consumers, whose marginal propensity to consume is presumably greater than zero, will respond fairly promptly to spend some of the income. But, just as in the case of the initial expenditure, the additional consumption spending creates further new income that initially is entirely saved (unless some of it is absorbed in taxes).

This principle is illustrated in Figure 7–9, where, for simplicity's

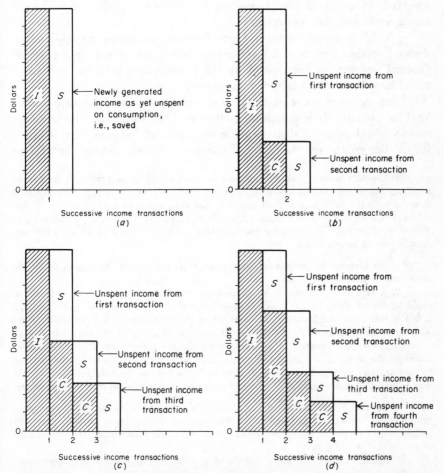

Figure **7–9.**   The constant equality of investment and saving during the operation of the multiplier process.

sake, it is assumed that all increments of income are eventually distributed to households and that all income recipients tend *ultimately* to spend 70 percent of the increments of income on consumption. Diagram *a* indicates the situation immediately after an increment in investment spending has occurred. At this point there has been only one expenditure or income transaction, and none of the newly generated income has yet been spent on consumption; it is all being saved, at least temporarily. In diagram *b* we have a second, somewhat later snapshot of the multiplier process. By now the consumption of the initial income recipients has begun to respond, thereby initiating a second round of income transactions, and a second round of increased income and saving. In diagram *c* the expansion process has continued, and in *d* the consumption of those who received the first increment in income has about fully responded (if our MPC assumption is correct). But some of the response of later-stage recipients has not yet occurred. Throughout the process there is constant equality of additional saving and additional investment.[13]

3. While actual saving and actual investment always are equal in the demand model, they are in equilibrium only when actual saving equals "normal" saving, as determined by the consumption function, and when actual investment equals intended investment.[14]

As we noted a few pages ago, the concept of planned saving is a little hard to swallow. It is stretching matters a bit to assume that passive consumers would program their negative consumption decisions very thoughtfully. But consumers do *react;* the essence of the consumption-function

[13] The text asserts that *any* increase in total spending generates an immediate matching increase in saving, assuming no rise in tax collections. It may be asked how increments in the categories of final demand other than investment, which the chart considers, would affect the $S - I$ relationship. First, remember that the full relationship is $S + T = I + G$. Then consider the following alternative ways in which additional spending could be generated:

1. An increase in government purchases: S rises to match the rise in G, in the same fashion as described above.

2. A rise in C occasioned by an increase in DPI relative to GNP: such a rise could be caused either by (*a*) a fall in gross retained earnings (business saving) or (*b*) a fall in taxes. In the first case, business saving simply is converted to personal saving with no overall change in S. In the second case, the rise in S offsets the decline in T.

3. A rise in C caused by an autonomous upward shift in the DPI consumption function: the saving newly generated by the additional income produced by the increase in consumption exactly offsets the amount of saving out of the previous level of DPI that was displaced by the upward shift in the consumption function; total saving is unaffected.

If, in Fig. 7-9 or in any of the above cases, the no-tax-change assumption were dropped and taxes were assumed to absorb some of the increased income, these tax increments, of course, would exactly offset losses to the saving increments that the change of assumption would entail.

[14] Again, "always are equal" if there is a continuing balance in governments' consolidated budgets.

hypothesis is that, in the short run, consumption-saving behavior *responds* to changes in current incomes in a fairly predictable manner. However, these reactions are never instantaneous. When total spending (and total income) changes, the actual division of this new level of income between consumption and saving initially diverges from that which the consumption function would indicate as normal. This divergence, however, results in a temporary condition of disequilibrium; that is, consumers are not spending the proportion of income that they would normally want to spend. Consequently, forces are set in motion to restore equilibrium.

Figure 7–10 illustrates the major aspect of this equilibrating process. As in our previous charts, *CC'* is the assumed consumption function. When income rises from *MM'* to *NN'* because of an increase in nonconsumption spending from *AM'* to *BN'*, at first there is no change in consumption; all the increased income accrues as saving; and actual consumption moves off

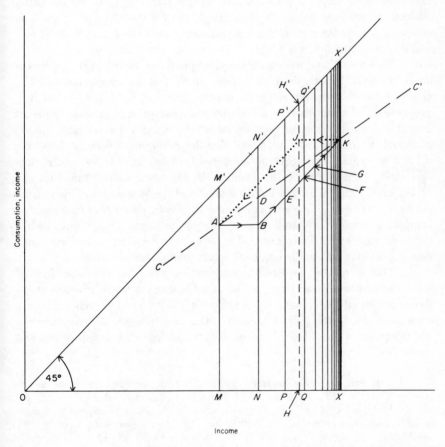

Figure **7–10.** The equilibrating process set in motion by an autonomous change in spending.

the consumption-function line from A to B. This step corresponds to the first diagram in Figure 7–9. If the consumption function is a valid generalization of consumer preferences, however, B is not an equilibrium position. Consumers increase their consumption from NB to ND, or by BD. But this increment in consumption itself adds to total spending and income, raising income by the same amount, or its identity, $DE = NP$. Thus, at this new PP' level of income, we still have a condition of disequilibrium; consumption is only PE, which is less than the consumption function tells us it would normally be. The gap between actual and normal consumption, while narrowed, is not fully closed. Thus consumers have an incentive to raise their spending further. The equilibrium-regaining process, increasing income by the smaller and smaller increments represented by the diminishing distances between the solid vertical lines in the figure, continues to point K, where actual saving and consumption again are normal. The new equilibrium income is XX'. In the event that nonconsumption spending thereafter declined as much as it initially rose, the downward route of saving and consumption would, for similar reasons, run along the dotted track from K to J and thence eventually back to A.

To sum up this finding, the consumption (or the saving) function is never properly hypothesized as a rigid track that consumption-saving decisions invariably travel; rather it is a tendency or, as Keynes called it, a propensity. The fact that actual consumption and saving temporarily depart from the normal as income changes decisively explains the constant equality of actual saving and of investment plus the government deficit. Likewise, it helps to explain the frequently observed tendency of changes in consumption to lag behind changes in income. However, normal consumption and saving exert a magnetic pull upon actual C and S whenever they depart from the norm, and it is this which constitutes the motor power that multiplies an instigating change in spending into a larger total change. While, with a balanced government budget, actual investment and saving always are equal, demand is never in equilibrium until actual saving also is normal.[15]

That is one of the equilibrium conditions for the short-run demand model we are here considering. The other is that the actual investment for the period equal the amount of investment spending which entrepreneurs are content to do as the period unfolds. The one category of investment in which serious discrepancies between actual and intended spending can and

[15] For simplicity's sake, in this exposition we have sloughed over the distinction between GNI and DPI. There are two elements in the lag of C behind GNI: (1) the lag of DPI behind GNI and (2) the time it takes for consumers to respond to changes in DPI. Thus, if a chart like Fig. 7–10 shows C as a function of GNI, the curve ABK should belly out farther to the right, and KJA farther to the left, of CC' than would be the case if CC' were drawn as a function of DPI.

do frequently arise is that of inventory accumulation—a topic we shall explore rather extensively later on.

Meanwhile, if we leave aside the possibility of changes in the government sector, we can summarize the essential conditions for short-run equilibrium as equality between intended and actual investment, including inventory investment, and between normal and actual saving.

CONCLUSIONS

Consumption theory is an impressive, albeit a rather simple, structure of ideas, and it obviously has a great potential importance for applied business conditions analysis. For not only does it purport to explain the behavior of the largest major component of final demand; because of the relationship it asserts between consumption and nonconsumption spending, it supplies our aggregative economic model with the basic mechanisms it needs for explaining the process through which total demand changes. In so doing, consumption theory explains the total demand effects of investment and government spending.

For this reason, as soon as one grasps the consumption-function hypothesis, he is moved to hurry on to the problem of what determines nonconsumption spending. For, if we accept the hypothesis, that is the payoff question as far as demand determination is concerned. First, however, it is well to think much more carefully about whether we *should* accept the hypothesis. Just how reliable is the consumption-income relationship that has been presented in this chapter? How well does the empirical evidence support it? That is the subject of the next chapter.

8

LONG-RUN BEHAVIOR
OF THE CONSUMPTION
FUNCTION

It should be a solace to all of us who would rather speculate than correlate that the Keynesian consumption-function hypothesis, one of the most influential concepts in modern economics, was strictly an armchair construct to begin with. John Maynard Keynes was a man of many talents and interests. In addition to being a teacher and writer of professional economics, he was an eminently successful businessman and banker, intermittently a leading civil servant, always an active and trusted adviser to his and other governments, an indefatigable contributor to weekly and fortnightly journals of opinion, a patron of the arts, and the husband of a principal ballerina of her time. He had neither the temper nor the time for the grubby business of statistical research. Thus, although the propensity to consume generally conformed to a number of studies of family budget behavior then available, it was originally propounded as nothing more than an intuitive induction about how people in general behave.

Almost as soon as *The General Theory* was published, however, economic statisticians on both sides of the Atlantic, taking advantage of the coincidental appearance of the first modern national accounting estimates, leaped to the task of testing and verification. As such things go, their endorsement was a ringing one. When, adopting the format of the consumption-

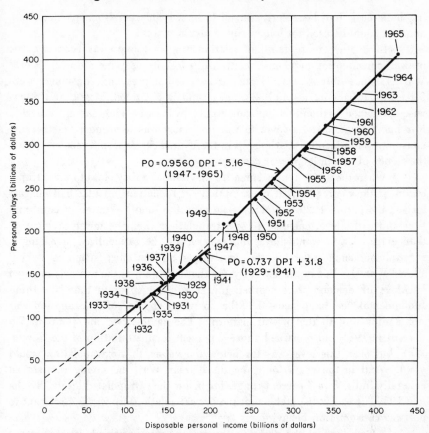

Figure 8–1.   Relationship between disposable personal income and personal outlays, 1929–1941 and 1947–1965, in 1958 dollars. Note: Personal outlays deflated with implicit price deflator for PCE. Source: *Survey of Current Business*, U.S. Department of Commerce.

function diagram, they plotted, in the manner of Figure 8–1, the scatter of points for which annual aggregate consumption and income data were available, they found that in both the United States and Britain the historical data fitted a straight line that resembled the hypothesized, static consumption function quite closely.[1] By the time World War II broke out, the short-run Keynesian consumption function was widely regarded not only as a challeng-

---

[1] This paragraph contains a little literary license. Almost from the beginning, many of the statistical verifiers tested more elaborate consumption functions, i.e., those including more variables, than the simple $C = a + bY$ formulation around which the present discussion has revolved. For a definitive treatment of this matter, cf. Robert Ferber, *A Study of Aggregate Consumption Functions*, National Bureau of Economic Research, Inc., Technical Paper no. 18, New York, 1953.

ing hypothesis but, because it seemed to be a highly persistent phenomenon, one that could be used for longer-run analyses as well.

Like other more familiar relationships in the prewar economy, the prewar consumption-to-income relationship lost its usefulness during World War II, since output was diverted from civilian uses and consumers were forced by price controls and shortages (and were orated, kissed, and otherwise persuaded by bond-selling campaigns) to increase their saving radically. For many economists, a favorite wartime sport was to wonder whether the consumption-to-income relationship in the United States would reemerge from the clouds of war in its prewar shape and position.

When the 1946 figures came in, they landed fairly close to an extrapolation of the aggregate real consumption–DPI relationship that had characterized the period 1929 to 1941.[2] And even the small deviation of consumption above the level calculated by extrapolation (i.e., the lower saving rate than extrapolation would have indicated) could be rationalized as a temporary phenomenon reflecting the constraints on consumer spending during World War II. But in the several years that followed, as the war-accumulated backlogs of demand were worked off, it became apparent that something fundamental had happened—that the postwar behavior of consumption was not conforming to the prewar pattern. The saving rate did jump to 7.6 percent in 1951 and remained above 7 percent for the duration of the Korean War, but even this level was far below the values that extrapolation would yield. And in the years following the Korean War, the saving rate stayed generally in the 5 to 7 percent range, far below the extrapolated level. By the late 1950s, it was indisputable that the prewar relationship was not relevant to postwar consumption behavior.

As we look at the data for the entire postwar period, it is apparent that two things happened during World War II. First, the *slope* of the historical consumption-disposable income line of relationship changed (see Figure 8–1). The prewar line of relationship had a slope of 0.737. The postwar line of relationship has a slope of 0.956—fairly close to unity. Second, the prewar regression line had a sizable Y intercept ($31.8 billion), which meant that the *average* propensity to consume would decline with increases in DPI. The postwar regression line, however, had a Y intercept of almost zero (−$5.16 billion), which meant that consumption would rise proportionately with income.[3]

This prewar and postwar experience raises two important questions. First, what is the significance of the fact that, whereas in the prewar period

[2] These words are written with the benefit of several revisions in the consumption, saving, and DPI figure made since 1946, notably the 1965 revision. The data actually available in 1946 showed an even closer fit to the extrapolated prewar consumption-income regression.

[3] In view of the inevitable margin of error in the data, no significance should be attached to the negative sign of the Y intercept. About all that we should conclude is that the intercept is approximately zero.

the regression of consumption on income over time (a decade or so) seemed to conform pretty well to hypothesized notions of the static, or short-run, relationships between consumption and income, in the postwar period it did not? And second, if the answer to the first question implies a shifting short-run consumption function, what causes it to shift? And are the shifts erratic and unpredictable, or can we count on fairly orderly, and therefore predictable, shifts in the consumption function in the future?

The answer to the first question is fairly clear. Whereas in the prewar period the slope of the consumption-income relationship over time (i.e., for the 1929–1941 period as a whole) might well have been reasonably representative of the slope in any particular year (or other short period of time), in the postwar period this similarity could apparently no longer be assumed. With the benefit of hindsight, we can now conclude that the prewar similarity between the historical consumption-income relationship and the hypothesized static consumption function was probably a coincidence and reflected the fact that the years under analysis were years of heavy unemployment and depressed incomes. The shape of the postwar relationship made necessary a clean distinction between static, or short-run, and long-run historical consumption-to-income relationships.

This distinction is illustrated in Figure 8–2. Each of the CC' lines

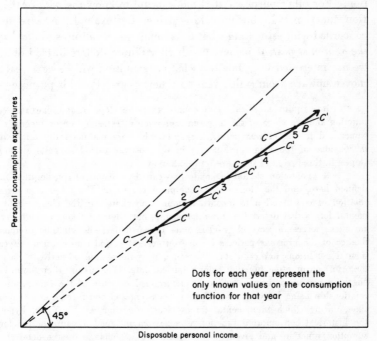

Dots for each year represent the only known values on the consumption function for that year

Disposable personal income

Figure **8–2.**   Hypothetical consumption functions for five consecutive years of steady expansion and a regression line fitted to known values for income and consumption in each year.

represents the hypothetical aggregate consumption function appropriate for each of several successive *points in time,* say, a year apart. We do not know, of course, the precise dimensions of the consumption function at any point in time. The shape and slope of the function can be only estimated, using reasoning based on studies of household behavior, the behavior of aggregate consumption during unusual periods when a sudden change in income has occurred, and common sense. But we do know (assuming accuracy in the statistics) one point on the static consumption function, if we are willing to stretch the "static" concept into a period of time as long as a quarter or a year. This is the actual value of income and consumption in that quarter or year, illustrated by the points 1, 2, . . . 5 on Figure 8–2.

Then, if we fit a regression line to these known points, we get a measure of the *path* of the consumption function as it shifts upward over time.[4] The regression line, shown in Figure 8–2 as an arrow, may be called the "historical consumption function."[5]

For certain purposes, we need to know the shape of the consumption function for a given point in time. For example, if the Congress is contemplating a tax increase that could be imposed on either low- or high-income persons, it would be useful in assessing the economic impact in any given year of alternative tax changes to know the shape of the static consumption function. For other purposes, it is more useful to know the *path* of the consumption function. In business forecasting, for example, we are usually not concerned with estimating what consumption expenditures *would have been in the year just past,* if income had been y billion dollars instead of x. Rather, we are interested in estimating what consumption will be *next* year if income moves upward from x this year to y next year. For this purpose—if we can

---

[4] It is quite conceivable, of course, that the slope of the short-run consumption function and the slope of the long-run regression of consumption on income could be the same, and in the prewar period they probably were not markedly different. But the 0.956 slope of the long-run function in the postwar period suggests strongly that the slopes, in this period of time, are quite different.

[5] A distinction should be made between the "historical consumption function," as defined here, and the "long-run consumption function." The latter is a measure of the relation of consumption to income, assuming no change in the character of the fundamental forces that determine this relationship, but allowing a long enough period of time for these forces to work themselves out—in particular, enough time to remove the influence of the *previous* period's income on current period consumption. Because fundamental conditions never do stay the same, it is impossible to derive a measure of the long-run consumption function from empirical data. The historical consumption function, on the other hand, is an empirically determined measure of the consumption-to-income relationship using known values of actual consumption and income over a long period of time, during which fundamental forces clearly do change. We might hypothesize that the historical consumption function is a reasonably good measure of the long-run consumption function, and given moderate and gradual changes in the determinants of the consumption-to-income relationship, it may well be. But it is not necessarily so. See Gerald Sirkin, *Introduction to Macroeconomic Theory,* Richard D. Irwin, Inc., Homewood, Ill., 1961, pp. 63–72, for a further discussion of this point.

assume that the economy will continue to grow and that scales of living will continue to rise—the historical consumption function is the more useful concept.

The second question (Why does the consumption function shift and are the shifts predictable?) requires a more elaborate answer. We need to examine, in some detail, the determinants—other than income itself—of consumption and how they operate over time.

DETERMINANTS OF THE CONSUMPTION TO INCOME RELATIONSHIP

In the next few pages we shall list some eleven (not entirely separate and distinct) actual or alleged determinants of the consumption-income relationships. Such a lengthy listing suggests a word of caution.

We should avoid the fallacy of pseudo quantification, that is, of letting the lengths of the lists of qualitative points on the opposite sides of the question decide the question. For example: Jones, on the one hand (1) is a thief; but on the other hand he (1) contributes to the Red Cross, (2) attends church, and (3) helps with the dishes. Therefore, on balance, he is a man of good character. The social sciences are rife with such nonsense, but certainly economists, who have superior opportunities for real quantification, should avoid it.

This preachment is particularly pertinent in the present instance. The length of the list may convey the impression that so many influences are at work to disturb the consumption-to-income relationship that no stable relationship could possibly exist. Yet, as we shall see, these forces usually exert their influences in a gradual and orderly way (World War II was clearly an abnormal period, from the point of view of this relationship), and in the absence of such exceptional circumstances, a rather stable and predictable long-run relationship between consumption and income is a reasonable expectation.

Population Changes

If, under the rationale of the consumption-function hypothesis, aggregate consumer behavior is simply an aggregation of individual behavior, it is rather obvious that changes in population, as well as changes in income, will affect aggregate consumption. A consumption function derived from per capita data should provide a more reliable statement of the consumption-income relationship than one derived from aggregate data. Or, alternatively, if two consumption functions, one on an aggregate and the other on a per capita basis, are calculated for the same period, and if the period is one during which both population and per capita incomes have been rising, the aggregate function should have a steeper slope than the per capita function. This obvious arithmetical point would not be important to our discussion if an increased population meant simply more of exactly the same people, but population growth may also be accompanied by a change in the age distribution of the population.

Changes in the age distribution of the population are unlikely to affect consumption as sharply as they affect the economy's productive capacity if they involve shifts of population into or out of the working ages; all live mouths eat, but not all live hands work. However, a change in age distribution can have a significant impact upon the saving rate and also upon the commodity composition of consumption. For example, a rise in the proportion of the population in the family-formation age range may raise the consumption function. Or again, a jump in the birthrate may have its quickest effect on the consumption of nondurable goods and services and may only register its full impact on the purchase of household durables some years later, when the new generation has reached marriageable age.

In an analysis of the effects of age distribution, it is important to distinguish between the age effect itself and the income effects, because incomes are correlated with age, typically rising as a person gets older, to a point, then declining gradually or abruptly. One interesting study showed that, after removing the effects of income, family saving as a percentage of income tended to rise with the average age of the wife.[6]

Similarly, a shift in the geographic location of the population, especially from rural to urban areas, may cause the consumption function to shift; households typically save less in urban areas. Both of these types of changes occurred during and shortly after World War II, and they go far toward explaining the shift in the consumption-to-income relationships during the war.

Changes in Income Distribution among Consumers

As we implied a moment ago, the distribution of personal incomes as well as their aggregate amount has an effect upon consumption, and also as noted earlier, numerous family budget studies bear out the fact that households' average propensity to consume declines as you go up the income scale. Some findings also have suggested, however, that the marginal propensity to consume is about the same for all income groups in particular periods;[7] this has led some analysts to conclude that a given stimulus to high personal income, e.g., via a tax reduction, will induce just as large an increment in consumption as would the same concession to low-income groups.

Many working economists remain unconvinced on this last point. They take the position that, even if it should be true that a sharp, sudden

---

[6] Dorothy Brady, "Family Saving, 1888–1950," in Goldsmith, Brady, and Mendershansen, *At Study of Saving in the United States,* Princeton University Press, Princeton, N.J., 1955, vol. 3, p. 193.

[7] See Harold Lubell, "Effects of Redistribution of Income on Consumers' Expenditures," *American Economic Review,* vol. 37, no. 1, pp. 157–170, March, 1947.

redistribution of individual incomes in the direction of equality would not change the slope of the short-run aggregate-consumption function, it probably would shift the whole function upward. On the other hand, sharp, sudden shifts in individual income distribution are most uncommon in the United States; even the significant move toward less income inequality achieved during and after World War II was relatively moderate. On balance, it may be safe to conclude that the distribution of incomes among consumers (remember that the distribution of gross national income between consumers, on the one hand, and business and government, on the other, is a very different story) does not vary rapidly enough to be an active determinant of consumption in such short periods as a year, or a couple of years, or maybe even a decade. An exception to this generalization would no doubt be the decade of the 1940s, when an important change in income distribution did occur, a change that presumably helps explain the prewar-to-postwar shift in the consumption-to-income relationship.[8]

Income Change

A number of studies[9] indicate that the magnitude and rapidity of income change over time have an effect on the proportion of income that is spent.[10] Households that have experienced a recent increase in income are likely to spend a smaller portion of their total income than those who have been enjoying this same level of income for some time. This, indeed, is what we would expect; consumers do not change their habits—their patterns of living—overnight. After a time, however, as consumers become accustomed to the higher incomes, especially if they consider the increase to be, not a temporary windfall, but a permanent and continuing addition to income, they are likely to adjust their living habits to reflect the higher level of income.[11] The reverse response—to a *decline* in income—is not entirely analogous. Again, consumers will tend to resist a sudden change in their patterns of liv-

---

[8] It should be emphasized that the variable of individual income distribution, properly construed, concerns only the relative income spread among households, not the absolute level of particular groups. Thus if all groups move up a notch, this probably seldom means that each inherits the lower average propensity to consume of the previous occupants of its new income stratum. See the discussion of the effect of rising living standards later in the chapter.

[9] See, for example, George Katona, "Effects of Income Changes on the Rate of Saving," *Review of Economics and Statistics*, vol. 39, May, 1949; and George K. Brinegar, "Short-run Effects of Income Change upon Expenditure," *Journal of Farm Economics*, vol. 35, February, 1953.

[10] Note that we are referring to the effects of various kinds of income change through time, not to alternative income points on a static consumption function.

[11] The effect of income change on consumption is partly a matter of varying responses to actual, experienced changes in income, and partly a matter of responses to changing expectations of future income. To the extent that the latter is involved, it is a special case of changes in consumer expectations, discussed below.

ing; they will wish to maintain their living standards in spite of the fall in income. They tend to adjust, however, more slowly to the decline in income as it persists over time than they do to a rise in income. It is easier, it seems, to raise one's scale of living than to lower it.

The Level of Liquid Holdings

The war and postwar experience brought into sharp focus the fact that the level of current consumption is conditioned by the extensiveness of consumers' current liquid holdings. If individuals acquire abnormally high amounts of liquid assets, as they did during World War II, then that part of their subsequent saving which is security-motivated tends to be diminished. This is part, but only part, of the explanation of the low saving rates in 1947 and 1949.

Interruptions in the Supply of Durable Goods

Another part of the explanation is that consumers did, during World War II, acquire backlogs of wants for durable goods that were in short supply. It is impossible to accumulate a backlog of needs for goods that are perishable or that are consumed quickly. But when the supply of durable commodities suffers a sustained interruption, a subsequent reaction in consumption is to be expected.

The Asset Components of Living Standards

This point is not entirely separable from the preceding two, but at least it casts them into a more systematic framework. Actually, consumer buying, which is the only thing that consumption statistics directly measure, is not an end purpose of economic activity. What consumers try to raise and maximize is their standard of living, an important aspect of which is their use of consumer goods.

Where living standards are low and thus almost all income is used for buying goods of little durability, the use of consumer expenditures as an index of current consumer welfare does not involve an important error. However, all living standards also have certain asset components. They include both the services of physical assets, such as houses and consumer durables, and the psychic services of liquid holdings. And as living standards rise, these asset components may well rise in relative as well as absolute importance.[12] Thus

---

[12] For example, during the six years 1935 to 1940, purchases of consumer durables accounted for 9.4 percent of disposable income in the United States; in the six years 1950 to 1955, consumer-durables buying absorbed 13.4 percent of DPI; in the six years 1957 to 1962, however, as the period of restocking came to an end, the proportion declined slightly to 12.7 percent. In 1963–1965, however, it rose again to 13.6 percent.

more and more current consumer spending and saving, some of which involves the acquisition of assets, is only an indirect measure of current consumer welfare and current living standards.

All this has little practical significance, so far as the consumption-income relationship is concerned, if incomes and living standards rise steadily and smoothly. But if the rise is discontinuous and lumpy, a distortion in normal consumption-income relationships can occur.

For example, during World War II consumers' liquid assets rose radically, beyond even the increasing liquid-asset requirements of their rising living standards, while their access to new durable goods including housing was sharply curtailed. Then, during the early postwar years, households rushed to bring their physical assets up to the level their radically higher income levels now justified, and there was a substantial shift from liquid to physical holdings. Then, in the early 1950s, once the initial consumer reaction to the Korean outbreak was over, consumers embarked on a campaign of liquidity replenishment as the shift toward physical assets combined with the intervening further rise in incomes and, particularly, with the intervening price inflation were found to have left personal liquidity at an inappropriately low level.[13]

Thus, it is only when the asset aspects of living standards are considered that the record of the saving rate and the consumption rate during the decade starting, say, in 1944, begins to make sense.

Personal Debt and Priority Saving

So far we have emphasized the residual definition of personal saving: the use of disposable personal income for purposes other than personal outlays. This is the national accounting definition and the one which keys into demand theory most readily. However, net personal saving may also be defined as any net increase in personal assets, either real or financial. This more direct, positive definition is the conceptual equivalent of the first and is employed by the Securities and Exchange Commission in its calculation of an alternative personal saving series.

Given the latter definition, it is easy to understand that any increase in personal indebtedness in the economy, which constitutes an increase in personal liabilities, can be treated as negative personal saving or, as the term goes, "dissaving." Similarly, any net retirement of personal debt is a type of saving. Thus there is nothing about the phenomenon of personal credit transactions that necessarily falls outside the framework of the consumption function. Net personal saving is *net*; that is, it is the difference between a much larger total of positive saving by some persons and negative saving by

[13] See John P. Lewis, "The Lull That Came to Stay," *Journal of Political Economy*, vol. 44, no. 1, pp. 1–19, February, 1955, for a fuller discussion of this experience. Also see text Chap. 15.

others. Expansions and contractions of debt are simply one minus or plus form that saving may take.

However, the terms of personal debt associated with particular kinds of purchases may have a subsequent impact upon the rate of buying in those areas and, if not offset in other commodity areas, may affect the total consumption-saving relationship. The comparative easiness of automobile credit, for example, certainly has some effect upon the rate of automobile sales. To some extent such easiness or tightness is a matter of interest rates, but the size of minimum down payments and the length of maximum retirement periods are of much greater importance.[14]

Moreover, any substantial change in consumer indebtedness sets in motion subsequent effects upon consumption and saving that are largely independent of succeeding changes in disposable personal income. For example, a sharp increase in installment buying guarantees a heavy rate of installment payments in the year or two immediately following and may tend to depress consumption in those years. Indeed, such an increase in installment buying may have a double-barreled effect, because not only will repayment obligations be higher, but also, after a period of rapid rise in consumer debt, consumers may be relatively well stocked with debt-financed consumer goods, thus bringing into play the asset effect discussed above.

There is a further related point. Conventional theory seems to suggest that saving is a more discretionary, postponable activity than consumption—that if income falls, saving will be the first thing to go. Actually, however, consumers are committed by installment loan, mortgage, pension fund, and life insurance contracts to continue much of the saving they are doing at any given time.[15] The extensiveness of such contractual or institutionalized saving means that, if saving actually is more squeezable than consumption when income is declining, the squeezability must be concentrated in only part of personal saving.

Interest Rates

It has been hinted already that some analysts think a rise in interest rates—i.e., higher prices for the use of loanable funds—tends to persuade consumers to increase not only the portion of saving they do in lendable form but their total current saving and, hence, to reduce their current consumption. The item is included here to make this list of possible determinants of con-

---

[14] It may appear that the impact of mortgage credit terms upon consumption and saving would be similar to those of automobile and other installment credit terms. However, this is not the case statistically in view of our convention of treating house buying as investment (and saving) rather than consumption. In the case of mortgage credit, easier terms may mean an increased purchase of new houses (saving) and a roughly offsetting increase in mortgage debt (dissaving).

[15] This matter will be explored more extensively in Chap. 20, which deals with the short-run forecasting of outlays on housing and automobiles.

sumption and saving as comprehensive as possible. However, although it must be granted that money interest rates can influence the *form* in which saving is done, there is little if any evidence that they have much direct effect on the total volume of saving in the United States.[16] As has been noted already, rising interest rates on personal debt can help to deter installment buying and thereby indirectly stimulate saving. However, this is an effect of personal credit terms in general; it is not peculiar to the interest rate, which is commonly less potent in this respect than either the minimum down payment or the maximum length of the repayment period.

Price Changes

The physical volume of total consumer purchases clearly is not so sensitive to price changes as are the sales of most particular commodities. Certain commodities are as price-elastic as they are income-elastic because they have close substitutes. It doesn't take much of a price hike on brussels sprouts to switch many housewives to broccoli or beans. But all that consumers can substitute for consumption as a whole is one or another form of saving, and, usually, changes in the retail price level that *do not alter the overall real income of consumers* probably do not cause alterations in their real consumption and saving.

The qualifying phrase in the preceding sentence is a necessary proviso for isolating the consumption effect of a change in prices per se. For if we did not include it—that is, if we considered a case where current-price disposable personal income failed to keep pace with the average change in retail prices and where, therefore, the price change caused a change in real consumer income—we could (and probably should) treat any resulting change in consumption as an income, and not a price, effect.

Such price-engineered changes in real consumer incomes are not uncommon. It is true that every rise in consumer prices is reflected in someone's income, for the familiar reason that there are two sides to every counter. But much of the initial impact is on the gross retained earnings of business and the net receipts of governments, not on disposable personal income. Thus price changes can have some important effects on real consumption that operate via their impact on real consumer income. They do not constitute a formal exception to the consumption-function hypothesis as long as the latter treats consumption as a function of DPI. But price changes can be a major cause of changes in real DPI. This is a matter to which we shall return at various later points, including Chapter 26.

As for the direct effect of price changes upon consumption—the case where, despite constant real incomes, consumers are led by price increases

---

[16] Note that this conclusion is quite the opposite of the classical, pre-Keynesian assumption that the volume of total saving responded directly and proportionately to changes in the interest rate.

to save more and consume less—some exceptions should be noted to our dismissal of it as ordinarily not important. The principal exception is the behavior of American consumers in intensely inflationary periods. Under such circumstances, they fortunately do have the habit, after scrambling for goods for a while, of backing down and accepting a higher rate of real saving. In addition, not only in such periods, but on other occasions as well, the Survey Research Center at the University of Michigan (our best source on consumer attitudes) now and then comes up with the finding that sizable numbers of consumers are refraining from buying simply because they find prices "too high." It is doubtful, however, that such findings prove that *total* consumption is significantly price-elastic in the ordinary sense. They may be only (1) reactions to certain conspicuous price increases, especially on "big ticket" items, which may for a time deter consumers in their purchases of those items, (2) responses to the recent rate at which prices have been rising rather than to the present height as such, or (3) reactions to implicit expectations concerning future price changes (see the section below), or (4) reflections of weakened real incomes owing to the failure of current-price DPI to keep pace with consumer prices.

Consumer Expectations

Consumer anticipation of sharp increases or decreases in commodity prices undoubtedly can have an effect upon current consumption that is not attributable to the current rate of personal income. However, this is a point properly listed under the heading of expectations rather than prices, for the same thing applies to a whole range of factors. Anticipations of future individual incomes, of general business conditions, of commodity shortages, and of international events—all can have impacts on current consumption that are in no sense a function of current income.

An interesting case in point is the alleged feedback effect of business forecasting. A general consensus among forecasters that a downturn in business activity, incomes, and employment was imminent might well—if consumers paid any attention to the forecasters—bring on the very downturn predicted through its impact on consumer spending. In practice, the effect of such a consensus is more likely to be transmitted via investment spending by businessmen, who are probably more alert to prevailing forecasts than are the mass of consumers. But the effect, whether on consumer or business spending, is no doubt sufficiently real to cause a widely read economic forecaster, such as the authors of the "Business Round-up" in *Fortune* magazine, to think twice before making a frank and forthright forecast of a business decline.

A second case in point is the mass scare buying in the months immediately following the Korean outbreak. In the fall of 1962, during the Cuban crisis, however, consumers responded much more phelgmatically—perhaps because the crisis came to an end before they had had time to act.

Institutional Changes

We lump under this heading a variety of changes in law, custom, business practice, and the like that may affect the consumption-to-income relationship over time. It is these institutional changes, in particular, which are usually assumed to be constant in discussions of the short-run consumption function. When we shift our attention, however, to the historical consumption function, such institutional changes must be taken into account.

A notable example has been the enormous spread, since World War II, of consumer and mortgage-debt contracts that provide for regular contractual amortization. A debt which a consumer is conditioned and obligated to pay off in regular monthly installments and which, as a result, is unlikely ever to present him with a liquidity crisis entails an entirely different burden and hazard than one of the same size that calls for a lump-sum payment at the end of, say, five years, as was typical in the 1920s. The dampening effect of the postwar personal debt expansion upon consumption doubtless has been much less than it would have been without this institutional change. Another example is the adoption, since the 1930s, of a variety of income-stabilizing devices, such as unemployment compensation and old age, survivors, and disability insurance. Although it is not clear that these devices have shifted the consumption function upward, they have added an element of stability to both the short-run and the long-run consumption-to-income relationship.

THE PERMANENT-INCOME HYPOTHESIS

In recognition of these determinants of a changing consumption function, economists in recent years have devoted a great deal of time and attention to the development of hypotheses that take some or all of them into account. One of the most important of these is the somewhat inadequately labeled "permanent-income" hypothesis, advanced at about the same time in similar, though not identical, frameworks by Franco Modigliani in collaboration with R. E. Brumberg and Albert Ando, and by Milton Friedman.[17] The Modigliani and associates' hypothesis, first, defines consumption, not as total current consumer expenditure, i.e., PO, but as current expenditures for nondurable goods and services (net of any changes in consumer stocks of nondurables) plus the rental value of consumer stocks of consumer durable goods. The hypothesis then identifies the determinants of consumption in any given period, thus defined, as: (1) current nonproperty income; (2) the present value of expected future nonproperty income; and (3) the net worth of con-

---

[17] See, for a recent exposition and empirical testing of the former, Albert Ando and Franco Modigliani, "The 'Life Cycle' Hypothesis of Saving: Aggregate Implications and Tests," *American Economic Review*, vol. LIII, no. 1, part 1, pp. 55–84, March, 1963. For a statement of the latter, see Milton Friedman, *A Theory of the Consumption Function*, Princeton University Press, Princeton, N.J., 1957.

sumers at the beginning of the period. This elaboration of the conventional consumption-function hypothesis gives explicit recognition to several behavior responses of rational consumers: (1) The definition of consumption takes into account the fact of durability of consumer durable goods. A given increase in income would elicit a different expenditure response from consumers who are well stocked with consumer durables than from those who are not. (2) The definition of income tends to reduce the significance of transitory income in consumption expenditure decisions by adding, as a major determinant of current consumption, the present discounted value of expected future income that presumably would not be affected by one-shot, nonpermanent income. (3) The addition of consumer net worth as a determinant of consumption takes recognition of the fact that the financing of consumption is not limited to current income, that consumers whose net worth position is strong can maintain their consumption at a fairly steady pace in spite of fluctuations in current income, and that conversely consumers whose net worth is low or negative have no similar room for maneuver and, indeed, if they have sizable repayment commitments on debt, may be forced to curtail their consumption expenditures drastically when income declines only moderately. (4) The addition of expected future income as a determinant takes into account the fact that *rational* consumers do not live for this day or this year alone, but presumably plan their consumption to reflect their expected income over their remaining lifetime.[18] As we noted earlier, the consumption response of young households, with a forty- or fifty-year lifetime of income to look forward to, is likely to be quite different from that of the couple approaching retirement even at the same level of *current* income.

Such consumption-function hypotheses—if the premises on which they are based are valid—are valuable additions to our kit of analytical tools for understanding the behavior of consumption in relation to income, especially as regards individual households. And as applied to aggregate consumer behavior, they attempt to quantify some of the influences we have analyzed only in verbal terms. Their operational usefulness for such purposes as business forecasting, however, has yet to be demonstrated. As a practical matter, the statistical problems of measuring consumption (as defined in these hypotheses), consumer net worth, and "expected future income" are formidable.[19] Nevertheless, the logic of the hypotheses suggests that we would do well, when we undertake to forecast PCE and PO, to make a clean distinction between nondurable goods and services, on the one hand, and durables—certain durables, at least—on the other.

---

[18] This does not necessarily mean that consumers plan their affairs so that they can enjoy a *stable* level of consumption over their lifetime; their utility functions are presumably such that they give a higher priority to current consumption than to future consumption.

[19] But see Ando and Modigliani's efforts in this direction in the article cited.

CONSUMPTION THEORY'S TIME DIMENSION

Assuming that there is something in the historical consumption function as estimated for the United States economy in Figure 8–1, how durable can such a consumption-income relationship be expected to be? Are changes such as that which occurred during World War II to be expected every now and then? Or is the long-run function a dependable relationship that we can use for analytical purposes?

The Secular-stagnation Hypothesis: Naïve Version

Actually, much of the debate among demand theorists has revolved around the other extreme of this durability issue. There has been a good deal of attention to the possibility that it might be *too* durable, or more precisely, that a particular consumption function involving a less-than-proportionate relationship of consumption to income might persist secularly. A historical consumption function with a positive and substantial Y intercept, similar to that which apparently prevailed prior to World War II and similar to the usually assumed shape of the short-run consumption function, if it were to be permanently fixed in the web of our economic institutions, of course, would have the most profound impact on the economy's growth prospects. For it would mean that, from here on, in order to grow steadily and to prosper, we should have to devote an always-rising share of our output to capital formation and government uses because of our unwillingness to consume more than an always-declining share of total output. The chances of maintaining prosperity under such circumstances would appear rather dismal. In a profit-seeking economy, where the main reason for increasing private investment is to serve expanding markets, it would be difficult to achieve a sufficient secular rise in nonconsumption spending relative to consumption spending—unless technological developments should require just the right "deepening" of capital relative to output, or unless, as a people, we were ready to accept a steadily rising proportion of total output in the form of government services.

The idea that we may have such a fixed and nonproportionate historical consumption function can be called the naive version of the so-called stagnation or mature-economy thesis. Keynes and Hansen dramatically popularized a different version of that thesis in the late 1930s. Impressed by the dogged persistence of the Great Depression, they suggested that advanced Western economies like Britain and the United States might be encountering an era of their history in which insufficient aggregate demand would be not merely a periodic "cyclical" problem but a characteristic, secular one. Events since 1940 have certainly seemed to belie the stagnation thesis, and it has been a principal sport of many economists and business commentators to lambaste it. Most of this criticism, however, has been misdirected in that it has assumed that Keynes and Hansen rested their conclusions on the premise of a secularly fixed short-run consumption function. Actually neither of them did, at least not predominantly. What they argued was that, for certain reasons, it may be increasingly difficult to maintain even a proportionate rise in investment spending as economies such as those of the United States and the United Kingdom get older and richer.

In later chapters we shall have occasion to consider whether there still is anything in this line of reasoning, so far as the United States is concerned. For our present purposes, the point simply is that neither Hansen nor Keynes accepted the idea of a historical consumption function that implied a secular rise in the saving rate. For one thing, there is statistical evidence against it. Simon Kuznets, going back with his national income estimates as best he could to the third quarter of the nineteenth century, found that from then up to the end of the 1930s (when the government's share of output began to rise significantly) the average propensity to consume national income was relatively constant in periods of high employment.[20]   Later studies by Raymond Goldsmith[21] have confirmed this finding.

For another thing, the idea does not make good sense. If the same historical consumption function that characterized the United States in the late 1930s had been in effect throughout the nineteenth century, when national income and product were far lower—even if the function were adjusted for population changes—consumption would have consistently exceeded income and output. This, of course, is nonsense; if such uninterrupted net capital consumption (rather than capital formation) had been our early history, the American economy would have burned out like a cinder long before the twentieth century ever rolled around.

Experience since World War II, especially when viewed with the benefit of the hindsight provided by the 1965 revision in the consumption and saving statistics, seems to provide the answer to the dilemma posed by the secular-stagnation theorists. It is clear that the shape of the historical consumption-function characteristic of the 1930s not only could not possibly have been characteristic of the pre-1930 decades, it has in fact not been characteristic of the post-World War II period.

The historical consumption function of the 1930s was definitely atypical. The shift in the consumption function that occurred during World War II would no doubt have come in due time in any event, but World War II accelerated the necessary changes so that by 1947 or 1948, a more logical historical relationship between consumption and income had been reestablished.

Since then, it seems clear that the short-run consumption function has gradually shifted upward, for the reasons discussed in the last several pages, somewhat as illustrated in Figure 8–2. Indeed, in a steadily growing economy

[20] Simon Kuznets, *Uses of National Income in Peace and War*, National Bureau of Economic Research, Inc., New York, 1942.

[21] Raymond Goldsmith, *A Study of Saving in the United States*, Princeton University Press, Princeton, N.J., 1955.

in which consumers increasingly expect and increasingly realize rising living standards, a relatively smooth secular rise in the consumption function would seem to be well-nigh inevitable—at least until that distant date when substantial numbers of consumers become so satiated that no further rises in living standards are desired.

One qualification, however, is in order. Such a steady secular rise in the consumption function is postulated on the assumption of a steadily growing economy. What happens, however, when expansion does *not* predominate —when employment and incomes turn down? In this event, the historical record suggests that consumption, rather than retracing its path down the historical function, may move down the short-run function, which has a lesser slope. The first writer to state this point clearly was James Duesenberry, who did so in a monograph published in 1949.[22] Consumer spending, Duesenberry concluded—and subsequent experiences during the 1949, 1954, 1958, and 1960 recessions seemed to bear him out—is strongly conditioned, not only by current incomes, but by the highest income levels that consumers have previously experienced. As we noted earlier, consumers respond somewhat slowly but, after a lag, quite certainly to a rise in income, but they resist adjusting to declines in income. This means that in all probability the secular rise of the consumption function is of a ratchet character. It is not reversible. This effect is illustrated in Figure 8–3. If, after income has risen to Y_4, the econ-

[22] J. S. Duesenberry, *Income, Saving and the Theory of Consumer Behavior*, Harvard University Press, Cambridge, Mass., 1949.

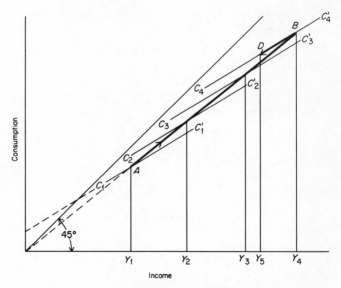

Figure **8–3.**   Consumption behavior with sustained income growth and during an interruption in growth.

omy should encounter temporary difficulties and income should slump to Y_5, consumption would not retrace the line BA. Instead, the short-run consumption function would come into its own, and consumer spending would move in the direction of D. Then, when recovery came, consumption would regain and renew its climb up the secular AB curve.

CONCLUSIONS

The concept of the historical consumption function, modified by the "Duesenberry effect," provides a useful tool for forecasting. As we shall see when we get to the chapters on forecasting, certain additional modifications are in order for operational purposes; the chief modification relates to the fact that consumer responses to changes in income are somewhat different for nondurable goods and services than for durables, notably automobiles. We shall conclude that, for forecasting purposes, it is useful to subtract automobile expenditures from other personal outlays, and relate the large remainder to DPI. Automobiles will be treated as a quasi-autonomous category of demand, influenced *in the short run* by disposable income only in a very general way. And we shall find that the problem of lags must be given more specific attention than the simple consumption-function thesis would require. But these are matters of detail that we can set aside until we reach that part of our study.

9

THE INDUCEMENT TO INVEST

While consumption is not the sole purpose of economic activity, it is such an obviously important purpose that in economic analysis we can usually take it for granted that people are universally motivated to consume. And although consumption and consumer buying are not identical, they are so closely related that the explanation of consumption determination can lean heavily upon those factors, notably income, which enable consumers to translate their inherent inducement to consume into effective demand. Investment, however, is a different story. Ordinarily, the acquisition of capital assets is not an end in itself. Consequently, any plausible treatment of the causes of investment spending must deal more centrally and pointedly with the motivations of decision makers than is necessary in the case of consumption theory.

This emphasis on motivation is most obviously true of the largest segment of United States gross private domestic investment: fixed-capital spending by business, or, as it is called in the national income accounts, business fixed investment (BFI). BFI is the remainder left when expenditures for private residential construction and for net changes in business inventories are

191

deducted from gross private domestic investment.[1] While new residential construction and inventory investment have characteristics common to all kinds of private capital formation, both are relatively specialized activities. The determinants of house buying are probably more analogous to those of other consumer-durable purchases than they are to those of fixed-capital formation by business. Inventory change is the one form of investment spending that can occur inadvertently and involuntarily so far as the investor is concerned, and it is spending oriented to a much shorter run than is most private investment. In Part Four we shall give explicit attention to the determinants of residential construction and inventory change. Meanwhile, the present discussion will refer predominantly to fixed-capital formation by business enterprise.

THE GENERAL THEORY OF INVESTMENT DETERMINATION

Most economic theory assumes that businessmen who invest seek profit. It is true that profit maximization is too simple a description of business motivation. Firms are interested in self-preservation, and in this concern they may substitute the more prudent, if less ambitious, objective of satisfactory profits for the goal of maximum profits. Firms also are interested in increasing their holdings of capital assets and in the aggrandizement of the social power that accompanies such holdings. Moreover, business decision making is influenced by the individual objectives of the salaried managers who inhabit the corporate bureaucracies of modern American industry. And certainly, many contemporary American firms have a public relations (or, depending upon your point of view, a public-interest) ingredient in their motivational patterns. Nevertheless, it serves reality reasonably well to assume that businessmen ordinarily invest either to attain future profits or to enhance the future position of the firm in some dimension the management regards as a substitute for profit in the simpler sense.

It cannot be emphasized too much that the demand for investment goods depends upon expectations of *future* developments. Insofar as investment is profit-oriented, it depends upon expectations of future returns. Present rates of return are logically significant only as indicators—symptoms—of what future returns may be.

THE MARGINAL EFFICIENCY OF CAPITAL

In the usual model of private investment determination, the first picture we get is of the entrepreneurs of the economy constantly appraising all

---

[1] Being a residual, the GNP version of business fixed investment includes a little nonbusiness buying—namely, capital goods purchases by private nonprofit institutions. Further, it includes farm fixed capital spending. This and other differences between the GNP business fixed investment series and the familiar plant and equipment series that is jointly compiled by the Department of Commerce and the Securities and Exchange Commission will be emphasized in Chap. 19.

existing opportunities for investment of which they are aware and which have any pertinence to their business interests. Either consciously or unconsciously, this canvass takes the following form: the investor evaluates each investment possibility within his scope of attention by translating it into a series of expected returns over successive periods of the future. Every such series is, of course, a highly subjective thing. Whenever an actual capital purchase is made so that the validity of a given series of expected returns can be explored over time, the expectation may turn out to have been a will-o'-the-wisp. Nevertheless, it is on a tissue of such expectations that investment decisions inevitably are based. And a key step in the investment decision process is the evaluation, by the investor, of this expected series of returns.

At this point, it may be well to digress momentarily to remind the reader of the arithmetical process by which such a series of expected returns over time is evaluated. A dollar due a year from today is worth less than a dollar today, even if we ignore the risk involved in waiting a year for the dollar, and any rational person presumably has in his mind some rate of discount at which he calculates the value to him of this deferred dollar. If we express this percentage rate of discount as r, the value of the dollar due a year in the future would be $\$1/(1 + r)$. For example, if the rate of discount were 5 percent, the value of the dollar due a year in the future would be $\$1/1.05$, which equals $\$0.95238$. A dollar due two years in the future would be worth even less. It would have a present value of $\$1/(1.05 \times 1.05)$ or $\$1/1.05^2$, which equals $\$0.90703$. And obviously, the value of $\$2$, the first due one year in the future and the second due two years in the future, would be $\$1/1.05 + \$1/1.05^2$, which equals $\$1.85971$. We can generalize this process and say that the present value V of an expected series of annual returns R_1, R_2, R_3, . . . , R_n, for n years, can be computed from the equation

$$V = \frac{R_1}{1 + r} + \frac{R_2}{(1 + r)^2} + \frac{R_3}{(1 + r)^3} + \cdots + \frac{R_n}{(1 + r)^n}$$

Now let us see how this equation may be used in the investment decision process. Let R_1, R_2, R_3, . . . , R_n be the series of annual returns attaching to an investment opportunity. These yields represent the excess of the expected gross returns, including the necessary amounts to cover depreciation costs, over the current expenses of operating the asset in question. Each series of hypothetical yields has a limited time dimension. Either because the asset itself is expected to wear out, become technologically obsolete, or otherwise reach the end of its useful life in a limited time, or because the potential investor who contemplates it has a greater preference for earlier than for later returns, or for a combination of these reasons, the series of relevant expected yields into which each investment prospect is translated is of limited duration.

The investor already knows, or can estimate, the cost of the asset; what he is interested in is the rate of return to him of the series of Rs. In other words, the r in our equation becomes the unknown. If we substitute in the equation the symbol B, meaning the present cost (or supply price) of the asset, for V, the equation becomes

$$B = \frac{R_1}{1 + r} + \frac{R_2}{(1 + r)^2} + \frac{R_3}{(1 + r)^3} + \cdots + \frac{R_n}{(1 + r)^n}$$

Given the Rs and B, the rate of return r can be calculated.

One other consideration must be taken into account before we use this equation to generalize about the investment determination process. This has to do with an allowance for risk and uncertainty. Most investors, aware of the infirmities of human judgment, want to hedge against risk and uncertainty. To be on the safe side, they want something more than a 50-50 probability of success. We could inject this allowance for risk and uncertainty into our calculation in several ways. For example, we could subtract from the calculated r a percentage allowance for risk and uncertainty. Or, what amounts to the same thing, we could add it to the money interest rate, the cost of capital. For our purposes, it is more convenient to subtract it from the series of expected dollar returns, the Rs in our equation. For example, if the prospective investor realistically estimates the dollar returns at \$50,000 a year for ten years, he might reduce this to \$40,000 in his calculation of the expected rate of return, just to allow for risk and uncertainty. Another practice used by many business firms is to adopt arbitrary "payout" periods in their evaluation of investment projects. For example, an asset may normally be expected to have a useful life (not only physically but also by not becoming obsolete) of, say, ten years. Yet the business firm as a matter of policy may adopt a rule that it will be interested in the project only if it has a payout period of five years. In effect, what they are saying is that R_1, R_2, R_3, R_4, and R_5 are all the returns they will take into account in calculating r. The rationale for requiring a five-year payout period might be that, during the first five years, the possibility of a lesser return than estimated, or an actual loss, due to risk and uncertainty is relatively small, and to the extent that it exists, it is offset by the possibility of returns in years beyond the fifth year.

For our purposes, we will assume that any allowance for risk and uncertainty takes the form of a deduction from the Rs, the expected annual dollar returns. Out of what remains, the investor must expect to recover the supply price of the asset as well as to earn whatever net return he foresees. The calculated rate of return is called the *marginal* efficiency of capital because it concerns the expected return to a possible increment in the investor's existing capital, not the average return to his total capital including that which he already has. The marginal efficiency of capital will presumably vary widely among various investment projects.

Why, it might be asked, should there exist, in an economy that is generally highly competitive, investment opportunities varying significantly in their expected profitability. Of the many reasons that could be cited, three are obvious. The first pertains to the time dimension of the economic process.

Growing population and rising real incomes generate, over time, expanding markets and therefore new investment opportunities. The expansion in markets, however, can vary substantially from one to another. Consequently, in one line of business, economic expansion may open up many highly profitable investment opportunities, whereas in another line of business, profit prospects change little or perhaps decline. Second, as a result of changing technology and changing relative prices (e.g., prices of capital goods and wage rates), investors will constantly be revising their calculations of the optimum combination of capital and labor. Such recalculations affect the estimates of expected profitability. For example, a technological improvement in a production process, or a change in wage rates, may lead an investor to raise his estimate of the profitability of substituting machinery (investment) for labor. Third, it must be recognized that business investors are imperfect forecasters. They do make mistakes. Experience gained from the passage of time may suggest that a given potential investment, once considered of low profitability and therefore not made, has in fact a higher marginal efficiency of capital than was previously reckoned.

To continue with the outline of investment determination, one must next imagine that all the investment projects each potential investor has appraised are ranked according to their marginal efficiencies. Each such ranking can then be cast into an individual investor's demand schedule for investable funds—one that relates marginal efficiencies (expressed in percentage rates) to the volume of investment that would be undertaken in a given time period. Similarly, the sum of these individual investment appraisals by all the individual entrepreneurs in the economy can be thought of as arranging themselves into an economy-wide investment demand schedule.

The investment demand schedule for the economy as a whole might look something like the downward sloping line in Figure 9–1. The negative slope of the curve indicates that the volume of investment opportunities that will be considered highly profitable, i.e., have a high marginal efficiency of capital, is typically smaller than the volume of less profitable ones.[2] Thus, at point 1 on the II' line a volume of investment spending equal only to OI_1 would be expected to yield a marginal return of r_1. A much larger volume (OI_2), however, would be considered to have a marginal efficiency of capital equal to r_2. The fact that the line crosses the X axis at point 3 says that, at a given point in time, there is a limited volume of new investment (OI_3) that is considered to be profitable at all, i.e., that there is some volume of investment at which the marginal efficiency of capital falls to zero.

There are several reasons why we can expect the investment demand

[2] The phrase "volume of investment" refers to investment during a given time period or to investment per unit of time. The marginal efficiency calculation, however, is made as of a point in time—the day on which investors make their appraisal of investment opportunities. We are therefore concerned with static analysis, a schedule as of a point in time.

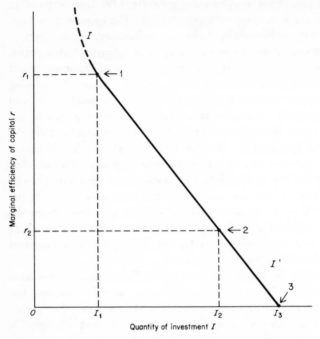

Figure 9–1. The investment demand schedule at a given level of GNP.

curve to slope downward to the right; we point out a few here. First, an increasing stock of capital of a given type and quality is subject to diminishing returns as increments are added to it. It is a traditional and reasonable tenet of economics that the proportions in which productive factors are combined affect their efficiency. More specifically, if we can assume a given collection of productive techniques, additions of one factor without proportionate increments in other factors will yield diminishing *increments* in output. Therefore, at any given time, with a given population, technology, etc., we would expect successive increments of capital to yield diminishing rates of return.

Second, at any given time, we would expect the increase in demand for capital assets in general, resulting from successive increments in investment, to raise the supply price of a particular capital asset, the B in our equation. Similarly, successive increments of investment at any given time might well raise costs of operation of the capital asset (e.g., wage rates) and thus reduce the Rs in the equation. Both of these effects would tend to lower the rate of return r.

Third, the demand schedule for the *output* of the capital asset is presumably negatively sloped; that is, as more units of a given end product are produced, the price at which they can be sold can be expected to decrease. If this happens, the series of revenues, the Rs, is diminished, thus reducing the rate of return r.

Let it be noted that what we are concerned with at this point is the slope of the investment demand *schedule* at a given point in time. We are not concerned with shifts in the schedule over time—a matter to which we shall return shortly. But at a given point in time, it seems reasonable to conclude that the investment demand schedule is clearly negatively sloped.

The precise *shape* of the curve is a matter of speculation. Following convention, we have drawn it as a straight line except for the upward tilt as the curve approaches the vertical axis, which is intended to suggest that, in the economy as a whole, there is no precise upper limit to the marginal efficiency of capital. There may be a very few potential projects of enormous estimated profitability. It can also be argued that the curve becomes nearly vertical (i.e., the demand schedule becomes highly inelastic) at very low rates of return.[3] Actually, for most analytical purposes, the shape of the curve at the extremes is not relevant. We are usually interested in the central portion of the curve, which covers the range of investment opportunities that, given the cost of capital most likely to prevail at any given time, are likely to be marginal. We do not violate the facts of life significantly, therefore, if we focus on the central portion of the curve and make life a bit simpler for ourselves by assuming that it is a straight line.

The foregoing reference to the cost of capital reminds us that every new investment expenditure must be financed, and this involves a cost that has not been mentioned so far—that of using money. A price, also usually expressed in percentage terms, must be paid to those who can supply the needed funds by parting with their liquidity, i.e., for accepting less negotiable assets (such as the IOUs of investors) for more negotiable assets (such as bank deposits). The cost of capital is a cost which any thoroughly rational investor must take into account, even if the funds he uses for an investment expenditure are his own, because by tying up his funds in his own investment project, he loses the interest he could earn by lending them to someone else.

It is customary to call this cost of using money "the money rate of interest." To speak of a single money rate of interest, when we know that in fact many interest rates are being charged at any given time, sounds like another piece of unrealistic abstraction, and to a degree it is. Actual market rates of interest include, not only a reward for parting with liquidity, but also an allowance for risk and uncertainty that the *lender* incurs when he entrusts the administration of his assets to someone else, and an allowance for the administrative costs of making and servicing the loan.[4] We are concerned

---

[3] See Norman F. Keiser, *Macroeconomics, Fiscal Policy, and Economic Growth,* John Wiley & Sons, Inc., New York, 1964, pp. 101–103.

[4] They may also include an element of monopoly profit if the lender is in a non-competitive position.

here, however, with the effects of changes in the supply of and demand for liquidity on the investment-determination process and therefore abstract from these nonliquidity-related components of market rates of interest. It is also true that different rates of compensation may be demanded for different durations of liquidity loss; for example, different rates per annum may be charged for equally risky short- and long-term loans. However, it does not distort reality badly to imagine that, with an organized money market, a single liquidity premium will characterize a given economy at a given time. In the United States, for instance, the interest rate on medium-term government bonds (which are as riskless as any credit instrument with a fixed face value can be) approximates the "pure" rate of interest pretty closely.

The money interest rate is the connecting rod that links the supply of money and financial institutions into the income-determination process. It symbolizes the whole problem of financing investment. We shall consider these matters in the next chapter. For the moment, it is sufficient to know that the going money interest rate serves as a limit upon the volume of investment spending. Investors proceed along the collective marginal-efficiency-of-capital schedule to the point that is just short of that project whose expected return over cost, allowing for risk and uncertainty, just fails to cover the cost of borrowing money. Or, to use our symbols, investors wish to invest in projects with progressively lower marginal efficiencies of capital to the point where $r = i$. Thus, in Figure 9–2, where the II' line represents the marginal efficiency of capital schedule, the volume of investment undertaken will tend to be I_1 if the cost of capital is i_1. If the cost of capital at the same point in time should be i_2, the volume of investment undertaken will tend to be I_2. And at a rate of interest of i_3, the volume of investment would be only I_3.

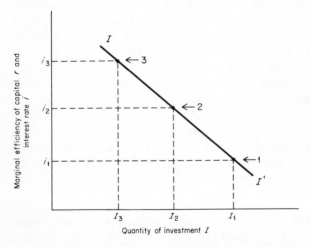

Figure 9–2. Determination of the volume of investment at a given time.

THE SIGNIFICANCE OF THE MARGINAL-EFFICIENCY-OF-CAPITAL CONCEPT

The theory of investment determination just summarized has helped to clarify a branch of economic theory that had long been muddled in the minds of many economists. Specifically, it drew a clear distinction between the monetary and the other determinants of capital formation. This distinction has had a particularly helpful policy effect in many Western countries. It has helped to clarify the relationship between the money rate of interest and investment and therefore between these key variables and GNP. At the same time, it has put the purely monetary determinants of investment more nearly in their places so far as public policy is concerned. Given the theoretical formulation we have just described, it is clear not only that the monetary and nonmonetary influences are distinguishable but also that the latter typically are far more volatile and variable than the former. On the one hand, the money interest rate is the product of an elaborate institutional mechanism, and it usually varies, at most, within a relatively narrow range. On the other hand, the marginal efficiency of capital, a creature of expectations, is subject to rapid and extreme shifts. In a severe depression most of a nation's marginal-efficiency-of-capital schedule may well drop below a zero rate of expected returns. Conversely, a sharp fillip to business expectations, such as might be provided by a major technological breakthrough or a sudden change in international relations, may lift most of the marginal-efficiency-of-capital schedule well out of reach of the highest rate of interest that can reasonably be imagined.

Thus the model just inspected implicitly challenges the feasibility of interest rate cutting as a means of stimulating investment when the latter is in the doldrums, or of restraining investment by interest rate manipulation when profit expectations are soaring. It suggests that the most active wellsprings of investment determination lie in the complex of factors determining the marginal efficiency of capital. It suggests that the effectiveness of monetary policy as a stablizing device is greatest when the stabilization issue is fairly close—when demand is deviating only moderately from its average or typical level and when no violent changes in business expectations are occurring.

But having said this much in favor of the marginal-efficiency-of-capital concept and the rest of the theoretical apparatus that centers around it, it is hard to sustain the applause. For the question, What determines the *actual* marginal efficiency of capital today, and next month, and next year? immediately raises a host of other questions about why the marginal-efficiency-of-capital schedule shifts, sometimes violently, from time to time. And to these questions, neither Keynes, who originated and gave currency to the marginal-efficiency-of-capital concept, nor the theoretical literature that has followed him supplies a systematic or decisive answer. The reason for this deficiency is not that the problem has not received the attention of economists, nor because it is difficult to identify determinants of the marginal efficiency of capital. Rather, it is because there are so many of them that one can never be sure that one has exhausted the list or has weighted the items properly.

DETERMINANTS OF SHIFTS IN THE MARGINAL-EFFICIENCY-OF-CAPITAL SCHEDULE

To say that entrepreneurs' desire to invest depends upon their expectations of profit is not in itself very illuminating, nor does it convey the full scope of the factors that influence investment decisions. A reasonably comprehensive list of such influences would have to include at least the following: (1) technological and other innovations, (2) factors involving the market positions of particular firms, (3) changes in price expectations, (4) tax laws, and (5) a collection of forces and circumstances, including the four influences just enumerated, that combine to influence expectations concerning the relationship of future demand to capacity. There is some overlap among these headings, but they are separable enough to constitute a framework for the ensuing discussion.

THE STIMULUS OF INNOVATIONS

In an advanced economy such as that of the United States probably no determinant of business' desire to invest is more important than the pace of current technological innovation. Innovations in the form of new products, improvements and modifications in existing products, new materials for old products, new machines, new productive processes, new forms of energy, new or modified transport and communications media, distributive innovations like the shopping center—all these induce investment spending.

It is true that an advanced economy whose technology had become static but whose population continued to grow and/or move around geographically would continue to have an incentive to expand its capital stock. And even if the population of such an economy became static in size and stationary in domicile, there would be a continuing need for a substantial amount of replacement investment. But in an economy where technology *is* forever shifting, experimenting, reaching out—in short, innovating—innovations interact with and profoundly leaven these other inducements to invest.

It should be noted particularly that the pace and character of innovations are major determinants of the rate of replacement as well as of expansion investment; for it is technological change rather than literal wear or tear and aging that terminates the economic life of most producers' durable equipment and of much industrial and commercial construction in the United States. By shortening the life of capital, innovations add to the rate of replacement investment.

Technological change and innovation can also be capital-saving in the sense that they lower the requirement of additional capital per unit of additional output. Historically, in the United States, innovations seem to have had this effect. To say, however, that the capital requirement per unit of output has been lowered is not to say that the demand for capital has necessarily been dampened. For this very capital-saving effect, by buoying the marginal productivity of capital, can buoy expectations of return to investment. In more specific terms, the killing-off effect that innovations exert on existing capital usually may more than outweigh the capital-saving effect, so far as the total current investment demand is concerned. It is probably safe to conclude that, in the United States in the postwar years through 1957, the killing-off effect of innovation did in fact outweigh the capital-saving effect. It is less clear, however, that the same conclusion can be drawn from the period since then. Investment demand in the 1957–1963 period was in fact sluggish, and Bert G. Hickman of The Brookings Institution argues that this sluggishness could be attributed in important part to a pronounced decline in the amount of capital needed for a given output, i.e., to the capital-saving effect of technological change, and that the decline would have occurred even if full employment had prevailed. His projections to 1970 suggest that the decline in the amount of capital needed for a given output, again assuming full employment, can probably be expected to continue.[6] He is careful to qualify his conclusions to allow for the inevitable margin of error in such projections, and the sharp rise in capital spending in 1964–1966 may give rise to some second thoughts, but at a minimum his analysis suggests that the issue is not closed.

Economics already has produced some major philosophers of technological change; the greatest so far is the distinguished Austrian-American scholar, the late Joseph Schumpeter. Schumpeter built his theory of capitalist development around the pulse and surge of the innovation process and around the willingness of venturesome entrepreneurs to break risky new technological trails. According to Schumpeter and others, major business fluctuations are traceable primarily to the fact that, historically, not only has the rate at which investors have exploited new innovations been an irregular, lumpy thing, but the innovational process itself, while never entirely subsiding, has moved in fits and surges.

Most innovation-induced investment appears historically to have been bunched around the emergence and expansion of a few major industries. In the United States in the nineteenth century there was, above all, the building of the railroads during the middle quarters of the century. At about the turn of the century, the construction of street railway systems and the first major expansion of the electric power industry provided a similar, although less pronounced, capital surge. Then the 1920s brought the peaking of expansion

[5] Bert G. Hickman, *Investment Demand and U.S. Economic Growth*, The Brookings Institution, Washington, D.C., 1965.

in the automobile industry. In each case, growth in the primary-expansion industry brought secondary or complementary expansion in a number of related areas—in equipment, materials, and parts suppliers, and in producers of complementary products, e.g., oil in the case of automobiles. Typically, these clusters of technological change coupled with increasing urbanization also have induced major public investments—e.g., again in the automobile case, heavy investments in street and highway systems.

If one wishes to speculate in the Schumpeterian framework about recent and current capital formation in the United States, one may be somewhat puzzled by the period since World War II. Except possibly for television, the period has not witnessed the expansion of any *major new* industry of anything like the importance of the railroads in the nineteenth century, automobiles in the 1920s, or even street railways and electric power in the first decade of this century. A disciple of Schumpeter might nevertheless satisfy himself that the 1945–1957 period could be explained as an exceptional era, involving a prolonged whittling down of a backlog of miscellaneous postponed investment opportunities built up during the preceding fifteen years, first during the Great Depression of the 1930s, and then during World War II. And he might well sense, in the 1960s, the stirrings of a great new innovational surge of the classic pattern, centering around accelerated adoption of more highly automatic self-controlling production equipment, nuclear-energy generation and the expansion of atomic chemistry, the revolution in military technology, desalination of sea water, space travel, and eventually, perhaps, techniques for control of the world's weather.

However, the fact is that the economic science of technology has mostly yet to be developed. We cannot be sure that, because the innovational process has proceeded in fits and starts in the past, it will do so in the future. The innovational process has become far more organized, more ubiquitous, more institutionalized, and far better financed during the past generation; there has been a rapid accumulation of major continuing research activities in business and of heavy research spending by the Federal government.

At the very least, it is likely that the institutionalization of research will cause innovations to accrue at a more orderly pace. Some observers, moreover, are confident that the average rate of innovation will accelerate. But this is not a conclusion that should be adopted casually, as we shall suggest at later points—especially in Chapter 25, which considers the United States economy's long-term growth prospects. All that we really need to say now, is that, in the United States, innovations have been and probably will continue to be the most pervasive and dynamic of all stimulants to investment.

THE MARKET POSITIONS OF FIRMS

One of the recurrent themes of *Fortune* magazine articles is the story of a corporation whose share of the market and whose profits are slipping or failing to keep pace with those of competitors, which thereupon launches a major investment program to modernize and expand its facilities for the manufacture of an improved product, in the hope of arresting and reversing the decline.[6] Chrysler Corporation's $300 million, bank-loan-financed investment program in 1954 in the face of collapsing markets for Chrysler automobiles is perhaps the classic example of such sink-or-swim tactics. Such heroic actions reflect an interest in future profit; the investments they involve can be interpreted as efforts to forestall adverse changes in future demand, and many of them involve the adoption of innovations. But more simply and directly, they reflect the insistent effort of firms in certain market situations to make whatever investments are necessary to protect their shares of the market.

Market share is an obvious consideration in the decision making of investors only in markets where most of the business is done by a relatively few sellers. But in such cases it clearly is important. A firm that settles for a declining share of such a market usually finds it hard to make money; internal financing is harder to come by; usually it is considerably harder to recruit outside capital; and frequently it is much harder to recruit desirable managerial personnel. At any rate, a firm that accepts such a fate loses caste in terms of our operative business values; elaborate and uneasy explanations to boards of directors become necessary; and frequently the sense that a product is slipping seems to communicate itself very rapidly to the clientele. A slippage in the market share may quickly get out of hand and snowball; always there is the fear that a mild slippage symptomizes causes that will persist. All in all, given the fact that markets dominated by a few sellers account for a very considerable portion of the American economy, it is easy to see why the impulse to protect or recoup market shares deserves, in its own right, to be listed as one of the more dynamic stimulants of investment in the United States.[7]

THE IMPACT OF PRICE EXPECTATIONS

Both current and expected price changes clearly have pervasive effects upon investment decisions. While such price influences may be implicit in

---

[6] See, for example, "Big Steel Wants a Bigger Share," in the January, 1965, issue.

[7] This point, with its implication that oligopolistic markets make for progressive investment behavior, will not go down well with those more extreme antitrust enthusiasts who would like to see the government enforce policies that would restore markets to the point of satisfying the conditions of "workable," if not pure, competition. They would argue that oligopoly, by inhibiting the entry of new firms and by colluding to retard the pace of capital-destroying innovations, suppresses more investment than it stimulates. This point, it appears to us, is moot—although the comparative investment and growth records of more as against less concentrated manufacturing industries during this century provide little support for the pure competition school. The present point simply is that, given the character of existing markets, the effort to protect market shares *is* a stimulant to investment, and it constitutes a stimulant that would be absent in the case of thoroughgoing monopoly.

the other influences already discussed, some explicit reference to them is appropriate.

The prices that concern us here are all commodity, service, and factor prices excepting the money rate of interest, the latter being reserved for special treatment. For present purposes, it will suffice to classify this enormously varied range of prices in two ways.

First, the prices that relate to an investment decision may be classified chronologically as to whether they are (1) current prices or (2) expected future prices. Second, prices, as they relate to investment decisions, may be classified in the following functional sense: Are we talking about (1) the cost-price of the capital asset that an entrepreneur is deciding whether or not to buy, or about (2) the price of another factor of production that would account for some of the expenses of operating the asset in question and/or that might serve as a substitute for it, or about (3) the price of the product that the asset would help to produce?

As we noted a few pages back, current prices of the new assets, of other factors, and of the product of the asset, all play a role in determining the investment demand schedule. More precisely, they serve as indicators of prices that will prevail when the investment is undertaken and in operation. This does not necessarily mean, of course, that investors assume that prices will be unchanged if they proceed with the project. A currently high or rising price may create expectations of still higher prices in the future. On the other hand, a currently high price may also be interpreted as abnormal, the result of transitory forces, and hence may prompt expectations of lower prices in the future. And, again as we noted earlier, the fact of the investment itself should have some effect on all these prices. Current prices are therefore relevant to the investment decision process only to the extent that they play a role in determining the price expectations used in constructing the marginal-efficiency-of-capital schedule.

The important point for our present purposes, however, is that these price expectations can *change*, sometimes drastically, and when they do they tend to shift the entire investment demand schedule. For example, if investors should reestimate their position and collectively come to the conclusion that costs of relevant capital assets are likely to rise, the changed expectation would tend to stimulate current purchases of the capital assets as investors try to beat the anticipated price rise. And in the event of a change in expectations on the downward side, the opposite would hold. Similarly, expectations of prices of other factors of production, such as wages, can change; when they do, they shift the investment demand schedule. The fact that these shifts can occur means that, to forecast investment spending, the forecaster must not only estimate *current* expectations (which expectations, it should be remembered, are determined in part by current prices), but he must also estimate how these expectations are likely to change over time and thus shift the schedule. The latter estimation is especially precarious business.

The Influence of General Price Changes

For the most part, the investment effects of general price movements can be indicated by a simple aggregation of the particular price relationships noted. However, changes in expectations of prices in general have one broad impact upon investment that deserves explicit emphasis. Since to anticipate a general inflation of prices is also to anticipate a depreciation in the value of money, the expectation of a rising price level heightens the value of all real assets (including newly produced real assets) relative to money and other assets the value of which is fixed in terms of money. The marginal-efficiency-of-capital schedule is shifted upward. For example, the change in price expectations between 1939 and 1945 clearly had the effect of shifting the investment demand schedule positively and radically.

However, this is not necessarily to say that an expectation of general price inflation will invariably stimulate investment. For the same expectation that raises the marginal efficiency of capital may prompt lenders to demand a higher premium for parting with their liquidity; by lending they lose the option of getting out of cash into real assets themselves, while accepting assets with a value fixed in terms of money. It is perhaps no coincidence that the upsurge in investment spending after World War II subsided markedly in the late 1950s, coincident with a rise in interest rates—a rise partly engineered by the Federal Reserve but partly a reflection of expectations of chronic inflation.

THE IMPACT OF TAXES

The fourth item on our list of nonfinancial investment determinants is changes in taxes.[8] Here, as before, we are concerned with the impact, not upon entrepreneurs' ability to finance investment, but only upon their desire to invest. It is the so-called incentive effect of taxation that is pertinent.

What the net impact of taxation is in this respect is far from clear. Businessmen regard all taxes—not just those which, like excise taxes, are levied upon units of sales—as costs that must be deducted from gross revenues before estimating returns on investment. The most common assumption is that a rise in tax rates dampens investment incentives by reducing expected returns over cost. This effect is neutralized, however, to the extent that producers expect to be able to shift the higher taxes to their buyers in the form of higher selling prices. The extent to which they can in fact do this is a complicated, highly debatable issue. It depends partly on general demand conditions, partly upon the price elasticities of specific products. The experience of the 1963 investment credit offered to corporations via a revision in

---

[8] The simplifying assumption of this sentence is that tax laws are effectively enforced. While this is a much more realistic assumption for the United States than for most other countries, it is by no means completely realistic here.

the tax laws and of the 1964 cut in corporate income tax rates would suggest that *changes* in taxes do have a direct effect on the inducement to invest.

Whatever may be the merits of this issue, it can be safely concluded that changes in tax laws that discriminate between alternative investment opportunities have a significant impact upon the *pattern* of total investment. Laws that favor particular industries—here the notable examples are the generous depletion allowances and dry-well write-offs accorded the oil and natural gas industries—do encourage investment in those industries. Second, tax laws can effectively discriminate against riskier investment opportunities. Such is the result when, with a progressive system of taxation, the high earnings that riskier investments make in their off-and-on good years cannot be spread forward or backward to proximate bad years in which losses were incurred. Third, experience with the rapid-amortization provisions which have been introduced into the Federal tax code since the Korean War indicates that changes in tax laws that discriminate between differently timed investments can affect at least the chronological pattern of capital formation (as well as the interindustry pattern, where such concessions are selective in that respect).

Under the rapid-amortization arrangements, firms are privileged to depreciate newly acquired assets at a faster rate for tax purposes than is customarily allowed. This means lower taxable profits until the speeded-up amortization period has run its course. The principal effect of such provisions upon investment is probably financial: they allow firms to replenish their liquidity out of current revenue faster than otherwise would be permissible and, thereby, to accelerate the retiring of indebtedness or the self-financing of new investment. But the extent to which firms have taken advantage of the rapid-amortization provisions suggests that their inducement to invest also has been stimulated—perhaps by the expectation that either tax rates will be lower or capital goods prices higher by the time the period of accelerated depreciation has expired.

DEMAND AND CAPACITY

American business managers have an almost instinctive impulse to adjust their firms' productive capacities to meet demand. Their efforts in this regard, of course, can be interpreted as simply a mode of profit seeking —on the principle that to profit one must first sell. Often, however, the decision to invest to meet an anticipated change in demand has no indirection about it; it is well-nigh automatic, and management does not have to traverse any explicit or conscious profit-maximization calculus to reach it. Rather, the impulse to alter capacity to meet demand is prompted by such simple and direct pressures as the wish to retain customer loyalty and the desire to maintain one's share of an oligopolistic market.

As noted already, the demand that is logically relevant to current investment decisions lies in the future. This means that investors rest their judgments on whatever clues to future demand they identify and take seriously. One set of such clues is provided by current levels of, and changes in, demand.

The Impact of Current Demand: The Acceleration Principle

The discussion of one effect that current sales experience exerts on current investment—namely, the impact of sales upon the ability of firms to finance investment—belongs in the next chapter. Another effect was noted earlier and requires no further explanation: current sales experience strongly conditions the forecasts of future markets that all systematic investment programs reflect. No matter how sophisticated and scientific business forecasting may become, this always will be true to some extent. Current sales are therefore one of the determinants of the investment demand schedule at any point in time.

It is the manner in which current demand can shift the investment demand schedule, however, that has particularly captured the interest of business cycle theorists. This is the process that, in the literature, goes under the name of "the acceleration effect" or "the acceleration principle." The term implies that responses of investment to changes in the demand for finished goods accelerate the final-demand changes associated with fluctuations in finished goods sales. The acceleration principle describes changes in current finished goods sales as directly inducing—in fact, as virtually forcing—changes in the derived demand for capital goods.

Some writers have become so preoccupied with the kind of capital-output problem to which the acceleration principle refers that they seem to suggest that *any* change in current finished goods sales *necessarily* forces a change in current fixed-investment spending. This is not so. The problem that the acceleration principle posits is actually only a special case among several that can arise within the general framework of capital-output relationships. For an increase in demand directly and more or less mechanically to induce an increase in its fixed-capital spendings, three conditions must hold:

First, at the time the demand for its products rises, the industry or firm in question must not have sufficient excess capacity to handle the advance in sales.

Second, the advance in sales cannot have been sufficiently well anticipated so that, as it occurs, the new capacity needed to meet it already is coming on the line as the result of past investment decisions. (If firms were capable of perfect forecasting, this condition never would be met.)

Third, the advance in product demand cannot be regarded as a flash in the pan; it must be expected to persist at least somewhat longer than it will take to acquire additional effective capacity.

Under these circumstances, and only under these circumstances, a current rise in finished goods demand can be counted on to induce a current rise in the demand for capital goods. Most of the literature on the acceleration effect has been concerned to identify the general characteristics that can be attributed to such an investment response. Table 9–1, representing the effects of the rise in a hypothetical industry's sales from one stable level to another, sheds some light on this question. Since the increment per period and therefore the rate of change in sales is zero at the beginning and end of the illustration, it is reasonable to assume that during the upswing the *rate* of increase in sales first gradually rises from zero, then gradually falls back to zero. Since it is the sales increment per period, not the level of total sales, that under the acceleration-principle assumptions induces investment in additional capacity, we can already deduce one feature of the investment response: during a rise in sales from one relatively stable level to another, expansion investment will first rise, then fall.[9]

In our illustration the amount of induced expansion investment depends, in addition to the sales increment per period, upon the incremental capital-capacity ratio that obtains in the hypothetical industry. When we are dealing with the total economy we usually expect a ratio of capital to output (or capital coefficient) of more than 1—estimated coefficients of 2 to 3 are common. But if we therefore assumed that our hypothetical industry's investment-output ratio exactly reflected a national average of, say, 2, it would not follow that the industry's investment-incremental *sales* ratio would be 2. Rather it would be less than 2 because only part of the industry's sales—the part representing its value added—constitutes its own output. Table 9–1 assumes an investment–incremental-value-added ratio (as well as a total-capital–total-value-added ratio) of 2. And it assumes that value added uniformly represents two-thirds of sales. Thus the ratio between incremental capital, i.e., net or expansion investment, and incremental sales is $2 \times \frac{2}{3}$, or 1.33.

Given these assumptions, it can be seen in the illustration that when sales (column A) and value added (column C) begin, in period 3, to rise above their previously stable levels, expansion investment (column F) rises from zero. Expansion investment peaks in period 5 when the rates of increase in sales (column B) and in value added (column D) peak, and falls back to zero in period 8 when they too subside to zero. Thus the change in expansion

---

[9] One of the simplifying assumptions the illustration reflects is that, despite the snugness of capacity, the industry succeeds in translating the expansion in demand into actual increases in sales in the same periods in which demand expands. Aside from the possibility of product price increases (which would make the numerical relationships between sales and investment indeterminate), such success could be explained as the result either of (1) the newly purchased capacity's coming into operation early enough in the same period in which its purchase was induced to satisfy the increment in demand that induced it (a rather unrealistic hypothesis unless the periods are construed as quite long) or (2) supernormal-capacity operations involving overtime and the like.

Table 9-1. The Acceleration Principle: A Hypothetical Illustration of the Response of Investment to a Change in Sales (In millions of dollars)

Period	Sales		Value added		Capital stock at start of period (E)	Expansion investment (increment in capital)		Replacement investment (H)	Total investment	
	Level (A)	Increment (B)	Level (C)	Increment (D)		Level (F)	Increment (G)		Level (I)	Increment (J)
1	300		200		400	0		20	20	
2	300	0	200	0	400	0	0	20	20	0
3	309	9	206	6	400	12	12	20	32	12
4	327	18	218	12	412	24	12	20.6	44.6	12.6
5	354	27	236	18	436	36	12	21.8	57.8	13.2
6	372	18	248	12	472	24	−12	23.6	47.6	−10.2
7	381	9	254	6	496	12	−12	24.8	36.8	−10.8
8	381	0	254	0	508	0	−12	25.4	25.4	−11.4
9	381	0	254	0	508	0	0	25.4	25.4	0

investment is positive during the first half of the upswing in sales and output, negative during the second half of the rise as the rate of increase in production and sales is slowing down.

It will be noted that in the illustration the absolute fluctuation in net investment (column F) exceeds the absolute fluctuations in sales and value-added increments (columns B and D). Appeal to such (not unrealistic) illustrations has led to the common textbook assertion that swings in finished goods sales necessarily lead to larger swings in capital goods production. Whether this is true in an absolute sense, even under the special accelerator-actuating conditions specified above, depends on the particular combination of investment-to-value-added and value-added-to-sales ratios involved.[10] However, we can say that the *relative* change in expansion investment under accelerator conditions is almost sure to be considerably greater than the relative change in finished goods sales.

It is this principle, basically, which underlies the familiar belief that the business of such capital goods suppliers as the machine tool and construction industries is almost bound to be more volatile and to experience wider relative fluctuations than that of consumer goods industries. It is true, of course, that the more durable any commodity is, the less closely current consumption of it is tied to current purchases of it, and the more susceptible to fluctuations, other things being equal, purchases of the commodity are. However, before the accelerator story is accepted as proof of the inevitable relative volatility of capital goods buying, these points should be considered.

First, within the framework of the accelerator model, the volatility of total investment relative to sales may be moderated (although not eliminated) when we add replacement investment to the picture. This addition has been made in Table 9–1, on the assumption that the capital stock in the industry has an average life of twenty years and that in each period (assumed to be one year) one-twentieth of the stock owned at the beginning of the period is replaced.[11]

Second, and more important, an underlying assumption of the whole accelerator model must be remembered. Events occur in this way *only* if investors, having failed to foresee changes in demand and to prepare capacity to meet them, are in the position of belatedly responding to the unexpected. Such a belated response would be a less-than-realistic description of the nature of modern American investment planning, particularly in view of the systematic capital budgeting now being increasingly practiced in many industries.

The accelerator story, taken alone, conveys a much too hectic and dis-

---

[10] See W. J. Baumol, "Acceleration without Magnification," *American Economic Review*, vol. 46, no. 3, pp. 409–412, June, 1956.

[11] This assumption, of course, is an unrealistic one because it takes no account of the average age of the capital stock, which, in a period of heavy expansion, tends to fall. Conceivably, age-dictated variations in replacement could partially offset fluctuations in expansion investment.

organized picture of investment decision making. On the other hand, in the United States, we have by no means achieved a state of imperturbable investor omniscience. Thus the acceleration principle provides a helpful explanation of some of the variability that can be observed in our current investment experience—particularly that residue of variability which other determinants of investment may fail to explain. Whenever conditions like those posited in Table 9–1 apply to any considerable portion of the economy, the accelerator concept clearly signals the possibility of unstabilizing swings in investment.[12]

Specifically Anticipated Shifts in Demand

Investment decision making is not simply a scramble to react to the unexpected; many investment expenditures are based upon expectations of changes in demand that have not happened yet. Entrepreneurs usually are alert to whatever specific indications of change may come to hand. For instance, successive international crises in recent years have typically triggered sharp jumps in investment spending, well before the government could get around to placing the orders occasioned by an expanding defense program. An indispensable skill for many business investors is the ability to identify new products and new fads as quickly as possible after their appearance, to judge with some accuracy which will catch on and which will not, and to decide which will persist in public favor long enough to justify an adjustment in productive capacity.

Projections of Full-capacity Gross National Product

While any and all clues concerning the future are fair game for investors, a random catch-as-catch-can canvass of specifics is really not a very satisfactory methodology for investment planning. Particularly in modern professionalized corporate management, there is a demand for something more orderly and scientific. Many firms are, of course, increasingly making or availing themselves of systematic forecasts of general business conditions. However, it is a fact, which we shall have occasion to appreciate more fully in Part Four, that general forecasts of *actual* demand or sales in the economy cannot be made to reach with much reliability far enough into the future to

[12] It should be noted that the term "accelerator" has been applied here only to the phenomenon of unexpected induced changes in investment with which it is most familiarly associated in economic literature. Some writers, e.g., William Fellner, *Trends and Cycles in Business Activity*, Holt, Rinehart and Winston, Inc., New York, 1956, chap. 4, use accelerator simply as a synonym for the investment-incremental-capacity ratio. In this sense, of course, the concept is an integral element in any growth theory. Just as a matter of semantics, however, it confuses matters to tag the investment requirement per unit of additional capacity—a concept that is pertinent to any kind of investment planning—with a label that has become heavily associated with a special case of demand and capacity interaction.

serve the needs of investors, who want to know what the world is going to be like five or ten or fifteen years hence. On the other hand, it is possible, by taking account of probable trends in the availability of labor and in productivity, to project with much greater confidence the approximate growth in the size or normal capacity of the economy some distance into the future.

This set of circumstances has led to an incomplete but nevertheless dramatic and important revolution in American private investment programing in recent years. More and more businesses are embodying their investment decisions in capital budgets based upon projections of the economy's probable size in future periods, with appropriate adjustments made for the shares of particular industries in the total, and for the share of a firm within its industry.

Implicitly such investment programing involves a basically optimistic forecast of demand—namely, that the projected capacity of the economy will be largely used. Thus, in effect, a major segment of American business now is casting an annual vote of confidence in the continuing comparative stability of the economy. In part, at least, these votes imply confidence in the future ability of government to help check and reverse major slumps—in itself a remarkable social phenomenon, considering the nearly total lack of such confidence a generation or so ago.

We shall want to consider in Part Three the extent to which these changes in business investment policy appear to have affected the economy's stability characteristics. Most present business conditions analysts probably would argue that the following statement, made by Dexter Keezer, Chairman of the McGraw-Hill Publishing Company's department of economics, to the U.S. Department of Agriculture's Outlook Conference in November, 1955, is too strong.[13] But most of them also would follow Keezer part way toward his conclusion.

> "Historically the most unstable element in our economy has been business investment in new producing facilities. . . . But that's all over now. Over the next few years business investment in new plant and equipment will be expanding and at a relatively stable rate. Two new . . . elements in the economy will make important contributions to this state of affairs. One is the growth of long-range planning of investment by American business corporations. . . . Along with this increased emphasis on long-range investment plans has gone a greatly increased determination to stick to the plans, and thus be in a position to take advantage of the greatly expanded markets which lie ahead. . . .
>
> "Another major force in stimulating business investment in

[13] Including even Mr. Keezer himself, as judged by his later publications, e.g., *Are We the Slaves of Some Defunct Economist?*, Claremont Graduate School and University Center, Claremont, Calif., 1963, pp. 88–89.

new processes and equipment is provided by the tremendous volume
of research of one kind and another being done these days. . . . New
products, new processes, new equipment come tumbling out of the
research laboratories at a rate and a volume which made the price
of survival for most business firms an aggressive investment program. . . ."

If Keezer is approximately correct in his diagnosis, it means—to use
the terminology of investment theory—that the static investment demand
schedule is now a more rational construct, and therefore a more dependable
one. And by the same token, major shifts in the investment demand schedule
are less likely.

CONCLUSIONS

The general influence that the existing stock of capital plus those
increments of capital already on order have upon current investment has been
implied in the last few pages. There is no need to belabor the argument. We
have also observed that an increasing stock of capital of given type and
quality is subject to diminishing returns as increments are added to it. This
fact, obviously relevant to analysis of the operation of economic forces in
a timeless world (i.e., static analysis), led many able economists, including
Lord Keynes, to fear a declining marginal efficiency of capital *over time.*

At this writing the number of American economists losing sleep over
this anxiety is much smaller than it was in the late 1930s. This sanguine view
in part reflects empirical studies indicating that since 1900 the unit productivity of capital, despite a big increase in capital stock per worker, has risen
significantly, not fallen.[14] More generally, it reflects increasing awareness
that the "quality" of capital does not in fact remain constant; it improves.
Our productive techniques are not fixed; they change constantly. New technology is forever resisting the encroachment of the diminishing returns that
our increasing stock of capital relative to labor might otherwise cause. In
effect, the decline in the marginal efficiency of capital that static analysis
would lead us to expect has been more than offset by dynamic shifts, attributable to technological change, in the marginal efficiency *schedule* over time.

In this chapter, we have tried to identify the determinants of the marginal efficiency of capital and to show how it relates to the cost of capital at
any point in time. We have also described some of the factors that cause the
marginal-efficiency-of-capital schedule to shift from time to time. Such an
itemization and description is essential if the theory of investment determination is to have any realistic content. But it does not leave us with a theory
that has much analytical value in business forecasting.

[14] See the reference in Chap. 5 to John Kendrick's findings on this point.

Economists are probably years away from knowing enough about the relative importance and interaction of the numerous influences upon investment incentives to weight and combine them into a functional relationship that would have any great predictive value. By dint of multiple-correlation analysis, it is possible to come up with a quantitative function that employs some such list of variables as that just reviewed and seems to describe fairly well the determination of investment in some past period. But the variables are so numerous and in many cases so evidently unstable over time that there is little sense in projecting any given historical determination pattern into the future.

We shall not conclude our general inspection of the theory of investment determination until we have considered the finance side of the issue in the next chapter. On the nonfinancial side, then, all we wind up with is a checklist. As we shall see when we reach Part Four, our models may not need to be quite so loose-ended as this in the cases of house building and inventory investment. But in the majority case of fixed-capital spending by business, the investment-determination model terminates in an unweighted checklist of significant influences.

There are two ways in which practicing analysts of business conditions and prospects can react—and have reacted—to the theoretical indeterminateness of the inducement to invest. The first is to accept current investment as an independent, largely unexplained, and largely unpredictable variable. The analyst who follows this course may view investment as a bellwether of the economy, and certainly he is concerned with sharpening the statistical perception of investment's current movements. But he does not attempt to divine its future course.

Increasingly, however, it has become apparent that economists who adopt this, and only this, posture toward investment changes are denying themselves valuable and available information. For although the factors that motivate investment decisions may not be susceptible of sufficiently rigorous analysis to permit prediction, we can, by modern sampling techniques, canvass the decisions themselves. Realization of this rather simple point has given rise since World War II to some invaluable forecasting aids, mentioned a time or two already and to be examined further in Part Four: periodic surveys of investors' spending intentions. These surveys are not completely reliable, if for no other reason than that they are always at least a little out-of-date, so there is no escaping some measure of direct analysis of the determinants of investment. But they do compensate for many of the deficiencies in our theoretical framework and usually reduce the errors in forecasting investment to tolerable proportions.

10

THE FINANCING
OF INVESTMENT AND
THE ROLE OF MONEY

Our order of business in the next two chapters is, first, to spell out the mechanics of contemporary (neo-Keynesian) interest rate and monetary theory. That is, what are the determinants of the demand for and supply of money? And how do the demand for and supply of money equate? Then, in the following chapter, we shall try to integrate the investment-determination theory, developed in Chapter 9, with the interest rate and monetary theory developed in this chapter. Next, we shall note some necessary qualifications and amendments to this integrated theory, particularly to inquire whether it is realistic to make the slender stem of money interest carry the full burden of the problem of investment financing. We shall also observe that monetary policy has an effect, not only in investment determination, but also in consumption determination. And finally, we shall discuss the relevance to the problem of the role of money of the recent emergence of various nonbank intermediaries which do not create money, narrowly defined, but do participate extensively in the credit creation process.

215

INVESTMENT FINANCING

When the money rate of interest is thought of as the price paid for loss of liquidity, it can be viewed as jointly determined by the community's demand for liquidity (represented by its liquidity-preference schedule) and its supply of liquidity, i.e., of money.[1]

THE SUPPLY OF MONEY

It may be well at this point to remind the reader of how the supply of money is created and its amount determined in advanced countries, particularly in the United States. The mechanism operates, for all practical purposes, via the creation and liquidation of demand deposits, because demand deposits and currency are immediately and readily convertible into each other at commercial banks, and by commercial banks at the Federal Reserve banks. Further, it has consistently been the policy of the Federal Reserve to permit expansion or contraction of the supply of currency in accordance with the needs of trade, i.e., to insulate bank reserves from fluctuations in currency in circulation. The impact of Federal Reserve control has therefore been on bank deposits, which account for the bulk of our money supply and for an even larger percentage of the total volume of transactions.

Banks that are members of the Federal Reserve System are required by law to maintain reserves in the form of deposits at the Federal Reserve banks or in vault cash (usually a minor amount).[2] The volume of reserves required is a calculated figure, derived by multiplying the demand and time deposits of the member bank by certain percentages. These percentages are set by the Federal Reserve within limits prescribed in the law.[3] The Federal Reserve is thus able to set a limit to the volume of demand deposits that the banking system can create through its lending and investing activities by: (1) varying the percentage reserve requirements, or (2) adding to, or sub-

---

[1] In the Keynesian system, the demand for money and the demand for liquidity are considered identical. We shall have more to say about this postulated identity later in the chapter.

[2] In the discussion that follows, we are ignoring the fact that about 17 percent of the demand deposits of commercial banks are in banks not members of the Federal Reserve System. These nonmember banks are governed by the banking laws of the various states, which invariably require the holding of some reserves. These reserves are typically held in other banks, which in the main are members of the Federal Reserve System. Interbank deposits come under the reserve requirements of the Federal Reserve. Deposits in nonmember banks are thus indirectly, though somewhat loosely, controlled by Federal Reserve policy.

[3] The limits for demand deposits are, for "reserve city" banks, 10 and 22 percent, and for "country" banks, 7 and 14 percent. For time deposits, the limits are 3 and 6 percent for all member banks, though different percentages for the two classes of banks may be established within these limits. At the time of writing, the effective requirements were, for demand deposits, $16\frac{1}{2}$ percent and 12 percent, and for time deposits, 4 percent for both classes of banks.

tracting from, the actual volume of reserves available to member banks. In equation form, where D is the volume of member bank deposits, r is the percentage of deposits that the Federal Reserve requires be held as reserves, and R is the dollar volume of required reserves:

$$R = rD \text{ and } D = R \times \frac{1}{r}$$

The Federal Reserve can influence D by varying either R or r.[4]

   Change in the reserve ratio r by the Federal Reserve has been termed the "blunt instrument" of control. Although conceivably the ratio could be changed frequently and by small increments, in practice the Federal Reserve has chosen to confine the use of changes in r to those infrequent occasions when a major change in policy is indicated. It has relied mainly on actions that affect the actual volume of reserves available to member banks.

   In the main, two actions, both of which involve extension of central bank credit, have been used. The first is changes in the discount rate.[5] Banks are permitted to supplement their reserves by borrowing from the Federal Reserve bank of the district in which they are located. They are required to pay interest on the loans, the rate of interest being the discount rate. Presumably banks are influenced in their willingness to borrow by the cost of borrowing, i.e., by the level of the discount rate in relation to rates currently earned by banks on their loans and investments. The reason is that any member bank, if it finds its reserves deficient or likely to become so, has the option of borrowing from the Federal Reserve bank or of selling or liquidating some of its assets (e.g., Treasury bills).[6] If the deficiency is expected to be temporary, the bank may well decide to borrow rather than sell assets in order to eliminate brokerage commissions and to avoid disturbing portfolios—even though the discount rate may be significantly higher than the rate being

---

[4] As noted in the previous footnote, reserve requirements apply to both time and demand deposits, though the ratios are different. Although this dual reserve requirement complicates the control process, because deposits are sometimes shifted by their owners from demand to time and vice versa, the principle of control is the same. See Lester V. Chandler, *The Economics of Money and Banking*, 4th ed., Harper & Row, Publishers, Incorporated, New York, 1964, pp. 97–108, for a method of analyzing the effects of deposit shifts and currency drains on the control over demand deposits exercised by the Federal Reserve. See the same source (pp. 108–111) for an explanation of the fact that, although the banking system as a whole can expand the deposits by $1/r$—under typical requirements about 6—times an increment in reserves, an individual bank can expand its own deposits by an amount only roughly equal to the increment.

[5] Sometimes called the "rediscount rate"—a carry-over from the days when a substantial volume of member bank borrowing took the form of rediscounting customer loans held by the member banks. In recent decades, most member bank borrowing has taken the form of a direct loan (advance) from a Federal Reserve bank secured by United States government securities.

[6] Individual banks may borrow from the Federal Funds market, which means that banks with reserve deficiencies borrow reserves from other banks with excess reserves.

earned on the liquid assets that could be sold. If the deficiency is expected to be of a longer run, however, the banks will be likely to weigh carefully the cost of alternative means of meeting the reserve deficiency. One means is to sell liquid assets. For the banking system as a whole, reserve positions can be improved by sales of assets only if the sale is to nonbank buyers.[7] If banks choose this method, incidentally, they may well find that the very economic circumstances (e.g., a vigorous rise in business activity) that caused the banking system to want to supplement its reserves may also cause nonbank institutions to be unwilling buyers, i.e., the assets could be sold only at declining prices, which would mean taking capital losses. In this event, banks may feel "locked" in their present bond portfolio.

Another means of meeting the pressure on reserves is to reduce the volume of outstanding loans, probably by refraining from making new loans as old ones are paid off. Both techniques liquidate deposits for the system as a whole by about an equal amount, thus releasing reserves by an amount approximately equal to r times the amount of the sale or loan reduction.

Conversely, if the central bank adds to member bank reserves, banks have the option of buying assets or expanding loans (both of which create customer deposits) or of reducing their indebtedness at the Federal Reserve bank. Their choice of alternatives will be influenced by the relative profitability of the available alternatives. It is for this reason that the level of the discount rate in relation to yields obtainable on other assets exercises an influence on the lending and deposit-creating activities of member banks. Just how big an influence is a matter of some debate. There are those who argue that the tradition against borrowing and the often-repeated policy of the Federal Reserve that banks should not borrow just because it is profitable, but rather only to meet the legitimate needs of their customers, are sufficient to reduce the significance of the discount rate to minor proportions. Others, who note that the distinction between meeting the legitimate needs of customers and making a profitable loan is often an extremely subtle one and that the volume of borrowing is in fact positively correlated with the profitability of borrowing, attach more significance to the discount rate.[8]

Whatever may be the merits of this debate, the primary instrument of central bank control, as exercised by the Federal Reserve, is open-market operations, i.e., purchases and sales on the open market of United States government securities. When the Federal Reserve buys a government security from a bond dealer, it pays for it with a check drawn on itself, which the dealer deposits in a commercial bank. The bank thereupon deposits it in its reserve account at the Fed. Bank deposits and reserves are thus increased by

[7] The sale does not increase the volume of reserves available to the system, but it reduces their deposits and therefore the volume of reserves required.

[8] For a further discussion of this point, see R. C. Turner, *Member Bank Borrowing*, Ohio State University Press, Columbus, Ohio, 1938.

equal amounts. Reserve requirements rise by r times the increase in deposits. The remaining portion of the increase in reserves, $1 - r$ times the amount of the purchase, is unencumbered. A *sale* of securities will, of course, have the opposite effects.

Open-market operations are used by the Federal Reserve as their primary instrument of control chiefly for two reasons. First, the technique is an extremely flexible one. Securities can be bought or sold in any quantity desired (within broad limits) and on very short notice, thanks to an active and continuous market for government securities. A reserve-injecting policy can be pursued one day and a reserve-absorbing one the next if circumstances require, as they sometimes do when the purpose of Federal Reserve policy is primarily to offset unusual flows in reserve funds associated with holidays, international gold flows, and other unique events. Second—and perhaps this is the same reason in different garb—open-market operations are an unobtrusive instrument of control. No public announcement, such as is required for a change in reserve requirements or in the discount rate, is needed. All that is required is a confidential instruction to the trading desk in the Federal Reserve Bank of New York to buy or sell according to some generally worded criteria. If the Federal Reserve is not entirely certain about its proper policy posture, or if it is uneasy about the effects of pursuing a certain policy, it can, through open-market operations, feel its way, hour by hour and step by step, and it can reverse its policy just as unobtrusively when the time comes to do so. Only after the event, when the Federal Reserve statement is published each week, does the public know what transactions have taken place. And even then, it is difficult for all but the most expert to disentangle open-market operations taken for technical and seasonal reasons from those taken for economic policy reasons.

To these formal instruments of Federal Reserve control, it is customary to add a fourth, sometimes called "moral suasion." Moral suasion can take many forms. The Chairman of the Board of Governors may make a speech in which he admonishes the banks to follow different lending policies. News stories about Federal Reserve Board reaction to current bank lending policies can be deliberately inspired. Or at the other extreme in the officialdom of the Federal Reserve, the officer at the discount window in the Federal Reserve bank, under the authority of "Regulation A" of the Federal Reserve Board, may bring pressure on individual banks to reduce their borrowing—or deliberately refrain from doing so.[9] By its very nature, the effectiveness of moral suasion cannot be measured, but in monetary policy as elsewhere it is generally believed to be not very significant.

By using these four techniques of credit control in combination, the

---

[9] If such pressure extends to the point of actually closing the discount window, it probably exceeds the definitional limits of moral suasion.

Federal Reserve is able to hold a fairly tight rein on bank deposit creation.[10] Two reasons for inserting the word "fairly" in the previous sentence should be noted. First, because member banks cannot make perfect forecasts of their reserve requirements or of the movement of reserve funds in and out of the bank, they typically carry a small cushion of reserves in excess of requirements. Thus they are usually able, for days or even weeks, to escape the consequences of Federal Reserve policy actions by using their cushion, or by borrowing some other bank's cushion via the Federal Funds market. In the late 1930s, this cushion of excess reserves took on large proportions, but for different reasons growing out of the depths of the Depression and the impact on banker attitudes of the collapse of the banking system in the early 1930s. During that period, excess reserves were so large that the effects of Federal Reserve policy on deposit creation were minimal.[11] Under more normal circumstances, however, the effect of excess reserves is only to smooth out, and perhaps postpone slightly, the consequences of Federal Reserve policy.

The second reason has to do with the borrowing privilege of member banks. As we noted earlier, banks may through borrowing meet the pressure brought on them by, for example, open-market operations. The borrowing privilege inserts a rubber link in the chain of Federal Reserve control. But, as we implied earlier, it is a stout rubber link. Efforts by banks to escape the consequences of Federal Reserve policy by borrowing may be costly, and in any event the Federal Reserve can, if it chooses, take up the slack provided by the rubber link by pulling even harder on the chain, i.e., by additional open-market operations. We do little violence to the facts, therefore, when we conclude that under reasonably normal circumstances, the Federal Reserve has the power to limit fairly precisely an expansion in the supply of money, defined again as bank deposits plus currency outside banks.[12]

The power of the Federal Reserve to limit a *contraction* in the money supply is less certain. A decline in business activity and in incomes is likely to lead to a decline in the demand for bank credit. As the volume of bank loans and investments declines, the money supply tends to be reduced. If the decline is a moderate one, i.e., if the circumstances are reasonably normal, a

[10] In addition to these credit control powers, the Federal Reserve establishes margin requirements for loans on securities by brokers and dealers and by banks. It has also been given the power, during and after periods of military emergency, to exercise direct controls over consumer and real estate credit.

[11] The experience during World War II and the immediate postwar years was of a different character. During this period the Federal Reserve deliberately refrained from exercising its controls for monetary stabilization purposes. Instead, it used its control techniques (chiefly open-market operations) to maintain government bond prices at a fixed support level.

[12] The dilution of the economic consequences of Federal Reserve control by the existence of various near-moneys, such as savings and loan shares, is another problem, to which we shall return shortly. Our concern here is simply to define the Fed's ability to control the money supply, narrowly defined.

large part of the potential decline can be offset, and probably reversed, by a Federal Reserve injection of reserves into the banking system sufficient to reduce interest rates to the point where loans will again be attractive to borrowers. If the decline should be a drastic one, however, accompanied by a general impairment of confidence, no action by the Federal Reserve would be likely to prevent a decline in the money supply.

The question of the power of the Federal Reserve to prevent a contraction in the money supply is probably less relevant than it was a generation or so ago. Today, in the event of an impending serious decline in business activity, the fiscal powers of the Federal government would almost surely be brought to bear in support of monetary policy. That is, the power of the Federal Reserve to limit and reverse a contraction in the money supply is not so likely to be tested as it was some years ago. Under present-day conditions, therefore, we may conclude that the effective monetary power of the Federal Reserve in the instance of a contraction is, though not so obvious as in the instance of an expansion, not inconsiderable.

It may not be inappropriate to note that the Federal Reserve exercises its monetary control powers even when it does nothing. Suppose, for example, that business activity is expanding vigorously and that the demand for money is therefore also expanding. If the Fed simply sits tight and refrains from taking action to increase reserves (needed to permit banks to enlarge their lending and thus expand their deposits), or even if it does take action to expand reserves but by a lesser amount than needed, it is exercising a restrictive monetary policy. To say that the tighter lending policies of commercial banks and the higher interest rates that would ensue in such a situation are the result solely of market forces is to say that price is determined solely by demand and that supply has nothing to do with it—to say, in Alfred Marshall's words, that one blade of the shears does all the cutting. A so-called neutral monetary policy—meaning by that term a Federal Reserve policy that neither augments nor diminishes the supply of funds—is not, in fact, neutral.

Public monetary and credit policies are so seldom neutral and are potentially so generally effective in regulating the money supply that it is the habit of modern theorists to treat credit policies as an autonomous variable fully controllable by the monetary authorities.[13] Thus in a diagram such as Figure 10–1, where the supply of liquidity (or money) is plotted against different interest rates, any M that the authorities set (M_a or M_b in the figure) must, on this assumption, be shown as wholly inelastic to any changes that may occur in the interest rate.

[13] The choice of criteria according to which the money supply is actually controlled, in the United States and other countries, is another matter, which we cannot go into here. Among the obvious criteria, in addition to stabilization of the general level of economic activity, are maintaining a low level of unemployment, price-level stabilization, balance-of-payments considerations, maintaining "orderly" conditions in the capital markets, etc.

Figure **10–1.** The supply of liquidity—if exclusively determined by central bank policy.

THE DEMAND FOR MONEY

The public's demand for liquidity actually is a composite of two types of need or desire for money. The first type has to do simply with the use of money—currency plus demand deposits—in usual day-to-day, week-to-week, and month-to-month business operations. If the expenditures of every spending unit in the economy were timed exactly to match its receipts, there would be no need for money as a medium of exchange for day-to-day business transactions. Incidentally, the growing use of credit cards, installment buying, and similar devices for shifting expenditure dates closer to income receipt dates is gradually moving us in the direction of such coincident timing of expenditures and income. But a large volume of business transactions still does not benefit from such coincident timing. A substantial money supply is therefore needed to bridge the gap. Further, spending units seldom attempt to budget their income so that, at the instant before the paycheck arrives (or at the moment before sales receipts arrive in a business firm), cash on hand and on deposit in the bank are down to exactly zero. Our ability to forecast expenditure needs is imperfect. We like to hold some balances, both of cash and of bank deposits, for unforeseen spending needs. For some people, incomes as well as expenditure needs are not predictable, even in the relatively short run, and they may wish to maintain idle balances to smooth out these irregularities of income. The first of these motives for wanting money is called the "transactions motive," the second the "precautionary motive." Both motives for wanting money are related to the spending unit's volume of transactions. And for the economy as a whole, they are related to the total volume of current money transactions, which means, for the most part, to the level of final demand in current price terms, i.e., GNP.[14]

This first portion of the demand for money is virtually inelastic with respect to interest rates at normal interest rate levels. It can be argued that at very high rates of interest, holders of money might be persuaded to lend

[14] For this linkage to hold, duplicative and financial transactions must not change disproportionately to income and output transactions. In addition, the statement in the text assumes that business customs that affect the need for transactions cash, such as the duration of payroll periods and the frequency of bill paying, do not change.

their precautionary idle balances to reap the interest return. Or very high rates of interest might persuade business firms and individuals to devise new techniques for making more efficient use of money for transactions purposes (thus raising its velocity) so that they could lend the difference. But any such shift of asset form involves both trouble and expense—at minimum brokerage commissions and similar transfer costs. In the range of interest rates relevant to most economic forecasting, therefore, it is probably safe to conclude that interest rate changes have little or no effect, and that the transactions and precautionary demand for money is almost entirely a function of aggregate demand. Following tradition, we shall call this transactions and precautionary demand the "L_1 demand." The L_1 demand can be shown either as a function of the interest rate (an inelastic relationship, illustrated in Figure 10–4 to which we shall come in a moment) or as a function of aggregate demand (GNP), illustrated in Figure 10–2.[15]

   The other portion of the demand for liquidity—L_2—involves what Keynes called the "speculative" motive. Individuals and businesses like to hold some liquid assets so that they may be able to make profitable use of them when the proper investment opportunities arise.

   Why, you might ask, would anyone want to hold idle cash, a nonearning asset? The answer lies in the fact that, although holding idle money involves a cost—loss of earnings—investing money in bonds and other securities also involves a possible cost—loss of capital value, and the loss of value can easily exceed by a considerable margin the interest earnings in any given year or other interest period. When interest rates rise, bond prices go down, and the holder would therefore take a loss if he were to liquidate his investment. Practical investors observe that, although interest rates fluctuate from time to time—generally rising in periods of strong business activity and declining in periods of falling business activity—the range of fluctuations is

---

   [15] It should be noted that we have said nothing about the precise shape and form of (i.e., the equation for) this L_1 curve. In Fig. 10–2 it is arbitrarily drawn as a linear function with a positive Y intercept. We could just as well have drawn it as nonlinear, with varying slopes and varying intercepts. Although for purposes of policy making and for some analytical purposes the character of the L_1 curve is of importance, for purposes of the present general discussion of interest theory, the precise equation is not crucial, so long as it is positively sloped.

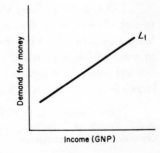

Figure 10–2.   The transactions and precautionary demand for money (the L_1 function).

fairly narrow, and there seems to be no perceptible long-term trend. At least, if there is any long-term trend of interest rates, it is so gradual as to be of little interest to mortal investors. Practical investors also observe that interest rates seldom hold steady at any given level—high or low—for any very prolonged period of time. When they deviate markedly above or below the long-term average, it is only a matter of time—months or at most a few years—until they will move toward, and perhaps beyond, the historic average. Or the matter might be expressed in terms of probabilities. When interest rates are significantly below the average—near the lower end of the normal range of variation—the probability that they will rise (which would produce a capital loss) is considered to be higher than the probability that they will fall even further (a capital gain). And vice versa when interest rates are near the upper end of their normal range of variation.

A prudent investor will normally want to diversify his portfolio, dividing it between relatively high-return investments, which, however, involve a considerable likelihood of capital gain or loss, relatively low-return investments such as short-term government securities, which involve very little risk of capital loss, and cash, which is entirely risk-free. Some investors will be disposed to maximize their return at the risk of large capital losses. Other more conservative investors will be more inclined to minimize their risk and will hold a larger portion of their portfolios in money and near-money. Both types of wealth holders will be influenced by the level of interest rates in the relative emphasis they place on interest return, on the one hand, and avoidance of risk, on the other. If interest rates are low relative to historic levels and are considered more likely to rise than to fall (i.e., if bond prices are considered more likely to fall than to rise), investors will tend to shift their portfolio distributions in the direction of money. Some will want to become highly liquid. Most will simply want to hold a somewhat larger proportion of their wealth in liquid forms. A few, for whom risk bearing, in and of itself, yields a positive utility, will be unaffected by the low level of interest rates. In total, however, the speculative demand for liquidity will tend to be high at low interest rates and low at high interest rates.[16] In other words, at any given point in time, the speculative demand for liquidity is a function of the interest rate and the slope is negative. Graphically, the function may look something like the L_2 curve in Figure 10-3.

One peculiar thing about this L_2 curve, which we have not anticipated in our discussion, is that at the right-hand end it is parallel to the X axis. What this says is that interest rates do not have to go to zero for asset holders to want to become virtually 100 percent liquid. At some very low level of interest rates, the return is so small, and the probability of a capital loss is so large, that everyone will want to convert his assets into cash. Whether or

[16] See James Tobin's classic article, "Liquidity Preference as Behavior towards Risk," *Review of Economics Studies*, vol. XXV (2), no. 67, February, 1958, for a full exposition of this argument.

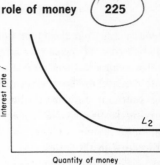

Figure **10–3.** The speculative demand for
money (the L_2 function).

not there really is such a "liquidity trap"—though its existence seems logical
on a priori grounds—is a matter of some debate. We shall note but refrain
from entering into this debate, however, because—barring another Great
Depression or some other equally unlikely event—this portion of the curve is
of little interest to us in practical forecasting. The relevant portion, it seems,
is clearly negatively sloped.

One final, if obvious, point should be made about these L_1 and L_2
curves before we attempt to combine them. This is that both functions may
shift from time to time. The L_1 curve may shift as a result of technological or
other changes in methods of making payments (e.g., the credit cards to which
we adverted). A prolonged period of steadily rising incomes may persuade
businesses and persons to reduce their precautionary balances. Higher price
expectations, as we noted in Chapter 8, if the change in expectations is substantial, may cause money holders to reduce their precautionary balances.
Conversely, an actual, experienced rise in the general price level may tend to
reduce consumer spending and cause consumers to try to increase their cash
balances, because the real value of their liquid holdings has been reduced.[17]
Similarly, changes in investor notions of what constitutes a normal, or average, range of interest rates may cause the L_2 function to shift. Also, attitudes
about the probable range of variation in interest rates may change. And if
the Federal Reserve should follow, as it did from 1941 to 1951, a policy of
stabilizing United States government bond prices, investor attitudes toward the
risk of capital loss will be affected—just how much will depend on how likely
they think the Federal Reserve is to hold to that policy.

An analysis of business conditions over time must make necessary
allowance for any such shifts in these functions. At the moment, we are
engaged in static analysis: What determines the demand for money at a particular point in time? For purposes of such analysis, we can assume that
the two functions are fixed.

To recapitulate briefly, we have said that one portion of the demand
for money, transactions and precautionary demand, is a function of *aggregate*

---

[17] This type of behavior is called the "Pigou effect," after its identifier, Prof. A.
C. Pigou of Cambridge University.

demand and that the other portion, speculative demand, is a function of the *interest rate*. How can we add these two disparate functions? The answer is that we can add them only if we hold one of the independent variables, aggregate demand or the interest rate, constant. That is, we can determine (assuming that our functional diagrams are correct) the demand for money at varying levels of GNP, *given the interest rate;* or we can determine the demand for money at varying interest rates, *given the level of GNP.* Let us proceed with the latter.

Given our assumption that the speculative demand for money is entirely a function of the interest rate, the diagrammatic presentation of the L_2 function describes the speculative demand for money at *any* level of GNP at any given point in time. The diagrammatic presentation of transactions and precautionary demand, the L_1 function, however, must be changed to show the relationship between the demand for money and the interest rate, *at a given level of GNP.* Because we assumed that the transactions and precautionary demand for money is not affected by the interest rate (except slightly, perhaps, at very high rates of interest), i.e., is inelastic with respect to the interest rate, the line of relationship will be a vertical straight line, in the manner of Figure 10–4. (The slight, leftward bend in the line is a concession to our exception at high rates of interest.) The dashed L_1' and L_1'' lines are added to show what the L_1 demand for money would look like at *other,* higher, levels of GNP, which we might call GNP' and GNP''.

Now we are prepared to add the two demands for money at a given level of GNP. Figure 10–5 shows the combined effects of the transactions and precautionary demand for money and the speculative demand *at a given level of GNP.* The $L_1 + L_2$ curve describes the total demand for money at the given level of GNP. Obviously, we could make such a calculation for numerous possible levels of GNP (such as the dashed lines in Figure 10–4), which would yield us a series of $L_1 + L_2$ curves as shown in Figure 10–6.

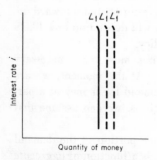

Figure **10–4.** The transactions and precautionary demand for money at a given level of GNP.

Figure **10–5.** The total demand for money at a given level of GNP.

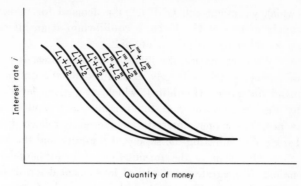

Figure **10–6.**   The total demand for money at successive levels of GNP.

MONETARY EQUILIBRIUM

We are now in a position to compare the total demand for money (at any given level of GNP at a given time) with the supply of money which, you will recall, we said was effectively determined by the central bank (Figure 10–1). Figure 10–7 simply superimposes the M function in Figure 10–1 (without the alternative dashed line) on Figure 10–6. This chart tells us that at the lowest level of GNP postulated, where the demand for money is represented by the $L_1 + L_2$ curve, the demand for money and the supply of money would be equal (i.e., demand and supply would be in equilibrium), if the interest rate were i_a. At an alternative and somewhat higher level of GNP

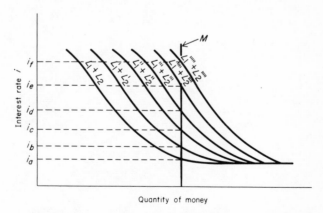

Figure **10–7.**   Demand for and supply of money at successive levels of GNP.

(which we might call GNP'),[18] the demand for money $(L_1' + L_2')$ and the supply of money M will be in equilibrium at an interest rate of i_b. And so on for other possible levels of GNP.

To summarize, the money rate of interest is a function of the supply of money, which is largely determined by the central bank, and of the demand for money (liquidity), which, at a given level of GNP, is determined by the transactions and the precautionary and speculative demands for money. The money interest rate therefore reflects both changes in central bank policy affecting the supply of liquidity and the level of GNP.

One step in the formulation of investment-determination theory remains: to integrate the model of investment determination, *given the interest rate* outlined in Chapter 9, with the model of interest rate determination outlined in the present chapter. This integration is the subject matter of Chapter 11.

---

[18] Note that we are referring to an alternative, higher level of GNP at *the same point in time*, not a higher GNP at some later date when the L functions would probably have shifted.

11

THE FINANCING
OF INVESTMENT AND
THE ROLE OF MONEY
(Continued)

In Chapter 9, we developed the Keynesian static equilibrium concept that *investment* is a function of the interest rate. The functional relationship was graphically illustrated in Figure 9–2. In Chapter 10, we developed a similar static equilibrium concept of the demand for *money* as a function of the interest rate. This is about as far as Lord Keynes went in investment theory per se. It remained for the post-Keynesians, in particular, J. R. Hicks in England and Alvin H. Hansen in the United States, to interrelate these two equilibrium concepts and to combine them into a total investment-market–money-market equilibrium concept.[1]

THE EQUILIBRIUM OF SAVING AND INVESTMENT
AND OF THE SUPPLY AND DEMAND FOR MONEY

This connection can be made by deriving the so-called IS (for investment and saving) and LM (for demand for liquidity and supply of money) functions. Let us proceed first with the LM function.

[1] See J. R. Hicks, "Mr. Keynes and the Classics: A Suggested Interpretation," *Econometrica*, vol. V, 1937; and Alvin Hansen, *Monetary Theory and Fiscal Policy*, McGraw-Hill Book Company, New York, 1949, especially chap. V.

Figure 11–1.   The LM function.

The LM Function

The derivation of the LM function is fairly simple. Figure 10–7, the concluding diagram in the previous chapter, it will be recalled, showed: (1) a vertical line M representing the supply of money (assumed to be controlled by the central bank and therefore fixed at any given point in time, regardless of the level of GNP); and (2) a series of $L_1 + L_2$ curves, each representing the demand for money at some level of GNP. The points $(a, b, c, \ldots, f)$ at which these $L_1 + L_2$ curves intersected the M line were the points at which the demand for and the supply of money would be in equilibrium. By reading from the diagram the i value for each equilibrium point, and associating that i value with the level of GNP that the $L_1 + L_2$ curve pertained to, we can now construct a table of values showing for each of the several levels of GNP the interest rate, given the supply of money, at which the demand for money would be exactly equal to the supply of money. And the paired values (i and GNP) in this table could be plotted, and the values between the selected points could be interpolated, as in Figure 11–1. The LM function illustrated by this curve, to repeat, describes the alternative values of GNP and the interest rate at which, at a given time, the demand for and supply of money would be in equilibrium. We might call it the "money-market equilibrium curve."

The IS Function

In earlier chapters, it was stressed that (assuming the balance in the government and exports-imports components of the GNP accounts to be zero), saving must, by definition, be equal to investment $(S \equiv I)$. And at any given time, the economy will be in equilibrium only when the complex of saving-determining forces yields a volume of saving equal to the volume of investment yielded by its complex of determining forces. And we said that, with a given consumption function and again assuming away government and exports-imports, the volume of saving is a function of income, i.e., roughly of GNI (GNP).

We need to qualify this latter statement a bit when we are referring to the *total* saving of the economy rather than to net personal saving only. Net personal saving is clearly a function of DPI, and DPI, in turn, is (with some

Figure 11–2. The saving function.

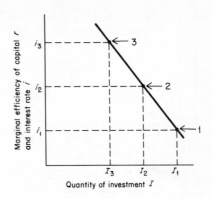

Figure 11–3. Determination of the volume of investment at a given time.

qualifications that we shall discuss in some detail in the forecasting chapters in Part Four) a function of GNP.   Total saving, however, also includes business saving, i.e., undistributed corporate profits and capital-consumption allowances.   The former, undistributed profits, is of course related to total profits, and total profits are importantly influenced by the level of GNP, or more precisely, by the level of GNP in relation to capacity GNP.[2]   Capital-consumption allowances, however, are related to GNP only in a very general, long-term manner.   The main component of capital-consumption allowances, depreciation allowances, is determined in each firm by multiplying the value of the firm's depreciable capital at the beginning of the accounting period by a somewhat arbitrary depreciation rate (itself heavily influenced by occasional changes in the tax laws and regulations).   The value of depreciable capital is (assuming constant capital-output ratios) a function of the level of potential output, but it is a function of *actual* GNP only to the extent that actual output correlates with potential.[3]   In somewhat less precise but perhaps more understandable words, what we are saying is that depreciation allowances are a function of the long-run trend of GNP but do not significantly reflect its cyclical fluctuations.   This fact will be more readily apparent when, in Part Four, we develop a technique for short-run forecasting of capital-consumption allowances; the technique comes close to being linear extrapolation.

In spite of these qualifications, it is not unreasonable to postulate that total saving is a function of GNP and that the relationship is approximately linear and positively sloped, as in Figure 11–2.

Next, to preclude having to turn pages back and forth, let us repeat here Figure 9-2, the diagram illustrating the determination of the volume of investment, and give it a new number, Figure 11–3.   This chart, it will be

[2] See Chap. 23 for a defense of this statement.

[3] Note that we have used the term "potential output" rather than "capacity" to mean a measure of output in which the limiting factor is the stock of capital, not the labor force.

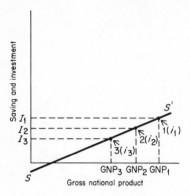

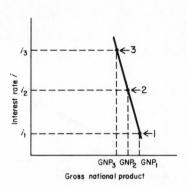

Figure **11–4.** The saving func-   Figure **11–5.** The IS function.
tion and investment at various
rates of interest.

recalled, illustrates the volume of investment (given the marginal-efficiency-of-capital schedule) that would be undertaken at various money rates of interest.

The question to which we now address ourselves is this: Under what conditions will the volume of saving (a function of GNP) be in equilibrium with the volume of investment (a function of the interest rate)? How can we combine these two functional relationships? Figure 11–4 represents such a combination, and it is important to understand how this chart is derived. The SS' line is the saving function, lifted without change from Figure 11–2, and the ordinates along the two axes are the same. Point 1 on the saving function is opposite the volume of investment (I_1) that would be undertaken at an interest rate i_1, read from the horizontal axis of Figure 11–3 (point 1 on that figure). Or, to put it the other way around, Figure 11–3 tells us that at an interest rate i_1, investment would be I_1; because $S = I$, the relevant point on the saving function, where $I = S$, is point 1. The vertical coordinate of point 2 is the volume of investment that would be undertaken at i_2, again read from Figure 11–3. And so on with point 3 and various possible other points.

We are now in a position to project (the vertical dashed lines in Figure 11–4) down to the GNP axis and read the values of GNP at which, for each of the postulated interest rates, saving would be equal to investment. Thus, if the interest rate is i_1 (point 1), saving would be equal to investment at a level of GNP equal to GNP_1. If the interest rate is i_2 (point 2), saving would be equal to investment at GNP_2. And so forth for as many rates of interest as we wish to postulate. Given this set of paired values (i and GNP), we can now plot them on a chart that shows the respective values of the interest rate and GNP where saving and investment will be in equilibrium. Such a line is shown in Figure 11–5. Thus, looking at point 1, the diagram says that at an interest rate of i_1 and a GNP of GNP_1, saving (determined by GNP) would be equal to investment (determined, given the marginal-

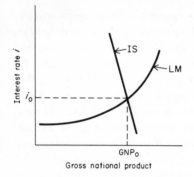

Figure **11–6.** The LM and IS functions.

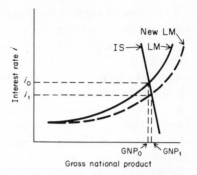

Figure **11–7.** The IS and LM functions before and after a change in the money supply.

efficiency-of-capital schedule, by the interest rate); that is, an equilibrium condition would prevail. Or, at point 2, if the interest rate were i_2 and if GNP were GNP_2, saving and investment would be in equilibrium. And so forth for other points. The relationship described by all such possible values (within relevant limits) of the interest rate and GNP *at which the saving and investment forces in the economy would be in equilibrium* is customarily called the IS function.[4] It is comparable to the money-market equilibrium diagram that we developed early in this chapter, the LM function, which showed the values of GNP and i at which the supply of money and the demand for money would be in equilibrium. Thus, by superimposing the two diagrams, we can identify the *one* point at which *both* markets—the saving-investment market and the money market—would be in equilibrium, which, of course, is the point at which the two curves intersect. Such a combining of the two functions is shown in Figure 11–6. Thus, in Figure 11–6, both markets would be in equilibrium, at a given time, if GNP were equal to GNP_0 and if the interest rate were i_0. If either GNP or the interest rate were at some level other than its equilibrium value, the disequilibrium would set into motion forces in both markets that would tend to restore equilibrium.

Such a diagrammatic presentation of the LM and IS functions is useful in tracing out the possible economic impact of various autonomous events that might occur. Suppose, for example, that the central bank were to increase the money supply. With a more abundant money supply, *ceteris paribus*, the LM function would shift to the right. (Go back to Figure 10–7 and draw a vertical line for the larger money supply and note how such a shift changes the values of $a, b, c, \ldots, f$.) Thus, Figure 11–6 would be changed as shown by the dashed line in Figure 11–7. The forces set in motion to restore equilibrium would tend to raise GNP from GNP_0 to GNP_1, and to reduce the interest rate from i_0 to i_1.

---

[4] Needless to say, these diagrams are highly stylized and are not meant to be graphically or mathematically precise.

Second, suppose that there should be an autonomous change in investor expectations resulting, perhaps, from some major technological breakthrough, raising the marginal-efficiency-of-capital schedule. Such a change would tend to shift the IS function to the right. (Go back to Figure 11–3, raise the marginal-efficiency-of-capital schedule with respect to the rate of interest, then transfer the new values of I for points i_1, i_2, and i_3 in Figure 11–5, and note the change in the values of GNP that would correspond with each of these new I values.) In this case, our diagrammatic presentation of the IS and LM functions would look as in Figure 11–8. The shift in the marginal-efficiency-of-capital schedule would set in motion forces that would tend to raise GNP from GNP_0 to GNP_1 and to raise the interest rate from i_0 to i_1.

And so on. It would be a helpful exercise for the student to postulate various other autonomous events and to trace out the direction of change in i and GNP of the equilibrating forces.

SOME NECESSARY QUALIFICATIONS AND AMENDMENTS

The theory just summarized probably goes too far in downgrading the financial influences upon aggregate demand in two principal respects. First, the availability and the distribution of money and of other highly liquid assets undoubtedly do have effects upon other-than-investment forms of spending. This we shall deal with later in the chapter. Second, and worthy of immediate attention, is the fact that the effects that the stock of investable funds exerts upon the magnitude of investment are not, as Keynesian model implies, limited to those which the stock of funds indirectly exerts through its impact on the money rate of interest. In addition, the quantitative availability and location of investable funds frequently are direct determinants of the amount investors spend.

THE QUANTITATIVE AVAILABILITY OF FUNDS

The point that the availability of funds is an important determinant of investment becomes nearly self-evident as soon as it is made. Institution-

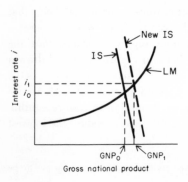

Figure **11–8.** The IS and LM functions before and after a shift in the marginal-efficiency-of-capital schedule.

ally, it is evidenced by the fact that central banking controls operate directly upon the quantity of credit that commercial banks are free to extend to business and other borrowers.   These controls affect the rationing of bank loans. In part, of course, the controls achieve this effect by affecting interest rates and thereby altering the attractiveness of borrowing.   For the most part, however, when the banks' reserve position is narrowed, banks ration the reduced volume of available credit simply by raising credit standards, screening loan applicants more closely, and reducing the size of their loans.   Among the major monetary controls, only adjustments in central bank rediscount rates are designed primarily to affect interest rates.   With this one exception, the *immediate* effect of central bank control is on the availability of funds, and only indirectly on interest rates.

The significance of the quantitative availability of loanable funds as a direct determinant of investment follows, theoretically, from the stickiness, especially upward stickiness, of interest rates.   In the event of a sharp rightward shift in the demand for, or a leftward shift in the supply of, loanable funds, lenders may *not* raise their rates of interest to a level that would clear the market under the new demand-supply conditions.   Instead, as a result of law, convention, or other influences, the rise in the interest rate may effectively bump into a ceiling.   In this case, the market is not cleared.   A gap between the demand for and the supply of funds exists; in the absence of adequate market adjustments in the interest rate, the gap must be closed via direct rationing by the lender.   Similarly, interest rates on certain types of loans are sticky on the downside.   Lenders of residential mortgage loans, for example, may resist lowering interest rates below the conventional level, in spite of an abundance of loanable funds.   In this event, the market is again not cleared.

The imperfections in the money market are not limited to interest rate inflexibility.   In fact, the market actually is a whole collection of partially compartmentalized markets through which not all funds flow with equal facility.   Some major lenders, e.g., life insurance companies, are cut off by law or custom from major groups of borrowers.   And some would-be business borrowers, e.g., small firms whose securities are not listed on the major securities exchanges, lack effective access to important concentrations of lenders. These are matters of mounting significance in the United States as more and more saving is channeled into income-seeking private pension, welfare, and insurance funds, which typically are inhibited in their acquisition of equity securities, particularly those of smaller and newer enterprises.[5]

[5] The present discussion of the provision of loans to investors is intended to embrace the purchase of new shares of stock as well as of other securities more nearly fixed in dollar value.   It seems more realistic to regard the stockholder—at least the small stockholder—as a *lender* who chooses an uncertain instead of a contractual interest rate in the hope that the former will exceed the latter than to view him as a purchaser of real assets, i.e., as an investor in the economic sense.

THE SIGNIFICANCE OF INTERNAL FINANCING

It is partly because of the market imperfections just mentioned that the feasibility of internal, as against external, financing of investment projects has a much heavier bearing upon the volume of investment activity than the simple investment model implies. The latter, emphasizing the principle of opportunity cost, suggests that it makes little difference whether the would-be investor happens to have the necessary liquid assets himself, and hence "borrows" from himself, or whether he borrows from someone else. The model assumes that in either case the investor must anticipate a rate of return from his new capital goods expenditure that exceeds the going market interest rate. It further assumes that *at* this interest rate he will find funds available in the external money market.

This last, as we have just seen, often is not the case. If a company has funds of its own, it can use them. If it does not have funds of its own, it may encounter roadblocks in the money markets even though its inducement to invest may be very high. Furthermore, the retention of earnings by firms usually does not diminish the availability of investable funds to other (outside) investors so much as it increases their availability to the incident firms. For when corporations shift income from retained earnings into dividends, stockholders can be expected to channel some of their increased dividends into consumption and into forms of saving that are insulated from the loan markets.

Thus the greater the liquidity of industrial and marketing corporations, the greater, other things being equal, the economy's *total* supply of investable funds is likely to be. Nor is this the only influence upon investment that corporate liquidity has. In addition, high corporate liquidity often prompts investment expenditures with lower expected returns than would be required if all investment were externally financed. This is because it is *not* a matter of indifference to the typical corporate management whether internally held funds are employed in the firm's own investment projects or are lent to outsiders. There is a strong preference for the first of these uses. Management's persistent drive to expand its own business volume and to protect its share of the market pushes in this direction. The fact that a substantial portion of gross retained earnings (charges to depreciation) are earmarked for internal investment adds to the effect. And it is augmented still more by the fact that a management decision to retain earnings for reinvestment in the business (instead of distribute them) is much less likely to encounter stockholder opposition than is a decision to lend retained earnings to outsiders.

The result is that the implicit interest rates corporate investors charge themselves when they self-finance projects are substantially lower than those outside lenders demand. The marginal efficiency of a firm's real capital usually must fall well below the external interest rate before it will farm out its internal funds.[6]

[6] Cf. Edgar M. Hoover, "Some Institutional Factors in Business Investment Decisions," *American Economic Review*, vol. 44, no. 2, pp. 201–213, May, 1954.

These significant differences between internal and external corporate financing have a number of important consequences. They have resource-allocation implications; they mean that, in choosing among investment projects, the economy as a whole does not always assign priorities in the sequence that a perfect capital market would dictate. They create a competitive disadvantage for new firms attempting to enter a market. Probably they provide an important part of the explanation for the recent flurry of corporate mergers in the United States. The expansion, especially the diversification, of a corporate unit increases the opportunity for internal investment in particular phases of an enterprise of earnings that accrue elsewhere in the business.

However, the point to emphasize in the present context is that the differential between internal and external interest rates plus the frequent scarcity of external financing make the relative extensiveness of corporate liquidity an important determinant of the volume of investment spending. It is nothing like a sole determinant, mind you; the inducement to form real capital must still be there. But with abundant internal funds, marginal projects are more likely to evoke affirmative decisions.

It is this circumstance which probably explains most of the very buoyant effect upon plant and equipment spending that accelerated tax-amortization concessions seem to have had in the United States in recent years. There were the equally striking converse results in Canada during the Korean War when, as an anti-inflationary measure, the Canadian government placed a moratorium on the amortization of new plant and equipment for tax purposes. Together these experiences suggest that a corporate tax law that allowed Federal stabilization authorities some discretion to vary amortization provisions might, with good forecasting and intelligent use, offer a technique for regularizing business investment that would be indirect and impersonal, would not undertake to control the composition of private investment, and yet would be reasonably effective.

THE TOTAL IMPACT OF FINANCE

Many economists have a habit of going to extremes in their appraisals of the financial influences upon economic behavior. Either they tend to have eyes for little besides the financial factors, or they are inclined to regard all financing problems as something quite subsidiary to the essential determinants of the economy's performance.

Hoover distinguishes among three significant interest rates—the external, the implicit internal rate corporations charge themselves for the use of net retained earnings, and a still lower implicit rate that is charged for self-use of depreciation reserves.

The very intimacy with which financial and nonfinancial factors inter-mesh in a monetized economy makes such biases easy to maintain. The only significant means of increasing the money supply is that of bank credit ex-pansion, and almost none of the latter would ever occur in the absence of decisions to spend. Yet in many cases the new spending could not occur without the new credit, i.e., the new money. The single-track analyst is left free to assert that either the spending decision or the monetary expansion is the prime mover of demand—and he is bound to be wrong in either case. Each is an essential cause, but neither is a sufficient one. An adequate analy-sis must comprehend both.

In its good effect of upending the monetary extremism that preceded it, the original Keynesian theory of finance somewhat overshot the mark, not only by rendering an excessively narrow account of finance's impact upon investment, but by implying that investment is the only demand sector that financial phenomena significantly affect. The availability and cost of funds to other than business borrowers are also important; in addition, the financial markets exert some direct influence upon business expectations.

LIQUID ASSETS AND CONSUMPTION

It is now generally accepted that monetary and credit conditions have some effect upon consumers' spending behavior. The nature of the effect is usually discussed, as it was briefly in Chapter 8, in terms of the reaction of consumption to the size of consumers' stock of liquid assets. The greater are consumers' liquid holdings, the more, other things being equal, consumers can be expected to spend. While this statement is probably correct, unhap-pily it seldom explains the kind of consumer behavior that the working analyst needs to diagnose. For what typically must be explained are *changes* in con-sumption, which would need to be attributed to *changes* in consumer liquidity. And usually the latter are only by-products of the consumer income-spending-saving process itself, not phenomena that are distinguishable from it.

This is a point worth understanding, for those who are fuzzy about it often draw spurious policy inferences about the effect of monetary policy on consumption. They imply that an easy-money policy, by some mysteriously direct mechanism, can build up cash balances relative to income all over the economy and thereby stimulate consumption relative to saving. However, the only way an easy-money policy can get additional money into the economy is by persuading someone to borrow and spend. And the only way anyone but the original borrower can get any of this new money is by receiving it as income. And the latter's liquid assets will rise relative to his income (this being the phenomenon that is supposed to induce him to save less and spend more), only if he spends less than the usual proportion of his income (i.e., if he first saves more and spends relatively less). The most likely event is that changes in the money supply—particularly gradual changes—will, through the spending-income process, induce changes in consumer liquidity that are roughly porportional to the changes in consumer incomes and will, as a consequence, exert no independent effect upon consumption spending.

This does not mean that the so-called liquid asset effect has no significance in practical consumption analysis. First, there are times (World War II was the classic case) when, for special reasons, gains in income lead to abnormally high or low rates of personal liquid saving, which in turn lead subsequently to spurts or slumps in spending. Second, significant changes in the face values of consumers' liquid or semiliquid holdings occasionally do accrue from sources other than liquid saving. For example, major gains or losses in the market value of outstanding shares of common stock may have some impact upon consumption, *if* the stocks are widely enough held by consumers and *if* they are regarded as highly liquid assets. Third, there is the point we noted earlier, the "Pigou effect." A change in the consumer price level may tend to stimulate an opposite change in real consumer spending because of its impact upon the real value of consumers' liquid holdings.

These special circumstances under which changes in consumer liquidity can directly affect consumption are not inconsequential. However, the manner in which monetary conditions affect noninvestment demand can be explained more simply and more persuasively in another way.

THE CREDIT-DEPENDENT AREAS OF DEMAND

In an economy such as that of the United States, tight money means scarce credit—this and nothing more or less. The money market can be tightened only by decreasing the availability of loans relative to the demand for loans. Thus the primary impact of changed monetary policies upon demand extends to, and does not extend much beyond, those types of spending which are significantly dependent upon debt financing.

Purchases can be financed in only three ways: (1) out of current revenues or incomes, (2) out of existing assets that are liquidated or have been accumulated in liquid form, or (3) out of borrowing. Except for its roundabout effects upon other spending and hence upon incomes, the state of the money markets cannot greatly affect the first type of purchases.[7] As just discussed, it is possible for monetary conditions to affect the rate of liquid asset accumulation and hence subsequently to affect purchases made out of liquid holdings. However, it is debt-dependent buying that monetary changes mainly influence.

---

[7] The text sentence bypasses these possibilities: (1) Easier credit, by stimulating the purchase of items financed partly through borrowing but also partly out of income, e.g., automobiles, may reduce the availability of income for other typically income-financed expenditures, e.g., apparel. (2) By stimulating purchases of debt-financed items, e.g., houses, easier credit may also stimulate complementary income-financed purchases, e.g., minor house furnishings.

Original Keynesian theory was correct, of course, in holding that significant portions of investment demand are debt-financed and hence sensitive to monetary changes. But it erred in denying the impact of credit availability and terms upon other subsectors of demand that also are heavily dependent upon debt financing—within the consumption sector, particularly automobiles and other large-ticket durables, and within the government sector, bond-financed projects of state and local governments.[8]

The roster of the demand segments in which debt financing is important is, to a considerable extent, a matter of commercial convention. At present in the United States, for instance, installment-financing arrangements are spreading to new commodity and service areas. If debt-financed buying continues to account for a rising fraction of the purchases of clothing, food (through frozen-food plans), vacation travel, and even college education, we shall have to subject demand prospects in these areas to the same kind of credit-oriented analysis that is presently appropriate for automobiles and appliances.[9] It is only by such a segment-by-segment inspection, and not by a global relation of liquidity either to aggregate consumption or to aggregate investment, that the impact of finance upon spending can be adequately appraised. We shall make such an inspection of the monetary and credit influences upon particular GNP components in Part Four.

THE FINANCIAL MARKETS AND BUSINESS EXPECTATIONS

Up to this point our analysis of the effects of finance upon demand has concerned only the supply side of the loan markets. But the state of the financial markets also can influence the demand for loans—i.e., as far as investment is concerned, it can shift the marginal-efficiency-of-capital schedule —through its effect upon spenders' expectations.

It should be emphasized at once that this reverse-causation effect is usually a marginal consideration. It implies, in effect, that prospective real investors regard the current condition of the financial markets[10] as a significant indicator of future business conditions. At present in the United States this is a doubtful contention. In years past, levels and trends of prices in the

[8] The Federal government also borrows, of course; but except as it is restricted by the congressionally imposed debt limit, it always has access to unlimited credit, if necessary via borrowing from the Federal Reserve. Nor is it realistic to regard Federal deficit financing as ever being inhibited by high interest rates in the same way that state and local borrowing often is. For, given Federal monetary controls, such high interest rates are, in effect, self-imposed.

[9] The reference in this sentence is primarily to installment loans, the accessibility and terms of which are much more directly and sensitively linked to relative easiness of bank credit than is the case with ordinary retail charge accounts.

[10] This purposely vague term is meant to suggest the whole array of markets that traffic in financial claims and are populated by commercial bankers, investment bankers, brokers, mortgage lenders, and other specialists in financial trading.

financial markets, particularly in the stock market, were taken much more seriously as economic outlook indicators than they are now. Their own poor record in this respect plus the increasing availability of more systematic forecasting techniques have weakened the hold of the financial markets upon business expectations.

This may be the place for an explicit word on the stock market. It can almost be said nowadays that the American economy is one thing and the stock market is something else. The latter responds sensitively to changes and expected changes in the economy, in tax laws, in politics, in international affairs, and in nearly everything else including itself. But the economy frequently seems to respond little, if at all, to changes in the market. In 1962, for example, Standard and Poor's index of industrial common stock prices tumbled more than 20 percent in three months without causing a noticeable tremor in business investment spending, let alone in the other segments of final demand. The analysis and prediction of stock price changes is a fascinating, extraordinarily complex, and, for some people, highly utilitarian subject. But it is not, as we conceive it, the subject of this book, except as it bears significantly upon general business developments. Because that bearing is usually so slight, you will not find very much more on the matter in the pages that follow.[11]

With these disclaimers duly recorded, the presumption remains that the trend and tone of the financial markets still do have some conditioning effect upon the expectations of real investors. There was, as will be noted in Chapter 14, a massive effect of this sort in the Great Depression of 1929–1933, and it would be presumptuous to conclude that the economic impact of radical changes in the financial markets could not occasionally still be substantial. In the more routine short run, moreover, it is obvious that changes in Federal Reserve policies have some direct impact upon business' appraisal of the near-term outlook. For such policy changes are recognized both as active conditioners of the outlook and as indicators of what the central banking system's appraisal of underlying business prospects is.

CURRENT ATTITUDES TOWARD FINANCE

It has already been indicated that the majority views of American economists about the role of finance in the economy have been subject to rather modish swings in recent decades. In the twenties, in the heyday of the

---

[11] Lest this paragraph offend or disappoint those readers whose vocational or avocational objective is to become a securities markets analyst, it should be noted that the position taken in the text does not mean that they are on the wrong track in their present study. A rather detailed and comprehensive understanding of general business conditions is a necessary preliminary for the more specialized analysis of securities markets. Our point, simply, is that a detailed and comprehensive understanding of the securities markets is *not* essential to business conditions analysis.

quantity theory of money, it was fashionable to regard the cost and availability of funds as a potent determinant of the price level and of business conditions. By the forties, in the heyday of pure Keynesianism, the fashion had swung to the other extreme, and the independence and stature of the financial variables had been greatly diminished in the average aggregative analysis. The fifties, so far as the fashions are concerned, were a decade of comeback for the financial aspects of business conditions analysis. And the 1960s have witnessed a swing part way back to aggregate-demand-oriented analysis. These swings reflect in significant measure changing political fortunes. A Republican administration is more likely to listen to, and thus give prominence to, the ideas of economists who emphasize the importance of financial variables and the usefulness of monetary policy that operates (presumably) impersonally via the banking system. A Democratic administration, on the other hand, may be more willing to give effect to economic ideas that rely on the use of fiscal policy (including, at times, deficits in the government budget) to influence aggregate demand. But the swings also reflect changing economic events and institutions and the efforts of economists to incorporate these changes into their theoretical constructs. One such development—an important one—is the dramatic growth in recent decades of the nonbank intermediaries.

THE NONBANK INTERMEDIARIES

One preoccupying topic in the recent literature on finance has been the role that financial intermediaries other than commercial banks play in the United States money and credit system. The variety and, at least in absolute terms, the scope of such intermediaries as life insurance companies, pension, health, and welfare funds, investment funds, savings and loan associations, credit unions, mortgage bankers, and personal finance companies have grown remarkably during the past two or three decades. A very large part of all household liquid saving now flows into these institutions, and they do most of the private lending in the economy. Yet most of the briefer textbook expositions of the influence of money and credit treat the nonbank intermediaries elliptically—as, indeed, we have in this chapter. We have emphasized that the money supply can be altered only through expansions and contractions of commercial bank credit; have tacitly recognized the fact that many business and other borrowers, however, borrow from institutions other than commercial banks; and therefore have left the implication that changes in the availability and cost of bank credit tend somehow to spread their effects through the loan markets generally. At the same time, there has been mention of the substantial imperfections in our financial markets that deny certain classes of borrowers access to certain types of lenders and make some interest rates stickier than others.

The net impression that the chapter creates is of a complex of lending institutions whose loan policies are heavily but not exclusively influenced by the commercial banking system. They operate in a complex of loan markets among which funds flow extensively but not always freely, and with interest rates significantly but not perfectly articulated with bank rates. This, we believe, is a substantially accurate picture, but it leaves many details undeveloped. Much remains to be filled in about the interconnections between the banks and the other intermediaries, and this ellipsis is not peculiar to the present exposition.

Financial economists' recent spurt of interest in the nonbank intermediaries has involved more than a generalized impulse to research a little-investigated subject. Debate has been sharply drawn over whether the upsurge of the nonbank intermediaries in the United States since the late 1930s has significantly weakened the Federal Reserve's control over money and credit conditions. Some writers—particularly the team of Edward Shaw and James Gurley in a series of articles published from 1955 to 1957 followed by their monumental book in 1960[12]—strongly affirm this position. The essence of their view is that, although the nonbank intermediaries cannot technically expand the money supply, they can largely enervate the effect of a tightening of Federal Reserve monetary policy by speeding up the conversion of their existing assets, especially government securities, into new loans and hence accelerating the velocity of monetary circulation. The Shaw-Gurley thesis has been sharply disputed, notably by Ross M. Robertson, writing in the *Monthly Review* of the Federal Reserve Bank of St. Louis.[13] Robertson's key counterclaim is that, since a tight-money policy certainly is effective in creating a general upward pressure on interest rates and therefore in depressing prices of the long-term securities that nonbank intermediaries typically hold, it restrains the nonbank intermediaries from lending by "locking" them in their existing securities portfolios. The intermediaries will not, he argues, ordinarily accept the capital losses entailed in converting existing assets into new loans; and because of the essentially long-term character of their assets they are especially sensitive to changes in the long rate of interest.

The key point at issue in this exchange is a behavioral one that extends

---

[12] J. G. Gurley and E. S. Shaw, "Financial Aspects of Economic Development," *American Economic Review*, vol. 45, no. 4, pp. 515–538, September, 1955; "Financial Intermediaries and the Saving-Investment Process," *Journal of Finance*, vol. 11, no. 2, pp. 257–276, May, 1956; "The Growth of Debt and Money in the United States, 1800–1950: A Suggested Interpretation," *Review of Economics and Statistics*, vol. 39, no. 3, pp. 250–262, August, 1957; and *Money in a Theory of Finance*, The Brookings Institution, Washington, D.C., 1960.

[13] Ross M. Robertson, "The Commercial Banking System and Competing Nonmonetary Intermediaries," *Monthly Review*, Federal Reserve Bank of St. Louis, vol. 39, no. 5, May, 1957.

See also J. M. Culbertson, "Intermediaries and Monetary Theory: A Criticism of the Gurley-Shaw Theory," *American Economic Review*, vol. 48, no. 1, pp. 119–131, March, 1958; and a reply by Gurley and Shaw in the same issue, pp. 132–138.

far beyond the scope of this book. Before leaving the matter, however, we should record three observations. First, the often-repeated contention that the activities of the intermediaries can never be inflationary because they lend only savings is plainly specious. This should be obvious within the analytical framework established in preceding chapters. If the economy faces a significantly inelastic aggregate-supply path, any loan that facilitates additional spending is inflationary regardless of the pedigree of the funds loaned. The activation of inactive cash balances can have exactly the same effect as the activation of new (bank-credit-created) cash balances. Second, the thesis that in times of high interest rates the operations of nonbank intermediaries can accelerate monetary velocity makes good sense in at least one case: individuals may be persuaded to transfer their superfluous checking account balances, which exceed their needs for transactions purposes, to savings and loan associations, for example, which are pursuing more liberal lending policies than the banks. Or the same effect can be achieved by shifts within commercial banks themselves, thanks to the development since the early 1960s of a new financial instrument, the negotiable certificate of deposit (CD).[14] Business firms in particular are able to economize on their checking account balances, and thus increase velocity, by switching their funds into and out of negotiable CDs as their needs fluctuate.[15] Third, the rise of nonbank intermediaries and the development of a variety of highly liquid short-term instruments, such as negotiable CDs, may mark a transition in American financial habits whereunder, eventually, Americans will choose to hold only their absolute minimum transactions cash in the form of actual (demand deposit) money and will hold a portion of their transactions cash and all their speculative and precautionary cash in the near-moneys offered by some of the other intermediaries. To the extent that the latter becomes the case, the assumption of an identity between the demand for money and the demand for liquidity in the Keynesian model ceases to be valid. Liquidity preference can be satisfied by shifting funds from long-term instruments, not to money, but to these highly liquid near-moneys on which the risk of capital loss is negligible. The demand for *money* (as distinct from liquidity) therefore ceases to be significantly interest-elastic with respect to interest rates. Control of the central bank over the rate of interest is thus weakened. Indeed, Prof. Lawrence S. Ritter argues that under certain circumstances the demand for money might

[14] A certificate of deposit is a commercial bank time deposit on which interest is paid if the deposit is not withdrawn prior to the maturity of the certificate, usually one year. If the terms of the certificate permit it to be sold to third parties, it is a negotiable CD. Although CDs are not new, their use did not become widespread until the Federal Reserve's Regulation Q was amended on Jan. 1, 1962, raising the rate of interest that member banks were permitted to pay on savings deposits, especially on those with a maturity of one year or longer.

[15] The same effect can be achieved with nonnegotiable CDs, though less conveniently and often only after a considerable lag.

become completely inelastic, and conceivably even perversely elastic; that is, an increase in the demand for money could lead to a *decline* in interest rates.[16]

This, however, is an unlikely event. The demand for money and the demand for liquidity are not yet, at least, becoming disassociated rapidly. For one thing, market rates of interest typically do reflect the difference between highly liquid near-moneys and long-term instruments. Shifting to near-moneys usually involves some loss of return. Further, the recent historical record demonstrates that, in spite of the prevalence of near-moneys, interest rates are still quite sensitive to central bank actions affecting member bank reserves. Perhaps as far as we should go in this book is to suggest that the issue is an open one and refer the reader to the continuing dialogues in the current professional journals.

[16] See Lawrence S. Ritter, "The Role of Money in Keynesian Theory," New York University School of Business Reprint Series no. 13, New York, n.d. (presumably 1965).

12

THE ROLE OF
GOVERNMENT

Any realistic business outlook analyst will, at a very early stage in his analysis, attempt to assess the impact of government on economic activity during the period he is studying. From the earliest days of this Republic, government has played an important economic role. It has served as maintainer of civil order, enforcer of contracts, and proprietor of the currency. It has facilitated internal trade; regulated, protected, subsidized, advised, and promoted particular industries and producer groups; collected taxes; acted as employer, customer, and enterpriser; and supplied the private economy with transport and communication facilities and with essential social services. Effective government was a prerequisite for American economic development, and government always has been an influential conditioner of that development.

Moreover, events of the past generation have broadened and deepened government's economic role in the United States. For one thing, the sheer magnitude of governmental economic operations has grown enormously. Government activities now exert a powerful, overt, often scale-tipping impact upon the level of economic activity in the short as well as the long run—

exert it willy-nilly, whether or not governments consciously pursue stabilizing and growth-stimulating policies. In addition, as we shall emphasize in Part Three, the national government has become politically responsible for promoting stability and growth. Because government has assumed this responsibility, its economic behavior is distinctly different from that of any other sector of the economy. Government may, and often does, for example, take actions that are directly counter to its own economic interests, if such actions are in the *total* public interest. This is a responsibility that can be assumed only by government; government is the only sector of the economy that represents, and is responsible to, *all* citizens of the state or nation.

Thus it now is essential for the business conditions analyst to be able to identify the principal effects that the extant congressional, executive, and central bank policies exert—or that possible changes in those policies would exert—upon the level of economic activity. Some of those effects already have been touched upon in earlier chapters, but it will be useful to knit all the more important ones into a single summary statement. That, and only that, we shall try to do here.

THE OUTLOOK ANALYST'S NEED (HERE UNREQUITED) FOR POLITICAL INSIGHTS

It is important to make clear the restricted scope of the present chapter. The business outlook analyst obviously needs to comprehend the stability and growth consequences of public policies. But if he would be a self-sufficient economic forecaster, he also needs something else: the ability to forecast crucial changes in government policies. And for competence of the latter sort there is no substitute for the kind of full-blown, penetrating study of the government decision-making process that this book cannot begin to supply.

One intriguing way around this conclusion appeals to some politically illiterate economists. They reason that twenty or thirty years ago it did indeed take a political analyst to figure out what economic policies the government was going to undertake. But, they argue, now that government pursues purposeful stabilization and growth objectives and knows pretty well how to achieve them, the causes of economic policy changes have become mainly endogenous to the economic system itself. Public economic policy has become a virtual feedback mechanism, which, detecting business conditions that are deviating from those desired, responds with offsets calculated to counteract the deviations. Thus nowadays, the argument runs, the economic forecaster can rely upon nothing but economic know-how for the political forecasting he needs to do.

As a description of a *direction* in which our politicoeconomic institutions are moving, there is something to be said for this view. But it constitutes a very unreliable premise for concrete business forecasting. In part this is because governments often are not as decisive, alert, and efficient in adjusting their stabilization and growth policies as the feedback thesis implies. But the main trouble with the thesis is that it illuminates the public-policy arena only with the half-light of the business conditions analyst's own specialty. That specialty focuses upon only two social objectives—stability and growth. These, to be sure, *have* become vital goals of contemporary national governments. But governments also have other equally or more important and perhaps conflicting objectives to pursue. Sometimes it is the essence of responsible policy making to advance programs that, although they are in the interests of national security or some other public purpose, make the nation's attainment of stable growth more, not less, difficult.

Consequently, while any would-be diviner of public-policy changes may find it useful to know what the sound course for a single-track stabilization policy would be, he will be in no position to forecast policy changes until he has steeped himself in the identity of, and the interrelationships among, government's entire collection of major objectives and has carefully studied the whole public decision-making and administering process. To repeat, these latter subjects lie beyond the scope of this work. To the business outlook analyst who is unable or unwilling to fortify himself with the knowledge essential to forecasting the results of the political decision-making process, we can only suggest that he *assume* the relevant public-policy actions, and make his assumptions explicit!

GOVERNMENT'S IMPACT UPON AGGREGATE DEMAND

The effects of government programs on the level of economic activity can be classified in many ways. For our purposes, a classification that derives directly from the aggregative economic model we have been building should be the most convenient. Moreover, the use of such a breakdown will further a secondary function that this chapter can serve because of the extraordinary pervasiveness of government's economic impact: it can afford a comprehensive review of the whole aggregative economic model that we have constructed so far. Accordingly, we shall consider first, and at greatest length, government's various influences upon aggregate demand. Then we shall turn briefly to government's influences upon the other major determinants of aggregative economic behavior—namely, the aggregate-supply path, the size of the labor force and working hours, and productive capacity per man-hour.

The most natural classification of government's demand effects is the familiar GNP breakdown. We shall consider, first, the direct contributions of government to final demand—i.e., government purchases of goods and services—second, its effects upon personal consumption spending, third, the effects upon net exports, and fourth, those upon domestic investment expenditures. Finally, as a supplement to this basic classification of government's demand effects, a few pages will be added under the general heading of surpluses, deficits, and the public debt.

GOVERNMENT PURCHASES OF GOODS AND SERVICES

The most direct, and often the most important, effect that government exerts upon final demand is supplied by its own contributions to final demand. In proper GNP style, we should count as final demand only those government expenditures which are classified as purchases of goods and services. The remainder, which are generally of the transfer-payment type, will be treated as altering the shares of disposable income that private purchasing groups receive, and thus as affecting private buying.

Important as government purchases of goods and services are quantitatively, there is nothing analytically that really needs to be said on the subject, except to emphasize their highly autonomous character. This autonomy has both substantive and procedural origins. With respect to the latter, the procedures by which government expenditures are budgeted, authorized, and made (to be described in more detail in Chapter 18) are cumbersome and time-consuming. This is perhaps even more true of state governments than of the Federal government, since many states have only biennial legislative sessions. And even where there are annual legislative sessions, lasting long enough to make feasible occasional supplemental appropriations, as in the case of the Federal government, the entire process is so formal and deliberative that changing economic events seldom significantly affect actual expenditures within the next six months to a year. This attribute of government spending is in contrast, of course, to the behavior of both business investment spending and consumer spending, which, as we have seen, are usually quite responsive to income and other economic changes.

But government purchases are independent and autonomous for a more fundamental reason. It is government's responsibility, as determined by the political process, to meet certain needs of its citizens—for national defense, education, police and fire protection, streets and highways, hospitalization and public health, general government, and many others. In the main, these needs are unaffected by short-run fluctuations in national income, interest rates, profit expectations, or psychological reactions to the latest automobile models. This is not to say that the magnitude of these needs does not change; national defense expenditures can fluctuate widely depending upon international events; highway expenditures will reflect our changing assessment of the urgency of a fast and safe interstate highway network. But changes in these needs and in the priority we attach to them reflect, not current economic conditions, but deep-seated, noneconomic or quasi-economic developments, such as population growth, changing technology, changing cultural and political attitudes, and political, social, and economic developments in other countries.

Further, if needs and income do not match, government—in contrast to persons and business firms—has the option of changing, by mandate, its income.[1] Or, if it determines not to change tax rates, it has the further option of borrowing. This option is also available to persons, but not in a degree comparable to government, the Federal government in particular. The Federal government not only has the power to tax and to create money; it can manage its borrowing and debt management affairs in a different time perspective than can households and even, under some circumstances, business firms. The mortal family needs to manage its financial affairs so that its debts, undertaken early in the family's life, will be paid off within a few decades. Government, on the other hand, is presumably perpetual. It is not compelled by a finite existence to amortize its debt in any given time period. In this respect, government resembles large, presumably perpetual business firms, who enjoy a freedom to borrow and carry debt not available to real persons.

A word of qualification is in order. Certain types of government expenditures are at times significantly affected by short-run economic events. State and local governments may temporarily defer debt-financed public works projects, such as school buildings, if interest rates are high. Government-owned business enterprises, such as TVA or a municipal water company, will be influenced—in greater or lesser degree depending on the statutory purposes of the enterprise—in their expansion programs by changing profit expectations. And state and local governments, especially those which have exhausted their legal borrowing authority, may be constrained to curtail expenditures by a decline in economic activity and hence in tax revenues. But these are exceptions. In the main, and especially in the short run, governments are relatively immune to the purely economic determinants that so largely influence private spending.

GOVERNMENT'S INFLUENCE UPON PERSONAL CONSUMPTION

The effects of government programs on consumption can be conveniently grouped under three main headings: (1) effects government has as an instigator of the multiplier effect, (2) effects of government's impact upon the relation of disposable personal income to gross national income, and (3) effects flowing from the governmental impact upon the relation of consumption to disposable personal income.

---

[1] Strictly speaking, government mandates, not its income, i.e., tax revenues, but tax rates. The revenues to be derived from any change in rates, however, can usually be closely estimated.

Consumer Response to Changes in Government Purchases of Goods and Services: The Multiplier

To the extent that consumers have a marginal propensity to consume in excess of zero, changes in government purchases of goods and services, of course, induce changes in consumer spending. The response of consumption to changes in government spending may be expected to differ from the response to any other change in spending only as there is a difference in the proportion of total expenditure that becomes disposable personal income, or only as the marginal propensities to consume (MPCs) of the original recipients of government outlays differ from the MPCs of those who first receive other outlays. There is no reason to believe that government expenditures as a class differ significantly from aggregate private expenditures in these respects. But significant differences may exist among particular types of government expenditures. For instance, a billion dollars spent on a work-relief program, mainly in the form of wage payments to low-income workers, should induce more consumption spending than a billion dollars spent for space vehicles or for the purchase of electric power from private or municipal power companies.

In order not to clutter up our subsequent discussion with repetitive references to the multiplier, it may be well to note, once and for all, that all government-caused changes in private spending also must be expected to exert multiplier effects of a magnitude determined by the shape and character of the relevant consumption function.

The Impact on the Relation of Disposable Personal Income to Gross National Income

Among the most powerful influences that government brings to bear upon personal consumption (and, as we shall see, also upon private investment) are those which impinge upon the receipts side of the Nation's Economic Budget, i.e., on the *distribution* of income. Once the initial effect on the receipts side of the Nation's Economic Budget has registered, however, it may quickly lead to a change in *total* spending and in total income because of the differing dispositions to spend income that the various purchasing groups have.

As far as consumption is concerned, the biggest income-distribution question concerns the share of gross national income that is available for consumer expenditures. Government affects the relationship of DPI to GNI through two general means: (1) by the taxes it collects from individuals and the transfer payments it makes to them, and (2) by the influences it exerts upon the structure of factor and commodity prices in the private market.

Personal Taxes and Transfers. The problem here is the economic effects of changes in the personal taxes and other payments that government collects from individuals, and in the transfer payments it makes to them.[2] If other variables in the economy remain unchanged, a rise in government's net receipts from persons will dampen consumption spending. Of course, other things may not remain unchanged. The effect of a change in personal taxes or in government transfer payments may be offset by an opposite shift in the propensity to consume. However, it is unlikely that such offsets would be the joint effects of the same measures that changed the government's share of total income.

Thus a gain in government's income share at the expense of consumers is likely to retard total spending unless its effect is offset by an advance in public spending. Such parallel increases in public revenues and public expenditures are not at all uncommon. But in the case of most national governments and specifically of the United States government, as we noted earlier, there is not any necessary short-run linkage between the trend in revenues and the trend in government expenditures. Federal government spending, in other words, is not a function of Federal government income to anything like the extent that personal consumption is a function of consumer income.

When the economist evaluates the consequences of a change in the Federal tax take, he therefore has no a priori reason for expecting counterbalancing changes in Federal expenditures. As a matter of fact, in logic, his expectation might be the opposite. In practice, as the classic 1963–1964 tax cut debate made clear, political considerations may necessitate changes in government expenditures that offset the effects of changes in taxes. But insofar as governmental policies are designed to compensate for fluctuations in private spending, one would expect to find the anti-inflationary impact of a decrease in the tax take not neutralized by a decrease in Federal spending.

The same view, however, should not be extended to state and local governments in this country. The latter do not have anything like the Federal government's credit resources. Even if they have the constitutional abilities to borrow, they must compete for private loans with corporate and other private securities. Moreover, the capacity of their tax systems is, in the aggregate, much less flexible than that of the Federal government. The fact

---

[2] For the kind of demand-effects analysis we are pursuing here, the term "transfers" is rather misleading. (For present purposes, we shall extend it to all outlays for which the government does not receive currently produced goods and services, thereby including such transferlike payments as interest on the public debt as well as those payments, like social security benefits, which national income accountants call transfer payments.) The term suggests that transfers are simply income that government takes away from one group in the economy and gives to another, and so they are, if we think of government as a kind of final, last-word overseer of the disposition of total national income. But transfers are not, as the term may appear to suggest, necessarily income that is *taxed* away from one group and handed out to another. Unless legislation specifies the contrary, transfer payments, like other public expenditures, may be either tax-financed or debt-financed. Thus they may rise or fall independently of changes in revenues.

that financing ability effectively limits state and local spending is particularly evident in the present era, when needs for schools, streets, highways, water and sewage systems, educational, health, and recreational services, and the like are pressing insistently upon the financial resources of many states and municipalities. Under these circumstances, it is very likely that a rise in state and local revenue will lead to, and will be a necessary condition for, a rise in state and local spending at least as large as the private spending that may be deterred by the higher taxes. But, to repeat, the same assumption is improper in the case of the Federal government.

The most obvious measures of public policy by which the ratio of governmental net receipts to gross national income can be altered are changes in tax rates and in transfer payments. Such changes can be the result of explicit, discretionary government decisions. In addition, however, there can be changes in the shares of both gross revenues and of transfers, which occur *automatically* under existing programs, as existing tax and transfer programs respond to changes in current business conditions. Such arrangements are among those which now go under the name of "built-in stabilizers." One example is the interaction of progressive income tax rates with rising incomes. A further example is the tendency of certain transfer payments—notably unemployment compensation and welfare payments—to rise as incomes fall.

Changes in taxes and transfers have not only direct effects, but also indirect effects. An increase in defense expenditures, for example, adds to government expenditures but also, because the expenditures generate private incomes, adds to government tax revenues. A $10 billion tax cut—meaning a reduction in tax rates that, at levels of incomes that would prevail in the absence of the tax cut, would cause a $10 billion loss in tax revenues—would probably result in an actual revenue loss of less than $10 billion; the spending of private income released by the tax cut would generate income, which in turn is subject to taxation. In the lingo of government economists, there is a feedback to Treasury revenues from a tax cut that partially offsets the direct revenue loss of the tax cut. Or—to take still another example—a government program to raise employment in a given industry or area that has been suffering from unemployment could cause a significant decline in transfer payments and thereby provide an additional stimulus to governmental net receipts. Any careful analysis of the impact of government policy upon the DPI/GNP relationship must canvass all these more roundabout effects as well as the direct impacts of changes in the laws governing personal taxes and transfers.

The Influences on Price-Wage-Profit Relationships. In addition to the impact of its tax and transfer programs, government affects the DPI/GNI ratio through its influences on the before-tax distribution of income between businesses and individuals. This distribution is determined by the relationships among factor and product prices; for the most part it depends upon wage-price-profit relationships. For example, either an increase in money wages relative to money profits or a decrease in consumer prices relative to money wages will tend to raise individuals' share of private income.

Except in emergency periods, government policies play a distinctly subordinate role to private decision making in this area. However, a great many government measures affect the interrelationships among factor and product prices one way or another. Among them are antitrust policies that influence the character of market organization and of competitive practice (and therefore influence the flexibility of prices and profit margins); regulation of prices, costs, and/or profits in such regulated industries as public utilities; more general controls over prices and wages in periods of defense emergency; regulation of maximum working hours (beyond which premium wages must be paid) and minimum wage rates; the support, through such techniques as farm price supports and tariffs, of the market prices of certain commodities at levels above those they would otherwise seek; regulation of certain product and factor prices through the stipulations of government contracts; and various suasive (e.g., presidential) influences over price and wage making. Another government influence upon the split of gross private income between businesses and individuals is supplied by tax laws and regulations governing the amount of revenue businesses can charge to depreciation; for gross income allocated in this fashion is not available for distribution as earnings to the factors of production.

This whole matter of cost-price-profit relationships is an important and fascinating subject for the business conditions analyst. We shall return to it in this and succeeding chapters, especially in Chapter 26.

It is neither very easy nor very helpful to generalize about what the total spending effects of shifts of income between business and household income may be. This follows from our discussions of consumption determination in Chapters 7 and 8 and of investment determination in Chapters 9 to 11. The effect will depend upon whether consumption is more or less responsive to disposable personal income than investment is dependent upon internal business financing. This will vary from period to period and will turn heavily upon which groups of consumers and investors are mainly involved. About all that we presently are in a position to say is that, when the economy is operating at a level appreciably below its full-employment capacity, the response of consumption to an increment in DPI is a more reliable phenomenon than is the response of investment to increased retained earnings. This issue will be explored further in subsequent chapters.

The Impact upon the Relation of Consumption to Disposable Personal Income

Finally, among government's effects on consumption expenditures, there are those which are exerted upon the height and shape of the consumption function—construing the latter term as the relationship of consumption to disposable personal income. The only influence of this sort that is sufficiently decisive and swift to be chosen as an intentional instrument of short-run stabilization policy is that provided by government controls over consumer credit. Consumer borrowing, like other private borrowing, is affected by the general credit controls operated by the central banking system. These, discussed in the preceding chapter, we shall return to briefly here. In addition, as noted in Chapter 10, the Federal Reserve Board from time to time has possessed the authority to regulate the terms of installment credit and by this means has exerted effective control over the volume of automobile and other big-ticket consumer-durables purchases.

Also, government policies and activities bring somewhat more subtle but, in the long run, perhaps equally important pressures to bear on the height and shape of the consumption function. In the first place, government tax and transfer programs can have a substantial impact upon the distribution of spendable incomes among individuals, with the significant but rather elusive spending consequences that were considered in Chapter 8. In the second place, it is generally assumed that social security and other public programs that diminish the economic hazards of old age, unemployment, widowhood, accidents, illness, and physical disability dampen some of the motives for individual saving and thereby tend to nudge the consumption function upward.[3] In the third place, government may influence consumers' disposition to spend through the effects that its overall economic activities have upon the course of consumer prices and certainly through its influence upon consumer expectations of price changes, shortages, and prosperity or depression.

GOVERNMENT'S INFLUENCE UPON NET EXPORTS

Since a nation's international trade balance is the resultant of a whole web of forces active both inside and outside the country, almost everything that government does to or for the domestic economy may be said to register some effect upon net exports. There are also, however, a number of public policies that have a more specialized bearing on the flow of international exchange. Among these are tariffs, quotas, and other regulations of imports; foreign assistance programs that stimulate production and income in other countries and hence induce demand for our own economy's exports; and whatever encouragements and protection our national government provides for the export of private capital.

[3] It is worth noting, however, that in the United States the great surge in purchases of private life insurance and annuities came *after* the introduction of social insurance. The argument is sometimes advanced that enactment of the social security program, by making people more conscious of the need for providing for dependents and for old age, led them to seek a more adequate protection program than that afforded by the rather meager benefits of Old-Age and Survivors Disability Insurance (OASDI). It is impossible to test this thesis, of course, because no one knows what would have happened to purchases of private insurance if OASDI had not been enacted.

In terms of the United States–oriented aggregate-demand model we are trying here to build, this is about all the attention that net exports quantitatively deserve; and this, for the time being, is all that we shall give. If net exports were allowed to stand unamended, however, such a truncated treatment of international economic developments not only would make the model inapplicable to other economies with relative trade balances typically larger than in the United States; it would outrageously underrate the full importance of world markets and international economic affairs for present and future United States business conditions. Accordingly, we shall have more to say in a later chapter in which we discuss the forecasting of net exports.

GOVERNMENT'S IMPACT UPON THE DESIRE TO INVEST AND INTERNAL FINANCING

The theory of government's influence upon the rate of investment must be virtually as complex as the overall theory of investment determination itself. It seems best to break the problem down via approximately the same dichotomy as that employed in Chapters 9 and 10. There we distinguished between, on the one hand, all those factors which determine the demand for investment financing and, on the other hand, those which influence the financing of investment demand. Here it will be useful to draw the line a little differently. Many government programs affect both the desire to invest and investors' resources for internal financing, and it often is impossible to separate the one effect from the other. Thus it will be well to treat these subjects concurrently and then, in the next section, to consider policies that affect the external financing available to investors, as well as to other credit-dependent buyers.

Investors' Responses to Changes in Government Purchases of Goods and Services

As the first of government's investment effects, one can note the operation of that intellectual twin of the multiplier, the acceleration principle: certain changes in private investment expenditures are more or less predictably and mechanically induced by changes in government purchase programs.

When government steps up the purchase of armaments, for example, some of its orders typically go to firms that, at the time of the contracts, do not have enough of the particular capacities required for filling the contracts satisfactorily. The fact that firms do find themselves in this posture is evidence that the situation fulfills one of the conditions for the operation of the cyclical accelerator, namely, that the increase in demand has not been sufficiently anticipated so that new capacity already is coming on the line to meet it. And the very fact that such firms seek and accept the contracts is proof that the second condition also is fulfilled, namely, that entrepreneurs decide that the increase in orders is large enough and the time available for filling them is long enough to make investment in the necessary capacity worthwhile. Under such circumstances, government contractors tool up for the jobs they have undertaken to do.[4]

Just as in the case of the multiplier, such accelerator reactions magnify the total impact that changes in government spending exert upon final demand. An additional and distinguishable point is that the timing of the impact on total demand, as reflected in the national income accounts, is affected by the fact of, and behavior of, business inventories. Governments typically do most of their paying for purchases at times of delivery, and the transactions are so recorded in the national accounts. However, much of a government's total commodity purchases from business are goods and structures made to order. In the process of filling such government orders businesses build inventories, first of purchased materials, then of goods in process, and finally of finished goods—until the latter are delivered and the transaction is recorded as a government purchase. When such inventory building occurs, this is what first registers government's direct (noninduced) impact on final demand. Subsequently, when finished goods are delivered to government and the transaction is recorded as a government purchase, the increase in the "government purchases of goods and services" category of GNP tends to be partially offset by a reduction in business investment in inventories.[5]

The Impact upon Business Earnings and Their Distribution

As we saw in Chapter 9, almost any stimulant to the desire to invest may be construed as exerting its effect upon investment demand through its influence on profit expectations. However, we shall confine our attention for the moment to the investment effects of government programs that impinge directly upon only the fraction of their gross receipts that entrepreneurs currently retain, or in the future expect to retain, for their own disposition.

Here, as in the comparable portion of our discussion of government's consumption effects, we are considering policies affecting the split of gross

---

[4] It is interesting to note, however, that during World War II, extensive industrial installations were built at government expense (and government-owned), largely because the relevant business firms were not confident that demand for the output of the facilities would persist for a long enough time to amortize the cost of the facility. This was true, not only of armament industries per se, but of industries producing basic industrial materials, notably steel and aluminum. Again, during the Korean War, government financing of some war-related types of facilities was required. Since 1953, however, government financing and ownership has been necessary only for certain highly specialized facilities.

[5] There is a reduction, that is to say, in the particular business inventories that have been built up to fill the particular government orders under discussion. Other changes in inventory, for example, other accumulations in response to other subsequent government orders, may, of course, offset and camouflage this one aspect of inventory developments.

income on the receipts side of the Nation's Economic Budget. And here, as there, the most obvious and usually the most important instruments of such policy are tax laws—particularly, in the case of American business, corporate income tax rates and those provisions of the corporate tax law determining the rate at which business may allocate revenue to the depreciation of its existing fixed capital. In addition, governments pay direct subsidies to selected industries and firms; these are roughly analogous to transfer payments to consumers. Finally, there are the various influences—by means of price, wage, promotion of competition, and other market policies—that governments exert upon private factor and market prices. In this area, as already was noted with respect to the consumption effects, government policies ordinarily are not dominant, but they are extensive and important.

In private investment decisions, the consequences of all these tax, subsidy, price and wage, and other public distributional policies are ambivalent. They not only affect the magnitude of current business earnings and hence the amount of internally financed spending that business investors can undertake if they want to, but they also affect profit expectations and thereby alter the incentive for investment. As we saw in Chapter 9, this incentive aspect of governmental distribution policies is not easy to pin down. The investment tax credit enacted in 1962, and the administrative revision in the depreciation provisions of the internal revenue code in the same year, were based on the explicit assumption that increasing business' disposable income relative to the government and consumer shares would stimulate aggregate investment. The extent to which this result was actually achieved, however, is difficult to prove.

But it is plain that favored treatment to particular industries, in the form of tax concessions, subsidies, and the like, does stimulate the inducement to invest in the favored industries. Whether such concessions also raise aggregate investment depends upon whether they deter offsetting amounts of spending elsewhere. This they might do if the total present supply of investable funds were closely limited, or if favored treatment to a particular industry had the main effect of permitting it to take business away from another industry producing a comparable product (e.g., oil versus coal), or if it is reasoned that such concessions must be made up for, or matched, by extra taxes on unfavored groups. If none of these restraints operates, the extension of special concessions to favored industries would, at any given time, seem to add to the aggregate inducement to invest. But if the restraints do apply, the granting of such favors would tend to worsen other investment opportunities, and aggregate investment would rise correspondingly less or not at all.

It would appear, on the basis of Chapter 10, that the internal financing side of the investment effects that governments exert through their distributional policies is somewhat clearer. Here, partly because of the compartmentalization of the loan market and partly because of the differential between the internal and the external interest rates, it seems plain that government action resulting in higher gross retained earnings will tend to yield higher business investment, and that this is true in the aggregate as well as the favored industry case. But this does not justify the conclusion that the higher gross retained earnings necessarily mean higher aggregate demand. For the allocation of an increment in gross retained earnings away from disposable personal income or away from the revenues of state and local governments may force a curtailment of spending in those sectors that exceeds the resulting increase in business spending.

Other Influences upon the Inducement to Invest

In addition to their effects upon the distribution of private income, governments also profoundly influence the volume, location, and character of private fixed investment by the manner in which they provide, or fail to provide, the basic underpinnings of public facilities and services—highways, streets, schools, health facilities, water, sewage disposal, police and fire protection, and, in many cases, power and local transport—that are essential complements to private fixed capital in the operation of any going business concern. That an adequate base of such "social capital" is a requisite for vigorous private investment, and hence for healthy productivity gains, is certainly an economic fact that one can prove without turning to the experience of underdeveloped countries. It is a fact to which the chambers of commerce of many American communities will ruefully attest. Most business executives recognize that the level of local tax rates is an inadequate criterion for determining new plant location; rather, what counts is the balance between local tax rates and public facilities provided. In addition, public investment may not only supply complementary facilities for private plant and equipment; it may, for example, by providing large quantities of low-cost power, directly affect business cost prospects and, thereby, sales and profit expectations.

Further, as discussed later in the chapter under the heading of productivity effects, government—both now and historically—has had a very considerable influence on the course of technological innovation in the United States. In recent years, over two-thirds of the nation's scientific research and development budget has been provided by government. Through its immigration policies the United States government has influenced the pace of population growth. And during the nineteenth century, of course, it presided over the nation's territorial acquisitions. In all these respects it has strongly influenced the generation of new investment opportunities. Finally, and in short-run terms, government actions and policies—a decision to intervene in Vietnam, the decision of a President to run for reelection, the business conditions forecast signaled by a Federal Reserve decision to raise the rediscount rate—are the most dramatic conditioners of the general climate of business expectations in which particular firms work out and revise their specific investment programs.

GOVERNMENT'S IMPACT UPON THE VOLUME AND THE COST OF PRIVATE BORROWING

Some types of private spending typically are partly or wholly financed by borrowing (or sometimes by the drawing down of private liquid balances) rather than out of current incomes. As we saw in the preceding chapter, such credit-dependent spending is particularly characteristic of private investors. It accounts for much inventory investment, for a majority of residential construction, and for a large part of plant and equipment spending. Even where internal finance is available to those contemplating investment expenditures, the opportunity cost of funds influences decisions of whether or not to spend.

Moreover, as we also saw in the preceding chapter, the influence of the factors that determine the availability and cost of credit extends beyond the investment sector to other credit-dependent areas of demand, notably to consumer durables and state and local government spending. Government policies, of course, are among the most potent and adjustable of these factors. It remains only to list the principal types of such policies, elaborating a bit on those which have not been considered explicitly already.

The Central Bank's General Credit Controls

The role played by the national government's basic instruments of monetary policy—the so-called general credit controls that in the United States are operated by the Federal Reserve System and take the form of open-market operations, changes in the Federal Reserve bank rediscount rate, and adjustment in member-bank reserve requirements—has already been explicitly considered. It should not require reiteration to establish the importance of these policies.

The Management of the Public Debt

When the Federal Reserve Open Market Committee wants to stimulate business activity, it buys government bonds, thereby retiring certificates of the government's indebtedness from private hands and putting cash in their place—cash which, when it is deposited in commercial banks, builds up the latter's reserves and, other things being equal, paves the way for an expansion in private debt. Conversely, when the Open Market Committee wants to dampen private spending, it sells government securities with the opposite effect. These are very familiar facts; yet many people who know them perfectly well fail to transfer their implications to the national government's overall public debt operations—operations that in the United States are conducted by the Treasury Department.

The fact is that the impact upon private finance when a government security is sold to or bought from a private party is exactly the same whether that security is sold or bought by the Treasury or by the New York Federal Reserve Bank under instructions from the Open Market Committee. The only difference is that the Treasury deals in a greater variety and a far greater volume of government securities, for it is the original seller and final buyer of all the Federal government's general obligations, from shortest to longest term. This function keeps it heavily involved in the securities market, not only when the total size of the public debt is being expanded or contracted, but when particular maturing issues of the existing debt have to be refunded, i.e., paid off with the proceeds of a new loan floated for the purpose.

The Treasury's problem of debt management concerns the forms in which government's indebtedness should be held. The Treasury has to decide, among other things, the duration of specific issues, the par value interest rates and other terms at which they should be offered, the timing of offerings, and the selection of particular issues for prematurity retirement. In every such decision there is an impact upon the private-loan market to be considered. For, to the extent that government demands loans (sells securities) in the same credit markets that supply private borrowers, it inevitably competes with them. And because a national government, as sovereign and proprietor of the currency, has a higher credit rating than any other domestic borrower, and because (with congressional authorization) it can pay whatever interest rates it needs to pay,[6] government borrowing can easily shoulder some private borrowers out of the money market and choke off some credit-dependent private spending. Conversely, every Treasury acquisition (retirement) of an outstanding government obligation, whether at or before maturity, tends to bring some new funds seeking placement into the private capital market.

Consequently, public debt management must be construed as an integral part of a national government's total monetary and credit program, and particular care must be taken to see that the impact of public debt operations on private finance does not enervate the general stabilization program (or the balance-of-payments program) the government is trying to pursue. To this end, national governments, for one thing, usually try to adjust the timing and character of their purchase and repayments of loans to the needs of the private-loan market. For instance, the date of a government bond issue may be put off for a few months to accommodate a seasonal demand for residential mortgage credit; or government may decide upon short-term borrowing instead of a long-term bond issue to avoid competing in the long-term capital market with business borrowers who are trying to finance plant and equipment programs. A classic example of the latter is the so-called twist program, begun in 1961, when the Treasury, in cooperation with the Federal Reserve, succeeded in raising short-term interest rates (for balance-of-payments reasons) without significantly raising long-term rates (for domestic investment reasons). This was done chiefly by taking advantage of both new issue and refunding operations to lower the average maturity of the Federal debt, thus shifting demand from the long to the short end of the market.

A more powerful set of techniques, however, that the United States

---

[6] Subject currently to the statutory $4\frac{1}{4}$ percent interest ceiling on long-term debt, which can, of course, be changed by the Congress.

Federal and other national governments can use for offsetting the unwanted financial effects of public debt operations involves the monetary and banking policies that can be brought to bear upon the supply side of the loan market. If government borrowing will, without such an offset, absorb too much of the existing credit supply, the financing of the debt can be coupled with monetary policies designed to increase the availability of bank credit. And government, to make sure it does not step on the toes of private borrowers who do not have ready access to more than a restricted portion of the credit market, can do its borrowing from the banks. Or, if it is the buoyant effect that debt retirement will tend to have upon private finance that needs offsetting, an effort will be made (1) to channel the debt repayment to the banks and (2) to tighten up monetary controls sufficiently to dissuade the banks from relending these funds to private borrowers. It is the need for such backstopping of debt management by central bank policies that, in Washington, makes careful coordination between the Treasury and the Federal Reserve Board so essential to a smoothly running stabilization program.

Other Influences on the Private-loan and Securities Markets

American governments—principally the Federal, but also state and local—exercise a number of supplementary effects on the availability and terms of credit to private borrowers. For particular industries and activities, e.g., residential construction, farming, small businesses, and private capital exports, the scope of credit has been greatly broadened and the cost of borrowing reduced by government loan-guarantee programs and, to a lesser extent, by direct government loans. Also, when they have been so empowered, Federal monetary authorities periodically have engaged in specific anti-inflationary controls of certain types of credit, notably installment loans and residential mortgages. In addition to these temporary control powers exercised during emergencies, the Federal Reserve Board has permanent power to fix the minimum margins of cash that purchasers of securities must put up in stock market transactions. Also, Federal and state regulation of banks, Federal regulation of securities and commodities markets, state regulation of insurance companies, and Federal and state regulation of the financing activities of railroads and public utility companies—all have significant effects upon the types and quantities of loan transactions open to particular groups of borrowers and lenders.

THE EFFECTS OF SURPLUSES, DEFICITS, AND THE PUBLIC DEBT

This discussion of government's impact upon aggregate demand is rather novel in that it has proceeded this far without once using the words "deficit" and "surplus." This omission has been intentional. The great popular focus upon the phenomenon of so-called deficit spending[7] during the past several decades tends dangerously to oversimplify and frequently to distort the effects of fiscal, i.e., governmental taxing and spending, policies.

Let it be said at once that there are perspectives from which our characteristic preoccupation with budgetary balances as such is proper. Certainly, it is altogether proper for those who appraise the adequacy of government programs principally in terms of the requirements for financially responsible public administration. The latter include the abhorrence of waste and the search for efficiency in governmental operations, the development of effective financial accountability by public servants to their political superiors, and the need for educating political authorities—including the electorate—to weigh the (easily overlooked) costs of public expenditure programs against the advantages of such programs. These are wholesome objectives that need to be knit effectively into the web of government. They properly dominate the professional viewpoint of those public administrators who are budgetary specialists, and of legislators who have a special interest in the government's financial efficiency; traditionally they also have dominated the thinking of many economists specializing in the field of public finance. These objectives provide the chief, and an important, justification for the rule of thumb of annual budget balancing: it greatly facilitates financial accountability.

For the economist who is trying to figure out the final-demand consequences of a change in fiscal policies, however, an exclusive or even a principal focus on the size and sign of the budgetary balance can be very dangerous. It involves two principal risks. First, it may cause him to overlook the fact that the magnitude and composition of the government spending and taxing programs, and the directions in which each is changing, may be most inadequately revealed by the residual that remains when one side of the budget is subtracted from the other. For instance, it is altogether possible for a shift from a surplus to a deficit to depress aggregate demand, if the deficit is brought about by a drop in tax collections that only slightly outstrips a sharp drop in public spending. At the end of this section we shall return to one illustration of this point upon which the literature has dwelt at some length: the so-called balanced-budget multiplier. But the point itself simply is that, as we have seen, the consequences of both tax and spending programs are exceedingly diverse, and one cannot safely size up the joint effects of a combined tax and spending program until he has appraised the effects of each of its elements.

A second and sillier error into which preoccupation with budgetary balances occasionally traps analysts is that of thinking that the fiscal impact of a deficit or surplus can somehow be divorced from, and then added to, the effects of the tax and spending programs which it reflects. This, of course, is a plain and simple case of double counting. If, as we have tried to do in

---

[7] The redundancy of the term is revealed when we try to identify its opposite; it would presumably be "surplus nonspending."

this chapter, you analyze, first, the full spending effects of government expenditures and, second, the spending effects of taxes, you cannot then go on, third, to discuss the spending effects that the deficit or surplus exerts as a fiscal phenomenon. You have already discussed them, and more fully than you could have by focusing on the deficit or surplus per se.

For this reason deficits and surpluses as such have a logical place in the present discussion only if they have certain intrinsic effects that are actually distinguishable from those of the taxes and expenditures that bring about the budgetary balance. As it happens, there are such intrinsic effects in the United States, deriving from the manner in which deficits are financed and from the financial disposition made of surpluses. It will become evident, however, that even these have been largely anticipated in the foregoing analysis.

SURPLUSES, DEFICITS, AND PRIVATE FINANCE

Some years ago, a leading business conditions consultant argued, in a privately circulated appraisal of the economic outlook for the following twelve months, that the Federal budget surplus then in prospect should, in one sense at least, be counted as a bullish factor. For (he said) as the government used the surplus to retire some of the public debt, several billion dollars of funds would be turned loose in the private-loan market, thereby easing some of the scarcity of funds that was inhibiting private investment.

In an economy where every sophomore had come to know that "surpluses are deflationary and deficits are inflationary," the contention that a Federal surplus could, in any sense, stimulate business seemed novel. In the light of our discussion of debt management's impact upon private finance, however, the consultant's point appears perfectly sound—*provided* he was talking only about the intrinsic, financial effects of the surplus itself, and elsewhere in his analysis already had taken account of the effects of the tax programs and the spending programs that jointly yielded the surplus.

Arrangements are conceivable under which the financing of a government deficit or the disposition of a surplus would have no intrinsic effects at all. For example, if business in the economy were done principally through the circulation of currency rather than of demand bank deposits, the national government could simply run its printing presses when it decided to spend more money than taxes brought in, and, in other periods, it could remove from circulation any excess of tax money over public expenditures. Or, if demand deposits were the principal circulating medium, government could achieve the same results by giving non-interest-bearing notes to, and redeeming them from, the central banking system. Under such financing arrangements the entire effect of a deficit or surplus would be that which inheres in the tax, transfer, and spending programs that bring it about.

In the United States, however, it happens that governments finance deficits by borrowing, not simply by printing new currency, and dispose of surpluses by retiring indebtedness rather than currency; that they usually borrow, not from the central banking system, but from the public including individuals and all manner of nonbanking financial institutions as well as commercial banks; and that they pay interest on their debts. These are the circumstances that cause the generation of a deficit or surplus to have some intrinsic demand effects of its own.

The nature of the impact upon private financial markets is that already indicated under the heading of debt management. The financing of a deficit by the sale of government securities tends to compete with private borrowers and thereby exerts a dampening effect upon private spending. The degree of the dampening effect depends on a variety of circumstances, including notably the strength of demand for investment funds. At one extreme, funds siphoned out of the market by the financing of the deficit could preclude an equivalent amount of private investment spending. At the other extreme, when investment is at a low ebb and investment funds are plethoric, financing the deficit would absorb funds that would otherwise have remained idle.[8] The more typical situation, of course, is somewhere in between. In general, perhaps as much as we should conclude is that the expansionary effect of the "excess spending" that causes a deficit will tend to be offset by the contractionary effect of financing the deficit only in minor degree at low levels of business activity, but significantly at boom levels. The surplus case is symmetrical. The expansionary effects of the disposing of a surplus (i.e., making funds available to the investment markets via retiring government securities) will in greater or lesser degree offset the contractionary effect of the excess of tax revenues that caused the surplus. In times of depressed business activity, injecting funds into the money markets via debt retirement would lead to little or no increase in private spending. In times of boom, however, when business investment is limited by the supply of available funds, an injection of funds into the money markets via debt retirement should lead to a more or less equivalent increase in private investment spending. Seen in this light, it is plain why debt operations must often be coupled with central bank policies designed to offset the former's financial impact.

THE BURDEN OF THE PUBLIC DEBT

Not only does our mode of financing deficits and disposing of surpluses in this country tend to affect private spending through the impact upon the

---

[8] The reader may object that in a perfectly competitive market the supply of and demand for funds are equated at *some* interest rate, and therefore the supply of funds is never, in an absolute sense, plethoric. If this were true, financing a deficit would always preclude an equivalent amount of private spending. In the real world, however, as we have noted in previous chapters, markets—even markets for funds—are imperfect, and absolute surpluses or shortages do occur. That is, the *availability* of funds, as distinct from their cost, is often a determinant of private borrowing and spending.

private-loan market at the time a net change in the public debt is occurring, but also the total level of the public debt, given the type of government indebtedness we have in the United States, has a distinguishable effect upon business activity in its own right, although in most popular thinking this is vastly exaggerated.

Probably more misleading folklore attaches to the public debt than to any other variable of overall economic behavior. For example, such beliefs as these are still popular in the United States: the indebtedness of the United States government to United States nationals "mortgages future generations"; the aggregate public debt (as well as the particular issues that compose it at any given time) must necessarily, sooner or later, be paid off; and any further significant rise in the public debt necessarily threatens us with something called "national bankruptcy." If you share these views, you owe yourself an exposure to the kind of dispassionate debunking of them that can be found in most introductory economics texts these days. The present context does not afford room for an explicit, full-dress assault upon all the erroneous beliefs about the public debt that so stubbornly persist. Rather, there is space only for sketching the possible effect that the cost of carrying the debt has upon private spending.

Since government always has the choice of financing the repayment of a particular maturing debt issue either out of taxes or by borrowing anew, it is now generally recognized that there is never any necessary reason why the United States government, any more than the Union Pacific Railroad, must reduce its total indebtedness. Accordingly, the debt burden—the unavoidable burden—is a phenomenon that relates not to the retirement of the debt but only to the costs of carrying it. That there are such carrying costs in the United States follows from the fact that the debt is interest-bearing. The burden of the debt derives from the interest bill, the size of which may be varied by a change either in the total size of the debt or in the average interest rate attaching to it.

The net payment of interest on Federal public debt in the United States presently entails an annual disbursement of more than $9 billion to private persons and businesses. State and local governments add, roughly, another billion. It is not this payment per se that imposes a burden. The burden arises from the fact that the recipients of the interest payment are free to spend it, in which case it may be necessary for the rest of us, who are not receiving government interest payments, to move over—to forgo purchases to make room for the entry of this increment of purchasing power into the market place. If markets are slack, very little or none of this moving over may be necessary, and the debt may be virtually burdenless. However, when there is not enough slack in the economy to accommodate the spending that results from the interest payments without forcing price increases, the rest of us have to move over one way or another. Either government charges us higher taxes than it would otherwise charge to squeeze our disposable private incomes enough to make room for the interest received by the government's creditors, or we suffer inflation; we pay the costs of carrying the debt in the form of higher market prices.

Either way, the payment of government interest in high-employment periods requires some shift of real disposable income from government's non-creditors to its creditors, and the tax way is the neater and presumably the more equitable way. Hence it is customary to regard the cost of carrying the debt as those taxes which *must* be collected to pay the interest bill.[9]

Thus, the effect of the debt burden on aggregate demand depends upon the combined spending responses to a shift of income from taxpayers to debt holders. Economists often have opined that this effect is somewhat dampening. They reason, first, that partially because debt holders may on the average represent higher-income groups than do taxpayers, their marginal disposition to spend out of income may be less than that of taxpayers. Second, because part of the tax cost of interest payments is imposed on business, the impact of higher taxes on net profits probably dampens business investment incentives in a fashion that is not offset by the accrual of a matching amount of government interest payments, even if these should accrue to the business that pay the taxes. It is doubtful, however, that these contracts are very pronounced. At best—or worst—the net impact upon aggregate demand involved in a $9 or $10 billion transfer from taxpayers to debt holders is fairly marginal.

THE "HIGH-EMPLOYMENT SURPLUS" AND THE ROLE OF THE FEDERAL GOVERNMENT IN A GROWING ECONOMY

For a half-dozen years before the enactment of the Revenue Act of 1964, the American economy, as will be discussed in Chapter 15, experienced chronic excess unemployment and underproduction. In the course of probing for reasons for this persisting economic slack, economists more explicitly examined the behavior of the United States Federal budget in an economic growth framework than they had ever done before, and in the process they popularized the concept of the so-called high-employment surplus.

The Tendency toward Fiscal Drag

By the early 1960s it had become apparent that the American economy had for several years been suffering from a severe, but curiously surreptitious, case of fiscal drag. It had a Federal tax structure with rates high enough to have generated, under full-employment conditions, revenues substantially in

---

[9] More complete discussions of the debt burden usually and properly go on to point out that the *relative* size of public debt burdens in different economies or for the same economy in different periods can be sensibly compared only in terms of the ratio of the interest bill to the national income. It is in this sense that the public debt burden in the United States has declined significantly since World War II. In 1946, net interest on the Federal debt was 2.3 percent of national income; in 1965 it was 1.6 percent.

excess of the expenditures that the Federal government was making. But in the face of these high tax rates, private propensities to spend were not strong enough to produce full-employment levels of aggregate demand. As a result, the personal and corporate income tax base was held below full-employment levels; actual revenues and the actual balance in the Federal budget fell short of their potentials; and the economy limped along, as it were, with a missing cylinder.

The diagnosis of this problem did not require any brand new economic concepts or insights. But it was only in 1960 and 1961 that the problem was identified and formulated in a way that commanded widespread attention.[10] This diagnosis made two points: first, that for several years prior to the tax cut of 1964, Federal tax rates had been too high relative to public and private spending propensities because the tax system had been structured during the early postwar and Korean War periods when there were extraordinary pressures of both government and private demand.

But the diagnosis emphasized a second point of more lasting significance—namely, that in a growing economy *any* given set of Federal income tax rates has an inherent tendency to generate a progressive fiscal drag on economic activity unless the growth of Federal outlays is at least proportionate to the growth of the economy's productive capacity. This is because, with fixed tax rates, the annual growth of Federal revenues is at least proportionate to the annual expansion of gross national income.[11] Indeed, because our

---

[10] Intellectual antecedents of the high- or full-employment surplus concept may be found in the publications of the Committee for Economic Development (e.g., *Taxes and the Budget,* 1947) and in the writings of William H. White (e.g., "Measuring the Inflationary Significance of a Government Budget," *IMF Staff Papers,* vol. 1, April, 1951) and E. Cary Brown (e.g., "Fiscal Policy in the Thirties: A Reappraisal," *American Economic Review,* vol. XLVI, December, 1956). One of the earliest uses of the concept as an analytical device, in this case to measure the excessive restraints built into the 1960 tax structure, was by David W. Lusher in a paper presented at the University of California at Los Angeles in May, 1960 [subsequently published in J. A. Stockfisch (ed.), *Planning and Forecasting in the Defense Industries,* Wadsworth Publishing Co., Belmont, Calif., 1962]. Charles L. Schultze and Herbert Stein argued in testimony before the Congressional Joint Economic Committee that the budgetary programs existing in 1960 would produce surpluses at full employment that were so high as to impede private demand from coming up to the full-employment level (*Current Economic Situation and Outlook, Hearings before the Joint Economic Committee,* 86th Cong., 2d Sess., Dec. 7–8, 1960, pp. 114–122). The Council of Economic Advisers (then Walter W. Heller, Kermit Gordon, and James Tobin) included a comprehensive exposition of the same thesis in their testimony to the Joint Economic Committee in the spring of 1961 ("The American Economy in 1961: Problems and Policies," Statement of the Council of Economic Advisers in *January 1961 Economic Report of the President and the Economic Situation and Outlook, Hearings before the Joint Economic Committee,* 87th Cong., 1st Sess., Feb. 9, 10, Mar. 6, 7, 27, and Apr. 10, 1961, pp. 310–392). The 1962, 1964, and 1965 *Economic Reports of the President* further elaborated this point.

[11] In a typical year in the mid-1960s, for example, if income keeps pace with the growth in potential and if tax rates are unchanged, the *annual increment* in Federal tax liabilities will amount to $6 billion to $7 billion.

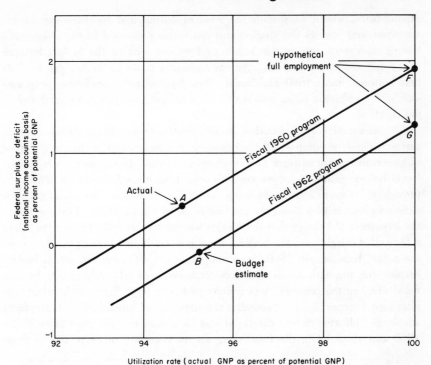

Figure **12–1.**   Effect of level of economic activity on Federal surplus or deficit, 1960 and 1962.   Source: *Economic Report of the President,* January, 1962, p. 79.

Federal tax system is a progressive one, in a growing economy with fixed tax rates, the proportion of GNP taken in taxes tends gradually to rise.[12] Unless tax rates are reduced—or unless private spending propensities alter—this withdrawal from the disposable income stream must be matched by additional government expenditures if the expansion in total demand is not to fall short of growth in capacity.

The High-employment Surplus

This analysis leads to the conclusion that instead of the actual budget balance, the calculated balance that the Federal budget would generate at full employment should be adopted as an approximate gauge of the government's net fiscal impact on the economy. Thus, the Council of Economic Advisers in its January, 1962, *Report* illustrated the theory of this high-employment surplus with the chart we are reproducing as Figure 12–1. In such a chart, any year's fiscal program—under which revenues, and to a lesser extent,

---

[12] Conceptually, this conclusion would not be true in an economy in which prices *fell* enough to offset completely the increase in output per man, so that current dollar income per man actually held steady or declined.

expenditures, would vary with the level of output and income—can be interpreted, not just as the single-figure estimates presented in the President's budget document, but as a schedule or function relating the budget balance to the fullness of production. An expansionary move in the budget, such as that between fiscal 1960 and fiscal 1962, by raising expenditure programs and/or by reducing taxes would shift this budget function downward and to the right.

As we have argued earlier in the chapter, no surplus or deficit concept can adequately encompass all the economic effects implicit in the composition of government expenditures and revenues and in the directions each is taking. Nevertheless, estimates of successive annual high-employment surpluses do provide a far more significant economic indicator than do the actual surplus-deficit figures, with which they are compared in Figure 12–2. For one thing, the hypothetical balance that the budget would show at full employment offers a far better insight into the Federal fiscal posture in any given year than does the actual balance—in 1960, for example, when, although the actual budget surplus (on the national income account basis) was relatively small, the true fiscal drag on the economy was represented by a large high-employment surplus (see Figure 12–2). Secondly, the sequence of annual high-employment surpluses indicates clearly the rapid way in which, in such periods as 1958–1960 and 1962–1963, the fiscal drag on the economy tends to mount from

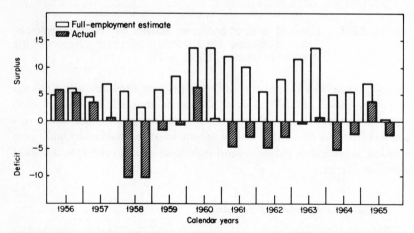

Figure 12–2.   Federal surplus or deficit: actual and full-employment estimate (national income accounts basis), 1956–1965, by half-years, seasonally adjusted. Note: Calculations of full-employment surplus assume continuous full employment, with unemployment tax revenue and benefits held to those which would have prevailed at 4 percent unemployed. They exclude the temporary extension of unemployment benefits from expenditures and repayment from revenue. Source: Unpublished data supplied by Council of Economic Advisers. Data for 1965 are preliminary.

year to year unless and until it is offset by such budgetary changes as the dramatically expansionary tax reduction of 1964.

In passing, it is interesting to note the use of the high-employment-surplus concept that the Council of Economic Advisers made in a summary statement of the requirements for a stabilizing budget policy contained in its January, 1964, *Report*. "The economic impact of a given budget program," the Council remarked once again, "is best measured by its surplus or deficit at full-employment income levels." Then the *Report* went on to emphasize the need for relating budget policy to the strength of private demand and to the remainder of the stabilization policy mix:

> ". . . The surplus in the full-employment budget is too large when the Government demand contained in the budget, and private investment and consumption demands forthcoming from after-tax incomes, are insufficient to bring total output to the full-employment level. The actual budget will then show a smaller surplus or larger deficit than the full-employment budget.
>
> "If the fiscal structure is biased in this direction, it can be corrected either by expanding Government purchases to employ idle resources in satisfying public needs; or by expanding private business and personal after-tax incomes through reduced tax rates or increased transfer payments to employ idle resources in satisfying the demands of the private sector. When the budget is too expansionary, the combination of public and private demands will eventually exceed productive capacity, and excessive upward pressure on prices will develop. In this event, sound fiscal policy calls for lowering expenditures or raising tax rates, or both.
>
> "The appropriate size of the surplus or deficit in the full-employment budget depends on the strength of private demand and its responsiveness to fiscal policy. The budget must counterbalance private demand. The weaker the underlying determinants of private demand, the more expansionary the budget should be; the stronger these determinants, the more restraining the budget should be.
>
> "Whether a given budget is too expansionary or restrictive depends also on other Government policies affecting private spending, of which monetary policy is the most important. Other things being equal, a strongly expansionary monetary policy permits a larger surplus by strengthening business investment, residential construction, and other expenditures that are sensitive to the cost and availability of credit."

THE BALANCED-BUDGET MULTIPLIER: AN ADDENDUM

In the mid-1940s the assertion that an increase in government spending that was fully matched by an increase in taxes would nevertheless increase aggregate demand caused a minor furor within the economics fraternity.[13] It did so only because of analysts' previous bad habit of acting as though the demand effect of fiscal policies could be inferred simply from the size and trend of the deficits or surpluses prevailing.

The balanced-budget-multiplier contention usually has been presented with rigorously simplifying assumptions. It may be summarized as follows. In the case of a $10 billion increase in government expenditures exactly matched by a simultaneous $10 billion increase in tax collections, assume that all the increased spending is for goods and services rather than transfers; assume, secondly, that all the increased spending is paid out directly to consumers; assume, thirdly, that tax collections are unchanged except by the amount of the postulated tax rise, $10 billion in our example; and assume, finally, that the marginal propensity to consume characterizing those consumers who pay the increased taxes is exactly the same as the marginal propensity to consume characterizing those who supply the increased goods and services to government. Let us label this ratio b. Then the increased spending generated over successive income-turnover periods by the increased government spending would be $10 billion $+ b$ ($10 billion) $+ b^2$ ($10 billion) $+ b^3$ ($10 billion) $+ \cdots + b^n$ ($10 billion).

On the tax side, however, because the initial spending impact of an increased $10 billion in taxes would be not that full amount but only the fraction of it represented by the marginal propensity to consume, the total deterrent effect of the tax increase over successive income periods can be represented as b ($10 billion) $+ b^2$ ($10 billion) $+ b^3$ ($10 billion) $+ \cdots + b^n$ ($10 billion). Thus the *induced* effects upon consumption just offset each other, and aggregate demand, over time, would be raised by the amount of the initial $10 billion increase in government spending. Hence, the common conclusion that the balanced-budget multiplier is 1.[14]

Our previous analysis, both here and in Chapter 7, where we examined the multiplier concept with some care, generates a critique of the balanced-budget-multiplier thesis almost automatically.

---

[13] H. C. Wallich, "Income-generating Effects of a Balanced Budget," *Quarterly Journal of Economics*, vol. 59, no. 1, pp. 78–91, November, 1944; T. Haavelmo, "Multiplier Effects of a Balanced Budget," *Econometrica*, vol. 13, no. 4, pp. 311–318, October, 1945 (see also comments by G. Haberler et al. and reply by Haavelmo in the April, 1946, issue of the same journal, vol. 14, no. 2, pp. 148–158); R. Turvey, "Some Notes on Multiplier Theory," *American Economic Review*, vol. 43, no. 3, pp. 275–295, June, 1953; W. J. Baumol and M. H. Peston, "More on the Multiplier Effects of a Balanced Budget," *American Economic Review*, vol. 45, no. 1, pp. 140–148.

[14] If the third assumption (that tax collections, except for the postulated cut, are fixed) is dropped and instead it is assumed that they are a function of income, then the balanced budget multiplier is somewhat less than 1. It would be $(1-b)/(1-b+cb)$, where b is again the marginal propensity to consume and c is the marginal tax rate. (See Barry N. Siegel, *Aggregate Economics and Public Policy*, Richard D. Irwin, Inc., Homewood, Ill., 1960, p. 116.)

First, it *is* quite evident that the model just outlined is an oversimplification. The marginal propensities to consume of those who would pay increased taxes and those who would receive increased payments from the government probably would not be the same. Moreover, the model bypasses the gap between gross national income and disposable personal income. In reality, some of the increased taxes probably would come from gross retained earnings of business rather than from disposable personal income, and some of the increased government spending would accrue to the income shares of business and of government rather than to individuals. (In the literature about the balanced-budget multiplier these issues usually are discussed under the heading of leakages.) Furthermore, the simplified model does not specifically make allowances for lags, including the sizable lag between changes in government spending and changes in disposable personal income, the sometimes significant lag between changes in DPI and resulting changes in personal consumption expenditures, and possible lack of synchronization between changes in government spending and in tax collections. Finally, the model errs, if it purports to be a practicable device for business conditions prediction, in that it makes no allowance for the possible collateral demand effects that such a combination of government spending and taxing policies might exert upon business and consumer expectations or upon the availability of investment financing.

Second, however, the balanced-budget-multiplier model does underscore the fact that a change in the level of government spending that involves no change in the budgetary balance *may* nevertheless exert a stimulating or a dampening effect upon total activity. It is sure to do so if it is not fully offset by an opposing change in private spending, and, before one assumes such offsets, it is important to recognize that increased government spending may add to the consumer income stream as much as, or more than, an equal increase in taxes takes from it.

But, third, there is nothing in the balanced-budget-multiplier case that is necessarily peculiar to government. An almost exactly similar case might be hypothesized for business, for example. A rise in business investment spending that was fully matched by increased gross retained earnings—let's say in the form of increased undistributed corporate profits taxed away from consumers in the form of higher profit margins—might have the same consequences. The balanced-budget multiplier is just a specific, and, from a public-policy viewpoint, an interesting, illustration of the general relationships that obtain among groups that receive and spend income in the economy.

Lastly, the point made at the beginning of this section bears repetition: an analysis that never explicitly considered the budgetary balance at all but that instead examined, first, the effects of an increase in government expenditures and, second, the effects of a matching tax rise, would arrive at the same net conclusion as that yielded by the balanced-budget-multiplier model—except that such reasoning would take more seasoned and explicit account of leakages, lags, etc. If this had been economists' standard frame of reference for fiscal policy analysis, no one ever would have gotten very excited about the balanced-budget multiplier in the first place.

GOVERNMENTAL INFLUENCE ON NONDEMAND FACTORS

The four factors identified in Chapter 5 as major determinants of the economy's overall performance happened to be listed in the following order: productivity, labor input, the aggregate-supply path, and aggregate demand. This chapter, in attempting to analyze the impact of government on the econ‑ omy, has attacked the last item on that list first. We may as well continue the procedure, taking up the remaining three in inverse sequence.

THE IMPACT ON PRICE-OUTPUT RELATIONSHIPS

Government affects the level and shape of the aggregate-supply path in two categories of ways. First, as we noted in our discussion of the aggregate-supply path, the pattern of price-output responses depends on the rate at which demand changes relative to capacity; a slow, gradual expansion in demand, relative to capacity growth, will have a quite different price-output effect than a sudden expansion in demand. It follows, then, that those government measures which affect total spending (already considered in this chapter) and those which affect capacity (yet to be considered) both have an influence on price-output relationships. A tax cut, for example, that went into effect by steps, over a two- or three-year period, would be likely to have less of a price effect, and more of an output effect, than would a tax cut of the same size that went into effect all at once.

Second, however, government can have a more specific and direct influence on the level and shape of the aggregate-supply path. Through legis‑ lation or administrative action, it can influence pricing practices. Among the factors affecting pricing practices are such characteristics of product market organization as the numbers of buyers and sellers, the degrees of product differentiation, and the degree of interfirm collusion in price and other de‑ cision making; also the distribution of bargaining power among producer groups in general and the character of intergroup bargaining; and, more specifically, the costing, pricing, and margin policies of business managers, the wage policies of management and union negotiators, those practices which determine the method of price quotation, the duration of price-quotation periods, and the presence or absence of discounts, "extras," transportation charges, and price discrimination in particular markets. All these may be influenced by government. Moreover, the decisions of regulatory commissions in regulated industries and laws that determine minimum wages, maximum hours, working conditions, and the height of supported prices in selected industries are even more direct influences.

This list has a familiar ring. The fact that we have encountered substantially the same collection of factors more than once before in the present chapter illustrates the basic complexity of our subject matter. Earlier in the chapter, the point was made that pricing practices heavily determine the distribution of real income among purchaser groups and hence affect the size of aggregate demand. Now we are concerned with the additional and distinguishable fact that pricing practices also obviously affect the price level and, hence, that portion of changes in aggregate demand that translates into changes in prices rather than in real output. The influence of government on pricing practices therefore affects the economy via two routes: (1) via the distribution of real income and hence aggregate demand, and (2) via the shape of the aggregate-supply path and hence the relative degree to which changes in aggregate demand are reflected in prices and in output.

GOVERNMENT'S INFLUENCE ON THE LABOR SUPPLY

American governments, the Federal government in particular, are beginning to exercise an influence on the birthrate through the dissemination of birth control information and materials. Through public health programs, American governments exert an important continuing restraint on the death rate; and, if we wanted to take the rather superficial view that the Federal government is responsible for, or gets us into, wars, we might say that it also occasionally causes a rise in the death rate. Generally, however, governmental influences on the size, age, and sex distribution of the native-born population in the United States are sufficiently subtle and/or constant to be overlooked in anything but the longest-run analysis. The Federal government does possess one positive and direct control on the size of the total population: its immigration policies. However, these have for many years been set to admit only a trickle of immigrants into this country. The 1965 overhaul of the immigration laws changed the criteria for admission, but it did not increase substantially the number of immigrants to be admitted. Immigration policies, therefore, can probably be regarded as a constant factor and can be safely overlooked in most aggregative labor market analyses.

Where government does significantly affect the labor supply in the United States is in the matter of the labor-force participation rate. As a major source and conditioner of final demand, government influences the labor-force participation rate insofar as the latter is responsive to demand. In this respect, and as a civilian employer itself, government's role in the labor market is similar to that of private buyers and employers.

However, in its determination of the size of the Armed Forces, the

Federal government exerts a unique influence on the ratio of the civilian labor force to the total age-eligible population. The effect is not so obvious as it might seem, however, because many in the Armed Forces are individuals who would be outside the total labor force, e.g., in school, if they were not in service. In addition, during emergency periods, government makes strenuous efforts to recruit into the labor force persons not normally in it to replace those who have been transferred from the civilian labor force to the Armed Forces.

In addition, both our social security system and public education programs affect the participation rate significantly. Both tend to reduce it—the first by lowering the average retirement age, and the second by raising the average age of entry.

In the matter of working hours, since we are concerned with the available (but not necessarily employed) labor supply as one of the determinants of normal capacity, it is the normal, not the actual, workweek or work year that particularly interests us. Government's impact upon normal working hours depends upon the influence of maximum-hours legislation (of the forty-hour-a-week type), and this depends, in turn, upon how much such legislation is leading or lagging the length of the customary workweek.[15] When Federal legislation established the forty-hour week as a maximum for nonovertime compensation back in the 1930s, the move was a step ahead of the evolutionary decline in the workweek in many industries; clearly it contracted the labor supply. But once this adjustment was completed, the forty-hour law probably fixed a norm that has somewhat retarded the progressive reduction of the industrial workweek since.

GOVERNMENT'S IMPACT UPON PRODUCTIVITY AND CAPACITY

Every increase in the economy's capacity to produce that is not explained by increases in the available supply of man-hours of labor is, by definition, due to increased ability to produce output per man-hour. Government's influences on labor productivity are almost as numerous as its influences on social behavior. However, it seems reasonable to group the more important ones under five headings.

First, through its effects upon demand, government can affect aggregate labor productivity by causing shifts in the output mix among industries with different value outputs per man-hour. This point was spelled out in

[15] Government could be said to have another (at least statistical) influence upon normal working hours if it were judged to exert a positive or negative effect upon the rate at which workers shift out of agriculture into the nonagricultural labor market, since average hours are substantially higher in the farm sector.

Chapter 5. There is nothing unique, of course, about government's ability to cause such aggregative productivity changes, but in recent American experience they have been most noticeably associated with changes in defense spending, for which government is directly responsible, and with the rate of the farm-to-city migration, which agricultural and general stabilization policies may significantly affect.

Second—and from here on we deal with impacts that register directly on particular industries and do not depend upon a reshuffling of activity among them—certain government policies exert an underlying and conditioning effect upon the competence and morale of individual workers and managers. Most important in this respect, undoubtedly, is the public education system, but the public health and social security programs and policies affecting working conditions and labor organization also are significant. It is apparent that governmental influences upon this dimension of productivity are of a highly gradualistic, long-run character.

Government affects productivity, third, by engaging in, subsidizing, and otherwise directly encouraging invention and innovation. Among the generators of such influence are the patent system, the government's military and agricultural research organizations, the National Bureau of Standards, the National Science Foundation, atomic-energy and space research, government contracts with business, and governmental research contracts with universities and other private organizations. Beginning at least as early as the Army's contract with Eli Whitney and Simeon North for the design and production of muskets in 1803, the fulfillment of which marked the first introduction of interchangeable machined parts into American industry, and continuing through and beyond the development of atomic energy, governmental contributions to the development of American technology have been numerous and substantial.

Fourth, and of most obvious importance, government affects the rate of productivity and capacity changes through its influences upon the scope of private investment. These influences, including government orders, taxes, credit policies, and the general impact of public policies upon business expectations, are the same ones that were considered when we viewed investment as a component of aggregate demand. But the bearing such measures exert on our economic future is greatly magnified when we consider their capacity effect as well as their demand effect.

Finally, as already discussed earlier in the chapter, governments powerfully affect private productivity by their provision of social services and facilities. Some of these, such as the local schools that are necessary if a business firm is to be able to recruit and hold a work force, are essential complements of private productive facilities if the latter are to have any output at all. Many others affect the efficiency with which, in firms that are operating, labor time can be used.

SUMMARY

The process by which public economic policies are formed is a vital subject that lies beyond the bounds of this discussion. But the nature of the principal impacts that public policies do or can exert on general business conditions is a subject from which no applied economist, qua economist, can turn away. Of this subject the present chapter has developed the following view:

First, governmental actions have an exceedingly varied impact upon final demand, affecting all four of its major categories. Government purchases of goods and services, obviously, are directly determined by government decision. These expenditures, especially those of the Federal government, differ markedly from private expenditures in their autonomous character. Personal consumption responds to changes in public spending; is influenced by tax, transfer, and market policies that affect the share of gross national income accruing to consumers; and is affected by public policies—particularly, in the short run, those concerning consumer credit—that influence the portions of given disposable incomes that consumers are disposed to consume and save. Government affects private domestic investment both by the impact of government spending, taxes, market and other policies upon the expectations of investors and their capacity to finance investment projects internally, and by the impact of credit- and debt-management policies upon the availability and cost of private credit. And by a variety of policies we have scarcely touched on here, government pointedly affects the size and trend of net foreign investment. We have noted that the effects of budget balances are, for the most part, not additional to those which flow from the government expenditure, transfer, and tax programs already cited. However, if government chooses to finance deficits by selling interest-bearing securities to the public and to dispose of surpluses by retiring such securities, changes in the public debt do have intrinsic effects upon private finance that frequently are perverse, so far as general stabilization objectives are concerned; and the carrying of the debt requires a shift of income from taxpayers to the government's creditors, which may have minor spending consequences.

Second, government, through its numerous influences upon pricing practice in the economy, as well as through its impact upon the rate of change in aggregate demand and upon the rate of change in capacity, exerts a variable but always significant effect upon the shape of the economy's aggregate-supply path.

Third, government influences the size of the labor supply principally through its effects upon the labor-force participation rate. The sharpest of these effects are those resulting from governmental control of military manpower, but more subtle influences also are exerted by such nonmilitary programs as public education and social security.

Fourth, government profoundly conditions the rate of productivity improvement, and hence of capacity expansion, in the economy. In the relatively near term, the most clearly revealed instrumentalities in this regard are government's influences upon private investment. However, the long-run influences exerted by the provision of a social services and facilities base for private investment, by public stimuli to research and innovation, and by the impact of the public educational system upon the workers' talents and morale may be no less significant.

13

A GENERAL THEORY OF AGGREGATIVE ECONOMIC BEHAVIOR: Conclusion

We have about finished our inspection of the concepts and behavioral hypotheses that make up the basic framework of contemporary aggregative economic theory. The present version of that theory is not entirely conventional. Bits of disputation have been injected into the exposition, and here and there the latter has been somewhat novel. But most of the concepts and relationships that have been expounded here are anything but original with the present authors; they are the stock in trade of contemporary macroeconomic theorists; they are the basic conceptual tools that aggregative economics presently offers the working business conditions analyst. Before we proceed, in the rest of the book, to consider what use can be made of these tools, a few general remarks on the theoretical framework itself are in order.

THE MODEL

The preceding chapter not only contained an analysis of the governmental influences on the economy's stability and growth performance but also afforded an opportunity for a fairly detailed review of the whole theoretical terrain we had traversed up to that point. Indeed, the scope and variety of government's economic impacts made such a review unavoidable. As a result, very little summarizing remains to be done. But three general characteristics of the body of theory we have been considering should be emphasized.

In the first place, the hypotheses and concepts examined in the foregoing pages are not a loosely connected collection of discrete doctrines. They are knit together into a single, integrated, and, for the most part, internally coherent web of theory. At some points we have found the internal articulation imperfect; there are some fuzzy spots, many loose ends; and here and there particular reputable hypotheses may appear in conflict. But by and large contemporary aggregative theory does offer a single comprehensive model of economic behavior—a simplified model, to be sure, but one that pretty well hangs together. This obviously is as it should be, for the economy that the model imperfectly represents is, despite its enormous complexity, an integrated social organism, not a random collection of bits and pieces. When the model is used as a framework for applied analysis, its built-in feature of logically connected parts safeguards the careful analyst from inconsistent conclusions about the business situation and outlook. It will be argued in Part Four that a forecaster can have no more valuable protection than this.

In the second place, the aggregative economic model does not submit to neat, crisp summaries that, at the same time, are reasonably exhaustive. Highly streamlined versions of the determination of the economy's stability and growth performance deserve always to be viewed with suspicion. The complexity of the real economy simply is too great to support highly facile representations. In Chapter 5, four variables were identified as the major determinants of growth, production, employment, and price-level performance, but, as we hastened to point out there, these are scarcely more than shorthand labels for the arrays of more specific determinants standing back of them.

The fact that to remain workably realistic the aggregative model must be kept reasonably complex needs to be urged, particularly in the face of the efforts of some popularizers of Keynes to oversimplify his system. At one point in the chapter where he summarized the outline of his theory, Keynes made this statement:[1]

> "Thus we sometimes can regard our ultimate independent variables as consisting of (1) three fundamental psychological variables, namely the psychological propensity to consume, the psychological attitude to liquidity and the psychological expectation of future yield from capital-assets, (2) the wage-unit as determined by the bargains reached between employers and employed, and (3) the quantity of money as determined by the action of the central bank. . . ."

[1] John Maynard Keynes, *The General Theory of Employment, Interest, and Money,* Harcourt, Brace & World, Inc., New York, 1936, pp. 246–247. Keynes uses the term "wage unit" here to mean the price of labor.

There has been a tendency in simplified transcriptions of Keynes to lift this conclusion out of context. Some writers, after presenting streamlined versions of the consumption function, the marginal efficiency of capital, liquidity preference, and the quantity of money (the wage unit is dropped from the list on the ground that it represents only Keynes's atypical mode of valuation), have gone on to reassure their readers that these four concepts are all there really is to the aggregative model. But the man who seeks in theory a framework and discipline for practical business conditions analysis must register these exceptions: (1) that the determination of each of these "ultimate" variables requires—and, at least in part, submits to—further analysis; (2) that the variables cited are not, as the statement would appear to imply, uniformly independent of one another; (3) that the statement, reflecting the unrealism of Keynes's two-sector (consumption and investment) demand model, grossly underplays the role of government; and, worst of all (4) that the statement assumes as given a number of variables that the working analyst seldom can afford to so treat. Most important of the latter are the determinants of the aggregate-supply path, the size of the labor supply, and all the many factors determining labor productivity. Holding all these things constant, the model that the statement bespeaks represents a physically arrested, not a physically growing, economy of the kind we actually have.[2]

In the third place, however, while the model outlined here is complex, it is not a maze; it is not an unclassifiable snarl of minute interrelationships. Rather it is largely composed of a few distinct branches, a few dominant subtheories, which, while they intertwine and overlap rather disconcertingly, nevertheless do allow the total problem of the economy's behavior and prospects to be broken down, at the beginning of any analytical exercise, into a few relatively manageable pieces. This is as helpful a characteristic of the model, grossly underplays the role of government; and, worst of all, (4) that when, at a later stage in analysis, the pieces of a problem are fitted together.

The major branches of the theory we have examined can be enumerated in various groupings and sequences. But at this point let us itemize them as six subtheories, listed in a somewhat different sequence from that in which they were originally discussed.

We have considered, first, the theory of the economy's physical growth —the growth of its productive capacity as determined by such factors as the emergence of technological and other innovations, the investments that are made partly in response to such innovations, and changes in the availability of other resources, including labor.

Because of the heavy role played by investment in determining capacity growth, it is appropriate to list, second, the theory of investment determination, which also, of course, is an important part of aggregate-demand theory.

[2] Keynes himself was careful to make explicit and pointed reference to all these factors which his oversimplified summary seems to bypass.

A third major branch of the model deals with the problem of how capacity and aggregate demand interact. This is the theory of the aggregate-supply path. It is here that the whole issue of prosperity or recession comes into focus, for it is here that one can see most precisely that the adequacy of demand must be measured against a changing-capacity yardstick. And even with capacity fixed, it is the shape of the aggregate-supply path that determines the production and price results of variations in aggregate demand.

A fourth branch of the model is the theory of consumer behavior, with particular attention to the responsiveness of consumer spending to consumer incomes. By supplying a nexus between consumption and nonconsumption spending, the consumption-function hypothesis supplies a pivot around which the whole of demand theory tends to swing.

We have considered, fifth, the theory of the economic role of public monetary policies, including public debt management, and of phenomena which those policies heavily affect, namely, the money supply and the availability and cost of private credit. These variables not only partly underlie the subject of investment determination but also heavily influence the debt-dependent portions of consumption and of state and local government spending.

Finally, we have examined briefly the theory of the distribution of spendable incomes among purchasing groups, especially among the major groups—governments, business, and consumers. This issue, which depends partly on tax and transfer arrangements and partly on interrelationships within the commodity- and factor-price structures, links closely with the theories of consumption and investment determination, and it overlaps with aggregate-supply theory.

A FEW OBSERVATIONS ON THE MODEL

In addition to what has been said about its integral characteristics, the following observations on the model constructed are appropriate as we leave the subject of theory as such.

1. The analytical framework erected here is one of an economy on the move. Its keynotes are growth and change. That, generally, is what an economist means when he says that such a model is "dynamic." The term has been badly overworked. In some current writing it has become little more than a word of art, vaguely equated to "progressive" or "vigorous," that authors use to distinguish the merit of their own concepts from the less realistic and potent (more "static") qualities of other ideas. We have largely avoided the term up to now, partly for this reason and partly because dynamic analysis has the reputation of being a more difficult second stage of economic reasoning that one can successfully handle only after he has mastered the simpler ideas of static analysis.

However, the fact is that, carefully used, the word "dynamic" does have a precise, unemotional meaning in economics. It attaches to any model that explicitly incorporates the dimension of time or, more concretely, that specifies time lags in some or all of the relationships it asserts. And a further fact is that, because such time lags characterize so importantly the real world, dynamic models are the only ones applied analysis can properly employ. All forecasting problems, for example, are essentially dynamic. This is true of very short-run as well as long-run probings of the future, for some of the most important determinants of next month's business conditions are developments that occurred some distance in the past. In laying up a theoretical framework for practical business conditions analysis, therefore, the most reasonable procedure is not to go through any two-stage static-dynamic explanatory sequence. It is simply, without particular fanfare, to build from the beginning a model that is dynamic in its conception. This is what has been done here.

2. Anyone undertaking to use an economic theory as a tool for explaining and predicting concrete economic events is vitally interested in how quantifiable the theory is. The more fully its concepts can be safely converted into numbers and mathematical relationships, the more precise are the conclusions that can be drawn from it. On this score the modern aggregative model gets high marks, although not so high, we shall later suggest, as the more dedicated econometricians appear to give it. With the resources that national income accounting and the other economy-wide statistical series noted in this part now afford us, the aggregative model is highly quantifiable in one sense. For any given present or past period its qualitative concepts, like consumption, taxes, plant and equipment spending, average working hours, and labor productivity, can be very largely converted into numbers; and where economic statistics are as well developed as they are in the United States, these quantifications can, for the most part, be accepted as fairly reliable. It is in this sense that the Nation's Economic Budget for any particular period is an imperfect but highly usable quantification of the major variables in aggregate-demand theory.

More ambitiously construed, however, satisfactory quantification of a conceptual model requires that not only its variables be expressible statistically but that the model's assertions of persisting relationships among the variables submit to rigorous mathematical statement. Ideally, every asserted relationship—e.g., between consumption and its determinants, between investment and its determinants, between DPI and its determinants, and between labor productivity and its determinants—should be capable of statement in a concrete functional equation. To be concrete, such equations must have all their absolutes and coefficients—for instance, both a and b in the conventional consumption-function hypothesis $C = a + bY$—reliably expressed in specific numbers. A mathematician would say the same thing this way: for a model to be fully quantified, all of its parameters must be made explicit.

As we have seen, the aggregative economic model does not meet this test. The matter of investment determination is only one of several in which the argument of foregoing chapters dictates this conclusion. All the same, while the relationships in the model we have examined are seldom precise, neither are they shapeless. There are many structural regularities that, in a particular era of a particular economy, give distinct orders of magnitude, if not exact values, to such relationships as those expressed by the marginal propensity to consume, the capital-output ratio, and the marginal tax rate. Thus many of the relationships as well as most of the variables in the model are *roughly* quantifiable. It is this conclusion that sets the stage for much of the applied analysis we shall be investigating from here on.

3. This is a somewhat atypical book about business conditions in that it has had so little overtly to say about business cycles. Not many years ago— and even today in some quarters—it was popular to think of variations in business activity as more or less rhythmical ups and downs about a rising average trend, often characterized as "normal" and usually calculated by fitting a least-squares trend line to the relevant time series. In highly stylized form, this notion is illustrated in the upper half of Figure 13–1. The assump-

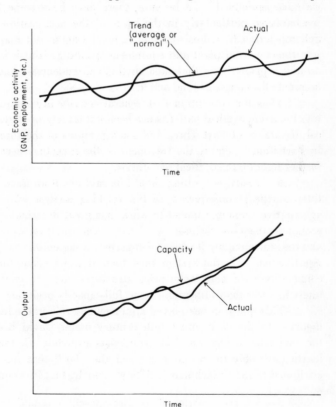

Figure 13–1.   Two concepts of the nature of business fluctuations.

tion, implicit or explicit, behind this kind of thinking was that there are certain mechanisms, either existing within the economy or impinging upon it from outside (e.g., sunspots), that tend to induce fairly regular, recurrent *cycles* in business activity above and below its average (and therefore more typical) level.

In recent years, this concept has been generally discarded by economic analysts.[3] As should be obvious from what has been said in previous chapters, most economic analysts now think of business fluctuations as deviations in output below (or occasionally slightly above) its estimated full-employment growth path, in the manner of the chart in the lower half of Figure 13–1.

Actually, the theoretical groundwork we have been laying is mainly neutral on the issue of whether or not fluctuations in economic activity are cyclical. The model could be used to contrive a causal explanation of *any* change in the level of business activity, including changes that a cycle theorist might construe as a cyclical phenomenon. The idea of regular, self-repeating fluctuations, however, is not an essential element of the theoretical apparatus we have assembled. To be sure, there have been some hints of recurrent mechanisms, particularly in the cases of the acceleration effect and of the Schumpeterian hypothesis of innovational waves, that may inject pulsations into the course of plant and equipment spending. But it is far from obvious on any a priori basis that such rhythmical tendencies should be expected to dominate the course of total activity.

Thus the contention that general activity in capitalist economies falls into recurrent cyclical patterns has been left largely in abeyance. The historical discussion of Part Three and some portions of the forecasting discussion in Part Four—notably the treatment of the inventory cycle—will shed some further light on the cyclical hypothesis.

4. Finally, something should be said about an issue that, while it is of little practical consequence to the working analyst who wants to put the aggregative economic model to work, has great doctrinal significance among economic theorists themselves. That is the question of whether the model and the real economy it tries to represent are susceptible to "underemployment equilibrium." Is the system such that, if it were not for rigidities in the commodity-price and factor-price structures, activity could stagnate indefinitely in a less than full-employment, full-capacity position?

This question has played a momentous role in the history of economic theory. In the early nineteenth century under David Ricardo's leadership the majority of the classical economists overrode Thomas Malthus's half-inarticulate objections and embraced the "law" that has been historically attributed to the Frenchman J. B. Say: namely, that in a competitive economy

---

[3] However, the remnants of the idea are still discernible in a foldout business cycle chart widely circulated, under a syndicated arrangement, by various commercial banks. The chart covers a hundred years or so and shows various measures of business activity fluctuating above and below their long-term "trend."

with flexible pricing, the aggregate supply of employable resources tends to create the aggregate demand necessary to employ those resources fully. It was this rejection of the possibility of persisting underemployment, more than anything else, that for a century turned the attention of most British and American economists away from the problem of general economic stability and stunted the development of macroeconomics. The important questions, it appeared, concerned the parts and pieces of the economy; if they were in good running order the whole would take care of itself. Hence the bankruptcy of the major Anglo-American economic tradition when it came to diagnosing the causes of the Great Depression, and hence Keynes's feeling that the essence of his new economics was a frontal assault on Say's law.

In the realm of pure theory, however, Keynes's analysis did not decisively dispose of the underemployment-equilibrium question, and neither does the neo-Keynesian aggregative economic model that we have built here. To say the least, the model readily accommodates the possibility of prolonged periods of underproduction. Indeed, it supplies the essential analytical machinery for explaining how such misfortunes can come about in the theories, first, of an aggregate-supply path that is relatively elastic at less than full-employment levels of activity and, second, of the direct, sympathetic dependency of changes in consumption spending upon changes in nonconsumption spending. The latter of these doctrines displaces the serene confidence of the classical economists that when investment or other nonconsumption spending fell off, consumption would take up the slack. And the aggregate-supply hypothesis warns that the general slumps in demand that can result from the cumulative interaction of declining consumption and nonconsumption expenditures will cause slumps in output and employment, not just price reductions.

As Keynes claimed, therefore, the modern aggregative model, unlike the rudimentary classical model, is a *general* theory; it applies just as matter-of-factly to the affairs of the economy in those numerous instances when demand is either deficient or excessive as it does to the special case of stable full employment. But there is an ultimate theoretical question that the model as it has been expounded here does not answer: suppose, as the result of a collapse in demand, economic activity comes apparently to rest in a position on the aggregate-supply path far short of full capacity. And suppose that all factor and commodity pricing were thoroughly free and competitive. Would this be a true equilibrium position, in the sense that without new autonomous increases in spending or other external changes, underemployment would forever persist? Or, instead, would it prove only a pseudo equilibrium in which the competitive erosion of wages and other factor prices would eventually return the economy to full employment at a lower level of aggregate money demand?

As an abstract exercise, the debate on this point is as interesting as it is heated, and we are loath to pass it by. But given our present objectives, bypassing is the only reasonable course, for the whole underemployment-equilibrium issue is nearly irrelevant in the area of applied analysis. This is so, for one thing, because the premise of thoroughgoing price and wage flexibility from which the debate proceeds is, as we have seen, notoriously inapplicable to modern Western economies. Moreover, the other premise of the debate—namely, that all autonomous factors including government policies should remain in neutral once a condition of underemployment is reached—is equally unrealistic. Even in the cause of scientific inquiry, popular governments today are not likely to test the proposition that if a deflating economy is left alone long enough, it will eventually, via a deflationary wage and price spiral, dig itself deeply enough into the mire to extricate itself. It is a political axiom of the mid-twentieth century that a government that conscientiously pursued this policy would not be around to observe the outcome.

Given the utilitarian motives with which we undertook this investigation of contemporary aggregative economic theory, the underemployment-equilibrium issue, therefore, is one facet of the subject from which we can safely turn aside. But there have not been many such facets. The bulk of what we have encountered is highly utilitarian. Without further delay let us move on to some of the concrete uses that can be made of it, first in interpreting an economy's past, then in anticipating its future.

PART THREE

READING THE RECORD

14

THE AMERICAN ECONOMY IN TRANSITION: The Thirties and Forties

The working business conditions analyst cannot avoid being something of a historian. He must turn to the past for testing his analytical hypotheses and for insights that may illuminate the present and future. This chapter and the next are meant to illustrate the kind of minimal historical knowledge that is conducive to effective current analysis and forecasting. We reach back for a quick impression of the American economy in the era before 1930, then sketch the outlines of the two great dramas of depression and war that occupied the next decade and a half, and finally treat the post-World War II period in somewhat greater detail.

All history is a mixture of continuity and change. Either historians tend to focus mainly on the mutations, the innovations, the new departures that always keep the past from literally perpetuating itself, or they preoccupy themselves with those deeply conservative properties of human institutions that channel most events along familiar routes. There is no way to avoid being somewhat willful on this matter. Our deliberate emphasis will be on the enormous changes that have dominated the history of the American economy since 1929. These have not been random. Nor do they represent any complete break with the past. But they have left the United States economy of 1966 a radically different social organism than was the economy of 1929.

The emphasis upon change will contrast with the excessive attention that many business cycle historians have paid to the repetitive features of our business conditions history. The cyclical theme in contemporary economic history writing is largely a legacy of the period before the nation's traumatic experiences of the 1930s and 1940s, and it was, perhaps, a proper theme for the aggregative economic history of that era. But it seems a singularly inappropriate preconception to enforce on the events of the new economy that has since emerged.

THE OLD ECONOMY: ROUTINE OSCILLATION

It would be foolish to suggest that up through the 1920s the performance of the American economy, either from the beginning of the Colonies or of the Republic, or even from the middle period of the nineteenth century, was all of one piece. During these long stretches of time the country's product grew from virtually zero to the world's highest; the nation received large injections of European population and capital; it inhabited and began developing an enormous and rich geographical territory; it became a predominantly nonagricultural economy; it originated and adapted radical technological innovations; it enormously expanded its effective energy, transport, and communications resources; it established a scheme of decentralized economic organization that, while its origins were West European, became in its adaptations, peculiarly American; and the country fought several wars, particularly the Civil War, which instigated profound changes in its industrial structure. But at least from the mid-nineteenth century through the 1920s the record can be said, for our purposes, to have had three substantial constants.

One was vigorous secular growth in productive capacity. Production estimates extending long periods into the past are highly uncertain things. However, it probably is safe to say that during the three-quarters of a century ending in 1929 the nation's ability to produce had an average annual growth of 4 percent, and that the expansion of output from one normal full-employment peak to another was reasonably steady. Much of this vigorous rate of growth, especially during the nineteenth century, was attributable to a rapidly rising population, the consequence of relatively high birthrates and heavy immigration. Output capability per capita, however, also rose respectably by an average for the period as a whole of nearly $1\frac{1}{2}$ percent a year, despite something on the order of a two-fifths reduction in normal working hours. The old economy was dynamically progressive in the ability it manifested to produce.

Another constant, as of the twenties, had been the absence—except during major wars—of attempts on the part of government to assume responsibility for the general level of business conditions. Throughout our history there had been a good deal of government regulation and ownership of business. But public economic policy had been largely particularistic, focusing on problems or fortunes of specific industries, groups, or regions. The Federal government, like everyone else, had become concerned in times of business panic, and there had been unending disputes about monetary policy. But such issues either arose only because of the government's special constitutional responsibility to manage the currency, or they were of a transitory type in which most people lost interest once the economic weather had cleared a little.

The general policies adopted were designed, as in the case of banking or antitrust legislation, only to provide a more constructive climate for private decision making. Or, as in the case of tax, expenditures, and tariff policies, they were almost wholly inadvertent with respect to their impact on stability. All of this, of course, was in line with the dominant strain of American economic ideology, which held that the total performance of the economy, like that of its parts, was something properly left to the direction of the decentralized private market; that the aggregate supply of resources, if left to its own devices, inevitably would create the demand for its product; that the private competitive enterprise economy was incapable of sustained malperformance; and, therefore, that any government attempt to evolve a positive, active, and continuing stabilization strategy would only befoul the natural and benign workings of the market. It should be added that prior to the 1930s, except in war periods, Federal expenditures and revenues were, in any case, such tiny fractions of the national product and income that changes in them were scarcely capable of exerting a major impact on general business conditions.

A third characteristic of the United States economic system as far back as our records reach had been an extraordinary degree of routine instability— extraordinary, that is, by today's standards. From the end of the Civil War to 1929, leading historians of American business conditions count six major business cycles and eleven more minor cycles, mostly scattered through the upswings of the majors. Many of these seventeen fluctuations were violent. The five major declines in durable goods production from 1865 to 1929 reduced output an average of 33 percent below the preceding peaks. Moreover, total underproduction during these declines was substantially greater than this because of continuing increases in capacity. Throughout the period, underproduction in all manufacturing appears to have averaged nearly 10 percent. Full employment prior to the thirties normally was a passing, boom phenomenon, to be followed faithfully by financial or other crisis and slump.[1]

---

[1] Cf. Alvin H. Hansen, *Business Cycles and National Income*, W. W. Norton & Company, Inc., New York, 1951, part 1, pp. 3–39; Ross M. Robertson, *History of the American Economy*, 2d ed., Harcourt, Brace & World, Inc., New York, 1964; Edwin Frickey, *Economic Fluctuations in the United States*, Harvard University Press, Cambridge, Mass., 1942; and A. F. Burns and W. C. Mitchell, *Measuring Business Cycles*, National Bureau of Economic Research, Inc., New York, 1946.

The years from 1922 to 1929, aside from a couple of minor interruptions, were years of high-level activity. But this was almost a record. The economy's average performance, as far as stability is concerned, was one that today's American electorate would not begin to tolerate. Pre-1929 Americans, however, were rather fatalistic about it. Radical instability was regarded as a necessary concomitant of vigorous long-term economic growth. It was thought to be something that neither business itself could correct nor government cure without interventions so extreme as to sap the vitality of the whole private enterprise system.

This state of mind was terminated by an economic collapse of outlandishly unnatural proportions. It turned out that the old economy's latent capacities for instability were far more demonic than anyone had suspected. In the crumbling of old ideas that this disaster touched off, it was revealed that most of the old routine instability probably had been unnecessary.

THE ECONOMY LAID LOW: THE PATHOLOGY OF DEPRESSION

Judged by the sheer volume of human torment it produced, the Great Depression[2] was probably much the greatest catastrophe, other than the Civil War, ever visited on the American people. In the four years from 1929 to 1933, gross national product in current prices declined 46 percent from 103.1 billion to $55.6 billion. Gross national product in constant prices declined 30.5 percent. The Federal Reserve Board's industrial production index fell 45 percent from 1929 to 1932. The wholesale price index spiraled downward 32 percent, industrial wholesale prices fell 23 percent, and the consumer price index, 20 percent. Working hours in manufacturing fell off from an average of 44 in 1929 to 38 in 1933; and hourly earnings in manufacturing dropped 21 percent.

These losses were unprecedented, and they were unevenly distributed. The nation was victimized as never before by unemployment. Civilian employment fell 18.6 percent, and unemployment rose from about 1½ million to something on the order of 13 million by 1933. By that time one-quarter of the civilian labor force was completely out of work, and this does not include the very extensive part-time unemployment. Moreover, the statistic does not convey the full tragedy of massive unemployment. For one thing, it persisted; men out of work stayed out of work. Many lost their skills or the opportunity to develop them or to use them in occupations for which they

[2] Good general accounts of United States business conditions in the 1930s include *National Income, 1954 Edition: A Supplement to the Survey of Current Business*, U.S. Department of Commerce, 1954, part 1; and R. A. Gordon, *Business Fluctuations*, rev. ed., John Wiley & Sons, Inc., New York, 1961, pp. 428–450. An extremely interesting general history of the period is Dixon Wector, *The Age of Depression*, The Macmillan Company, New York, 1948.

were best fitted. Many people almost irretrievably lost faith in themselves. The psychic wounds of the Great Depression were nonmeasurable but enormous.

Another thing that the aggregate unemployment figure failed almost totally to reflect was the distress in agriculture. Farm prices crumpled relative to other prices, and with them, farm incomes. Net income per farm from farming fell, by 1932, to less than a third of the 1929 level. Many midland farm families burned corn and wheat in their stoves in the winter of 1932–1933 because grain was not worth so much as coal.

The United States was a desperately sick economy by the beginning of 1933. It is not easy to dispute those social historians who say that it was on the verge of revolution. Hordes of the indigent fought over the dumpings of the produce markets in our metropolitan areas. In the Southwest, hungry farmers broke into grocery stores for bread.

The country began to rescue itself from the psychology of defeatism with the inauguration of Franklin Roosevelt in 1933. At about that time most of the economic indicators began a gradual upturn that extended to the middle of 1937, when there was a short but violent relapse, from which, in turn, another gradual recovery began about a year later.

Much more significant than these ups and downs in activity, however, was the persistently unsatisfactory character of the economy's performance. Just as one unprecedented dimension of the Great Depression was its depth, another was its length. The duration of severe underproduction and unemployment did not fit the old cyclical stereotypes. The economy did, after a fashion, continue to cycle, but at intolerably submerged levels. Short of World War II, no adequate cure ever emerged or was contrived. Meanwhile, from 1929 to 1941, the cumulative shortfall of output below normal full-capacity levels totaled about $680 billion in 1965 prices—more, that is to say, than the total output used for war purposes during all of World War II.

Such, in very broad strokes, was the problem of the thirties. We shall do well to examine its character and consequences a little more closely.

THE ORIGINS OF THE 1929 DOWNTURN

The disaster of the early thirties has created a great retrospective curiosity about the 1920s.[3] It would appear that the forces that set such an extraordinary downturn in motion must have been peculiarly malignant. Actually, however, they seem to have been relatively conventional.

It is true that by 1929 the economy had become exceptionally vulner-

[3] See, for example, J. A. Schumpeter, "The Decade of the Twenties," *American Economic Review*, vol. 36, no. 2, pp. 1–11, May, 1946; and *Business Cycles*, McGraw-Hill Book Company, New York, 1939, vol. II, chaps. 14–15; also R. A. Gordon, "Cyclical Experience in the Interwar Period: The Investment Boom of the Twenties," in Universities–National Bureau Committee, *Conference on Business Cycles*, National Bureau of Economic Research, Inc., New York, 1951.

able to deflation, chiefly as a result of securities and real estate speculation and of the weaknesses thereby induced in the financial structure. But similar developments had preceded previous panics. The unique aspect of the 1929–1933 downturn was less its origins than its progress. In Joseph Schumpeter's suggestive phrase, defeat was turned into a rout. Once the economy was started downhill, a succession of weaknesses emerged to keep the decline going; the infection of deflation spread, aggravating itself as it went, and time and again, just as a particular set of depressive forces seemed about played out, something else contracted or collapsed to renew the general downslide.

The majority view among careful analysts of the period seems to be that the problem of the 1920s that led most directly to the downturn was overinvestment. By the standards of "routine instability," the United States had enjoyed an unusually long stretch of substantial prosperity from 1922 to 1929 in a period featured by an exceptionally high rate of capital formation. House building rose to a pronounced peak in the middle twenties, substantially in excess of the economy's sustainable annual requirements for new houses at that time.[4] The innovational stimulus to business investment was unusually strong, particularly in the case of the automobile. Car sales expanded from 1.7 million in 1919 to 4.6 million in 1929 as autos invaded the mass market. This meant huge plant and equipment outlays not only in the automobile and auto parts industries themselves, but in such complementary areas as oil, tourism, housing (as suburban development accelerated), and government outlays on streets, highways, and the like. The twenties also were an era of enormous expansion in electric power production and distribution, of great expansion in chemicals, and of initial major expansion in the radio industry. New techniques and processes requiring new equipment and plant were widely adopted throughout manufacturing.

Some of the particular elements in this surge of capital formation were clearly unsustainable. The bunching of the innovational stimuli to investment, particularly those contingent upon the penetration of the mass automobile market, was bound to end, and no equal new stimulants came forward. In addition, the increasingly lush market for securities and the feverish visions of limitless prosperity resulted in some business investment that was not soundly grounded in sensible projections of demand. This was particularly apparent in commercial construction in the latter part of the decade and also, to a lesser degree, in industrial construction.

Moreover, the tendency to build excess capacity was aggravated by the pattern of income distribution that evolved. Productivity gains during the decade were sizable, especially in manufacturing, where output rose 53 percent from 1919 to 1929, while employment remained approximately constant and hours fell 6 percent. However, on the income side of the Nation's Economic Budget, the distribution of the labor-cost savings from these productivity

---

[4] The normal physical requirements for new housing together with other determinants of house demand are discussed in Chap. 20.

gains did not meet the requirements for sustained growth. Both consumer and wholesale prices were substantially stable during the last two-thirds of the twenties, while money-wage rates rose distinctly less than labor productivity in manufacturing. To a disproportionate extent, benefits accrued to property incomes and profits. This had two adverse effects on the sustainability of expansion. It inflated the current profit stimulus to capital outlays, thereby aggravating the tendency toward overinvestment. And, secondly, it inhibited the growth of mass markets for the wares of mass-producing industries where, on the production side, the productivity gains were occurring.

Thus there was a tendency toward what some business cycle theorists call underconsumption. Some market expansion that, with a different income distribution, could have narrowed the appearance of excess capacity as the decade drew toward a close did not occur. Although some axe-grinding accounts of the twenties exaggerate this problem, it evidently was a factor.

On top of all of these drags on further fixed investment, inventories were accumulated, during the last push of the boom in 1928 and 1929, at a rate that now appears clearly to have been unsustainable. All told, it is not surprising that enough slack in the new orders for capital goods and for inventory developed in 1929 to level out general business activity and begin to tip it downward about midyear. With the government in its old neutral, or, in fact, collaborating posture so far as fluctuations in aggregate demand were concerned (a sharp decline in public construction, for example, coincided with that in private construction), there is no doubt that the factors we have noted lowered the marginal efficiency of capital enough so that, even without other complications, the slide in general activity would have been a major one. But now came the cluster of aggravations that turned defeat into rout.

VIRULENT DEFLATION

The first, most dramatic and symbolic, and probably the most crucial of the aggravations was the collapse of the stock market, beginning in September, 1929, reaching a crescendo in late October and early November, and then continuing as an intermittent crumbling for three years. A wild, speculative rise in securities values had been the economic and indeed social hallmark of the late twenties. It was in the securities and real estate markets (the temper of the period had first been displayed in the comic-opera Florida real estate boom of 1925–1926) that the virulent inflation of this boom occurred. Instead of creating excess demand for commodities, the decade's expanding profit and property incomes, together with much of the capital gains accruing, were sucked into the securities and real estate markets by the speculative spirals of those areas. The values of such assets were bid up far out of line with the productive potential they represented, while commodity prices remained relatively stable.

The spiral reached manic proportions in 1928–1929, even more in the financial structuring that was contrived to facilitate the boom than in security prices themselves. From the mid-1920s to a peak in 1929, there was something like a fivefold expansion in brokers' or call loans, as more and more speculators bought securities on the margin, proving their sole preoccupation with capital gains by their willingness to pay interest rates that frequently rose to 12 percent and more during 1929. These lush returns on what, as long as the market was rising, appeared to be almost riskless loans, brought a flood of funds to the call-loan market. Banks borrowed from the Federal Reserve Board at 5 or 6 percent (the latter being the highest the rediscount rate reached) and lent at 8 to 12 percent. American capital that had been attracted overseas in the earlier twenties, thereby supplying foreigners with some of the dollars needed for American exports, was enticed home to get in on either the call-loan bonanza or the securities appreciation itself, and much foreign capital came along with it. Many corporations channeled increasing portions of their working capital into the call-loan market. And some actually floated extra stock issues to raise funds for investing in a call-loan market that had been generated to facilitate the speculative up-bidding of old and new stock issues. For a time it looked as though the problem of perpetual motion finally had been conquered.

Along with the enormous overhang of stock-purchase debt and the overextensions into such debt and into inflated mortgage loans that had weakened much of the commercial banking system, the financial house of cards of the late twenties included pyramiding holding company structures, particularly in the public utility field, and a remarkable proliferation of investment companies (or "investment trusts"). The latter, which sold shares in their business of buying other companies' securities, frequently invested mainly in the stocks of other investment companies, which in turn invested in other investment companies. At the height of the boom the market value of investment trusts' own outstanding securities typically far exceeded the value of all of their holdings, and, like those of holding companies, their financial structures frequently were designed to maximize the leverage of common stock mainly held by the organizing group. This last feature pyramided the gains for insiders when everything was rising, but it was calculated to wipe them out and accelerate the collapse when things started down.

These financial facilitations of the stock market boom were not its causes, but they were outrageously imprudent. They virtually guaranteed that a decline, when it came, would be disastrous. The Federal Reserve System's general monetary controls provided no adequate protection—not even against the excesses in call loans, in view of the heavy premium being paid for that kind of credit. It is obvious in retrospect that certain specific controls were required and these, in large measure, we got in the 1930s with the regulation of stock issues, the Public Utilities Holding Company Act, and Federal Reserve regulation of the marginal requirements for stock purchase.

As J. K. Galbraith persuasively argues in his fascinating book, *The*

Great Crash, the speculative madness of the late twenties must, in the last analysis, be put down to the mood of the times.[5]   That mood required an underpinning of prosperity in the real dimensions of the economy, and it was abetted by a general monetary policy that probably was somewhat easier than it should have been.   But there had been periods of real prosperity and easier money before, and never anything quite like this nationwide flight into get-rich-quick fantasy.   As it was, although the vast majority of Americans never bought a share during the boom, an ever-rising stock market became for most of them the talisman of the New Era in which they believed. "The striking thing about the stock market speculation of 1929," says Galbraith, "was not the massiveness of the participation.   Rather it was the way it became central to the culture."[6]

This was a time, then, when our generalization in Chapter 11, to the effect that business conditions sometimes govern the stock market but that the stock market seldom governs business conditions, did not hold.   The collapse of the market was made doubly violent as leverage worked in reverse, call loans were called, and many financial institutions found their portfolios heavily committed to rapidly depreciating assets.   It shattered the public's confidence, not only in Wall Street, but in the large industrial corporations whose securities lost value so swiftly, in bankers, and in the business system as a whole.   The crash went a long way to shatter the system's confidence in itself.   The explosion of the New Era myth dealt a further body blow to long-term investment expectations, and the latter and the stock market began a dreary and it seemed almost bottomless downward chase.

We have dwelt on the stock market aggravation of the 1929–1933 decline, but there were a number of other aggravations.   For one thing, almost from the beginning, the general downturn was accompanied by a very sharp decline in farm prices.   This stemmed partly from the worldwide farm surpluses that had been gradually building for several years and now cropped out as production tapered off in the industrial countries.   Here at home, sliding farm prices lowered farm incomes and purchasing power, increased the demands for trade barriers against imports, began to produce a wave of farm mortgage foreclosures, and, by eroding farm real estate values, froze more bank assets.

International factors also accentuated the domestic decline.   The economy showed some signs of rallying a little in early 1931.   But this possibility was thoroughly done in by an epidemic of financial collapses and currency devaluations in Europe.   These marked the culmination of weaknesses to which American trade barriers and the volatility of American capital export

---

[5] J. K. Galbraith, *The Great Crash,* Houghton Mifflin Company, Boston, 1955. This book, like all Galbraith's works, is written in such a wholly delightful, irreverent style that in the eyes of many of his professional peers it suffers the grave fault of making economics fun. It is warmly recommended.

[6] *Ibid.,* p. 83.

during the twenties had contributed significantly. The present result for the United States, particularly after Britain was driven off the gold standard in September, 1931, was a run on the dollar, a flight of gold and short-term capital from this country, a rise in interest rates, more currency hoarding domestically, and a sharp rise in bank failures.

Bank failures were an aggravating element throughout the decline. Some came quickly after the stock market crash. Some were a by-product of the farm depression. They became increasingly common as the economy ground downward through a long and especially severe siege of general liquidation from 1931 to 1932. And then at the beginning of 1933, just as some wan signs of recovery again began to emerge, a final wave of financial panic prompted the new Roosevelt administration to close all the banks in the United States by the end of the first week in March. With its whole financial system temporarily immobilized, the performance of the economy was reduced to its lowest recorded state relative to its productive potential.

Some aggravating factors were inevitable concomitants of so deep a plunge. The slide in industrial prices, although not so radical as that in farm products and raw materials, picked up momentum, creating expectations of further declines and thereby feeding on itself. Wage rates, likewise, began to fall in 1931 and 1932, eroding incomes and generating expectations of further depression.

Throughout the decline, government appeared virtually helpless to do anything about it. President Hoover's initial policy impulses—to do what he could to talk down the psychology of deflation, to advocate a cut in the personal income tax, and to urge businessmen to maintain wage rates and their plant and equipment spending—were in the right direction, but they were pitifully inadequate. The Federal tax take was so small that reducing it could do little to stimulate private spending. Business self-restraint in cutting investment and wages was, at most, a delaying tactic that could work only if a general recovery came along rather quickly to vindicate it. And the downturn swiftly carried beyond the point where moral suasion could have any real impact.

Moreover, most of the reputable economic advice the Federal government received was perverse. Orthodox economists advocated wage reductions to clear the labor market, and stern measures, including reduced government spending and tax increases, to wipe out the anemic Federal deficits that emerged in 1931 and 1932. The achievement of a quick balance in the Federal budget was a major plank in the 1932 Democratic platform. Although the Federal Reserve System for the most part kept its general controls in a position of "active ease," there was no willingness to adopt—aside from the activation of the helpful but wholly inadequate Reconstruction Finance Corporation in 1932—the radical financial reforms needed to bolster the banking structure and arrest the spiral of liquidation. Total government spending, Federal, state, and local, actually was lower in 1932 and 1933 than in 1929.

The traditional view that there was no central or decisive role that government could properly play in arresting and reversing the "natural" forces of deflation continued for the time being to prevail.

THE POLITICAL REVOLUTION OF THE 1930s

The presidential election of 1932 marked a convulsive reaction against the idea that government ever again should adopt a posture of detached help-lessness in the face of substantial contraction. This was not a reasoned decision. There was no agreement in the country, or even in the victorious party and the new administration, about what measures the government should have adopted to curtail the 1929–1933 downturn or should now adopt to generate recovery. There was simply a ringing endorsement of the need for some kind of energetic antidepression program.

This almost visceral and—it now is safe to say—irreversible shift in political expectations, not the development of any enduring strategy of stabili-zation policy, was the great contribution of the early New Deal era to our business conditions history and prospects. It would be more than a decade after 1932 before a working consensus had evolved in the United States on what the rudiments of a stabilizing Federal fiscal and monetary policy should be. It would be four years even before the theory of aggregative economic behavior, which was to supply the rationale for such a policy, had begun to claim wide attention within the professional economics fraternity.

But meanwhile the necessity for vigorous action had been decided, and without delay the new administration began to act vigorously, improvising in many often conflicting directions. It moved decisively to open the banks and restore confidence in the monetary system. It rapidly expanded emer-gency relief programs for the unemployed and for the indigent in agriculture, proceeded somewhat more deliberately to activate programs of useful public works, and adopted schemes designed to quarantine farm surpluses and support farm prices and income. What appeared at the outset to be the most ambitious vehicle for recovery measures, the National Recovery Administra-tion, proved more directly concerned to soften industrial competition, stabilize or raise industrial prices, and further unionization than to stimulate output and employment. But at least for a time the NRA blue eagle symbolized some improvement in business expectations. In addition, intermixed with these and other recovery efforts was a spate of long-term economic and social reforms, some of which we shall refer to shortly.

The landslide election of 1936 makes it clear that action was what people of the period wanted. Certainly the overwhelming majority accorded the Democratic party in that year did not reflect the brilliance of the recovery the New Deal had engineered. Business activity had, it is true, improved rather steadily throughout the first Roosevelt term. But in 1936, real gross national product still was 5 percent below the 1929 level and perhaps 20 or

25 percent below current normal full capacity. A sixth of the labor force still was unemployed. It was a grudging, disappointing upturn by historical standards. Nor was it any developing clarity or coherence in the administration's antidepression program that commanded such ardent support. The nearest thing to a central theme in the steps actually taken was that of deficit spending. But the administration still was paying earnest lip service to the doctrines of orthodox budget-balancing public finance.

Nor could the enormous popularity of the early New Deal be put down to the particular reform measures it had enacted, although these, while controversial, on balance won votes. Most of all it seems simply to have been the unprecedented vigor of the public-policy assault on the problem of depression that commanded widespread approval. It is significant that the 1936 campaign was the last in which either major party made the traditional argument that government should not meddle with the problem of instability.

Besides this basic political shift toward a much greater continuing antideflationary role for the Federal government, however, the 1930s had other lasting impacts on future United States business conditions. Many specific, mostly helpful, adjustments in the economy's capacities for resisting future deflations accrued as by-products of reform measures. The social security system, particularly its unemployment compensation component, and farm price supports provided some automatic cushioning of disposable personal income, and hence of personal consumption spending, against future declines in total spending. As already noted, banking reforms, including particularly the institution of Federal bank deposit insurance, greatly reduced the possibility of a wave of panic-induced bank failures comparable to that of 1929–1933. The establishment of regulatory legislation and machinery for securities exchanges, public utility holding companies, and margin trading in the securities markets limited the chance that the speculative excesses of the late twenties ever would reappear in full-blown form. And before the thirties were over, the institution of government-guaranteed mortgage programs provided a device, first widely exercised after World War II, that would permit some stabilization of the housing market if authorities were of a mind to use it. Even government sponsorship of labor organization probably had some lasting antideflationary effect. The upsurge in the strength of organized labor following the Wagner Act of 1935 increased the chance that wage earners in the future would share the fruits of rising productivity more quickly than they had in the late twenties, and the chance of downward spirals in wages when business activity slackened was reduced.

THE LESSONS OF 1936–1938

The striking thing about the United States economy's performance during the 1930s was its lack of adequate comeback throughout the decade. In a moment we shall suggest an explanation of this inadequacy. First, however, there are several points to be made about the submerged cycle that occurred within this consistently slack period. The sharp relative boom in activity from early 1936 to mid-1937 and the even sharper drop during the next year had many appearances of a traditional cycle. Yet this episode served only to underscore the fear of many observers that the economy had emerged from the worst ordeals of the Depression in a permanently weakened form. For here the system was fluctuating in the old manner, but apparently around a trend far below full-production and full-employment levels. To put the matter in technical language, the 1936–1938 boomlet and bust dramatized the possibility of underemployment equilibrium in the United States. For many economists the latter was the haunting fear of the late thirties. Subsequent events, as we shall see, did not discredit this fear so much as they outmoded it. But certain aspects of the 1936–1938 experience have continuing pertinence. Four, in particular, should be cited.

First, the economy put on a disturbing performance in the realm of price-output relationships. Prices rose briskly during the latter half of 1936 and early 1937. This more than anything else attached boom symptoms to the period and prompted authorities to adopt restrictive measures. Yet, as just noted, there was still much underproduction and unemployment. There were, to be sure, some special circumstances that helped explain this particular outbreak of inflation amid unemployed resources. The unionization drive created unusual pressures on wages. And the very depth and duration of the Depression had caused such prolonged curtailments of investment, even replacement investment, in some industries that more bottlenecks than usual may have been encountered as production began to recover. But many of the forces pushing upward on suppliers' costs and prices in 1936 and 1937—substantial increases in farm prices and some international raw materials from the earliest stages of recovery, the effort of manufacturing corporations to return quickly to full-cost pricing, and the continuing pressures on wages generated by powerful unions—were due to become routine in the postwar era. At least in retrospect it appears that 1936 to 1937 was the time when one of the postwar American economy's greater domestic dilemmas—the possible inconsistency of its full-employment and its price-stability objectives—first was sharply revealed.

Second, the 1936–1938 record vividly illustrates how a fluctuation in inventory investment can instigate a general business fluctuation and, in particular, can trigger a major decline in activity if other sectors of demand are susceptible. The 1936–1937 acceleration in buying was largely a restocking boom. Business had been buying inventory on a hand-to-mouth basis throughout the depth of the Depression. With some improvement in conditions, there was a natural tendency to replenish commodity stocks. In addition, rising commodity prices added a price-rise-beating incentive to inventory buying, and, by stimulating incomes, purchases for inventory gave a fillip to retail as well as raw material and manufacturers' sales. But this spurt could not be long sustained unless other advances in spending came along to replace the unsustainable rate of inventory investment and vindicate the higher levels to which inventories had been built by mid-1937. This did not happen. Fixed business investment remained in the doldrums, bogged down by dreary long-term expectations, limited in its access to credit, and discouraged by cost squeezes on profits. As we shall see in a moment, government fiscal policy, instead of fortifying the expansion, helped to undermine it. Thus during the middle quarters of 1937, prices and orders for inventory, interacting with each other, leveled off, but inventories continued to pile up until the end of the year as production for past orders outran sales. This brought a sharp curtailment in business buying for stock replacement, which, with fixed investment weak and fiscal policy perverse, tipped farm prices steeply downhill, reversed short-run expectations decisively, and caused very abrupt reductions in industrial activity.

Third, the 1936–1938 experience underscored the difficulties of administering a stabilizing monetary policy, particularly during a period of chronic slack when a problem of price inflation is superimposed. Throughout the halting recovery to mid-1936, money had been kept exceptionally easy, both with respect to interest rates and to the excess reserve position of commercial banks. However, the marginal efficiency of capital had fallen to such low levels that easy money had very little visible effect on investment. But then, in the midst of this situation, the monetary authorities became concerned about the price rise that began in 1936. Given the large excess reserves of the commercial banks, the authorities were in the unenviable position of a fisherman who finds that he has many fathoms of slack in his line just as he decides his quarry is about to make a run for it. In order to reel in the slack in a hurry, the Federal Reserve Board resorted to two violent shifts in that most indelicate of its control mechanisms—the fixing of member-bank reserve requirements. Reserve requirements were doubled in the space of nine months.

The effect on money rates was not particularly noteworthy, but that on the availability of bank credit was. Not only was banks' lending ability radically curtailed, but many were forced to make heavy sales of government securities, thereby absorbing some of the existing nonbank credit. There was a sharp adverse shock to the ability of corporations to finance new investment.[7] Thus the nagging dilemma of American monetary policy—one to which we shall have to revert in our discussion of the 1950s and 1960s—was starkly revealed: the anti-inflationary weapons of the central banking system are exclusively demand weapons; their function is to restrict spending. But to restrain prices in this fashion may exact a painful cost in terms of produc-

---

[7] Although students of the period differ over how much blame the Federal Reserve System should be assigned for the 1938 recession, the most careful of them conclude that the System cannot be entirely absolved. Cf. Kenneth Roose, *The Economics of Recession and Revival*, Yale University Press, New Haven, Conn., 1954.

tion and employment, a cost that was particularly hard to justify at the peak of a boom that found a sixth of the labor force still out of work.

Finally, if the monetary policy adopted during the 1936–1937 boom was dubious, the fiscal policy of the Federal government was miserable. Indeed it was so bad it taught Washington a powerful practical lesson that led, thereafter, to swift official acceptance of the doctrines of modern stabilizing budget policy. But in 1936, as we have noted, the Roosevelt administration still was apologizing for the moderate deficits it had been running. In 1937, partly at least as an orthodox budget-balancing effort, Federal outlays were curtailed and taxes raised, lowering the conventional budget deficit. Moreover, outside the conventional budget, the government's trust fund accounts received their first sizable intake of social security taxes (far outbalancing the immediate outflow of social security benefits). As a result, from calendar 1936 to calendar 1937 the Federal deficit as measured in the national income accounts dropped more than $3 billion.

Plainly, this adverse shift in fiscal policy contributed heavily to the ensuing reduction in GNP. With this experience, and with Keynesian economics providing a new rationale for a deliberate use of the government budget to supplement private demand in slack periods, the administration finally learned the fiscal policy lesson in a rush. In 1938 there was a shift toward a stimulating budget program. For the first time, deficit spending began to be advanced officially as a legitimate and reputable antirecession tactic. It was not, however, until the 1940s that Federal fiscal policy played a truly significant role in stimulating economic recovery. With respect to the decade as a whole, E. Cary Brown concludes, "Fiscal policy, then, seems to have been an unsuccessful recovery device in the 'thirties—not because it did not work, but because it was not tried."[8]

THE THREAT OF STAGNATION

Earlier in the chapter, three constants of the old, pre-1929 United States economy were cited—a lack of government responsibility for conditioning aggregate demand, routine oscillation, and dynamic growth. During the thirties the first of these was decisively reversed, and a good deal of the groundwork was laid for our current defenses against the second. The issue that most plagued observers in the late thirties, however, was whether the economy emerging from the trauma of the Great Depression might not also have lost the third of its traditional characteristics—that of dynamic self-generating growth.

The circumstances of grievously inadequate recovery that gave rise to the hypothesis of secular stagnation are obvious and already have been cited.

[8] E. Cary Brown, "Fiscal Policy in the 'Thirties: A Reappraisal," *American Economic Review*, vol. XLVI, no. 5, pp. 863–864, December, 1956.

Moreover, there was no mistaking the demand sector that, in terms of previous full-employment demand patterns, remained persistently inadequate throughout the decade. It was private fixed investment. In 1929 the plant and equipment component of gross national product and private residential construction together amounted to $14.5 billion and accounted for 14.1 percent of GNP. During the 1930s such private fixed investment averaged only $6.6 billion (or 8.6 percent of the GNP), ranging from a low of $3 billion (or 5.3 percent of GNP) in 1933 to a high in 1937 of $9.2 billion (or 10.2 percent of total spending).

Alvin Hansen, who was the principal American expositor of the secular-stagnation, or mature-economy, thesis near the end of the decade, attributed this lethargic investment record to a permanent attrition of the inducement to invest.[9] Put very sketchily, his argument went like this: that among the principal sources of American private investment opportunities in the past had been (1) population growth, (2) the opening and settlement of new territories in the West, (3) the industrial expansion associated with wars, and (4) technological innovations; that population growth was declining and evidently was due to cease, the continental frontier was gone, it could be hoped that wars were a thing of the past, and it was unrealistic to expect enough acceleration of innovation to offset the loss of these other sources of investment opportunity.

Although Hansen's argument made a good deal of sense at the time it was first advanced, history very quickly upset his premises. World War II, of course, broke out almost immediately, and the postwar era imposed a vastly greater continuing requirement for defense production on the American economy than the economy had ever known before. The postwar birthrate utterly shattered the projections of the prewar population forecasters. And it has become plain that opportunities for the intensive development of geographic regions may be quite as numerous as were those for extensive development. Moreover, as was remarked at one point in Part Two, it now is clear that the rationale of the other chief late-thirties secular stagnationist—Keynes himself—was almost equally vulnerable. For his fear that a continuing slippage in the marginal efficiency of capital would accompany the continuing accumulation of capital relative to other resources did not make adequate allowance for the offsets to diminishing returns to capital that would continue to be supplied by technological innovations.

Nevertheless, the fact that arguments advanced in behalf of the secular-stagnation thesis in the late thirties have not aged well does not necessarily mean the thesis was wrong. Although some of the investment drought of the thirties may have been due to a bunching of innovations in the preceding period, and although some of it certainly was due to the abnormally heavy

[9] *Investigation of the Concentration of Economic Power, Hearings before the Senate Temporary National Economic Committee*, 76th Cong., 1st Sess., May 16–26, 1939, part 9, pp. 3538–3559.

private construction of the twenties, the basic difficulty seems rather to have been psychological. The 1929–1933 plunge was an unprecedented blow to the country's confidence in business and to business' confidence in the country. The impact on investors' long-term expectations was prolonged, if not potentially permanent. For many businessmen the standard American vision of vigorous secular growth was shattered. Fears that the economy had become permanently mired were aggravated by the heavy overhang of unused capacity and by the dampened population trend (itself partly induced by the Depression). And, of course, the severe demoralization of business, by discouraging spending, tended to be self-confirming and -perpetuating.

In this connection there has been an interesting but irresolvable debate about whether the New Deal, by contributing via its reform programs to adverse business expectations, did more harm than good, as far as recovery was concerned. There is no question that, once the brief 1933–1934 honeymoon was over, many leading business decision makers developed a more violent antipathy for the Roosevelt administration than for any other before or since. With considerable reason, they regarded the administration as basically antagonistic to the corporate community, and no doubt some avoided the undertaking of all major risks as long as That Man was in the White House. But it is easy to exaggerate the impact the national political scene has on concrete business decisions. Probably the shattering collapse of confidence at the beginning of the decade did more to undermine expectations throughout the decade than anything that happened subsequently. It seems rather unlikely that all the adverse impacts of the New Deal on private investment deterred as much spending as expanded government programs added— or even as much as the private investment such programs induced.

Be that as it may, history offers no assurance that the deficiency in private demand would not have remained chronic had not World War II come along to give the American economy a kind of shock therapy—demonstrating the system's enormous productive potential, boosting incomes and income expectations up to a new full-employment growth path, reversing the trend in birthrates, renewing and intensifying industry's research and technological development, and demonstrating once and for all the antideflationary effectiveness of fiscal policy (if taken in adequate doses). It may be contended, of course, that even without the war the expectational wounds of the Great Depression sooner or later would have healed and full recovery have been achieved. But this we don't know. The self-perpetuating character of dreary long-term expectations might, at least, for a very long time, have kept the economy, although fluctuating and experiencing a sluggish net growth in activity, languishing far below its potential.

The one sure thing is that the heady experience of World War II and its aftermath restored the United States economic system's confidence in itself. To say this is not to condone or glorify war, nor is it to state that the economy today requires an underpinning of high defense spending to be healthy. It simply is to admit that as a matter of historical fact it was a second traumatic shock which undid some of the adverse effects of the earlier Great Depression shock.

THE ECONOMY AROUSED: THE WARTIME SURGE

The economic performance of the United States during World War II was a truly great national accomplishment.[10] From 1940 to 1945 the country's real output increased by more than one-half. For national defense reasons, total Federal outlays rose from 6.6 percent to 45.8 percent of the gross national product. And yet, despite more than a doubling of aggregate demand, the price level as measured by the GNP deflator rose only 36 percent between 1940 and 1945. The consumer price index increased only 28 percent. And from 1942, when a comprehensive program of wartime anti-inflation policy was first mounted, to 1945, the advances in the GNP deflator and in the consumer price index were, respectively, only 13 and 10 percent.

The problem of economic mobilization for total war in the early forties had three basic facets: (1) Total production had to be expanded. (2) There had to be a radical reallocation of resources and a shift of production from civilian to war purposes. (3) In spite of these first two requirements, and insofar as was consistent with them, price inflation needed to be fought. In barest outline the figures just recited reflect the remarkable record that was made on all three of these counts—expansion, reallocation, and stabilization.

EXPANSION AND REALLOCATION

The World War II record demonstrated the theoretically persuasive proposition that the cure for underproduction is an increase in aggregate demand—a sufficient increase—and that this advance can take the form of government spending. As we suggested earlier, the inadequate recovery of the 1930s did not prove the failure of government spending as an antidepression expedient. All that it proved was that public outlays of the period had been too small to achieve full recovery. As soon as those outlays were expanded radically after Pearl Harbor, underproduction and unemployment were wiped out forthwith.

Throughout the war the government contract remained by all odds the principal policy instrument by which continuing production expansion was achieved. Outside the uniformed services there was little formal resort to mandatory directives to work and produce. Patriotism and social pressures, to be sure, provided strong stimulants to production, causing firms to view

[10] The wartime economic experience has been elaborately documented in a number of official histories, one of the more general and competent of which is *The United States at War*, U.S. Bureau of the Budget, 1946.

government requests for output as virtual commands.   Along with public recruitment and placement programs, such pressures also partly accounted for the abnormal expansions in the total labor force and in average weekly hours.   (Each rose about 10 percent.)   But there is no question that the expansion in government spending and the gains thereby induced in private spending were principally responsible for driving output upward.

The attack made on the reallocation problem in World War II was, in some respects, the most fascinating aspect of the mobilization, but it had relatively little continuing relevance to nonwar circumstances.   Very briefly, the policies adopted contrasted sharply with those used for expanding production: for reallocation, the chief reliance was upon centralized controls.   The desired result was achieved by the detailed and rigorous allocation of just a few critical materials—notably, the key metals, steel, aluminum, and copper—and of a number of fabricated components, coupled with limitation or prohibition of production of certain clearly nonessential items, e.g., automobiles.   These controls would have been well-nigh unenforceable, however, if they had not been sweetened a little by the provision of some premium wage and profit incentives for war-related work.   In combination, the controls and inducements achieved a radical redirection of output without much reliance on outright commands to private industry to produce this or that commodity and without direct allocation of the labor force.

The rationale for relying primarily on centralized controls rather than on the decentralized private market as the key allocating mechanism during World War II was that the market, left to its own devices and guided only by government bidding for scarce materials, would not have been sufficiently swift and decisive in meeting war requirements; that, at least in the early stages of the emergency, uninhibited free market allocation would have been positively perverse because expectations of civilian shortages would have caused more feverish rises in consumer and business spending than in government's national security outlays; and that, even if government buyers of war-related output could eventually have spent enough to outspend would-be private low-priority buyers, the desired reallocation could only have been achieved in company with vastly greater price inflation than actually occurred.

THE STABILIZATION BATTLE

Price stabilization was, by definition, not the nation's primary economic objective during World War II.   On the contrary, it was the radical increase in spending generated by the pursuit of the primary objective—namely, to increase selected types of output—that largely created the inflationary pressures in the first place.   However, from the outset of the mobilization effort, well before Pearl Harbor, the minimizing of inflation was recognized as an important secondary wartime objective, not only because of the intrinsic hardships and inequities associated with inflation, but because a violent, uncontrolled inflation could have disrupted the price and income structure so seriously as to interfere with the expansion and reallocation of production.

Part of the wartime price problem was to exert specific restraints on the prices and wage rates paid for particular strategic commodities and skills in critically short supply. Much of the full story of the stabilization concerns the development of effective techniques for directly controlling prices—first selectively, in these critical commodity areas, and then much more generally. However, for our purposes it will be well to bypass the problems of selective price pressures and of price-control techniques and focus on the broad policies adopted to deal with the general imbalance between civilian incomes and civilian supplies. Looked at from another perspective, the same set of issues can be subsumed under the heading of wartime finance.

The United States gross national income, of course, increased hand in hand with total spending from 1940 to 1945, while physical supplies available to consumers and business rose relatively little. The key stabilization question was how to absorb, impound, or otherwise neutralize the excess of civilian incomes over civilian supplies. The orthodox answer offered by the "new (aggregative) economics" was to raise taxes, and, indeed, taxes were lifted radically. The net receipts of Federal, state, and local governments rose from $13.3 billion in 1940 to $44.7 billion in 1944, or from 13 to 21 percent of GNP. But this was far from enough to close the inflationary gap. Only some 45 percent of total Federal outlays during the war were offset by Federal tax collections, whereas, as we saw in the discussion of the balanced-budget multiplier in Chapter 12, even a 100 percent tax offset probably would not have been enough fully to eliminate the inflationary effect of expanded government spending.

A second element in the stabilization effort was the government's sponsorship of a so-called voluntary saving program. A heavy barrage of propaganda and moral pressure was mounted to persuade private income recipients greatly to increase their purchases of government bonds, the stabilization purpose being to get consumers and businesses to channel after-tax income gains into a form of liquid saving that did not increase the availability of private credit. Such liquid saving did, of course, rise enormously during the war. The volume of government securities held by individuals and non-financial corporations increased almost sevenfold from $12.6 billion to $86.3 billion. However, by no means all of this accumulation of liquid savings can be viewed as representing the success of voluntary saving as a causal element in the stabilization effort. Most of it, rather, must be counted an effect of a third and crucial facet of the effort: deliberate reliance upon what J. K. Galbraith has aptly called a disequilibrium system, which was premised upon effective enforcement of economy-wide controls of commodity and service prices.[11]

[11] J. K. Galbraith, "The Disequilibrium System," *American Economic Review*, vol. 37, no. 3, pp. 288–302, June, 1947. See also his *A Theory of Price Control*, Harvard University Press, Cambridge, Mass., 1952.

Basically, the unprecedented volume of voluntary liquid saving during World War II is accounted for by the combination of physical supply shortages and general price controls that denied would-be spenders the opportunity to fritter away their income gains simply by bidding up prices. With prices prevented from clearing the market, a rationing system for major consumer supplies was adopted to reinforce retail price controls and to prevent gross inequities in distribution. Similar instances of interpolicy reinforcement can be pointed to throughout the whole array of the World War II mobilization policies. The vigor of productive expansion somewhat eased the problem of reallocation by reducing the amount of civilian belt tightening necessary for meeting military requirements. Controls of materials eased the pressures on prices of scarce materials. Price controls on such materials, by curbing the competitive bidding for them, facilitated their direction into priority uses. Tax increases and the promotion of bond buying helped to keep down to manageable proportions the pressures price controls had to regulate. And the degree of success achieved in that regulation facilitated the sale of bonds.

However, when all such interactions have been noted, the fact remains that general price control was the pivotal element in the World War II stabilization program. Such control is a messy, meddlesome, ponderous, pressure-besieged, enormously difficult, thankless operation. It is one which, beginning shortly after its start, becomes increasingly difficult and decreasingly effective as cost pressures accumulate and products change. It is an operation that no one, least of all the price controller, enjoys. Yet during the war it was crucial; it happened to attract highly gifted and dedicated personnel; and it was, everything considered, remarkably successful.

THE LEGACY OF LIQUIDITY

While in subsequent economic discussions of the war years there has been little throbbing enthusiasm for the accomplishments of the Office of Price Administration, it generally has been admitted that these accomplishments were considerable. But it is common for contemporary economists to assume that the whole disequilibrium system of wartime stabilization was, in terms of aftereffects, a vast mistake—that if only it had been possible, a pay-as-you-go brand of war finance would have been ideal. This is by no means certain. For one thing, to deprecate the amount of tax raising accomplished during the war is to evince a political opaqueness of which economists are all too frequently guilty. It is hard to study the political history of the period without concluding that the public's tolerance for tax increases was, in fact, strained to the limit. And significant further increases, even had they been within the limits of legislative possibility, might have had adverse effects on incentives to work and hence on production.

Quite aside from this point, however, there is the strong probability that a large part of the overhang of liquidity that, as a result of disequilibrium stabilization, private spenders carried out of the war was an essential factor in propelling the economy onto its postwar growth path. It is well to remember the psychological depression that had still crippled private investment at the end of the thirties. The buoyant wartime performance proved the enormous productive vitality of the American economy. But it by no means convinced everyone that aggregate demand would hold up once the war was over. On the contrary, a wholly unprecedented decline in national security spending was in prospect, and during the later war years the air was thick with forecasts of a major postwar depression. If these somber expectations had been borne out, who is to say that investors would not have been confirmed in their 1930s-style view of the economy's long-term peacetime prospects? They might have settled into a pattern of conservatism that could have given us a substantially different postwar period.

But instead of reflecting the bearish forecasts, private domestic investment jumped from $10.6 billion in 1945 to $30.6 billion in 1946. This investment performance, probably more than anything else, was responsible for the surprisingly easy transition out of the war and for setting the economy on its high, if inflationary, postwar road. Five factors seem to have accounted for it.

One was the extremely effective public relations job that some business leaders and economists did in countering the bearish forecasts with carefully prepared but challenging projections of postwar possibilities for civilian market expansion. This work, partly inspired by business conditions analysts in the Department of Commerce, was spearheaded by the newly constituted, highly progressive business organization, the Committee for Economic Development.

A second was a program launched by the War Production Board (WPB) about a year before the end of the war to permit and assist industry to plan the reconversion from war to peace, and to do a limited amount of tooling up for peacetime production. Although the war ended somewhat sooner than the WPB's officials anticipated, the reconversion process was considerably shortened by these advance preparations.

A third factor encouraging investment was increased confidence in the ability and determination of the Federal government effectively to resist and soon reverse any recession that might develop. The war experience demonstrated that the government had such power, and as hostilities drew to a close there was an increasing chorus of official, including congressional, voices suggesting that the power should and would be used.

A fourth reinforcement of the transition was provided by the three- and four-year backlogs of unrequited wants for many durable goods, including good housing, with which many consumers emerged from the war. Similarly, many firms reached the end of the war with their capital replacement programs badly in arrears, not only because of wartime shortages, but also because of the long investment drought of the thirties.

However, the most important of all the factors influencing businessmen to invest boldly may have been the extreme liquidity of both households and corporations.   Whatever the long-term outlook, it was plain that consumers not only had backlogged wants; they had enough loose money in their pockets to promise a lively market for many items for a considerable period.   And the impulse of businesses to do the retooling and rebuilding necessary to get a piece of that market was fortified by the fact that they too, typically, had the liquid wherewithal needed for financing such investment.

In a perfect world, perhaps, taxes would have been enough higher during the war to have left the postwar overhang of liquidity sufficiently lower to have still given the economy an effective transitional boost without generating quite so much price inflation.   But too much liquidity probably was distinctly preferable to too little.   Almost certainly, pay-as-you-go finance during the war would have guaranteed a painful aftermath.

THE LATE FORTIES: APPROACHING A NEW NORM

THE LAPSE IN NATIONAL SECURITY

In addition to vigorous secular growth, minimal government intervention in aggregate-demand management, and routine oscillation, the old, pre-1929, United States economy had another crucial characteristic that, while less obviously economic, had major economic consequences.   That was the strategic isolation of the pre-1929 economy and, in consequence, the very low levels of peacetime national security outlays.   The United States had become a first-rank world power, but it had not, despite Woodrow Wilson's efforts, become the leader of a major international coalition.   Instead it typically kept all European power blocs at arm's length, rested its national security on its comparatively costless natural geographic defenses, and, except in time of war, kept its armed-forces-in-being at what were radically low levels by European standards.

Until the aftermath of World War II, therefore, the strategic history of the United States was pretty much an either-or proposition—either total war or total peace.   Europeans had lived most of the preceding thousand years in an in-between condition of heavily armed insecurity fraught with tensions and usually teetering on the brink of major conflict.   This was such an unfamiliar situation to Americans that, when we finally found ourselves plunged into it after World War II, we had to invent a new name for the condition: the cold war.

World War II clearly was a major watershed in United States strategic history.   The country emerged from it established as the leader of the free world coalition, with all the onerous military responsibilities that role entailed, and our traditional geographic defenses plainly were in the process of being rendered obsolete.   In retrospect it is easy to see that an old-style demobilization was no longer appropriate, and the country's political leaders were not blind to the changed situation. While most Americans hoped wishfully that some of the camaraderie that had characterized our wartime dealings with the Russians might carry forward into the peace, official Washington actually was quite quick to recognize the fundamental antagonism to the West of the power bloc the Soviet Union was building. And the war was not long over before the United States government began to devise and mount a series of resourceful measures to contain that threat.

Nevertheless, when it came right down to the matter of demobilization in 1945 and 1946, the political pressures to get the boys—just about all the boys—home and out of uniform were enormous. Not one of the country's principal political leaders felt able to resist these pressures. As it happened, it was possible to resort to one highly reassuring rationalization: namely, that the United States had a long lead over the rest of the world, notably the U.S.S.R., in developing and producing atomic weapons. This, it was felt, justified a much more radical reduction in conventional military strength than otherwise would have been feasible.

Thus immediately after the war the United States disarmed as rapidly as it ever had and, it is now clear, cut back to strength levels well below its cold-war strategic requirements. From 1945 to 1947, the Armed Forces were reduced from 11.4 million men to 1.6 million, and national defense spending was cut from a high of $87 billion in 1944 to a low of $9 billion in 1947. The defense program stayed in this radically lower range during the remainder of the forties.

Viewed from a business conditions perspective, this exaggerated lull in the national security effort invites two comments. First, the plunging drop in national security spending after the end of the war and the pouring of nearly ten million young adults back into the civilian labor market maximized the risk of recession as the economy tried to reconvert to peacetime activities. However, as we have partly discussed, this danger was bypassed extraordinarily well. It looked as though the bottom was dropping out of the stock market for a while in 1946, but the rest of business scarcely seemed to notice. Total spending, incomes, output, employment, and working hours all dropped sharply from their wartime super-full-employment levels. But there were enough withdrawals from the labor force and enough veterans took advantage of their educational GI Bill benefits so that the civilian labor force rose less than 4 million from 1945 to 1946 (yearly averages) despite an 8 million decline in the size of the Armed Forces. Less than 4 percent of the civilian labor force failed to find jobs in 1946, as private investment surged forward and consumers began to liberate some of their backlogs of liquid savings.

Second, it can be argued that the late-forties' lapse in national security, as long as it did not precipitate a recession, was a mighty good thing from a domestic stabilization point of view. Even with defense outlays in 1946–1948 far less than would have been advisable on strategic grounds, the boom in consumption and investment generated heavy demand pressures on prices. With adequate national security expenditures, price inflation would have been much worse, unless the government had adopted an extremely austere tax program or had managed the political and technical miracle of keeping effective general price controls in force throughout the decade. Of course, if one wished to counter this point with the claim that without this lapse in national security we might never have had to contend with the inflationary and other consequences of the Korean War, he might be right.

CONSUMERS' APPETITE FOR FIXED ASSETS

One of the most remarkable things about World War II was what happened to consumer incomes. Between 1940 and 1945 total dollar disposable personal income approximately doubled; even after allowances for price and population increases, real disposable personal income per capita rose 31 percent. This provided the average household with the income entitlement to a radically improved standard of living. However, the supply shortages meant that the fixed asset aspects of such a higher living standard—increased ownership of new houses, automobiles, furniture, household appliances, and the like —had to be largely postponed while the war was in progress, and households, thanks to the forced-saving effect of retail price controls, accumulated unprecedented volumes of liquid savings. Thereafter, as fast as new durables and housing supplies permitted, there was a spring-back of fixed asset purchases to or beyond the old relationship to income. There was a pronounced relative shift from liquid to fixed asset accumulation. Outlays on consumer durables and new housing, which had averaged $10 billion a year during the five years from 1937 to 1941 and had slipped to an average annual rate of about $8 billion during the war, soared to an annual average of $32 billion for the four years of 1946 to 1949. Meanwhile household financial saving, which had amounted to $41 billion in 1944, slumped to less than $3 billion in 1948, and to an even lower figure in 1949 and 1950.[12]

From the time of the immediate postwar reconversion, when business investment had supplied the decisive momentum, to the outbreak of the Korean War, this stocking-up boom in consumer hardware dominated the late forties. The surge was facilitated by institutional developments in the credit sphere—the increasing popularity of installment credit and of regularly amortized mortgages, and a rapid expansion in government-guaranteed mortgage debt. But essentially the boom was a reassertion of income-asset relationships. While there is no precise way of determining how long the pent-up demand lasted, probably, in the case of durables, it was pretty well satisfied by early 1950. In that year, however, a heavy round of scare buying after the Korean outbreak added to consumer stocks, and there was an extraordi-

[12] Note that the reference is to financial saving. Net personal saving dropped from $37 billion in 1944 to a low of $7.3 billion in 1947.

nary amount of house building, thanks partly to a marked liberalization of government mortgage-guarantee provisions legislated in 1949. It was not surprising that thereafter consumers eased their buying of new fixed assets and sought to replenish their liquidity.

THE INFLATION PROBLEM

What was to be the leading domestic economic anxiety of the 1950s in the United States first became widespread in the years 1946 to 1948. This was the fear that the economy had acquired a chronic inflationary bias. Part of the explanation can be found simply in the price indexes of the period. The United States wholesale price index rose 14 percent from 1945 to 1946 and made gains of 23 percent and 8 percent in the two succeeding years. The advance in the consumer price index during the same three-year period was 34 percent and in the GNP deflator, 33 percent. Observers' long-term expectations always are somewhat colored by current short-term developments, and perhaps this was enough short-term inflation to explain fully the new fears of secular inflationary bias. But to reason this way is to attribute a good deal of naïvety to economists of the period. For the United States had experienced such inflationary episodes before, especially during and immediately after wars. Yet during the remainder of its history, the economy, thanks partly to its vigorous physical growth, had evinced a great capacity for absorbing demand stimulants without major price-level reactions.

Superficially, at least, the 1946–1948 experience had most of the earmarks of one of those historically exceptional and temporary periods in which there had been a general excess of demand over supply at existing prices. The labor market was tight and many commodities, particularly durables, were in short supply. From 1946 to 1948 current-price GNP rose $49 billion while capacity in constant dollars advanced no more than $15 billion. Moreover, thanks partly to the temporary postwar bulge in the European demand for American farm products, inflationary pressures were especially heavy on farm prices, which are particularly volatile and particularly pervasive in their impact on the rest of the price structure. All this was historically familiar. In fact it might have been argued that the whole 1946–1948 inflation was nothing but a somewhat elongated and dampened repetition of the 1920 surge in commodity prices after World War I.

AN EXCESS DEMAND BIAS?

However, the spreading anxiety about secular inflation in the late forties was rooted in something more than the current-price indicators. For one thing, as noted earlier, the Federal government had assumed a new commitment to do all in its power to avoid and resist recession. This commitment, made on a *de facto* basis in the thirties, had been formally enunciated in the Employment Act of 1946. Aggressive Federal antirecession policy, it was reasoned, might tend to inject a secular inflationary bias into aggregate demand on several counts. First, if it worked, it would largely eliminate the principal occasions on which the general price level had receded substantially in the past; prices still would go up sharply now and then, but there would be little chance for them to reverse themselves. Second, the violent political repugnance for deflation with which the Great Depression had left the country would cause fiscal and monetary policy makers to err if necessary on the side of too much rather than too little demand. And third, this tendency in general stabilization strategy would be compounded by the fact that, from the perspective of individual congressmen, the antirecession fiscal policy prescription— lower taxes and more government spending—typically was more palatable back home than was its anti-inflationary opposite. Although compensatory fiscal policy might be economically symmetrical, it was politically asymmetrical.

Those economic observers of the late forties who argued in this fashion may well have been relying more on inference than observation. Throughout the worst of the inflation the Federal government ran a significant cash surplus —not large enough to represent a robust anti-inflationary policy, but at least on the side of the angels. Even the cut in the personal income tax which Congress passed over a presidential veto in 1948 and which was widely regarded as inflation-aggravating at the time of its enactment, really began to take hold only in time to help nip the 1948–1949 recession in the bud.

The one policy sector in which the events of 1946 to 1948 appeared to confirm fears of a new inflationary bias in aggregate-demand management was that of monetary policy. Here the authorities continued the war-born policy of supporting government bond prices at par. This had the effect of minimizing the interest bill on the public debt, but it virtually immobilized the potential anti-inflationary restraints of the central banking system's general credit policies. As a result, interest rates remained low and private credit was readily accessible to borrowers.

As was suggested in Chapter 11, this course of action can be partly explained by the swings of fashion in economic thinking about the effectiveness of monetary policy. Those who counseled against strong anti-inflationary monetary policies in the late forties were not unconcerned about inflation; they simply doubted that such policies would do enough anti-inflationary good to offset the costs to the Treasury in terms of carrying charges on the debt and to the economy in terms of needed kinds of capacity expansion.

Most American economists have now come to feel that this skepticism about the efficacy of monetary policy was exaggerated. It is noteworthy, however, that even with the easy-money policies of the period, the money supply did not expand much. From 1946 to 1948, while GNP was growing $49 billion, or 24 percent, total demand deposits and currency held by the public increased from $108.5 to $110.5 billion, or less than 2 percent. It was the activity of the extraordinary liquid balances in corporate and household hands, not an expansion of bank credit, that mainly financed the 1946–1948 boom. Thus the boom was less than ordinarily susceptible to central bank restraints. Coming at the unusual period that it did, the rejection of general monetary policy as an important stabilizing device may have added very little expansion to aggregate demand.

AN UPWARD COST BIAS?

But the worriers about long-term inflation were not just concerned about a lack of demand discipline. They thought they also spotted institutional changes that were tending to make the aggregate-supply path turn upward at levels of output and employment appreciably short of capacity. The most obvious of these changes was the sharply increased power of organized labor. It appeared that this might be the explanation for the unusual alacrity with which wage rates participated in the postwar inflation. From 1945 to 1948 current-dollar average hourly earnings in manufacturing increased 31 percent compared with a rise of 34 percent in the consumer price index. From labor's point of view this was better than its record in most previous inflations. But it was achieved only by successive jumps in dollar-wage rates that well exceeded any currently accruing gains in average real output per man-hour and which consequently added importantly to many manufacturers' unit costs.

Believing (1) that the balance of power in collective bargaining was such as usually to generate wage rises in excess of productivity gains and (2) that manufacturing corporations were showing an increasing commitment to cost-oriented rather than demand-oriented pricing policies and typically had the market power to pass on cost increases as price increases, many observers feared that the economy had stumbled into the grip of a vast escalating mechanism. No one had planned it; few wanted it; but no one quite knew how to arrest it as long as output and employment were being sustained at reasonably satisfactory levels.

The one concrete development of the period that seemed best to symbolize this danger was the introduction of the so-called cost-of-living escalator into the labor contract between the General Motors Corporation and the United Automobile Workers in the spring of 1948. This device was to spread very rapidly in the fifties. From the viewpoint of an individual union or the individual worker looking at his paycheck, it made eminently good sense. But from the viewpoint of the economy, it was a device perfectly designed to add momentum to the economy-wide cost-price escalator.

While the late forties thus bequeathed a problem that was to hang heavy over the long-term business outlook in the United States, the events of 1946 to 1948 by no means proved the worriers' case. They could, as we have pointed out, be ascribed very largely to a conventional excess demand boom, and by late 1948 it seemed to many that perhaps, after all, they should be.

By then spending had slowed up, chiefly because supplies had improved enough to satiate business' appetite for inventories, and the economy was heading into its first postwar recession. The lapse in demand quickly took most of the upward pressure off prices. Crude materials prices broke rather sharply, the general wholesale price index fell about 5 percent from 1948 to 1949, and even the consumer price index eased 1 percent.

THE 1948–1949 TEST

The fame of the 1948–1949 recession lies in its timing. This was the country's first postreconversion downturn after World War II, and inevitably it was viewed as the first important test of the new postwar economy's antirecession resiliency.

Actually the test was not a particularly severe one. The downturn proved to be little if anything more than an inventory recession. After two years of scrambling to build their inventories as sales continued to outrun supplies, sellers in 1948 rather suddenly began to find the supply situation easing. Inventory investment climbed to a peak annual rate of $6.1 billion in the third quarter of 1948, and efforts to check further accumulation put a damper on sales. This occasioned some further, unwanted, inventory accumulation until the first quarter of 1949. By then businesses were sufficiently overstocked that they cut output and purchases below sales; they disinvested inventories throughout the rest of 1949. From the fourth quarter of 1948 to the fourth quarter of 1949 there was a net shift of $9.6 billion (seasonally adjusted annual rate) in inventory investment.

Consumers' appetite for fixed assets, however, had not yet been satisfied, and it was not notably dulled by this slump in business purchases for resale. Expenditures on new automobiles jumped sharply from 1948 to 1949, and those on other consumer durables and on new houses held up very well. Purchases of producers' durable equipment declined only $1.4 billion, or less than 8 percent, from their very high 1948 level, and private nonresidential construction receded only $0.3 billion. Plainly, the long-term expectations of business continued strong, and its capital programs were not seriously compromised by adverse short-run markets.

This strength in private durable goods buying was supported by factors of recently increased importance. A sharp expansion in installment credit facilitated the consumer-durables outlays. Government-guaranteed mortgages supplied most of the credit for the new house buying. And the spread of serious long-term capital budgeting by corporations may have explained some of the resiliency of plant and equipment spending. On the other hand, a skeptic could discount these points and argue that the strength in private durables was largely a matter, still, of backlogged wartime wants and of abnormal private liquidity—factors that represented no lasting change in the economy.

There were other critical aspects of the 1948–1949 record, however, that would have been much less likely to have cropped up in the economy's pre-1929 history. For one thing, despite the setback in general business activity, disposable personal income rose slightly, thanks to sharp reductions in personal taxes. The latter declined from $21.1 billion in 1948 to $18.6 billion in 1949. Undistributed corporate profits were squeezed down from $15.6 billion to $11.3 billion. Secondly, government purchases of goods and services, despite the decline in revenues, jumped over $6 billion—somewhat over half of this in the Federal government and the remainder in state and local governments. From 1948 to 1949 the net balance in the Federal government's transactions with the rest of the economy, on a national income accounts basis, shifted from a surplus of $8.4 billion to a deficit of $2.4 billion, a swing of over $10 billion. Here was a pattern of fiscal policy far better than that which helped precipitate the 1937–1938 recession.

Admittedly, most of these helpful adjustments in fiscal policy were not accomplished consciously for stabilization purposes. Much of the tax reduction was attributable to Congress's 1948 cut, which became law on April 2, 1948, well before the downturn was evident. The administration had resisted the cut on the ground that it would add to inflationary pressures. Moreover, a good part of the increase in Federal spending reflected the new Marshall Plan economic aid to Europe, which first involved substantial outlays in 1949. Much of the counterrecessionary change in the budget was due to the operation of the built-in stabilizers.[13] But the total change, inadvertent or not, gave the future a new peacetime lesson in the effectiveness of a decisive adjustment in fiscal policy.

The combination of deflation-resisting supports confined the 1948–1949 recession to narrow limits. From peak to trough month (November, 1948, to June, 1949), the industrial production index fell only 13 percent; and from peak to trough quarter, current-price GNP declined only 3.3 percent. On a year-to-year basis, the GNP fell scarcely at all, from $257.6 to $256.5 billion. The slow-up was sufficient, however, to prove that, in an economy with persisting physical growth, leveling business activity is enough to produce a discernible recession in economic health. Profits were lowered substantially, and unemployment rose from 2.3 million, or 3.8 percent of the civilian labor force in 1948, to 3.7 million, or 5.9 percent of the civilian labor force in 1949.

The peak unemployment month of the 1948–1949 recession did not come until February, 1950. By that time, however, recovery already had gathered momentum. With inventories back in line with sales, businessmen began again to buy for stock on a replacement basis, housing and automobiles both began to head into a record year, and plant and equipment buying resumed its upward march. A new expansion clearly was underway before the outbreak of war in Korea caught the economy completely by surprise in mid-1950.

[13] See Wilfred Lewis, Jr., *Fiscal Policy in the Postwar Recessions*, The Brookings Institution, Washington, D.C., 1962, pp. 91–130.

THE THIRTIES AND FORTIES IN RETROSPECT

The American economy in June, 1950, was a very different system than it had been twenty-one years earlier. It was, of course, physically larger. Normal productive capacity had increased by three-quarters, and real capacity per capita was half again higher than it had been in 1929. But in addition, two decades of crisis had subjected the system to extraordinary stresses. First, there had been a tragic experience of unprecedentedly harrowing, stubborn, and non-self-correcting depression. This produced a revolution in political expectations as to the depression-avoiding responsibilities of the Federal government. It generated a rash of public-policy expedients and reforms. Some of these proved ill-conceived and were abandoned. But others survived and, in so doing, introduced permanent alterations into the economy's stability characteristics.

The Depression also generated corrosive suspicions that the traditional progressiveness of the economy had been permanently lessened. These were not effectively countered until the second crisis, World War II, came along to prove that all the economy needed was sufficient aggregate demand to prosper and expand as abundantly as it ever had in the past, and until the postwar boom suggested that there was no need for peacetime demand to recede to depressed levels. Viewed in the large, the economic mobilization of World War II was a brilliant performance. Even the financing of the war effort, while less than ideal in its inflationary impact on the years that followed, had the great merit of assuring private postwar demand sufficient buoyancy to offset adequately the staggering drop in military spending.

The scant five years from V-J Day to the Korean outbreak were a period in which many of the characteristics of the new economy began to come into focus. In a sense it is remarkable that the violent experiences of total depression and total war had wrought so little change. The nation's constitutional and political forms were undisturbed, and so, to a surprising extent, was its economic organization. There had been some redistribution of private power, most notably in favor of organized labor, and there had been considerable extensions of governmental programs to regulate, promote, or protect particular groups or industries. But compared with almost any other economy of record, the noteworthy thing about the United States government's intervention into detailed economic determinations continued to be the narrowness, not the breadth, of its scope.

Yet some profound changes had occurred and were beginning to sort themselves out. The foregoing account has not dwelt upon all of them. For example, there had been a very substantial improvement in personal economic security, and the relative inequality of income distribution had been reduced. By 1950 the scope of those changes we have discussed was not yet distinct. Despite the increased confidence (which the 1948–1949 record partly justified) in the antideflationary effectiveness of the Federal government, it certainly was too early to say that the economy had completed a shift from routine oscillation to routine prosperity.   Similarly, while the late forties seemed to suggest that the growth potential of the new economy was unimpaired, it was too soon to be sure that the early postwar performance had not been a transitory, backlog-supported phenomenon.   Nor could one be certain whether the alleged new danger of secular inflation was serious.   Nor had the full peacetime consequences of the nation's changed strategic situation yet been felt.

But the new trends were now in sight.   The events of the fifties were to establish them in sharper relief.   However, before this could happen the country had still to negotiate the third of the three crises that featured in the three decades beginning in 1929.   It had yet to experience its first modern exposure to the peculiarly confusing problems of limited war.

15

THE NEW AMERICAN ECONOMY: The Fifties and Sixties

Six months after the start of the 1950s, the outbreak of a small but costly war in Korea inflicted on the American economy a shock even more unexpected than Pearl Harbor. The ensuing three years, besides encompassing a limited mobilization and a violent but temporary and brief inflation, introduced the country to the economics of cold war. During the remainder of the fifties, while achieving unprecedented affluence and a new self-consciousness about its growth potential, the economy encountered another bout of disquieting inflation, suffered two recessions, and began to exhibit a widening gap between its potential and actual output and employment.

Six months after the start of the "soaring sixties," the United States was again in recession—for the third time in a half-dozen years. It began to be evident that the country's fiscal system, in the very process of becoming more cyclically benign during the past generation, had acquired characteristics that were secularly perverse in the absence of deliberate antidotes. Following the trough of the 1960–1961 recession, however, the nation's dominant business conditions story was one of prolonged expansion unprecedented in its endurance, orderliness, and balance. One can argue persuasively that the period was blessed by a combination of enlightened self-interest in private decision making and a new sophistication in public fiscal and monetary policies. But the early sixties were also etched with new or newly appreciated problems: the persistence of slack in the face of vigorous expansion; the newly publicized specter of "structural unemployment," in part, a by-product of automation; and the country's first serious balance-of-payments anxieties in this century. During the first four years of the long expansion, on the other hand, the price level was remarkably well behaved.

Chronologically organized accounts of economic developments have a particularly unfinished, nonilluminating quality for periods most recently at hand. They are apt to miss the pattern of events that longer hindsight reveals; tend often to make too much of the very recent past; and offer little bridging to the future. Accordingly we propose to organize this discussion of the fifties and sixties around six themes or issues. Each was in the foreground during much of this decade and a half, and each was implicit throughout all of it. Taken up in the order indicated, a review of the following issues can supply a sufficiently comprehensive perspective on the period:

defense expansion
"cycles" and recessions
growth and employment
fiscal drag, stagnation
inflation
balance of payments

DEFENSE EXPANSION

The Korean outbreak had a double impact on American national security requirements. The first was the immediate need for men, weapons, and logistics for prosecuting the Korean War itself. But second, the outbreak in one stroke crystallized popular support for a radical shift in the nation's long-term strategic posture, a shift that had substantial economic implications. The news of the explosion of the first Soviet atomic bomb in August, 1949, proved that the Western lead in nuclear weapons had narrowed, a point underscored in January, 1950, by the knowledge that the British physicist Klaus Fuchs, who possessed much Western thermonuclear know-how, had defected to the Communists. The grave significance of these events did not escape leading United States strategists. Their planning eventually led not only to much stronger United States standing forces but also to the North Atlantic Treaty Organization (NATO), the mutual-security aid program, and the rest of an international free world defense system. This planning—done in great secrecy before June, 1950—was largely unknown to the public and encountered profound inertia within the United States government, particularly with respect to the defense budget.

With the unexpected onset of hostilities in Korea, however, two undertakings, that of fighting the war at hand and that of achieving a lasting major buildup in the nation's defense strength, were suddenly fused in popular and official thinking, and there was an almost universal and instantaneous acceptance of both. The economy was unprepared for such a radical shift. Moreover, many Americans, unaccustomed to thinking in limited-war terms, assumed that the invasion of South Korea was a near prelude to World War III, and, as bidders for commodities, acted accordingly. Under this combination of circumstances, the outbreak of a relatively small war produced violent reactions in the United States economy. Yet fifteen years later, that economy has adjusted—with characteristic adaptability—to the seeming permanence of levels of defense outlays and total Federal budget unthinkable before World War II.

THE SURGE IN PRIVATE SPENDING

The Korean outbreak's first and heaviest impact on expenditures was concentrated in the private sectors of the economy. Washington was a beehive of mostly purposeful activity in the summer of 1950, and the deployment of forces and supplies in the Far East, the planning and provision of funds for defense expansion, and the letting of new military contracts all proceeded apace. But it took time before major acceleration in the national security program could show up in government purchases of goods and services. By the fourth quarter of 1950 national security outlays were at a seasonally adjusted annual rate only $4 billion (but 30 percent) higher than a year earlier and accounted for only 8 percent of the year's $50 billion rise in GNP. The big increase in defense spending did not occur until 1951, when the seasonally adjusted annual rate of national security outlays more than doubled, reaching $42 billion by the fourth quarter of that year and accounting for 77 percent of the rise in GNP.

The surge in private spending that accounted for a major part of the accelerated rise in GNP in 1950 represented a scramble for commodities by both consumers and businesses. At the start of the war consumers stocked up on items, particularly durable goods, they feared would disappear from the market as defense expansion proceeded. A second splurge, this time especially for soft goods, followed the full-scale intervention of the Chinese in Korea in late 1950. Meanwhile businesses were scrambling for inventories, partly also in anticipation of shortages, partly to beat expected price rises, and partly to stock up on materials and components that would be required for filling defense contracts. Inventory building was somewhat checked by the soaring volume of sales in the two quarters of heaviest consumer buying, the third quarter of 1950 and the first quarter of 1951. But in each of the succeeding quarters inventory investment surged upward, and in the second quarter of 1951 reached the wholly unprecedented seasonally adjusted annual rate of $15.2 billion.

Laid on top of the gradual acceleration of national security spending and of already high and rising trends in private fixed investment, this consumer and business scramble for commodities during the early months of the war created a classic example of demand pressures on prices. And rising prices, in turn, accelerated the growth in demand as they were reflected in rising incomes and served to accentuate expectations of further price increases. For the first eight months after the Korean outbreak, the economy was victimized by a full-blown inflationary spiral. By February, 1951, the Bureau of Labor Statistics daily index of spot primary-market prices had soared 46 percent above its prewar level, the wholesale price index had climbed 17 percent, and even the sluggish consumer price index had risen 9 percent.

The frothy, undisciplined inflation that dominated the business scene from mid-1950 until early 1951 classically illustrated the manner in which the aggregate-supply path in the United States can become sharply inelastic when the economy is caught off-balance by a sudden surge in demand and in income and price expectations. A month or two after the start of 1951, major inflation stopped almost as suddenly as it had begun, and comparative price stability characterized the whole remaining two years of the Korean War. As we shall see, the explanation of this second, remarkably docile phase of the 1950–1953 price experience traces back in part to some of the elements of the first phase that we have just discussed.

THE SHAPE OF LIMITED MOBILIZATION

Meanwhile, by the end of 1950, the process of defense procurement was beginning to have a more visible impact in the GNP statistics. But beyond the actual achievement of these heightened purchases lay unresolved issues whose resolution would importantly influence the economic significance of the mobilization. With worsening war news from Korea, there was a stock saying within government circles in Washington that a 10 percent mobilization suddenly had turned into a 25 percent mobilization. This phrasing had no real quantitative significance, but it does suggest some of the unfamiliar perplexities that surrounded the programing of a partial military effort. A shifting tactical situation in Korea created difficulties in determining military requirements, but chiefly the new problems of limited mobilization related to the scope and pace of the buildup in permanent defense strength.

Rather surprisingly, the design and engineering of limited mobilization proved a thornier problem than total mobilization. For one thing, economic policy needed to be directed to a broader range of objectives than during previous all-out wars. Then the single overriding objective had been early victory. Compared with this, long-term economic strength and stability had been distinctly secondary purposes. But now there had to be as much concern for building a base of fundamental capacity appropriate for long-run mobilization as there was for weapons production in the short run. This indicated a need for stimulating rather than curtailing private investment in many basic industries. Similarly, in weapons development and production itself, speed and volume of weapons output were less important—compared with their scientific sophistication and the pace of scientific advance—than would have been true if there had been an all-out war.

In the second place, the very nature of the defense buildup's targets generated difficulties. The universally accepted need was radically to raise the nation's level of military strength. But just how much of a rise was needed was not dictated by immediate combat requirements, and just how soon it *had* to be accomplished was debatable. Ideally it should have been done yesterday, but that being impossible, who could say for sure that it was essential to accomplish the desired buildup in two years instead of three or four? Decisions in these regards had major economic significance, since a more gradual as well as a lower total buildup in military spending promised less disruption of the civilian economy. A rise from one strength level to another tended to require a large but temporary bulge in defense spending. (And, of course, the costs of fighting in Korea intensified this bunching of expenditures in the near term.) But just how much of an expenditure bulge there had to be depended on the rate of the buildup.

Limited mobilization also generated awkward operational problems. Under little-war circumstances, the government had a hard time recruiting outstanding executive and specialist personnel for emergency agencies. The scope of the need for such emergency agencies itself became a bone of contention. And there were pronounced civilian-military frictions—notably over the professional military tendency, in a situation where mobilization targets remained so abstract, to delay production decisions on particular weapons in order to allow for the incorporation of design improvements. There also, of course, were some serious economic control problems, including the nature and operation of stabilization controls and whether a full apparatus of materials-allocation controls, à la World War II, was needed or whether greater reliance upon the private market was feasible. These issues, however, lie off the main track of our interests.

Of more central concern, in retrospect, are the ensuing shifts in the total volume of defense outlays, their relation to GNP, and certain shifts in their composition. From early 1951 through the second quarter of 1953, defense spending, as measured in the national income accounts, accelerated to a peak annual rate of $49.5 billion. With the subsidence of the speculative burst of private spending, this expansion in defense outlays carried them from 4.6 percent of GNP just before the Korean outbreak to 13.5 percent. In sharp contrast with World War II experience, private investment also rose during this period, providing the enlarged mobilization base required by the expanding defense establishment and by the rapidly evolving technological changes in defense requirements. Private consumption was the end-use category that was squeezed in proportion to GNP during this period, declining from 68.3 percent in early 1950 to 62.6 percent by mid-1953. Also, unlike in World War II, this curbing of consumption outlays was not achieved primarily by rationing and price controls, but by tax increases and, to some degree, by credit controls. Following the Korean conflict, defense outlays remained markedly higher, both absolutely and relative to GNP, but their significance changed in several important ways.

THE POST-KOREAN ROLE OF DEFENSE SPENDING

With the closing of Korean hostilities—following newly elected President Eisenhower's dramatic Korean trip—and with the beginning of a new political administration, defense outlays fell sharply from mid-1953 to the end of 1954. National security remained, however, a preeminent concern, and the continuing advances of Russian nuclear and space technology spurred renewed efforts in this country. Thus in 1955, following the post-Korean cutback, the defense budget (in GNP account terms) was $38.6 billion, which amounted to almost 10 percent of an essentially full-employment GNP. Subsequently, defense outlays rose unevenly to a new peak of about $51.6 billion in 1962, or a little over 9 percent of GNP.

The composition of these outlays shifted significantly from that during the Korean period. The adoption of "massive retaliation" as the central element of United States military strategy focused the highest priority on advances in the technology and scale of nuclear weaponry, the means for delivering these weapons, and the systems for warning of attack. The explosion of the H-bomb demonstrated that the atom bomb of Hiroshima was not the ultimate in terror. The launching of the Soviet sputnik in 1957 officially ushered in the space age. Although rocketry was already well advanced in this country and the launching of a satellite, in itself, was of debatable military significance, the Soviets' feat did illustrate beyond doubt their gains both in accuracy of rocket control and in rocket thrust. Thus, the race for military supremacy was run as much in the laboratory as in the munitions plants or the garrison.

The shift of focus toward research and development has considerable economic significance because many of the technological advances had civilian by-products if not direct civilian applications. Among the more obvious examples are the application of advances in radar to civilian aviation, the use of computer technology in feedback systems for industrial and business controls (automation), and the use of satellites for television and civilian communications.

The rapid pace of advance in military science was not without its liabilities. Apart from any problems of adjustment to changing levels of defense spending, there were problems of adjustment to changes in the structure of defense requirements. Perhaps the most dramatic was the shift in emphasis from aircraft to missiles. This was a primary factor in the abrupt decline of the airframe industry on Long Island, New York, and the burgeoning of the electronics and missile industries on the West Coast, resulting in a doubling in the population of San Diego during the decade of the fifties.

Following heated debate concerning military strategy, during the 1960 presidential campaign, another bulge of defense outlays occurred. Repeated crises in Berlin, Southeast Asia, and elsewhere prompted evaluation of the ability to fight brushfire wars as well as the capacity for massive retaliation. Airlift capacity and the equipment and troop capabilities for guerrilla action received new attention in the early days of the Kennedy administration. Once again, however, the outlays needed to achieve this addition to the overall level of military strength were higher than the outlays needed to sustain it. Meanwhile, cautious recognition by the major powers that a balance of power to annihilate had been achieved—a recognition implicit in the nuclear test ban treaty signed in 1963—served to place a ceiling on other types of defense spending. Thus, when Lyndon B. Johnson assumed the Presidency, the combination of circumstance and the extraordinary administrative abilities of Secretary of Defense Robert McNamara combined to produce new possibilities for curbing defense spending. In fiscal year 1965, it registered the first decline—though quite small—since 1960 and only the second in a decade.

The higher level of defense outlays since 1950 has served to put a floor under Federal budgets. The proportion of these expenditures to the budget and to GNP has not fluctuated directly, however, with their absolute level. As previously discussed, the level of aggregate demand was pushed up to—or beyond—the supply potential of the economy during the Korean War and the volume of real consumption was squeezed. Subsequently, the economy was not always operating at its full capacity, as will be discussed below, and the requirement that guns be substituted for butter was sometimes suspended. Thus, defense spending has by no means always squeezed out private (or state and local) spending because of an absolute ceiling on supply. Indeed in years of recession, 1958, for example, the relatively high and stable level of defense outlays served as a built-in stabilizer in the economy helping to resist the cumulative decline in private outlays. At other times, however, political decisions, on the part of either the administration or Congress, have assigned higher priority to limiting the total economic role of the Federal government in the economy (as realized in the budget) than to Federal civilian expenditures. Thus, it seems fairly clear that in many budgets of the late 1950s and early 1960s, Federal civilian programs were squeezed by the demands of national security during a period of cold war. Regardless of the nature of such political decisions in the near future, it seems likely that the economic requirements of national security not only have become but will remain large enough to impose some limitations on the flexibility of budget policy.

The smaller proportion of the budget accounted for by defense outlays in 1964—about 76.5 percent of Federal purchases of goods and services as measured in the national income accounts compared to 81.4 percent at their peak in absolute level in 1962—stands out, nevertheless, as an important accomplishment. Having achieved a greatly enlarged defense establishment, rigorous application of computerized budgeting techniques and cost-benefit analysis resulted in paring the costs of maintaining a strong defense posture. A reverse squeeze in budget allocations was achieved in the budgets for fiscal 1965 and 1966, when a deliberate effort was made to shift funds to high-priority civilian programs. Before the 1966 fiscal year had much more than begun, however, events in Vietnam forced another substantial increase in defense spending. And the fiscal 1967 budget, submitted at a time when the United States military engagement in Vietnam was expanding and when the economy was operating at a relatively high level, reflected a reversion to a policy of squeezing civilian programs in favor of defense.

Looking into the longer-run future, it would be foolhardy to predict a declining level of defense spending. Furthermore, in the absence of a radical change in the entire philosophy of diplomatic relations, it is clear that any major new international crisis carries with it the potential for large new military claims upon the economy; in the event of crisis, the government will spend what is deemed necessary. Nevertheless, since the Korean buildup, defense outlays constitute one major part of the Federal budget that has not grown in pace with the growth of the economy. Moreover, the time may also be past when defense spending exerts an automatic, top-priority claim on the budget. It has become more widely recognized that no matter what the level of the Federal budget found consistent with preferences of the public concerning the economic role of the government, or found necessary—in combination with tax policies—for stabilization purposes, expenditure programs should meet two criteria: their benefits should match or exceed their costs, and the benefits relative to costs for those programs included in the budget should exceed those excluded. The newly flexible and critical attitude now in evidence toward all types of budget outlays, including defense, is a particularly significant indication of increased economic sophistication in the Federal government.

"CYCLES" AND RECESSIONS

The post-Korean War period provides the first opportunity for observing, under quasi-normal circumstances, the net outcome of extensive but limited business conditions change brought by a quarter century dominated by depression and war. The late date and mild nature of the 1949 recession provided a pleasant surprise for those who had predicted a return to the stagnation of the thirties following demobilization from World War II. Yet so many fortuitous circumstances occurred then that the "depression-proof" character of the economy was not really tested. The years following the Korean War suggest that the economy might, indeed, have become immune to depression on the scale of the 1930s, but clearly it has by no means become immune to the internal imbalances that generate milder recessions.

THE "ENCOURAGING" RECESSION OF 1953-1954

The downturn in demand and production and later in employment that began in mid-1953 was probably the most thoroughly forecasted recession in American history. First discussed officially in the January, 1953, *Economic Report of the President*, submitted by outgoing President Truman, it was almost universally anticipated in the business and general press at that time. There was no mystery about this sudden flowering of prescience. The factor that was to trigger the downturn—the decline in national security spending associated with the end of accelerated defense expansion—had been publicly spelled out in the government's budgetary program. The attainment of a new plateau in defense strength meant the elimination of what might be called the expansion component of military outlays. The cessation of hostilities in Korea in 1953 accentuated this effect, and so did the cutting of the national security budget below previously planned levels when the new Eisenhower administration came to power in 1953. But the basic pattern of an over-the-hump drop in national security expenditures had already been inherent in the government's financial planning for some time. Its precise timing remained uncertain, but the probability that it would generate a significant stabilization problem was widely recognized.

Nevertheless the 1953-1954 downturn was not without its surprises. The chief one to many people was that the slump did not go further than it did. Unfortunately the question of just how severe a test of stability the 1953-1954 episode really was got badly befogged in political invective. The incumbent party had a natural tendency to minimize the seriousness of the downturn, was inclined to suggest that the decline was essentially just an inventory recession, and charged that certain Democratic "doom-and-gloomers" in Congress were irresponsibly undermining business confidence for the sake of narrow partisan advantage. And some of the legislators in early 1954 did seem exaggerated in their pessimism.

Invective aside, the 1953-1954 decline was, clearly, a major test of the economy in no sense comparable to that of 1948-1949. Potentially alarming weaknesses developed simultaneously in many sectors of demand. National security outlays themselves dropped $1.9 billion from the second to the fourth quarters of 1953 and an additional $10 billion by the end of 1954 (both seasonally adjusted annual rates), providing an exogenous disturbance that did not seem likely to be offset by any force comparable to the pent-up demands of the late-1940s. After advancing in late 1952 and early 1953, both new house buying and the consumer-durables outlays seemed likely to sag, or at least not to resist any reduction in general activity originating in the national security sector. Further, plant and equipment spending was expected to drop as the fast tax write-offs and other special stimulants to industrial expansion provided by the mobilization program tapered off.

In short, at the beginning of the 1953-1954 recession the economy was beset by a concurrence of weaknesses in demand. In the days of routine instability this would have been just the sort of situation calculated to launch the various downward cumulators in the economy—the multiplier, the accelerator, self-confirming price expectations, and credit contraction—into a progressive, interacting erosion of demand. Thus the holding of this recession to approximately the proportions of the downturn in 1948 to 1949 was a much more convincing stabilization achievement than the one five years earlier. In particular, the experience was more reassuring on this count: the snubbing and reversal of the downturn in 1953–1954 did not depend so much on happenstance factors as that in 1948–1949.

One thing that helped was the steady up-push of state and local spendin—at a rate of about $3 billion per year. This was an expression of urgent community needs for public educational, health, highway, and other facilities. While some of these needs had been accumulating since the outbreak of World War II, they were not just a temporary backlog phenomenon. With an increasingly numerous and prosperous population, such requirements would continue to be pressing for a long time to come.

Another vital factor was the striking resiliency of fixed-capital spending by business. Here the record was even better than in 1948–1949. Despite the tapering in government stimulants to invest, private nonresidential fixed-capital formation declined, at a seasonably adjusted annual rate, only $1.2 billion, or about 3.5 percent from peak to trough quarter. Then it rose almost 10 percent in the succeeding year. This strong performance—and the even stronger rise to come—obviously betokened a high business confidence in economic prosperity, which was largely unshaken by the 1954 decline in sales. It also seemed to reflect, in part, an accelerated pace of technological innovation and of obsolescence in existing fixed capital, and in part, a continuing trend toward a higher share of equipment in the plant and equipment mix.

The most important and striking of all the resistances to recession displayed during 1953–1954, however, was that in consumption. Durables buying, as we have noted, did weaken some, but with respect to soft goods and services consumption, the multiplier, as usually construed, did not function at all as an aggravator of the downturn. This was not mainly because of abnormal consumption relative to income. It was because of the excellent manner in which disposable personal income remained insulated from the decline in total spending. During the year following the second quarter of 1953, all the decline in total income was absorbed by the gross retained earnings of business and the net receipts of government, which together fell $4.7 billion while disposable personal income was creeping up $1.3 billion. Then during the second half of 1954, DPI claimed $7.7 billion of the $11.4 billion rise in the seasonally adjusted annual rate of national income.

Much of this gain in the consumers' share of spendable incomes was the result of automatic, or at least well-established, institutional processes including the payment of unemployment compensation benefits, the progressivity of the income tax structure—known as the built-in stabilizers—a continuing rise in wage rates, and the squeezing of profits as business slowed. By themselves, however, these factors serve more to stem the decline in consumer income than to turn the tide. A crucial additional margin of some $3.25 billion for consumers was provided by the timely reduction of the Federal personal income and excise taxes at the beginning of 1954. Happenstance accounted for the fact that these reductions, provided by the lapsing of temporary Korean War tax rates, already were on the books and therefore could take effect without specific legislative intervention. But Congress still had to decide whether to let the reductions take effect, and it decided the question essentially on stabilization grounds.

There were two other important moves in Federal stabilization policy. After a sharp and singularly inappropriate tightening of monetary policy in early 1953, general credit- and debt-management policies were shifted decisively to a position of "active ease" in mid-1953, at the very beginning of the recession. Secondly, in 1954, the permissible terms on Federal government-guaranteed mortgages were greatly liberalized.

Private spending had enough bounce in it so that, despite sharp reductions in Federal spending, these policy steps proved sufficient to arrest the downturn and create an opportunity for recovery. By the fall of 1954 both the inventory liquidation and the reduction in national security outlays had largely run their course, and, with these down-pushing factors eliminated, the general outlook was for a business revival. A new burst of fixed asset buying by consumers spearheaded the recovery and helped to make it exceptionally rapid. A swift rise in house buying, triggered by the mortgage-guarantee policies just noted, demonstrated a strong underlying demand for housing, and the 1955 automobile models sold at a phenomenal rate. The strength already noted in plant and equipment spending and soft goods and services consumption brought a decisive recovery in final demand accompanied by the emphatic turnaround in inventory investment that is characteristic of the early phase of cyclical recovery. Output returned to full-capacity levels with a rush in 1955, gross national product rising, at seasonally adjusted rates, $34 billion or 9.4 percent, in four quarters from the $360 billion level at which it had stood in the second quarter of 1954.

BUILT-IN DESTABILIZERS? FIXED INVESTMENT

With the period of sharp fluctuations in defense spending and of pent-up private demand largely completed, the economic history of the next few years proved to be dominated more strongly by fluctuations in the strength of various types of private spending. Yet the fast-acting, cumulative processes of the downward consumption multiplier and of credit contraction remained largely absent from the scene. The hypothesis to be developed in the next few subsections of this chapter is that the numerous possible recession triggers that can operate in the private sector of today's economy can, by and large, be grouped under the heading of "accelerator mechanisms" or "stock adjustment processes."

For example, by the end of 1955, there was some fear that full-blown prosperity would be short-lived. Rather clearly, the extraordinary volume of automobile sales that year had borrowed customers from 1956, since consumers had acquired a stock of cars that would last them for a while. Similarly, it looked as though the stepped-up rate of private residential construction was not wholly sustainable since the rate of additions and replacements to the housing stock appeared to be faster than could be supported by the forces of household formation and income growth. Thus, consumers began another minor swing toward liquidity replenishment, and the seasonally adjusted annual rate of expenditures on consumer durable goods and new housing fell $5 billion between the third quarter of 1955 and the third quarter of 1956. Instead of causing any lapse in prosperity, however, this only made room for an equal increase in fixed-capital formation by business at a time when the remainder of consumption also was rising vigorously.

Soaring plant and equipment outlays featured the two years of high prosperity that followed the American economy's 1955 return to full-capacity operations. After a decade of heavy business investment following World War II, nonfarm plant and equipment outlays were already at a new high that year. Nevertheless, they soared 22 percent higher in 1956 and another 6 percent in 1957.

Most of these increases in spending were indicated in advance in intentions surveys, although their timing had to be shifted somewhat as the capacity of equipment industries came under pressure. The pattern of these outlays did not suggest any massive speculative scramble but, rather, carefully considered long-term capital expansion and modernization programs. (These matters are discussed at greater length in Chapter 19.) Nevertheless, it was quite clear, even at the time, that the 1956 rate of *increase* in plant and equipment outlays could not be continued. The slowdown and final peaking out in the third quarter of 1957 are easily recognized to have followed the classic accelerator formula. It became equally clear late in 1957, however, not only that the rate of increase in plant and equipment spending could not be sustained but that—given the developments in the rest of the economy—the volume of capacity created by new investments had become excessive. As soon as the pressure on the equipment industries—created by the investment itself—slackened, underutilization of capacity became prevalent in manufacturing industries.

Federal policies played a significant role in the slackening pace of expansion in 1956 and 1957. The Federal national income account budget, after swinging sharply from deficit to surplus as revenues recovered from the effects of the 1954 recession, registered a growing surplus in 1956 and early 1957. Federal expenditures increased very slowly while revenues continued to grow with the economy. In addition, monetary policy became increasingly restrictive, prompted by a renewed bout of inflation. The "independence" of the Federal Reserve to use monetary policy in a countercyclical fashion had been reestablished in 1951 by the Treasury-Federal Reserve "accord." This accord ended a period of tense controversy (documented in the lengthy hearings conducted by Wright Patman, Chairman of the House Banking and Currency Committee) over the appropriate role of the Federal Reserve System with respect to the World War II policy of support for the prices of Treasury securities. The Korean hostilities and the ensuing recession did not give the Federal Reserve System an environment conducive to the use of its newly won freedom but the 1954–1957 expansion provided the opportunity. Following a period of years during which the supply of bank reserves had been dictated by a commitment to support the price of a rapidly growing volume of Treasury securities, it was natural that some increase in interest rates should occur. But the sharp increase in rates, particularly in 1957 when the forces of expansion were already slackening, went beyond such reasonable expectations. After rising by 2 percentage points from the end of 1954 to the end of 1956, short-term rates rose by another one-third of a point in 1957 while long-time Treasury bond yields rose by the same amount.

It remains debatable whether other public policies than those actually followed could have maintained a rate of advance in total demand that would have justified the volume of productive capacity created in 1956–1957. If public policies could have achieved this feat—which would have required considerable flexibility and daring—it is possible that the economy's subsequent expansion and growth would have been significantly more rapid. As it was, a sharp decline in fixed investment in 1957–1958 became inevitable, owing to the imbalance that had developed between the expansion of capacity and the expansion of demand. Not only were foreseeable needs for additional plant capacity adequately met for the time being, but the rate of growth of other components of demand slackened relative to existing capacity, slowing the rate of replacement and modernization. Thus, the accelerator mechanism operated even more vigorously than called for by the classic recipe, inducing a marked instability into the economy.

By the fall of 1957 there already had been enough dampening of consumer-durables outlays, of the expected revival in housing, and of debt-dependent state and local construction projects to widen the gap between output and capacity noticeably and to initiate an up-creep in unemployment. In November, the Federal Reserve Board began to reverse course and the launching of the Soviet sputnik in October touched off an intensification of national security efforts.

Nevertheless, the 1957–1958 recession was the deepest of the postwar period. When the GNP peaked in the third quarter of 1957, production already had slipped significantly below the economy's rising normal capacity. In the two succeeding quarters the seasonally adjusted annual rate of the current-price GNP dropped $11.6 billion. This, together with the further growth in real capacity and further increases in average prices, meant that the gap between output and capacity far exceeded the highest rate of underproduction during the 1953–1954 recession. Thus, it was not surprising that seasonally adjusted unemployment rose to its highest postwar rate—7.5 percent of the civilian labor force—in April, 1958.

In this recession too, however, it was the comparative resilience of the economy that was remarkable by prewar standards. From the peak quarter to the trough in the first quarter of 1958, the total net decline in the seasonally adjusted annual rates of gross private domestic investment, net exports, and consumer-durables outlays plunged a total of $18.7 billion. If the same linkages between GNP and personal income, between personal income and disposable personal income, and between DPI and soft goods and services consumption that typified the prewar economy had prevailed at this time, there is no question that there would also have been a sharp sympathetic decline in soft goods and services buying. The recession would have been worse than 1937–1938. And had such a decline been accompanied by a credit collapse, the recession would, instead, have been a depression. In fact, however, soft goods and services buying actually *rose* moderately during the downturn—chiefly because, just as in 1953–1954, disposable personal income remained largely insulated from the fall in gross national product. Although there was not the same helpful cut in personal tax rates as in 1954, the principal factors cushioning consumer incomes against declining gross income—rising transfer payments and shrinking corporate tax collections and a tight squeeze on retained corporate earnings—reappeared. Thus the events of 1957–1958 brought further support to the hypothesis that the economy had become depression-proof though remaining subject to instabilities bred of the stock adjustment mechanism.

BUILT-IN DESTABILIZERS? INVENTORIES, STRIKES, AND STRIKE THREATS

The 1957–1958 "business cycle" could be characterized as V-shaped. Just as the decline in economic activity from 1957 to 1958 was the sharpest of the post-World War II recessions, so the 1958 recovery was quite rapid. Added to the continued rise in consumption of nondurables and services was a new, sharp spurt in residential construction activity as the credit faucets were again turned on. As interest rates declined below the ceiling rate on mortgages insured by FHA, moderate-income households, in particular, took advantage of credit availability to move to their own homes or to better homes, many of them in the burgeoning suburbs. Furthermore, not only was the decline in incomes stemmed by a $6.3 billion decline in Federal revenues, but Federal outlays were also lifted by a $2 billion rise in "discretionary outlays" as well as by the $2.4 billion rise in unemployment insurance and other social insurance payments. These forces combined in 1958 to produce the largest

Federal budget deficit since 1945. Increases in housing activity and in Federal, state, and local purchases resulted in more substantial gains in household incomes; consumer durable goods purchases rose accordingly, although new car sales remained sluggish throughout 1958. Plant and equipment outlays also registered a modest comeback, turning up two quarters after the general recovery began.

Midst this normal marshaling of recovery forces, a swing from inventory decumulation to accumulation was natural. A significant "plus" from inventory investment, however, was not registered until the fourth quarter of 1958. Hard upon the heels of this recovery upswing in stocks, however, came a buildup in steel inventories in anticipation of a summer strike. July 15, 1959, marked the beginning of the longest steel strike in United States history. Recognition by producers that the strongly anti-inflationary bias of Federal policy makers created an unfavorable environment for passing on wage increases, unwillingness of the union to accept the burden of an anti-inflationary policy or implicitly to accept blame for previous price increases, and unwillingness of the administration to step into the situation in view of the prevailing opinion that intervention had frequently led in the past to settlements at the expense of consumers, all led to prolonging the dispute. Regardless of where blame lay for the lengthy dispute—and it must certainly be shared—the mills remained closed until November 8 when they were reopened under a Taft-Hartley injunction. By this time 500,000 steel workers had been out of work 116 days and almost as many other workers had been out of work for various lengths of time, primarily during late September and October, as operations were curtailed in other industries by shortages of steel.

Following reopening of the mills, steel output accelerated more rapidly than had been believed possible. The near quadrupling of iron and steel production from September to December surprised many observers who believed that repairing and restarting cold furnaces would be a far slower process. Nevertheless, disposable income failed to rise at all between the second and third quarters of 1959. This curtailed the expansion of consumption generally. Some demand for high steel-content products was simply deferred and was registered in soaring sales of automobiles, machinery, heavy construction, and other durable goods during the early months of 1960. Some sales of both durables and nondurables, however, were probably "lost" permanently. Thus, sales were disappointing. These developments were coupled with the improvements in inventory management that permitted a downtrend in inventory-sales ratios and with a waning of "inflationary psychology" following nearly two years of stable prices. In combination, they made inventory accumulation that had seemed reasonable in 1959 seem superfluous in 1960.

Meanwhile, in anticipation of excess pent-up demands following the steel strike, in a zealous eagerness to maintain the newly won price stability, and out of a desire to curb the role of the Federal government and the Federal deficit, both monetary and fiscal policy swung to sharply restrictive positions in 1959–1960. Interest rates reached the peak of the basically upward trend they had exhibited since the "accord." Short-term bill rates, at their peak in December, 1959, were 3 percentage points above the 1951 average of 1.5 percent and long-term Treasury bond yields went above 4 percent for the first time, except for a brief period in 1932, since 1924. The swing in the Federal budget was equally marked. The large 1958 deficit in the income and product account was replaced by a surplus of $3.5 billion in 1960, a net swing of $13.7 billion. In view of this generally restrictive policy, it is not surprising that the advance in housing activity was short—housing starts plummeted 22 percent from July, 1959, to July, 1960—and the advance in consumers' after-tax income and their consumption spending was snubbed. Consequently, the buoyance of the economy during the poststrike catch-up proved short-lived and the economy slumped into its fourth postwar recession in mid-1960.

INSTABILITY AND PUBLIC POLICY

The postwar recessions were mild by "normal" prewar cycle standards, let alone the Depression of the 1930s. But their frequency, at least until 1961, was an ample reminder that the components of private spending still do not always advance in step, that imbalances can develop between existing stocks of durable goods and the growth of income that prompts demands for new additions to stocks, and that the growth of productive capacity is not automatically balanced by the growth of demand for its output. The built-in stabilizers—an income tax system responsive to pulsations in the income base, sizable and *cyclically* stable government expenditures, social security and unemployment insurance, insurance of deposits in banks and savings institutions—served admirably in the postwar period to prevent cumulative downswings and financial collapse. But the propensity of the economy to generate mild fluctuations remains a well-documented characteristic. Indeed, some officials of the Kennedy administration that came to office in 1961, at the trough of the 1960–1961 recession, were wont to refer to the "dismal arithmetic" of 45-35-25—this being the dwindling series of months from postwar cyclical troughs to the ensuing peaks.

The Kennedy administration can claim little credit for the early turnaround in business activity that occurred within two months after it took office. Government policy certainly played a significant role, however, in sustaining the ensuing, relatively vigorous expansion that reversed the tendency for increasingly frequent recessions and achieved record peacetime length. President John F. Kennedy was assassinated in Dallas, Texas, three months before enactment of the massive tax cut provided for by the Revenue Act of 1964—certainly one of his crowning economic achievements—but the economic expansion had taken on new life in the fall of 1963 before the President's fateful trip.

The credit for the length and strength of the business expansion that began early in 1961 must be shared by the private and public sectors. The preceding mild recession had resulted from a combination of inventory imbalances and monetary and fiscal policy restraints, and by early 1961 there were no overhanging surpluses of durable goods to restrain the expansion of demand. Consequently, the 1961 recovery was strengthened not only by the customary swing in inventory spending and by substantial increases in government purchases (partly defense outlays, as previously discussed) and transfer payments, but also by simultaneous increases in *every* major component of gross national product.

By 1962, the initial upsurge in inventory spending had run its course and the pace of expansion slowed markedly. From the first quarter of 1961 to the first quarter of 1962 real output grew by 7.7 percent; from the first quarter of 1962 to the second quarter of 1963, the annual rate of growth of real output was only 3.8 percent. Nevertheless, in view of the cautious and balanced expansion of private investment outlays, the continuation of an accommodating monetary policy, and the stimulants to investment (an investment tax credit and liberalized depreciation guidelines) that became effective in mid-1962, there was nothing to trigger a new decline. The economy had sufficient strength to withstand the gradual shift in the Federal budget from a strongly expansionary to a much less expansionary posture. The slowdown in the advance was disappointing, but the widespread fears in some quarters of recession in mid-1962 were not validated.

Then in 1963 the Kennedy administration's tax reduction proposal added a new factor to business calculations. Dissatisfaction with the slow expansion and with the failure of the unemployment rate to fall below 5.5 percent prompted the administration's request to Congress for a massive tax reduction and reform measure. The proposal broke new ground. It marked the first time in United States fiscal history that a tax reduction had been requested when the country was not in recession and the budget was in deficit. It is not surprising that more than a year of debate was required before this measure became law. Meanwhile, however, as the continued expansion bred confidence in itself, growing expectations that the tax reduction would indeed be enacted prompted an acceleration in investment outlays.

The Revenue Act of 1964 became law in February. It reduced personal income tax payments for the year by $8 billion (annual rate), as the withholding rate was dropped immediately from 18 to 14 percent. The act also provided for a second-stage reduction of $2 billion in 1965 tax liabilities that would offset catch-up payments required by some underwithholding in 1964; and it further provided for a $3 billion reduction in corporate tax liabilities, the effects of which would be spread over several years as tax payments were shifted from a deferred to a more current basis.

The massive fiscal stimulus given to the economy during 1964 undoubtedly was a decisive factor in the strong advance of output during that year. Gross national product, in constant dollars, rose by 4.4 percent between the fourth quarters of 1963 and 1964, and personal consumption expenditures, the spending component expected to be most quickly and directly responsive to the tax cut, accounted for an unusually large 83 percent of the overall rise.

Although the tax cut was a major landmark whose significance it is difficult to overestimate, the continuation of strong expansion not only throughout 1964 but during 1965 owed much to the balanced character of the entire expansion.[1] State and local government spending rose steadily in the first half of the 1960s. Total Federal expenditures continued to increase, although at a declining rate that amounted to only $1.0 billion between mid-1964 and mid-1965, compared with the spurt of $3.6 billion (annual rate) in the first quarter of 1961. New car sales, stimulated by the growth of suburbs and the increasing numbers of youngsters reaching driving age, scored an unusual record of four consecutive years of increase. An accommodating monetary policy and intense competition among financial institutions in mortgage lending created a favorable environment for residential construction activity. Housing starts increased for an unusually long three-year period before turning down in early 1964. Surprisingly, the decline following this long upswing was quite mild—possibly reflecting public policies that enlarged the effective demand of lower-income households and stepped up the rate of demolition owing to increased urban renewal and highway construction. Inventory accumulation, although exhibiting fluctuations resulting from strikes and strike threats, was extremely moderate. Finally, fixed investment was stimulated both by the rapid pace of technological change and by tax measures that, in combination, reduced corporate income tax liabilities by nearly 20 percent. Yet increases in business plant and equipment outlays remained well short of the unsustainable surge experienced in 1956. Consequently, accumulations of durable goods and productive capacity remained justifiable by the continuing growth in after-tax income and in demand, and spending of practically all types moved upward or at least remained relatively steady.

The stabilization accomplishments of the first half of the 1960s should not be interpreted as indicating that institutional factors within the economy have made it recession-proof. The mildness of the recessions of the 1950s suggests that the tax and transfer system and the relative insensitivity of total employee compensation to fluctuations in demand greatly weaken the link between declines in aggregate expenditures and in disposable personal income, thus robbing the multiplier of much of its downward force. On the other hand, the stock adjustment process, as it has operated from time to time on automobile expenditures, housing activity, and business fixed or inventory investment, remains a potential source of instability.

---

[1] In addition, key elements contributing to the sustained advance in 1965 were the liberalization of social security benefits enacted that year and the phased excise tax reductions, the first phase going into effect in June and the second in January, 1966, when it helped offset the scheduled rise in social security tax rates.

Certain positive conclusions, however, can be drawn from the first half of the 1960s. First, the stability of consumer disposable incomes and consumer spending serves to reduce, though not eliminate, the degree of instability inherent in business capital spending and consumer expenditures for durable goods. If the overall economy is strong, mild setbacks in one sector or another can occur without triggering a downturn; and continued advances in private incomes can help to prevent or minimize the extent of sectoral imbalances. Second, in large measure public policy can be used to sustain advances in total private income even though it may have quite limited power to restrain excesses or to offset declines in particular sectors. The accomplishment of this policy objective, however, requires not only a generally correct assessment of the underlying strength of private demand but also careful planning within the government sector so that potential disturbances from one source (e.g., changes in military outlays or social security taxes) can be offset elsewhere. Thus complete avoidance of recession remains a difficult public-policy goal. But because of the weakening of the downward cumulators, the consequences of error in public stabilization policies are likely to be less devastating on the downside than they were a generation ago. And the chances of retrieving and correcting errors before they snowball out of control are much greater than they used to be.

GROWTH AND EMPLOYMENT

Two emerging problems of the 1950s generated vigorous, sometimes acrimonious, debate among both theoretical economists and practical politicians. These were, first, an apparent slowdown in the secular growth of the United States economy, and second, a generally rising level of unemployment.

RATE OF GROWTH

As has often been remarked by persons who find economic growth statistics being used to their disadvantage, different figures on the rate of growth can be obtained by selecting different beginning and ending years. For example, if one starts in a boom year and terminates in a recession year, a lower growth rate will result than if a boom-year to boom-year comparison is made. And even in the latter type of comparison, it sometimes makes a difference which boom years are chosen. The following calculations of average annual growth in real output in the United States illustrate the point.[2]

---

[2] The year 1947 is the earliest postwar year included because the closing months of 1945 and most of 1946 were clearly a period of reconversion from wartime to peacetime production, and therefore atypical. Indeed, in some industries the reconversion period extended into 1947.

Period	Average annual rate of change in real GNP (1958 $)
1947–1953	4.9%
1947–1955	4.4%
1948–1953	5.0%
1948–1955	4.4%
1953–1960	2.4%
1953–1959	2.4%
1955–1960	2.2%
1953–1962	2.8%
1955–1962	2.8%
1960–1965	4.5%
1962–1965	4.7%

No matter which years are selected, however, it is clear that during the later 1950s, much of the momentum of the earlier postwar years was lost. This loss was particularly distressing in view of the fact that, during the same time interval, every other major economy, excluding the United Kingdom but probably including the U.S.S.R., was experiencing rates of growth in real output substantially in excess of that of the United States.

Explanations of this unwelcome phenomenon were many and varied. One version was to the effect that the first eight years after the war were the beneficiaries of unique influences associated with World War II and the Korean War (e.g., rapid adoption of previously deferred technological developments). A growth rate of the order of 2½ percent, it was argued, was more nearly normal and more in line with long-run prospects for growth in the capacity of the economy. Other analyses focused on the inadequacy of profits to induce investment and to reward the risks entailed in the development of new products and new processes of production. In part, such commentary had its roots in the sharp fluctuations in profits that accompanied the mild ups and downs in business activity in the 1950s. Thus, the tendency already noted for profits to absorb the impact of fluctuations in demand and to shield personal income, while in the short run improving the stability of the economy, could tend to discourage investment and business initiative in the long run.

Somewhat paralleling the questioning of the adequacy of profits as an incentive to investment were questions concerning the responsiveness of investment to interest rates and the extent to which the postwar uptrend in interest rates was dampening the growth potential of the economy. Some observers attributed the sluggishness of fixed investment spending by business from 1957 through 1961 to the higher level of interest rates. Others were inclined to minimize this effect. They noted that corporate cash flows, which included depreciation and depletion allowances (untaxed, since they are a bookkeeping expense), showed a steadier and faster growth than did corporate profits. The increasing proportion of investment financed during the entire postwar period by corporate cash flow lessened the dependence of business corporations on borrowing to finance capital outlays, and hence lessened the significance of the higher level of interest rates.   Nevertheless, the probable effect of the shift toward internal financing was largely to add flexibility to the timing of borrowing relative to investment spending, not wholly to shield the business community from the effects of monetary conditions.   And, as we have seen in Chapter 11, the trend in interest rates may well have a significant influence on the capital intensity of the economy, particularly in the long run.

Although there was merit in these arguments, they did not provide an adequate explanation of the slowdown in the economic growth rate.   But before we pursue the matter further, it may be well to summarize the parallel developments on the employment scene, because the two problems were integrally related.

EMPLOYMENT AND UNEMPLOYMENT

The data on the overall unemployment rate are illustrated in Figure 15–1.   Unemployment rose sharply in each of the recession years of 1949, 1954, 1958, and 1961.   The behavior of the unemployment rate in the non-

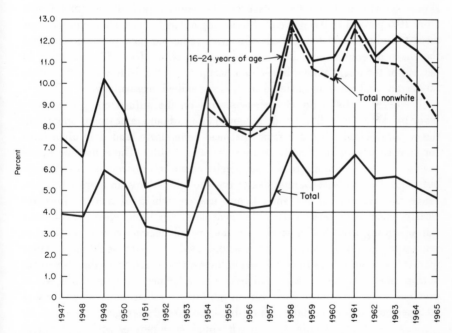

Figure 15–1.   Unemployment rate among all civilian workers, nonwhites, and young workers sixteen to twenty-four years of age, annual averages, 1947–1965.   Note: Owing to changes in definitions and coverage (inclusion of Alaska and Hawaii in 1960), data before and after 1953, 1960, and 1962 are not strictly comparable.   Source: U.S. Department of Labor.

recession years, however, is more significant. In 1947 and 1948, the unemployment rate averaged less than 4 percent, and during the Korean War years of the early 1950s, it averaged close to 3 percent. After the 1954 recession, however, the average annual unemployment rate failed to get back to 4 percent. Then, in the recovery years following the 1958 recession, unemployment failed to go below 5½ percent. Not until 1965, on an annual basis, did unemployment again go below 5 percent.

The incidence of this rising "prosperity level" of unemployment during the 1950s was uneven by industry and by area. The rapid shifts in the composition of total output and the swift adoption of technological change resulted in marked changes in the nature of employment opportunities. The shift from coal to oil and electricity as sources of power for many uses was a major factor in the economic decline of West Virginia. The development of synthetic fibers and the economic forces that tended to draw industry into the Southern states spelled decline in many New England textile towns. Equally striking were the shifts in the industrial and occupational mix of job opportunities. From 1953 to 1964, manufacturing output grew by 45 percent while payroll employment in manufacturing industries fell by more than 1½ percent. Meanwhile, the steep rise in labor productivity in agriculture and the slower growth in demand for its products reduced agricultural employment from 10.6 percent to 6.8 percent of total employment. The change in management techniques and the growth of service industries and professions raised the share of employment in white-collar occupations from 38 percent to 44 percent of the total; among blue-collar occupations, the decline was from 40 to 36 percent and was concentrated in the least-skilled occupations.

These shifts imposed serious strains on the adjustment processes in labor markets. It is difficult for a man to know about employment opportunities a considerable distance from his local community, and it is often hard for him to uproot his family to move to a new job. There may be heavy psychic costs in changing from a physically active job to one that is sedentary but requires speed and manual dexterity—though perhaps no more schooling. These impediments to the smooth and easy matching of men to jobs are clearly reflected in various unemployment data. In 1955, when the economy was operating near full capacity and the overall unemployment rate for the year averaged not far above 4 percent, there were as many as 20 major labor market areas out of 149 in which unemployment averaged more than 6 percent during most of the year. Similarly, unemployment among those whose previous work experience had been in the lowest skilled blue-collar jobs was 10.2 percent, or 6 percentage points above the overall average.

Other types of failures to match would-be employees with employment opportunities are evident in the much higher than average rates of unemployment among young workers and nonwhites. (See Figure 15–1.) These structural problems assumed increased importance in the 1960s because of the revolution in civil rights and because of the rapid rate of entrance of teenagers into the labor force as those born in the high birthrate period following

World War II reached employable age. In these instances, the failure of the market adjustment process can be traced in part to inadequacy of job training, in part to sociological factors, and in the case of teen-agers, primarily to the slow adjustment of attitudes on both sides of the market to a rapid increase in the supply of a particular type of labor.

The failure of the overall unemployment rate to fall to tolerable levels in the late 1950s and early 1960s, and the heavy incidence of unemployment on certain types of workers and geographic areas, made inevitable a focus on technological change and automation as causes of unemployment. Many attributed the persistence of high unemployment rates, even in expansion periods, to the problem of structural unemployment. Clearly, technological change has always been one source of unemployment. But if higher unemployment rates after 1955 than before were attributable to an *increasing degree* of structural unemployment, the unemployment rates of the particularly disadvantaged groups (such as the unskilled) should have been rising relative to the overall average. And this was not the case. It is true that group unemployment rates do bear a cyclical relationship to the overall rate such that, for example, when the overall rate rises, the rates of disadvantaged groups rise more rapidly. But the converse is also true; when the overall rate falls, the rate for the disadvantaged groups falls more rapidly. In the 1950s and early 1960s, the unemployment rate among disadvantaged groups did not rise more than could be accounted for by this cyclical phenomenon. The evidence is not that rising technological unemployment caused a rise in general unemployment, but rather the other way around—that higher general unemployment increased the incidence of what appeared to be structural unemployment.

THE COST OF SLUGGISH DEMAND

We started this section by noting two anxieties that dominated economic thinking in the late 1950s and early 1960s. One was that the slower rate of actual economic growth was "normal" and more in line with probable growth in capacity. In fact, the rate of growth of the population of working age was slightly higher in the 1953–1960 period than in the preceding postwar years. The downtrend in the length of the workweek continued, partly because higher hourly earnings made it possible for workers to afford more leisure, but the average *rate* of decline diminished. The growth of man-hour productivity, however, did slow down. Whether or not the decline in the rate of productivity increase was "normal," i.e., reflected fundamental technological and other influences, is a matter of debate. The argument could be made that technological developments of the late 1930s and early 1940s, not fully utilized in production for reasons of depression and war, were exploited in the 1947–1953 period, but that by 1953 the backlog of such developments had largely been worked off. On the other hand, the resumption of vigorous increase in output per man-hour after 1961, when aggregate demand again rose rapidly, casts doubt on the normality thesis.

The other anxiety was that technological change was proceeding so rapidly as to generate an increasingly indigestible structural unemployment problem. In view of the fact that technological change is one of the main sources of productivity increase, some reconciliation in the logic underlying these two anxieties would seem to be in order. As we have just argued, the recurrent recessions and incomplete recoveries are a much more persuasive explanation of both sources of anxiety.

It is clear that much of the reduced growth of actual output following 1953 is attributable to the sluggish expansion of demand, which left available labor unemployed. If the rate of potential growth is calculated by compounding the rate of change of actual output per man-hour, actual average working hours, and the actual labor force (rather than the number of persons employed), the result is 2.8 percent for the 1953–1960 period. The difference between this estimate of potential growth in the 1953–1960 period and the 2.4 percent growth in actual output is an indication of the output lost due to rising unemployment.

Even this latter comparison, however, does not represent a sufficient adjustment for the impact of demand. The growth in actual capacity during the late 1950s and early 1960s still suffered from hidden losses attributable to slack demand. The growth of the labor force was restrained as some persons became discouraged and ceased to look for work, and the rate of growth of productivity was lowered as overhead capital and labor were less effectively utilized. Furthermore, in the long run, the rate of investment in new equipment embodying new technology was probably retarded and fewer opportunities were provided to the labor force for on-the-job training. Analyses of the rate of expansion that the economy could have achieved had aggregate demand risen vigorously enough for it to operate at full capacity suggest that the rate of growth of supply potential from 1953 to 1960 was clearly above 2.8 percent, possibly close to 3.5 percent.

FISCAL DRAG, STAGNATION?

It has just been noted that the trends in supply and demand diverged during the second half of the 1950s. And the two trends converged only gradually during the first half of the 1960s. Thus, the post-Korean period as a whole demonstrates that even when oscillations in economic activity are mild, the trend around which these oscillations occurs is not automatically consistent with reasonably full employment.

DIAGNOSIS OF THE 1950s

A number of reasons have been adduced for the persistence of inadequate demand during the late 1950s. One argument was that the economy had returned to a state of stagnation similar to that which may have prevailed in the 1930s.　According to this line of argument, the propensity to save in the American economy tended to be high, owing to the level and distribution of income.　Meanwhile, the propensity to invest was relatively small owing to the large capital stock or possibly to a dearth of major capital using innovations such as the advent of electricity or the automobile.　As we said in Chapter 8, the evidence lends little or no support to the portion of this argument pertaining to consumer behavior.　And as we suggested in Chapter 9, and shall discuss further in Chapter 25, experience since 1961 indicates that there are good reasons for questioning the investment portion of the argument, at least as a continuing phenomenon.

　　The most persuasive diagnosis of the creeping sluggishness of demand that appeared in the late fifties had to do with the fiscal system.　According to the proponents of this view, the built-in stabilizing characteristics of the revenue system, useful as they were in a contracyclical sense, tended to impose a progressive fiscal drag on the economy.　The stabilizers withdrew less revenue when the economy was declining but also withdrew substantially more revenue as the economy expanded, thus tending to choke off the expansion.

　　In Chapter 12, we discussed the meaning of the full- or high-employment surplus, and made the point that this concept is the most useful measure of the economic impact of any given Federal tax and expenditure program.　In the late 1950s, full-employment growth would have generated an increase in revenues between $5 billion and $6 billion per year.　During the same period, the rate of growth of total Federal expenditures was slow. Consequently, as we saw in Chapter 12, the high-employment surplus, which had been about $4 billion in 1955, rose sharply in 1959, and in 1960 reached the very high level of almost $14 billion.

　　No one level of the high-employment surplus can be assumed to be appropriate for all periods.　During the period when pent-up demands were unleashed following World War II, for example, a substantial high-employment surplus imposed a desirable restraint on excess private demand. Since the Federal surplus or deficit is one component of aggregate saving, however, a substantial high-employment surplus is appropriate only when private saving out of full-employment income is small relative to investment demand at full employment.　If investment fails to match saving at full employment, neither full employment nor the full-employment surplus is achieved.

　　It is quite possible that the high-employment surplus of the late 1950s would have been appropriate if the distribution of income and other social conditions had, for example, made effective the latent demand for much improved housing or if a major technological innovation had sharply stimulated investment demand.　Given the private spending propensities that were actually in effect, however, a deliberate fiscal policy action to reduce the high-employment surplus was needed to sustain an adequate level of employment.

THE POLICY REVOLUTION OF THE 1960s

When the Kennedy administration took office, the 1960–1961 recession clearly dictated a resort to deliberate measures to reduce the high-employment surplus. The slowdown in economic expansion beginning in mid-1962, however, posed a different kind of problem. An actual decline in business activity had not occurred and, though predicted by some analysts, was not clearly on the horizon. Unemployment, however, stubbornly refused to return to an acceptable level. At that time it became more widely recognized among Federal policy makers—with Council of Economic Advisers Chairman Walter W. Heller in the lead—that the current fiscal system, the fundamental trends in private demand, and the goal of full employment were not mutually consistent. This analysis led to the major step of reducing taxes substantially during a period of expansion—a step that was major both in its size and because it could not readily be reversed.

The revolution in fiscal analysis and practice that occurred in the early 1960s did not end, however, with the Revenue Act of 1964. The analysis that resulted in that act implied that in any year when Federal expenditures did not rise by the $7 billion annual growth in full-employment revenues (the approximate amount that would be generated by the economy by the mid-1960s), the Federal budget would automatically become restrictive. In any year when the economy was not pressing against capacity and when private demand was unlikely to become stronger relative to full-employment income, such restriction would be inappropriate. Recognition of these fiscal facts led to the more delicate juggling of excise tax reductions and adjustments of social security taxes and benefits in 1965 that contributed to sustaining the expansion.

By the same token, the built-in growth of revenues could be a welcome offset to substantial rises in Federal expenditures, such as those sometimes necessitated by defense requirements. And, should outright fiscal restraint be required, it could be desirable to supplement automatic revenue growth with actual tax increases. Early in 1966, for example, strong private demand dictated rescinding certain excise tax reductions previously made and accelerating personal and corporate tax payments to neutralize the fiscal effect of rising defense outlays.

INFLATION

Misbehavior—or at least, nonclassical behavior—of the price system has been a recurrent event during much of recent American economic history. The simplest theory predicts that prices, including the price of labor, should remain constant or decline when economic resources are underutilized and rise when excess demand exists. This static concept and a more sophisticated dynamic analysis have been presented in previous chapters. Several characteristics of price behavior in the American economy have been noted: wages do not fall during recessions, thus thwarting the downward force of the multiplier but also imparting a stickiness to the price system; prices tend to rise abruptly when the economy is subjected to a sudden increase in aggregate demand, because output cannot be expanded rapidly enough to accommodate the increase in demand. These characteristics have been amply demonstrated in the postwar years. In addition, the economy has also experienced a period of inflation that was not associated with generally excessive demand or any sharp jolt, and later a period when prices were exceptionally well behaved despite strong increases in demand, albeit from a deficient level. These various patterns tend to obscure a systematic relationship among some of the variables that should be expected, a priori, to determine prices. Yet several important aspects of post-World War II price behavior are worth exploring.

KOREAN INFLATION AND THE SUBSEQUENT LULL

As we have seen, an urgent need for restraints on classical price inflation occurred in the early months of the Korean War. It was generally agreed that the stabilization strategy should not rely on the kind of disequilibrium system that had been employed during World War II. In a situation that contained no prospect of a subsequent radical reduction in defense spending, it appeared that the excess of overall civilian demand over civilian supplies should be sopped up by tax increases, not temporarily dammed away from the market by general price controls. And there was more than lip service to this principle. Within a fortnight after the North Korean attack, congressional leaders, following the initiative of the Joint Economic Committee, had combined with the administration in sponsoring tax increases that were quickly enacted to yield $5 billion or more of annual revenue. Thereafter, although revenue increases associated with rising incomes did not quite keep pace with rising Federal outlays, the Korean War saw a far closer approach to pay-as-you-go finance than had World War II. Fiscal policy's anti-inflationary record was a robust one.

General monetary policy was another story. The administration, still not greatly impressed by the anti-inflationary effectiveness of general credit controls in a period of high private liquidity, and still concerned to hold down the costs of servicing the public debt, found an additional reason for discouraging the Federal Reserve System from exerting strong general restraints on credit during the early months of the war. It was feared that, being indiscriminate in their impact, such restraints might interfere with the expansion of vital defense production. Subsequently, in March, 1951, the accord between the Federal Reserve Board and the Treasury freed the former to pursue more restrictive general credit policies. But this new era in monetary policy began a month after the back of the initial, surging Korean inflation already had been broken, and it can scarcely be held responsible for that turn of events. Selective credit controls, inaugurated in the fall of 1950, clearly did have an impact, however. These controls fixed high minimum down payments and low maximum durations for installment loans on consumer durables and for government-guaranteed mortgages and, after lags of a few months, took substantial bites out of automobile and new house sales.

In addition to these classical remedies for a classical, excess demand inflation, there was a quick disposition in official circles—both executive and legislative—to institute selective price and wage controls over strategic commodities and skills in particularly short supply. The desirability of general price and wage controls, however, was highly controversial. Some private advisers, like the venerable Bernard Baruch, and some members of Congress called for an economy-wide wage and price freeze almost as soon as the fighting started. However, the administration feared that an immediate across-the-board freeze might prevent some price and wage flexibility, which, in the early stages of mobilization, would be conducive to stimulating additional output and to attracting scarce supplies and labor into priority uses. Moreover, there was great doubt that a mobilization so limited would generate the popular acceptance and support necessary for administering an effective general control system. In retrospect, it seems that this last consideration was the most cogent. Direct controls of prices and wages are sufficiently unpopular in the United States—especially with the business, labor, and farm producer groups whose selling prices they restrain—and at the same time are sufficiently complex in their administration that they require a long line of political credit to operate effectively. During much of World War II, in the patriotic fervor of an all-out conflict, there was enough public support to make tough general price controls workable even in the face of substantial price pressures. During the Korean War there probably never was that support.

At the end of 1950, with the Chinese onslaught in Korea and the renewed surge of prices, it was decided that resort to comprehensive direct controls could no longer be delayed. General price ceilings were imposed the last week of January, 1951 (under powers established in the Defense Production Act the preceding summer) and, as we shall see, this act in itself contributed significantly to the reduction of inflationary pressures. The fact that the pressures on prices subsided almost at the same time and that the ceilings imposed were high meant, however, that the ceilings never had a severe testing. One can scarcely avoid the judgment that the controls apparatus could not have withstood effectively the far more violent pressures to which it would have been subjected, had it been in place a few months earlier.

At the beginning of 1951, it was widely assumed that the inflationary forces then so evident would continue strong throughout the mobilization period. When the daily primary-market spot price index and the wholesale price index stopped rising in February, 1951, and the advances in the consumer price index shortly began to slow up, everyone began talking about the "lull" in inflation. The implication was that the relaxation of price measures must be highly temporary.[3]

Actually the lull lingered throughout the remainder of the Korean War boom. In part this was easily explained by stretch-outs in the defense program. Even so, the second phase of the Korean War boom, from the first quarter of 1951 through the second quarter of 1953, was a period of very rapid expansion in demand and output. During these two and one-quarter years the seasonally adjusted annual rate of the gross national product increased at an annual rate of 6.2 percent; total real output increased at an average annual rate of 4.8 percent. The economy already was operating at full normal capacity or better at the beginning of the period, and it maintained most of the symptoms of drum-tightness. Working hours, for example, stayed high and unemployment averaged little more than 3 percent of the civilian labor force. Yet while demand and output were burgeoning, the wholesale price index declined 5.5 percent between the first quarter of 1951 and the second quarter of 1953, and the consumer price index, despite continuing advances in rents and other service charges, rose only 4.1 percent.

Some of the sources of relative stability after early 1951 were of a kind to provide encouragement for the long-term normal peacetime future. Labor productivity rose vigorously, showing annual gains averaging more than 4 percent for the 1950–1953 period, implying that the economy can operate quite efficiently at high levels of capacity utilization. Similarly, the experience suggested that ideas about the margin of unemployment needed simply to lubricate frictions in the labor market probably had been exaggerated. In addition, the robust character of anti-inflationary tax policy augured well for the responsibility of congressional stabilization policy in the future. Finally, the effective use of selective credit controls created a precedent for policies that might again be useful in future booms.

These projectable features of the 1951–1953 record by no means account for the full measure of price stability, however. Much of the anti-inflationary job appears to have been done by factors peculiar to that particular period. For one thing, the existence of operating price and wage controls, even though their application was not especially vigorous, was not inconsequential. In addition to the impact of the introduction of controls on business and consumer expectations (noted below), their operation did prevent or slow up rises in a good many particular prices and wage rates.

Second, and more important, much of the lull in prices after early 1951 reflected reactions to the violently inflationary period that had just preceded. Several of these can be enumerated.

---

[3] The subject matter of this section is treated more fully in John P. Lewis, "The Lull That Came to Stay," *Journal of Political Economy*, vol. 43, no. 1, pp. 1–19, February, 1955. Some of the present discussion is condensed from that source, and we are grateful to the editors of the *Journal of Political Economy* for the privilege of so doing.

1. The largest concrete and measurable offset to inflation was provided by the swing in inventory investment after the first year of the war. Businesses, as we have seen, joined in the initial commodity scramble after the Korean outbreak, and inventory investment finally rose to an all-time peak in the second quarter of 1951—part of this final surge of commodity stocking being the involuntary consequence of the slowdown in consumer buying. The internal logic of inventory fluctuations (with which we shall deal at length in Chapter 21) made a sharp drop in this category of spending virtually inevitable. This provided a full offset to the climb in national security spending during the next four quarters.

2. As a result of two waves of abnormal stocking, consumers started the 1951–1953 period in an unusually comfortable commodity position. Since they were able to maintain it, and were progressively reassured by the fullness of retail shelves, they were relatively impervious to further shortage and inflation scares.

3. Some of the statistical stability of 1951–1953 simply represented the recoil of the prices of many raw materials and unprocessed commodities from the untenably high levels to which they had been bid during the first feverish months of the war. The point here is the one made in Chapter 6 when we were discussing the nature and behavior of the price structure. During the initial phase of the war, prices of unprocessed commodities in general rose far more than those at the manufacturing, let alone the retail, levels. As a result, manufacturers' and distributors' margins got badly squeezed. As soon as the commodity scramble slowed down and expectations of further inflation were dampened, the resiliency of the distorted price structure reasserted itself; businessmen sought to regain something corresponding to their pre-Korean margins. And while this effort involved some pass-through of increased costs at the manufacturing and retail levels, it showed up most dramatically in the bidding down of prices in the competitive primary markets, where quotations had to work their way back down to levels justified by the sustained expansion in demand. It was not until August, 1952—by which time the daily spot price index had fallen 29 percent, and the general wholesale price index 4 percent, below their 1951 peaks—that the price structure approximately regained its pre-Korean shape at a new, higher level. And then, just as this factor had about worked itself out, the decline in average wholesale prices was extended by the fact that farm prices tailed off into an accelerated decline of their own, for reasons of their own.

4. The introduction of general price controls in early 1951 curbed the impulse of both businessmen and consumers to buy to beat further price rises. Certainly this was the case with business buying, which is highly sensitive to price expectations. Nothing can generate expectations of further price increases as effectively as an experience like that of the second half of 1950; and no single event is better calculated to break the back of such expectations

than a general imposition of price ceilings. Moreover, while consumer opinion research seems to indicate that consumers usually are much less sensitive
to price expectations than are purchasing agents, surely by the end of 1950
many households had strong enough anticipations of continuing price rises
to affect their buying decisions. As consumers became progressively aware
of the imposition of retail price controls in early 1951, these expectations were
weakened, and the public was left free in its buying to register considerable
distaste for the new heights to which retail prices already had surged.

   5. Some of the specific idiosyncrasies of the 1951–1953 price lull
traced all the way back to the late forties. The most puzzling aspect of the
period to economists at the time was the way in which the personal saving
rate, after suddenly jumping from its average of about 5 percent during the
first three quarters of the Korean War to 8.9 percent in the second quarter of
1951, stayed close to or above 7 percent throughout the rest of the emergency,
well above its average level of the late forties. In retrospect these superficially
inconsistent pieces of behavior both appear to have been parts of a single
spending-saving pattern. The factors involved, as we have noted elsewhere,
were the asset components of living standards.

   Emerging from World War II with a relative surfeit of liquidity and
hungry for real assets, consumers during the late forties stocked up on durables and did abnormally little liquid saving. But by mid-1950, with most of
the backlog demand for consumer durables satisfied, and with heavy buying
and price increases both having taken their toll of the real value of personal
liquid assets, it probably was about time for a shift back toward liquid asset
accumulation. The outbreak of war touched off a violent new scramble for
real consumer assets and another, exceptionally steep drop in the value of
liquid assets. It is not surprising that, as soon as the scramble subsided, consumers began to replenish their liquidity in earnest and kept at it for some
time.

   In summary, the Korean inflation and subsequent lull provide an
illuminating example of the characteristic behavior of the economy when subject to a sudden shock, but these characteristic reactions were combined with
some circumstances peculiar to that particular period. The characteristics
that the period seems to demonstrate are the lagged though remarkably
efficient adjustment of supply to increased demand pressures and the suscepti-
bility of the price structure to expectational factors. In combination these
characteristics imply that inflation can get rolling fast while supply is moving
toward its maximum possible adjustment. If fears of sustained shortages
prove unfounded, inflationary forces may subsequently lose much of their
strength as the pressures from scare buying subside. Nevertheless, the expectation of price increases and the behavior that such expectations cause may
continue for some time if external forces, such as price controls, do not intervene. During the Korean period, however, not only did the adoption of price

controls intervene but the simultaneous and fortuitous waning of demand pressures, built up in the 1940s, did much to relieve the overall pressure of demand against aggregate supply. A much different sequence of events occurred during the next serious bout of inflation.

PROSPERITY'S INFLATION DILEMMA

After four years of stability provided by the 1951–1953 lull and the 1953–1954 recession, industrial wholesale prices began to rise in mid-1955. By January, 1957, they had increased by 8.4 percent and after leveling out in most of 1957 and early 1958, they rose more mildly by $2\frac{1}{2}$ percent between mid-1958 and January, 1960. This price performance, and its reflection in consumer prices, offered the occasion for a good deal of alarm and posed, in sharper relief than ever before, the economy's nagging dilemma of how to curb full employment's inflationary propensities without undermining full employment itself.

The price experience of the late 1950s invited the interpretation that enough frictions existed in the economy to make it infeasible to reduce unemployment rates to 4 percent, or even somewhat above that figure, without incurring unacceptable inflationary pressures. It is much less clear, however, just what these frictions were and whether the expansion of demand was an actively inflationary force or merely a permissive one.

In no convincing sense did this inflation have the excess demand characteristics of the inflations of 1941–1945, 1946–1948, or 1950–1951. There were no symptoms of drum-tightness in the economy. Unemployment after the 1953–1954 recession never receded to the $2\frac{1}{2}$ to 3 percent range in which it had been from 1951 to 1953. Average working hours in manufacturing declined throughout 1956 and 1957. Despite an apparently sluggish growth in productivity, the normal capacity of the economy grew faster than real output. Thus, it appears that rising total demand was more likely to have been a permissive than an active factor in the "nonclassical" inflation of this period.

As we noted in Chapter 6 in discussing price-output relationships, certain structural characteristics of the American economy tend to give it an inflationary bias. The following characteristics were apparent in the late 1950s:

First, prices and wages in particular industries tended to be flexible only in the upward direction. If excess demand pressures develop in a few industries, prices rise in these industries. In the absence of generally excessive demand, it might be expected that prices would decline elsewhere. The stickiness of the price structure means, however, that this does not generally occur. Consequently, rising prices in a few industries raise the overall price level, both through their direct effect on the total and through their role as costs in other industries. This pattern appears to have had considerable importance in the 1955–1957 period when demand rose exceptionally rapidly in a few industries, such as machinery and machine tools. Pressure on capacity was created in these industries resulting in price increases of about 20 percent for metal-working machinery, general industrial machinery, construction equipment, and steel.

Second, noncompetitive elements in both the labor and product markets were evident. In a favorable environment of rising demand for products and labor, prices and wages were raised in many industries even before demand pressures raised costs, owing to above-optimal capacity utilization, and before labor supplies became tight at going wage rates.

Third, price increases tended to breed expectations of further increases.

In combination, these three characteristics were able to spread inflationary pressures from one sector of the economy to others and perpetuate upward price-wage spirals even in the absence of generally excessive demand. Price increases initiated in a few sectors were not offset elsewhere. As costs to other industries, they triggered further price hikes. And as inflationary expectations developed, prices in noncompetitive industries were set high enough to preserve desired profit margins even in the face of expected future increases in costs. Meanwhile, generally rising prices eroded the purchasing power of wages, leading to enlarged wage demands accentuated, in turn, by expectations of further price increases. The increasing use of cost-of-living escalator clauses in wage contracts during the 1950s was symptomatic of the whole process. It dramatized the contest over shares in real national income that developed during that period.

The type of inflation experienced in the late 1950s poses extremely difficult problems for policy makers. Few stabilization instruments are selective enough to curb excess demand in just a few industries without curbing total demand and thus undermining prosperity. Furthermore, persuasive arguments can be raised against attempting to operate a large battery of selective instruments, since this might tend to distort resource allocation and retard economic growth. The structure of industry cannot be quickly changed, and as the price stabilization experience of two wars demonstrated, it is difficult to break into an inflationary spiral without the appearance, at least, of inequities to particular industries or bargaining parties. The inflationary spiral of the late 1950s was broken by two recessions in quick succession. But this "cure" for inflation imposed very high costs on the economy as a whole.

PRICE STABILITY IN THE EARLY 1960s

In view of the experience in the late 1950s, fears were repeatedly and forcefully expressed, following the 1960–1961 recession, that pursuit of aggressively expansionary policies would generate renewed inflation. The facts belied these concerns. Wholesale prices of industrial commodities rose less than 1 percent between the recession trough in early 1961 and April, 1965. Except for a brief period of rapidly rising agricultural prices, consumer prices edged up quite steadily and slowly, at only slightly more than 1 percent per year.

A major factor in this sharply improved record was the final demise of the inflationary expectations that had prevailed a few years earlier. It is still too early to tell whether *the* major factor was the fact that the rapid expansion of the first half of the 1960s began from a base substantially below full capacity. Despite the judgments subsequent histories may render on this question, it seems quite likely that several other factors were also important.

1. The expansion was quite well balanced. Consequently, few bottlenecks developed, as is demonstrated in the generally low level of order backlogs relative to shipments. On average, the backlogs-to-shipments ratio remained one-third or more below the levels that occurred in the latter part of the 1950s.

2. Changes had evolved in the structure of industry as a result of technological developments that increased the range of substitutability among products and as a result of heightened competition from the imports made available from resurgent foreign economies.

3. The Kennedy and Johnson administrations devised and strongly endorsed a set of wage-price guideposts that established voluntary standards for good behavior. These guideposts, first presented in the 1962 *Annual Report* of the Council of Economic Advisers, were derived from analysis of how prices and wages would behave in the absence of deviations from the competitive norm. They stated that prices should be stable except in industries where productivity growth was substantially above or below the average for the private economy (in the former case prices should be cut and in the latter they could rise) and that wages should rise by the amount of the trend advance in average productivity (thus keeping unit labor costs constant on average) except for unusual circumstances that were detailed in the 1962 *Report*. It is difficult to judge just what effect these guideposts had. But it seems quite likely that public opinion was mobilized and a framework of analysis was established for government officials that focused pressures against price increases at certain key points. Outstanding examples were the specific pressures mounted by President Kennedy against steel price rises in 1962 and by President Johnson against aluminum price increases in 1965. The forestalling of such price increases undoubtedly slowed inflation.[4]

Whether or not this record of price stability can be reasonably sustained in a period of full-capacity utilization is, as we write these words, an unresolved question.

---

[4] See Chap. 26 for a fuller discussion of the wage-price guideposts.

BALANCE OF PAYMENTS

We shall examine in some detail the determinants of the balance of payments, as they relate to the problem of forecasting net exports, in Chapter 22. We cannot close this review of United States economic history of the 1950s and early 1960s, however, without a brief summary of balance-of-payments experience during that period.

The net export component of the gross national product accounts amounts to less than 2 percent of GNP. Taken alone, this might seem to be reason for treating the United States economy as if it were a "closed economy" —at least for business analysis purposes. The events of the 1930s amply demonstrated, however, that the national economies of the world's major countries are importantly linked, by trade and by the international monetary mechanism. Looking at the gross figures combined to derive net exports we find that both exports and imports of goods and services in 1964 were slightly larger than residential construction outlays. Thus, movements in either side of these accounts can have considerable impact on business developments unless they are largely and immediately offset. Furthermore, the domestic economy can rarely be completely shielded from policy actions taken for balance-of-payments purposes.

BALANCE-OF-PAYMENTS DEFICITS AND
BALANCE-OF-PAYMENTS PROBLEMS

One of the most striking features of the balance of payments accounts since 1950 is that the United States has almost consistently run a deficit on its international accounts. This deficit did not pose a problem, however, until late in the 1950s. And then, as in the case of the inflation of that period, the balance-of-payments problem was not "classical" in nature. Conventionally, balance-of-payments problems are associated with an excess of imports above that amount that can be financed largely by export earnings. In such a situation, a nation sooner or later runs into a limit on its line of credit. The United States has not, however, lived beyond its means in the postwar period. It has fairly consistently run a substantial surplus on its current account. The deficit has occurred because of large military and aid expenditures abroad —only part of which return in the form of larger exports—and heavy overseas investments by American businesses and financial institutions.

The reasons for large military and aid expenditures are too well known to require discussion here. The reasons for foreign borrowing in the United States and American private investment abroad may be less obvious. In the post-World War II period, a large backlog of capital needs existed in most developed economies; in addition, the aspirations of the less developed areas added to world demands for capital. The demands for physical capital pressed against the production capabilities of these economies, spilling over into both inflation and rising imports, in part from the United States. Meanwhile, the need for financial capital pressed against available domestic resources and spilled over into substantial borrowings in the United States open capital markets.

In the earlier part of the post-World War II period, the dollars that flowed abroad—as a result of foreign lending and military and aid expenditures—and failed to return in payment for exports, served as a medium of exchange in international trade and finance during a period when most currencies were not convertible. They constituted a welcome addition to the world's foreign exchange reserves. Subsequently, however, several new factors entered the picture. First, as the Western European countries rebuilt their economies, they claimed a somewhat larger share of world exports and also posed sharper competition in domestic American markets (as already noted in the discussion of prices). Second, the formation of the European Economic Community (the Common Market) created a large potential market undivided by internal tariff barriers but still protected by a common external tariff wall. This expanding market was sufficiently promising to lure American firms to establish foreign branches or subsidiaries, thus engaging in a significant volume of direct foreign investment. A similar motivation led to increasing investment in Latin America, Asia, and Africa. As a consequence, the volume of dollar outflows rose significantly. Meanwhile, the currencies of the major nations again became convertible, so the rapid additions to the world's stock of dollars outpaced the desire of foreign authorities for additional dollar reserves. Thus, the balance-of-payments problem emerged when these dollar outflows turned into drains on the United States gold stock, which threatened, in turn, to undermine confidence in the dollar.

BALANCE-OF-PAYMENTS POLICIES

The conventional remedy for balance-of-payments deficits has been restrictive policies that curtail demand for imports, lower prices thus stimulating exports, and raise interest rates, thus restraining capital outflows. The United States balance-of-payments problem has not, however, been a conventional problem. It is undoubtedly true that the United States competitive position was eroded by the price inflation of the late 1950s, but that inflation proved resistant to policy restraints and gave way only in the face of recession. It also tends to be the case that weaker domestic demand reduces the volume of imports. Yet recession or chronic underutilization of capacity is a high price to pay for relatively small balance-of-payments gains. Furthermore, these gains are likely to be short run at best since underuse of capacity is likely to slow the advance of productivity and eventually to produce the same erosion of the United States competitive position as does inflation. Thus, the twin problems of inflation and international payments each raise the fundamental question of how to achieve solutions without undermining domestic prosperity.

This problem was approached on several fronts:

1. Expansion of exports was seen as the key to the long-run solution. Consequently, in the Trade Agreements Act of 1962, the foundation was laid for major steps in reducing world tariffs. Unfortunately progress is not achieved easily in this area and, at this writing, the outcome of the "Kennedy Round" of negotiations under the General Agreement on Trade and Tariffs remains to be seen. In addition, the Kennedy and Johnson administrations stepped up export promotion programs and restricted the dollar outflows associated with military and aid commitments through such techniques as tying aid to United States exports.

2. While attempting to maintain a favorable monetary environment for domestic expansion, the government took steps to raise *short-term* interest rates to curb the most volatile capital outflows.

3. As an interim step, a series of special measures was taken to restrict longer-term capital outflows without requiring major increases in long-term interest rates. These include the imposition of a tax, the Interest Equalization Tax, on longer-term foreign borrowings in United States capital markets and from banks, and voluntary credit restraint programs applying to financial institutions and domestic corporations. These programs do involve interference in the freedom of international capital movements—a step backward in terms of the long-run objective of greater freedom of trade and capital flows. They were deemed necessary in view of the failure of market adjustments to achieve a satisfactory equilibrium in a world where the structure of national economies differs radically.

REPRISE

The phase of United States economic history beginning with the Korean War can in many ways be seen as a return to normalcy following a long period marked by a world depression and a world war. Yet this "normalcy" is far different from that of the 1920s. The built-in stabilizers that had evolved in the interim have helped significantly to moderate the instabilities to which the economy had been prone. And the enlarged role that the Federal government has acquired, in an economy still predominantly characterized by free enterprise, has made it much easier to prevent sharp swings in economic activity through appropriate policy actions. On the other hand, the accompanying need for deliberate policy actions to prevent the Federal budget from accidentally exerting a restrictive force on the economy came to be appreciated only late in the period under discussion. Furthermore, although the good price record of the first half of the 1960s stands out in contrast to the marked price gyrations of earlier periods, this record is too short to be proof that the problem of inflation has been solved. Finally, the new status of the United States as a major world power has posed economic as well as diplomatic problems that remain to be sorted out.

Much of recent economic history can easily be written in terms of the accomplishments of public policy and the challenges that remain before it. Yet it is at least equally important to recognize that the history of this period is one of remarkably successful adjustment by the *private* economy to swift technological change, to rapid growth in the population, to the development of a new defense and space industry, to increased foreign competition, and to increased involvement in international finance.

Any such cataloging of the major trends and problems of a period is bound to be incomplete. Notable omissions from this discussion include the evolving pattern of income distribution and attempts to change it, and the economic aspects of such human concerns as health, education, and racial equality.

PART FOUR

SHORT-RUN
OUTLOOK ANALYSIS

16

GENERAL FORECASTING TECHNIQUES

What lies ahead for the economy is the one concrete problem that almost no general business conditions analyst can escape. Decision makers must have an answer to the outlook question—either an implicit answer that assumes no change in existing conditions or an explicit one that involves a self-conscious appraisal of the future.

If the practice of general economic forecasting is universal, however, the nature of the practice is anything but uniform. Many forecasters rely upon mental processes that are scarcely rational. Others who do try to "think through" the outlook problem employ insufficient evidence and faulty or excessively narrow reasoning. Even among the respectable majority of so-called professional business forecasters, there are sharp cleavages over technique, and always there is a sizable minority whom the rest of the brotherhood regard as crackpots, if not downright frauds. Some are just that. On the other hand, it is well to remember that some of the greatest developments of economics have been lineal descendants of so-called crackpot theories.

The fact is that economic forecasting is a long way from being an authoritative science. But it is also true that many major economic decision makers today believe that systematic economic analysis can shed a good deal of light on the outlook problem, and this, of course, is a premise on which this book rests.

Certain limits that will circumscribe the present discussion of forecasting should be reiterated. We shall focus upon the economy-wide business outlook rather than upon analysis aimed specifically at particular industries or firms. In any reasonably thorough general outlook analysis it is necessary, to be sure, to look at prospects in particular critical industries, but this is done as a means of illuminating the general outlook, not as an end in itself.

Moreover, we shall be mainly concerned with short-run outlook analysis—not as a matter of arbitrary choice but because of limitations imposed by the available forecasting techniques themselves. Most of these techniques cannot penetrate more than twelve months or so into the future. However, we shall also encounter some important exceptions to this generalization and, when we do, shall treat them.

This chapter surveys a variety of general forecasting techniques that are used, or that only lately have fallen into disuse, by economists. Then the next chapter will provide a more detailed introduction to the analytical approach that the remainder of this part will emphasize: so-called loose, relatively nonmathematical, or opportunistic model building. First, however, some remarks applicable to all systematic efforts to anticipate general economic developments are in order.

THE FORECASTING PROBLEM

SOME GENERAL CHARACTERISTICS OF THE TASK

The economic forecaster's chances of success are sorely limited by the fact that what he is trying to predict is a complex of human decisions largely conditioned by human behavior, not by natural forces. And human behavior is such an enormously complex matter that science gives no near-term promise of rendering it wholly predictable. Fortunately, however, the study of large numbers of people has taught us that it is much easier to predict the average or total decisions of an aggregation of individuals than to predict the behavior of any particular one chosen at random. Typically, the deviants tend to cancel each other out when some kind of average is struck.

This large-numbers point is particularly pertinent to forecasting in an economy such as the United States. For here the task is to predict the decisions, not of one or a few decision makers, but of a vast number, each of whom has considerable discretion. In some respects it might be easier to forecast business conditions in a relatively centralized economy such as the Soviet Union. It would be easier to the extent (1) that decision makers made advance plans, (2) that plans tended to be carried out, and (3) that forecasters were able to find out what the advance plans were. If a central planner's plans were unavailable, unreliable, or nonexistent, however, a forecaster probably could generalize better about what 100,000 major investors would do in the coming year than he could particularize the actions of a single ministry of industrial development.

One thing is certain: forecasting is inevitably complex in a decentralized economy. The relationship among the particular decentralized decisions that collectively determine overall business conditions is not simply additive. Many decisions cannot be accurately anticipated by the decision makers themselves, since they will be responsive or reactive to other people's actions. In an economy such as the United States a summation of decision makers' advance plans, no matter how earnestly intended, can never be a sufficient forecast. Account must also be taken of probable interactions among decision-making groups.

Economic forecasting is a thorny business in still another respect. Many of the factors that will determine business conditions in a coming period lie in subject-matter areas beyond the forecaster's professional ken. The outlook may depend upon whether a war starts or upon whether young people marry at earlier ages. But the business conditions analyst is likely to be neither an international strategist nor a qualified sociologist. The best that he can sensibly offer, therefore, is a qualified forecast premised upon assumptions about certain variables that he cannot conscientiously undertake to predict himself. Even in very short-run forecasts, where dependence upon such assumptions often is not made explicit, they are still there; it is tacitly assumed that noneconomic factors will not change rapidly enough to affect business appreciably during the period under discussion.

All forecasting starts from the premise that there are certain continuities running through the past and present into the future. In part, these may be continuities between decision makers' present plans and future actions. But in large part, reliance is upon continuities in actual economic behavior—especially in a decentralized economy, where the reactive or response type of decision is so important. A generally reliable refinement of this point is that, especially in a growing economy, we assume relative *relationships* among economic magnitudes to have more persistence than the absolute magnitudes themselves. For example, if an analyst finds that plant and equipment spending has averaged 10 percent of total output over the past thirty years, he is apt to adopt this—rather than the absolute annual average of such spending —as a significant datum for the future.

FORECASTING'S OWN IMPACT ON THE OUTLOOK

Except perhaps for the local effects of occasional cloud-seeding, weather forecasts have no effect on the weather. But business forecasters can and do affect the future course of business activity. Those who make business decisions adjust them in the light of what they understand to be the general outlook for the economy. Thus, if the forecaster is one to whom decision makers listen, he affects the outlook itself in some measure.

In the individual forecasts made by most private analysts, whether they be individual-firm economists, consultants, or academicians, the scope of such feedback effects is not very great. Collectively, however, even restricted-clientele forecasters may influence the behavior of the economy significantly if many of them tell the same outlook story. In the case of government forecasters and those private forecasters who have wide and attentive audiences, the influence of the analyst on the outlook is even more apparent.

The existence of these feedbacks additionally complicates the forecasting task; the sophisticated forecaster must regard the current tenor of influential forecasts as an additional determinant of actual future business conditions. And, in so doing, he must distinguish two quite different types of feedbacks. One is the reaction of decision makers who regard the general level of business activity as a datum over which they have no significant control but to which they try to adjust their own policies. The other is the reaction of the decision maker who consciously and deliberately tries to influence the overall level of business activity.

The first of these situations is that of almost all business managers, of most state and local governments, and of all consumers. For these decision makers the net effect of the feedback reaction to forecasting is probably to reinforce or accentuate the trends asserted by influential forecasters. When the latter are bullish, they are likely, on balance, to stimulate spending, and vice versa.[1] In this case, therefore, the feedback helps the forecaster but may hinder the economy by aggravating any instability there may be in the outlook.

In the other case—that of decision makers who believe they have the power and responsibility to improve the general business outlook—the feedback works the other way around. It may be a little rough on forecasters' reputations, but it tends to be good for the economy. Such decision makers, who, in the United States, are largely concentrated in the Federal government, are apt to respond to the prospect of inflation or recession with a program of policies designed to make the forecast come untrue—given the constitutional, political, and administrative feasibility of such action and assuming no enervating conflict with other policy objectives of the Federal government.[2]

---

[1] It is true that some decision makers, particularly mindful of the higher costs and delayed deliveries that may accompany rising economic activity, or of the opposite attributes of a declining situation, may decide to swim against the tide. But to do so, they must be relatively indifferent to the timing of their expenditures, must have the necessary financial reserves, and must be relatively immune to the expectations of a further movement in the same direction that a price or supply change tends to engender. Such decision makers are clearly in a minority.

[2] In addition, there have been some interesting cases of policy moves by particular large firms and labor organizations that have appeared to be—in part, at least—efforts intended directly to influence general economic activity.

Both of forecasting's feedback effects raise troublesome issues for influential practitioners of the craft. In terms of the first of the effects, should such forecasters cite unfavorable economic prospects candidly at the risk of inducing reactions that will aggravate the emerging problem, or should they tone down their pronouncements? In terms of the second effect, should they only forecast the outlook, given existing Federal economic policies? Or should they anticipate corrective adjustments in Federal policies and indicate only what the outlook is when these are taken into account? Or should they do a double-barreled job, indicating, first, the outlook under existing policies and, second (if the first is unfavorable), a revised outlook that allows for the effect of offsetting policies?[3]

We shall not linger over these problems since the present discussion is not addressed mainly to influential forecasters. There are three things, however, that it would be helpful for the rest of us to remember about the feedback phenomena. First, any forecaster should observe what influential forecasters are saying about the outlook; if their consensus is pronounced, it may exert a significant impact upon business decisions during the coming period. Second, since influential forecasts—particularly such official and prominent government statements as those contained in the *Economic Report of the President*—are written with a keen awareness of their feedback possibilities, it may be necessary to read between the lines to obtain a full impression of what the authors think the economy's prospects are. Finally, it is desirable to incorporate anticipations of changes in Federal stabilization policies into one's outlook analysis. But to do this effectively will not only require some political forecasting but a reasonably good knowledge of the time lags likely to intervene in the formulation and implementation of particular government programs.

THE EARMARKS OF GOOD FORECASTING

Beside being technically proficient, a good forecaster must understand and respect the limitations of the materials with which he works; he must appreciate the interests of his audience; he needs a sense of proportion; and he should display that essential requirement of all good art: good taste. These are very difficult things to write about convincingly, but they merit some attention before we start canvassing specific analytical techniques.

Every forecaster should ponder the question of how precise he should be in his estimates. The answer depends upon his purposes and upon the particular circumstances under which he is working. The kind of decision making that a forecaster services may set high or low requirements for pre-

[3] See R. C. Turner, "Problems of Forecasting for Economic Stabilization," *American Economic Review*, vol. 45, no. 2, pp. 329–340, May, 1955; also P. A. Samuelson, "Economic Forecasting and National Policy," in G. Colm (ed.), *The Employment Act: Past and Future*, National Planning Association, Washington, 1956, pp. 130–134.

cision. Relatively exact estimates of personal and corporate income are necessary for predicting whether, under existing tax laws, the increment in Federal taxes during the coming year will be sufficient to balance the budget. But all that the Open Market Committee of the Federal Reserve System may need to know to decide whether it should pursue a course of restraint, neutrality, or active ease in its operations during the next few weeks is whether the pace of business is likely to quicken or slacken.

The degree of precision that is appropriate in a forecast also depends partly upon how publicly it is to be displayed. It may be wise for a forecaster to spell out for himself a picture of the future that is just as quantitatively precise as he can reasonably make it. But there is a general hesitancy within the trade to spread the whole body of a quantitative analysis on the public record. Instead, most analysts consolidate their work sheets into relatively simplified breakdowns and convert many of their figures into adjectives or adverbs. This resistance to publicized precision is not simply a matter of self-protection. The systematic techniques that give rise to precise forecasts still are not exhaustive enough to displace the need for that elusive quality we call judgment. Very commonly a forecaster carries his number work as far as it will go, but then makes a qualitative revision in the apparent findings to take account of some mood or quality or drift in the situation that the analysis has not adequately reflected. If one's clientele, having been led through all the details of the quantitative analysis, had thereby been conditioned to expect that the full outlook would be revealed by such rigorous procedures, it might find this judgment jump a very disquieting one to make. And yet it may be the forecaster's responsible opinion that the jump should be made.

Furthermore, for those not fully cognizant of the uncertainties involved, a precise quantification of the outlook misrepresents the accuracy to which forecasting can pretend. Certain American news magazines have been known to specify their forecasts of the coming year's gross national product down to the last tenth of a billion dollars. Such precision would be scarcely justified even among the professionals within a particular forecasting shop. Published nationally, it projects nothing but the editors' naïvety.

As in most matters of taste, the other extreme—excessively timid forecasting—is equally bad. It is easy to qualify and hedge an analysis into a condition of utter uselessness. However erudite it may be, an outlook analysis that fails to indicate some rather clear probabilities for the future (such clarity, to repeat, may not require much explicit quantification) does not fulfill its announced purpose. A forecaster who is not content to go out on a limb is in the wrong business.

One reason for excessively timid, fuzzy forecasting is the inappropriately high standards against which the accuracy of outlook analyses often are measured. Like precision, the needed degree of accuracy depends upon the kind of decision making for which the forecasting is done. In some cases it may be sufficient to predict only whether, during the coming period, there will be a sharp rise in economic activity or a sharp fall, or neither. Even when greater delineation is needed within the middle range of possibilities, it may only be important to call the direction of the gradual trend that general business may follow. A good many professional forecasting groups have made a fairly good record in these terms.

Being able to live with, digest, and profit by one's mistakes is an indispensable qualification for good forecasting. The professional scene is littered with technically superior analysts who have been lastingly warped by their past errors. Some of these casualties have soured on forecasting *in toto*. Others have become men in search of vindication, looking always for new events to do what they did not do on an earlier occasion. If they had had thicker skins, they could have learned more from their errors. Indeed, the good judgment that is so valuable to the successful forecaster can be defined as simply the ability to bring to current situations positive insights gleaned from past experiences and particularly from past mistakes.

While there is no denying the value of good judgment, in the sense just defined, the idea that forecasting talent is mainly an instinctive faculty is largely pernicious. There is, among those who try to use systematic forecasting techniques, much rueful glorification of certain nonsystematic, "horseback" or "seat-of-the-pants" forecasters who seem to employ none of the accepted analytical techniques and yet have a surer feel for the general outlook than most able technicians. It would be foolish to deny that there are such individuals. But what can be denied is that there is something occult about their ability or that good forecasters are born, not made.

The fact is that observers who seem to be peculiarly endowed with a feel for the business outlook are almost always men of very considerable experience, and the mental processes by which they arrive at their hunches, even though cryptic, are essentially rational. They involve the reference of current observations to some kind of implicit scheme or pattern of analysis that the gifted forecaster has evolved from his own experience. The predictive abilities of such observers are admirable, but the enigmatic quality of their forecasting procedures is not in itself an earmark of competence. It is a bad habit that some good forecasters have but to which those attempting to learn the craft should not particularly aspire.

THE AVAILABLE TECHNIQUES

Of the explicitly articulated modes of forecasting, some are essentially unambitious. Sole reliance on them reflects a lack of confidence in the effectiveness of conventional economic analysis for penetrating the future. The following survey of systematic forecasting deals, first, with several such "agnostic" techniques; second with certain "barometric" techniques that rely upon selected current indicators to provide advance warnings of coming turns in business conditions; third, with canvasses of decision makers' advance plans and commitments; and, finally, with two general types of income and product model building.

THE AGNOSTIC TECHNIQUES

Projections of Present Levels and Extrapolations of Recent Trends

We have seen that decision makers' expectations of the future are strongly conditioned by the current business climate. For the most part this is simply a matter of human nature, not a deliberate forecasting methodology. But what about deliberately converting it into a forecasting methodology? What, in other words, about forecasting with a no-change hypothesis—either no change in present levels or no change in the direction of recent trends (the second being somewhat more sophisticated than the first but an essentially similar approach)? Some very literate economic analysts advocate this practice on the ground that we are ill equipped to do anything wiser.

Certainly the no-change hypothesis must be employed with respect to many particular elements of business outlook. In the most elegant forecasting the general procedure is to try to identify those aspects of the situation which appear most likely to change, to estimate the directions and magnitudes of such changes, and then to assume that all other elements of the present situation will remain unchanged in some important sense—either as to level or as to relationship with other variables.

Moreover, and more generally, the no-change approach highlights the concept of momentum in the economy, and, in so doing, supplies a healthy antidote to forecasting techniques that spot nothing but the cyclical zigs and zags in the economy's performance. Some ambitious forecasters automatically look for a downturn whenever business is improving. This reflects an unrealistically jittery stereotype of the current American economy. If business is good and if the forecaster must have an initial hunch, a normally sounder one for him to indulge is that it will hold course, not reverse course, during the coming year.

Granting all this, the no-change approach still does not merit serious consideration as a sufficient forecasting technique in an economy of which change is the very essence. Even if literal, slavish extrapolation of the past and present were scientifically the best forecasting procedure available, intelligent decision makers never would submit to it. The one thing that every executive knows the year ahead will *not* be is a simple repetition of the year just past, and he expects his forecasting staff to know as much.

Speeding up Statistical Reporting

The considerable effort that has been made in the United States during the past decade or two to speed up the reporting of the government's economic statistics may not seem at first sight to have much to do with forecasting. However, a principal reason for the effort has been to serve outlook analysts. Just as a football coach, despairing of his team's ability to forecast the opposition's offensive maneuvers, may rely mainly on training his defense to diagnose plays swiftly once they start, so a business conditions analyst, despairing of our ability to predict the future behavior of the economy, may emphasize the need for spotting changes as quickly as possible after they occur.

If the quality of data is not compromised by accelerated reporting, then accelerated reporting, of course, is a good thing for all active forecasters. But a preoccupation with it can cost too much in terms of accuracy. And, by inviting too much hovering and quivering over the very latest figures, swift reporting can lead to a sort of occupational nearsightedness. Moreover, the fact remains that the fastest possible knowledge of current developments is far from an adequate substitute for forecasting. In many cases even instantaneous recognition of a change in sales, unemployment, or consumer prices, for example, would not give decision makers enough lead time for making needed adjustments—just as a football defense, at times, may be seriously damaged if it is not set for a pass before the play starts.

Ascertaining the Consensus of Observers

One thing our puzzled football coach could do, if he had the time before each of the opposition's plays, would be to poll a sample of the spectators for their opinions about what was coming next, digest the findings, and relay a conclusion to his defensive captain on the field. Or, if he wanted to survey a somewhat more expert and restricted array of opinion, he could simply poll the press box. Such methods often are followed in economic forecasting. A number of agencies, including business consulting and reporting firms and business journalists, make periodic surveys to see what the consensus is about the economic outlook among either broad groups of businessmen and consumers or economists who are thought to be qualified as expert observers.

A forecaster who treats the findings of such surveys of expectations as being, in themselves, usable composite forecasts is, in effect, an agnostic. He displays little confidence in his own informational and analytical resources. This does not mean, of course, that cross-checking one's own view of the outlook with the opinions of other observers is ever disreputable. Indeed, any professional forecaster who does not do a good deal of this is an opinionated fool. But an exclusive, automatic reliance on the average of other people's opinions is not, as a way of disposing of the forecast problem, any wiser than it is daring. If everyone proceeded in this fashion there would be no "expert" opinions to survey, and all outlook analysis would reduce to the job of summarizing the general expectations of relatively uninformed lay observers.

Before we leave this point, however, it should be emphasized that there is a wholly legitimate—indeed, essential—use that can be made of surveys of general business expectations. This is to treat them as in themselves constituting important data among the many variables that jointly will determine the course of business in the months ahead. To evaluate the firmness of present business plans for plant and equipment spending in a coming year, for instance, it is important to know the sales and profits expectations they reflect. But the general expectations survey cannot safely be substituted for the forecasting process itself.

THE BAROMETRIC TECHNIQUES

Thus far we have reviewed techniques used by people who doubt their own ability to figure out what the economy is going to do next. Now we come to some techniques that do involve a positive attempt to answer this What question, but not to figure out Why. The situation is like that of the man who wants to know what tomorrow's weather will be. He neither assumes it will resemble today's, nor does he get up at dawn tomorrow to see, nor does he ask his neighbors what they think. He consults his barometer. He cannot explain the nature of the supposed linkage between a barometer and the state of the weather, but he is convinced by his own or others' experience that such a linkage exists. And he is content with this knowledge.

Business Cycle Analysis

Much empirical business cycle research has had a symptomatic focus; it has been concerned more to observe and measure business fluctuations than to explain them. Particular economic time series have been singled out because of the degree and regularity of their fluctuations or because of their apparent representativeness of time series in general rather than because of the functional importance of the variables they reflect. In such research, for instance, more attention may be given to stock prices than to government expenditures, or to less-than-carload freight shipments than to personal consumption expenditures.

Once recurrent and allegedly rhythmical fluctuations had been identified in particular series by means of techniques that removed seasonal and trend factors, the drive in the heyday of American empirical business cycle research was somehow or other to average together the individual pulsating series into some kind of generalized reference cycle or into a family of major, minor, and other cycles for which average durations could be calculated. It was at this point that business cycle research gave birth to its first, but now generally discredited, forecasting application: the idea that measurable fluctuations in general business conditions were sufficiently rhythmical that future turning points could be anticipated simply by reference to past tempos. For those who fully accepted this doctrine the only tools required for forecasting were a historical time-series analysis (which managed to identify a general cyclical pattern and which was sufficiently current to locate the latest turning point) and a calendar.

Even in the 1920s only the more naïve forecasters tried to operate on such a stripped-down basis, but there was an inclination to reason in this direction. Today there is almost none. While analysts continue to be interested in the rhythms of the inventory cycle and in the rather regular recurrence of fluctuations in particular industries, any notion that the general business outlook can be read off the calendar has been exploded by the profound and unprecedented changes through which the economy has passed since 1929. Only one book fully dedicated to an inflexible cyclical hypothesis has appeared in the United States since World War II and, as V Lewis Bassie aptly says, it quickly became "an intellectual curiosity of the postwar period."[4]

NBER Leading Series

The forecasting by-product of business cycle research that has survived and prospered is one that focuses upon the fact that economic time series do not literally march abreast through time. Although the series as a whole, according to this approach, are subject to herdlike movements, there are some leaders and some laggards. The forecasting task is to identify the consistent leaders and then watch for turns in these to indicate coming changes in general business.

Interestingly enough, this leads-and-lags technique also traces back to the twenties. Its practitioners of that period were almost as thoroughly engulfed by the disaster of the Great Depression as were those of the more naïve rhythmical technique. However, the leads-and-lags approach has regained a following, both because of its inherently greater merit and because of the diligent and skillful modern development of it by Geoffrey H. Moore and other personnel of the National Bureau of Economic Research who have followed in the footsteps of Wesley Mitchell and Arthur F. Burns. Moore, who completed his basic forecasting system in the late forties, drew upon and added to the meticulous analysis of some 800 time series made by the National Bureau for the period up to World War II. Of these he identified 21 series that had been most consistent either in leading the "reference cycle" (which

---

[4] "Recent Developments in Short-term Forecasting," in Conference on Research in Income and Wealth: *Short-term Economic Forecasting*, National Bureau of Economic Research, Inc., Studies in Income and Wealth, vol. 17, Princeton University Press, Princeton, N.J., 1955, p. 22. The book Bassie refers to is E. R. Dewey and E. F. Dakin, *Cycles: The Science of Prediction*, Holt, Rinehart and Winston, Inc., New York, 1947.

the Bureau generalizes from all its series), or in lagging behind it, or in coinciding with it as far as turning points are concerned. This work was continued in the 1950s, and other leading series were added. In 1961, the enormous statistical job of compiling data, adjusting for seasonal variation, computing various indexes, and current publishing was taken over by the Bureau of the Census of the U.S. Department of Commerce, under the leadership of Julius Shiskin. The results of this work now appear in the Bureau's monthly publication, *Business Cycle Developments.*

Business Cycle Developments provides (as of the date of writing) data on 87 economic time series. Of these, 30 are identified as "NBER leading indicators," 15 as "NBER roughly coincident series," and 7 as "NBER lagging indicators." Included are 28 "other U.S. series with business cycle significance," together with 7 international series.

The 30 leading series are:[5]

---

* Average workweek of production workers, manufacturing
* Accession rate, manufacturing
* Layoff rate, manufacturing
* Number of persons on temporary layoff, all industries
* Average weekly initial claims for unemployment insurance, state programs
* Value of manufacturers' new orders, durable goods industries
* New private nonfarm dwelling units started
* Construction contracts awarded for commercial and industrial buildings, floor space
* Contracts and orders for plant and equipment
  Newly approved capital appropriations, 1,000 manufacturing corporations
* Number of new business incorporations
* Current liabilities of business failures
* Number of business failures with liabilities of $100,000 and over
  Corporate profits after taxes
* Price per unit of labor cost index—ratio, wholesale prices of manufactured goods index to index of compensation of employees (sum of wages, salaries, and supplements to wages and salaries) per unit of output
  Profits (before taxes) per dollar of sales, all manufacturing corporations
* Index of stock prices, 500 common stocks
* Change in book value of manufacturers' inventories, materials, and supplies

---

[5] See *Business Cycle Developments* (back cover) for sources of the series.

Change in business inventories, farm and nonfarm, after valuation
  adjustment (GNP component)
Ratio of profits (after taxes) to income originating, corporate, all
  industries
* Index of industrial materials prices
* Value of manufacturers' new orders, machinery and equipment in-
  dustries
* Change in manufacturers' unfilled orders, durable goods industries
* Buying policy—production materials, percent reporting commitments
  60 days or longer
* Index of new private housing units authorized by local building
  permits
* Nonagricultural placements, all industries
* Change in book value of manufacturing and trade inventories, total
* Vendor performance, percent reporting slower deliveries
* Percent reporting higher inventories, purchased materials
* Index of net business formation

---

* Monthly data; others are quarterly.

The 15 roughly coincident series include, notably, GNP (in current
and constant dollars), personal income, and nonagricultural employment, the
unemployment rate, retail sales, and wholesale prices. The lagging series
include business expenditures for new plant and equipment, two indexes of
labor costs, manufacturers' inventories, consumer installment debt, and bank
rates on short-term business loans.

In addition to these 87 principal indicators, data are collected on over
300 component series, the exact number varying from month to month as new
series are added or old ones dropped.

Twenty-five of the leading series, indicated with an asterisk (*) in the
listing above, are estimated on a monthly basis without much calculation or
publishing delay. Thus, to the extent that they work as they are supposed to,
they serve as highly sensitive indicators of the very short-run outlook.[6]

Aside from the question of predictive accuracy, the leading indicator
approach has a major inherent limitation: it can signal only direction of
economic activity. It indicates little or nothing about the magnitude of the

[6] The original NBER series are represented most impressively in Wesley C. Mitchell
and Arthur F. Burns, *Measuring Business Cycles*, National Bureau of Economic Research, Inc., New York, 1946.

The most extensive explanation of the current system is contained in Geoffrey
H. Moore (ed.), *Business Cycle Indicators*, Princeton University Press, Princeton, N.J.,
1961, and in Julius Shiskin, *Signals of Recession and Recovery: An Experiment with
Monthly Reporting*, National Bureau of Economic Research, Inc., Occasional Paper no.
77, New York, 1961.

coming changes. For some decision makers, this leaves the most important part of the issue unanswered.

Even with respect to indicating direction of change, the National Bureau's barometric technique encounters some difficulties. The leading series are subject to a number of wiggles, and many of the turns in them prove after the fact to have been false signals of turns in general business activity. Thus, it requires, in addition to the month or so needed to collect data, at least another two or three months' confirmation time before an apparent change of course in the leading series can be regarded as significant, and this, of course, greatly diminishes the one unique advantage the technique has. Moreover, there are frequent differences among the leading series themselves. Some signal a turn when others do not. The National Bureau and, more recently, the Bureau of the Census have attempted to meet this problem by two devices. One is the calculation of weighted, composite indexes, amplitude-adjusted by standardizing the month-to-month percentage changes in each series so that all the series are expressed in comparable units. The other is the calculation of "diffusion indexes," which show the percentage of 80 subseries of certain of the leading series that are experiencing rises over some given time interval (e.g., three months). Both of these devices tend to reduce, but by no means eliminate, irregularities and diversity of movements. In Figure 16-1 (see pages 378–379) such a composite of 8 leading series[7] and a comprehensive diffusion index over a three-month interval of 80 leading component series[8] are plotted against the Federal Reserve industrial production index and quarterly (seasonally adjusted) gross national product.

It can be seen from the chart that both the composite index and the diffusion index gave advance warning of the recession of 1953–1954, although the signals given by the former were ambiguous until after the decline had actually begun. The diffusion index, which declined sharply in the first half of 1953, actually reached its nadir and started up again before the beginning of the decline was evident in either industrial production or GNP. Both series gave clear signals of the rise in business activity that started in mid-1954, the upturn in the composite series index preceding the upturn in industrial production by about three months and the upturn in GNP by about six months. In the last half of 1954, while the composite index continued to rise, the diffusion index misbehaved, dropping sharply for a month, then rising again. It reached a peak in February, 1955, and thereafter, for two years, followed a sawtooth downward course that induced schizophrenic symptoms in

---

[7] Average workweek, manufacturing; manufacturers' new orders, machinery and equipment industries; new building permits issued, private housing; commercial and construction contracts, floor space; number of new business incorporations; price per unit of labor cost index; index of stock prices, 500 common stocks; and index of industrial materials prices.

[8] Including 21 average hours worked in manufacturing, 23 new orders, 23 stock prices, and 13 industrial materials prices components.

forecasters of the period. The composite index, on the other hand, continued upward, reaching a double peak in December, 1955 (115.2) and April, 1956 (115.3). GNP continued its rise through the third quarter of 1957, and the industrial production index, except for a steel-strike-induced drop in the summer of 1956, continued to rise through February, 1957, followed by a leveling off through August of the same year. If the decline in the leading indicators in early 1956 is to be interpreted as a true advance indication of the drop in GNP that began in the fourth quarter of 1957, then the lead was an exceptionally long one.

The upturn in GNP in the second quarter of 1958, and in industrial production in May, was not anticipated by the leading series index; movements in this index almost exactly paralleled those of the industrial production index. The diffusion index gave clear signals of a recovery late in 1957 and early in 1958. The diffusion index peaked, however, in July, 1958, when the business recovery of 1958–1959 was only nicely started. In the summer and autumn of 1959, all the series behaved erratically, reflecting the long steel strike of that year. In December, 1959, and early in 1960 the composite index moved definitely downward, anticipating the downturn in industrial production by about one month and the downturn in GNP by about six months. The diffusion index, in 1960, again behaved erratically, signaling a sharp decline in January–February, an equally sharp recovery in March–April, and another decline in May–October. The upturn in GNP and industrial production that began early in 1961, however, was presaged by both the composite index and the diffusion index, although the lead was a relatively short one.

After March, 1961, and continuing with some irregularities through July, 1962, the diffusion index gave a sequence of false signals of recession. The composite index also gave false recession signals beginning in April, 1962. The indicated recession did not occur. GNP continued to rise without interruption throughout 1962. Industrial production, it is true, leveled in the last half of 1962, but did not decline significantly, and resumed its rise early in 1963.

Late in 1962, the diffusion index reversed itself, endorsing the strong rise in GNP then under way. In early 1963, however, it again gave signals of economic trouble that did not materialize. The composite index, in the meantime, moved upward.

In the last half of 1963 and the first half of 1964, the diffusion index changed its mind almost every month. The composite index, however, moved quite steadily upward, as did industrial production (except for a one-month decline due to the automobile strike) and GNP. Later in 1964, the diffusion index rose steadily if not spectacularly, only to turn sharply downward early in 1965. And in mid-1965, the composite index leveled off, adding some credence to the warning of the diffusion index of a downturn that did not occur.

By way of comparison, one might claim the following record for fore-

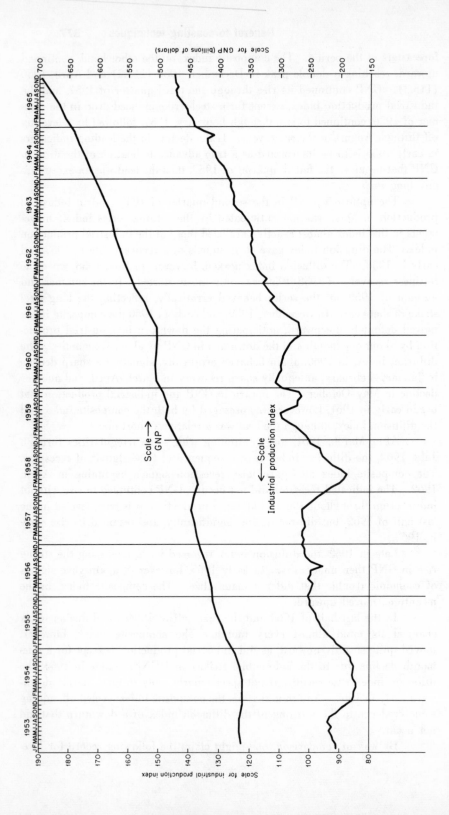

Scale for GNP (billions of dollars)

Scale for industrial production index

Scale → GNP

Scale ← Industrial production index

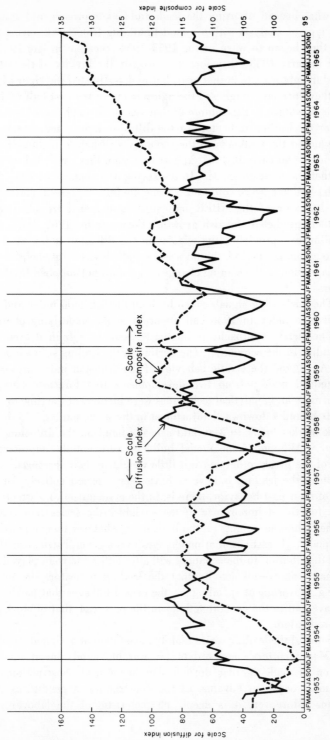

Figure 16—1. Comparison of the NBER diffusion index and amplitude adjusted composite index with the Federal Reserve index of industrial production and GNP. Source: Bureau of the Census, *Federal Reserve Bulletin*, and *Survey of Current Business*, U.S. Department of Commerce.

casters who, instead of using the leads-and-lags approach, did a more generalized type of analysis within a model-building framework during the same period: they began to warn of the 1953–1954 recession in late 1952 and insistently in early 1953; they foresaw correctly the brevity of the 1954 recession, and the upturn late in that year, but underestimated the vigor of the 1955 boom; they correctly diagnosed the aging boom in the first half of 1957, and called the downturn in the autumn of that year with much more precision than did either the leading indicators or the diffusion index; again early in 1960, they diagnosed the weakness in the economy well before it showed up in the GNP figures, and early in 1961, almost to a man, they predicted correctly the upturn that was soon to ensue. In the spring and summer of 1962, however, the model builders, were confused. Some, unduly impressed, perhaps, by the striking behavior of the NBER indicators, anticipated trouble later in the year; others predicted sluggish growth. Forecasts for 1963, 1964, and 1965 were uniformly optimistic; the wiggles in the diffusion index were ignored. And throughout the period, the forecasts supplied reasonably helpful estimates of the magnitude of the coming changes—a datum not supplied by the leading indicators.

The misleading signals given by both the diffusion index and the leading indicators index in 1956 call attention to the underlying characteristic of the barometric approach: it implicitly assumes a high degree of structural rigidity in the economy. The decline in the leading series index, beginning in April, and the erratic behavior of the diffusion index throughout the year stemmed mainly from two developments that forecasters using more comprehensive and analytical techniques were inclined at the time to discount: a steel strike and a downward adjustment in the stock market. Again in 1962, the stock market break in May laid a heavy hand on the diffusion index, in particular. Although some model builders were unduly impressed by the severity of the break, others gave it little weight in their forecasts.

Since the leading indicators have been selected entirely for the uniformity of their past behavior, there is, in the system itself, no attention to the inherent functional importance of the variables the series represent. As a result, the technique weights all the indicators, whatever their intrinsic importance, equally. It assumes that no changes in the general structure of production and distribution in the economy will alter either the roles played by those determinants of overall activity that the leading indicators do not directly reflect, e.g., government spending, or the causal linkages that particular indicators have had to the general activity in the past, e.g., that of stock prices to future production.

Some of the leading series plainly have inherent anticipatory characteristics. Manufacturers' new orders for durable goods inevitably lead the production of made-to-order durable equipment, and construction contracts awards must occur in advance of the construction expenditures following therefrom. Moreover, it is deeply characteristic of the labor market for working hours to respond more sensitively than employment to fluctuations in demand. However, the leading series that the National Bureau and, more recently, the Bureau of the Census have selected by no means exhaust the inherently foreshadowing indicators in the economy.

A conclusion to which few practicing forecasters would demur is that the modern leads-and-lags technique deserves credit for reawakening a healthy and systematic interest in foreshadowing indicators; that the barometric approach provides a helpful supplement to any general kit of forecasting tools; and that, at the same time, it is in no sense a self-sufficient technique.

CANVASSING ADVANCE PLANS AND COMMITMENTS

The most obvious business forecasting technique of all was touched upon early in the chapter. There it was noted that if economic decision makers already have plans or commitments concerning their future actions, and if they tend to stick to these plans reasonably well, and, finally, if the plans are accessible to the forecaster, then he certainly should find out what they are. Our football forecaster of a few pages back would have a hard time infiltrating the opposing team's huddle, but in the economic case an appraisal of advance plans and commitments is an essential part of any sensible forecasting procedure.

Most of the useful quantitative indicators of plans, commitments, and preliminary decisions upon which general forecasters nowadays rely in the United States are of relatively recent origin. This is because decision making is so decentralized in most sectors of this economy that a complete canvass of all plans would use up more time and manpower than most forecasting exercises could spare. Consequently, adequate exploitation of the plans-canvassing technique has had to await the development and application of reasonably satisfactory sampling procedures. With these available, however, there has been a swift multiplication of such "foreshadowing indicators," as they have been aptly called.

Among the more important of such indicators now available to American forecasters should be listed (1) the budget and appropriation documents of the Federal government (the availability of which, of course, is *not* dependent upon sampling procedures), (2) the surveys of business intentions to spend upon plant and equipment made by the Department of Commerce and the Securities and Exchange Commission and by the McGraw-Hill Publishing Company, as well as the surveys of corporate plant and equipment appropriations conducted by the National Industrial Conference Board, (3) surveys of consumers' intentions to spend conducted periodically by the Census Bureau, (4) surveys made by the National Association of Purchasing Agents of businessmen's plans regarding changes in their inventories, (5) the Department of Commerce monthly series on new orders of durable goods manufacturers (much of whose business is done on a made-to-order basis, which means that new orders substantially lead output and sales), (6) *Fortune* magazine's semi-annual survey of capital goods producers and their quarterly survey of inventory intentions, (7) the Department of Commerce survey of manufacturers' sales and inventory expectations, and a complex of indicators that foreshadow construction expenditures including (8) applications to the Veterans Administration and the Federal Housing Administration made in connection with the government's mortgage-guarantee programs, (9) the F. W. Dodge Company series on residential and nonresidential construction contract awards, and (10) the Department of Commerce series on new housing units authorized by building permits.

The foregoing are, without exception, helpful indicators, and the uses that can be made of them will be discussed in the chapters addressed to the analysis of prospects in particular spending sectors. For reasons indicated at the beginning of this chapter, however, one cannot, simply by adding them together, convert plans and commitments data into a general outlook appraisal. Some spenders don't know their own minds; others will change them arbitrarily or will respond either to external events or to changes in other sectors that they cannot now anticipate. Hence the desirability of surveying the general expectations of planners as well as the plans themselves, and hence the fact that use of the foreshadowing indicators does not in itself constitute a sufficient forecasting methodology.

QUANTITATIVE MODEL BUILDING: GENERAL

Of all modern systematic forecasting techniques, the most ambitious, most intellectually satisfying, most fashionable, and probably most fruitful are those which fall under this heading. Yet it is misleading to imply that the relationship between the model-building approach and the others we have surveyed is predominantly one of rivalry. While model building does not permit an exclusive reliance on any of the other techniques, it is basically a means for exploiting the others, not for abandoning them. It makes some use of the no-change hypothesis and of extrapolated trends; it treats general business expectations as determinants of future decisions; and, most certainly it employs data on decision makers' plans and commitments. Moreover, the approach is assisted by rapid statistical reporting and by the cross-checks that can be provided by leads-and-lags analysis and by surveys of expert opinion. It provides a common framework for integrating these and other insights into a comprehensive, more or less internally consistent, picture of a coming period.

In essence the term "model building" means here exactly what it meant in Part Two. In both cases "model" refers to a simplified representation of reality that leaves out enough of the confusing detail to be understandable and manipulable and yet retains enough reality to afford significant insights into real events. The model building of Part Two, however, was a more abstract and generalized process than that which shall occupy us here. There the model and submodels (or theory and subtheories) did not have any specific dates attached to them, and, although heavily oriented to American institutions, were not exclusively relevant to any one country. The model-building forecaster, on the other hand, constructs a simplified picture of a concrete economy in an explicitly dated future period.

The work of such an analyst is distinguished, for one thing, by its comprehensiveness. The approach requires the forecaster to survey the total business situation. This makes the technique rather cumbersome and laborious. By the same token, however, it guards against errors that can arise from too single-tracked a focus upon particular aspects or sectors of the economy.

For another thing, the model-building approach is, in a stricter sense than the others, analytical. It is concerned not only with symptoms of change. It assumes that the process of change is analyzable and tries to reason from identified causes to predictable effects. It is this characteristic of model building that marries aggregative economic theory to the forecast problem.

A third general characteristic of outlook models is their essentially quantitative character. Their direct products are numerical pictures of the future expressed in concepts for which there are extant historical time series. Presently, model builders' basic statistical vocabulary is that of national income accounting. It is for this reason that this type of forecasting often is spoken of as national income, or income and product, or gross national product model building.

While quantification injects certain risks into forecasting, it can have powerful advantages. It necessitates an effort, however rough, to forecast the magnitudes as well as the directions of changes, and for many decision-making purposes this is invaluable. It injects a healthy discipline into the analysis. After surveying the whole diverse array of on-the-one-hand and on-the-other-hand factors in the situation, the forecaster must eventually fish or cut bait; he must synthesize all the influences upon the outlook into a relatively small set of numbers that expresses his net appraisal. Furthermore, quantification is the one ready means by which the component factors in the outlook can be properly weighted together. Without quantification it is altogether too easy to assume, for example, that a (relatively) severe drop in inventory investment will offset a (relatively) violent rise in defense spending.

A fourth characteristic of model building in general is its comparative flexibility. Because it attends explicitly to the structure of demand and incomes and to the institutional structures underlying them, no model-building technique is so inflexibly committed to an assumption of structural rigidity in the economy as are the purely barometric techniques. As we shall see, however, this is a point upon which there are very substantial differences between alternative types of model building.

Finally, it should be emphasized that there is nothing occult about the approach. It can generate no knowledge about the future that is not fed into the models. Its results can be no better than the assumptions and the series of specific judgments that compose the analysis. What it does is force the forecaster to organize his opinions into an internally coherent pattern. It guards against inconsistencies and gaps in the appraisal. Careful model building is no substitute for good intuitive judgment about the direction in which the economy is moving; but at the very least, it offers a man with bad judgment the opportunity to be consistently wrong and, by so doing, affords him more opportunities for recognizing the weakness in his position.[9]

ECONOMETRIC MODELS

An econometrician is a man who tries to express economic theories in strictly mathematical forms,[10] tries to gain new economic insights through the manipulation of those forms, and uses historical statistics for purposes both of testing his mathematized hypotheses and converting them into concrete descriptions of an economy. A good econometrician, therefore, is a good economic theorist, a good statistician, and a competent mathematician all rolled into one package. Most of us who need to do some forecasting do not have all these qualifications. But we can admire the effort that the econometricians have been making to render forecasting a thoroughly scientific and objective pursuit even if we remain skeptical of its complete feasibility.

A Simplified Example

The distinguishing feature of a simon-pure econometric forecaster is his insistence that his forecast derive from nothing but the answers produced by a rigorously designed quantitative model of economic behavior. Ordinarily econometric models take the form of a collection of simultaneous behavioral equations. For instance, to adopt a very simplified example, assume that a theory of aggregate-demand determination could be expressed in just two equations, the first being the familiar (and truistic) national accounting assertion that in a self-contained economy

$$Y = D = C + I + G$$

[9] During its relatively short life—less than a quarter century—the technique has established a record of many successes, but it has also recorded some resounding public failures. Perhaps the most famous were the much, and somewhat unfairly, maligned forecasts of heavy unemployment after World War II that some government economists made late in the war period. While there is not space here to undertake any adequate critique of those forecasts, it can be said that their basic error lay in assuming too uncritically that many of the economy's prewar structural characteristics would be projected into the postwar period. See the paper by Michael Sapir, "Review of Economic Forecasts for the Transition Period," in Conference on Research in Income and Wealth *Studies in Income and Wealth*, vol. 11, National Bureau of Economic Research, Inc., New York, 1949, vol. XI, part 4, pp. 275 367.

[10] The mathematical forms, however, typically need not involve any more advanced mathematics than that covered in the usual college algebra course.

where Y represents gross national income, D gross national product, C personal consumption expenditures, I gross private investment, and G government purchases of goods and services; and the second, a simple consumption function in the form

$$C = a + bY$$

No self-respecting econometrician would be content to work with such a simple model, but if he were, he could consolidate the two equations into one:

$$D = Y = I + G + a + bY$$

For econometric purposes, such a generalized model must be converted into a specific form. That is, the constants in the equation(s)—those which are given generalized expression by the lower-case letters a and b in the equation at hand—must be converted into numbers.

To find out what the values of such constants may be in a particular economy in a particular period, econometricians inspect historical data. In the case in point they would determine, by means of a correlation analysis, what constant values for a and b make the conventional consumption-function hypothesis most descriptive of consumption-income relationships that have pertained during a specified past period in the economy they are studying. It is always possible to develop a single best answer to such a question even though, as we shall emphasize shortly, it may not be a very satisfactory one.

Suppose that our hypothetical econometrician emerges from an analysis of the sort reflected in Figure 8–1 at the beginning of Chapter 8, with the conclusion that, expressed in 1958 prices, the equation $C = \$25$ billion $+ 0.7Y$ is an adequate description of consumption determination during the past decade in the United States. He knows that he would have come up with different values for the constants if he had studied past periods of different duration. But he decides that it is reasonable to project the particular constants he has identified to the future period he wants to forecast. This latter is a crucial and vulnerable step in the econometric method of forecasting, and we shall need to return to it.

But to carry the example a bit further, our man now needs estimates of what investment spending and government spending will be during the forecast period. In terms of the model he is using, he must get both of these figures from external sources. They are exogenous to the model, in contrast to future consumption, which, given the exogenous variables, is determined by the character of the system the model describes. Assume that our man adopts the view, perhaps on the basis of surveys of plant and equipment intentions, that in the forecast period gross private investment will amount to $\$90$ billion. Further, after extrapolating state and local government purchases and making a careful politicoeconomic study of the latest Federal budget document, he concludes that purchases by all American governments will amount to $\$130$

billion. Then, plugging these figures into his model, he comes up with the forecast that gross national product in the coming period will be

$$Y = \$90 \text{ billion} + \$130 \text{ billion} + \$25 \text{ billion} + 0.7Y = \$817 \text{ billion}$$

Reasons for Complex Models

In practice, as we have said, no competent econometrician would work with so simple a forecasting model as that just described. To appreciate both the character and the limitations of mathematically rigorous model building, it is necessary to understand practitioners' motives for complicating their models. Basically, they do so for three reasons.

In the first place, a model may be so simple that it fails to forecast the right thing; its findings may not convey a meaningful picture of future conditions. This is the case with our example. If a forecaster relied exclusively upon it he would, in the language of Part Two, be aggregate-demand happy. He would express the outlook only for total demand without indicating the prospects for real output and the degree of underproduction, for unemployment, for price stability, and for growth in capacity. At the very least, then, an adequate algebraic forecasting model would need to add equations that would show these more fundamental dimensions of business activity as functions of aggregate demand *and* of such other determinants as the labor supply, labor productivity, and price-output relations.

A second reason for elaborating the model is to make it more accurately descriptive of past economic activity. In the case in point, for instance, the equation $C = \$25 \text{ billion} + 0.7Y$ may not fit very well the historical data from which it has been derived. The analyst is apt to find that for many of the years of the historical period the figure for consumption that he can calculate from the equation misses the actual consumption figure rather widely. If so, much of the variability in consumption has been attributable to something other than variations in gross national income; the simple consumption function oversimplifies the record to the point of introducing serious inaccuracies.

Under such circumstances the analyst tries to identify and add new variables that, together with gross national income, can provide a more exhaustive statement of consumption determination. We would expect him, for example, to note that consumption has been much more closely a function of disposable personal income than of gross national income. But to introduce this refinement, he will need to add to his model the relationship of the two income concepts. Beyond this, he may well want to introduce a number of nonincome variables such as net consumer credit extensions, liquid asset holdings, recent consumer price changes, and consumer expectations as ascertained by certain surveys. Still further, his investigation of the historical relationships between consumption and its several determinants may reveal that some of the relationships are lagged, and the same circumstance is apt to arise at many other points in his model before he gets through. Consequently, he must begin dating all his variables.

Finally, so far as elaborations made to improve the historical fit of the model are concerned, the analyst may decide that the variable an equation is intended to explain is not sufficiently homogeneous to have its behavior accurately described by a single functional relationship anyway. He may find, for example, that two separate equations, one for consumer nondurable goods and services and the other for consumer durables, jointly achieve a closer fit with past experience than can any single total consumption function.

A third reason for complicating econometric forecast models is to make them more determinative—i.e., to render endogenous to the model the determination of variables that simpler constructs must view as exogenous. In our example, for instance, investment spending was treated as such a given, but no good econometrician would be content with this. He would try to add to his system an equation or equations purporting to describe investment determination.[11] And he would try to do the same for as many as possible of the new variables that he had added to his system in the course of improving the fit between the consumption function and the historical data from which it was derived.

Every time a previously exogenous variable is rendered endogenous, at least one equation is added to the system. Of course, each of these new equations may itself sprout new, more specific exogenous variables. But this does not mean that the econometrician is on an analytical treadmill in his quest for determinacy. For one thing, the more specific exogenous variables may be less imponderable. Moreover, as new equations explaining the determination of determinants are added, by no means all the variables in them are new to the system. Instead the model builder keeps encountering what in Part Two we called back-circling relationships. He finds, for example, that whereas future demand will be partly determined by future investment, future investment will be partly determined by current demand. To the extent that the model ties back into itself, its loose ends are in this way reduced, and there is a net gain in the balance between endogenous and exogenous variables.

Not only is the econometrician, as a scientist, naturally inclined to make these efforts to reduce the unexplained variables in his model but, as a forecaster, he is forced to. For the more the performance of the system depends upon unexplained variables with future dates, the less predictive power it has. A forecast that can say no more than that GNP in a coming year will be $800 billion *if* investors and government jointly spend $220 billion is not much of a forecast. As an analyst dedicated to taking the guesswork out of forecasting, the econometrician must try to reduce all the exogenous variables to one or two types: (1) variables with future dates that

---

[11] He might very well evolve separate equations for each of several components of investment such as plant and equipment spending, residential construction, and inventory change.

can be reliably estimated from current canvasses of decision makers' advance plans, and (2) variables with present or past dates that in the past have proved to be reliable leading indicators of particular types of subsequent activity.

In practice, econometricians use both these methods, though often with a preference for the first. Daniel B. Suits, for example, in his widely known econometric model, treats the increment in plant and equipment spending over the preceding year as a function of the increment in after-tax corporate profits and of the previous period's plant and equipment spending. Expressed in billions of dollars, his equation is

$$\Delta PE = .605\Delta(P^*_{-1} - T_{fc-1} - T_{sc-1}) - 0.124\,PE_{-1} + 4.509$$

where PE = plant and equipment spending, including producers' durables, nonfarm nonresidential construction, and all farm construction

P^*_{-1} = the preceding year's corporate profits

T_{fc-1} = the preceding year's Federal corporate income taxes

T_{sc-1} = the preceding year's state corporate income taxes

PE_{-1} = the preceding year's PE

The rather large constant in the equation, 4.509, suggests that a certain amount of replacement investment would proceed regardless of increments in profits or of the preceding year's level of PE spending.[12]

But Suits does not rely entirely on this equation for PE spending. If he has available a recent figure derived from a survey of investment intentions, such as that yielded by the McGraw-Hill survey, he "frequently" plugs this figure into his model rather than use the equation.[13]

Difficulties with the Method

Admirable as are its objectives and erudite as are its procedures, strictly econometric forecasting suffers from certain shortcomings.

In the first place—and this is a difficulty that gets worse as the technique becomes more sophisticated—rigorous model building is for many purposes inordinately ponderous. The computations involved in manipulating a system of a dozen or more simultaneous equations are enormous, but this is not the worst of it, particularly in an era of electronic computers. What are really time-consuming are the construction and upkeep of an elaborate model —upkeep in the sense of the continuing analysis of newly accruing historical data to check the adequacy of the variables and the accuracy of the model's parameters (or constants). Moreover, the basic time series used to derive the

---

[12] The constant can be interpreted as an offset of the PE_{-1} term, reflecting the fact that part of PE_{-1} did not add to capital stock, but replaced real depreciation.

[13] See Daniel B. Suits, "Forecasting and Analysis with an Econometric Model," *American Economic Review*, vol. LII, no. 1, pp. 104–132, March, 1962.

parameters frequently are subjected to significant retroactive revisions by the issuing agency. Whenever this happens, the econometrician is forced to reconstruct a substantial portion of his model. For these reasons heavy continuing use of the technique tends to be feasible only for rather elaborately staffed forecasting groups.

The second difficulty with the technique is much more fundamental. That is its structural rigidity. Any rigorous model, no matter how elaborate it has been made, will overlook variables that turn out to be important in the future. Empirically derived functional equations are never more than approximate expressions of causation. They always leave out some of the pertinent variables that may have had little effect in the past, but may take on added significance in the future. If so, a model-bound forecast has no way of responding to them. The forecaster must shun them as long as he denies himself the privilege of exercising his judgment, either consciously or unconsciously, to react to novelties in the emerging situation. Some econometric forecasters, to be sure, do *not* deny themselves the use of judgment; they deliberately introduce a "judgment factor" into their calculations. When they do this, however, they cease (according to our terminology) to be simon-pure econometric model builders.

Essentially the same point can be made another way. The assumption that all the constants in a model will remain literally constant in the future is excessively narrow. It should be emphasized that, since only rather detailed *functional* relationships are inflexible in the econometric models, the models do not imply so severe a structural rigidity in economic events as does the leads-and-lags technique. But the rigidity still is there, and it is bound sometimes to be unrealistic.[14]

OPPORTUNISTIC MODEL BUILDING

Business Week, in a rather famous and irreverent article on forecasting, contrasted "elegant" (econometric) model building with what it called "the lost horse method."[15] The latter term was more amusing than enlightening ("the way to find a lost horse is to go where the animal was last seen and figure out what you would do if you were a horse"). It referred to what some have called the looser forms, and others, quasi-mathematical or arithmetical modes of model building. We prefer a still different label that may be no more edifying than the others: opportunistic model building. This refers to a forecasting procedure, at least somewhat less rigorous than the econometric approach, which borrows liberally from most of the other tech-

[14] See Edwin Kuh, "Econometric Models: Is a New Age Dawning?" *Papers and Proceedings of the Seventy-seventh Annual Meeting of the American Economic Association, American Economic Review*, vol. LV, no. 2, pp. 362–369; May, 1965, for a scintillating discussion of the current status of econometric model building for forecasting purposes.

[15] "Business Forecasting," *Business Week*, Sept. 24, 1955, pp. 110ff.

niques we have reviewed—including the econometric approach—and which has an appetite for any and all kinds of outlook information.[16]

This other form of model building actually is many forms. Opportunistic model building covers a whole range of possibilities; some are very close to what has been described as pure econometric analysis; others are very remote from it. But the variants have two common characteristics. All such analyses are conducted within a national accounting framework; this qualifies them as model building. And all allow some room for the introduction of judgment, hunches, the views of other observers, or various considerations not explicitly formulated in the economic theories upon which the models largely rely; this distinguishes the opportunistic model-building approach from the purely econometric one.

The least ambitious of the forecasting procedures that this definition accommodates involves the mere aggregation of independently arrived at estimates of how particular expenditure categories are going to move in the forecast period. Such forecasting depends upon no more elaborate a demand theory than the accounting truism $D = C + I + E + G$. Such a technique does not recognize any interdependence among the expenditure categories and does not hypothesize any of the functional relationships that are the core of an econometric model.

At the other (ambitious) extreme of the range of opportunistic model-building techniques, an analyst may work with virtually as elaborate a set of functional hypotheses (rooted in just as sophisticated a theory of aggregative economic behavior) as does the econometrician. He may even render them all into specific simultaneous equations and solve them with an electronic computer. Still there is this narrow but deep difference between him and the pure econometrician: the opportunistic model builder will not allow his equations to be bound by historical experience; while he will be greatly influenced by such experience, he may change the constants and add variables he believes have become newly important.

Most of the major economic forecasting exercises now being conducted in the United States by corporate staffs, consulting firms, trade associations, labor union groups, and government agencies fall somewhere within the opportunistic model-building range, and it is this general approach to the outlook problem that will occupy us in the remainder of Part Four. The range is so broad, however, that to avoid an encyclopedic treatment we shall have to concentrate upon a particular model-building procedure that is reasonably representative of the general approach. The next chapter will be a kind of cookbook proposition, outlining the steps in a model-building analysis to which subsequent chapters on particular sector forecasts will then relate. The

[16] Professor John Lintner, of Harvard University, in conversation with one of the authors, good-naturedly protests the use of the term "opportunistic," chiefly because of the connotation of unethical or at least undignified behavior that the word "opportunistic" has acquired.

procedure recommended will adopt a nation's economic-budget statistical framework and will invoke a considerably more elaborate abstract model than $D = C + I + E + G$. On the other hand, the procedure does not entail the development of anything like the number of explicit determinative functions that an average econometric model would employ, and consequently it does not involve elaborate computations.

SUMMARY

Not only is business forecasting a nearly universal activity among economic decision makers and a crucial one for many, but its practice is so varied even among the noncrackpot experts that a general overview of the subject must necessarily cover a lot of ground. In this introduction to the outlook problem we touched initially on its character, its setting, and some of the moods and folklore surrounding it.

Then, undertaking an inventory of those forecasting techniques that are relatively systematic and reasonably respectable, we noted, first, a group of approaches that are distinguished chiefly by their analytical unambitiousness: projections and extrapolations of things as they are or recently have been; efforts to speed up the nation's statistical reflexes; and opinion surveys —expert and otherwise—concerning the outlook.

Second, we considered the barometric or symptomological mode of forecasting, of which the best-known variant at present is the National Bureau of Economic Research leads-and-lags procedure for anticipating very near-term turns in business. This is a procedure that has certain evident merits but also some severe limitations.

Attention was given, in the third place, to the gratifying progress recently made toward supplying American outlook analysts with representative canvasses of decision makers' advance plans and commitments. These have become an invaluable resource for any adequate contemporary forecasting exercise, but they do not, by themselves, provide a sufficient insight into coming events.

Finally, the last third of the chapter has been devoted to various model-building possibilities. A sharp distinction was drawn (mainly for expositional purposes) between (1) the purely econometric approach, wherein the analyst expends all his discretion and judgment on the construction of a rigorously mathematical model, the specific characteristics of which are derived from historical time series, and thereafter faithfully cranks his forecasts out of his model, and (2) the less elegant but more flexible techniques that we have lumped under the heading of opportunistic model building. One great virtue of the latter kind of model building, of which we shall now begin a detailed examination, is the readiness with which it embraces the insights that any and all sensible forecasting procedures have to offer.

17

COMMENCING AN OPPORTUNISTIC OUTLOOK MODEL

A meaningful general economic forecast must estimate the prospects for real output, for capacity growth, for unemployment, and for the general price level. These can be found only by examining prospective changes in the supply of productive resources as well as in the demands for them, and by integrating these analyses. It follows that to do an adequate job of forecasting within what we are calling an opportunistic model-building framework involves three major steps.

One is to estimate the economy's normal *capacity* during the period in question. Such a supply estimate represents the volume of real demand that will be needed for full employment.

A second step is to predict *actual demand* during the forecast period. Each of these first two steps requires a framework of protective assumptions about external circumstances, and the two may be taken in either the indicated sequence or its opposite.

In the third place, the results of the supply and demand analyses must be *compared and evaluated*. The analyst must decide whether the outlook as analyzed contains a promise of either a significant excess of prospective capacity over prospective demand or an opposite imbalance. If it does, as this underlying aspect of the outlook begins to take shape, the analyst must then decide whether the reactions of decision makers (including public-policy makers) should be expected to alter his original estimates of the capacity and demand prospects. And finally, once a net, revised view of those prospects has been adopted, what forecasts of employment-unemployment and of price behavior are consistent with it?

The present chapter treats capacity forecasting and provides an overview of the procedures involved in preparing a demand forecast. The latter constitutes the most laborious part of an outlook analysis. It usually is built up, to begin with, on a sector-by-sector basis. Thus the six following chapters concern problems encountered in forecasting critical demand sectors—government spending, fixed-capital formation other than residential construction, new housing and automobile buying, net exports, inventory investment, and the remainder of personal consumption. Thereafter, the concluding steps in a demand analysis plus the comparison and evaluation of the capacity and demand estimates are considered in Chapter 24.

FORECASTS VERSUS PROJECTIONS: A SEMANTIC ASIDE

In current business conditions commentary, while the words "forecast" and "projection" sometimes are used as synonyms, it is evident that writers often mean to distinguish them. Sometimes it would appear that any short-run outlook analysis is a forecast and any long-run analysis a projection, or, again, that forecasts are estimates of the demand outlook while projections relate only to the capacity outlook. The most reasonable usage, however, is that which defines a projection as an outlook analysis that is more conditioned (protected) by operating assumptions than is a forecast. This is a useful distinction, even though it cannot be an absolute one, since a forecaster always must make some assumptions about things that lie beyond his professional competence.

One certainly can come much closer to an unconditional estimate of demand prospects for the coming year than for the long run. But, as we shall suggest in the following section, there is some reason to believe that our ability to forecast average capacity changes during the next ten or fifteen years may be as good as, and perhaps even better than, it is during any given next twelve months. However, some of the analysts who make long-run capacity forecasts have also been interested in the possible income and demand dimensions the economy may have when it obtains the physical size their capacity forecasts indicate. And lacking the demand-forecasting techniques that are available for the short-run future, these analysts accordingly project various hypothetical demand patterns to fit their long-run capacity forecasts.[1]

---

[1] Excellent examples of this type of analysis are Gerhard Colm's *The American Economy in 1960*, National Planning Association, Washington, 1952, and the *National Economic Projections*, issued annually by the National Planning Association on a subscription basis beginning in 1959. Also of considerable historical interest is the hypothetical demand model which, in 1952, the U.S. Department of Commerce, Office of Business Economics, built to fit its capacity forecasts for 1955 in its *Markets after Defense Expansion*, 1952.

They quite properly prefer to call these composite long-run analyses projections rather than forecasts. Moreover, the GNP projections upon which business planners increasingly are grounding their capital budgets are indeed projections, since they invoke the quite hypothetical proposition that actual demand five or ten years hence will closely approximate forecasted capacity growth.

But here—in this and the succeeding chapters of Part Four—we are concerned with *forecasting* in the sense just established. In the case of capacity, such forecasting can be fairly long-term, extending ten to fifteen years into the future. In the case of demand prospects, the forecasting range is very limited. But the limits are set by the forecasting tools, not by arbitrary time differences that distinguish forecasts from projections.

FORECASTING NORMAL CAPACITY

To forecast a nation's normal full-employment output it is necessary to predict the values of three variables that, as we saw in Part Two, can be viewed as the determinants of productive capacity: the labor force, average working hours, and labor productivity. Very much the same techniques have to be used in estimating these variables for any single coming year (including the one coming next) that are used in forecasting the average changes in them over an extended series of future years. However, the appropriateness of the techniques differs in the two cases, and it will be well to distinguish between them.

ESTIMATING CAPACITY FIVE TO FIFTEEN YEARS HENCE

That forecasting the United States normal productive capacity five, ten, or fifteen years hence is thought to be a feasible procedure is witnessed by the frequency with which reputable economists and economic staffs have popped up with such forecasts since World War II. A trail-breaking exercise of this sort was conducted by a group of economists for the National Planning Association (NPA) in 1945. It yielded a capacity forecast for the year 1950 or thereabouts that was adopted as a bench mark for a set of income and expenditure projections incorporated in the NPA pamphlet *National Budgets for Full Employment*.[2] Gerhard Colm's *The American Economy in 1960*, prepared under the same auspices in 1952, proceeded along similar lines.[3] Also in 1952 the President's Materials Policy Commission (the Paley Commission) projected the capacity of the economy in 1975 as a framework for estimating the nation's future materials requirements.[4] In the fall of 1954

---

[2] National Planning Association, Washington, 1945.

[3] Colm, *op. cit.*

[4] *Resources for Freedom*, U.S. Department of Commerce, President's Materials Policy Commission, 1952, vol. II, chap. 22, pp. 111–116.

the staff of the congressional Joint Economic Committee published a careful normal full-employment, i.e., capacity, forecast for 1965.[5]   At about the same time similar estimates for 1970, calculated by one of the authors of this book, provided national bench marks for certain regional and state estimates made along essentially similar lines.[6]   These early estimates have since been revised and updated, and others have been offered by an increasing number of long-run model builders.   Today, it is standard practice in many large corporations (e.g., AT&T) to prepare, usually for internal use, long-run projections that serve as a basis for long-run company planning.   The National Planning Association offers a regular service containing such long-run projections, giving demand estimates by state, by consumption category, etc., for business firms that prefer not to do their own projections or to check their own estimates against those of an outside body of experts.   Studies of national public-policy problems are often introduced by a long-run GNP estimate, which sets the economic framework for the study.[7]

Although such long-run estimates usually are expressed as a prediction of capacity in a particular future year, they actually are forecasts of average annual capacity changes during the intervening period.   The forecaster knows very little, for example, about what the change in capacity between the fourteenth and fifteenth year ahead will be.   But he believes that over the fifteen-year period annual changes will average a rate that, when compounded, will produce about the level indicated for the most distant year.   Even a quite abnormal change in that last year will not throw off the forecast very badly if the average change throughout the period is correctly estimated.

The fact that such estimates depend upon the abnormal years averaging out means that, in one sense, the estimates become less reliable as the target date is moved nearer the present.   But in another sense, of course, their reliability diminishes as the target date is extended.   The two influences at work are these: (1) The greater the remoteness of the forecast period, the less trustworthy are the clues that current and past evidence provide; thus a prediction of capacity changes during the second five years from now is less trustworthy than one for the next five years.   But (2) reliability tends to be positively correlated with the duration of the forecast period; for instance, a prediction of the total or average annual capacity change during the period from five to fourteen years in the future is apt to be very much better than a forecast of the change in the particular middle year of that period.

The combined effect of these two influences probably is to make the

[5] *Potential Economic Growth of the United States during the Next Decade*, U.S. Department of Commerce, Joint Economic Committee, 1954.

[6] R. C. Turner, "The American Economy in 1970," *Appraisal Journal*, vol. 24, no. 2, pp. 165–172, April, 1956.   Also, see *Indiana's Economic Resources and Potential: A Projection to 1970*, Indiana University Bureau of Business Research, Bloomington, Ind., 1956, vol. I.

[7] See, for example, H. H. Landsberg, L. L. Fischman, and J. L. Fisher, *Resources in America's Future*, published for Resources for the Future, Inc., The Johns Hopkins Press, Baltimore, 1963, pp. 69–87.

quality of forecasts of average annual changes in capacity for periods extending not less than, say, five years into the future or more than ten to fifteen years distinctly superior to forecasts either for substantially longer periods or for single years immediately impending.

The Labor Force

It is mainly a labor force consideration that prompts the choice of fifteen years as the upper limit of the range through which medium long-run capacity forecasts can be most safely extended. The two formal determinants of the labor force, identified in Part Two, are the age-eligible population, i.e., the noninstitutional population fourteen years of age and older, and the labor-force participation rate. The age-eligible population, in turn, is determined by net immigration, the birthrate, and the death rate. Net immigration has for many years been very small and even sizable percentage errors in predicting future net immigration would not affect the total significantly. For periods up to fourteen years, future changes in the birthrate will have no direct effect on the age-eligible population. The size of the age-eligible population, for periods of a decade and a half, is therefore almost entirely a function of mortality rates. And as Figure 17–1 suggests, the trend of the latter is far more stable and predictable than is the course of that most quixotic of population variables, the birthrate.

It is harder to predict the path that the labor-force participation rate will follow during a coming five- to fifteen-year period. However, for purposes of long-run capacity forecasting, minor year-to-year fluctuations in the participation rate can be ignored on the averaging-out principle. Moreover, the only source of moderately sharp variations in the participation rate in the

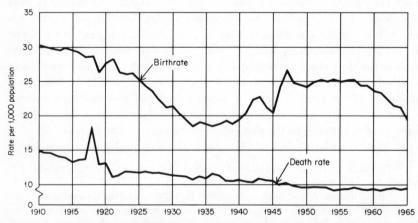

Figure 17–1.   United States birthrate and death rate, 1910–1965. Note: The birthrate is adjusted for underregistration prior to 1960.   Source: U.S. Department of Health, Education, and Welfare.

past—the impact of wars and of major defense emergencies—usually is screened out of the problem by a protective assumption about the international situation.

The only other major influences on the participation rate are, first, the age composition of the age-eligible population and, second, such institutional and sociological factors as the duration of schooling, customary marriage and retirement ages, and conventions concerning mothers and housewives working. During any coming fifteen years the age composition, like the size, of the age-eligible population will depend upon mortality. It is sufficiently predictable so that the U.S. Bureau of the Census feels free to make periodic official forecasts (discussed further in Chapter 25). The various institutional and sociological determinants of the labor-force participation rate, moreover, are slow-moving things that can be more or less confidently extrapolated from the experience of the recent past. The Bureau of the Census, therefore, also makes projections of participation rates by age group and by sex which, coupled with the age-sex composition projections, yield estimates of the labor force.[8] Long-run model builders typically use these Bureau of the Census estimates although anyone who is willing to undertake the labor involved can start from scratch and make his own projections.[9] Actually, it is a brave man who would attempt to improve upon the Bureau of the Census age composition estimates. With respect to the participation rate estimates, however, the projector can legitimately make his own assumptions about trends and perhaps come up with different figures. In this event, it is relatively easy to multiply the age composition estimates by the relevant participation rate estimates and derive projections of the labor force.

Working Hours

The prospects for normal full-employment working hours are considerably more elusive than those for average changes in the labor force. Here, too, however, the elimination of fluctuations associated with short-run variations in demand and with national emergencies greatly simplifies the problem. The remaining variation in the duration of normal workweeks is determined by gradually evolving commercial customs, conditioned and modified by maximum-hours legislation and by collective bargaining. There is no very trustworthy way of telling just how far the secular decline in average working hours will proceed in a particular decade or two. Looking at very long-run trends, we might expect the average workweek to decline by as much as 10

[8] See, for example, Bureau of the Census, *Current Population Reports*, ser. P-25, no. 286, or the *Manpower Report of the President*, March, 1966, pp. 215–216.

[9] For a description of the techniques involved, see Harold Wool, "Long-term Projections of the Labor Force," in Conference on Research in Income and Wealth: *Long-range Economic Projection*, National Bureau of Economic Research, Inc., Studies in Income and Wealth, vol. XVI, Princeton University Press, Princeton, N.J., 1954, pp. 43–66.

percent a decade. Looking only at the experience of the 1957–1965 period, however, we might conclude that the workweek will decline only slightly, if at all. The truth probably lies somewhere between these two extremes; a guess that in normal times working hours in the United States will fall off by roughly ½ percent a year on the average probably may be as reasonable as any that can be made. It should not be inferred from this rather cavalier guess, however, that the choice of a number is unimportant. The difference between an average decline of zero and 1 percent a year will make a difference of roughly $100 billion in the GNP projection of fifteen years hence. We dismiss the matter this abruptly simply because we have no authoritative figure to offer.

Productivity

Somewhat ironically, our techniques for forecasting this most important source of capacity growth are extremely crude. The practice that virtually all forecasters presently follow is simply to extrapolate a historical, constant-dollar productivity trend—sometimes doctoring it up a little to reflect the forecaster's judgment that in the coming decade or so it is apt to accelerate or decelerate moderately.

This sounds like a rather unreliable procedure, given the fact, emphasized in Part Two, that labor productivity is only an intermediate or summary variable that reflects the impact of many underlying determinants, such as the quantity and quality of capital, the efficiency of production processes, and managerial and labor skills. There seems to be little a priori reason why the causal pattern underlying productivity should remain constant through time. Nevertheless, there are some persuasive defenses for the simple extrapolation procedure *if* it is an average annual, rather than a specific year, estimate of future productivity that is desired, and if the forecast period is not more than a decade or a decade and a half.

For one thing, the procedure makes good sense historically. The empirical evidence, partly reviewed in Chapter 5, is that, apart from short-term fluctuations, the pace of productivity gains has been fairly steady during the past half century. Furthermore, there are reasons for believing that this past persistence of productivity trends has been more than coincidence.

In the first place, such major determinants of productivity as managerial and labor skills and technological innovation are not usually subject to jagged fluctuations over relatively short periods. Secondly, even the unstabilizing impact of one determinant that is subject to sharp fluctuation— namely, net new capital formation—is moderated by its combination with a large, relatively steady volume of replacement investment. This replacement investment, despite its name, actually affects productivity significantly through the incorporation of new designs and processes.

In the third place, the gains achieved in the economy's resistance to downturns in recent decades have tended to stabilize productivity growth.

An extrapolation of productivity growth during the 1920s into the 1930s yields figures markedly at variance with those which actually prevailed, partly because the rate of new capital formation implicit in such an extrapolation was not forthcoming and partly because the secular shift of labor out of relatively low-productivity agriculture into relatively high-productivity non-agricultural activities was temporarily reversed.   Both of these forecast-defeating factors were by-products of the long and deep depression in aggregate demand.   If the danger of such long, deep depressions has in fact now been greatly reduced in this country, these particular threats to productivity extrapolations have also diminished.

Finally, there is this reassuring possibility: there may be some reciprocal relation between productivity changes and average working hours in the medium-long run.   That is, if under conditions of high employment, productivity should fail to grow as fast as the historical rate that forecasters extrapolate, pressures in the economy for a continuance of the accustomed rate of rise in real incomes may induce labor market conditions that discourage average hours from falling at their secular rates.   If so, there would be a tendency for a forecaster's errors concerning productivity to be offset by his errors concerning working hours and for his general capacity forecast to be protected.   It is for this reason that some long-run model builders combine the two determinants, average hours worked per year and output per man-hour, into a single variable: annual output *per man*, the trend of which they extrapolate in some fashion.

All told, then, the popular method of forecasting productivity growth during coming five-, ten-, or fifteen-year periods makes pretty good, if crude, sense.   However, the technique is peculiarly subject to the ravages of time as it is extended into the more distant future.   The longer the forward period in question, the more probable it becomes that the variables underlying labor productivity and not directly canvassed by the forecasting technique will shift. Chapter 25 will reinforce the conclusion that no particular slope of the nation's productivity curve necessarily is knit into the fabric of our history.   At the same time, it seems unlikely that changes will occur rapidly enough to leave a straight-line extrapolation of annual percentage productivity gains far off the mark if the extrapolation is not extended much beyond a decade.

Rather than calculate their own estimates of past labor productivity trends, most capacity forecasters draw the data they extrapolate from such standard studies of the matter as those of the Bureau of Labor Statistics, mentioned in Chapter 5.[10]   But the analyst must rely on his own judgment in two respects.   First, he must decide what duration of past experience to extrapolate.   The average annual productivity gain in the United States private economy since 1909 has been about $2\frac{1}{3}$ percent; during the period since World War II, however, it averaged about 3 percent, and from 1960 to 1965, it averaged about $3\frac{1}{3}$ percent.   Second, the forecaster must decide whether to bend

[10] See pp. 109–112.

his extrapolation to fit his ideas about changes in some of the determinants of productivity that may be in the offing during the forecast period.

The productivity data cited above, it should be emphasized, refer to the private economy, i.e., they exclude government workers and their output. The reason for this exclusion is that, lacking a market transaction, there is no known method of correcting the data on the output of government workers for price change. Any increase in average payments to government workers per man-hour of input is arbitrarily attributed to a price increase rather than to an increase in productivity. Thus, by definition, the productivity of government workers is a constant.

Accordingly, if capacity forecasts are correctly made, they entail the formulation, first, of estimates for the private economy only. This involves projecting the size of the civilian labor force less government employment, working hours of private workers only, and the productivity of workers in the private economy only.[11] Compounding these projections and applying the total percentage to the base-year capacity will yield an estimate of gross *private* product capacity in the target year. To this, then, must be added a figure for government output that should be related, of course, to the number of government workers assumed in making the projection of the private civilian labor force, and to the gross private product figure that the initial projection yielded. For example, one could assume that the proportion of the civilian labor force employed by government in the target year will be the same as in the base year and that the percentage of GNP accounted for by government will also be the same in the target year as in the base year. In this way, the problem of the productivity of government employees is finessed. The extent to which the increase in the dollar value of government output is attributable to increased real output per worker, or to a (partially or wholly spurious) increase in the cost per unit of output of government workers, is left unspecified.

ESTIMATING CAPACITY CHANGES DURING A COMING YEAR

Not all model builders even recognize the need for making short-term capacity forecasts, but those who do simply use some variant of the extrapolation technique just discussed. Usually, because the published data on productivity, man-hour input, etc., are available only as index numbers rather than as absolute values, model builders calculate from the index numbers an estimated *rate* of change in the relevant variables, compound these several rates into a single total rate, and then apply this total rate of change to a capacity

---

[11] If $I + r$ is the multiple which capacity in any given year is expected to be of capacity in the preceeding year, then $I + r = (I + r_l)(I + r_h)(I + r_a)$, where r_l indicates the average annual percentage change in the civilian labor force, r_h the average annual relative change in working hours, and r_a the average annual percentage change in labor productivity.

estimate for some base year. If a fairly recent year can be found when the economy was operating at capacity, the actual GNP figure for that year can be used as the base. Thus, the Council of Economic Advisers has used mid-1955, when unemployment was close to 4 percent, as the base of their capacity estimates.[12] The Council extrapolated this base-year figure at different rates of change for subperiods since 1955, the differences reflecting breaks in the rates of change in the determinants of capacity, notably the labor force. This method is no doubt the best method if unemployment was down to the full-employment level in a recent year. The further back into the past one has to go to find a full-employment year, however, the larger is the potential error in compounding the rate of capacity growth.

In recognition of this problem, Arthur Okun, prior to his appointment to the Council of Economic Advisers, suggested an alternative method.[13] Okun noted that, at a given time, "each extra 1 percent of real GNP means a decrement, on the average, of about one-third of a percentage point in the unemployment rate." This generalization, dubbed by the forecasting fraternity as "Okun's law," may be used to estimate capacity in the current year (if unemployment is above 4 percent), by increasing the GNP figure by three times the differential between actual unemployment and 4 percent. For example, if actual GNP in a given year was $800 billion, and the unemployment rate was 4.7 percent, estimated capacity would be $800 billion multiplied by $1 + 3 \ (0.047 - 0.040)$ or approximately $817 billion. This method, it will be noted, ignores the government versus private output problem discussed above.

With respect to the rate of change in capacity, because productivity is expected to rise, on the average, x percent per annum during the coming decade, it is usually assumed that it will do so during the coming year. Much the same attitude is taken with respect to the labor force and working hours unless some specific influences, such as the delayed effects of the postwar "baby wave" or a change in the defense program, can be identified.

---

[12] *Economic Report of the President*, January, 1965, pp. 80–85. Note that it is the level of unemployment, not physical plant and equipment, that is used by the Council in determining capacity, and 4 percent unemployment is defined as "full" employment. "The potential GNP of the U.S. economy measures the volume of goods and services that our economy could produce if the unemployment rate were at the interim target of 4 percent." (p. 81) "The Council's estimate of potential GNP reflects the belief that the economy could operate at a 4 percent unemployment rate today without substantial strains on either labor supplies or plant capacity." (p. 83) The 4 percent figure is, of course, a matter of judgment. Further, under certain circumstances, plant and equipment, rather than manpower, could be the effective limiting factor on potential output.

[13] Arthur M. Okun, "The Gap between Actual and Potential Output," in Arthur M. Okun (ed.), *The Battle against Unemployment*, W. W. Norton & Co., Inc., New York, 1965, pp. 13–22. This article is an abbreviated version of a paper originally published in the 1962 *Proceedings* of the Business and Economic Statistics Section of the American Statistical Association.

Usually round-number estimates are all that the roughness of the procedure justifies. A rule of thumb for the last half of the decade of the 1960s, for example, might be somewhat as follows: United States output per man-hour is apt to rise about 3 percent in any given normal year; the labor input (labor force times hours) is likely to make a net gain of about 1 percent (varying this sometimes to allow for reactions to abnormally large or small changes in the preceding year); as a result, a real-capacity increment of approximately 4 percent probably is in store for the coming year.

The basic danger in this procedure, rather obviously, is that in a forecast for any particular year there can be no reliance upon the averaging-out phenomenon. All the determinants of normal full-employment capacity are subject to short-run deviations from secular trends. During the eighteen-year period 1947–1965, for example, annual United States gains in gross private product per man-hour averaged 3.3 percent but ranged from a low of 0.1 percent to a high of 8.8 percent; annual gains in the total labor force, although averaging 1.2 percent, fell as low as −0.6 percent and went as high as 2.6 percent. And annual changes in working hours varied from +0.75 percent to −1.50 percent, averaging −0.5 percent. Some of this variation can be attributed to the Korean mobilization, and some of it, in the other direction, to recessions. But even if we discard the figure for years when these abnormal influences were present, the remaining variation is still considerable.

Such variations can badly upset model-building forecasters, especially if two or more of the determinants of capacity happen to deviate from normal in the same direction at the same time. Suppose, for example, that, relying upon an increase of capacity in line with the secular trend, a forecaster concludes that the upcoming year will be afflicted with a demand deficiency of $15 billion. If capacity, instead of rising 4 percent, however, should increase only 2 percent, the problem would be wiped out.

Although such possibilities clearly threaten short-run model builders, the situation is not so bad as it initially appears. To a considerable extent, actual variations in the rate of change of the labor force, hours, and productivity reflect, not basic, long-run trends, but short-run changes in the level of aggregate demand relative to capacity. For obvious reasons, the average length of the workweek tends to fall during periods of declining business activity and to rise (or decline only slightly) during periods of boom. For somewhat less obvious reasons, the size of the labor force also is influenced by the level of aggregate demand. As we noted in Chapter 5, the labor force age group includes a substantial number of marginal participants—housewives, oldsters, youngsters—who are not normally in the labor force but who may be attracted into it temporarily if jobs are readily available.

Further, actual output per man-hour (as opposed to capacity output per man-hour) also is fairly responsive to the direction and rate of change of aggregate demand. Productivity tends to rise vigorously during a period of rapidly rising aggregate demand and to rise relatively little or to decline absolutely during periods of decline (as it did, for example, in 1930–1932). On the other hand, during the late stages of a boom, when aggregate demand is high absolutely but not rising relative to capacity, productivity increase may be quite small. And conversely, in the late stages of a decline, just before the upturn, productivity increases may be considerable.[14]

Fluctuations in the labor force, in hours, and in productivity that are the result of fluctuations in aggregate demand, however, *ought* to be left out of the forecaster's initial capacity calculations anyway.[15] It seems clear that the prediction that any given year's normal capacity will rise at the secular growth rate is, at the very least, a far better forecast than an assumption of no change would be. The no-change assumption, which is the implicit forecast embodied in analyses that ignore the capacity problem, dismisses the fact that in the near term some productivity gains almost always are in the offing as the result of investment expenditures already made, and some expansion of the normal labor force is almost inevitable.

FORECASTING AGGREGATE DEMAND

In forecasting aggregate demand, opportunistic model builders rely essentially on a basic idea that was stressed in Part Two of this book, namely, that the various categories of aggregate demand (components of GNE) vary considerably in their degree of dependency upon the total. Some are almost totally dependent on the level of aggregate demand and income; some are highly autonomous; and some lie between these two extremes.

The problem, in converting this idea into an operating procedure, is how to get started. For the very interdependency of the various sectors of demand seems at first blush to keep the analysis from getting off the ground. The volume of total demand in the forecast period will be the sum of the demand sectors. But, at the same time, the volume of every part will be dependent to some degree on the size of the whole.

In order to break out of this enervating circle the model builder must, for the time being, virtually neutralize the interdependent reactions among the GNP components by subjecting all of them to a uniform total demand and income hypothesis. This initial step in the analysis clearly must be a revisable one, since it assumes away the very problem that the forecaster is trying

[14] See John W. Kendrick, *Productivity Trends in the United States*, Princeton University Press, Princeton, N.J., 1961, pp. 72–78.

[15] Later on, if the analyst identifies a prospective tendency toward excessive or deficient demand, he will have to circle back through the model and consider what modifications in capacity behavior as well as in spending behavior the underlying excess (or inadequacy) of demand may cause. But to begin with, what he wants is an estimate of what the capacity would be if demand were just right to yield normal frictional unemployment.

to answer in this major phase of his work. The way to find out what gross national product and gross national income will be in the forecast period is to start by making believe you know. You hypothesize, that is, tentatively assume, the answer.

We shall return to the question of what the nature of this initial, revisable total income assumption should be. Whatever the figure, it is used in greater or lesser degree in estimating spending in each individual category of demand, depending on the degree of dependency upon aggregate demand that the analyst thinks is characteristic of that category. In the case of a highly autonomous category of demand, for example, the analyst will make no signifi- cant use of his preliminary total demand and income assumption. In the case of another, still largely but not entirely independent of changes in total de- mand, he will give some weight to the effect of his assumed aggregate demand, but will rely largely on other indicators of probable spending in that category. And so on down the line. It is useful, if not essential, for the analyst to pro- ceed in that sequence which will give him a reliable feel of the total situation as quickly as possible. Seldom, if ever, will this mean starting with personal outlays and going from top to bottom down a conventional listing of the GNP components. For, of all the categories of demand, the soft goods and services segments of consumption are among the most consistently dependent upon total income. It is better to start with those sectors in which changes typically are least dependent upon overall activity, in which buyers have a relatively good record of carrying out their advance plans, and in which such advance plans or other leading indicators of autonomous change are relatively accessi- ble. A sequence chosen in this light probably should begin with government spending, move next to nonresidential construction and producers' durable equipment (considered jointly), follow this with expenditures on new private housing and on automobiles (these being subject to similar patterns of causa- tion), net changes in business inventories, and net exports, and wind up with the remainder of consumer expenditures.[16] This is the order of topics that will be adopted in succeeding chapters.

The sector forecasts obtained while the initial total income hypothesis is in effect can be called the "first-approximation demand estimates." Even when a full roster of these has been established, much remains to be done be- fore a competent aggregate-demand forecast is achieved. But this is as far as we need to follow the step-by-step procedure at the moment. However, several important things remain to be said concerning the steps already outlined.

---

[16] It might be wise, in order to avoid misunderstanding, to anticipate here a point that will be made more fully in Chap. 23. By the time the analyst has made forecasts for all the sectors *except* consumer expenditures excluding automobiles, he will have sufficient information for forecasting this last category without using the initial demand hypothesis. He will, that is, on the assumption that expenditures for nonautomotive goods and services are *completely dependent* on total income, an assumption that we shall analyze later.

THE INITIAL TOTAL INCOME HYPOTHESIS

Theoretically, the question of what initial income assumption a forecaster should adopt for getting his analysis under way is not a momentous one. If the assumption turns out to be wrong, most of the first-approximation sector-by-sector estimates will be distorted—some will be badly distorted. But the autonomous changes in spending that are foreseen as resulting from other than total income influences will be unaffected by the assumption, and consequently the sum of the first-approximation estimates will not vindicate the initial assumption. In this event, the analyst should start over again, employing a new initial income hypothesis, which, judging from his experience with the first one, should prove to be more accurate. (In selecting the second income hypothesis, incidentally, the analyst should make a point to err, if at all, in the opposite direction to the error in his first hypothesis, because the first hypothesis "pulled" the forecast in the direction of the hypothesis. For example, if the analyst assumed $750 billion and his forecasting exercise yielded a figure of $810 billion, it should be assumed that the "correct" figure is *greater* than $810 billion. His second income hypothesis should therefore be, say, $815 billion.) Not until the initial hypothesis is validated by the final forecast can the analysis be considered a good one.

Actually, this successive-approximation procedure is far from foolproof. In practice, a bad initial total income hypothesis can inject a bias into the analysis that may never be wholly eradicated. Thus choosing the hypothesis is a matter of some consequence.

Some opportunistic model builders begin their sector-by-sector demand analyses with the assumption that total income will remain at the level existing at the time of the forecast. This is respectable practice and should not lead a careful analysis into serious error. Nevertheless, in the contemporary American economy, except perhaps when business activity is clearly turning downward, such a no-change assumption about overall activity inadvertently injects a slightly pessimistic slant into the analysis. Our experience since World War II suggests that the most normal behavior for demand in the United States is not to level but to grow more or less in line with rising capacity.

Consequently, in forecasting periods that promise to be reasonably normal, it is probably best to assume (initially) that demand and income will rise in line with the predicted capacity growth. If a recession is clearly under way, it would probably be more sensible to choose a lower working hypothesis.

WHAT ABOUT FINANCE AND PRICES?

The general manner in which credit and financial considerations should be factored into the construction of an aggregate-demand model can be described rather simply. The costs and availability of credit in various financial markets are among the major nonincome influences on demand that must be included in the appraisals of the sector-by-sector spending prospects. Thus our attention to the financial variables in forecasting will come principally in the succeeding chapters on particular sectors. In addition, the money and credit outlook may also require explicit treatment in the final stages of a model-building exercise. For instance, if the underlying prospect for the economy turns out to be inflationary, it is necessary then to consider the probable reactions of the central bank and, in turn, their probable impact on spending. Indeed, if the analysis is an ambitious one (and if the analyst is backed up by a competent statistical organization), it would be well to parallel the forecast's Nation's Economic Budget format with a flow-of-funds analysis, which would formalize and quantify credit influences.

The question of how price changes should be handled is a harder one, and there is no perfect answer to it. However, the following is one reasonably satisfactory procedure.

The price issue arises, in the first place, in connection with capacity forecasting. The initial capacity forecast is normally expressed in constant prices, perhaps prices prevailing during the year or quarter immediately preceding the period being forecast, since there is no way of predicting at the beginning of the analysis what current prices during the forecast period will be.

But where does this leave us when we get to the demand side of a comprehensive outlook exercise? Obviously, if the ultimate quantitative finding of the investigation is to be a comparison of capacity and demand prospects, both must be expressed in terms of the same price level. Yet many of the indicators of sector-by-sector spending prospects that must be used in building up a forward estimate of total demand reflect price as well as physical changes. For instance, it may be that the best independent estimate that can be made of auto purchases during a coming year is that sales will rise some $2 billion but that this will include a 3 percent price hike. It should be noted that in automobiles and in many other administered-price industries such a price prediction is not primarily a premature forecast of the operation of impersonal market forces. Rather, it is a prediction of discretionary behavior by decision makers who have considerable power to make good their decisions. Indeed, in such a case, one could conceivably feel surer of the price forecast than of the volume forecast associated with it. But the question remains, Should the model builder include such specific anticipated price increases in his first-approximation estimate of aggregate demand, or should he screen them out, i.e., put his demand estimates in deflated, constant-price terms?

The latter practice is the easier way of keeping the capacity and demand forecasts comparable. However, it has some serious disadvantages. For some purposes (notably for judging the adequacy of the money supply and the role of financial factors in the forecasting period) it is important to keep current-price demand in the forefront of the analysis. Moreover, it is very difficult to examine the prospects for changes in consumer, business, and government incomes in other than current-price terms. For example, you may feel that wage rates are due to go up 5 percent during the coming year and that this is one of the most important insights you possess into the outlook for disposable personal income. But if the personal consumption figures in the model are in constant dollars, it could be quite wrong to let the full 5 percent increment in money wages register on the model's disposable personal income figure. For not all the wage increase may be in real wages. Yet at those intermediate stages in a demand analysis where one is wrestling with disposable personal income and consumption prospects, the outlook for consumer prices is not yet clear enough to warrant converting a money-wage-rate forecast to real terms.

Accordingly, the best procedure is probably to build up one's aggregate-demand model in current-price terms, recognizing however, that the general pressures on prices cannot be precisely identified at the time one is beginning to make first-approximation estimates of sector expenditures. The initial sector demand estimates should reflect only whatever specific price changes are rather firmly anticipated in particular markets, especially ones of the administered-price type.

This means that the first tentative GNP forecast that emerges once the initial sector-by-sector expenditures have been totaled may not contain anything like the full price-level change that the analyst will wind up predicting if, for example, he should decide that a significant narrowing of the gap between demand and capacity is in prospect. But, at the same time, the inclusion of specific price changes in the sector demand estimates means that the initial forecast of aggregate demand will not be in terms of quite the same price level as that in which we left the capacity forecast. Accordingly, it will be necessary to inflate the capacity figure enough to match the limited price changes incorporated in the demand estimate before the two are compared. We shall return to this point in Chapter 24.

SUMMARY

In this how-to-do-it introduction to opportunistic model building we have seen that the construction of a full-blown forecast involves three steps—the making of a capacity forecast, the making of a demand forecast by successive approximations, and a revision phase in which the two are compared, evaluated, and, if necessary, modified.

It happens that the maximum feasible ranges for capacity forecasting and demand forecasting are very different. It is possible to make a relatively unconditional forecast of demand (as opposed to a relatively conditional set of projections) only for periods up to the next year or thereabouts. Conversely, it appears that the extrapolation techniques available for predicting changes in capacity are better suited to forecasting average annual capacity changes over periods up to a decade or a decade and a half hence than they are to predicting capacity change in a specific coming year.

This discrepancy has two consequences. It means, first, that the forecasting range of an overall opportunistic model-building exercise is limited to that of its short-range portion. It means, second, that in such short-run forecasting there must be reliance upon capacity-predicting techniques that are less well adapted to that purpose than they are to the extension of long-run capacity trends. However, while there is evident need for efforts to develop improved methods of near-term capacity forecasting, and particularly of productivity forecasting, the imprecision of presently available techniques is by no means so great as to rob short-run opportunistic model building of all utility.

On the demand side of the issue we have seen that the analyst's initial methodological problem is how to break out of a trap; namely, that, in the forecast period, the whole of spending will depend on its parts while, at the same time, the parts will, in greater or lesser degree, depend on the whole. The answer is to adopt an initial and revisable total income hypothesis, to test it out with sector forecasts based, as appropriate in each case, upon both the assumed total income and other indications of probable spending, to revise the total income hypothesis as necessary, and to repeat the process until the final result agrees with the initial income hypothesis.[17]

With this overview of the forecasting process, we are now at the point where we should look at techniques for forecasting the individual sectors of total demand. Before actually starting on the sector forecasts, however, the analyst would do well to equip himself with a forecasting work sheet, similar to that shown in Figure 17–2. The figure provides for an orderly array of recent historical and forecast data for the various sectors of demand, together with certain ratios that will be needed in the forecasting exercise. (The abbreviations and symbols, to the extent that they are not obvious, will be explained as we go along.)

---

[17] In case our reference to "repeating the process" may have alarmed you, and have suggested a never-ending sequence, it might be well to say that if the analyst starts with a reasonably good hypothesis—as any experienced forecaster is almost sure to do—one repetition is usually all that is necessary. (A discrepancy between the assumed total demand and the result of the forecasting exercise of anything less than a billion dollars or so—in the United States—can be ignored.) And this repetition is normally much less time-consuming than the initial calculation, because much of data gathering and data analysis have already been done. In practice, what the repetition amounts to is a revision of the previous estimates.

Figure 17–2. Forecasting work sheet: sector forecasts. (Current dollars; quarterly data at seasonally adjusted annual rates.)

Actual........ (Year) .... Forecast........ (Year)

	Year	Year	Qtr. I	Qtr. II	Qtr. III	Qtr. IV	Qtr. I	Qtr. II	Qtr. III	Qtr. IV	Year
Preliminary income hypothesis											
GPGS (G)											
Federal											
Defense											
Other											
State and local											
GPDI (I)											
Business fixed investment											
P & E											
Other											
Residential structures											
Inventory investment											
Net exports (E)											
PCE autos (C_a)											
Transfers by persons (T)											
$G + I + E + C_a - T$											
$u = \text{PI}/\text{GNP}$											
$v = \text{DPI}/\text{PI}$											
$w = C_o/\text{DPI}$											
$1 - uvw$											
Personal income (PI)											
Disposable PI (DPI)											
$C_o = \text{PO} - C_a$											
Personal outlays (PO)											
$\text{PCE} = C_o + C_a - T$											
GNP											
Net personal saving											
NPS/DPI											
Capacity (_____$)*											
Implicit price deflator											
Capacity (current $)											
Gap											

*Same year as base year (=100) for implicit price deflator.

18

THE OUTLOOK FOR GOVERNMENT SPENDING

During the past generation in the United States, government purchases of goods and services have fluctuated more violently than either personal consumption or domestic investment expenditures. Yet government purchases usually have constituted the most predictable major segment of final demand in the short run. Of all the major categories, they are the least dependent upon the general level of economic activity. And because governmental budgeting and appropriation processes are matters of public record, more is explicitly known about the Federal government's advance spending plans and commitments than about those of any other major spending group.

It makes both statistical and analytical sense for the forecaster to deal separately with Federal spending, on the one hand, and state and local spending, on the other, and that will be our procedure here.

FEDERAL EXPENDITURES

The course of Federal outlays has been too erratic to justify reliance upon trend analysis, and government spending is so largely independent of short-run changes in total economic activity that it would make little sense to treat it as a function of other variables in the economy. Consequently, almost all forecasting of Federal expenditures relies initially upon the publicly proposed, debated, legislated, and budgeted spending intentions of Federal authorities.

But this does not mean that all this forecasting is equally competent. Good workmanship in the area depends upon an understanding of certain rather specific matters—for example, the difference among such concepts as budget requests, new and unused obligational authority, and expenditures, which have precise meanings in the Federal spending process; the sequence of the various budgetary and appropriations documents, and their comparative reliability as advance indicators of Federal spending; the degrees to which different components of the budget are variable and subject to discretionary control in the short run; and the differences among the various formulations of the Federal budget.

THE TERMINOLOGY AND DOCUMENTATION OF THE FEDERAL SPENDING PROCESS

United States government spending programs typically are proposed by the Chief Executive, but they must be enacted—and in the course of enaction often are modified—by Congress. Thereafter, of course, they actually are carried out by the executive branch. The sequence of steps through which a plan to spend gets translated into cash outlays reflects these facts. Because the Federal budgeting-appropriating-spending process is administratively and politically complex, as well as because many of the things the government buys require a long lead time, the process is a lengthy one. In many respects this is unfortunate; it reduces the flexibility of public policy. But from a narrow forecasting perspective it is a great advantage. The attenuated character of the Federal spending process means that plans have to be formed well in advance of expenditures.

Federal spending plans are made for fiscal years that run from July 1 through June 30, and adopt the year number of the calendar year in which they end. Thus, the fiscal year 1968 runs from July 1, 1967, through June 30, 1968. The various departments and agencies of the executive branch typically start planning their budget requests about eighteen months in advance of the fiscal year in question, usually in the light of some general guidance supplied by the President through the Bureau of the Budget, a staff agency to the President.[1] During the ensuing months, through a process of negotiation be-

---

[1] The procedures used in the preparation of the budget and the timing of the several steps, as well as details of government accounting, vary somewhat from one President to another, and even from one budget director to another. The description of the process given here corresponds to recent practice at the date of writing, but subsequent modifications can be expected.

tween departments and successively more authoritative Budget Bureau person-nel, these departmental budget requests are revised, refined, and usually lowered. They are consolidated into the budget of the United States govern-ment, which, including the President's Budget Message, is sent to the Congress in January. The President has been kept generally informed of the progress of budget preparation throughout the fall, has established policies regarding the general dimensions of the budget, and has been discussing the more criti-cal issues with his Cabinet, the National Security Council, and other advisers. He becomes most actively engaged in the final stages of the process, usually having to settle certain disputes that cannot be resolved at lower levels. Nom-inally, the President approves every "mark" in the budget and when it is completed it is officially *his* budget, not that of the agencies concerned or of the Budget Bureau.

Increasingly, as the transmittal date for the budget approaches, alert business conditions analysts can pick up in the press indications of what the general proportions and some of the detail of the new budget will be. By the end of December, such journalistic anticipations—provided one chooses his sources carefully—usually are fairly comprehensive and complete.[2] Never-theless, the transmittal of the budget is the first authoritative and compre-hensive revelation of the administration's new spending program. It is there-fore a key event for the forecaster.

The budget is a multivolume document. The main document, from the forecaster's point of view, is given the all-inclusive title "The Budget of the United States" and is an ordinary book-size volume of around four hundred pages that contains, in addition to the President's Budget Message, several chapters of summary information about budget receipts and budget expendi-tures by function and by agency for the previous, the current, and the upcom-ing fiscal years. It also contains several special analyses that provide useful information on certain aspects of the budget. The special analysis that con-tains information on Federal activities in the national income accounts is of particular interest to the economic analyst. The second volume of the budget document rivals the Manhattan telephone directory in size, weight, and num-ber of numbers. It contains all the detail of the agency-by-agency budget requests that the appropriations committees of the Congress need. It is not of much use, however, to the economic forecaster. A third volume repeats the special analyses included in the main document and adds several others of less general interest. In addition to these documents a much more popularized and abbreviated digest is provided by the Budget Bureau in a little pamphlet,

---

[2] The analyst who relies on press reports should be warned, however, that it is not unknown for a newspaper story to be "planted" by the agency concerned, in the hope of influencing presidential or congressional decisions. Also, news reporters sometimes get bad information, or information that is not up to date. An example is the bad forecasts made by news reporters just prior to the release in January, 1964, of President Johnson's fiscal 1965 budget.

The Budget in Brief, released at the time of budget transmittal. The budget is explained at length in administration press conferences; there is extensive press coverage of the budget itself; and at about the same time,[3] its proposals are subject to an economic evaluation in the widely circulated and reported *Economic Report of the President.* The February issue of the *Survey of Current Business* also usually contains an article analyzing the budget data.

What the President, in his budget, actually asks Congress to do is not to spend (he and his subordinates have to do the spending) but to appropriate; that is, he requests the creation of new authority to "obligate" funds for specified purposes. However, in order to explain what the effect of such congressional action would be, the budget document sets forth not only the requests for new obligational authority but the program of spending that, contingent upon receipt of this authority, the executive branch plans to carry out during the coming fiscal year. It is the latter that ordinarily is headlined in the press.

The distinction between new obligational authority (a term that covers both appropriations and other authorizations to obligate funds) and budget expenditures would be less important to the economic analyst if obligational authority were provided only for single fiscal years and resulted in cash outlays in those years. In fact, however, much of the money appropriated endures from year to year. This is necessary because of the long lead time involved in procuring many of the things the government buys—notably public works, the larger types of military equipment, and space vehicles. Consequently, of the funds Congress provides in any given fiscal year, some already have been spent by the end of the year; some have been obligated but not yet spent; and usually some, not yet earmarked by the writing of contracts, are still unobligated. The latter, unless provided by appropriations specifically written to expire at the end of the year, are added to the government's backlog of unused obligational authority—for military aircraft, foreign economic aid, Bureau of Reclamation projects, or whatever the object of the appropriation may have been. Because expenditures as a whole lag behind appropriations as a whole, it is possible for the two to move in opposite directions in any given year. And it is also possible to obtain from currently proposed appropriations some insight into the long-run future of Federal spending, beyond the fiscal year for which the budget formally spells out the spending program. The relationship between new obligational authority and expenditures is illustrated in Figure 18–1.

It should be emphasized that the expenditure figures in the budget document are estimates, prepared by the Budget Bureau. These estimates assume that the President's program will be enacted by the Congress *as recom-*

---

[3] The *Economic Report* usually follows the budget by a few days, but in some years (e.g., 1964) the *Economic Report* is issued first in which case, to avoid "scooping" the budget, the *Economic Report* contains less detailed information about the budget figures than can be incorporated when it follows the budget document.

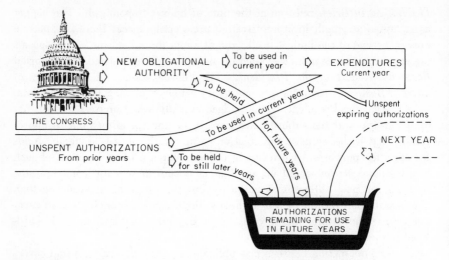

Figure 18–1. The relation of new obligational authority to expenditures.

mended. Typically, the President's program calls, not only for the appropriation of funds to finance ongoing programs, but for the enactment of new, substantive legislation for new or enlarged programs (or the termination of old ones). Such substantive (or enabling) legislation may or may not be subsequently enacted by the Congress. In the early 1960s, for example, programs for aid to secondary education were repeatedly recommended to the Congress and the expenditures that would ensue after enactment of the legislation were repeatedly included in the expenditure estimates, but year after year the basic legislation failed of enactment. The estimates also assume that expenditure programs, duly authorized by law, will go forward at a certain rate. In practice, however, the expenditure rate may vary from the advance estimate. In some cases, relatively uncontrollable events determine the rate at which expenditures occur. Expenditures under agricultural price support legislation, for example, are importantly influenced by the weather and other factors influencing crop yields and farm product prices. The rate of expenditure of Department of Defense appropriations is importantly influenced by international events. In the case of some programs, such as urban renewal and interstate highways, actual expenditures are largely determined by the speed with which state and local governments act to use funds available to them. Further, because there is such a long lead time between the submission of the budget document and actual expenditure of funds, the executive branch may change its plans before the fiscal year to which the estimates apply has expired—or perhaps even begun. This is particularly likely when there is a change of administration. In early January, 1961, for example, President Eisenhower submitted a budget after the election in which his party had been defeated. On January 20, President Kennedy assumed office and proceeded, in the next two or three months, to overhaul the Eisenhower budget. No new, formal budget, however, was issued by the new administration; revised budget figures could be obtained only from press releases and from testimony of the new administration officials before congressional committees.

In spite of all the imponderables involved in making expenditure estimates, the estimates for the current fiscal year and even for the first half or so of the upcoming fiscal year are usually not likely to be very far off the mark, simply because of the inertia of the government spending process. New programs, especially if they involve substantial amounts of money, are inevitably slow to get off the ground. New public works programs require extensive engineering work and contract negotiations. Even for nonconstruction types of programs, staff must be recruited and specific plans must be decided upon before any significant volume of funds can be expended. Contracts are often let months and even years before delivery date, which is the time at which (except for "progress payments" in the case of certain contracts) expenditure occurs. A decision to cut back an expenditure program (e.g., defense or a public works project), therefore, unless the government is willing to bear the money cost of contract liquidation damages, and the economic cost of idle, partially finished projects, is not likely to reduce actual expenditures until many months after the decision is made. Later in the chapter, we shall look at the record to see how well the budget document and other documents produced in the course of the budget-appropriating-spending process have stood up in this respect. But for the moment let us continue with our review of the process itself.

In the Congress the budget gets pulled to pieces and, in a sense, never gets put back together again. Appropriation bills corresponding to the various organizational and functional segments of the budget are considered by the various subcommittees of the appropriations committees in the two houses, hearings are held, revised bills are reported by the appropriations committees, and the usual steps of legislative procedure are followed as appropriations, piece by piece, get enacted into law. At the same time, spending authority other than appropriations (e.g., contract authorizations, public debt financing) may emerge from the deliberations of committees other than the appropriations committees.[4] This period of congressional action, beginning in late January or in February and often extending well beyond the start of the new fiscal year, is a difficult one for the forecaster who is trying to keep track of changes in the government's total spending program. It is particularly difficult, even exasperating, when the Congress drags out the appropriations process until the fiscal year to which the appropriations apply is nearly half gone, as it did in 1962 (fiscal 1963 budget) and 1963 (fiscal 1964 budget). However, a careful reading of the press usually permits one to follow the

---

[4] Such spending authority, which bypasses the customary appropriations committee process, is referred to in popular parlance as "backdoor spending." A more accurate title would be "backdoor authorizing."

progress of new substantive legislation and of the larger appropriation bills—particularly defense appropriations—reasonably well.

It is fortunate for the business conditions analyst that, after the Congress has gone home, the Budget Bureau undertakes to piece together all that has happened to the expenditure program and comes up with a revised statement of the overall spending plan that conforms with the actual appropriations Congress has made. The resulting document, the so-called Budget Review, sometimes issued in August but more often later, is not widely distributed and does not receive the prominence in the press it deserves.[5] Copies, however, are available on request from the Budget Bureau, and no careful analyst should fail to study this document. For the fiscal year now started it presents a spending forecast from which most of the legislative uncertainties have been removed.

Finally, so far as official forecasts of expenditures are concerned, the following January, in the new budget document presenting the proposed spending program for the next fiscal year, the Budget Bureau publishes re-revised estimates of budget expenditures for the current fiscal year, now half over. If the analyst wishes to follow the progress of actual budget expenditures more closely than the Budget Review and the January budget's current-year estimates allow, he may watch the daily and monthly Treasury statements. However, adequate interpretation of these requires a good knowledge of the details of budget accounting, together with a recognition of whatever seasonal patterns may affect Federal expenditures, and these are not of sufficiently general interest to the average forecaster to justify discussion here.

ALTERNATIVE BUDGET CONCEPTS

So far we have been discussing the conventional or administrative budget. This is the formulation of Federal spending data that is most widely quoted in the press and that is used in computing the Federal government surplus or deficit upon which so much public attention is focused. Also, the figures that emerge from the congressional appropriations committee hearings typically pertain to the administrative budget.

The administrative budget, however, is not an adequate formulation of Federal receipts and expenditures for economic analysis purposes. It falls short of our needs in several respects. First, it is incomplete. It includes only about four-fifths of the total activities of the Federal government, and the criterion of inclusion and exclusion is a legal rather than an economic one. It includes, on the receipts side, only those receipts into the "Federally owned funds," i.e., funds that are not held in trust in a fiduciary capacity by the

---

[5] In some years, when the congressional appropriations process has been concluded so late that there would be only a few weeks interval between the release of the Budget Review and the January budget document, the Budget Review has been omitted.

government.[6] It includes, on the expenditure side, only expenditures from these Federally owned funds. It excludes the receipts and expenditures of the trust and deposit funds. The original reason for excluding these funds— such as the Social Security Trust Fund—was that such funds represent fiduciary activities of the government, comparable to private insurance or pension funds; the revenues were held in trust for future generations and did not "belong" to the government. Payments out of the fund were not costs of government in the usual sense. Because they were of this character, expenditures from these funds were determined by the provisions of the basic legislation; annual review by the usual appropriation process was not needed. The Congress therefore established trust funds that removed both tax receipts earmarked for these programs and expenditures for them from the conventional budget. One of the more recent of these, oddly enough, was the Highway Trust Fund, established in 1956 to finance the new interstate highway program.[7] Since 1956, receipts and expenditures pertaining to the highway program have not been reflected in the administrative budget at all. Whether or not exclusion of this and other trust funds from the administrative budget is appropriate for legal or policy purposes, it is inappropriate for economic analysis purposes. Social security and gasoline taxes affect the private income stream just as much as do income and other excise taxes. And expenditures out of the trust funds add to the income stream just as do expenditures from the General Fund. For this reason, the economic analyst needs a tabulation that includes the trust funds, the receipts and expenditures of which were budgeted at $41.6 and $37.9 billion, respectively, for fiscal 1967.

On the other hand, the administrative budget includes certain types of transactions that, for economic analysis purposes, should be excluded. It includes *both* purely financial transactions (e.g., loans) and purchases of goods and services. A loan to a veteran, scheduled to be repaid, is counted as a current expenditure the same as an outlay for a veteran's hospital care. For economic analysis purposes, the distinction between a loan and a purchase of goods and services is important. The first generates no current income; the second does. Such purely financial transactions should therefore clearly be excluded. The administrative budget also includes purchases and sales of existing assets. These reflect a swapping of assets, not payment for current

---

[6] In the main, the receipts included in the administrative budget go into the "General Fund" and are available for unrestricted appropriation by the Congress. The administrative budget also includes, however, receipts into certain special funds where they are earmarked for certain purposes (e.g., 25 percent of the money received from the national forests is paid to the states for public schools and roads of the county in which such forests are located).

[7] We say "oddly enough" because the Highway Trust Fund is much more comparable to the other earmarked special funds, which are included in the administrative budget, than it is to the trust funds. The decision to classify the highway fund with the trust funds was apparently made, not on grounds of accounting logic, but to permit the addition of some $3 billion a year of expenditures (and receipts) without increasing the popularly noted administrative budget totals.

production of goods and services. For economic analysis purposes, as we noted in Chapter 3, transactions in existing assets among sectors should be shown as offsetting entries so they will not affect the nation's total income and output. The inclusion of such transactions in the budget tabulation is therefore appropriate, but their net amount should be identified so that it can be subtracted (algebraically) from appropriate other sector accounts.

The administrative budget also usually includes only the net operating receipts and expenses of government-owned enterprises, such as the TVA or the Post Office. With this treatment we have no complaint. As we noted in Chapter 2, for national income accounting purposes these enterprises are treated as private businesses as regards their current operations. Only their capital expenditures, net interest paid, and their net surpluses or losses are treated as a government expenditure or revenue. Subject to the adjustments discussed in the paragraph immediately above, therefore, administrative budget treatment of operations of government-owned enterprises is consistent with national income accounting.

The administrative budget makes no distinction, incidentally, between investment and current operating expenditures of the regular agencies of government (i.e., other than government-owned enterprises). Money spent on a public building that will yield benefits for many years is tabulated as a current expenditure, just as are the wages of government employees or a purchase of paper towels for the washrooms in government buildings. Both of these generate income and therefore for economic analysis purposes should be included in our tabulation of Federal government expenditures, and they are so included in national income accounting. For certain other purposes, it might be desirable to classify separately current and capital expenditures—as any business firm does and as the Department of Commerce does in its tabulation of private spending. But this is another problem that need not concern us here.

Third, the administrative budget, with a few minor exceptions, is on a cash rather than an accrual basis. It records tax receipts when the cash is received by the Treasury, and expenditures when payment is actually made. If business activity moved along at a steady pace, and if there were no significant changes in the volume of Federal spending, this characteristic of the Federal budget might not be a serious deficiency. When there are swings in business activity, however, recording tax receipts in the time period in which they are received by the Treasury rather than when the tax liability is incurred tends to give a distorted picture of the effect of taxes on incomes and hence on spending.[8] In the past, this has been particularly true of the corporation income tax, where the lag between the incurring of tax liability and the actual payment of taxes has been considerable. The Tax Adjustment Act of 1966, however, removed a large part of this lag.

---

[8] Actually, because the wage and salary component of personal income, as we noted in Chap. 3, is calculated on a cash rather than an accrual basis, *personal* income taxes are recorded on a "when paid" rather than on a "when accrued" basis. Personal

CONSOLIDATED CASH BUDGET

To correct the *first* of these deficiencies—the exclusion of the trust funds—the so-called consolidated cash budget was devised by economists in the Bureau of the Budget and the Federal Reserve during the 1940s. The consolidated cash budget (called "Receipts from and Payments to the Public" in official government documents) simply consolidates the Federally owned funds and the trust funds, eliminating transactions between them. It gives a tabulation of total cash transactions between the Federal government and the public; hence, the surplus or deficit in the consolidated cash budget is a measure of the Treasury's needs for borrowing from the public or its ability to repay indebtedness (assuming no change in operating cash balances of the Treasury).

Figure 18–2 illustrates schematically two things: first, the difference in coverage between the administrative budget and the consolidated cash budget; and second, the way in which both budgets treat the transactions of government-owned enterprises. With respect to the latter, as we noted above, both budgets include only the net transactions of the government-owned enterprises. Thus, in Figure 18–2, the arrows labeled 5 and d, reflecting respectively gross expenditures and receipts between the enterprises and the public, are not included in either budget concept. All that is included (in both budget concepts) is net expenditures (arrow 3) resulting from surpluses or losses of these enterprises and capital expenditures financed by appropriated funds.

The difference between the conventional budget and the consolidated cash budget is indicated in Figure 18–2 by the two types of boundary lines. Thus, the consolidated cash budget adds to the conventional budget the transactions between the trust funds and the public (arrows 4 and c) and eliminates transactions between the trust funds and the General Fund (arrows 2 and b). Arrow 2, incidentally, reflects chiefly interest payments by the General Fund to the trust funds on their investments in government securities, and arrow b reflects payments by the trust funds to the general government for administrative or other services. The consolidated cash budget, it should be

---

income tax *withholdings* are withheld (paid by the taxpayer) in the same quarter in which the tax liability is accrued, and reflect quarter-to-quarter variations in current earnings. The quarterly payments for nonwithheld taxes, however, are based on estimates of income earned during the year as a whole, not during the particular quarter when the payment was made. Further, these quarterly payments are not spaced one to a quarter: two occur in the second quarter (April and June), one in the third quarter (September), none in the fourth quarter, and the fourth (January) payment is made in the first quarter of the following year. These quarterly payments and the final settlement are recorded in the accounts in the quarter and year when payment was actually made. It may well be that this timing of personal income tax payments reflects more accurately the economic impact of the personal income tax than would strict accrual timing; in contrast to corporations, many personal income taxpayers are not very foresighted about setting aside reserves for delayed tax payments, and in fact have to make these delayed payments out of current income.

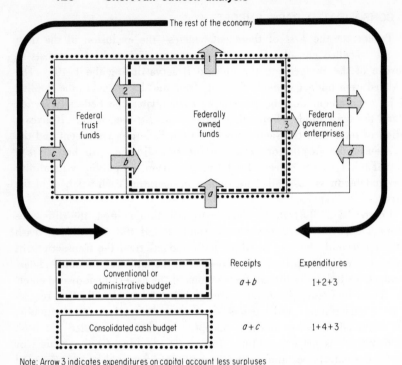

	Receipts	Expenditures
Conventional or administrative budget	$a+b$	$1+2+3$
Consolidated cash budget	$a+c$	$1+4+3$

Note: Arrow 3 indicates expenditures on capital account less surpluses (or plus losses) on current account.

Figure 18–2.   The relationship between the United States government's conventional and consolidated cash budgets.

noted, is a "cash" budget in the same sense that the conventional budget is: it reflects transactions accounted on a cash rather than an accrual basis. If we were to be consistent about it, we should refer to the two budget formulations as the "administrative cash budget" and the "consolidated cash budget."[9]

THE NATIONAL INCOME ACCOUNTS BUDGET

The two versions of the Federal budget just discussed are Budget Bureau calculations. A third, which resolves the two remaining deficiencies (for economic analysis purposes) of the administrative budget, is a concept of the National Income Division of the Department of Commerce. This tabulation, variously called the "income and product budget," the "Federal budget, national income basis," and the "Federal sector of the national income accounts," is based on the same primary data as the consolidated cash budget, but with revisions to make them fit national income accounting concepts and classifications. Thus, it is on an accrual rather than a cash basis. It includes only the transactions that directly affect the current flow of income and output,

[9] There are a few minor exceptions to this statement, the only one of any consequence being interest on savings bonds, which is recorded when the interest accrues in the conventional budget and when it is paid in the consolidated cash budget.

except that it also includes net transactions in existing assets (other than land) with the other sectors of the economy (an amount that is offset with opposite entries elsewhere in the national income accounts). It excludes purely financial transactions. Also—a minor point—the national income accounts budget classifies the District of Columbia in the category of state and local governments, rather than as a part of the Federal government.

Since 1962, forward budget data on an income and product basis have been published in the January budget documents. Somewhat later, in an article in an issue of the *Survey of Current Business,* the same data are given in greater detail. The *Survey* and *Economic Indicators* also give past data on a quarterly basis, adjusted for seasonal variation.[10]

Table 18–1 shows data for years 1961–1967 for each of the three budget concepts. In the case of the administrative budget, data are published on a fiscal year basis only. Past monthly data are also supplied in *Economic Indicators,* so that calendar year figures can be calculated if the analyst has any need for them—which we do not. Past data for the consolidated cash budget are published on both a fiscal and a calendar year basis, but forward data are available for fiscal years only. The same is true of the national income accounts budget. This means that the forecaster, who is often working with calendar years and indeed with quarters within years, has to invent his own forward quarterly and calendar year data. As Table 18–1 reveals, it is not safe to assume that the calendar year figure will be the average of the two fiscal years that overlap it. This would be a good estimating procedure if the trend of expenditures and receipts were a straight line, but often—especially in the case of receipts—it is not. In prorating the fiscal year data over the four quarters, therefore, there is no substitute for the use of judgment based on the best available information as to probable changes during the year in the rate of expenditures and receipts.

Table 18–1 shows two variants of the national income version of the Federal budget: gross and net. The gross version covers all receipts and all expenditures, including both purchases of goods and services, and transfers and transferlike payments that affect the private income stream but do not result in a claim by the Federal government on the current output of the economy. The net version subtracts these transfers and transferlike payments from gross receipts, yielding a figure for net receipts, i.e., the total tax take of the Federal government less the net amount of income that it returns to the economy to be spent for currently produced goods and services by private persons, business, and state and local governments. The net figures are the ones we shall need for our overall forecast in a Nation's Economic Budget (NEB) format. The gross figures, which include transfers and transferlike

---

[10] Seasonally adjusted data for the consolidated cash budget are also shown in *Economic Indicators.* Past monthly data are available for the conventional budget, but for some reason—perhaps because economic analysts have so little interest in the conventional budget—a seasonal adjustment of conventional budget data has not been attempted.

Table **18-1**. Alternative Budget Concepts for the United States Federal Government, 1961–1967 (In billions of dollars)

Budget	1961 Fiscal	1961 Calendar	1962 Fiscal	1962 Calendar	1963 Fiscal	1963 Calendar	1964 Fiscal	1964 Calendar	1965 Fiscal	1965 Calendar	1966* Fiscal	1966* Calendar	1967* Fiscal	1967* Calendar
Conventional or administrative budget:														
Receipts	77.7	78.2	81.4	84.7	86.4	87.5	89.5	88.7	93.1	96.7	100.0		111.0	
Expenditures	81.5	84.5	87.8	91.9	92.6	94.2	97.7	96.9	96.5	101.4	106.4		112.8	
Surplus or deficit (−)	−3.9	−6.3	−6.4	−7.2	−6.3	−6.7	−8.2	−8.2	−3.4	−4.7	−6.4		−1.8	
Consolidated cash budget:														
Receipts	97.2	97.9	101.9	106.2	109.7	112.6	115.5	115.0	119.7	123.4	128.2		145.5	
Expenditures	99.5	104.7	107.7	111.9	113.8	117.2	120.3	120.3	122.4	127.9	135.0		145.0	
Surplus or deficit (−)	−2.3	−6.8	−5.8	−5.7	−4.0	−4.6	−4.8	−5.2	−2.7	−4.5	−6.9		0.5	
National income account:														
(A) Gross:														
Receipts, total	95.3	98.3	104.2	106.4	110.2	114.3	115.1	114.5	119.6	124.1	128.8		142.2	
Personal tax and nontax	43.6	44.7	47.3	48.6	49.6	51.5	50.7	48.6	51.2	53.9	54.8		60.5	
Corporate profits tax accruals	20.3	21.8	22.9	22.7	23.6	24.5	25.3	26.0	27.0	28.3	29.3		31.1	
Indirect business tax & nontax accruals	13.3	13.6	14.2	14.6	15.0	15.3	15.6	16.1	16.8	16.7	15.9		16.5	
Contr. to social insurance	18.1	18.2	19.9	20.5	22.1	23.0	23.6	23.7	24.6	25.2	28.8		34.1	
Expenditures, total	98.0	102.1	106.4	110.3	111.4	114.0	117.1	118.3	118.3	123.3	131.0		142.7	
Purchases of goods and services	55.5	57.4	60.9	63.4	63.4	64.4	65.8	65.3	64.5	66.6	70.7		74.4	
Transfer payments	25.6	27.0	27.2	27.7	28.6	29.2	29.6	29.9	30.3	32.1	34.2		39.2	
Grants-in-aid to state & local govts.	6.9	7.2	7.6	8.0	8.4	9.1	9.8	10.4	10.9	11.4	12.8		14.7	
Net interest paid	6.8	6.6	6.8	7.2	7.5	7.8	8.1	8.4	8.6	8.8	9.0		9.7	
Subs. less current surplus of govt. ent.	3.2	3.8	3.8	4.0	3.6	3.6	3.8	4.3	4.1	4.5	4.3		4.7	
Surplus or deficit (−)	−2.7	−3.8	−2.1	−3.8	−1.2	0.3	−1.9	−3.8	1.2	0.7	−2.2		−0.5	
(B) Net:														
Receipts	52.8	53.6	58.8	59.6	62.2	64.7	63.9	61.5	65.7	67.3	68.5		73.9	
Purchases of goods and services	55.5	57.4	60.9	63.4	63.4	64.4	65.8	65.3	64.5	66.6	70.7		74.4	
Surplus or deficit (−)	−2.7	−3.8	−2.1	−3.8	−1.2	0.3	−1.9	−3.8	1.2	0.7	−2.2		−0.5	

* Estimated.

Source: *Economic Report of the President, Economic Indicators,* and *Budget of the United States.*

payments, are useful in analyzing the disposable incomes of other sectors of the economy and hence their probable expenditures. It should be noted, incidentally, that one of these transferlike payments is grants-in-aid to state and local governments. If, in our NEB, we consolidate Federal and state and local governments into a single set of entries, as is usual, these grants-in-aid need to be added to state and local tax receipts.

FORECASTING FEDERAL GOVERNMENT EXPENDITURES

With these different budget concepts clearly in mind, we are now ready to forecast Federal government expenditures. The principle involved in such forecasting is simple; in practice, a number of statistical barriers have to be surmounted. The principle is to start with the published forward estimates on a national income accounts basis, convert them to calendar years or quarters, and then adjust them upward or downward to correspond with the judgment of the analyst as to influences that will cause actual expenditures to deviate from the Bureau of the Budget estimates. These estimates, it will be recalled, are based on the President's recommended program. This program may not—probably will not—be enacted by the Congress exactly as recommended. Proposed enabling legislation for new or expanded programs may not be passed, or may be passed later than assumed in the Bureau of the Budget estimates. Appropriations may be less (or sometimes more) than the President requests. And nonlegislative events, as we noted earlier, may affect the rate of actual spending.

An immediate statistical difficulty is encountered, however, because detailed data on expenditures by program are available in the budget documents on a conventional budget and consolidated cash basis but not on a national income accounts basis. Therefore, we are forced to reverse the procedure: start with the consolidated cash budget, estimate the effects of congressional and other events on *the purchases of goods and services component* of each consolidated cash budget category, and then adjust the national income accounts estimates by the net amount of such changes. If the analyst prefers, he can—for present purposes—start with the conventional budget, rather than the consolidated cash, in view of the fact that virtually all Federal government purchases of goods and services are covered by the conventional budget. There may, indeed, be some advantage in using the conventional budget because press reports of congressional actions are consistently in conventional budget terms.

Estimating the needed revisions in the official estimates requires, of course, that we know how much of the expenditures estimated for each functional category reflects purchases of goods and services, and how much reflects transfers and transferlike payments and purely financial transactions. Careful study of the budget will reveal much of this needed information. Defense expenditures, for example, are almost wholly purchases of goods and services, the only important exception being military retirement benefits, which (except when a change in basic law is made) are a very stable though secularly rising component of the total. Net interest paid by government, on the other hand, is, of course, 100 percent transfers (under Commerce's peculiar definition of transfers). Most other programs are mixed. The Veterans Administration, for example, builds hospitals and provides hospital care to veterans, but it also pays pensions and makes loans to veterans (and receives repayments on loans). There is no substitute, therefore, for detailed analysis of the character of Federal government expenditures programs. Fortunately, the highly variable expenditures are concentrated in a relatively few programs, notably defense, space, and agriculture. Most of the goods and services expenditures in other functional categories are relatively stable and, in comparison with national defense, relatively small.

It is also necessary to make allowance for the fact that, whereas the conventional and the consolidated cash budgets are on a cash basis, the national income accounts figures are on an accrual basis. One should remember, however, that the official expenditure estimates on a national income accounts basis already reflect this difference and that on the expenditure side of the budget the difference between cash and accrual is usually not very large in any event. This distinction can therefore usually be ignored, unless the analyst contemplates a major revision in the President's proposed program.

The record of the period since World War II suggests that a general outlook analyst in the United States could usually get along tolerably well, as far as predictions of conventional budget expenditures are concerned, if he did no more than adopt the global estimate for upcoming fiscal years contained in the President's January budgets. Table 18–2 compares, for each of the fiscal years 1948 to 1965, both this estimate and the later revised estimates contained in the Midyear Budget Review and in the succeeding Executive Budget with the actual after-the-fact expenditures record. As the percentage columns in the table indicate, the later estimates were generally—but not always—better than earlier ones. But for a majority of the postwar years the original budget estimates, published a half year before the fiscal year began, proved to be reasonably reliable forecasts.

During the period covered by the table, the largest errors in the President's original budget estimates were for the fiscal years 1953 and 1954. The outbreak of fighting in Korea at the beginning of fiscal 1951 widely outmoded the military budget proposed for that year, but, partly because of downward revisions in nondefense spending, this was not enough to throw off the total expenditure estimate that had been made in January, 1950, by more than 5 percent. The Korean War, however, continued to be a disruptive factor so far as the predictive power of the President's budget estimates was concerned. The continuing stretch-out of defense targets kept the military build-up lagging behind original plans, a situation that reached a climax in fiscal 1953. The discrepancy for 1954 is largely explained by the termination of the Korean War, which was not assumed when the budget was submitted in January, 1953.

Table **18–2.** United States Administrative Budget Expenditures: Adjusted to Original Estimate, Fiscal Years 1948–1965

Fis-cal year	President's original estimate		Budget Bureau's revised estimate, Midyear Budget Review		Rerevised estimate in succeeding January budget		Final budget expendi-tures
	In billions	% of actual	In billions	% of actual	In billions	% of actual	
1948	$37.5	103%	$37.0	102%	$37.7	104%	$36.3*
1949	39.7	91	42.8†	98	43.5*	100	43.7*
1950	41.9	104	43.5	108	43.3	108	40.2
1951	42.4	95	None issued		47.2	106	44.6
1952	71.6	108	70.0	106	70.9	107	66.1
1953	85.4	114	79.0	106	74.6	100	74.6‡
1954	78.6	115	72.1	105	71.5‡	105	68.4‡
1955	65.6	102	64.0	99	63.5	98	64.6
1956	62.4	94	63.8	96	64.3	97	66.5
1957	65.9	94	70.2§	100	70.0§	99	70.4§
1958	71.8	100	72.0	100	72.8	101	71.9
1959	73.9	92	79.2	98	80.9	100	80.7
1960	77.0	100	78.9	102	78.4	102	77.2¶
1961	79.8	97	80.8ᵃ	98	79.9¶ᵃ	97	82.5¶ᵃ
1962	80.9	92	89.0	101	89.1	101	87.8
1963	92.5	100	93.7	101	94.3	102	92.6
1964	98.8	101	97.8ᵇ	100	98.4	101	97.7
1965	97.9	101	97.2	101	97.5	101	96.5

* Includes refunds of receipts and capital transfers.

† Includes capital transfers.

‡ Includes payments of employment tax receipts to railroad retirement fund.

§ Includes expenditures of the highway trust fund.

¶ Includes interfund transactions.

ᵃ Includes expenditures for states' administration of unemployment claims and employment service.

ᵇ Estimate given by the Director, Bureau of the Budget, in testimony on the debt limit.

Note: On many occasions over past years, changes in Federal budget accounting have been made, administratively and pursuant to legislation. Sometimes such changes are made in the middle of a fiscal year so that the budget totals shown in the Budget Review are not comparable to those shown in the preceding January budget. Whenever such a change is made, past year's figures are also revised to assure year-to-year consistency. The present table, however, does not include such retroactive revisions. Instead, each year's figures are revised so that all the data for that year will be consistent with accounting definitions in effect when the initial January budget estimate was issued. This means, however, that the data are not consistent from year to year. For such data on actual receipts and expenditures, the reader should consult the historical tables in the most recent budget document. The footnotes indicate changes in concept or coverage occurring after the first data for the fiscal year were released.

Source: Bureau of the Budget.

During the remaining years of the Eisenhower administration, the January expenditure estimates rather consistently underestimated actual expenditures. The later estimates, however, in the Budget Review and in the succeeding January budget, were not far off the mark. The 8 percent error in 1962 reflects a change of administration. The outgoing Eisenhower administration in January, 1961, left for the incoming Kennedy administration a legacy of an extremely tight budget. Indeed, President Kennedy charged, shortly after assuming office, that the Eisenhower estimates were unrealistically low on the expenditure side and unrealistically high on the revenue side, even assuming President Eisenhower's own program. In addition, President Kennedy launched a number of new programs that added to the expenditure total. The 1964 overestimate reflected partly President Johnson's economy program, but largely the refusal of the 1963 Congress to enact in full President Kennedy's recommended program. Again in 1965, the final figures reflected economies, chiefly in the defense program, not fully anticipated earlier.

Although blind acceptance of the President's original estimates would not have led a general forecaster very far astray during the 1948–1965 period, a more penetrating analysis of the budget would have stood him in good stead. That this is true becomes apparent when we examine a functional breakdown of the conventional budget. The character of the breakdown has shifted considerably over the years, but the following listing, which was used for fiscal 1967, and is shown with the dollar expenditures proposed for that year, is representative:

Budget items	Proposed expenditures*
National defense	$ 60.5
International affairs and finance	4.2
Space research and technology	5.3
Agriculture and agricultural resources	3.4
Natural resources	3.1
Commerce and transportation	2.7
Housing and community development	0.1
Health, labor, and welfare	10.0
Education	2.8
Veterans' benefits and services	5.7
Interest	12.9
General government	2.6
Allowance for contingencies	0.4
Interfund transactions	−0.7
Total expenditures	$112.8

* In billions of dollars.

It is apparent from this table that a relatively few categories account for the bulk of the total. National defense alone accounts for over 50 percent.

Interest on the national debt and veterans' benefits and services, both of which reflect largely the current costs of past wars, account for another one-sixth of the total; the space program and the costs of international affairs and finance, both of which are civilian programs but are closely related to defense, account for another 8 percent. Agriculture (chiefly price support programs and other subsidies, euphemistically called "farm income stabilization" in the budget) accounts for 3 percent.[11] Health, labor, and welfare account for 9 percent, about two-fifths of which is grants to states for public assistance programs. All the remaining functions, including "General Government" (the general administrative and law-enforcement activities of the legislative, judicial, and executive branches of the Federal government), account for 10 percent.

This concentration of expenditures indicates the categories on which the analyst should focus in forecasting government expenditures. First, the dollar figures suggest that he should spend about half of his time and energy on the defense program. Indeed, he might do well to spend more than half of his time on this category, because this is a budget category that has been extremely variable over the years, and in which big changes can be made if sudden changes in international events or in defense policy require. Moreover, virtually all expenditures in this category are purchases of goods and services, the only important exception, as we noted earlier, being about $1.5 billion a year of military retirement pay. Also, the congressional debates on defense expenditures are extensively reported in the press, so that the analyst can readily acquire a good feel for probable congressional action, bearing in mind, however, that a heavy proportion of the defense budget is composed of long-lead-time items that are financed out of appropriations made in prior years.

The two next largest categories, interest on the Federal debt and veterans' programs, should probably take a good deal less than the one-sixth of the analyst's time that the figures indicate, for two reasons. First, since these outlays are largely determined by previous legislation and previous contractual commitments, both are remarkably stable and predictable (except occasionally, in the case of veterans' benefits, when a veterans' bonus or other major change in the law is enacted). Second, about three-quarters of veterans' benefits and services are transfer payments, not included in purchases of goods and services, and all government interest payments are excluded by the Department of Commerce from national income and from purchases of goods and services.

In the case of expenditures for international affairs, the highly variable item is foreign economic aid and contributions to international agencies, but here again most of these expenditures are not included in Federal purchases of goods and services. The space program, on the other hand, is not only a

---

[11] The "Food for Peace" (now renamed "Food for Freedom") program ($1.5 billion), which covers mainly foreign assistance in the form of concessional exports of agricultural products, was included in "Agriculture" prior to 1965. It now is included in "International Affairs and Finance."

large and changing category of expenditures; it is also very largely composed of purchases of goods and services. Agriculture programs, as we noted earlier, are largely various direct or indirect subsidy programs. However, in the main, these subsidies involve the making of nonrecourse loans to farmers, for which agricultural products are used as collateral for price support purposes. The loans are usually not repaid, in which case the Commodity Credit Corporation (CCC) of the Department of Agriculture acquires the collateral. National income accounting ignores the fiction of the loan, and records the transaction as a government purchase of goods and services when the loan is made, not as a transfer payment.[12] Therefore, the analyst should follow closely the progress of farm legislation, as well as the weather and the amounts of fertilizer that farmers are pouring on their fields, and make the best estimate he can of any probable deviations from expenditures as estimated by the Budget Bureau.

About half of conventional budget expenditures for health, labor, and welfare are grants to states, and most of these become transfer payments by the states to public assistance recipients. Another important item in this category is the research activities of the National Institutes of Health, for which the Congress often appropriates more money than the President recommends. A significant proportion of the remaining items in this category are transfer payments of one kind or another (e.g., unemployment compensation for Federal employees and ex-servicemen, school lunch and special milk programs, the food stamp program, etc.). Unless something truly important is pending in this area, the analyst would do well to accept the official expenditure estimate and focus his attention elsewhere.

The same is true, with occasional exceptions, of the other functional categories of expenditures. Housing and community development programs are largely loan and grant programs and hence do not involve purchases of goods and services (except for administrative costs). Note that the budget for fiscal 1967 was only $0.1 billion, i.e., it was estimated that loan repayments and sale of previously acquired mortgages, plus other receipts, would about offset anticipated current outlays. Commerce and transportation is a stable item. A change in postal rates, when made, can affect administrative budget expenditures for the postal service (i.e., the deficit) by several hundred million dollars, but the deficit shows up in the national income accounts as a part of "subsidies less current surpluses of government enterprises." Certain public works programs are included in this category, and these can swing quite a bit one way or the other, depending upon congressional action.

---

[12] This is true even though the loan may be made by a private bank, under an arrangement whereby the loan is fully guaranteed as to principal and interest by the Commodity Credit Corporation.

For some reason, tobacco loans are classified as a bona fide loan transaction, not as a purchase of goods and services. In addition, CCC payments to exporters for purchases of foreign currency are included in the national income accounts only when the foreign currencies are spent.

Most public works, however, are included in the category of natural resources (e.g., projects of the Corps of Engineers, the Bureau of Reclamation, and the Forest Service). The analyst will want to watch, therefore, the progress of the annual public works legislation, remembering again, however, that because these are long-lead-time items, congressional action on these projects will usually not affect expenditures until a year or so later. Expenditures for general government cover such a wide variety of activities, and are so stable, that the analyst would do well to rely on the Budget Bureau estimate.

After the analyst has gone through this process of estimating how much expenditures for goods and services will be affected by congressional actions and other influences on conventional (or consolidated cash) budget appropriations and expenditures, the rest is simple. We simply add (algebraically) the necessary revision to the official estimate of total expenditures in national income accounts terms. But two questions remain.

What does the analyst do if he is making a full-year forecast at a time of year (say, November) when there is no official estimate for the upcoming fiscal year (which would cover the last half of the upcoming calendar year)? To this question we have no good answer. A private telephone line to the Budget Bureau would help. Lacking this, the analyst can only guess, using his own good judgment and press reports on the probable dimensions of the new budget. This much we can say: barring a change of administrations or some other major event, the inertia of Federal expenditures is such that a simple extrapolation of the first half (calendar) year figures, bent only slightly to reflect the analyst's own judgment of the probable course of future events, would not miss the mark very far.

Second, where does the analyst get all the information he needs to revise the official (national income accounts) budget estimates, even when the latter are known? The answer is simple: hard work and good political sense. The news media are full of stories on the appropriations process and the probable fate of proposed legislation. The trend of national and international events can be detected by the astute observer. This is the essence of forecasting. Experience and a good knowledge of the details of government programs will improve the accuracy of the predictions, but even the beginner, if he works at it, can do a respectable job.

STATE AND LOCAL GOVERNMENT SPENDING

Until the strategic revolution of the 1930s and 1940s, state and local governments did most of the peacetime spending in the United States. They still account for the great majority of domestic civilian government outlays. Even with the new level of national security spending that has become normal since World War II, state and local governments account for about half of all government purchases and for about a tenth of total purchases of goods and services.

While, in principle, the forecasting problem in the state and local case might appear to be closely analogous to that for the Federal government, it differs substantially. On one hand, the readily available data on plans and commitments are vastly inferior. On the other hand, state and local expenditures submit much better than do Federal expenditures in the short run to analyses that treat them simply as extrapolated trends or as functions of other observable variables.

A FORECASTING GAP: STATE AND LOCAL GOVERNMENTS' INTENTIONS SURVEYS

As an eminent authority has noted in one of the best available discussions of the problems the general outlook analyst encounters in forecasting state and local government expenditures,[13] theoretically there are two ways one can attack the sector. One can go directly to the annual and biennial budgets, appropriations, and other fiscal documents of the governmental units, interpreting them as reports of spending intentions. Or one may evaluate the trends that are conditioning the overall level of lower government outlays and factors that can be expected to influence particular segments of total expenditures.

Actually, however, the first of these approaches lies beyond the reach of all but the most generously staffed forecasting agencies at present. This is because the governmental units involved include 50 states and more than 100,000 local jurisdictions. Although virtually all have advance plans and commitments that are matters of public record, there is now no agency that regularly collates or adequately samples this multitude of records and reports a single summary record of state and local spending intentions. This is a gap in our inventory of forecasting data that some public or private research organization should undertake to fill, perhaps by sampling state and local spending programs at a postappropriations stage corresponding to the Federal government's Budget Review. The feasibility of such an undertaking is indicated by the fact that the Department of Commerce's Office of Business Economics already has done the job on a one-shot basis—in 1952 in the course of preparing its *Markets after Defense Expansion* projection noted in the previous chapter. But until a continuing public series on state and local government spending intentions is developed, the average forecaster has no choice but to fall back on other techniques for anticipating final demand in this sector.

FACTORS INFLUENCING THE STATE AND LOCAL SPENDING TREND

Figure 18–3 juxtaposes to the comparatively erratic course of Federal purchases of goods and services the relatively steady rise in state and local

[13] G. W. Mitchell, "Forecasting State and Local Expenditures," *Journal of Business*, vol. 27, no. 1, pp. 17–21, January, 1954.

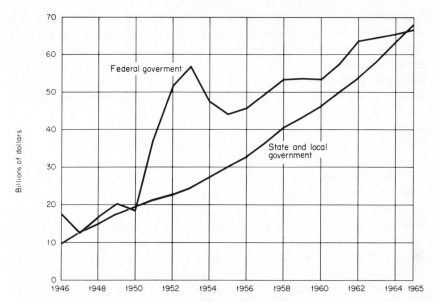

Figure **18–3.** Federal and state and local government purchases of goods and services in the United States, 1946–1965. Source: U.S. Department of Commerce.

government purchases during the postwar period. Most year-to-year fore-casting of state and local spending involves little more than a simple extrapo-lation of this trend. Fortunately there are some significant justifications for the practice, in addition to the negative one that superior techniques are hard to come by. For one thing, during the forties and fifties a heavy backlog of generally recognized unrequited needs was built up in the state and local government sector. In part, this backlog was the product of competition from other resource uses—defense programs, particularly during World War II and the Korean War, and heavy private spending during most of the first postwar decade. In part the needs backlog was, and continues to be, asso-ciated with the soaring demands for state and local government services that have been produced by such factors as the impact of the postwar birthrate upon public education, the flight to the suburbs, the mushrooming of automo-tive traffic, and the growing public awareness of mental health problems. During the 1960s, at least, none of these pressures shows any sign of leveling off, let alone declining.

There are financial reasons, moreover, why the continuing backlog of needs for state and local services and facilities cannot be suddenly met in one fell swoop—could not be, even if other demands upon resources were suddenly to abate. The year-to-year growth in state and local spending is held in check by a system of state and local taxation that, partly because of its heavy de-pendence upon real property taxation with laggard assessed valuations, does not easily keep pace with the growth of real income in the economy. In the aggregate, state and local revenues keep getting cranked upward from year to year, but this is a politically arduous, painful, and relatively slow business, and there is no reason to think that it will be otherwise for some years to come. In brief, then, the case for extrapolating recent trends in state and local purchases is that the pressure of needs for services will for some time continue to force all the spending for which finance can be found, and that the finding of new state and local tax revenues is as likely as not to continue at recent rates.

This very argument, however, calls attention to circumstances that should cause a forecaster to adopt a modified rather than a literal extrapolation as his estimate of prospective state and local spending. The important moderating factors enter, again, on the revenue side of the issue.[14] For one thing, although state and local tax receipts are sluggish in their response to changes in general business activity, a pronounced change in activity, by curtailing or stimulating tax collections, can affect spending programs. The 1957–1958 recession was not very far advanced, for example, before a number of states and municipalities, which had been counting on a steady growth in revenues, found themselves in financial difficulties. Conversely, the stimulus to business activity provided by the 1964 tax cut contributed significantly to state and local revenues. Whether such considerations are pertinent to the stage in the forecasting exercise that we are now discussing depends upon what initial income hypothesis underlies the analyst's first-approximation demand estimates. If his initial assumption is that aggregate demand during the forecast period will grow in line with capacity, then the effects that a change in demand would have upon revenues and hence upon spending would only become pertinent later in the exercise if the prospect of such a change were revealed by further analysis. But an analysis made at the beginning of a forecast period, such as 1954 or 1958, when a recession already is under way, presumably would adopt a less optimistic initial income hypothesis. In this event, the prospective drag of sluggish tax receipts upon the growth in state and local expenditures should be recognized from the outset. And a forecast made at the beginning of 1964, when the tax cut was a virtual certainty, should have clearly recognized the effect on state and local revenues and hence on expenditures.

Moreover, the forecaster must consider the availability of nontax financing for state and local government outlays. In addition to receiving

---

[14] There are also some modifying factors that are significant in the short run on the needs side of the matter. However, these notably affect only the requirements for welfare payments, which, alone among the needs state and local governments serve, are outstandingly responsive to fluctuations in general business conditions; and such payments are not accounted as part of government purchases of goods and services. Moreover, in all his first-approximation demand estimates, the opportunistic model builder is assuming a satisfactory level of general economic activity. On both counts, a short-run variation in the need for welfare payments can, at the stage of analysis presently under discussion, be disregarded.

taxes, state and local governments sell bonds and receive Federal grants-in-aid. Accordingly, one's forecast of state and local outlays may be varied from the extrapolated trend by expectations (1) that the Federal grants will be significantly larger or smaller than in recent years or (2) that bond financing will be either abnormally high or low. The first circumstance can be readily ascertained from the Federal budget, although the analyst must learn enough about the particular program involved so that he does not exaggerate the speed with which state and local outlays will respond to congressional acts that change the authorizations for grants-in-aid.

The second circumstance, that involving state and local bond issues, largely affects construction expenditures, and it is harder to forecast. Something can be told from the summary results of referenda authorizing borrowing as reported in the financial press after general elections. However, such authorizations may remain unused for months or even years. A great deal depends upon the interest rates at which state and local borrowers can sell their securities. The supply of state and local offerings is peculiarly interest-elastic, both because of the tightness of many state and local budgets and because the legal authorization for bonds may prescribe the maximum interest rates at which they can be offered. Consequently, the credit-dependent segment of state and local government purchases is not one for which the model builder's first-approximation estimate can be very firm. A figure can be put down in the light of current credit conditions, but at a much later stage in the analysis, when the likelihood that those conditions will continue can be better appraised, the estimate must be reconsidered.

CONCLUSION

Viewed overall, the government sector of the gross national product is one in which the forecaster is apt to feel somewhat apologetic for his craftsmanship. But there is this solace: it is also an area in which he is unlikely to make very serious mistakes—providing he can avoid the stupid mistakes that can be generated by inadequate attention to such comparatively simple matters as the differences among various Federal budget concepts, the sequence of stages in the governmental budgeting-appropriating-spending process, and the rather deliberate pace at which the process ordinarily moves. If he avoids such pitfalls, the forecaster can come up with a very serviceable first-approximation estimate of prospective government outlays by adopting the Federal budget as an intention-to-spend survey and by extrapolating the recent trend in state and local spending—cross-checking and refining each of these basic estimates as much as his accumulating knowledge of particular government programs and of particular credit conditions permits.

19

FORECASTING BUSINESS
FIXED INVESTMENT

The next logical step, following government expenditures, in a sequence that proceeds roughly from the most autonomous category of total spending to the least autonomous, would be investment spending. Total investment spending—gross private domestic investment in the national income accounts —however, is a broad category that includes components with quite different determinants. We would do well, therefore, to consider the major components separately. Investment in inventories is a wholly different subject from the remainder of private capital formation and will not be treated until Chapter 21. Decisions to buy residential houses are made mostly by households rather than by businesses and mostly with different motives than are business fixed-investment decisions. These are considered, along with the buying decisions that households make about automobiles, in the next chapter. The predominant remainder of gross private domestic investment (GPDI) is the matter at hand—a residual loosely called business fixed-investment expenditures. This is the concept—one that had a value of about $70 billion in 1965—for which our model builder wants a figure. Our next step, therefore, is to find out just what is included within this term and to break the total down into subcomponents with which we can work.

The breakdown of business fixed investment (BFI) given in the global GNP accounts is simply: (1) nonresidential structures and (2) producers' durable equipment. This distinction is useful to the analyst whose interest is that of the supplier of capital goods; new construction and equipment are typically produced by quite different business firms. But from our point of view, that of the analyst of general business activity, a breakdown by buying groups is needed. Decisions to buy, not decisions to supply or sell, are the things that primarily concern the business analyst. Further, we should like a breakdown that matches, definitionally, the widely quoted surveys of business plans to spend on new plant and equipment, to be discussed shortly. Unfortunately, data currently published preclude achieving these objectives completely, but we can come fairly close.

A farm versus nonfarm breakdown of each of these components (nonresidential structures and producers' durable equipment) of business fixed investment is easy to obtain. To go further than that, however, requires digging deep into the national income accounts, and unfortunately, some of the needed data are published only on an annual basis, in the July "National Income Number" of the *Survey of Current Business,* or not at all. Another series (the so-called Commerce-SEC series) on new plant and equipment expenditures, not a part of the national income accounting system, is published in the *Survey of Current Business* and other standard sources. The industry coverage of this series, however, is narrower than the National Income Division's nonresidential structures and producers' durable equipment series. Further, because the two series are prepared by different divisions of the Department of Commerce (in one case in cooperation with the SEC) by somewhat different statistical procedures, a perfect reconciliation is not possible.[1] In 1964, for example, business fixed investment in the GNP accounts amounted to $60.5 billion, of which $4.3 billion was farm and $56.2 billion nonfarm. Total plant and equipment expenditures in the Commerce-SEC series were $44.9 billion, all of which was nonfarm, leaving $11.3 billion for nonfarm items not covered by the Commerce-SEC series. The largest separately identifiable item in this $11.3 billion remainder was plant and equipment expenditures by nonprofit institutions, which amounted to $3.6 billion in 1964. Two other important items were business purchases of passenger cars not covered by Commerce-SEC survey ($2.3 billion in 1964), and equipment outlays for oil and natural gas well drilling charged to current expense, not

[1] Such a reconciliation is completely infeasible from data published at this writing, and even using unpublished data available on request from the National Income Division, only a partial reconciliation can be obtained. The Division advises that a reconciliation may be published in the July "National Income Number" of the *Survey of Current Business* after the revision of the Commerce-SEC series, under way in 1966, is completed, but that even after this revision, a discrepancy between the two series may remain.

covered by Commerce-SEC survey ($1.5 billion in 1964). The remaining $3.9 billion was accounted for by plant and equipment expenditures of the real estate industry, of forestry and fisheries industries, of insurance agents and brokers, equipment expenditures by professional persons (doctors, dentists, etc.), net transfers of assets to or from government (usually a negative number), exports of used equipment (negative), margins on used equipment, scrapped equipment (negative), and a statistical discrepancy reflecting the absence of a complete reconciliation, noted above.

FORECASTING PLANT AND EQUIPMENT EXPENDITURES

Almost to a man, opportunistic model builders use plant and equipment intentions surveys as the starting points of their analyses of the short-run outlook for fixed-capital spending by business. This approach is not a logical necessity. Opportunistic model builders could, instead, follow the example of the econometric model builders and treat future plant and equipment spending as being determined by such observable and measurable past quantities as profits, prices, and interest rates. But if they did so, it was our judgment in Chapter 10 that they would overstrain existing knowledge of the nature of investment determination.

Accordingly, while the careful opportunistic model builder considers the conditioning factors upon which the econometrician depends, he does so as a means of cross-checking, evaluating, and perhaps shading upward or downward an initial estimate that he gets from another source. He starts with the reported spending plans and commitments of potential business buyers of plant and equipment. Given this approach, skill in formulating the plant and equipment outlook depends very largely on two things: (1) how well the analyst knows the sources of information on advance plans and commitments in this field, including their forecasting records, and (2) how good he is at deciding, in the light of various conditioning factors, whether to accept or modify the estimates that the intentions surveys supply.

The two principal sources on plant and equipment intentions are the surveys made by the Securities and Exchange Commission and the Department of Commerce jointly, and by the department of economics of the McGraw-Hill Publishing Company. Findings of both of these surveys are blown up to represent the entire statistical universes that the surveys sample, and the two now employ comparable concepts of plant and equipment spending; they mean to cover just about the same spending groups. Thus, McGraw-Hill's forward estimates can readily be compared with the historical series that Commerce and SEC publish and to which they link their own reports of business intentions to spend in the future.

Both the Commerce-SEC intentions survey, started in 1947, and the McGraw-Hill survey, inaugurated in 1948, are based on relatively limited samples.[2] Of the two, the Commerce-SEC sample is larger and more representative of the size distribution of business firms. McGraw-Hill, in an attempt to give its restricted sample a relatively large dollar coverage, has tended to concentrate on larger firms. This makes the findings of the two surveys not entirely comparable, for the capital programs of the larger companies have appeared to be somewhat less sensitive than those of smaller firms to short-run fluctuations—particularly declines—in sales.

These two surveys, it should be noted, are not the only sources on business plant and equipment intentions in the United States. *Fortune*, for example, makes occasional surveys of its own; and the National Industrial Conference Board does a quarterly canvass of business plant and equipment appropriations. The conceptual distinction between appropriations, in this sense, and the intentions to spend reported in the other surveys is essentially the same as that between appropriations (or new obligational authority) and expenditures in the United States government's financial process.

THE SEQUENCE OF INTENTIONS RELEASES

A fall issue of *Business Week*, usually early in November, carries the findings of a McGraw-Hill canvass of plant and equipment spending plans for the coming year as a whole. This survey typically is made at about the beginning of the fourth quarter. In December, Commerce-SEC releases its regular quarterly report on plant and equipment intentions for the coming two quarters. It is not until March that the government agencies release (first to the press and then in an article in the March issue of the *Survey of Current Business*) their findings as to capital-spending intentions for the whole of the year now begun. These are based upon a survey in late January and early February. Since Commerce-SEC at this time reports a revised estimate for the first quarter (now nearly finished) and one for the upcoming second quarter, the release of these two estimates also implicitly contains an estimate for the second half of the year. Then, usually in the latter part of April, McGraw-Hill comes along in *Business Week* with the results of a new survey taken in late March or early April. Thereafter in the third month of each quarter Commerce-SEC releases quarterly surveys showing spending planned for the current quarter and for the coming quarter. Moreover, in both its fall and spring surveys, McGraw-Hill usually reports in general terms the tentative plant and equipment plans business seems to have for the years following the year with which the survey is primarily concerned.

[2] In this respect they are distinctly inferior to the very comprehensive survey that the Canadian government conducts annually. O. J. Firestone, "Investment Forecasting in Canada," in Conference on Research in Income and Wealth: *Short-term Economic Forecasting*, National Bureau of Economic Research, Inc., Studies in Income and Wealth, vol. 17, Princeton University Press, Princeton, N.J. 1955, pp. 113–259.

This sequence of surveys and the periodicals in which they are published are summarized in the following timetable:

Month released	Survey by	Publication	Period covered
November (prior year)	McGraw-Hill	*Business Week*	Entire year
December (prior year)	Commerce-SEC	*Survey of Current Business*	Fourth quarter and first two quarters
March	Commerce-SEC	*Survey of Current Business*	First two quarters and year
April	McGraw-Hill	*Business Week*	Year
June	Commerce-SEC	*Survey of Current Business*	Second and third quarters and year
September	Commerce-SEC	*Survey of Current Business*	Third and fourth quarters

Obviously, the later a particular survey is, the firmer are the spending plans and decisions it reflects. In most firms capital budgets for periods starting a year or a year and a half hence are still subject to very extensive change. But for many, and particularly for a number of larger firms, the fall McGraw-Hill survey, taken about three months before the new calendar year begins, is late enough to catch the results of the annual capital-budgeting exercises which review, revise, and spell out earlier and more tentative capital planning. Such exercises set the outlines of the coming year's plant and equipment spending programs in reasonably firm form. By February, when the Commerce-SEC annual survey is taken, and even more so some six weeks later, when McGraw-Hill makes its spring canvass, most current-year budgets are well into their operating phase. Management now can make fairly sure forecasts of its outlays for the remainder of the year in the light of such specific factors as contracts let and the supply situations confronting it.

THE RECORD

Forecasters take the McGraw-Hill and the Commerce-SEC surveys seriously because they have accumulated respectable forecasting records. Since the inauguration of the surveys a considerable literature has grown up commenting on their methodology and experience and on possibilities for improving them.[3] This continuing critique of survey techniques is altogether

[3] See Arthur M. Okun, "The Predictive Value of Surveys of Business Intentions," *American Economic Review*, vol. LII, no. 2, pp. 218–225, May, 1962. Also Robert Eisner, "Interview and Other Survey Techniques of Investment," in National Bureau of Economic Research, Inc., Studies in Income and Wealth, vol. 19, Conference on Research in Income and Wealth: *Problems of Capital Formation*, Princeton University Press, Prince-

healthy, and it has had some salutary effects on the actual surveys already.[4]

The results of the two McGraw-Hill annual surveys and the Commerce-SEC March survey are compared with actual expenditures on new plant and equipment in Table 19–1. (Data for the McGraw-Hill surveys are shown only for years since 1960; prior to that year, the definitions employed by McGraw-Hill were not identical to those used in compiling the actual data, so that, even though the survey results were useful in predicting percentage of change, they were not strictly comparable to the dollar totals.) In the past ten years, the Commerce-SEC surveys have missed the actual expenditures by more than 5 percent only twice, in the boom year of 1955 when it undershot the actual figure by 6 percent and in the recession year of 1958 when it overshot the actual figure by 5 percent. The McGraw-Hill spring surveys, beginning with 1960, have missed actual expenditures by more than 5 percent only once, in the recession year of 1960. The fall surveys, however, have been less reliable. In some years the surveys have been phenomenally accurate.

We shall proceed in a moment to the interpretation that the forecaster should put on reported capital-spending intentions. But first it should be remarked that both Commerce-SEC and McGraw-Hill in their more recent surveys have been soliciting collateral information from their respondents that is calculated to facilitate the interpretation of the findings as to planned expenditures.

First, respondents have been asked to indicate whether their programed expenditures allow for expected changes in capital goods prices. Information on this point permits the model builder, if he treats price changes in the manner advocated in Chapter 17, to retain a current-price rather than constant-price estimate for plant and equipment expenditures but, at the same time, to correct his capacity forecast for any specifically expected price changes incorporated in the first-approximation demand forecast.

Second, respondents are asked to indicate the expectations as to their

---

ton, N.J., 1957, pp. 513–584. Comments by James N. Morgan, Charles B. Reeder and Walter E. Hoadley, Jr., and Michael Gort, and reply by Mr. Eisner, pp. 584–596.

Also see Irwin Friend and Jean Bronfenbrenner, "Business Investment Programs and Their Realization," *Survey of Current Business*, U.S. Department of Commerce, vol. 30, no. 12, pp. 11–22, December, 1950; and "Plant and Equipment Programs and Their Realization," in Conference on Research in Income and Wealth: *Short-term Economic Forecasting*, National Bureau of Economic Research, Inc., Studies in Income and Wealth, vol. 17, Princeton University Press, Princeton, N.J., 1955, pp. 53–98. Comments on the last by E. M. Hoover and George Katona, and reply by authors, pp. 98–113.

[4] For example, rather early in the game it was discovered that the spending plans business would report tended to be systematically understated—presumably because not all, particularly the smaller, items of capital spending are anticipated well in advance and also because businessmen, despite the fact that their reports are kept anonymous, are somewhat reluctant to reveal projects which they are contemplating but for which decisions have not yet quite jelled. The identification of this characteristic led to the introduction of a compensating adjustment into the calculation of the intentions estimates.

Table 19–1. Results of Plant and Equipment Expenditure Surveys

Year	McGraw-Hill fall survey	Commerce-SEC February survey	McGraw-Hill spring survey	Actual
1954		27.23		26.83
1955		27.06		28.70
1956		34.89		35.08
1957		37.36		36.96
1958		32.07		30.53
1959		31.79		32.54
1960		37.01	37.87	35.68
1961	35.07	34.57	35.35	34.37
1962	35.84	37.16	37.98	37.31
1963	38.15	39.10	40.07	39.22
1964	40.72	43.19	44.08	44.90
1965	46.86	50.17	51.67	51.96
1966	54.87	60.23	61.64	

Source: *Survey of Current Business*, U.S. Department of Commerce, and *Business Week*.

own sales and/or as to general business conditions upon which their reported capital programs are premised. The responses to the sales anticipations questions, unfortunately, have a rather poor record for accuracy. Because these same sales anticipations presumably influenced the business firms' plans to invest, however, the survey results are not irrelevant. If the analyst feels that the sales anticipations are demonstrably high or low, he may want to modify the plant and equipment expenditure figure accordingly—but with caution, as we shall note in a moment.

Third, incorporated in the surveys are questions pertaining to the present and preferred rates of capacity utilization. "Economists might be stunned into silence by the overwhelming conceptual problems if they had to answer such questions; but the survey respondents calmly supply figures which produce a meaningful time series."[5] Presumably, such data should give the analyst some clue as to possible accelerator effects of anticipated plant and equipment spending. Whether or not they actually do provide such a clue has yet to be determined. Other questions are introduced from time to time. Questions have been asked about factors affecting cash flows. In the 1963 and early 1964 surveys, the respondents were asked to what extent tax and depreciation rate changes had been considered and to what extent future changes in these rates would affect their reported decisions. Some of the

[5] Arthur Okun, *op. cit.*, p. 225.

survey findings have contained indications of how much respondents think that their plant and equipment programs would alter if general conditions fell short of or exceeded their expectations by specified degrees. Questions have also been included to determine the proportion of planned expenditures that is a carry-over of projects already started, as opposed to new projects that have yet to be started. Although the reliability of the responses to such questions is uncertain, such information provides the only insight that the surveys offer into the firmness of the spending intentions they report. Although, as we have noted, it is almost invariably true that, in the October prior to a given year, capital programs for the year are less firm than they will be the following March but firmer than they were the preceding April, this is not the end of the matter. There also can be a lot of difference in the firmness of coming-year capital budgets in different Octobers. Anything that can help the analyst to decide whether the intentions for a particular year are more or less resilient than usual is of great value.

ADOPTING AN INITIAL PLANT AND EQUIPMENT ESTIMATE

Grateful for the boon that reasonably good surveys of business investment intentions provide, many forecasters do not look a gift horse in the mouth. They adopt the latest survey results as their own first-approximation estimates of plant and equipment spending and ask no questions. While this is by no means reprehensible forecasting practice, a careful craftsman will not be satisfied with it. Instead he will cross-examine a survey estimate on various counts and may revise it significantly before he adopts it as a working forecast.

THE CROSS REFERENCES PROVIDED BY ORDERS AND CONTRACTS DATA

Some of the plans to spend that intentions surveys report already have been partially implemented; in some of them contractual commitments to spend already have been undertaken. In the United States we have some separate indicators of such commitments. These are the monthly series showing the new orders and order backlogs of durable goods manufacturers, and those showing the contracts for nonresidential construction awarded to building contractors. These data certainly are well worth the plant and equipment forecaster's inspection. But for several reasons the cross bearings they provide on the intentions surveys are not nearly so invaluable or conclusive as might appear at first blush.

In the first place, it is not easy to identify which commitments data pertain to the plant and equipment expenditures sector as such. The Department of Commerce series showing the dollar volume of new orders on manufacturers of durable goods reflects orders for producers' durable equipment. But it also includes new orders for consumer durable goods, for durable goods and components that the buyer plans to process or assemble and resell, and orders placed by governments.

A second difficulty with the orders data stems from the fact that they are supplier-derived rather than buyer-derived figures. Custom in many industries allows business buyers, in the event of a short supply situation, to place orders with several suppliers and then to cancel the remainder without serious penalty when delivery on one of the orders is received. Consequently, figures for the new orders and the unfilled order backlogs gathered from suppliers may include a significant amount of padding.

A third, much more fundamental, difficulty with using orders and contracts data as any kind of precise check upon the reliability of business' investment-intentions surveys turns upon the unknown character of the average lags that intervene between purchase commitments, production or construction, and buyers' outlays. Suppose, for example, that you want to use contract awards to anticipate the volume of commercial and industrial construction outlays in the first half of the upcoming year. What months in the awards series should you look at? Some in the fall of the current year? Or maybe in the spring of the current year? Or even earlier? The answer is that in the case of aggregate construction, we really do not know. The same applies to the average lag between total commitments and total outlays for producers' durable equipment.[6]

In most cases the time that elapses depends upon three things: (1) the lag between the supplier's receipt of the order and his starting of work on it (Does he have a backlog of unstarted orders?); (2) the length of production, which depends upon the availability of materials, labor, and other inputs as well as upon the basic technology of the process; and (3) the pattern of payment (Does the buyer make partial-plan payments as the work progresses or only after delivery?). All these factors can vary for given types of equipment or structures. They vary even more among different types. Thus the average lag can fluctuate radically for plant and equipment totals of a changing composition.

Particular business investors presumably know the nature of these lags in their own particular capital projects and reflect this knowledge in their responses to surveys of their intentions to spend. But the available aggregative data on new orders for durable goods and on contract awards scarcely equip the outside analyst to cross-examine the reliability of the aggregated spending intentions. If new orders for durable goods and construction contract awards are tapering off sharply at the same time that business reports

[6] See Thomas Mayer and S. Sonenblum, "Lead Times for Fixed Investment," *Review of Economics and Statistics*, vol. 37, pp. 300–304, August, 1955.

rising capital-spending programs, there is ground for suspicion, but that is about as much as one can say.

If data on current commitments are accompanied by figures on the commitments backlog or by comparable data on current sales, more can be inferred. In the United States such companion series are available for durable goods manufacturers. The existence of a backlog suggests a certain momentum to capital goods output (and therefore expenditures) which may carry part or all the way through the forecast period. But there, too, it is easy to err. The mere existence of an unfilled-orders backlog—say, for machine tools —several times the current volume of monthly deliveries does not promise a buoyant outlook for purchases. It promises this only if the multiple by which unfilled orders exceed current monthly deliveries is greater than the number of months in the average production period. For example, an equipment firm with current sales of $10 million a month, an order backlog of $30 million, and a production period of four months faces a declining sales prospect.

The average general forecaster does not know enough about the production periods involved in business capital formation to be able to tell much about the investment outlook from a single reading on the orders backlog in industries, such as machinery manufacturing, which specialize in producers' durable equipment. But a rising backlog in a period when suppliers seem to be operating at full capacity is another matter. This indicates a clear probability that equipment expenditures will continue strong some months into the future. The same evidence is provided by the circumstance that causes such a rise in the order backlog—namely, a more or less sustained recent excess of new orders over full-capacity shipments (and sales).

In summary, the conclusion we can draw from the foregoing discussion is as follows: data on contracts awarded for nonresidential construction cast nothing more than a very impressionistic light on any estimate of plant outlays in a specific near-term period, since the lags involved in such construction are so sizable and varied and since most of the awards data are accompanied neither by data on the contract backlog nor by comparable figures on current deliveries. The commitments data for durable goods manufacturing do not suffer from all these faults; they include comparable figures for the order backlog and for sales. Unfortunately, however, their coverage does not match the private purchases of producers' durable equipment at all closely. All told, the immediate assistance that contracts and order data can give the plant and equipment forecaster is extremely limited.[7]

Earlier in the chapter we mentioned the National Industrial Conference Board (NICB) surveys of capital appropriations of 1,000 manufacturing corporations. The survey reports both newly approved and the backlog of

[7] Arthur Okun (*op. cit.*, p. 224) concludes: "But for a quantitative prediction of plant and equipment over the short horizon covered by the quarterly anticipations data, I cannot find any profitable use of the orders and contracts data. Other researchers may be able to show that this reflects my limitations and not those of the series in question."

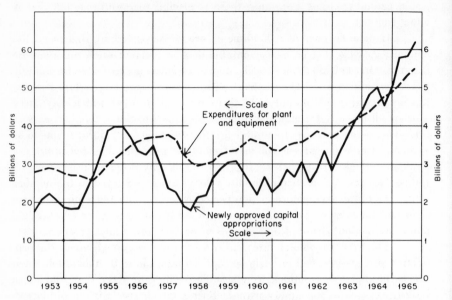

Figure 19–1. Expenditures for new plant and equipment (seasonally adjusted annual rates) and newly approved capital appropriations (seasonally adjusted), 1953–1965. Source: U.S. Department of Commerce and National Industrial Conference Board.

capital appropriations.[8]   These series are somewhat similar (for manufacturing only) to the Commerce-SEC and McGraw-Hill surveys in that they tend to reflect investment intentions.   But they differ in two important respects. First, the NICB reports funds appropriated by company boards of directors, as of a given date, without any indication of when these funds will be spent. The Commerce-SEC and McGraw-Hill series, on the other hand, are estimates of probable actual expenditures in each of the future time periods specified in the survey.   Second, however, the NICB series reflects formal actions—appropriations—by the companies surveyed, whereas the McGraw-Hill and Commerce-SEC surveys of expenditure plans or anticipations are not limited to capital programs on which formal action has been taken.   The NICB series therefore presumably represents investment programing when it has reached a firmer stage of planning but, for the same reason, it may miss investment programs that, though not approved at the time of the survey, will nevertheless go forward.   Also, to repeat, the NICB survey covers manufacturing only.

The new capital appropriations series has been identified by the National Bureau of Economic Research as a leading indicator.   During the period 1953–1965, the series showed a rather clear tendency to lead the

---

[8] Data for these series are reported in the NICB's *Investment Statistics.* They are also conveniently summarized in *Business Cycle Developments.* The results of successive surveys are also currently reported in *Business Week.*

Commerce-SEC plant and equipment (P and E) expenditures series as is shown in Figure 19–1. The upturn in P and E at the end of the 1954 recession was anticipated by the appropriations series by four quarters. The appropriations series leads the P and E series at the downturn in the 1958 recession by six quarters, and again at the subsequent upturn by one quarter. Again in 1960, the appropriations series turned down two quarters ahead of the P and E series. In 1961–1963, however, the appropriations series, though trending upward, followed a sawtoothed pattern, whereas P and E expenditures rose steadily except for a mild, two-quarter dip in the last quarter of 1962 and the first quarter of 1963. From then, both series rose rapidly, although the appropriations series indulged in one rather substantial wiggle in 1964.

The appropriations series gave relatively little indication of the magnitude of the swings in P and E expenditures except, perhaps, in 1962–1965, when the steepness of the rise presaged a vigorous rise in P and E expenditures—a rise that subsequently did occur. In general, the best use of the series is in identifying turning points. And even here, we run into the same problems that are involved in all leading indicators: variable leads and sufficiently erratic behavior, on occasion (e.g., 1961–1963), to make life very uncomfortable for the nervous forecaster. In spite of these deficiencies, the survey is a valuable supplement to the McGraw-Hill and Commerce-SEC intentions surveys, especially when a recent intentions survey covering the full forecast period is not available.

THE PHYSICAL FEASIBILITY OF BUSINESS' INVESTMENT PROGRAM

Plant and equipment intentions surveys are accumulations of individual investment programs. There is no a priori assurance that, when all these individual programs are added up, they will not constitute an aggregate bill of requirements for materials, engineering, capital goods-producing capacity, and labor that exceeds the total resources available for such production in the planning period. Thus one question that a careful forecaster certainly needs to ask in evaluating an intentions survey is whether, in the aggregate, business investment programs are physically feasible.

It should be noted that for demand-forecasting purposes, a negative answer to this question is not in itself a sufficient basis for rejecting the outlays estimate. If investment programs were primarily plans to spend specified amounts of money rather than to procure specified quantities of specified types of capital goods, an excess of total programed outlays over available supplies at existing prices would simply cause investors to buy a somewhat different batch of capital goods than they originally had intended, and to force up capital goods prices in the process. To some extent this is the way things actually happen in a tight supply situation. For the most part, however, corporate investment programs are plans to procure specified types of assets, and if supply shortages emerge, buyers do not just redirect expenditures; they actually forestall them for the time being. For this reason a finding that intended plant and equipment spending exceeds available supplies should cause some paring down of the demand forecasts an analyst derives from an intentions survey.

It cannot be assumed that the intentions survey reflects spending plans which already have been adequately adjusted and discounted for possible supply bottlenecks. Some large corporate buyers, who do highly refined capital programing and have preferred access to suppliers, may investigate the bottleneck possibility pretty thoroughly before they firm up their spending schedules. But this is not the general practice. Neither individual suppliers nor individual buyers are fully aware of what the buyers in the aggregate are proposing to do.

It is much easier to argue the need for evaluating the physical feasibility of reported investment programs than it is actually to make such an evaluation. There are no aggregative data to which the analyst can readily turn for this purpose. What he needs is a good deal of familiarity with the current demand and capacity situation in a number of specific industries. This is a kind of knowledge in which the veteran forecaster is likely to excel the erudite beginner, for the informal communications network through which the veteran acquires specific front-line impressions of conditions in particular industries and markets is apt to be more highly developed. However, anyone who is willing to read enough of the current periodical trade literature has access to a reasonable substitute for such personalized sources. Moreover, one scarcely has to venture beyond such general statistical sources as the monthly tables in the back of the *Survey of Current Business* to garner valuable insights into situations in a number of critical supply areas.

Of the latter, steel is the most obvious. By comparing current output with the output of past periods of critical supply adjusted for estimated changes in capacity and by observing the backlogs of representative types of steel, one can generally spot tight supply situations. Similar data are available for cement, lumber, and other building materials. Recent trends in average hours worked per week suggest the tightness of operations in these manufacturing industries for which capacity estimates are not directly available, and trends in construction workers' wages indicate a good deal about the current condition of that labor market. Rather elaborate information is available on the degree of order backlogging in the machine tools industry.

When the forecaster has done the best he can to check such information against the reported size and composition of the business investment programs, has made some allowance for what at this stage of his analysis he thinks may be the other-than-business-investment demands upon the same supplier industries, and has garnished his own thinking with the relevant current comment in the business press, he ordinarily will have little difficulty in spotting any serious physical infeasibilities in the investment program. Translating the degree of infeasibility into numbers is, as we intimated above, more a matter of experienced judgment than of statistical procedure.

THE FINANCIAL FEASIBILITY OF THE INVESTMENT PROGRAMS

We saw in Part Two that, to be carried out, investment projects must be financially feasible. Both the costs of using money (implicit internal as well as external market costs) and the quantitative availability of funds—internally within firms as well as externally in particular money markets—can exert telling restraints on investment. Moreover, it would seem that such restraints should be especially telling upon the plant and equipment portion of investment, where funds are committed for relatively long periods and where, of all investment categories, there is the hardest-headed profit and loss calculus on the part of buyers.

Yet there is a strong and apparently contradictory persuasion among many practicing business conditions analysts that the investment programs reported in the intentions surveys are likely to be fairly impervious to changes in the money and credit situation. They are probably right. The reason for this seeming paradox is, once again, the phenomenon of lags. The cost and availability of funds do affect plant and equipment activity. But their direct impact is upon decisions to buy, not upon actual expenditures, which typically lag the decisions by a number of months. It seems probable that, from the fall McGraw-Hill survey onward, the intentions surveys largely reflect investment programs that already have been adjusted in the light of financial circumstances. Comparisons of expected returns over the current cost of funds already have been made, and investors already have canvassed the availability of funds for the projects they plan.

In the light of these and other considerations, once a corporate board of directors has given final approval to a capital project, it takes a radical change in the financial situation to stop the project or slow it up appreciably. Before long, enough sunk costs will have been incurred to make it cheaper to pay a sizable unexpected premium for funds than to cancel or even delay the undertaking. And as far as the quantitative availability of funds is concerned, lenders—provided borrowers are willing to pay premium rates—are apt to record priority to the presumptive lines of credit that good business customers have established for their capital programs. Conversely, in the event of an unexpected easing of the credit situation, investors cannot rush immediately into new capital expenditures; much planning, contracting, and engineering must come first.

Current plant and equipment outlays are not absolutely impervious to quarter-to-quarter changes in the financial situation, of course. Some, particularly smaller, business borrowers may be turned away by the banks or other lenders when loanable funds are unexpectedly constricted. And programs whose progress is contingent upon the accumulation of retained earnings that do not fully materialize may be reluctantly delayed. But certainly it appears that the major plant and equipment impact of any significant change in the cost and availability of credit lies some distance in the future.

Obviously, the practical question is how far distant. As was implied a couple of paragraphs back, our own working hypothesis is that the remainder-of-the-year programs reported in the Commerce-SEC and McGraw-Hill spring surveys are very largely impervious to unexpected financial changes during the remainder of the year, and that even the coming-year programs reflected in McGraw-Hill's fall survey have a high degree of such immunity.[9]

Under this view, there seldom should be an occasion, in making first-approximation estimates of plant and equipment spending for periods running no more than twelve months into the future, for adjusting survey findings on the ground that they are financially infeasible. To justify such a revision it would take a more radical alteration in financial circumstances than the analyst ordinarily has any business assuming at the first-approximation stage of his work.

THE SENSITIVITY OF INVESTMENT PROGRAMS TO UNEXPECTED SALES EXPERIENCE

How much would business change its plant and equipment spending programs for the next six to twelve months if sales should behave differently than is currently expected? Later on in his analysis a forecaster may have to puzzle out the answer to this kind of question if the sum of his first-approximation estimates of sector-by-sector spending does not square with the initial income hypothesis with which he began his demand analysis. But at this stage of the analysis a similar issue is raised if the forecaster's own initial income hypothesis differs significantly from the sales expectations upon which businessmen have premised their investment programs. In practice, such a discrepancy is unlikely to be very large. But if there is one, the analyst in principle should adjust the survey finding before adopting it as his own plant and equipment forecast. He must decide how imperturbable current capital-spending programs would be in the short run in the face of unexpected sales developments.

Here, as in the case of unexpected financial developments, there are competing considerations. On the one hand, there is nothing more important

---

[9] The interesting analysis of Franz Gehrels and Suzanne Wiggins, "Interest Rates and Manufacturers' Fixed Investment," *American Economic Review*, vol. 47, no. 1, pp. 79–92, March, 1957, provides persuasive support for this assumption. For the period 1947–1955, they find a high degree of correlation between market interest rates and manufacturers' plant and equipment expenditures—lagged one year behind the interest rates.

to business planning than long-run sales forecasts and, at the same time, there are few things about which the average firm feels less confident. Thus, unexpected sales experience in the short run can tint the long-run outlooks that many firms see and thereby have a major impact on their investment decisions. But, on the other hand, there is the lag factor: the decisions primarily affected will be those regarding new orders and contracts, not expenditures under orders and contracts already placed or let. For this reason, revisions in sales expectations are likely to have a lagged effect on investment spending. After six or nine months, however, the effect can be substantial.[10]

The following appear to be sensible rules of thumb. First, any upward or downward revisions that are made on this count in plant and equipment forecasts for no more than the next twelve months should be made sparingly. Second, however, it is well to recognize that the present inertia of current plant and equipment programs will diminish during the forecast period. By the time the most distant quarter arrives, visible reactions to unexpected sales developments may be quite plain. Finally, the extent of investor reaction to unexpected sales developments almost surely will bear a progressive rather than a proportionate relationship to the size of the error in business' sales expectations. Whereas a minor sales-forecasting error is unlikely to faze investment decision makers much, an error twice as large may cause several times the alterations in investment plans. This is because current sales experience becomes important only when it gets far enough out of line with the expected to cause a real loss of confidence in the long-run sales forecast that business has been using.

COMPLETING THE PRELIMINARY FORECAST OF BUSINESS FIXED INVESTMENT

To this point, we have been discussing only business expenditures for new plant and equipment. There remain the other components of BFI, defined early in the chapter. The lazy man's way of forecasting these outlays is to note that, in combination, they have accounted for a fairly constant percentage of BFI, and then to extrapolate that percentage (or a small increase or decrease in the percentage as the trend may indicate) for one more year. The data for the years 1957 through 1965 are as follows:[11]

[10] Arthur Okun, in the article cited a few pages back, examined the correlation between the deviation of actual from expected sales of manufacturing corporations, on an annual basis, and the deviation from expected investment expenditures as reported in the Commerce-SEC spring survey, also on an annual basis, and found that from 1948 to 1961, the former accounted for nearly 80 percent of the variance in the latter series.

[11] BFI data are after the 1965 revision in the national income accounts. Data for P and E do not reflect a major revision in this series, scheduled for 1966. The analyst should calculate new percentages when the revised P and E data become available.

Year	BFI*	P & E*	Other*	Other as % of BFI
1957	$46.4	$37.0	$ 9.4	20.3%
1958	41.6	30.5	11.1	26.7
1959	45.1	32.5	12.6	27.9
1960	48.4	35.7	12.7	26.2
1961	47.0	34.4	12.6	26.8
1962	51.7	37.3	14.4	27.9
1963	54.3	39.2	15.1	27.8
1964	60.5	44.9	15.6	25.8
1965	69.8	52.0	17.8	25.5

* In billions of dollars.

Employing this easy method, however, implicitly assumes that the same influences that determine plant and equipment expenditures in the categories covered by the survey also determine the similar expenditures in the other categories, and in the same degree. This is probably a safe assumption to make in the case of a number of the items included in the "other" category, where roughly the same motivations and criteria could be expected to apply. But it is not necessarily safe to assume that farm enterprises and nonprofit institutions, in particular, are subject to the same influences.

In the case of farm enterprises, the determinants of fixed-investment expenditures are presumably to be found in circumstances peculiar to farming. First, the rate and degree of technological change in agricultural equipment would be a determining factor. Much of farm equipment expenditures in the post-World War II decades can be attributed to the revolution in the technology of farming which, coupled with a high degree of competition in agriculture, virtually forced the acquisition and use of modern equipment by any commercial farmer who wanted to remain in business. Variations in the level of farm income, however, clearly have had an effect on the rate at which farmers were financially able to acquire this capital equipment. The record since 1953 suggests that net farm income *per farm* reflects both of these determining influences, income and technology. A comparison of fixed-investment expenditures by farm enterprises with net farm income per farm of the *previous* year shows a positive correlation for the period since the Korean War.[12] The relationship, illustrated in Figure 19–2, though not entirely

[12] The lagged regression of farm construction and equipment outlays (1954–1965) on net income per farm including inventory change (1953–1964), using annual data, is described by the equation $Y = 0.836 + 948\,X$, where Y = outlays in billions of dollars and X = income in the previous year in thousands of dollars. $r^2 = .6746$. The coefficient of correlation achieved in this simple regression is, of course, partly attributable to the similar trends in the two (absolute dollar) series.

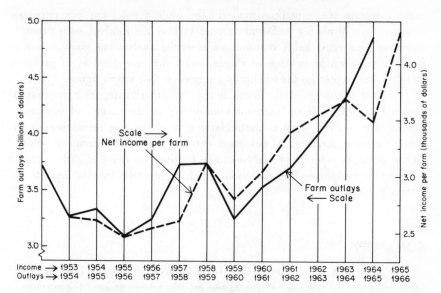

Figure **19–2.**   Net income per farm (including inventory change) and farm outlays for equipment and nonresidential structures lagged one year, 1953–1965.   Source: U.S. Department of Commerce.

reliable, would have given reasonably good forecasts in ten of the twelve years covered by the chart.

More sophisticated, but increasingly complex, devices for forecasting farm capital outlays can, of course, be developed.   One may consider such influences as the current-year farm income, prices of farm equipment, and changes in government farm programs.   Perhaps the simplest technique is to rely largely on the lagged relationship described above, and introduce allowance for these other influences on an intuitive or judgment basis, especially when converting the annual forecast yielded by the regression to a quarterly one.

The striking characteristic of expenditures by nonprofit institutions for new construction and equipment is their steady upward progression, with no indication of variation due to changing economic conditions.   Indeed, the only year in the post-World War II period to show a decline was 1952, and this probably reflected certain minor supply constraints imposed by the Korean War.   Until such time as the data or other information indicate that there is or is about to be a change in this trend, therefore, a simple extrapolation would seem to be an adequate forecasting device.

Expenditures for oil and natural gas well drilling charged to current expense could be forecast accurately only by a thorough study of the economics of the petroleum and natural gas industries—and presumably authoritative forecasts are sometimes made in the trade press. For our purposes, however, it is probably sufficient to observe that the total of such expenditures has been remarkably constant. Unless the analyst has good reason to believe, based on knowledge of the industry, that a change is in prospect, therefore, he cannot go far wrong by plugging in last year's figure.

Most of the remaining items in the "all other" category can safely be assumed to bear a fairly constant relationship to the plant and equipment expenditures series. This is particularly true of the one remaining sizable item, "business purchases of passenger cars not covered by Commerce-SEC." At this point, therefore, the analyst can be forgiven for being slightly lazy and lumping the remainder into one total, which he forecasts by relating it to the P and E series.

SUMMARY

The efforts of contemporary forecasters to anticipate business fixed investment during the next six to fifteen months center around the surveys of business intentions to spend on new plant and equipment. To make intelligent use of the surveys, it is necessary to know something of their character, record, and timing, and to understand the difference between the business plant and equipment concept and the total business fixed-investment component of the GNP accounts that the forecaster needs to estimate in his aggregate-demand model. Beyond these more or less mechanical matters, there is the question of how much the analyst should adjust reported intentions in arriving at a first-approximation forecast of overall plant and equipment outlays.

In this regard, we have argued that the careful analyst does need to do some second-guessing of the survey results. These results themselves are not forecasts but aggregations of individual investment programs, and there is no assurance that the programs in the aggregate are entirely feasible.

But, in practice, the forecaster should second-guess with a good deal of self-restraint. Only a very limited and tentative kind of cross testing can be accomplished with the data on advanced business investment commitments, i.e., new orders and contract awards, available in the United States. And because the process of business fixed-capital formation is a relatively time-consuming one, it is unlikely that, within the range of a short-run forecast, it will be notably affected by unexpected changes in sales or in the cost and availability of funds. If the sales projection that is implicit in the forecast is markedly different from business sales expectations, however, some modification of the plant and equipment forecast for the later part of the forecast period would be in order.

The one ground on which a model builder may need to make a substantial revision—a downward revision—in converting the survey results to a first-approximation plant and equipment forecast is that of physical feasibility. Supply bottlenecks may hold expenditures below their intended level.

With respect to the other components of BFI, we have suggested that they may be estimated by assuming that, in total, they will be the same percentage of business plant and equipment expenditures that they have been in recent years, or preferably that the more important ones be estimated separately. In the case of farm capital outlays, an analysis focusing on recent trends in net farm income per farm would seem to be in order. For construction and equipment expenditures by nonprofit institutions, and capital outlays changed to current expense in oil and natural gas well drilling, an extrapolation of trend should yield a good figure, unless there is some substantive evidence to indicate that a change in trend can reasonably be anticipated.

20

THE DEMAND FOR
NEW HOUSING AND
AUTOMOBILES

Outlays on new houses and on automobiles are treated as sharply contrasting things in the United States national income accounting system, but their similarities are more impressive than their differences. Both new houses and automobiles are bought by households, are wanted in their own right, and, because they last a long time, are purchased by particular households only infrequently. Thus outlays for additions to these stocks are both highly postponable and can vary greatly without affecting the total flow of services very much, particularly if there are offsetting fluctuations in the rates at which older items are retired from household commodity stocks. Both expenditure categories have in fact been relatively volatile fragments of the United States gross national product.

There are further similarities. In housing and in automobiles there are substantial used-commodity markets that powerfully condition markets for newly produced items. And both house buying and automobile buying are heavily dependent on the use of personal credit.

In neither the housing nor the automobile category of demand can there be the same reliance on plans and commitments data that is appropriate for forecasting Federal government expenditures and plant and equipment

454

outlays.   Intentions surveys are not lacking, but they do not provide very reliable forecasts.   Consumers typically do not plan their purchases even of fixed assets so thoroughly or so far ahead as do governments and business, and the plans they make are more subject to change.

Although current income is clearly among the determinants of housing and automobile expenditures, the past behavior of these two categories of demand suggests that, for forecasting purposes, it is appropriate to treat them as quasi-autonomous variables.   The opportunistic model builder therefore must develop his own initial estimates in the light of what he considers to be the pertinent determinants.   We shall find that a serviceable analytical procedure in these areas gives attention, more or less sequentially, to four partially overlapping questions:

1. What are the physical sources of the demand for new household fixed assets?

2. What is the impact of disposable personal income upon the ability of households to purchase fixed assets?[1]

3. What will be the impact of personal finance conditions—meaning by that the volume and distribution of consumers' liquid holdings, the availability of mortgage and installment loans, the sizes of minimum down payments, the influence of interest rates and of loan maturities on monthly payments, and the capacity of households to shoulder new debt?

4. Are other factors in evidence, including those of supply, cost, and price, which may augment or dampen the above influences?   In particular, what implications do the apparent trends in the used-house and the used-car markets hold for the sale of new houses and new cars?

While the following discussions, first of housing forecasting, then of automobile forecasting, do not parallel each other closely, each gives attention to the issues just enumerated.

PRIVATE RESIDENTIAL CONSTRUCTION

Around three-quarters of the outlays on private residential construction are expenditures for new "dwelling units"—this being the accepted term for all single-family houses, apartments, flats, or other spaces in which people can maintain separate households.[2]   This is the highly variable component of

---

[1] It is true that at the stage of the model-building exercise we are presently considering, the analyst would be holding the income factor "neutral" by hypothesizing a given level of overall activity and income in the forecast period.   However, unless he makes this initial income hypothesis a no-change-from-recent-levels proposition, he is going to have to decide immediately how much house and automobile buyers are likely to respond to the hypothetical income change that he is assuming.   And later on, when and if his further analysis forces him to abandon this initial income hypothesis, he will need to consider the income elasticity of consumer automobile and house buying once again. Thus he may as well make his basic examination of this relationship the first time around.

residential construction and is the portion of housing demand that the fore-caster is chiefly concerned to estimate. If he can do a good job on it, fairly rough and ready estimates of the sector's remaining components—expenditures for additions and alterations and for nonhousekeeping units plus a minor amount for real estate commissions and net transfers of structures to or from government—will not throw the total private new housing forecast off significantly.

THE PHYSICAL SOURCES OF DEMAND

The underlying physical requirements for new residential construction are essentially of two kinds—first, for net additions to the nation's housing

[2] At this writing, a statistical hiatus exists in the published residential construction statistics. The Census Bureau publishes (*Construction Reports*, series C-30) monthly figures for total nonfarm residential construction, and detail for new housing units and for nonhousekeeping units. However, the figure for the third component of nonfarm residential construction, additions and alterations, not shown separately but included in the total, is a *constant*, used for lack of adequate data. The constant number has been changed each year or two, to reflect revisions in the Census Bureau's rough estimates of average, recent expenditures for additions and alterations, but it is not intended to be a true measure of the current level of such expenditures. Commerce advises that surveys of residential additions and alterations under way may yield results that would permit substitution of a reliable figure for the constant, in which case the series will be revised.

It should also be noted that the nonfarm residential construction figure published by the Census Bureau, and republished in the *Survey of Current Business* ("Construction Put in Place") and in *Economic Indicators* ("New Construction"), differs from the non-farm residential construction component of gross private domestic investment in that the latter includes an amount for commissions on the sale of dwellings and net transfers of structures to or from the public sector. The total GPDI residential construction component also includes farm residential construction—not shown separately but calculable by subtracting the nonfarm figure from the total.

House trailers, incidentally, are not included in residential structures. They are classified as either automotive parts and accessories or producers' durable equipment, mainly the former. This classification, a carry-over from the days when most trailers were in fact automotive accessories and not dwelling units, is an unfortunate one. It introduces a significant element of error into the calculation of the physical sources of demand for housing, because each year the housing needs of an increasing number of households are being met by house trailers (mobile homes). Similarly, the inclusion of house trailers in automotive parts and accessories distorts that series, as we shall note later, to the point where the series fails to correlate with the obvious determinants of automotive parts and accessories as such. Moreover, the present classification understates GNP to the extent that the imputed rental value of owner-occupied house trailers, in contrast to the imputed rental value of constructed houses, is not included in the tabulation of GNP.

The problems created by the current accounting treatment of house trailers are discussed more fully in J. R. Becklin, "The Problems in Forecasting and Measuring GNP Created by the Treatment of Mobile Homes in our National Income Accounting System," unpublished as of the date of this writing.

stock and second, for replacement of units withdrawn from the stock. Most of the factors determining these requirements are slow-moving variables which are unlikely to change greatly in any one year. It therefore may seem unnecessary to expend much analytical energy on them for the purposes of year-to-year forecasting. But this is not so, for the physical requirements may be thought of as determining, at any given time, a normal band or range within which actual housing demand is likely to fall. The active determinants of short-run changes in actual demand usually are the more transitory variables—notably the credit variables—discussed below. But to appraise the degree of response that a change in the latter is likely to call forth in housing expenditures, it is important to know where actual outlays currently lie relative to what the physical requirements for housing presently indicate as normal. Once an analyst establishes such a view to his own satisfaction, he may not need to reexamine this problem so frequently as many others. But he does need an opinion about whether there is little or much unrequited demand for housing that, for example, increased credit availability could unleash during the forecast period.

Of the two sorts of physical requirements, the expansion category is both larger and easier to predict.[3] We shall consider it first.

Net Household Formation

According to U.S. Bureau of the Census definitions, the number of households in the United States is identical with the number of occupied dwelling units. Thus the factors determining net additions to the housing stock consist of those which determine net household formation, plus additional forces that cause changes in the number of housing vacancies (some of which are second houses).

Because an increase in households can be decisively checked by a failure of the housing stock to expand (just as a rise in the number of dwelling units relative to families can allow doubled-up families to separate and move into different households), the rate of net household formation is not entirely dependent upon demographic factors. However, the principal component of annual net household formation is the year's net increase in the number of families. A second component is the amount of undoubling (a positive entry) or doubling (negative) of families. And the third is the net change in single-member or other nonfamily households.

---

[3] Although, in the past, expansion demand for housing has been much larger than replacement demand, it does not follow that this will always be the case. A significant decline in the birthrate followed, twenty-odd years later, by a decline in the rate of net family formation, coupled with greatly enlarged urban renewal and highway programs, could completely reverse the balance between these two categories of housing demand determinants. Nevertheless, this would take some doing because of the average durability of houses.

The rate of net family formation is fairly predictable in the short run. It depends, for one thing, on the size and age composition of the population, and this, for the marriageable ages, is pretty well known for periods extending

Table 20–1. Number of Families and Households, and Annual Change, by Type of Household, 1940 to 1960, and Projections to 1970 and 1980* (In millions)

Year	Total households	Families Husband-Wife	Families Other	Primary individuals
Actual				
1940	34.9	26.6	4.9	3.5
1950	43.6	34.1	4.8	4.7
1960	52.6	39.3	5.6	7.8
Projections	A B	A B	A B	A B
1970	63.9 62.0	46.2 45.4	6.6 6.6	11.1 10.0
1980	76.5 73.6	55.4 54.2	7.4 7.6	13.6 11.8

Average Annual Change†

Year	Total households	Husband-Wife	Other	Primary individuals
Actual				
1940–1950	0.86	0.75	−0.02	0.13
1950–1960	0.91	0.52	0.08	0.30
Projections	A B	A B	A B	A B
1960–1965	1.21 0.92	0.66 0.51	0.13 0.13	0.42 0.27
1965–1970	1.05 0.97	0.73 0.71	0.07 0.07	0.25 0.19
1970–1975	1.23 1.14	0.88 0.85	0.08 0.09	0.28 0.20
1975–1980	1.29 1.17	0.97 0.92	0.09 0.10	0.23 0.15

* The two projections, A and B, are revisions of projections originally published in 1958 (*Current Population Reports*, ser. P-20, no. 90) to reflect actual experience since 1958, and to add Alaska and Hawaii, but are based on essentially the same assumptions. The differences between the two reflect differences as to the assumed annual change in the proportion of persons who will be household heads. Series A assumes that the average annual change from 1950 to 1956–1958 will continue to 1965, and then will drop to half that amount in the period 1965–1975 and to one-quarter of that amount in the period 1975–1980. Series B assumes one-half the average annual change of 1950 to 1956–1958 for the period 1957 to 1965, and one-quarter of that amount for 1965–1975, and no change after 1975.

† Calculated from unrounded data.

Source: U.S. Department of Commerce, Bureau of the Census, *Current Population Reports*, ser. P-20, nos. 123 and 124.

not more than fifteen years or so into the future. Moreover, the other principal determinants—the average age at which people marry and the percentage of adults who do marry—usually change only gradually. The Census Bureau accordingly publishes projections of the number of families and of households in the United States up to twenty years in the future. Table 20–1, for example, contains the projections of families and of households for 1970 and 1980 that the Census Bureau issued in April, 1963. The Bureau emphasizes that these are projections rather than forecasts and that, because they are based on somewhat arbitrary assumptions, the two series should not necessarily be interpreted as "high" and "low." As will be noted from the table, the range between the A and B series is not inconsiderable. Further, the projections of annual change are averages for the periods shown; the actual figures can fluctuate appreciably from year to year as is evidenced by the data shown in Table 20–2 for the years 1940 to 1965. Nevertheless, it is not unreasonable to treat the projected range for net increase in the number of households as an approximate forecast, providing one does not see on the immediate horizon any influence that would cause actual household formation to deviate markedly from the pattern indicated by quite predictable growth in adult population and by recent trends in attitudes toward marriage, in tendencies for families to double up, and in maintenance of households by nonfamily units, chiefly single individuals. A brief review of experience in recent decades may suggest some of the influences one should watch.

During the decade of the 1930s, the total number of households increased by 5,100,000. This, according to calculations based on census data by the Office of Business Economics of the Department of Commerce,[4] is just the amount of increase that the population gain of that decade would indicate (after allowance for change in age distribution). For the decade as a whole no increase at all came from undoubling or net increase in nonfamily households.[5]

The decade of the 1940s witnessed an increase in net household formation to 8,600,000, most of this occurring after the end of World War II in 1945. Of the 8,600,000 increase, only 6,300,000 is attributable to population increase alone. Some postponed marriages of the 1930s were no doubt consummated in the early 1940s. On the other hand, after the war mobilization began, many marriages were again postponed. For the decade as a whole, undoubling contributed nothing to household formation; the extensive undoubling that occurred after the war just about offset the doubling that was

[4] See L. Jay Atkinson, "Long-term Influences Affecting the Volume of New Housing Units," *Survey of Current Business*, U.S. Department of Commerce, vol. 43, no. 11, pp. 8–19, November, 1963. All the data in this historical review are from this source and do not reflect certain revisions in the data from 1955 on, made in 1965 (see Table 20–2).

[5] There was no doubt an actual shrinkage in nonfamily households, and an increase in doubling up, in the first half of the decade, followed by a reverse movement in the second half.

Table 20-2.   Net Household Formation, 1940–
1965 (In thousands)

Year*	Incre-ment	Year	Incre-ment
1940–1947 avg.	593	1960	1,364†
1947–1950 avg.	1,525	1961	665
1950–1955 avg.	850	1962	1,188
1956	942	1963	537
1957	771	1964	807
1958	801	1965	1,255
1959	961		

*Data are annual increments in the total number of households from March of the previous year to March of the year shown, or from April to April, when the surveys were conducted in the same month in consecutive years. In years when the survey month changed, data were adjusted to a twelve-month basis by linear interpolation.

† The figure for 1960 includes approximately 210,000 households added by the inclusion of Alaska and Hawaii in 1960.

Note: 1960–1965 figures are not strictly comparable with earlier years owing to inculsion of Alaska and Hawaii and a minor change in the household definition introduced in 1960.

Source: *Current Population Reports*, Population
        Characteristics, ser. P-20, no. 140, p. 4,
        July 2, 1965.

forced by housing shortages during the war. The major postwar influences on net household formation, in addition to the consummation of previously postponed marriages, was the drop in the average age of marriage that coincided with the return of members of the Armed Forces from active duty. The proportion of married males[6] in the twenty- to twenty-four-year age bracket rose from 27 percent in 1940 to 42 percent in 1950. For about three years after the war the rate of net family formation soared to a phenomenal 1.5 million.

In the decade of the 1950s, net household formation rose again to 9,100,000, only 6,200,000 of which could be attributed to population increase. The reasons for the 2,900,000 extra households were different from those of the prior decade. The average age of marriage continued to decline, but only slightly. Some further undoubling occurred in the first half of the decade. But the primary reason was the rise in the number of single-member (primary

[6] Defined as being married with spouse present; i.e., divorced and separated couples are excluded.

individual) households, particularly women and even more particularly, widows. The explanation for this rise no doubt lies in improved levels of income and employment opportunities for women and in the increase in eligibility for social security benefits and other annuity and pension plans that permitted many women, after the death of the husband, to continue to maintain separate households. The number of male primary individuals also increased more than population increase alone would indicate, although in the case of males the increase was primarily in the younger age groups rather than in the sixty-five and over bracket.

The Census Bureau projections, cited above, assume a continuation of the trends of the 1950s, but with a tapering off in the rise in the ratio of households to population after 1965, and a further tapering after 1970. They assume a further rise in the proportion of the population married, partly reflecting the rise of the 1950s in this proportion for the younger age brackets as these persons move into older age brackets, and partly reflecting some further decline in the average age of marriage. Consequently, for the 1965–1970 period, for example, the projected average annual net increase of 1,050,000 in households is explained only to the extent of 780,000 by population increase, 270.000 resulting from other factors. Even so, the assumed tapering off in the ratio of households to population is enough to indicate, in projection A, a reduction in net household formation between the first and second halves of the 1960s, from an annual average of 1,210,000 in 1960–1965 to 1,050,000 in 1965–1970. After 1970, nearly all the projected net increase in households is accounted for by population increase alone.

Atkinson, in the article cited above, suggests that the amount of tapering off in the increase in the proportion of households to population assumed in the Census Bureau projections may be too great, or more precisely, that it may not occur as soon as Census assumes. He suggests that this is particularly likely if the decade of the 1960s turns out to be one of vigorously rising incomes, if social security benefits are significantly increased, and if special housing programs for the elderly are expanded. He therefore offers a third set of projections of average annual net household formation which compares with the Census Bureau projections as shown in Table 20–3.

We leave it to the reader to decide which of these projections (if any) is the most reasonable. By the time these words appear in print, enough additional information may be available to permit a reasoned judgment. And in due course, revised projections will no doubt be published.

Vacancies

Because a household is defined as an occupied dwelling unit, housing construction in any given year must exactly equal net household formation plus withdrawals from the housing stock, plus (algebraically) mergers less conversions, plus (again algebraically) the change in the number of housing

Table 20–3. Projections of Average Annual Change in Number of Households, 1960–1980 (In thousands)

Years	Census A	Census B	Atkinson alternative
1960–1965	1,210	920	1,210
1965–1970	1,050	970	1,280
1970–1975	1,230	1,140	1,400
1975–1980	1,290	1,170	1,400

Source: L. Jay Atkinson, "Long-term Influences Affecting the Volume of New Housing Units," *Survey of Current Business*, U.S. Department of Commerce, vol. 43, no. 11, pp. 8–19, November, 1963.

units vacant. This statement of the identity, however, may seem to imply that vacancies are an independent variable, which could be predicted separately from the other variables. In practice, the number of vacancies is largely a residual and is determined by the net interaction of housing building, net household formation, and withdrawals. To the extent that this is true, vacancies can be ignored as an active determinant of housing construction. At times, however, the vacancy rate can get enough out of line with normal levels that builders or buyers may be significantly influenced in their plans and actions, and housing construction thus may be directly affected. And at any time, even when the vacancy rate is quite normal, the *possibility* of an excess of vacancies is something that the alert speculative builder never forgets for long.[7] This is especially true, of course, in particular local communities where past overbuilding (or underbuilding) may have reverberative effects on future building or on the ability of homeowners who want to trade up to dispose of their old houses.[8] Further, the vacancy total includes builders'

[7] In urban communities, the vast majority of housing units are built, not for or by the owner-occupants, but by speculative builders for sale or for rent during or after construction.

[8] An extreme example of underbuilding, on a national scale, is the condition that existed immediately after World War II. The construction of housing units was prohibited during World War II, except for limited numbers in and around defense installations. And the 1930s had been a decade of low home building. After the war, therefore, an acute physical shortage existed; vacancies were virtually zero. The consequent bidding up in house prices gave homeowners who, only a few years before, had been deeply in debt on their house, a handsome equity to use as a down payment on a new house. The shortage of houses thus had a double effect on residential construction: first, the direct effect of the shortage, and second, the indirect effect of enhancing, via shortage-induced inflation, the liquidity position of existing homeowners.

Table 20-4.   Housing Vacancy Rates by Condition and Type of Vacancy in the United States, 1959–1965 (First quarter data)*

	1959	1960	1961	1962	1963	1964	1965
Year-round housing:							
Sound or deteriorating	5.6	6.2	6.6	6.5	6.4	6.5	6.9
Available for rent	2.3	2.6	3.0	2.8	2.6	2.6	2.8
Available for sale	0.6	0.6	0.7	0.7	0.8	0.8	0.8
Rented or sold	0.4	0.4	0.4	0.5	0.4	0.4	0.4
Held off market	2.3	2.6	2.5	2.5	2.6	2.7	2.9
Dilapidated	1.3	1.2	0.9	0.9	0.7	0.7	0.7
Seasonal	3.2	2.8	2.7	2.6	3.3	3.2	3.1
Total	10.1	10.2	10.2	10.0	10.4	10.4	10.7

* Percent of total housing units.

Source: *Current Housing Reports*, ser. H-111, *Housing Vacancies*, U.S. Department of Commerce, Bureau of the Census.

inventories of new housing units built but not yet sold or rented.   Speculative builders are particularly sensitive to variations in this type of vacancy.   It is therefore necessary for the analyst to keep a wary eye on the vacancy rate figures published quarterly by the Bureau of the Census.   It is essential, however, to know how to interpret these figures; otherwise the wrong conclusions may be drawn.   Table 20-4 shows annual first-quarter data for recent years.

From 1959 to 1962, total vacancies were about 10 percent of total residential housing units, and increased to about 10.7 percent in 1965.   This gross figure, however, includes a number of categories that presumably have little or no effect on the housing market.   Seasonal units, for example, are chiefly cottages and other homes in resort areas; a rise in the number of seasonal units would reflect strength, not weakness, in the housing market. Dilapidated vacant units, the percentage of which declined in the period covered by the table and which may well continue to decline, should not properly be considered a part of the housing supply.   And housing units that have been rented or sold and are awaiting occupancy do not affect the current market.

The relevant vacancy data, therefore, are those pertaining to non-dilapidated housing units currently available for sale or rent.   Further, even within these categories changes may occur that would affect the significance of a given change in vacancy ratios.   For example, because of the virtual cessation of house building in the early 1940s (plus a low level of house building in the 1930s), the housing stock in the 1960s consists of two quite distinct classes of units: those built since World War II and those built prior to World War II, many of them in the 1920s or earlier.[9]   These prewar hous-

[9] In the first quarter of 1965, 59 percent of the rental housing units vacant and available for rent, and 36 percent of the homeowner units vacant and available for sale, were built in 1939 or earlier.

ing units lack many of the amenities of postwar housing, such as air conditioning, modern heating systems, elevators in the case of apartments, etc., and they are often located in areas that are no longer preferred. A rise in the total vacancy ratio may reflect largely an increase in vacancies in these prewar units, some of which are very close to the dilapidated category and are obvious potential candidates for withdrawal from the housing stock. An increase in vacancies in these units would therefore be much less significant than an increase in more recently built units.

Other information that the analyst should note in interpreting the significance of a change in vacancy ratios includes: (1) the regional location of vacancies; (2) the average duration of vacancy; and (3) the quality of vacant housing units as indicated by plumbing facilities, number of rooms, monthly rental or sales price, etc. The first of these—regional location—is especially important. A population not only needs houses but needs them in the right places. Much has been written about the rural-urban, urban-suburban, and interregional migrations that are in progress in the United States. The first of these, the population shift out of agriculture, keeps net nonfarm household formation running ahead of total household formation. While the exodus from agriculture has not been invariant and, in absolute terms, cannot go on indefinitely, for some years yet it will continue to add to the requirement for private residential construction, and the empty houses left behind will add to the vacancy totals (or possibly to withdrawals).

However, it is easy to exaggerate the impact of the urban-suburban and interregional migrations upon national housing supply and requirements. These migrations, of course, do affect the intensity of construction activity in different areas. But they cause a net increase in housing vacancies nationally, and therefore in national housing requirements, only if the net outflow of migrants from a population-losing area exceeds (1) the indigenous growth in households within the area, plus (2) the attrition of the existing housing stock within the area, plus (3) any migration-induced decline in vacancies in the population-gaining areas. There probably have been—and will be during the next decade or two—few instances of emigrations of this magnitude.

Difficult as the vacancy statistics are to interpret, their significance should not be underestimated. A change of 1 percent in the relevant vacancy ratio is more than 550,000 housing units—about one-third of the annual demand for new housing units in the mid-1960s. Properly interpreted, the vacancy statistics can be a sensitive barometer to the net interaction of household formation, housing construction, and withdrawals from the housing stock. Sherman Maisel uses this barometric quality of the vacancy data to formulate an econometric model of the housing market, in which one of the key variables is inventories of houses for sale and for rent.[10] The primary

[10] Sherman Maisel, "A Theory of Fluctuations in Residential Construction Starts," *American Economic Review*, vol. LIII, no. 3, pp. 359–383, June, 1963. See also Gary Fromm and Laurence R. Klein, "The Brookings-S.S.R.C. Quarterly Econometric Model of

determinant of short-run fluctuations in residential construction is to be found, he finds, not on the demand side of the market (income, credit, etc.) but on the supply side, and "the channel of causation appears to be through inventories."[11]

Second Houses

Theoretically, changes in the number of families owning two or more residences is another factor that could cause the national need for housing to deviate from the schedule of household formation. Presently, however, second houses still are too small an item in the aggregate to count for much; a generation hence it may be different. To the extent that it is presently a factor, it is measured in the vacancy statistics; if one household owns two housing units, one of them must be vacant at any given moment.

Family Size

Nothing can generate quite such a literal pressure on a family's supply of housing as several more children in the family. Thus it may appear that our concentration so far upon the numbers of households and families rather than upon the sizes of families could yield a badly distorted picture of the physical sources of housing demand. But it would be easy to exaggerate such a view. Families, not individuals, are the basic demanders of housing, and they have a good bit of stretchability and compressibility, vis-à-vis given units of dwelling space.

Nevertheless, developments set in motion after World War II will continue for some time to make family size a significant dimension of housing demand. Average family size rose fairly sharply during the first postwar decade, and many of the families in which this growth occurred bought their own houses when the parents were young by prewar standards. Moreover, partly because of the Federally underwritten mortgages which facilitated this earlier house buying, and partly because of income limitations, these young families typically bought small houses. Furthermore, the idea of living in and owning a series of houses, rather than living out one's life in a particular house, became much more of a commonplace during the postwar years. The population became more mobile; income expectations became buoyant; and rising prices disguised the depreciation of existing houses.

The result was a pronounced shift in the composition of construction demand in the fifties. The same couples who bought small houses in the late forties—by then five or ten years older with more and older children, con-

---

the United States: Model Properties," *American Economic Review*, vol. 55, no. 2, pp. 348–361, May, 1965.

[11] *Ibid.*, p. 376.

siderably higher incomes, and an equity accumulated in their old houses—reentered the market for larger, more valuable, second-of-a-series houses. The construction of houses, especially larger, single-family residences, was therefore fairly well maintained throughout the decade.

The 1960s, however, witnessed a shift in the type of housing demanded. The war babies were now getting old enough to go away to school or to get married and set up their own households. The population was "youthing" and aging at the same time, with very little increase in the middle-age brackets. Simultaneously, so it is reported, many persons became disenchanted with suburban living with its regimen of lawn mowing, home repair, and commuting. Consequently, newly married war babies teamed up with older, now-childless couples to demand apartments rather than houses. The result, in the first half of the 1960s, was a sharp rise in the ratio of apartment units to total new housing units constructed.

The late 1960s and early 1970s may again see a reversal of trend, when babies of the war babies reach the age where separate housing units and adequate play space become essential. Some forecasters identify 1967 as the year when the percentage of apartments to total new housing units will reach its peak. If this were purely a demographic calculation, one could be surer of the prediction, but as we have suggested earlier, income and sociological considerations also have an influence, and the latter, especially, are difficult to foretell.

Replacement Requirements

The demographic determinants of housing construction usually operate quite gradually, even predictably, and when marked deviations do occur, they tend to be self-reversing. But the replacement demand for housing, on the other hand, has no particular level that can be described as normal or natural. Few old houses literally wear out. If their owners and occupants are of a mind to provide the necessary maintenance and improvements, most residential structures can ke kept habitable almost indefinitely. Thus, while some of the annual replacement for housing is quite literally physical, in that it reflects accidental losses of existing structures, most of it is created by willful human decision.

Two kinds of decisions are involved. In the first place, occupants of existing houses must decide that they want bigger and/or better houses. Dissatisfaction with existing housing can be prompted by expanding families, by changes in incomes, and by innovations in construction and design. If such influences were the only ones governing the volume of replacement, it would be mistaken to think of them as, in any sense, a physical, underlying requirement analytically distinguishable from the income, credit, and other influences on housing demand that we have yet to examine. However, a desire for new houses by persons already housed is only one of the necessary ingredients for a heavy replacement requirement. If decisions to buy improved new houses are not to lead quickly to a rate of construction in excess of net household formation, someone else must decide to withdraw existing structures from the housing market. Otherwise the increase in vacancy rates will tend to push down the price of existing housing, thereby deterring would-be buyers of new housing, both by diverting their purchases to old houses and by reducing the equity they can transfer out of their present homes.

If the people who decide how many old houses to withdraw from the consumer stock could base their decisions simply on the depreciated value of existing structures, an increased desire for new houses would lead simply and readily, via declining used-house prices, to increased scrappage of old structures. But the trouble is that structures are tied to pieces of land, and land—particularly urban land—is valuable. Thus, aside from accidental losses by fire, etc., for dwelling units to be withdrawn from the housing stock, there must be demand for the land on which they stand. And such demand comes chiefly from businesses and governments, which want space for such things as gas stations, parking lots, stores, shopping centers, factories, office buildings, streets, freeways, highways, public buildings, parks, college campuses, hospitals, urban renewal projects, or other new residential developments, usually apartment buildings. For this reason the rate at which business and government acquire and withdraw residential properties from the housing stock is a powerful independent conditioner of the demand for new housing.

In addition to actual losses, the number of housing units available for occupancy is affected by the merging of small units into larger ones, and conversely, by the conversion of single large units into smaller units (e.g., the conversion of a large old house into an apartment building). Actually, in the decade of the 1950s, mergers and conversions were almost exactly offsetting; 962,000 units were converted into 1,966,000 smaller units, for a gain (in number of units) of 1,004,000, whereas 2,060,000 other units were merged into 1,005,000 larger units, for a loss of 1,055,000.[12]

Because there is no routine procedure by which losses to the housing stock are consistently reported to a statistics collecting agency, current data are almost nonexistent. Such information as is available is limited to that derived from the housing inventories conducted at infrequent intervals by the Census Bureau. On the basis of these studies, Atkinson, in the article cited above, estimated net withdrawals from the housing stock at 3,078,000 for the decade of the 1950s, and projects net withdrawals at 5,500,000 for the 1965–1975 decade. This projection assumes that mergers and conversions will continue to be offsetting.

THE ROLE OF INCOME

As a practical matter, a competent forecaster of short-run changes in housing demand is not apt to linger so long over income prospects as the underlying dependence of personal spending upon personal income would

[12] Atkinson, *op. cit.*, p. 18.

suggest.   On a priori grounds it is perfectly plain that changes in disposable personal income strongly condition actual housing demand.   First, income and employment are important determinants of marriage rates, doubling and undoubling, and the ability of single persons (e.g., widows) to maintain separate households.   That is, income affects the short-run and even the long-run operation of the demographic determinants of housing demand.[13]   Second, income is an obvious determinant of the size and quality of housing units that households are able to buy or rent and therefore of dollar expenditures if not of numbers of housing units.   Third, the general level of business activity (and of income) affects the rate at which housing units are demolished to make way for commercial construction and other new uses of land.   Nevertheless, studies of the relationship over time of housing construction to various relevant determinants fail to show any significant correlation between short-run fluctuations in housing construction and disposable income.[14]   The reason for this lack of significant correlation is probably that housing expenditures, more than any other category of consumer expenditures, involve commitments over a long period of time and are therefore likely to be influenced more by long-run *anticipations* than by current income.   The permanent income hypothesis, discussed in Chapter 8,[15] probably has its greatest relevance in housing.

The most reasonable course for the short-run forecaster, therefore, is to view disposable personal income as a general conditioner of housing demand, which, within the space of a year or so, is unlikely to exert any markedly distinctive influence of its own except on those occasions when a marked change of direction in incomes or income expectations appears to be in store.   If the general forecast indicates a recession in business activity, the consequent change in income expectations could be the decisive factor in determining housing activity.   Nevertheless, for purposes of short-run forecasting, there is little point in trying to generalize about the degree of responsiveness of residential construction to year-to-year income changes.

THE IMPACT OF FINANCE

More often than not, financial considerations are the ones that bring the short-run housing outlook into sharpest focus, and the aspect of housing finance that accounts for most of the finance-induced fluctuation in new house buying is that involving the supply of mortgage credit and the terms under which it is available to borrowers.   Two other broad aspects of the personal

---

[13] See G. H. Orcutt, M. Greenberger, V. Korbel, and A. Rivlin, *Microanalysis of Socioeconomic Systems: A Simulation Study*, Harper & Row, Publishers, Inc., New York, 1961, pp. 81–85.

[14] See Sherman Maisel, *op. cit.*; also J. M. Guttentag, "The Short Cycle in Residential Construction," *American Economic Review*, vol. LI, no. 3, pp. 275–298, June, 1961.

[15] See pp. 185–186.

finance picture are potentially important: the extent and distribution of consumers' liquid holdings and their ability and/or willingness to shoulder new mortgage debt. But, as will be explained below, neither begins to be so active an influence on the demand for new housing as does the supply side of the mortgage money market.[16]

Variations in Mortgage Terms

For the great majority of house buyers, who debt finance their new houses, the pertinent financial considerations are essentially ones of mortgage terms. In periods of tight money, would-be buyers occasionally encounter absolute shortages of mortgage funds in the lending institutions they visit. But almost always a new house buyer can get a 50 percent, ten-year loan on a new house at 6 or 7 percent interest if he can use it; tight money usually means adverse terms rather than no borrowing opportunities at all. The loan terms that really matter are just two: the minimum required down payment and the size of the monthly payments buyers must undertake to meet.

Two kinds of factors largely determine changes in terms that borrowers on residential mortgages have to meet. The first is general credit conditions, which are determined by the general level of business activity and, more immediately, by Federal Reserve policy. In periods of tight money, interest rates tend to rise on all types of debt instruments, including mortgage loans. The rise in mortgage interest rates itself probably has some restraining effect on the demand for mortgage funds, as potential homeowners or builders are deterred from borrowing by the higher cost. The evidence seems to indicate that this restraining effect, however, is quite nominal. Housing demand seems to be not very price-elastic to changes in interest rates that can be spread over the life of the loan.[17] Rather, the restraining effects seems to take the form simply of a reduction in the available supply of mortgage funds. Interest rates on mortgage loans, because they are long-term loans and because a well-organized, competitive, and impersonal market for mortgage loans does not exist, tend to be sticky. They fluctuate, but over a fairly narrow range and rather tardily as compared with other money market rates. The result is a tendency for mortgage loans to become relatively less attractive to lenders in times of tight money and more attractive in times of easy money. Diversified institutional lenders, such as life insurance companies and commercial banks, can shift their lending between the mortgage market and other markets with-

[16] Because our concern here is with the demand for new housing, i.e., consumer expenditures for residential construction, the discussion focuses on the impact of the supply of mortgage money for permanent financing of housing units. An additional impact that occasionally operates on the supply side of the housing market should be noted: variations in the supply of short-term funds available to builders to finance the construction of housing—so-called construction loans.

[17] See Sherman Maisel, *op cit.* Also J. M. Guttentag, *op. cit.*

out serious difficulty.   Even savings and loan associations, which deal primarily in residential mortgages, have the option, within limits, of changing the proportion of their portfolio in government securities.

The second set of factors is really a special case of the first and has its origins in short-run changes in the pertinent regulations of the Federal Housing Administration (FHA) and the Veterans Administration, the two agencies that administer the Federal government's mortgage-guarantee programs.   In the first decade or so following World War II the FHA and VA programs caused basic structural changes in the housing market.   They accomplished a lasting reduction in the liquidity qualifications and income qualifications required for home ownership in the United States.   This change, it should be noted, is not limited to mortgages insured by FHA or guaranteed by VA.   In the competition for business, lenders on conventional, i.e., non-government-guaranteed, mortgages have also eased their lending terms.   But now that they are in effect, these structural changes do not necessarily imply short-run variations in house-financing terms.   Such variations, however, do stem partly from these agencies' exercise of their authority to make administrative adjustments in down payment, maximum loan duration, and maximum interest requirements (or from failure to exercise their administrative authority when mortgage market conditions change), and from similar adjustments directly enacted by the Congress.   These are policy changes of which the forecaster needs to keep track as he appraises the mortgage market.

The impact of general monetary conditions on the availability and terms of government-guaranteed mortgages is even more emphatic than it is on conventional loans, but because of the interaction with the administratively fixed aspects of terms in these cases, more complicated.   The bulk of government-guaranteed mortgage money is supplied by large lenders (insurance companies, mutual savings banks, etc.) who make close calculations of the extra costs (servicing, home office expenses, possible closing costs, etc.) in mortgage loans.   If the differential in yield between a government bond and an FHA or VA mortgage is not sufficient to cover these extra costs, a shift in portfolio is indicated.   Thus, if the lender decides, for example, that a spread of $1\frac{1}{4}$ percent between government bond yields and mortgage interest rates is needed to make the latter profitable, and the maximum permissible rate on FHA and VA mortgages is, say, $5\frac{1}{4}$ percent, money from these lenders would tend automatically to shift into or out of the FHA and VA mortgage market as the yield on government bonds fluctuated below or above 4 percent.

If there were literally no way of modifying a legal requirement that the interest rate on FHA and VA mortgages not exceed the prescribed maximum, this mechanistic relation between Treasury bond yields and required net yields on Federally underwritten mortgages would mean that funds for government-insured and guaranteed loans would virtually dry up whenever the spread between the two yields fell below the calculated required amount.   To an extent this is literally how things work; some lenders do shy away from guaranteed mortgages when the spread between government bond rates and nominal VA and FHA mortgage rates narrows to an unacceptable degree. But for the most part, a similar effect is achieved somewhat differently. In a period of generally rising interest rates and falling government bond prices, the prices of guaranteed mortgages to secondary lenders do not remain fixed; rather, the mortgages are sold to such lenders at a discount, which raises the effective rate of interest received on the loan.

However, while this practice makes the behavior of insured and guaranteed mortgages, under changing general credit conditions, roughly comparable to that of conventional mortgages from the perspective of the ultimate lender, it does not make them comparable from the viewpoints of house buyers and house builders. For the discount paid the lender cannot legally be added into the interest charges that are to be spread over the duration of the loan; it must be paid in one lump sum at the time of the financing transaction. Under VA regulations the discount—which, for example, on a $10,000 mortgage selling at $9,500 would be $500—tends to be borne by the builder and, in a period of generally tightening credit, quickly dulls his appetite for marketing houses with VA financing. Under FHA regulations the discount is almost entirely borne by the buyer and adds substantially to the very dimension of price to which his decision to buy is most sensitive: the down payment.[18]

These two sets of factors go far toward explaining the approximate tendency for residential construction to fluctuate contracyclically in the 1950s. The Federal Reserve followed a policy of tightening money rather promptly in times of expanding business activity and easing it in times of recession. In consequence, mortgage funds were more readily available to borrowers (i.e., on more attractive down payment and maturity terms) in periods of declining business activity than in times of boom.[19] And because of the rigidities in the FHA and VA maximum rates, most of the variation in mortgage lending took place in the government-guaranteed market. Indeed, conventionally financed residential construction, despite substantial fluctuation in interest rates, was remarkably stable.

In the 1960s, however, after the Kennedy administration took office, changes in government policy produced a somewhat different result. First, the Federal Reserve, even after the recovery of 1961–1962 was well advanced, followed a policy described by some as one of "passive ease." More particularly, as we noted in Chapter 11, Federal Reserve authorities attempted to prevent long-term rates (including mortgage rates) from rising significantly while permitting short-term rates to move up for balance-of-payments reasons. And the FHA and VA attempted to put downward pressure on mortgage rates

---

[18] It is probably true that, in the long run, mortgage discounts on VA guaranteed mortgages, if they are persistent, are also passed on to the buyer via higher prices than would otherwise prevail—in spite of VA regulations and appraisal standards.

[19] This kind of contracyclical performance, it should be noted, could be expected to occur only in a period when declines in business activity are relatively minor. A major depression would no doubt shake the confidence of both lenders and borrowers and would lead to a curtailment of both borrowing and lending in spite of easy money.

generally by lowering maximum rates on FHA and VA mortgages and then holding them at this lower level during the subsequent expansion. The Federal National Mortgage Association supported this policy in its own buying policies. The result, as the logic of our above analysis would suggest, was a sharp drop in the volume of new FHA and VA mortgages. But on this occasion, the *total* volume of residential mortgage lending did not decline. Instead, conventional mortgage lending expanded by more than enough to offset the decline in FHA and VA mortgages. The reasons for this upsurge in conventional mortgage lending seem to be primarily the fact that, although FHA and VA mortgages were relatively unattractive to lenders, conventional mortgages were not. Further, there is some reason to believe that conventional lenders (chiefly savings and loan associations), via improved efficiency and the organization of private mortgage insurance companies, were able to compete more effectively with FHA and VA mortgages.

The implications of all this for the forecaster are that some indication of developments in residential construction can be gleaned from probable near-term trends in government bond yields relative to administratively prescribed FHA and VA nominal interest rates, or by doing the equivalent— anticipating trends in discounts on government-insured and -guaranteed mortgages. When the FHA and VA are largely out of the market, however, further reductions in the spread between bond yields and FHA and VA maximums are not likely to have much effect. In this event, the forecaster must appraise the effect of credit conditions on the availability of *conventional* mortgage money and this, as we have seen, is a much less simple and mechanistic matter. It is probably correct to say, however, that an abrupt and substantial change in yields on alternative forms of investment, including, notably, government bonds, could have a pronounced impact on the availability of mortgage funds and hence on residential construction.[20] A more gradual shift, however, is not likely to have the same degree of effect because, as we noted above, conventional mortgage rates do respond, though sluggishly, to changing money market conditions.

Financial Aspects of the Demand for Mortgage Money

In some discussions much attention is given to purely financial considerations on the demand side of the mortgage market, but if we are trying to

---

[20] To repeat, constraint on the availability of mortgage funds usually takes the form of higher down payment and maturity requirements, plus tighter screening of the credit rating of prospective borrowers. But occasionally, it is a direct constraint. Speculative builders need a financing commitment from a lender before launching a new residential construction project. In a tight mortgage money situation, lenders may simply reduce the number of units they will commit to finance. Or—and this practice is common in large-scale lenders dealing with large-scale builders—the lender may commit himself to finance, say, 1,000 housing units, provided that the money stops whenever the builder falls short of his sales schedule by a given number of units. Thus, an increase in local vacancies is promptly reflected in a drying up of mortgage money.

anticipate short-run *changes* in demand, such an emphasis can easily be exaggerated. It is true, of course, that variations in households' cash holdings alter their ability to make down payments. But consumers are likely to be superliquid in their own view only after the kind of forced liquid saving that occurred in World War II. In more normal times, to be sure, they may be uncomfortably illiquid after particularly heavy bouts of buying, and for this reason it is wise for the housing forecaster to check the available current data on personal liquidity.

Alarm often is voiced about the capacity of aggregate households to absorb additional mortgage debt in view of the way mortgage indebtedness has been rising relative to disposable personal income since World War II. A somewhat similar alarm has been expressed about an alleged deterioration in the quality of mortgage debt, caused chiefly by unduly vigorous competition among lending institutions for business. The first of these anxieties does not appear to have much relevance, at least to short-run analysis. Mortgage indebtedness has risen relative to income because at higher levels of real income, consumers have been able to devote a larger proportion of their income to luxuries and quasi luxuries, one of which is expenditures (mortgage payments or rent) for bigger and better housing. Other important contributing influences have been the shift toward lower down payments that the government-guaranteed programs have achieved and the pronounced trend in the post-World War II period toward increased home ownership. The first of these factors certainly is not going to be reversed, and the second, in spite of the shift toward apartments in the 1960s, will probably only be slowed. Further, the existing level of mortgage debt would appear in itself to have very little bearing on the future demand for new housing. Most households not making mortgage payments are paying rent. The carrying charges on existing mortgages do not displace anyone's ability to buy new housing and give new mortgages—unless it is that rare household that wants to own two households simultaneously. Indeed, to amortize one mortgage is the best means available to most households for building the equity they need for buying a better house and assuming a new mortgage. Unless they are assuming the calamity of general deflation, those who point with alarm to the mounting "overhang" of mortgage debt as a threat to the housing market seem to be building a bugaboo that the short-run forecaster can safely ignore.

The concern about the quality of mortgage debt has relevance only if the deterioration is in fact real—which is by no means proved—and if adverse economic conditions expose the deterioration in quality and thus affect the lending policies of mortgage lending institutions. While we do not mean to minimize the undesirable economic consequences that an actual and significant deterioration in the quality of outstanding mortgage debt could have in a period of deflation, this, again, is a possibility that the short-run forecaster—unless his prognosis indicates significant deflation—can usually leave out of his calculations.

THE SUPPLY AND PRICE SITUATION

In the usual short-run forecasting situation the outlook for private house building will depend largely on the factors already surveyed. However, there are several other considerations relating to the supply, and to the supply prices, of housing that a careful analyst will review before formulating his estimate of new residential construction.

In the first place, it is possible that shortages of construction materials or labor will hold house building activity below buyers' intentions. It is not often that such shortages cause other than local constraints on residential building, but occasionally they do. And when such shortages do occur, their origin can often be found outside the residential construction industry per se, because supplies such as lumber, cement, roofing, and plumbing materials are used in many other kinds of construction, and carpenters, electricians, plumbers, and masons can also take jobs in nonresidential construction or even in nonconstruction types of employment.[21] It is therefore necessary for the analyst to look beyond the residential construction industry itself to spot possible supply limitations on residential building.

In the second place, there is the matter of new house prices. Here we do not refer to price simply as a dimension of total outlays, which must be estimated in order to convert a units or starts forecast into an expenditures forecast; this step is mentioned below. Rather the reference is to price as a determinant of demand—to the price-elasticity-of-demand issue. And here there are several partially distinct considerations. The first is any clearly established trend in new housing costs, and hence prices, relative to general consumer prices. This is a matter about which the general forecaster should be slow to develop any firm opinion at the first-approximation stage of his analysis before he has any clear view of the economy's overall relationship between demand and capacity in the forecast period. Moreover, as already indicated, probably house buying is not nearly so responsive to changes in total house prices as it is to changes in the down payment and monthly payment dimensions of price. And the latter are apt to be more sharply altered in the short run by changes in credit conditions than in construction costs.

A second, more specific, aspect of the supply-price situation is the comparison between owner-occupant costs for new housing, on the one hand, and, on the other, rents. Since residential rents are quite sticky, any extant trend in this relationship may have significance for the coming year. Often it is assumed that a rise of buying costs relative to rents, by dampening purchases for occupancy, will slow down residential construction activity. After a time such a trend in relative prices, of course, should stimulate rental construction. But in the short run, a disequilibrium between rents and construction costs can have a significant effect on the demand for new housing.

A third, more significant, aspect of the supply-price situation involves

---

[21] For example, Detroit contractors report that a boom in automobile production invariably means a shortage of electricians in residential construction.

the comparative price changes for new and used houses. Unfortunately in this case, however, the analyst must rely upon his own and others' impressions and upon some extremely sketchy factual reporting. The Departments of Labor and Commerce maintain some serial information on new house prices, but in a form not adequately deflated for changes in average unit size and quality. The only published information comparing prices paid for old and new houses is of a rough, mostly qualitative character; it appears in certain publications of the United States Saving and Loan League and of the National Association of Real Estate Boards.

FRAMING A HOUSING FORECAST

It now will be useful to summarize the various phases of a residential construction outlook analysis that already have been considered and to note, additionally, certain other steps that are needed to complete and reinforce the forecasting procedure.

1. To begin with, it is well to build up a working estimate of the normal physical requirements for new dwelling units in the United States in the coming year. Just for illustrative purposes—the following numbers are arbitrary and are not meant to be estimates for any specified period—such a calculation might run like this:

	Housing units	
1. Net family formation	920,000	
2. Undoubling	0	
3. Net change in single-member and nonfamily households	200,000	
4. Equals: Net household formation	1,120,000	
5. Net change in vacancies	50,000	
6. Equals: Net expansion requirement		1,170,000
7. Accidental losses	70,000	
8. Demolitions, condemnations, and other business and government withdrawals from the housing stock	280,000	
9. Net change from mergers and conversions	0	
10. Equals: Replacement requirement		350,000
11. Total requirement		1,520,000

Estimates for 1, 2, and 3 may be made separately, or the forecaster may proceed to net household formation directly, using Census Bureau or other projections of net household formation, modified to reflect the analyst's judgment as to how past birthrates and economic and other conditions may affect marriage rates, doubling and undoubling, and nonfamily households in the particular year under consideration.

The estimate for the net change in vacancies should reflect a composite of variables. First, are current vacancy ratios enough out of line with normal levels to call for a correction? Second, how are migrations, especially from rural to urban areas, likely to affect the number of vacancies? (The analyst should remember that projections of vacancies, such as those in the Atkinson article cited earlier, already assume a migration from farm areas.) Third, is there likely to be a significant change in second houses that would affect the vacancy figure?

Again, steps 7, 8, and 9 may be taken separately, or the analyst may move directly to step 10, recognizing that the major determinants of changes in the rate of withdrawals from the housing stock are not losses from fire, etc., but government programs (e.g., urban renewal, highways) and the level of business activity itself. Because the necessary data for constructing an independent estimate of withdrawals are largely lacking, the analyst may again wish to rely primarily on official projections of average withdrawals, modified as necessary in his judgment to reflect forces at work in the particular year being forecast.

In reviewing the physical sources of housing demand, the analyst will, of course, compare his estimate of the normal housing requirement with the figure for actual housing starts in the current year as reported by the Bureau of Labor Statistics. The lower the latter is relative to the former, the stronger will be the response in housing outlays that a given improvement in the income situation or in buyers' access to easy mortgage money will be expected to evoke.

2. House building has a significant, but not a closely calibrated, relationship to disposable personal income. Therefore in the first-approximation phase of a residential construction forecasting effort in which a normal growth in incomes is being initially hypothesized, there is little point in lingering over the effects of the income variable. However, if a less buoyant initial income hypothesis is adopted because at the time of the forecast the economy's performance already has become sluggish, consumer incomes and expectations of income can be expected to dampen the vector of change running from actual current starts to what has been calculated as the physical requirement for starts in the forecast period. Moreover, if, later on in the analysis, a discrepancy crops up between the initial income hypothesis and actual income prospects, some adjustment in the housing forecast may be needed. But past behavior does not suggest any generalized rule for quantifying the relationship.

3. Usually credit factors are the ones that put the finish on a short-run housing forecast. The crucial influences are changes in down payments and monthly payments, and the determinants of these influences which bear particular watching are (a) changes in VA and FHA regulations and (b) changes in general credit conditions—especially, in the latter instance, the relationship of government bond yields to nominal maximum interest rates on government-guaranteed mortgages and to going interest rates on conventional mortgages.

Because of the intervention of other variables there is no fixed relationship between degree of change in mortgage terms and degree of impact on housing starts. However, some insight into this can be gathered from the records of past periods when credit conditions similar to those anticipated for the forecast period were in effect. Historical analogy also sheds some light on another element in the problem: the lag that should be assumed between changes in general credit conditions or in VA and FHA regulations and the impact on starts. This is bound to be at least a month or two and, in the aggregate—the record suggests—is apt to be something closer to six months.

4. As suggested just a few paragraphs back, it is well to decide at this point in the analysis whether to modify one's housing-starts forecast in the light of supply or supply-price considerations.

5. The forecast of housing starts must be converted into an expenditure estimate that can be incorporated into the demand model. In the first place, this means establishing an average unit-value figure for the period's new residential construction. The questions involved are (a) whether the average size and quality of newly constructed units are apt to change and (b) whether the prices of units of given sizes and qualities will change. One's preceding analysis is likely to have established a reasonably clear view of the first point. As noted already, only those cost and price changes—notably in construction wages—which are relatively impervious to short-run fluctuations in housing demand should be assumed at this first-approximation stage of the demand analysis. On the other hand, if the analyst foresees a significant change in the proportion of multifamily units to total units, he should divide his forecast into single-family and multifamily components, and forecast average values for each, because the cost per unit of multifamily units is typically significantly lower than it is for single-family residences. In converting the forecast to a dollar figure it also is desirable, although not vital, to allow for the lag of changes in construction outlays behind changes in housing starts. The average lag indicated by a comparison of the two series is about two months, with the interval somewhat more pronounced in upswings than downswings.

6. The forecasted outlay for new dwelling units must be supplemented with figures for additions and alterations and for nonhousekeeping units to obtain a comprehensive estimate for private residential construction. The latter of these items is sufficiently small that a simple trend extrapolation should not, as a practical matter, endanger the forecast. Or the forecaster could base his estimate on last year's figure modified to reflect observable trends in construction of hotels, motels, and the like. Outlays on additions and alterations, however, present a more significant problem. These expenditures are related, not to new construction, but to the existing stock of housing. Furthermore, because enlarging or improving an old house is an alternative to buying a new one, an a priori case could be made for a negative correlation between expenditures for additions and alterations and for new housing con-

struction. The current state of the data on past expenditures for additions and alterations, however, precludes any meaningful time-series analysis of the correlation between these two types of housing expenditures, or between expenditures for additions and alterations and other possible determinants of demand. Such evidence as there is seems to indicate that, although the demographic and credit determinants of new housing construction also have their effects on expenditures for additions and alterations, the primary short-run determinant—in contrast to new house construction—is income. If this conclusion is correct—and we emphasize that more research needs to be done as soon as the data permit—the forecaster can base his forecast primarily on his preliminary income hypothesis, to be modified later if his hypothesis proves to be in error. Some additional indication can be gained from the Department of Commerce's periodic survey of consumer buying intentions which indicates household intentions to make major expansions or improvements in existing houses.[22] Further, those general factors (including family-size considerations) which suggest a change in the real unit value of new construction may also indicate a trend in additions and alterations.

7. Also, to obtain the residential structures component of GNP, the forecaster needs a figure for real estate commissions and net transfers of structures between sectors. Fortunately, the figure is small enough and stable enough that no significant error is likely to be involved if he simply plugs in last year's figure.

8. The available cross bearings on the housing outlook should not be overlooked. The F. W. Dodge Corporation's series on new residential construction contract awards and the series on applications for FHA and VA loans suffer from the same difficulty noted for the series on commercial and industrial construction contract awards in the preceding chapter. The lags of expenditures behind the commitments appear to be very irregular. However, they often provide a sense of the direction in which residential construction activity is going that serves either to confirm the analyst's own impression or to challenge him to reexamine it. The National Association of Home Builders does periodic surveys of builders' intentions. Although these surveys pertain only to metropolitan areas and are incomplete in their builder coverage, they do provide a useful clue to the way in which the builders themselves are assessing the demand for housing in their own communities. In the same way, the findings of the survey of consumer buying intentions—with respect to the fraction of the households surveyed that contemplated, early in the year, new house purchases—should be considered. And, as usual, a general forecaster should give careful attention to what other analysts, particularly specialists on the housing market, are saying. A good starting point in this last respect is the formal forecast of the coming year's residential construction jointly prepared by the Departments of Labor and Commerce and usually published in the November issue of *Construction Review.*

---

[22] See *Current Population Reports*, ser. P-65, *Consumer Buying Indicators.*

AUTOMOBILES AND PARTS

The automobile is not only about the most expensive commodity that the United States National Income Division classifies as durable consumer goods but it is on several counts the most distinctive. It is the only one for which there is an extensive, highly organized used-commodity market. It accounts for a much higher proportion of total consumer durable outlays than does any other single commodity. And, most significantly, automobile purchases are by far the most variable of the major consumer durable components.

As Figure 20–1 indicates, total expenditures on consumer durables have been subject to year-to-year variation roughly comparable to those in new house buying and greater than the relative changes in nonresidential fixed investment. But the great bulk of the volatility in consumer durables as a whole has been concentrated in the purchases of new automobiles and parts. Consumer expenditures for durables other than automobiles have been quite stable; the relatively minor variations from year to year are correlated with variations in DPI.[23]   In this respect, they much more closely resemble non-durable goods and services than they do automobiles. Indeed, the stability of the relationship of consumer expenditures for nondurables and services to DPI is improved when we add durables other than automobiles to nondurables and services. For this reason, we shall reserve our consideration of techniques for forecasting consumer expenditures for durables excluding automobiles for the chapter covering nondurables and services, and confine our attention in the present chapter to the one item of consumer expenditures that, in the short run, has behaved as a semiautonomous variable: automobiles.

THE STATISTICS

Perhaps because the automobile is such a popular item of consumption and such a major source of employment, statistics about one aspect or another of the automobile industry are abundant and widely quoted. Indeed, there is probably no other consumer good for which there is such a wealth of statistical information. Some of the most current and reliable statistical series are not directly relevant to our task, which is to forecast the component of PCE, automobiles and parts. Nevertheless, a brief review of the relationship between some of these statistical series may avoid confusion and error in the forecasting exercise.

First, an obvious point: We are talking about automobiles, not motor

[23] The ratio of PCE for durables excluding automobiles to DPI has fluctuated within a narrow range and inversely with the ratio of nondurables and services to DPI, suggesting that consumers consider many durables other than automobiles to be substitutes for or alternatives to nondurables. Actually, the definitional line separating durable from nondurable goods is by broad groupings and therefore somewhat arbitrary. It is one with which some housewives would disagree. A fur coat, for example, is classified as nondurable, whereas inexpensive jewelry is classified as durable.

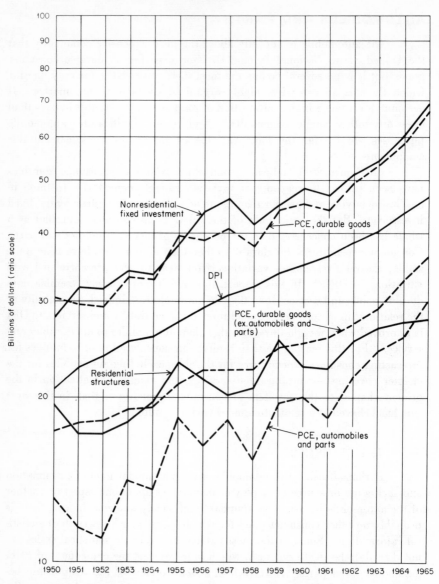

Figure **20–1.**   Expenditures for various types of durable goods, and disposable personal income by year, 1950–1965.   Source: *Survey of Current Business*, U.S. Department of Commerce.

vehicles, which would include trucks and buses. In the national income accounts, it is assumed that any trucks purchased by persons are for business purposes, not for personal consumption.

Second, as pertains to automobiles only, we need to understand the conceptual relationship between the frequently cited automobile production figure ("a 10-million car year") and our GNP component.   This relationship may be summarized as follows:

1.   Production (number of cars)
2. Minus: Increase in factory inventories (number)
3. Equals: Factory sales (number)
4. Minus: Exports (number)
5. Plus: Imports (number)
6. Equals: Domestic factory and import sales (number)
7. Minus: Increase in dealer new car inventories (number)
8. Equals: Domestic sales by dealers (number)
9. Minus: Sales to government and business (number)
10. Equals: Sales to consumers (number)
11. Times: Average price paid per car
12. Equals: Sales to consumers (dollars)
13. Plus: Sales of parts and accessories
14. Plus: Dealer markups (gross margins) on used cars sold to consumers
15. Equals: Personal consumption expenditures for cars and parts

The above conceptual tabulation is largely self-explanatory, but one or two comments are in order. (1) The tabulation above, through item 10, is in numbers of automobiles. It could also have been presented in value terms, in which case step 11 would, of course, be omitted. (2) The price paid per car is the gross price, not the balance net of trade-in. Further, the proper figure for inclusion in GNP is the actual price paid, not the manufacturer's list price. If Commerce were to tabulate at list prices, dealer markups on used cars could possibly be a negative figure because nominal trade-in allowances often exceed the resale price of the traded-in car. (3) The average price paid per car includes optional equipment and accessories incorporated in the car when delivered. This means that, even though prices of a fixed-equipment-specification car might not change, average prices paid would rise if consumers purchased cars equipped with more extras. Also, the average price paid will vary with the brand and model mix of current sales. For example, if consumers shift from standards to compacts, *ceteris paribus*, the average price paid declines. (4) Used-car sales, as such, are not included in PCE, automobiles, as indeed they should not be if the GNP accounts are to measure the current value of newly produced goods and services. However, Commerce reasons that when a dealer reconditions, warehouses, and sells a used car, he is "producing" a portion of the value (retail sale price) of the used car. For this reason, dealer *markups* (though literally a service) are included in PCE, automobiles. (5) Current data on numbers of cars sold to consumers are not available, partly because of the statistical difficulties created by the fact that cars are frequently used for both personal and business purposes. A Bureau of Public Roads survey made prior to 1958, however, indicated that 83 percent of the sales of new cars and gross margins on used cars, after deducting sales to government (roughly $0.1 billion in the mid-1960s), was allocable to personal consumption expenditures. This number was subsequently revised to 85 percent. At this writing Commerce allocates total expenditures for new cars and for used-car margins, after deducting government purchases, on this 85-15 basis. (6) An incidental point, the relevance of which will become evident later in the chapter: data on PCE for automobile parts and accessories are published on an annual basis only.

THE NEW AUTOMOBILE MARKET

Americans—persons, businesses, and governments—own about as many automobiles as they do dwelling units, and the numbers of annual net additions to the two stocks typically do not differ greatly. It is in the matter of replacement demand that the contrast is most marked. In automobiles, replacement demand not only is more volatile than expansion demand but quantitatively it vastly outweighs the other. Because the average house lasts so much longer than the average automobile, people usually buy several times as many new cars as new houses and typically spend about as much on the one as on the other.

Expansion Demand

The expansion demand for automobiles can be thought of as depending on net household formation and on changes in the ratio of the total consumer stock of automobiles to total households. In forecasting the ratio of automobiles to households, however, simple extrapolation is risky business. A number of relevant considerations need to be taken into account.

The determinant that one would naturally think of first is income. Disposable personal income obviously is a determinant of the demand for automobiles. However, as Figure 20–1 shows, between 1950 and 1965 relative fluctuations in expenditures for new cars were much greater than the almost imperceptible fluctuations in DPI. Further, the correlation between annual increments in DPI and in PCE, cars and parts, though positive, is not impressively high. Also, there is no clear evidence of a lead-lag relationship. It thus seems that, although variations in DPI give some indication of the general *zone* of consumer demand for new automobiles (and therefore are relevant for long-run projections), they are not very useful for short-run forecasting. We must look largely to other determinants for an explanation of annual and quarterly fluctuations in consumer demand for new automobiles.

One such determinant is income *expectations,* which are important because automobile purchases are so often credit-financed and installment loans must be amortized out of future income. The Consumer Research Center at the University of Michigan makes periodic sample studies of consumer attitudes toward the general business outlook, prices, and personal finances. Such attitudes are not synonymous with personal income expectations, but for consumers *in the aggregate,* it is probably safe to assume that optimistic expectations in general are rather closely translated into optimistic personal income expectations, and vice versa in the case of pessimistic expectations. These surveys seem to indicate that changes in consumer attitudes do explain a significant portion of changes over time in consumer demand for automobiles.[24]

Another such determinant is changes in the age distribution of the population. Teen-agers are notorious would-be or actual consumers of automobiles. An upsurge in the proportion of the population composed of teen-agers, such as occurred in 1963–1966, adds to aggregate demand for automobiles in two ways. First, a powerful stimulus to two-car (or three-car) ownership is provided when Junior brings pressure on Dad to put him on wheels. Second—a consideration more relevant to replacement demand that we shall discuss in a moment—teen-ager demand for automobiles is often satiable by a used car, perhaps even a jalopy. Prices of such old cars are therefore bolstered, making it easier for present car owners to trade for new cars.

Another consideration is the locational pattern of residency. The postwar shift to suburbia obviously was a strong inducement to two-car ownership, and as commuting distances became longer, the strength of the inducement increased.[25] Similarly, increases in the availability of high-speed highways have made commuting by automobile more attractive and, in many instances, feasible when it would otherwise be virtually impossible, given an eight-hour workday in a twenty-four-hour day. For this reason, the Interstate Highway Program, which produced little in the way of accumulated tangible results prior to about 1960, subsequently served as a significant stimulator of multiple-car ownership.

Still another determinant of the automobiles-to-households ratio is automobile prices. Automobile demand for replacement purposes is presumed to be quite price-elastic;[26] the demand for second cars is probably even more price-elastic. If it is, automobile producers (including foreign producers of such cars as the Volkswagen) go far toward determining the demand for second cars when they set their list prices.

One more determinant (not entirely distinct from those already discussed) is a complex of factors that determine the feasibility and desirability of "no-car" ownership. As late as mid-1965, an estimated 23 percent of the households in the United States owned no car at all. In substantial part, these households went without cars for income reasons. For some households, how-

[24] See F. Gerard Adams, "Consumer Attitudes, Buying Plans, and Purchases of Durable Goods: A Principal Components, Time Series Approach," *The Review of Economics and Statistics*, vol. XLVI, pp. 347ff., November, 1964. It is interesting that variations in consumer attitudes do *not* explain a significant proportion of the variation in expenditures for durables other than automobiles—a finding that is consistent with our forecasting plan of treating automobiles separately from other durables.

[25] Presumably, at some distance, the inducement should diminish, or alternative methods of commuting (e.g., trains) begin to look relatively more attractive.

[26] That is, a 1 percent change in car prices relative to other prices is apt, other things being equal, to induce an opposite change in unit sales of more than 1 percent.

ever, particularly those in congested areas in large metropolitan areas, it was a matter of voluntary choice. And it is quite conceivable that increased urbanization may swing the pendulum in the other direction, the disadvantages of automobile ownership to some families more than offsetting the advantages of multiple-car ownership to others.

After he has analyzed the impacts of these and perhaps other determinants of the number of cars per household, the forecaster can readily project the recent ratio into the forecast period, multiply it by the same household projection that he used in estimating expenditures for residential structures, and calculate probable expansion demand.

Replacement Demand

As in housing, the people who buy new cars seldom are the same people who decide to scrap old cars; and total decisions to scrap must match total replacement purchases if the used-car market is not to become glutted, thereby pulling down used-car values and tending to dampen new car sales.

But there is this important difference: in automobiles the scrappage rate is much more responsive to the replacement demand for newly produced items than it is in housing. Unlike old houses, old cars are not tied to valuable pieces of land that must be disposed of advantageously at the same time the vehicles are scrapped. Most decisions to scrap are made by dealers who have taken in aging vehicles in trade, and they are based on straightforward profit-maximizing considerations. Although the rate of physical deterioration obviously exercises a general influence on such decisions, most cars that are scrapped could run a good deal longer if they had adequate repairs. They are scrapped simply because, given current used-car prices, their resale value, less repair and other costs that would be involved in reselling them, falls short of their scrap value.

This means that when the replacement demand for new cars rises relative to the demand for used cars, thereby raising the used-car supply and exerting a downward pressure on used-car prices, scrappage picks up quickly. This flushes out more of the old vehicles, checks the downward trend in used-car prices, and limits the drag that used-car prices would otherwise place on new car demand. Thus in the automobile market the explanation of the volume of replacement demand centers much more exclusively than it does in housing around the desire and financial ability of owners of existing units to trade them for newly produced units.

Unhappily, the all-important remaining question of what determines decisions to trade up is an extraordinarily slippery one. Certainly income, in replacement demand as in expansion demand, is a part of the story, at least in the long run, and in the short run when there are sizable changes in disposable personal income. Price is again a factor although, as we suggested earlier, replacement demand may not be quite so price-elastic as expansion demand. And credit conditions, the impact of which is discussed below, are important.

But the foregoing by no means exhausts the list of major determinants. A number of other influences, much more difficult to quantify, affect the replacement demand for automobiles.

First, a negative point: consumer decisions to buy new cars are not planned very firmly or far in advance. Usually such decisions can be easily moved forward or backward through time, not only by households' income experience and expectations, but by the influences that are brought to bear on consumers from outside. It is probably for this reason that the Census Bureau surveys of intentions to buy automobiles have a rather limited horizon.

Second, there is the powerful factor of models and model changes. Upon no other commodity in the world is so much costly effort expended to create obsolescence, and there is no other for which the effort succeeds so well. But both the effort and the success vary from year to year.

Third, the intensity of the selling effort in a particular year often makes a good deal of difference. Selling effort is partly a matter of price, especially when the effective retail price is recognized as involving all the complex dimensions of discounts, trade-in allowances, service guarantees, and adjustments for optional equipment. But, in addition, the net sales pressure on consumers can be intensified by all manner of televised and other promotional activities, by salesmen's contests, and by the hungry competition of the auctions and of used-car dealers who bootleg and supermarket the new models.

Fourth—and this is a factor that partly determines the intensity of the selling effort just discussed—the organization and market structure of the automobile industry give manufacturers some degree of control over retail sales volume. With three companies accounting for more than 96 percent of domestic production, the industry is one of the most concentrated at the manufacturing level. Moreover, under existing franchise arrangements, manufacturers are in a position to threaten dealers with cancellation or nonrenewal of their franchises unless dealers pursue the marketing goals and objectives set by the manufacturers.[27] Put this structure together with the sensitivity of

[27] There are many other ways that the manufacturers can "encourage" dealers to adhere to their policies. These include: delays in processing dealer orders, mistakes in filling orders, delays in making reimbursements, and the ultimate threat—the appointment of a "stimulator" dealer in the dealer's territory. See *A Study of the Antitrust Laws*, Subcommittee on Antitrust Policy of Committee on the Judiciary, 84th Cong., 2d Sess., part 6, S.D. 67272, 1956, p. 2759; *ibid.*, part 8, p. 3845. See also Charles M. Hewitt, *Automotive Franchise Agreements*, Richard D. Irwin, Inc., Homewood, Ill., 1956.

Since the enactment of the *Automobile Dealer Franchise Act* (15 U.S.C. secs. 1221–1225) in 1956 the manufacturers must exercise caution concerning the degree and type of pressure exerted on dealers. Although the law has eliminated some of the abusive practices, it only penalizes the use of "coercion and intimidation" and does not reach the basic underlying disparity in bargaining power. In Galbraith's phrase the "countervailing" power of the individual dealer is still weak relative to the power of the manufacturer. For a discussion of the operation of this law see Charles M. Hewitt, "The Development of Automobile Franchises," Indiana Business Information Bulletin no. 37, Bureau of Business Research, Indiana University, Bloomington, Ind., 1960.

sales to the intensity of retail selling, and you have this possibility: manufacturers can raise production and, by pushing the extra output into retail inventories, thereby force a harder sell, squeeze dealers' unit margins, and raise retail sales.

Obviously such producer control of retail automobile sales does not begin to be absolute. For production to accelerate sales, consumers' incomes must be receptive; credit must be available (although with the producers owning or partially controlling a large portion of personal finance facilities, this is not an entirely exogenous variable); consumers must have some tolerance for further indebtedness; and if they have just been supersold last year or the year before, it may be harder to do the trick again.

THE IMPACT OF FINANCE

During the decade and a half prior to 1966, as Figure 20–2 shows, the proportion of disposable personal income devoted to personal saving and to automobile and parts expenditures has fluctuated considerably. But the fluctuation has been inversely related, so that the sum of the two has been more

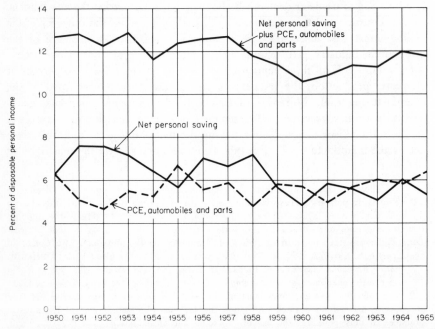

Figure **20–2.**   Net personal saving and personal consumption expenditures for automobiles and parts as a percent of disposable personal income, 1950–1965. Source: *Survey of Current Business,* U.S. Department of Commerce.

stable than either of the components.[28]   It often is hypothesized that, in consumer decision making, additions to real assets in the form of automobiles and household hardware are more closely substitutable with net additions to liquid assets, i.e., net personal liquid saving, than they are with purchases of consumer soft goods and services.   The chart provides some confirmation for this view.

There is nothing mysterious about this inverse relationship.   To buy major durables most consumers either must use previously accumulated liquid holdings or go into debt.   In both cases, given our classification of the purchases as consumption, they dissave.   Similarly, they save, largely at the expense of the more postponable items in their budgets, when they replenish their liquid balances; and they save when they pay off installment debt.

The primary causal relationship between consumer-durables buying and installment credit probably is that flowing from the former to the latter. Variations in consumers' desire to buy durables, particularly automobiles, cause fluctuations in new installment-credit extensions.   But credit conditions also have some causal impact on sales.   This is of two sorts.

In the first place, there is the matter of credit availability.   Installment-lending policies, particularly of commercial banks, are affected by the general monetary situation.   This exercises some dampening or stimulating effect on sales of consumer items that are typically credit-financed.   However, the responsiveness of consumer credit extensions to general monetary conditions is overrated.   For one thing, the flexibility of installment interest rates and consumers' comparative imperviousness to high rates makes consumer loans highly profitable outlets for funds in periods of tight money.   In addition, the capacity of the auto industry for aggressive merchandising plus its control of a segment of the personal finance business mean that even in periods when the overall money supply is tightest, funds can be made available—at a price— for just about as many new car buyers as the manufacturers want to finance.

Usually a more telling consideration than the availability of installment credit is the willingness and the ability of consumers to shoulder more such indebtedness.   This issue usually is discussed in terms of what total burden of consumer debt relative to disposable income can be safely and comfortably supported, but such speculations really are not of much practical help to the short-run forecaster.   On the one hand, he can see that the rise of total installment debt relative to income in recent years has not necessarily been bad or threatening.   Presumably it reflects the facts that (1) as their incomes grow, consumers prefer to spend relatively more of their incomes on big-ticket durables that are typically debt-dependent and (2) the much wider use of regu-

---

[28] It is significant, however, that the sum has not been entirely stable, declining in 1954 (a recession year), 1958–1960 (two recessions), and rising again in 1960–1964 (expansion).   We shall return to this point in Chap. 23, when we note that the ratio of consumer expenditures *excluding* automobiles to DPI behaves in the opposite manner; i.e., it tends to rise in recessions and decline in expansions.

larized amortization procedures has reduced the psychic burden associated with given volumes of debt relative to income. At the same time, it is hard to believe that net installment-credit expansion can keep on indefinitely at its rate of recent years. But such reflections only leave the analyst in a quandary as far as any given coming year is concerned.

A more practical approach to the issue of consumers' tolerance for new debt in a coming year may be the following. First, assume until it is proved otherwise that any level of debt already achieved is supportable. Second, assume that the capacity to absorb new debt depends simply on consumers' ability to make new monthly payments. Third, assume that the fraction of total disposable personal income that can be allocated to monthly installment payments in the future, whether on new or old debt, will not vary much from what it has been in the recent past. Under these assumptions, a rapid expansion of installment purchases and debt creates claims on future income and cuts down the room for new contract buying until the old contracts have run their course.

This view of the matter squares nicely with the picture of reciprocating fluctuations in durables buying and personal saving that Figure 20-2 presents. To the forecaster it means that any current period in which installment debt has been rising notably faster than disposable personal income must be suspected of carrying its own built-in aftermath. A bulge in new debt now, by causing a bulge in repayments in the months to come, automatically creates a drag on further new installment-debt extensions.

In following this line of reasoning, however, the analyst should be wary of assuming that there is an *annual* pattern to this extension-repayment cycle. Especially if the excess of extensions over repayments is moderate, it can persist for years. And in a period of strong and uninterrupted economic expansion, as in 1961–1965, installment credit extensions can exceed repayments by a substantial margin for quite long periods of time. Eventually, however, if the rise in debt has been significantly above the rise in incomes, the day of reckoning must come. But there is no substitute for the use of judgment as to when the burden of accumulated consumer debt has become so heavy that a correction is in order.

Framing an Automobile Forecast

What is a forecaster to make of all this when he is groping for a first-approximation estimate of consumer outlays on new automobiles and parts in a coming year?

First, it may be somewhat instructive, as in the case of housing, to calculate in units what a normal volume of sales would be. By normal volume we mean the number corresponding to the expansion demand estimated from household projections and automobiles-to-households ratios, plus the replacement demand that would appear if the average scrappage age of old cars withdrawn from the consumer stock during the coming year should, let's say, equal the average age of cars scrapped during the past five years. However, because of the almost exclusive dependence of the replacement "requirement" on the desire of owners of existing cars for new ones, this normal volume estimate does not have nearly the independent significance in the auto case that it does in housing. It is therefore necessary to revise upward or downward this normal volume estimate by considering a number of other influences.

One of these influences might be the level of sales relative to estimated normal volume in a recent period of time, say, the current model year or the one just past. If sales have been notably out of line with normal, this in itself may introduce what might be called a "reaction factor" into the forecast. If sales have been held substantially below normal by supply shortages, the coming period may have a positive reaction. We should warn, however, against taking the "what goes up must come down" theory of forecasting very seriously, here as elsewhere. The experience of the first half of the decade of the 1960s demonstrated that it is possible, in the automobile market if not anatomically, to put not just two but several good years back to back.[29]

Second, if he has not already done so in making his normal demand estimate, the forecaster should give consideration to income effects, particularly income expectations. Although, as we said earlier, income variations have not accounted for much of the short-run variation in automobile demand, part of the reason is that, in the 1950s and 1960s, income (DPI) fluctuations have been relatively small. If the forecaster foresees a significant change in DPI, as incorporated in his preliminary income hypothesis, due allowance should be made for it. Or a finding by the Survey Research Center surveys indicating change in consumer attitudes toward the economic future would provide a basis for modifying the "normal" forecast.

Third, the following should also be considered as modifying factors: the rumored extent of the coming model changes; consumers' intentions to buy cars, as reported by the Census Bureau (at least worthy of attention); the prospects for credit availability and consumer willingness to assume new installment debt; all available indications of the hardness with which cars will be sold in the coming year, including the current state of dealers' inventories and margins and any available indications of manufacturers' attitudes toward the latter; and any notable retail price changes that may be indicated by changes in manufacturers' prices or by evident trends in dealer markups.

Fourth, no general forecaster should leave the automobile outlook without considering carefully what Detroit is saying. Detroit almost always is saying something on the subject, and with a little practice the analyst can

[29] It can be argued—and reasonably so, we believe—that the "good" automobile years of the early 1960s were not *notably* out of line with normal, and the fact that they seemed to be abnormal to some forecasters resulted from a failure to estimate "normal" properly. The record production and sales figures of 1955 were used uncritically as a measure of "goodness," without adequate attention to a number of the variables we have been discussing, especially growth in the number of households, the effect of the teen-ager explosion on the cars-to-households ratio, and the effects of the highway construction program.

rather easily learn to discount systematic biases in the for-publication views of some industry spokesmen and arrive at a fairly accurate composite view of what the industry actually expects.

Finally, having established a unit estimate, the analyst must translate this into a dollar-volume forecast, allowing for any prospective changes in average unit values, either as a result of price changes or of shifts toward higher- or lower-price models and more or fewer optional features and accessories, that an appraisal of the automobile market may have turned up.

PARTS AND ACCESSORIES

In logic, consumer expenditures for parts and accessories—the most important single items of which are tires and batteries—would seem to be a function of the existing stock of cars, their age, disposable personal income, and new car sales.[30] The authors have experimented with multiple correlation analysis of annual fluctuations in consumer expenditures for auto parts and accessories with various combinations of the variables listed. Our net conclusion is that, from a practical forecasting point of view, such techniques are not worth the time and effort they require.[31] Essentially as reliable forecasts can be made by simple extrapolation of recent trend, adjusted slightly to reflect the preliminary income hypothesis on which the forecast is based and any special influences of which the forecaster may have knowledge. Indeed, if the new car forecast indicates a rise in expenditures about proportionate to the rise in parts and accessories that such a projection would have yielded, some economies of arithmetic can be achieved by lumping the PCE components for new cars and net purchases of used cars, and parts and accessories, into a single figure, and calculating the "price" per car by dividing this figure for the year just past by the number of new cars purchased by consumers in that year. Then, after making proper allowance for change in model mix, in amounts of optional equipment installed in new cars, and actual price changes, the forecast figure of consumer purchases of new cars, in numbers of cars, can be multiplied by the adjusted "price" per car to obtain a forecast of total consumer expenditures for automobiles, net used-car purchases, and parts and accessories.

[30] We said earlier that accessories incorporated in the new car at time of sale are included in "new cars" rather than in "parts and accessories." This is Commerce's intent. However, Commerce advises that their estimating techniques may fail to catch all of such accessories, in which case the omitted items would be reflected in the parts and accessories category. Some accessories, of course, are added to new cars shortly after purchase. These two considerations may account in part for the fact that new car purchases appear to be a partial determinant of expenditures for parts and accessories. An even more probable explanation is the point discussed in a footnote early in this chapter: the inclusion of house trailers in automotive parts and accessories.

[31] This is not to say that they would not be worth the time and effort of, say, a tire manufacturer who was interested in fairly precise forecasts of tire demand.

21

INVENTORY INVESTMENT AND ORDER-SALES-INVENTORY RELATIONSHIPS

We now have discussed the formulation of first-approximation short-run forecasts for all but two of the quasi-autonomous sectors of the gross national product—the change in business inventories (or inventory investment) and net exports. The latter will be considered in the next chapter. Both of these components of aggregate demand are small, in absolute terms, but both are relatively volatile and difficult to forecast. Inventory investment, in particular, although a flyweight among the major GNP components, at times throws that weight around, in relative terms, more violently than any of the others.

Figure 21-1 makes the familiar point that the time path of the United States gross national product is notably smoothed when inventory investment is deducted from the total. A 1962 study done for the Joint Economic Committee found that inventory changes accounted for about 70 percent of the declines in GNP during the postwar recession periods, and for 13 percent of the increases in GNP during expansion periods. During the early stages of an expansion in GNP, inventory changes were more important than later in the expansion, accounting for 25 percent or more of the change in GNP

491

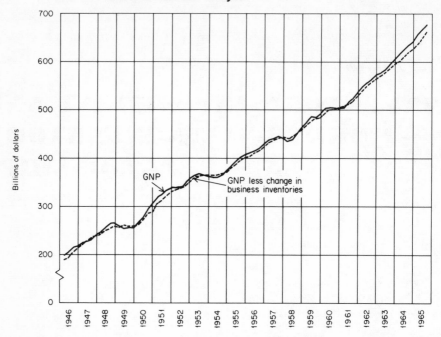

Figure **21–1.**   United States final demand, 1946–1965, including and excluding inventory investment.   (Seasonally adjusted annual
rates.)   Source: U.S. Department of Commerce.

during the first year of each postwar expansion.[1]   It does not necessarily
follow from this statistical evidence that inventory change *caused* fluctuations
in aggregate demand.   They may simply have augmented fluctuations initiated
by other events.   The sequence of events in an "inventory cycle" is a matter
to which we shall return later in the chapter.

The forecaster of inventory investment cannot make the same kind of
direct attack on his problem as is appropriate in most of the other demand
sectors.   There is no sector for which the projection of present levels or an
extrapolation of recent trends makes less sense.   And it is inappropriate to rely
simply on business intentions surveys, for, as we shall see, inventory changes
are not subject to the same degree of managerial control as are plant and
equipment outlays.   Indeed, since changes in inventories are so heavily
dependent on changes in sales, it is not possible to size up inventory investment
prospects until total sales prospects for the economy have begun to come into
reasonably clear focus.

Even then the analyst cannot attack his problem directly, for the GNP
component he is after—i.e., inventory investment—is a first difference of
something else: inventory levels themselves.   If he would understand inventory

[1] *The Role of Inventory Changes during Expansion and Contraction,* Joint Economic
Committee, 87th Cong., 2d Sess., 1962, p. 1 .

change, there is nothing for it but to dip rather extensively into the whole subject of the nature, functions, and behavior of business' commodity stocks. To begin with, he needs to know what the principal available factual sources are, and how they differ.

INVENTORY DATA IN THE UNITED STATES

THE AVAILABLE SERIES

There are two principal series of national inventory statistics in the United States. Both are calculated and published by the Department of Commerce. One, the GNP component already mentioned, reports the *changes* in business inventories, and can be found wherever a detailed breakdown of the gross national product is published. Like all national income series, it measures a flow or activity during a period, and like all the other GNP components, it is reported quarterly and annually and usually in the form of seasonally adjusted annual rates. It covers changes in the value of inventories held by *all* commodity-selling American businesses. Only a two-way breakdown of the GNP component is published quarterly—farm versus nonfarm. These inventory change series measure variations in inventory values after the inventory-valuation adjustment (IVA). That adjustment, you will remember, converts the value of inventory withdrawals during the period from a book- to a current-value basis.[2] Because inventory levels can either rise or fall over the course of a quarter or a year, the inventory change figure for a period can be either positive (accumulation) or negative (decumulation).

The other principal source of aggregative inventory data in the United States is the Department of Commerce's monthly series, both seasonally adjusted and unadjusted, on the dollar *level* of inventories in manufacturing and in wholesale and retail trade at the end of each month. Manufacturing and trade inventories do not cover agriculture, the other extractive industries, or construction. And the "wholesale" category covers merchant wholesalers only. The series reports business' own book valuations of its commodity stocks, not the revised valuations (i.e., after IVA) calculated by national income accountants.[3]

It would be a great convenience to the business forecaster if he were able to calculate for recent quarters, from currently published data, the change

---

[2] See the Appendix to Chap. 3.

[3] In addition to these conceptual differences in the two series of inventory data, two other statistical matters sometimes cause discrepancies between the two series: (1) revisions in the monthly end-of-month inventory series for recent years are often not incorporated into the NIA inventory change series until long after the revisions are made, and (2) the annual inventory change in the NIA series is based on seasonally unadjusted data, and the quarterly seasonally adjusted figures are not forced to this control.

from the end of one quarter to the end of the next in the book value of inventories, make the necessary inventory-valuation adjustment, and derive the National Income Division's (NIA) inventory change series, all on a seasonally adjusted basis. Such a calculation could provide a useful background for forecasting the quarters ahead. Unfortunately, this is not feasible for two main reasons. First, data on the inventory-valuation adjustment are published only once a year, for the previous year, in the July National Income Number of the *Survey of Current Business.*. Publication of these data, though invaluable for purposes of historical research, is often too late to be of much value in short-run forecasting. Second, as mentioned above, the coverage of the two sets of series is not identical. The differences in coverage may be summarized as follows:

| | Coverage of inventory data ||
	NIA change in business inventories series	End-of-month inventory level series
Manufacturing	Same	Same
Wholesale trade	All wholesalers	Merchant wholesalers
Retail trade	Same	Same
Farm	Included, but shown separately	Excluded
All other	Included, not shown separately	Excluded

Fortunately, however, the differences in coverage are relatively small. In 1964, for example, the total change in the book value of nonfarm business inventories was $5.7 billion. The net change in the book value of nonmerchant wholesalers' inventories was $0.3 billion, and the net change in book value of inventories in the "all other" category was $0.5 billion. No very large error is likely to result, therefore, if forecasts, based on past data, of the book value of inventory change are made for the categories for which inventory-level figures are published, and then it is assumed that "all other" and nonmerchant wholesalers' inventories will move in the same direction and by a similar proportionate amount.[4]

The series on inventory levels in manufacturing and trade is particularly useful because of the availability of breakdowns by industry, by market category, and by fabrication stage (purchased materials, goods in process, and finished goods). The series is also paralleled, in coverage and in timing,

---

[4] The problem of the *quality* of the inventory data is another matter, and is one that was the subject of extensive study in the late 1950s and the 1960s. See, for example, Elmer C. Bratt, "Availability and Reliability of Inventory Data Needed to Study Economic Change," in *Inventory Fluctuations and Economic Instability*, Joint Economic Committee, 87th Cong., 1st Sess., 1961, part III. Major improvements were made by the Department of Commerce in 1963 and 1964, and further changes may be made by the time these words appear in print.

by other series on manufacturing and trade sales and on manufacturers' new orders and backlogs of unfilled orders. Throughout much of the chapter we shall be preoccupied with the inventory-sales-order relationships for which this family of series supplies the principal American evidence.

One further, purely mechanical, point: the so-called inventory-sales ratios that figure heavily in the analysis of inventory behavior commonly are cited simply as unlabeled ratios, e.g., 1.5 to 1. But this requires a convention about what duration of sales (a flow through time) shall be compared with the inventory figure (a stock as of a point in time). The same problem arises in all comparisons of capital stock with output, income, or expenditures. In the case of plant and equipment the usual comparison is between capital stock and annual output. It happens that in inventories it is with monthly sales. Thus if, throughout a year, a firm has maintained an inventory valued at $160,000 and each month had sales of $100,000, making a yearly total of $1,200,000, it normally would be said to have an inventory-sales ratio of 1.6, not 0.1333. In the manufacturing and trade series, annual sales figures are expressed as monthly averages, not as annual totals.

THE STRUCTURE OF MANUFACTURING AND TRADE INVENTORIES

The forecaster should take time to observe the general pattern of inventory holdings that the subdivisions of the series on manufacturing and trade inventories show. The figures for almost any month will convey a faithful rough picture of the economy's inventory structure, for, although there are frequent and, from a stabilization point of view, highly disturbing minor fluctuations in stocks at the different processing and distributing levels, the general proportions of the pattern have a high degree of permanence. The pattern of average monthly sales and inventories in 1964, shown in Table 21-1, is reasonably typical. It shows a two-dimensional structure differentiated, on the one hand, among manufacturing, wholesale, and retail trade, and, on the other hand, between sellers of durable and of nondurable goods. The table invites several observations.

For one thing, the distribution of absolute inventory holdings among the manufacturing, wholesale, and retail series has a top-heavy hourglass shape. Manufacturing accounts for over one-half of the total, wholesale for less than one-sixth, and retail for somewhat less than one-third. This is the general pattern in both durable goods and nondurable goods industries, although the dominance of the manufacturing inventories is more pronounced in durables.

The height of manufacturers' inventories, compared with those in trade, is accounted for by two factors: (1) Manufacturers' sales include, in addition to those to distributors, sales to business and government end users and sales of commodities to other manufacturers for further processing. Thus the dollar volume of manufacturing business is much higher than retail busi-

Table **21–1.** Average End-of-month Book-value Inventories and Average Monthly Sales in United States Manufacturing, Wholesaling, and Retailing, 1964*

Distribution level and fabrication stage	Sellers of nondurable goods			Sellers of durable goods			Total (nondurable and durable)		
	Inventories†	Sales†	I/S	Inventories†	Sales†	I/S	Inventories†	Sales†	I/S
Manufacturing	24.2	17.9	1.35	36.8	19.2	1.91	60.9	37.1	1.64
Fabrication stages:									
Materials and supplies	(9.5)			(11.0)			(20.5)		
Work in process	(3.5)			(15.3)			(18.8)		
Finished goods	(11.2)			(10.5)			(21.7)		
Wholesale merchant	7.3	8.0	0.92	8.7	5.7	1.51	16.0	13.7	1.17
Retail	17.3	14.7	1.18	13.2	7.1	1.86	30.5	21.8	1.40
Total	48.8	40.6	1.20	58.7	32.1	1.83	107.5	72.6	1.48

* Details do not necessarily add to totals because of rounding.
† In billions of dollars.
Source: U.S. Department of Commerce.

ness, despite the intervening markups.   (2) Manufacturers' inventories include
not only finished goods, which are all that wholesalers and retailers carry, but
also stocks of materials and of goods in process.   That this tends to make for
a slower turnover of manufacturers' total inventories (or, what is the same
thing, a higher inventory-sales ratio) is evidenced most clearly by the figures
in the soft goods sector.   These two factors outweigh a third, which tends to
hold down total manufacturers' inventories relative to those at the wholesale
and retail levels: many manufacturers do business on a made-to-order basis,
and therefore typically do not maintain stocks of finished goods.   We shall
return to this point later.

In addition to added markups, two circumstances largely explain the
height of retail inventories compared with those at wholesale.   Many consumer
goods, especially durables, flow directly from manufacturers to retailers, bypassing the wholesale level.   In addition, wholesale inventories as a group turn
over somewhat faster than those at retail, where marketing conditions require
large numbers of small retailers to carry comparatively large varieties of slow-
moving items to meet the occasional demands of their small clienteles.

Table 21–1 reveals the characteristic heaviness of durable goods inventories, up and down the processing and distribution chain.   In 1964, durable
goods businesses held more than one-half of all inventories in manufacturing
and trade but accounted for much less than one-half of total sales.   At the
manufacturing level it takes longer, on the average, to make durable than
nondurable goods, and consequently much larger inventories are tied up in
the production process.   At the trade levels the reasons for the heaviness of
durable inventories relative to sales are more obscure.   Presumably they
include the fact that consumers, who on the average buy hard goods much less
frequently than soft, demand a wider range of choice when they do shop for
the former.   At any rate, the comparative top-heaviness of inventories in the
whole durables area suggests that here is where inventories are likeliest to get
out of hand in the eyes of business decision makers and where, as a result,
inventory fluctuations are apt to be centered.   This, in fact, has been the recent
American experience.

One further piece of structural information that the series on manufacturers' inventories provides and Table 21–1 reflects is the breakdown by
fabrication stages.   These, it should be emphasized, are classified from the
viewpoint of the firms presently holding the inventories.   Thus a sheet of steel
might show up among finished goods at the end of one month, when it is still
in the hands of a steel company, and the next month be counted among
materials and supplies held by a refrigerator manufacturer.   Note, in Table
21–1, the much greater importance of work-in-process inventories in durable
than in nondurable goods manufacturing, and, conversely because of the large
amount of made-to-order business the durable goods producers do, the lesser
scope of finished goods inventories in that area.

So much for the basic data.   The inventory forecaster's next need is for some understanding of the role that inventories play in the economy and of the kinds of decisions that determine their behavior.

INVENTORY DECISION MAKING

Businessmen often find themselves holding higher or lower commodity stocks than they want. But before an analyst can identify such a situation or figure out of its implications for future inventory change, he must have some idea of what levels of inventories businessmen do want, and why.

THE FUNCTIONS OF INVENTORIES

In ancient and primitive societies stocks of commodities traditionally were desired as stores of wealth, and people wanted as high inventories as they could get. With the development of well-established monetary and banking systems, however, money provided a more convenient, safer, and less perishable form in which to accumulate savings. And it was seen that other forms of real capital could be made to yield returns to their owners by being engaged in production, whereas isolated stockpiles of commodities could not. Thus it is a universal characteristic of modern businesses to prize inventories only as a form of working capital, a certain amount of which is necessary equipment for doing the firm's production and selling job, and a redundance of which is as bad as a deficiency.

The need for a "certain amount" of inventory in the production-sales process arises from two inescapable characteristics of any economy. One is that the production of commodities takes time. The other is that the pattern of production over time cannot be perfectly synchronized with the pattern of demand. The first of these circumstances alone creates the necessity for business to own what might be called "inventories in motion," i.e., goods in process in manufacturing, and commodities in transit from sellers to buyers who will resell them.

"Sitting inventories," on the other hand—sellers stocks of finished goods and manufacturers' stocks of unprocessed materials—are not economic necessities in the same sense that inventories in motion are. If the types, varieties, numbers, and sizes of the finished goods flowing off production lines and being transported to end-user outlets could be exactly synchronized with the demands for commodities which buyers register in the form of new orders, there would be no occasion for sitting inventories at all. Every time you walked into a clothing store to buy a shirt, a messenger from the manufacturer would be walking in the back door with exactly the shirt you wanted.

But such exact synchronization of production and demand obviously is impossible. Since production takes time, the current output always is largely controlled by production decisions made weeks, months, or even years before. Thus for current output to match current demand perfectly, producers would have had to do a perfect sales forecasting job. This they can seldom do and never can be sure of doing.

Moreover, even if producers and sellers could forecast their new orders perfectly, most of them could not or would not follow exactly matching production or buying schedules anyway. To do so might dictate production patterns so highly seasonal that they would entail exorbitant capacity and overtime labor costs; or retailers might be required to accept deliveries from suppliers every ten minutes. Thus in the case of all commodities there are bound to be discrepancies between buyers' current new orders and sellers' current output and purchases; production and purchases for resale are bound to lag demand as sellers try to bring them into line with it; and certain cushioning mechanisms must intervene. Broadly speaking, two of these cushioning mechanisms are possible: the sitting inventory and the backlog of unfilled orders.

ALTERNATIVE DEMAND-OUTPUT CUSHIONS

From a producer's viewpoint the simplest way of handling the necessary lag of production behind demand is to make the buyer wait while the item he wants is made or acquired. Almost all business used to be conducted on such a made-to-order, or custom, or jobbing basis, but it entails an obvious inconvenience for buyers and it ill comports with the requirements of mass production. Thus there has been a massive shift in all highly industrialized economies toward the selling of ready-made goods out of finished goods inventories that have been produced, not in response to, but in anticipation of demand.

At retail in the United States very few commodities still are fabricated on a made-to-order basis, although a fair amount of retail marketing is done by such inventoryless sellers as door-to-door salesmen and certain mail-order-house outlets. And a good deal of jobbing continues to be done in wholesale markets. But the great remaining concentrations of custom business in the United States are in the manufacture of producers' durable equipment and in contract construction. Only the latter, typically, is pure jobbing, in the sense that producers do not even maintain significant inventories of purchased materials between jobs. Manufacturers of machine tools, heavy electrical machinery, locomotives, and other major items of producers' equipment keep stocks of materials and inevitably some stocks of goods in process, but they produce only to order and carry virtually no finished inventory.

In such industries new orders reflect month-to-month changes in demand; sales tend to be synchronized with production; and the order backlog supplies the cushioning between demand and output. When demand outruns output, the backlog builds up, and in the reverse case it is drawn down for a time until production is adjusted downward or demand recovers. In industries that typically fill orders upon receipt, on the other hand, new orders and sales are virtually synonymous; there is no order backlog to speak of, and finished goods inventories do all the cushioning between demand and output. About three-fourths of the nondurable manufacturing business, for example, is done on this basis.

In between these two extremes, there are many manufacturing industries—particularly those producing such industrial materials as steel and lumber—whose operations characteristically involve both kinds of cushions. Orders queue up to some extent, but when they are filled, they are filled out of finished goods inventory, which permits a rate of shipments (sales) that is independent of the rate of production. In such instances the usual response to a change in demand involves a two-step lag, first of shipments (sales) behind new orders, and second, of production behind sales. This throws the cushioning burden initially on the order backlog, and then shifts it to the finished goods inventory.

Because durable goods manufacturing as a whole includes a lot of these "mixed-cushion" cases, while the rest of the category is a composite of made-to-order business (mainly in the case of producers' durables) and ready-made business (most consumer durables), the category as a whole generally is subject to the sequence just described: a downturn in new orders often has been followed in a few months by a leveling or decline in sales, with similar changes in production and inventories lagging somewhat further behind. Although there is nothing precise about it, this is a useful sequence for the inventory forecaster to keep in mind.

Having identified the principal function of sitting inventories, we should push on to the kinds of policies business adopts toward them. But first, there is one further comparison between finished goods inventories and backlogs of unfilled orders to be noted. That is the comparative impact of the two forms of demand-output cushioning on the stability of production and employment. Fluctuations in inventories tend to give production a more erratic course than that of sales to end users. The empirical evidence that inventories are an unstabilizing element already has been noted, and we shall find an explanation of this in the theory of the so-called inventory cycle.

On the other hand, industries where there is a large volume of made-to-order business, sales and production typically both increase and decline less sharply than demand as, via the order backlog, part of each spurt in new orders is used to cushion the next dip or slowdown in demand. Thus purely from a stability point of view, order backlogging is a benign kind of demand-output cushioning, while finished goods inventories are perverse.

INVENTORY POLICY IN THE FIRM

In the short run, there is very little inventory policy as such about the volume of goods in process; this is largely a function of production decisions.[5]

---

[5] This is strictly the case with continuous-flow production, and even with discontinuous processes the quantities of goods stockpiled at various work stations are likely to have a fairly close relationship to the output of the process.

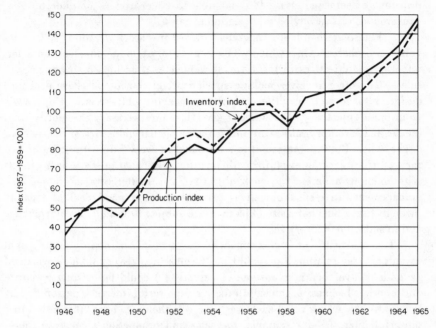

Figure **21–2.** United States manufacturers goods-in-process inventories and
production, 1946–1965. Production is measured by the
manufacturing component of the FRB industrial production
index inflated by the industrial prices component of the BLS
wholesale price index. Source: U.S. Department of Commerce, U.S. Department of Labor, and the Federal Reserve
System.

As Figure 21–2 indicates, manufacturing production and the price-deflated
value of goods in process usually move in close parallel. Moreover, manufacturers' inventories of purchased materials ordinarily account for less than one-
quarter of total sitting inventories in the United States. Hence inventory
decision making in the firm centers around the desired level of finished goods
inventories.

Such decision making contains an inherent element of frustration
because the finished goods inventory is one dimension of a firm's activities
that always is partly out of control. The behavior of the finished goods inventory is jointly determined by two things: (1) the firm's own decisions to produce and/or buy and (2) the firm's sales; and the firm has no strict control
over the latter.[6] Thus inventory decision making is a little like flying wing on
another airplane. The decisions involved are production or purchasing decisions, but the core of the problem is to maintain a desired relationship to the

---

[6] We do not mean to deny that marketing policies and efforts can influence sales.
However, such control of sales almost never is decisive enough to remove the indicated
uncertainty from the inventory problem.

decisions of someone else. It is possible to underproduce or underbuy or overproduce or overbuy only in relation to sales.

Put somewhat more concretely, firms' inventory decision making involves two phases. One, which we call "inventory policy," involves the determination of objectives in the form of wanted relationships of inventories to sales. The other involves making specific production or purchase decisions designed to correct deviations of actual inventory-sales relationships away from these objectives. For our purposes, it is not necessary to identify what the desired inventory-sales relationships in particular industries or firms are or ought to be. But it is important to realize that in every firm with sitting inventories, such objectives exist, formally or informally; that in every firm with its wits about it, adherence to such objectives is a matter of some moment to management; that such objectives probably have a good deal of tenacity through time; but that these objectives are subject to gradual secular change and to sudden temporary shifts.

The intensity of management's interest in maintaining the right inventory-sales relationship should not be obscure. Every dollar's worth of redundant inventory is a wastage of capital that could be earning a return, and in every business organization there are powerful interests, personified by the controller, which resist such wastage. On the other hand, there are other powerful interests—for example, the sales and production vice presidents—who are concerned to keep the finished goods and purchased-materials stocks comfortably high. Given such a contest within the firm, the hammering out of some sort of company policy or practice on inventory-sales relationships is necessary to avoid continuing internal bickering. And once such policies are established, they are not changed casually, for whenever they are, the energies of management may be dissipated again in intrafirm dissension.

At the same time, obviously no given inventory policy is inviolate. Over time it may be shifted gradually as the marketing arrangements, production processes, or product mix of the firm changes and, in particular, as capital-saving innovations occur that permit the conserving of inventory without loss of sales. In addition, inventory objectives are subject to rapid and sometimes radical short-run revisions for what are usually called speculative or precautionary reasons. If purchase prices are expected to rise, it may be decided that a higher-than-normal inventory-sales policy for the near future will minimize costs; an anticipated decline in prices may have the opposite effect; and there may be similar reactions to expected shortages or gluts of supplies.

AGGREGATE INVENTORY-SALES RELATIONSHIPS

THE SECULAR RELATIONSHIPS

If individual firms do try rather hard and somewhat successfully to adhere to particular inventory-sales objectives that are fairly stable through time, and if there is reasonable continuity in the industrial composition of total business activity, a normal relationship of aggregate inventories to aggregate sales should be discernible for the whole economy or for such major subdivisions as manufacturing and retail trade. The fact is that such secular relationships between inventories and sales are plainly evident in the United States.

The kind of relationships displayed in Figure 21–3 were first prominently noted by Louis Paradiso and some of his Department of Commerce associates in *Survey of Current Business* articles in the late forties and early fifties.[7] Such relationships are not necessarily proportionate; they do not necessarily assert secularly constant ratios between total inventories and total sales. But they do suggest that ratios of increments in inventory to increments in sales are steady over long stretches of time.

Secular trends of the ratios between total inventories and total sales are the product of many conflicting forces. The ratios may be pulled down, for instance, by outright capital-saving innovations; the substitution by many paint retailers of relatively small stocks of white paint plus tubes of pigment for large multicolored stocks of ready-mixed paint constitutes one neat example. The computerization of inventory control since the mid-1950s, coupled with improved managerial practices, has clearly tended to reduce inventory-sales ratios. The ratios may also be pulled down by changes in marketing organization, e.g., the rise of the rapid-turnover discount house, or by the simple statistical fact that as sales and inventories grow, a relatively smaller share of inventories is required to meet demands for commodities of unusual style, color, or size. On the other hand, the ratios can be pushed up secularly by a proliferation of product brands, styles, colors, etc., or by a shift of manufacturers from made-to-order to ready-made marketing. Again in manufacturing, the ratios may be pushed up by more pronounced leveling of production relative to seasonal fluctuations in demand. This matter of the secular drifts in inventory-sales ratios would be an interesting one to pursue further, but it is not a matter of primary concern of the short-run forecaster. For his purposes it is enough to know, as the data in Figure 21–3 indicate, that there are in the United States pronounced and observable normal relationships between aggregate inventories and sales of such character that in any short period the normal inventory-sales ratios usually change relatively little.

THE FORECASTING IMPLICATION

We now seem to be closing in on the forecasting problem. In view of the short-run volatility of inventories, which we began by noting, the short-

<hr />

[7] See particularly Louis J. Paradiso and Genevieve B. Wimsatt, "Business Inventories: Recent Trends and Position," *Survey of Current Business*, U.S. Department of Commerce, vol. 35, no. 5, pp. 9–15, May, 1953.

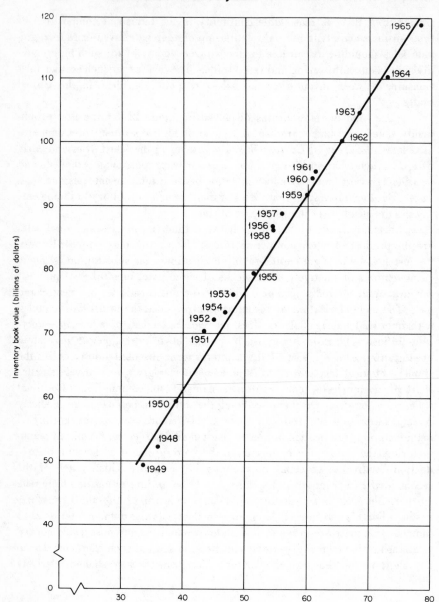

Figure **21–3.**   Secular inventory-sales relationships in United States manufacturing and trade, 1948–1965.   Source: U.S. Department
of Commerce.

run analyst clearly would not be justified in adopting the secular ratio between
the increment in inventory and the increment in sales as his sole forecasting

guide. The fact, for example, that in the United States during the ten years 1956 to 1965 inventory investment averaged 14.2 percent of the average annual increment in current-price gross national product does not justify the prediction that inventory investment is going to be that same percentage of the increase in GNP in the coming year.

But if the analyst has identified the normal trend and recent level of inventory-sales ratios in manufacturing and trade from either a scatter diagram, as in Figure 21–3, or from a time-series chart, as in Figure 21–4, and knows the actual current inventory level, can he not do this: (1) estimate that in the forecast period manufacturing and trade sales will increase or decrease in proportion to the overall change in the commodity segments of GNP that his first-approximation estimates of the other demand sectors indicate, and then (2) reason that the change in inventories will be such as to carry them from their actual level at the beginning of the forecast period to the level that would be normal for the expected level of sales? The rationale for this procedure involves two assumptions—first, that the inventory policy of firms will be to regain and/or retain normal inventory-sales relationships and, second, that they will succeed in this effort.

Very often the procedure just outlined will yield a satisfactory estimate of inventory change. But it is an incomplete forecasting doctrine because each of the assumptions just indicated can be fallacious. The difficulty with the first assumption—that the inventory policy of firms during the forecast period will be to seek normal inventory-sales relationships—is that inventory decision making may be affected by speculative or precautionary considerations. The forecaster has no business blindly assuming the normality of inventory policy in the coming period. He must decide as best he can, partly from extant market trends, partly from perusing the business press, and partly from such direct indications of business attitudes as the reports of the National Association of Purchasing Agents (cited in the final section of the chapter), whether firms strongly expect changing prices or altered supply conditions. There is no easy formula for estimating how much such expectations will shift inventory objectives above or below the normal level, but some insight can be had by considering the way business behaved in inflationary, deflationary, shortage, or surplus periods in the past.

The converse of the point just made is equally valid. A forecaster has no business blindly assuming that a currently abnormal set of objectives will persist. If a price or shortage scare has temporarily raised the preference for inventories, then inventory policies, if they are as tenacious as the strength of the secular inventory-sales relationships would indicate, are very apt to revert toward normal as soon as the expectation fever begins to subside.

The difficulty with the second of the above assumptions, namely, that business will succeed in achieving its apparent inventory objectives in a coming year, involves the final complicated subject with which we must deal in this chapter—that of the so-called inventory cycle.

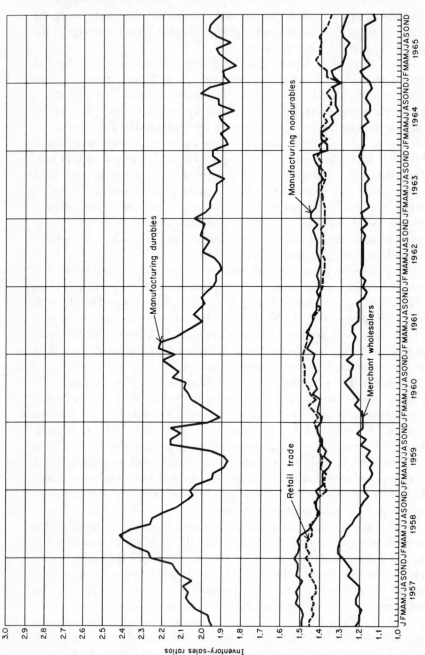

Figure **21–4.**   Inventory-sales ratios in manufacturing (durables and nondurables), merchant wholesaling, and retail trade, 1957–1965, seasonally adjusted.   Source: *Survey of Current Business*, U.S. Department of Commerce.

THE INVENTORY CYCLE

An outstanding business conditions analyst once said with exasperation that the only thing a forecaster can safely infer from the fact that inventory-sales ratios now are "normal" is that they are on the verge of becoming abnormal. Actually, as we shall see, this is not always so. But there is this element of truth in the statement: once the inventory-sales ratio has, for any reason, been pulled away from the desired level, it seems to have an inherent tendency, when it reapproaches the desired level, to overshoot the mark and then, doubling back, to overshoot again, and perhaps, indeed, to keep this up indefinitely.

Abramowitz clearly identified such inventory cycles in the aggregative American experience between the two world wars; to most observers' eyes they have reemerged in the years since World War II; and Ruth Mack has reported new documentation for what appears to be the same phenomenon by a different name.[8] Paul G. Darling, in his 1961 testimony before the Joint Economic Committee, summarized his investigation into empirical evidence in support of the inventory cycle concept, as follows:[9]

> "The overall conclusion of the investigation is that the recurrence of business recessions, four in number, during the postwar period, and the wavelike nature of postwar fluctuations in GNP, are both manifestations of inventory cycles. Periods of expansion and contraction were substantially contributed to by investment and disinvestment in inventories, and the decisive element in inducing reversals (turning points) in economic activity was the inventory mechanism described in this paper. Needless to say, this conclusion stands as a statement of probability. In my judgment the probability is high that it is a true statement."

The empirical evidence of inventory cycles is much too elaborate for the working forecaster to overlook, and certainly the theoretical documentation is also elaborate.[10] In fact, it almost seems that some of the aggregative theorists

[8] Ruth P. Mack, "Notes on Subcycles in Theory and Practice," *American Economic Review*, vol. 47, no. 2, pp. 161–174, May, 1957. Also see discussion by Edwin B. George et al., pp. 175–186.

[9] Paul G. Darling, "Inventory Fluctuations and Economic Instability: An Analysis Based on the Postwar Economy," in *Inventory Fluctuations and Economic Stabilization*, Materials Prepared for the Joint Economic Committee, 87th Cong., 1st Sess., 1961, part III, p. 66.

[10] See Lloyd Metzler, "Nature and Stability of Inventory Cycles," *Review of Economic Statistics*, vol. 23, no. 3, pp. 113–129, August, 1941; "Business Cycles and the Modern Theory of Employment," *American Economic Review*, vol. 36, no. 3, pp. 278–291, June, 1946; "Factors Governing the Length of Inventory Cycles," *Review of Economic Statistics*, vol. 29, no. 1, pp. 1–15, February, 1947; Ragnar Nurkse, "The Cyclical Pattern of Inventory Investment," *Quarterly Journal of Economics*, vol. 66, no. 3, pp. 385–408, August, 1952; J. S. Duesenberry, Otto Eckstein, and Gary Fromm, "A Stimulation of the United States Economy in Recession," *Econometrica*, vol. 28, pp. 749–809, October, 1960; and Shozaburo Fujino, "Some Aspects of Inventory Cycles," *Review of Economics and Statistics*, vol. 42, pp. 203–209, May, 1960.

have become disproportionately intrigued with the inventory cycle as a kind of fascinating theoretical microcosm without giving enough attention to how it fits into a general theory of inventory behavior.

THE THEORY OF THE CYCLE

There are just three essential ideas that underlie the cycle concept. Two of them we already have well in mind: (1) that in industries that sell out of finished goods stocks, production lags behind sales, so that inverse changes in inventories cushion unexpected changes in sales, and (2) that sellers try, in making their buying and/or production decisions, to maintain relatively constant inventory-sales ratios.

The third idea is a new one that applies only to the economy as a whole or to major segments of it. It is that, when a dominant portion of commodity sellers find themselves in a position of having underbought or -produced or overbought or -produced, their simultaneous efforts to replenish or pare their inventories tend to be partly self-defeating. For sales as a whole will themselves be stimulated (or dampened) by a concerted effort of business to build up (or liquidate) inventories, and this will cancel out part of the progress of the actual inventory-sales ratio toward the desired level. Moreover, the effect that a wave of inventory building or reduction has upon sales is not limited to the impact upon firms that supply other sellers. In addition, there is a multiplier effect: the increase in production that inventory accumulation calls forth generates increased income, part of which accrues as disposable personal income and stimulates increased consumption.

The manner in which these circumstances can lead to recurrent fluctuations in production, sales to end users, inventory investment, and inventories can be seen most readily by tracing through such a simplified graphic model as Figure 21–5. There it is assumed that, in the first period, production and sales to end users are equal, which means that inventory investment is zero and that the indicated relationship of inventories to sales—namely, 1.5 to 1— is the desired one. To upset such a balanced situation and start the cycle in motion there must be an unexpected disturbance, and—this deserves emphasis —it must affect a substantial segment of business in the same way at approximately the same time. Otherwise, many little contrapuntal inventory swings may be under way in different industries running in different directions at the same time and largely offsetting each other.

The inventory cycle can be touched off by a change in sales that, because it is unexpected, is not matched by an increase or decrease in production and therefore lowers or raises finished goods inventories. Or it can be triggered by an upward or downward shift in inventory objectives—away from normal for speculative or precautionary reasons, or back toward normal when the desire for unusually heavy or light inventory holdings has passed. The classic case of a disturbance that initiated an inventory cycle was the out-

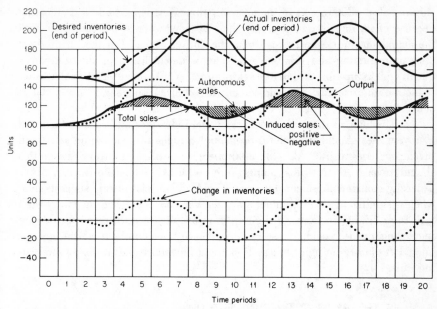

Figure 21–5. A schematic inventory cycle initiated by an unanticipated autonomous rise in sales. Assumptions: (1) Desired inventories equal 1.5 times preceding period's sales. (2) Output equals preceding period's sales plus the excess of desired over actual inventories at end of preceding period. (3) Induced sales equal 0.5 times the preceding period's increment in output.

break of the Korean War. That event had the effect both of raising sales unexpectedly and of causing a temporary rise in inventory objectives. All that is required to start the cycle is something to create, throughout much of the economy, a significant gap between actual and desired inventories.

When, in Figure 21–5, inventories are pulled down by an unexpected rise in sales, sellers are motivated to raise inventories not only to their old absolute level but enough higher to regain the preferred inventory-sales ratio. The orders they place for this purpose, either upon the suppliers or upon their own production lines, cause an increase in production as quickly as the latter can respond. But by creating additional disposable personal income, this advance in production induces an advance—though a lesser one—in end-user sales, which prevents part of the intended rebuilding of inventory. This prompts more orders for inventory and further stimuli to production, sales, and inventory until finally, in period 7 in Figure 21–5, inventories regain the desired level. But as soon as this happens, orders for inventory rebuilding cease, production declines, there is an induced decline in sales, and inventories rise further, this time unintentionally. So firms reduce production orders below current sales in an effort to cut inventories back to the desired relationship to sales. But just as in the upswing, this effort is partially self-defeating because of its impact on sales, and thus the downward swing continues until the actual inventories again overtake the desired level. But then firms start once more buying and producing on a replacement basis, production consequently picks up and stimulates sales, and there is an unintentional further reduction in inventories. And so on ad infinitum as far as the model is concerned.

The logic of the inventory cycle model indicates that peaks and troughs in inventories should lag behind peaks and troughs in production, sales, and inventory investment. Also the attainment of desired inventory-sales ratios should precede the turning points in inventories. The empirical evidence generally confirms these conclusions. This lead-lag relationship suggests that, when a significant cycle is under way, the very periods when inventory-sales ratios are "right" in terms of desired levels are the ones when inventories are increasing or decreasing most rapidly; hence the complaint of the analyst quoted at the beginning of this section about inventory-sales ratios as forecasting aids.

IS THE CYCLE A PREDICTIVE TOOL?

Now what about the forecasting implications of all this? Does not the cycle model finally provide the short-run inventory forecaster with the all-purpose device he needs? Since this particular variety of fluctuation is commonly alleged to have a fairly regular rhythm, once an exogenous disturbance sets it in motion, cannot the analyst identify the secular inventory-sales relationship and extrapolate it as the norm around which inventories will weave; then take note of recent fluctuations and decide where in the current cycle we are; and then simply project the continuation of the cycle into the near future, with, say, a six-month quarter-cycle rhythm? In other words, is not this one place where we can almost forecast from the calendar?

Before taking violent exception to this as a definitive forecasting technique, let us admit that there are occasions when an analyst must proceed in very much this fashion. If a pronounced inventory cycle already is under way as the result of a sharp disturbance of normal inventory-sales relationships and if the rest of the demand outlook is relatively neutral, so that it appears that the impact of inventory policy on business sales is not likely to be offset by much of anything else, then reliance on the inventory cycle is in order. But the procedure outlined above falls far short of being a generally reliable forecasting doctrine for the following reasons.

First, the short-run pulsations in inventories typically are much less hectic things than verbal, mathematical, or graphical inventory cycle models tend to suggest. It is seldom that business in a herdlike manner revises its expectations sharply enough, or gets surprised by sales violently enough, to set a heavy inventory swing in motion. The relative stability in inventory-sales ratios in 1961–1965, evident in Figure 21–4, is evidence on this point.

Moreover, when a swing does begin, certain dampening factors, which the simple model does not include, may intervene. For example, there may be some elasticity in inventory objectives, so that all firms do not attempt to recover normal levels immediately. The inventory cycle also is sometimes dampened by capacity limits on production. And, in particular, it is dampened by the cushioning that tends to insulate disposable personal income from changes in business gross receipts.

Second, a somewhat intuitive extension of the preceding point: although there is nothing in the cycle model necessarily to indicate it, American experience seems to suggest that, once instigated, inventory fluctuations become progressively dampened through time until some new major disturbance provides a new impetus. The unexpected shock of the Korean outbreak touched off a wave of inventory investment that finally reached an all-time high—seasonally adjusted annual rate of $15.2 million in the second quarter of 1951. An inventory cycle most certainly had been set in motion. But thereafter for several years there was no remotely comparable shock, and succeeding peaks in inventory investment were far more moderate.

Third, the tidy periodicity of the inventory cycle holds logically only as long as this implicit assumption of the model stands up, namely, that the only exogenous event that affects the system is the one that sets it in motion. But a steel strike can intervene and interrupt an upswing in inventories or, once it is over, replace a downswing with an upswing long before the latter is "due." And, more importantly, changes in sales can occur elsewhere in the economy that can cancel out or overwhelm the induced changes in sales that are supposed to keep the cycle cycling. Suppose, for example, in an upswing, when actual inventories reach the desired level, causing the reduction of orders for stock that is supposed to start a decline in sales, that government spending or plant and equipment expenditures or automobile sales spurt. Inventories may stabilize without further ado or the company may be carried directly from the first half of one inventory cycle into the first half of another.

The short of it is that inventory fluctuations do *not* have implacable rhythms, and they do not *have* to work themselves out. It is essential that an inventory forecaster understand the cycle theory and keep alert for its manifestations, but he is lost if he makes a fetish of it.

FORECASTING INVENTORY CHANGE

While the inventory forecaster needs to have in mind all the considerations we have been surveying, what he wants, in the final analysis, is a reasonably concrete and workable forecasting procedure. Something along the following lines suggests itself:

1. It is well, from the beginning of one's analysis, to recognize the distinction between sitting inventories and inventories in motion, even though

the analytical procedure one adopts may slough over it. Ideally the analyst should deal with the goods-in-process segment of total inventories separately and quickly by assuming that it will change just about in proportion to total production. Then, in focusing upon the remaining bulk of the inventory problem, he should use data limited to inventories of finished goods and purchased materials. In practice, general forecasters seldom work in quite so refined a fashion, since goods in process constitute a comparatively small fragment of total inventories.

2. The first essential thing is to inspect the present and recent condition of inventories, satisfying oneself on the following points:

a. What are the secular relationships between inventories and sales in total manufacturing and trade and its major segments? (Because of the tendency of inventory fluctuations to concentrate in the durable goods area, it is often useful to break out figures on that sector separately.)

b. What is the present location of inventory levels relative to these secular relationships? In this connection one refinement deserves mention. Although the secular inventory-sales relationships are calculated from book-value inventory figures, the periods involved are long enough and include sufficiently varied price experience so that discrepancies between book values and current values are pretty well washed out. In other words, long-term inventory-sales functions do not require any valuation adjustment. But the figures on present book values do invite such adjustment if there have been sharp price changes in the immediate past. Since a substantial portion of inventories are carried on a first-in-first-out basis, their book values at any given time are out of date, on the average, by about one-half the length of their average turnover periods. If we adopt the conventions about the latter that the National Income Division employs in figuring its inventory-valuation adjustments, this would suggest—as a very rough rule—that the latest-month figure on manufacturing and trade inventories can be converted to a current value by applying to it the percentage change in the industrial component of the wholesale price index during the immediately preceding month.[11] In nine situations out of ten this adjustment is a trifle that can safely be overlooked. But if substantial price movements are under way, it makes for a more valid comparison between existing and normal inventory-sales relationships.

c. How orderly or disorderly have inventory changes been during the past two or three years? Have there been major disturbances to inventory-sales relationships? Does a significant fluctuation in aggregative inventories seem to be in progress? If so, what have its magnitude and timing been thus far, and what has been the sequence of changes in sales and inventories and, in the durable manufacturing sector, the sequence of peaks and troughs in new orders, sales, and inventories? Does the current rate of inventory investment appear to be unsustainable? Or alternatively, does it take a magnifying glass

---

[11] *National Income, 1954 Edition: A Supplement to the Survey of Current Business,* U.S. Department of Commerce, 1954, pp. 135–138.

to identify the recent fluctuations? Has the notable thing, instead, been the comparative steadiness of actual inventory-sales ratios?

3. As discussed earlier in the chapter, the analyst must do the best he can to detect any upward or downward revisions of inventory policies that may be in store for the forecast period. Are the inventory-sales relationships in manufacturing, wholesaling, and retail trade likely to be moving away from or back toward the secular norms?

Here, of course, it is well to consider the presently available evidence of price and supply conditions that stimulate changed expectations. It is useful to listen to the tone of comment in the business press. And it is particularly helpful to examine the various reports that deal explicitly with current business intentions concerning inventories. The best of these are the frequent reports of the National Association of Purchasing Agents[12] and Commerce's quarterly surveys of manufacturers' sales and inventory anticipations reported in the *Survey of Current Business*. A survey of inventory intentions also is reported quarterly in *Fortune*.

4. Frequently the forecaster will conclude that inventory behavior recently has been orderly for the most part and that there is little or no evidence of either a currently active inventory cycle or a mass shift in the inventory objectives. In this event, if his other first-approximation demand estimates indicate a continuing growth in manufacturing and trade sales, his best course is to estimate that inventories will grow sufficiently to maintain the secular inventory-sales relationship, and to calculate what change in sales would be consistent with his preliminary income hypothesis. The latter will be a simple or a complicated job, depending on the composition of GNP as revealed by the forecast. If no significant change in the composition of GNP seems to be in prospect, the sales figure can be estimated by extrapolation of recent sales-to-GNP ratios. However, if a marked change in the composition of GNP is in prospect, more elaborate techniques are appropriate because retail sales, in particular, are associated, not with the totality of GNP, but primarily with consumer expenditures. An increase in government expenditures, for example, would probably increase manufacturers' sales but might not directly affect retail sales at all. If a radical change in the composition of GNP is in prospect, therefore, multiple correlation techniques that distinguish between components of GNP and categories of sales are essential.

If the sum of the first-approximation demand estimates indicates an interruption or decline in sales that, according to the available information on inventory intentions and manufacturers' new orders, business in general is not anticipating, the prospect may be for a cycle-initiating disturbance. The latter could cause, first, several months of unintentional inventory accumulation, followed by several more months of inventory reduction. In general, however, the general forecaster should be rather cautious in calling this kind of turn. There is a strong possibility that any slump in sales that he correctly

[12] *Bulletin of the National Association of Purchasing Agents*, New York.

anticipates is also being foreseen by many well-staffed firms who are adjusting their inventory ordering accordingly. In this case there need be little or no departure from desired inventory-sales relationships. There will still be a decline in inventory investment, but a quicker and less violent one.

5. If, instead of a comparatively orderly situation, the appraisal of recent developments indicates significant fluctuations already in progress, these must be taken into account. In particular, under these circumstances, one should avoid the trap of concluding that, because an inventory-sales ratio just lately has come back into line, it necessarily is going to stay in line. For his own guidance, the analyst should project any ongoing inventory cycle several quarters into the future on the assumptions that its rhythm will persist but its scope progressively dampen.

6. Before any forecast is read off of such a cyclical projection, however, the analyst should consider very carefully whether the remainder of the demand outlook, as he sees it, does not include changes in sales that may elongate, truncate, or virtually snuff out the fluctuation now in progress.

7. It is sensible to cross-reference the aggregative estimates that a procedure like the foregoing yields with whatever indications of inventory trend are available for specific major commodities such as steel and automobiles. While it would be virtually impossible to build up a useful general forecast of inventory behavior on a commodity-by-commodity basis, convincing signs that in a number of particular commodities inventories are moving in the opposite direction from one's overall forecast may signal a need for rechecking the forecast.

8. The procedure just outlined will lead to a forecast of the change in the current value of inventories in manufacturing and trade (if, provided there is a need for it, existing inventory levels have been converted from a book- to a current-value basis along the lines suggested in step 2*b* above). If subsequent analysis should disclose a prospect of greater general price change than the sales estimates employed in the inventory analysis have implied, it will be necessary to revise the inventory forecast to reflect higher or lower current values for the commodity stocks.

Another adjustment—one to account for the difference between manufacturing and trade inventories and the GNP series concept of nonfarm business inventories—is appropriate. As we suggested earlier, not much of an error is likely to be involved if the analyst simply assumes that inventory change for these industrial categories will be proportionate to inventory change in manufacturing and trade.

9. Thus all that remains to be done is to make some allowance for the change in farm inventories. During the 1956–1965 decade, farm inventories rose by an average of $0.2 billion a year. This is another of those items sufficiently small not to justify much investment of a general outlook analyst's time. If he cannot readily avail himself of expert opinion, he is justified in simply extrapolating the long-run trend.

22

FORECASTING NET
EXPORTS

Forecasting net exports presents as many difficulties as estimating inventory investment, if not more. The most obvious sources of change in the net export sector stem from different rates and sources of economic expansion and from different price level trends in the United States compared with the rest of the world.[1] These factors usually set the longer-run trend in our net export position. Other sources of change in net exports, such as strikes and crop failures or a technological breakthrough in an important export or import item, can cause a significant deviation from the trend in any particular month, quarter, or year.

Although forecasting net exports in many ways is like forecasting the other sectors of aggregate demand, the chances of relative error are much greater. On the export side, the demand in question is an amalgam of all other countries' composite demands for imports and of the competitive balance between our own country and alternative suppliers. Unlike the other GNP sectors, except inventory change, the quantity being forecast is the difference between two large totals; hence a small percentage change in either one of these underlying variables can cause a radical percentage change in net exports. Moreover, when forecasting the other demand sectors, we are, in the main, predicting the behavior of a large number of consumers and a relatively large number of firms. Exports and imports, on the other hand, are more strongly influenced by the actions of a few large firms and even more so by the policies of autonomous governments.

This last distinction is only one of degree, but it is important. Private decisions such as those which led to the introduction of the compact automobile and jet aircraft or a change in dividend policy of the major international

[1] The implications of this sentence could be the subject matter of a rather extensive book. For an excellent analysis of some of the theoretical problems involved, the advanced student is referred to chaps. III and IV of H. G. Johnson's *International Trade and Economic Growth*, Harvard University Press, Cambridge, Mass., 1961, pp. 65–119.

manufacturing companies, international events such as the Suez crisis, and government policies designed to affect trade either directly—e.g., changes in foreign exchange rates, tariffs, subsidies, or quotas—or indirectly through domestic price and income changes, may result in a significant quarterly change in total exports or imports.   Thus, the forecaster must be aware of possible policy changes as well as the traditional economic factors of price and income changes.   Although it is apparent that neither events such as the Suez crisis nor their effect on United States trade can normally be anticipated, the direction and possible magnitude of many government policies can be foreseen if one has a little experience and a rudimentary knowledge of the environment in which international trade and payments take place, including developments in the United States balance of payments.

In the first two sections of the chapter we shall survey recent developments in the international economy and the United States balance of payments for the purpose of gaining a basic framework for viewing policy changes.   We cannot go very far in this direction in this book; the reader is referred to recognized sources on international trade theory and practice for a more systematic treatment.   In the remaining section a method for forecasting exports and imports that emphasizes basic economic relationships will be described.   The method presented will provide a working forecast that can be adjusted for anticipated policy changes and other events.

INTERNATIONAL ARRANGEMENTS FOR PAYMENTS

Current attitudes toward international payments continue to be heavily influenced by the memory of the events that reached their culmination in the early part of the Great Depression of the 1930s with the general introduction of exchange controls, quotas and other import restrictions, and substantially increased tariff rates.   The consequences of restrictions and general reduction of economic activity were severe.   The value of world trade, which amounted to $55.9 billion in 1929, was reduced to $21.8 billion in 1932.[2]   These events were followed by a round of beggar-my-neighbor devaluations, which in Gottfried Haberler's words "inflicted upon different groups of countries protracted periods of over-valued currencies, causing deficits and losses, further trade restrictions, and more depressions."[3]

During the latter part of World War II, a movement began to reconstruct the world economy on the basis of the liberal ideals of free trade and

[2] *Finance and Development*, International Monetary Fund and the World Bank, vol. 1, no. 1, p. 3, June, 1964.

[3] Gottfried Haberler, "Integration and Growth of the World Economy in Historical Perspective," *American Economic Review*, vol. 54, no. 2, part 1, p. 9, March, 1964.

payments. On the payments side, the International Monetary Fund Agreement, signed in 1944, established a new monetary system with the International Monetary Fund as the administrative machinery. The system, as designed by its adherents, is based upon the following four underlying principles.

The first principle is that of exchange rate stability and cooperation. Article IV provides that member nations, which as of January 1, 1966, numbered 102 non-Soviet-bloc countries and Yugoslavia, are supposed to keep their exchange rates pegged within limits of 1 percent on spot transactions. Flexibility was given to the system by providing that a country may, without the consent of but with notification to the Fund, appreciate or depreciate its currency by 10 percent and, with the consent of the Fund, by a greater amount if the country is experiencing a "fundamental disequilibrium" in its balance of payments.[4] But until a fundamental disequilibrium is declared, members are expected to order their domestic policies with some consideration for the needs of external balance.

Second, with pegged exchange rates, additional international reserves are needed to finance possible deficits. The Fund is supposed to fill this need by its holding of a pool of member currencies. Members have primary responsibility, however, for providing their own sources for financing deficits caused by either fundamental or transitory forces; the Fund's resources can be used only as a secondary source. Each member has a limit or quota on the amount of currencies that can be purchased, and use of the Fund's resources within the quota is subject to progressively stricter conditions.[5] Thus, with the exception of the gold reserve or "tranche," the Fund's resources must be viewed as a source of funds for temporary borrowing by individual countries and not as a source of world liquidity.

Third, the framers of the agreement recognized that surplus countries as well as deficit countries have the responsibility for combating a sustained

[4] The characteristics of a country experiencing a fundamental disequilibrium are not identified in the Fund agreement. A country would certainly fall under this category if it experienced a persistent balance-of-payments deficit accompanied by inflation, overfull employment, and myriad restrictive trade measures taken to correct the deficit.

[5] The limit to borrowing or quota is also the amount subscribed to the Fund by each member and the basis for participation in the Fund's management. With minor exceptions subscriptions are made one-fourth in gold and three-fourths in the member's own currency. Members are virtually assured of receiving permission to borrow the first one-fourth of the quota, sometimes called the gold tranche, but the conditions for borrowing the remaining three tranches become progressively more severe.

The Fund's resources may be increased upon approval of a four-fifths majority of the total voting power. With a few exceptions, quotas were increased by 50 percent in 1959 and by 25 percent in 1966. The increase combined with the quotas of new members raised the Fund's total resources from $9.2 billion at the end of 1958 to $20.6 billion on Dec 31, 1966. The United States quota as of the latter date was $5.2 billion.

disequilibrium. This is the principle of joint responsibility, given substance by the scarce currency clause, Article VII of the Fund agreement. Under this clause, member countries may impose temporary exchange restrictions on the currency that has been declared scarce by the Fund.

The implications of joint responsibility and the scarce currency clause are very important and should be clearly understood. The clause was designed to provide an incentive for the surplus country to reduce its surplus by socially desirable means, such as expanding its income, reducing tariffs and other trade restrictions or export incentives, or by increasing long-term international investment and aid. The appropriate measure or combination of measures depends, of course, on the internal economic condition. In contrast, the deficit country, when faced with a falling reserve level, is forced into reducing its internal income and price level, diminishing its long-term international investments, or increasing trade and payments restrictions, which, by the way, are contrary to the establishment of free multilateral trade and payments. Because of the superior means available to the surplus countries, joint action both relieves part of the burden on the deficit country and tends to be less restrictive on international trade.

With the exception of payments restrictions taken by countries under the scarce currency clause, the Fund has the function of assisting members in the removal of exchange restrictions. This function is a part of the agreement's fourth principle, the establishment of a multilateral system of payments. Article VIII provides that, after a postwar transitional period, no member may impose payments restrictions on current international transactions or engage in any discriminatory or multiple currency practices without the approval of the Fund. For various reasons, primarily to control balance-of-payments deficits and to conserve funds for economic development, members have been reluctant to end the restrictions allowed during the transition period and accept the obligations of Article VIII. Only 10 North and Central American countries accepted the obligations in the first few years of Fund operations. The major Western European countries gradually gave up payments restrictions, but they waited until a clearly favorable turn in the balance of payments had developed before formally declaring convertibility in December, 1958. Even then the full obligations of Article VIII were not accepted until early in 1961.[6]

The international monetary system set up by the agreement, it should be noted, continues to use a commodity, gold, as the basic medium of interna-

---

[6] Japan's acceptance of Article VIII in April, 1964, brought the total to 24 countries that have accepted the full obligations of the Fund agreement.

We have pointed out that nations have been slow to accept the convertibility requirements of Article VIII. The requirements of Article VIII, however. call for only limited convertibility. Members may maintain payments restrictions on transactions of residents and on capital flows.

tional exchange. It did not create a new, alternative means of payment independent of gold. The decision to follow the traditional path of reliance on gold apparently rested on an assumption that actual payments would be made in the currencies of the major trading countries—currencies that would be of equal strength. In reality, equality of major currencies never came into being. Large sterling balances accumulated through ties to London, the traditional world financial center, together with sterling area wartime finance and the postwar dollar shortage, made the pound and the dollar the major trading currencies. These currencies, especially dollars, have been increasingly relied upon since the war because inflation and inadquate gold production have limited the availability of gold for monetary use. By historical accident and evolution of trade practices, therefore, the free world has returned to the gold exchange standard of the early 1930s. Almost the entire burden of the present system falls on the United States, and to a lesser extent on Great Britain, who, because of the widespread use of their currencies, have unwittingly assumed the role of world bankers.[7] It is the banker countries that must be ever mindful of the possibility of short-term capital movements and large-scale conversions and must order their internal economies in a manner that convinces the holders of dollars and sterling of the unfaltering strength of these currencies.

What implications for forecasting net exports can we draw from a knowledge of the international monetary system and its current problems? First, successive administrations and the Congress have persistently interpreted the Fund agreement's provision for devaluation as not applying to the United States, a reserve center country. This is not the place to argue about the correctness of the interpretation but rather to point out that this precludes the United States from using the most effective adjustment mechanism provided in the current monetary system. Thus, to relieve balance-of-payments difficulties, the United States is forced to pursue policies that may have undesirable domestic economic consequences and/or to impose *ad hoc* restrictions on payments and trade. *Ad hoc* arrangements have had an important effect on exports and imports in recent years, and in the absence of major changes in the international monetary system we can expect them to continue. Outstanding examples include the "tying" of foreign aid, i.e., making foreign aid grants and loans subject to the condition that, with some exceptions, the funds be spent in the United States; the "Buy America Act" and the directives issued pursuant to that act, notably by the Department of Defense, requiring government procurement from domestic rather than foreign suppliers unless there is a substantial difference in cost; special credit facilities for exports,

---

[7] During the nineteenth century and the early part of the twentieth, Britain played this role largely alone.

which are actually a disguised export subsidy; the President's program of voluntary restrictions on foreign spending by United States business and financial companies; and agreements with principal foreign exporter nations to limit voluntarily their shipments of textiles to the United States[8] (a similar agreement was gained with Japan's television manufacturers). Similarly, since 1958 the Federal Reserve has tended to follow monetary policies that undoubtedly are more restrictive than those they would have followed had there been no balance-of-payments problem.

If balance-of-payments deficits are to be overcome, so must surpluses. The counterpart of the United States deficit is, for the most part, the combined surpluses of the European countries and at times Japan and Canada. United States authorities have tried to induce the European countries to reduce their surpluses—i.e., pursue policies that would decrease United States imports or increase United States exports—but with only limited success, because the surplus countries have little incentive to cooperate. The scarce currency clause is not likely to be invoked unless the European currencies actually become scarce in the Fund's holdings. The determining influence on balance-of-payments policies of continental European countries appears to be, not equilibrium in international payments, but the adequacy of their own monetary reserves. If the administration in the surplus country believes reserves are inadequate, any threat to its surplus will be met by policies that will adversely affect United States exports and possibly increase United States imports. Only when the surplus countries regard a continued inflow of reserves as redundant are they likely to follow policies that increase United States exports.[9]

In addition to the influence of liquidity, there are undoubtedly strong political motives attached to European policies. In H. G. Johnson's words:[10]

"The European countries have a strong political motivation for preserving the U.S. deficit by preserving their collective surpluses. The weakness of the U.S. international financial position since 1957 has played a vital part in the economic and political upsurge of the Common Market and decline of the United States in world affairs, and it

---

[8] It is true, of course, that the impetus for protection came from the domestic textile industry, but the choice between domestic adjustment assistance and import controls had to be made with an eye on the balance of payments.

[9] Tibor Scitovsky has developed a convincing argument for this interpretation. The argument hinges on the fact that a balance-of-payments surplus involves a transfer of real resources. See his statement before the Subcommittee on International Exchange and Payments of the Joint Economic Committee, *International Payments Imbalances and Need for Strengthening International Financial Arrangements*, 87th Cong., 1st Sess., May 16, June 19, 20, and 21, 1961, August, 1961, pp. 175–176.

[10] H. G. Johnson, "The International Competitive Position of the United States and the Balance of Payments Prospect for 1968, a Review Article," *Review of Economics and Statistics*, vol. 46, no. 1, p. 31, February, 1964.

cannot be supposed that the European monetary authorities have been unaware of the interrelationship between monetary and political strength."

The complications caused by the present international monetary system are hard to understand, let alone predict, but the forecaster should at least be aware of them. In addition, the forecaster should be aware of any basic change in the monetary system, for it may have a profound impact on the policies of various countries and hence on our exports and imports.

THE BALANCE OF PAYMENTS

In Part One, we saw that the balance-of-payments series is a member of our social accounting system. The series is compiled by the Department of Commerce's Balance of Payments Division for the purpose of providing a systematic record of all economic transactions in a given time period between residents of the United States and foreigners. The data are collected on both a quarterly and a yearly basis and are published quarterly, along with an analysis of current developments, in the March, June, September, and December issues of the *Survey of Current Business*.

The series is based on the principle of double entry accounting—i.e., each transaction is shown both as a credit and as an equal, offsetting debit. As a result, the balance of payments must always balance in an accounting sense. Most analysts of the United States net international position proceed by selecting certain categories of debit and credit items to define the net balance of international payments, treating the others as balancing or financing items. The three most commonly used categories combine to form: (1) the net balance on goods and services; (2) the "liquidity balance;" and (3) the "official settlements balance." The three balances are shown for the years 1953 through 1966 in Table 22–1.[11]

---

[11] The balance-of-payments data prior to 1953 do not contain many insights useful to the business conditions analyst. From the end of World War II through 1949, United States international transactions were dominated by the effects of war devastation and our aid for redevelopment (mainly through the Marshall Plan). The United States emerged from the war as the only major supplier of manufactured goods, and this fact, when combined with large aid outlays, resulted in an average surplus of exports of goods and services for the years 1946 through 1949 of $8.0 billion with a peak of $11.5 billion in 1947. From the middle of 1950 to 1953 international transactions were again dominated by extraneous forces, this time arising from the Korean War. The export surplus was decreased substantially and so was foreign aid, although the latter remained high by historical standards. By 1953, most of the direct effect of the Korean conflict had ended, and we entered a new era that witnessed the reemergence of Europe and the continued evolution of the international monetary system toward a gold exchange standard.

Table **22–1.**   United States Balance of Payments, 1953–1966
(In Millions of dollars)

	1953	1954	1955	1956	1957
1. Merchandise exports	12,281	12,799	14,280	17,379	19,390
2. Merchandise imports	−10,990	−10,354	−11,527	−12,804	−13,291
3. Merchandise balance	1,291	2,445	2,753	4,575	6,099
4. Services, receipts	4,474	4,778	5,324	6,055	6,716
5. Services, payments	−2,956	−2,935	−3,367	−3,875	−4,245
6. Services, net*	1,518	1,843	1,957	2,180	2,471
7. Military sales	192	182	200	161	375
8. Military expenditures	−2,615	−2,642	−2,901	−2,949	−3,216
9. Military, net	−2,423	−2,460	−2,701	−2,788	−2,841
10. **Balance on goods and services**	**386**	**1,828**	**2,009**	**3,967**	**5,729**
11. Pensions and remittances	−644	−633	−597	−690	−729
12. U.S. direct investments	−735	−667	−823	−1,951	−2,442
13. Other U. S. L.T. investment	185	−320	−241	−603	−859
14. Foreign L.T. capital	228	274	390	593	399
15. Private L.T. capital, net	−322	−713	−674	−1,961	−2,902
16. U.S. private S.T. capital†	153	−660	−270	−455	−182
17. U.S. government grants and capital, net	−2,123	−1,554	−2,225	−2,402	−2,522
18. Errors and omissions	366	191	515	568	1,184
19. **Liquidity balance**	**−2,184**	**−1,541**	**−1,242**	**−973**	**578**
20. Increase in U.S. liquid liabilities other than to official agencies, etc.	N.A.	N.A.	N.A.	N.A.	N.A.
21. **Official settlements balance**	**N.A.**	**N.A.**	**N.A.**	**N.A.**	**N.A.**
Method of financing item 19 (1953–1959) or item 21 (1960–1966)					
22. Decrease in U.S. official reserves‡	1,256	480	182	−869	−1,165
23. Liquid liabilities to all foreigners, 1953–1959	928	1,061	1,060	1,842	587
24. Liabilities to foreign official agencies, 1960–1966	N.A.	N.A.	N.A.	N.A.	N.A.
25. Sum of items 10, 11, 15–18, 20, 22–24	0	0	0	0	0

   * Merchandise and service accounts exclude military transactions; military merchandise and service transactions which affect the balance of payments (military aid does not) are shown together in items 7 and 8.
   † Includes modest amounts of foreign-owned short-term capital.
   ‡ U.S. official reserves include gold, the U.S. gold tranche in the IMF, and holdings of convertible foreign currencies.
Source: *Survey of Current Business*, U.S. Department of Commerce, June, 1966, for 1953–1964; and March. 1967, for 1965–1966.

1958	1959	1960	1961	1962	1963	1964	1965	1966	
16,264	16,295	19,489	19,954	20,604	22,071	25,297	26,276	29,180	1.
−12,952	−15,310	−14,732	−14,510	−16,187	−16,992	−18,621	−21,488	−25,507	2.
3,312	985	4,757	5,444	4,417	5,079	6,676	4,788	3,673	3.
6,503	6,892	7,420	8,219	9,018	9,611	10,914	11,873	12,822	4.
−4,474	−4,925	−5,397	−5,463	−5,878	−6,514	−7,013	−7,667	−8,458	5.
2,029	1,967	2,023	2,756	3,140	3,097	3,901	4,206	4,364	6.
300	302	335	402	656	657	747	844	908	7.
−3,435	−3,107	−3,069	−2,981	−3,083	−2,936	−2,834	−2,881	−3,649	8.
−3,135	−2,805	−2,734	−2,579	−2,427	−2,279	−2,087	−2,037	−2,741	9.
2,206	147	4,046	5,621	5,130	5,897	8,490	6,957	5,296	10.
−745	−815	−698	−732	−757	−867	−879	−994	−992	11.
−1,181	−1,372	−1,674	−1,599	−1,654	−1,976	−2,416	−3,371	−3,363	12.
−1,444	−926	−863	−1,025	−1,227	−1,695	−1,961	−1,080	−213	13.
73	709	430	447	272	326	109	−149	1,912	14.
−2,552	−1,589	−2,107	−2,177	−2,609	−3,345	−4,268	−4,600	−1,664	15.
−205	−65	−1,438	−1,381	−659	−808	−2,033	907	−89	16.
−2,580	−1,971	−2,743	−2,695	−2,149	−3,195	−3,097	−3,178	−3,386	17.
511	423	−941	−1,006	−1,159	−352	−1,011	−429	−589	18.
−3,365	−3,870	−3,881	−2,370	−2,203	−2,670	−2,798	−1,337	−1,424	19.
N.A.	N.A.	479	1,023	−503	626	1,252	32	1,695	20.
N.A.	N.A.	−3,402	−1,347	−2,706	−2,044	−1,546	−1,305	271	21.
2,292	1,035	2,143	606	1,533	378	171	1,222	568	22.
1,073	2,835	—	—	—	—	—	—	—	23.
N.A.	N.A.	1,259	741	1,173	1,666	1,375	83	−839	24.
0	0	0	0	0	0	0	0	0	25.

THE NET BALANCE ON GOODS AND SERVICES

The net balance on goods and services corresponds to the net export component of the national income accounts. In Table 22–1 the balance is broken down further into three subtotals, merchandise, services, and military, the purpose of which will soon become apparent. A glance at the balance on goods and services in the table yields the immediate and important conclusion that it is subject to large annual fluctuations. Most of the change in 1956 and 1957 was caused by a large increase in exports associated with, first, a capital expenditure boom in Europe and, starting in the latter part of 1956, the Suez crisis that diverted petroleum purchases to the United States. Again in 1959 most of the change was associated with movements in the merchandise balance. However, this time imports increased substantially over 1958 while exports failed to move forward. The import rise was associated with the rise in business activity in the United States starting in mid-1958 and a steel strike that increased imports and reduced exports of steel. As if this were not enough, foreign orders switched from propeller to jet aircraft that were not yet ready for delivery and an announcement was made that the United States cotton export subsidy would be increased in the following year. Both these events had a depressing influence on exports in 1959 but reversed their influence in 1960. In that year, the net balance on goods and services surged upward by nearly $4 billion when a recession in the United States coincided with a boom in Europe. From 1960 to 1964, the balance on current account remained strong, rising from $4 billion in 1960 to $8.5 billion in 1964. In 1965 and 1966, however, the balance shrank as the war in Vietnam was superimposed on vigorously rising business activity in the United States.

Study of the table yields at least two positive conclusions. First, the net merchandise component is the major source of change in the United States balance on goods and services, and hence, net exports. Thus, the main forecasting problem reduces to finding a reasonably efficient method for predicting merchandise exports and imports. Second, and this is really the converse of the first conclusion, the net service component has been relatively stable and thus does not present the forecaster with as many difficulties. There are occasional exceptions, as in 1961 and 1964. Both these changes were associated with substantial increases in investment income receipts.[12] The 1964 increase, for reasons we shall describe later in the chapter, was apparently in part the result of the shifting of dividends of United States subsidiaries abroad from 1963 to 1964 in anticipation of the 1964 tax cut.

To one whose interest is in forecasting gross national product, those parts of the balance of payments which lie outside the confines of the net balance on goods and services (items 11–25 in Table 22–1) are not of primary interest. The reason, simply stated, is that the latter items are concerned with financial transactions between domestic and foreign residents which do not involve payments and receipts directly affecting the country's current production of goods and services. Most discussions of United States foreign economic and financial relations, however, center on broader measures of the balance of payments than the net balance on goods and services, and

---

[12] Investment income includes receipts of domestic residents from direct investments abroad in the form of branch profits, dividends, and interest; receipts from portfolio and short-term investments abroad in the form of interest and dividends; and receipts of government income from abroad, mainly interest from foreign loans.

therefore it is worthwhile to glance—if only briefly—at other items in the balance of payments and at the relationship between them and the net balance on goods and services.

THE LIQUIDITY BALANCE AND THE OFFICIAL SETTLEMENTS BALANCE

The two alternative concepts of "balance" presently being used to measure the United States balance of payments are the "balance on official settlements" (item 21 in Table 22–1) and the "liquidity balance" (item 19). The former concept of balance is the narrower of the two and defines the surplus or deficit in the balance of payments as the algebraic sum of changes in the government's officially held reserves (item 22) and in United States liabilities to foreign official institutions (item 24). Data for this narrower and newer concept of the balance are available only as far back as 1960 and were added to the official statistics as a result of long deliberation by experts in and out of government, highlighted by the publication in 1965 of a report by a Presidential Review Committee on Balance of Payments Statistics.[13] The basic logic supporting this concept is that since monetary authorities buy and sell gold and foreign exchange in the process of maintaining stable exchange rates for their currencies, net changes in officially held reserves are the best single indication of the strength or weakness of a currency and, therefore, are the best measure of a country's balance of payments.

The liquidity balance, in contrast, includes in its definition of the surplus or deficit changes in United States residents' liquid liabilities to private foreign owners as well as liabilities to foreign official agencies. This concept of the balance is more inclusive than the official settlements concept, and in recent years the United States deficit based on this definition has been somewhat larger than the deficit measured on the official settlements basis. Advocates of the liquidity balance point out that dollars held by private individuals and banks abroad can easily be turned over to the foreign monetary authorities of their owners' countries who can—unlike foreign private individuals—convert them into gold at the United States Treasury. Thus, because dollars held privately abroad are only one step away from being eligible for conversion into a foreign withdrawal of gold from the United States, it is argued that changes in these *private* short-term claims on the United States economy should be counted, along with changes in *official* claims, in measuring the balance of payments of the United States.

---

[13] *The Balance of Payments Statistics of the United States: A Review and Appraisal*, Report of the Review Committee for Balance of Payments Statistics to the Bureau of the Budget, United States Government Printing Office, Washington, April, 1965.

It should be noticed that, when *all* financial transactions between United States residents and foreign residents are considered in the framework of double entry bookkeeping, the books balance out to zero as shown in item 25 of Table 22–1. A balance in this purely technical sense is not very meaningful, however, and hence interest usually comes to focus on items farther up in the table where balances—or, strictly speaking, *imbalances*—of a more significant sort are to be found.

CAPITAL FLOWS AND NET EXPORTS

In Chapter 15, we observed that the deficit in the balance of payments did not pose a problem to the United States until the late 1950s—1958 to be more precise. With the benefit of hindsight, we can see that the change in the payments position actually started in the mid-1950s. This is shown quite clearly in Table 22–1 by the large increase in private long-term capital outflows, mainly direct investment, that took place in 1956. At the time, however, the newly emerging payments position was concealed in both 1956 and 1957 by the temporary increase in the balance on goods and services that more than offset the influence of capital outflows on the overall balance. Also, the increase in direct investment was itself judged as a transitory item associated with the Suez crisis; $800 million of the $1.1 billion increase in 1956 occurred in the petroleum industry. It is no wonder that many economists were caught by surprise when capital outflows remained high after the Suez crisis subsided.

The direction, as well as the volume, of private capital flows changed significantly in the late 1950s and early 1960s. Much of the change in direction and even in volume can be ascribed to the high growth rate and profit margins in Europe, the return to convertibility, and the fact that United States investment in the European Economic Community (EEC)[14] and the European Free Trade Association (EFTA)[15] countries provides a means of getting around the discriminatory tariff walls. For similar reasons, the proportion of capital outflows in the form of direct investments, especially in foreign manufacturing facilities, increased markedly.

In general, the other forms of private long-term capital flows, portfolio investment and long-term loans from financial institutions, have not been so responsive to the changed opportunities in Europe. These issues consist primarily of bonds, with Canada being the major borrower. The lower interest rates and ease of borrowing in the United States have apparently been the

---

[14] EEC: Belgium, France, Germany, Italy, Luxembourg, and the Netherlands.
[15] EFTA: Austria, Denmark, Norway, Portugal, Sweden, Switzerland, and the United Kingdom.

major factors influencing the volume of new foreign securities floated in the United States.

Although the effect that net capital outflows have on the overall balance is important, our purpose here is to relate them to the balance on goods and services. In general, net capital outflows create a stock of assets or claims against foreigners which, after a time lag, yield a return flow of income in the form of branch profits, dividends, and interest.[16] By 1966 the gross inflow of private investment income amounted to $5.6 billion, and *net* private income amounted to an impressive $4.3 billion. The large accumulation of foreign assets in the past few years and the prospect for continued high capital outflows suggest that net investment income will continue to gain importance as a component of the balance on goods and services.

In addition to their long-run influence on the balance of goods and services through income flows, net private capital outflows have an immediate impact on merchandise exports. Long-term bank loans, as well as short-term capital movements, may finance the purchase of United States goods that otherwise might be impossible; i.e., they may make up for a temporary shortage of reserves in foreign countries and thus have a stabilizing influence on United States exports. In addition, direct investment in foreign facilities may require a substantial quantity of United States capital equipment.

It is commonly remarked that there is great interdependence among many individual items in the balance of payments. The dependence of some parts of United States merchandise exports upon the outflow of United States private capital, as described in the preceding paragraph, is a good illustration of this interdependence. The interdependence has been of great significance in recent years as the United States government has sought to devise measures to eliminate—or at least reduce the size of—the balance-of-payments deficit. What the interdependence means is that a reduction in the size of some outflows of funds, such as private foreign investment or government foreign aid, will probably also involve an unwanted reduction in United States exports.

Net government grants and capital transactions are shown in item 17 of Table 22–1. The largest components of this item are current foreign aid extensions by the United States government, partially offset by repayments of past foreign loans extended by the United States government. Foreign aid is represented by disbursements under specific nonmilitary foreign aid programs authorized by Congress plus foreign aid-type transactions by agencies such as the Export-Import Bank and United States government contributions to international agencies. It should be noted in passing that military aid extended by

---

[16] Parent companies may receive additional income in the form of royalties and management fees from their foreign affiliates. These revenues, which are a part of miscellaneous services in the balance-of-payments accounts, amounted to more than $756 million in 1964 and over $893 million in 1965.

the United States government is ordinarily not included in the balance of payments. Official balance-of-payments statistics prepared by the Department of Commerce show two items, "Transfers under Military Grants" and "Military Grants of Goods and Services," of exactly equal size but of opposite signs, which of course have the effect of canceling each other. These military grants usually take the form of the direct shipment—without payment—of military equipment by the United States government to the military forces of its allies.

Like private capital, government capital and unilateral transfers also have a back-circling effect on the balance on goods and services. First, the government receives interest income from foreign loans. This income amounted to about $595 million in 1966. More important, government capital has a direct impact on merchandise exports. Most of the loans and grants given under AID require purchases to be made in the United States. About 30 percent of our agricultural exports are transferred under Public Law 480, and the Export-Import Bank extends some long-term loans to finance United States exports. Since 1960 the Department of Commerce has been estimating the value of exports financed by government grants and capital. In 1966 this amounted to $3.0 billion of the $29.2 billion total merchandise exports.

Generally speaking, a forecast of the net foreign balance component of GNP does not require very much attention to these financial transactions unless major changes are pending in one or more of them. Large changes in private foreign investment plans or in government transactions such as large-scale wheat sales to India should, of course, be carefully noted for their effect in subsequently increasing United States exports.

One whose interest is in forecasting the American GNP need not acquire expertise in balance-of-payments matters, but he should have at least a nodding acquaintance with the accounts. The large and thus far chronic deficit in the United States balance of payments, whether measured on the liquidity or the official settlements basis, is a weak point in the otherwise sturdy American economy and someday—for example, if foreign holders of dollars should "run" to convert them into gold—it might suddenly give rise to grave domestic and international economic difficulties.

DEVISING A WORKING FORECAST FOR NET EXPORTS

The conceptual and practical difficulties mentioned in the introduction to this chapter, combined with the fact that net exports seldom constitute much more than 1 percent of GNP, have led most general forecasters to pay only minimal attention to this sector. If a specialist's estimate is not available for use, most current practitioners use either the current value of net exports or a projection of the past trend as a forecast for the upcoming year, on the assumption that no significant error can be involved.

More sophisticated analysts recognize that it is not the absolute size of a sector but rather the extent of its quarter-to-quarter variation that is important for accurate forecasting.   Thus measured, the forecast of the net export component often equals in importance the forecast of many of the other sectors.   In these more sophisticated forecasts, with minor variations, the first-approximation estimates of some or all of the components of domestic demand are used as a basis for forecasting merchandise imports.   Merchandise exports are forecasted by relating them to some measure of economic activity in other countries.   The services components are treated separately, in some instances with payments and receipts netted, and are forecasted by extrapolation of recent trend adjusted for unusual developments that can be reasonably anticipated.   In the pages that follow, we shall suggest versions of these forecasting techniques that are simple enough to be useful to the average economic forecaster.   More elaborate econometric models have been developed, but these are normally used only by relatively well-staffed forecasting organizations with a special interest in the total balance of payments or in components of the balance of payments uniquely affecting their industry or business.

NONMILITARY MERCHANDISE EXPORTS

Contrary to the popular characterization of an advanced country, the United States is a large exporter of agricultural products which make up about 25 percent of our total exports.   Another 15 percent are industrial supplies and raw materials.   Of the 60 percent composed of finished manufactures, less than 10 percent are consumer goods.

The area destination of our exports is as revealing as their composition.   The highly industrialized countries provide our major markets.   Exports to Canada, Japan, Britain, and the six Common Market countries make up slightly over one-half, and almost two-thirds is accounted for if the remaining countries of Western Europe, Australia, and South Africa are added.   Canada and Japan are by far the most important export markets.

A complete analysis of the prospects for merchandise exports would require inspection of the myriad income, price, and composition changes in all the countries to which the United States economy sells.   Somewhat less ambitiously, the countries of the world could be grouped into a few major, relatively homogenous areas (e.g., Western Europe, Canada, Japan, Latin America, and the remaining underdeveloped countries), and economic developments in each of these areas as they relate to their purchases from the United States could be analyzed.   Agricultural exports should be given separate attention because they are largely affected by variables other than foreign business activity.   Changes in agricultural policies here and abroad, foreign crop failures, and agricultural exports under foreign aid programs are usually well known, sometimes even several quarters before they have an impact on

United States exports. Changes in foreign aid shipments of agricultural products can usually be projected ahead by using the Federal budget document.

In practice, a less complete analysis will usually suffice. A reasonable approximation of total merchandise exports, which can be adjusted later for special agricultural and other unusual developments, may be attained by a method somewhat similar to one originally developed by Walther Lederer of the Department of Commerce.[17] This involves relating our exports to the business activity of five of our major industrial customers, France, Germany, Italy, Japan, and the United Kingdom. (Canada, the United States largest single export market, was not included in this list because of its uniquely intimate relationship with the United States economy, which calls for special, separate consideration.) These five countries are among the few that can afford to hold significant reserve balances. For this reason, they are virtually the only countries in which the level of business activity is the major determinant of their demand for imports. In contrast, most of the remaining countries of the world, particularly the primary producers and underdeveloped countries, use their foreign exchange receipts within a short time period for imports, partly of consumption goods, but more importantly, of capital equipment. Their imports, then, are closely related to receipts of foreign exchange, derived principally from two sources: capital outflows from the developed countries and international organizations; and earnings from their exports.

Conceptually, the level of business activity in the advanced countries indirectly influences United States exports to the primary producing and underdeveloped countries.[18] A substantial rise in business activity in the major foreign industrial countries, for example, leads to increased imports from both the United States and other countries. These imports, in turn, supply additional foreign exchange for the underdeveloped countries, some of which is spent on imports from the United States.

For our purposes the best indicators of business activity in the five countries are their indexes of industrial production, because industrial supplies and raw materials and machinery make up such a large portion of our exports to these countries (only about 5 percent of our exports to Western Europe and about 2 percent to Japan are made up of consumer goods). In addition, the industrial production index is the only general business indicator compiled promptly and quarterly in all the above countries.

[17] See "The Balance of International Payments in the Fourth Quarter and the Year 1961," *Survey of Current Business*, U.S. Department of Commerce, vol. 42, no. 3, pp. 18–24, March, 1962.

[18] A significant statistical relationship between United States nonagricultural exports to third areas lagged by one-quarter, and deviations from the average growth rate in Europe and Japan were found by Francis G. Masson and John B. Bodie, "Factors Affecting U.S. Merchandise Exports," *Survey of Current Business*, U.S. Department of Commerce, vol. 43, no. 2, pp. 20–27, February, 1963.

To facilitate analysis, the individual country indexes must be combined. One method is simply to form a weighted average of the individual industrial production indexes, the weights being an average of the selected countries' respective yearly imports from the United States over a recent period.

The two series—a weighted combined industrial production index and United States merchandise exports—are plotted against each other in scatter diagram form (with quarters connected chronologically) in Figure 22–1. It will be observed at once that the correlation is by no means perfect, nor is it dependably linear. Nevertheless, it is clear that a definite relationship does exist.[19]

Because the relationship is imprecise, the production index should be viewed as a guide to orderly thinking and not as an adequate forecasting formula. An extrapolation of the line of relationship in recent years can provide a reasonable first approximation of merchandise exports. This first approximation should then be adjusted to reflect any relevant developments foreseen by the forecaster in the five countries included in the industrial production index and in other countries, especially Canada, the United States principal customer. Exports to Canada are positively correlated with industrial activity in that country which, in turn, is closely correlated with industrial activity in the United States. If the general forecast seems to be pointing toward a vigorous rise in business activity in the United States, the forecaster should adjust his merchandise exports forecast upward to allow for high exports to Canada, and vice versa if a decline seems to be in prospect.[20]

MERCHANDISE IMPORTS

Under the blanket label "total merchandise imports" the Department of Commerce distinguishes six distinct subcategories: industrial supplies and

---

[19] Part of the rationale for this relationship may lie in the possibility that the industrial production index serves as a proxy variable for both price changes and supply capabilities. Prices of manufactured items in many of the European countries and Japan have generally been relatively flexible compared with similar prices in the United States. Thus, when the production index expands less rapidly over a period of time, foreign prices have a tendency to decrease, which, in turn, results in the substitution of domestically produced goods for imports. Similar reasoning can be applied for an upturn when prices have a tendency to increase and imports may be substituted for domestically produced goods. It should be obvious that supply capabilities are also reflected in the index and that this effect works in the same direction to reinforce the price effect.

[20] In the actual use of the index for forecasting, the analyst must first project the industrial production indexes of the five countries. He will be helped by publications such as the International Monetary Fund's (IMF) *International Financial News Survey*, which contains summaries of the current economic situation and prospects for the upcoming year for most of the major IMF members. Industrial production indexes for the five countries are conveniently available each month in *Business Cycle Developments*.

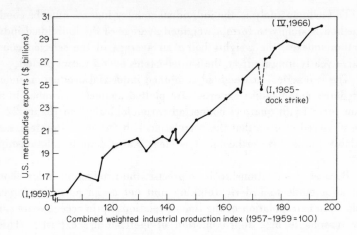

Figure 22–1. The relation between a combined industrial production index of United Kingdom, West Germany, France, Italy, and Japan, and United States merchandise exports, 1959 to 1966. (Quarterly data at seasonally adjusted annual rates.) Source: U.S. Department of Commerce.

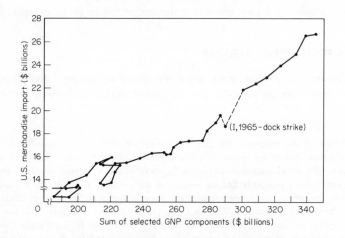

Figure 22–2. The one-quarter lagged relation between the sum of selected GNP components (government purchases of goods and services, gross private domestic investment, personal consumption expenditures for automobiles and parts, and total exports), IVQ 1956 to IIIQ 1966, and United States merchandise imports, IQ 1957 to IVQ 1966. (Quarterly data at seasonally adjusted annual rates.) Source: U.S. Department of Commerce.

materials (averaging 52 percent of the total during 1957–1965); food and beverages (22 percent); nonfood consumer goods (16 percent, three-fifths of which are manufactured durables); capital equipment (4 percent); materials used in farming (3 percent); and noncommercial and unclassified (3 percent).

Excepting the food and beverage component, which tends to be price- and income-inelastic, and the noncommercial and unclassified category, the level of the remaining 75 percent or so of United States merchandise imports (chiefly raw materials) is basically dependent on domestic goods output. The raw materials are either immediate inputs to the United States production machine or are induced ingredients as expansion raises the level of demand. Although, logically, we should relate the former grouping to one set of variables and the latter to another, the difficulty of obtaining balance of trade statistics in this detail, seasonally adjusted and up to date, forces the short-run forecaster to identify the factors that determine the broader merchandise imports total rather than its subdivisions. This, of course, introduces the probability of greater error into his calculations.

Because of their particular composition we would not expect merchandise imports to be related to GNP as a whole, but rather to the "autonomous" sectors. (This also dovetails with our model in which consumer nonautomotive expenditures are treated as determined largely by the sum of these sectors.) Figure 22–2 is a scatter diagram in which quarterly data (seasonally adjusted annual rates) for the sum of the autonomous variables, defined for present purposes as being government purchases of goods and services (Federal, state, and local); gross private domestic investment (business fixed investment, inventory investment, and residential structures); personal consumption expenditures for autos and parts; and *total* exports are plotted against quarterly data (seasonally adjusted annual rates) for merchandise imports *in the following quarter*. That is, autonomous domestic demand is assumed to lead imports by one quarter. Again, it will be observed that the relationship is not a precise one nor is it clearly linear. The very mild recession of 1960–1961 resulted in a more pronounced drop in merchandise imports than a linear relationship would indicate. And after the first quarter 1965, a break in the relationship is evident. Imports rose to a higher level than the prior relationship would have suggested. The reason for this phenomenon may lie in the fact that in 1965 and 1966, as the United States economy pressed against capacity limits, the lengthening of domestic delivery lead times made imports relatively more attractive. The reemergence of inflation in the United States, though moderate, may also have played a role.

The experience over this period of time suggests that, although there is a positive functional relationship between domestic demand and merchandise imports, it is not necessarily one that can be expressed by a single, least-squares linear regression line. The forecaster would do well to examine the relationship over the past several years, give attention to anticipated unusual events during the forecast period that could cause the relationship to alter, and then "free hand" a line of relationship that reflects these anticipated events. Alternatively, if the forecaster has the time and facilities, multiple correlation analyses introducing as independent variables the factors mentioned above and others might yield a better forecast. But for most general economic forecasters, the increased reliability of the forecast would not be worth the effort. In any event, the multiple regression should be updated frequently to reflect changes in the underlying relationship.

MILITARY EXPENDITURES AND SALES

Military expenditures in the current account are payments for the direct purchase of *foreign* goods and services under our defense programs, while military sales for the most part are shipments to foreigners of nonaid military goods arranged and handled by the Department of Defense. Military expenditures and sales, then, are actually the imports and exports, respectively, of government agencies for defense-related programs.

The bulk of military expenditures, which amounted to approximately $3.6 billion in 1966, represent costs for the support of United States military forces. Such costs include foreign expenditures of servicemen and post exchanges, the services of foreign nationals, and the foreign procurement of supplies and equipment. The remaining portion of military expenditures is made up of overseas payments for defense-related activities of agencies other than the Defense Department. We might add that, although military expenditures are conceptually an import item, in most cases even when foreign goods are purchased there is no physical flow into the United States.

As already indicated, military sales are cash sales of military equipment arranged and shipped by the Defense Department. Commercial shipments of military-type equipment are classified as a component of finished manufactures and are included in merchandise exports. The responsibility for procuring and shipping such items has been gradually shifted from commercial sources to the Defense Department. Thus, while most of the increase in military sales can be attributed to an actual increase in sales, at least a part of the rise has resulted from a shifting of accounts.

In an attempt to limit the balance-of-payments impact of our defense commitments, government programs that decrease military expenditures and increase sales have been deemed appropriate. The United States has carried out negotiations with several European countries for increased procurement in the United States. In addition, a series of measures designed to decrease foreign defense procurements and expenditures by military personnel have been undertaken. We may expect additional measures to decrease expenditures and increase sales, depending upon balance-of-payments pressures. Ample warning of upcoming moves is usually given in the press, and with these in mind the forecaster should be able to come quite close on his net military estimate.

SERVICES

The composition of this remaining and important component is shown in Table 22–2. For the most part, the information used in forecasting merchandise trade provides sufficient background for an educated extrapolation of the individual net service components once the entries are understood. Transportation services arise because merchandise exports and imports are valued f.o.b. (free on board) and the related costs of transportation are listed separately as a service. As with all components of the balance of payments, entries arise only when a domestic resident makes a transaction with a foreigner. Thus, the receipts of United States carriers transporting our merchandise exports (owned by a foreigner once they leave port) and other foreign goods or foreign passengers is recorded as a transportation receipt, as are the expenditures of foreign carriers for bunkerage, repairs, dock fees and wages, etc., in our ports. United States merchandise imports and other United States goods and residents transported by foreign carriers, as well as foreign port expenditures made by domestic carriers, give rise to payments in the transportation service account.

Changes in the volume and composition of foreign trade and passenger travel, carrier rates, and the degree of participation of United States carriers are the main determinants of fluctuations in transportation receipts and payments. Large changes in the net transportation balance are unlikely, however, because of the countervailing effect of port expenditures. For example, a large expansion of our merchandise imports would expand transportation payments because a part of the increased volume would be carried by foreign carriers. Part of this increase in payments would be offset by receipts from port expenditures made by the foreign carriers as they leave their cargoes in United States ports. The counterbalancing tendency of port expenditures is so important that it has been estimated that *ceteris paribus* if *all* United States imports and exports were carried by United States ocean carriers the net transportation balance would be plus $820 million, whereas if *all* were carried by foreign vessels the balance would be minus $300 million.[21] These relatively narrow limits represent very extreme circumstances and serve to indicate that a simple extrapolation should not be far off.

[21] Angelos J. Clones and Gary C. McKay, "Transportation Transactions in the U.S. Balance of Payments," *Survey of Current Business,* U.S. Department of Commerce, vol. 43, no. 8, pp. 23–28, August, 1963.

Net travel services can be handled similarly. Payments for travel include United States residents' expenses for food, accommodations, souvenirs and other personal purchases, and transportation within foreign countries (transoceanic travel expenses were included under transportation services). United States travel payments are closely related to United States DPI. Expenditures *per person* traveling abroad have generally decreased since the duty-free allowance was reduced from $500 to $100 in 1962, but *total* expenditures have risen steadily as an increasing number of middle-income persons have found foreign travel within their means. Presumably, foreign travel expenditures in the United States are influenced by DPI in each of the countries from which travelers come. If so, to the extent that business fluctuations in the United States and abroad are positively correlated, a rise in expenditures of United States residents abroad would be offset by a rise in expenditures of foreign residents in the United States. In any event, fluctuations in travel caused by changes in business activity are damped by the stability of DPI, relative to GNP, in the United States and abroad. Important sources of change remain in the form of policies for tourist promotion and reduction of tourist purchases, international political tensions, or even events such as the Olympic Games. At times such changes are possible to anticipate, but the relatively small degree of yearly fluctuation from the trend makes further analysis unrewarding.

In contrast, private investment income represents a difficult forecasting problem because of the possibility of rather large changes such as those experienced in 1961 and 1964. The main source of change comes from the receipts side where direct investment income in the form of dividends, interest, and branch profits dominates—$4.0 billion of the $5.6 billion total in 1966. The earnings of foreign *manufacturing* subsidiaries do not show up as an income receipt in the balance of payments until a dividend to the parent company has been declared. Thus a part of the quarter-to-quarter fluctuation in direct investment income is simply a result of changes in dividend policies. In contrast to domestic dividend policies, which in the aggregate seem to be quite predictable, dividend policies of major European companies and especially of wholly owned or largely owned manufacturing subsidiaries of United States companies are difficult to anticipate. This unpredictability reflects partly the smaller number of companies involved, but chiefly the fact that tax considerations, in the United States and abroad, may play a decisive role in the *timing* of dividend declarations. Prior to the tax cut of 1964, for example, dividend payments by foreign manufacturing subsidiaries of United States companies dropped, in anticipation of the cut. And as might be expected, they rose again after the tax cut.

Income receipts from the petroleum industry, however, are treated differently from manufacturing companies for tax purposes. Profits of foreign subsidiaries of petroleum companies are counted as "received" when earned—

Table **22-2.** Service Components of Net Exports, 1953–1966 (In millions of dollars)

	1953	1954	1955	1956	1957	1958	1959	1960	1961	1962	1963	1964	1965	1966
Transportation														
Receipts	1,198	1,171	1,406	1,617	1,967	1,638	1,646	1,752	1,805	1,964	2,115	2,317	2,415	2,585
Payments	−1,081	−1,026	−1,204	−1,408	−1,569	−1,636	−1,759	−1,915	−1,943	−2,128	−2,316	−2,464	−2,691	−2,903
Net	+117	+145	+202	+209	+398	+2	−113	−163	−138	−164	−201	−147	−276	−318
Travel														
Receipts	574	595	654	705	785	825	902	875	885	878	934	1,095	1,212	1,417
Payments	−929	−1,009	−1,153	−1,275	−1,372	−1,460	−1,610	−1,732	−1,735	−1,885	−2,090	−2,216	−2,400	−2,623
Net	−355	−414	−499	−570	−587	−635	−708	−857	−850	−1007	−1,156	−1,121	−1,188	−1,206
Income on investments														
Private:														
Receipts	1,658	1,955	2,170	2,468	2,612	2,538	2,694	3,001	3,561	3,954	4,156	5,003	5,389	5,585
Payments	−375	−361	−395	−414	−438	−530	−547	−667	−656	−717	−871	−952	−1,158	−1,311
Net	+1,283	+1,594	+1,775	+2,054	+2,174	+2,008	+2,147	+2,334	+2,905	+3,237	+3,285	+4,051	+4,231	+4,274
Government:														
Receipts	252	272	274	194	205	307	349	349	380	471	498	454	512	595
Payments	−86	−59	−94	−154	−201	−139	−281	−332	−278	−339	−400	−452	−488	−557
Net	+166	+213	+180	+40	+4	+168	+68	+17	+102	+132	+98	+2	+24	+38
Miscellaneous services														
Receipts	792	785	820	1,071	1,147	1,195	1,301	1,443	1,588	1,751	1,922	2,098	2,345	2,640
Payments	−485	−480	−521	−624	−665	−709	−728	−751	−851	−809	−838	−930	−930	−1,064
Net	+307	+305	+299	+447	+482	+486	+573	+692	+737	+942	+1084	+1,168	+1,415	+1,576
Total net services	+1,518	+1,843	+1,957	+2,180	+2,471	+2,029	+1,967	+2,023	+2,756	+3,140	+3,110	+3,953	+4,206	+4,364

Source: *Balance of Payments Statistical Supplement to the Survey of Current Business,* 1963 edition, for 1953–1959; *Survey of Current Business,* U.S. Department of Commerce, June, 1965, and March, 1967, for 1960–1966.

in the balance-of-payments accounts as well as for tax purposes—without regard to whether an actual remittance occurs.

From this information, a rough but workable method of forecasting net private investment income can be devised. Payments are sufficiently stable that they can simply be extrapolated. Receipts are a function of three variables: the accumulated volume of investment abroad; the level of economic activity which affects the profitability of operations in the countries where United States investments are primarily located; and the degree of repatriation of earnings. Information on the trend of capital investment abroad can be gleaned from the financial press. Because it is a cumulative figure, the total increases quite gradually. With respect to the profitability of foreign operations, the same information that was used in forecasting United States exports, i.e., forecasts of industrial production in the principal European countries and Japan, provides a useful clue. This clue is relevant, it should be noted, even for the petroleum companies whose operations are *not* located mainly in Western Europe and Japan, because a large proportion of the petroleum products produced by these companies is sold in Western Europe and Japan. With respect to the degree of repatriation, a distinction needs to be made between the petroleum companies, who typically repatriate a large percentage of their earnings for the reasons cited above, and other, chiefly manufacturing, companies in which the degree of repatriation is not only much lower but subject to sudden changes when changes in applicable tax laws are expected. This latter difference makes it advisable to make separate investment forecasts for petroleum companies and for other industries, with the prospect of tax changes being a more important determinant in the case of the latter.

Again, special attention should be given to developments in Canada which, in 1966, provided more than one-fifth of United States income from private investment abroad.

The second subcomponent of investment income is net government investment income. Although, as Table 22–2 shows, total receipts and total payments have been sizable numbers and have fluctuated considerably, *net* receipts have been quite small—usually less than $0.2 billion. Little error is likely to be involved, therefore, in simply using the net figure from last year or the average of recent years.

The remaining item in the services component of net exports in the national income accounts, "miscellaneous services," is a troublesome one simply because the transactions included in its are miscellaneous. The most important single item is royalties and fees, including royalties paid to parent companies by subsidiaries. Also included are management consultant fees, film rentals, the excess of insurance premiums over losses, and a variety of minor items. The difficulties of forecasting are compounded by the fact that, from time to time, items previously in the "errors and omissions" balancing item have been identified and measured with sufficient accuracy to be shifted to this miscellaneous category.   Thus, a part of the increase in previous years reflects an improvement in statistical coverage, not a real increase.

Fortunately, as Table 22–2 shows, the excess of receipts over payments —"miscellaneous services, net"—closely approximates a linear progression. In the absence of some major event, actual or anticipated, that would importantly affect one of the items included in this miscellaneous category, a simple extrapolation of recent trends in the net amount is likely to be not far from the mark.

Once the net service components listed in the table are established, they can be added to the estimated net military and net merchandise balance to arrive at a forecast for net exports.

23

CONSUMER DEMAND
(Excluding Automobiles)

We have now made preliminary forecasts of government purchases of goods and services, gross private domestic investment (business fixed investment, residential structures, and inventory investment), net exports, and personal consumption expenditures for automobiles. The remainder of GNP, consumer purchases of goods and services other than automobiles, constitutes much the largest expenditure component for which a model-building short-run forecaster must develop a first-approximation estimate. If it were necessary to build a forecast on the basis of a commodity-by-commodity approach, the difficulties would be almost insurmountable. Fortunately, however, an imposing case can be made for assuming that, in the United States, aggregate consumer purchases of goods and services other than automobiles can, for general forecasting purposes, be viewed as almost exclusively a function of aggregate disposable personal income. If, therefore, we can devise a method of forecasting, from the total of the components of GNP that have already been preliminarily forecast, an estimate of DPI, we can short-cut the segmental, commodity-by-commodity approach and get on with the job of making a *general*, short-run forecast.[1]

THE C_o/DPI RATIO

The basic rationale for streamlining the forecasting of personal outlays other than automobiles (C_o) was laid in our discussions of the consumption-function hypothesis in Part Two, but it began to take concrete shape at the end of Chapter 20. There we observed that, in recent years in the United States, automobile and parts outlays (C_a) and net personal saving taken together have maintained a considerably more stable relationship to disposable personal income than has either of them alone. The inverse of this proposition is that the relationship of consumer outlays for other than automobiles to aggregate disposable personal income also has been comparatively stable. The fact is, as Figure 23–1 makes plain, this relationship has been one of the most noteworthy regularities in the American economy during the past generation.[2]

The regression line plotted in Figure 23–1 (expressed algebraically in the equation $C_o = \$0.11$ billion $+ 0.8833$ DPI, where C_o represents personal outlays less automobiles and parts, and DPI $=$ disposable personal income, both in billions of current dollars) is a least-squares regression for the years 1946 through 1965. The secular relationship that the figure displays is an extraordinarily close one. For the years included in the calculation, nonautomotive outlays and disposable personal income in current prices have a coefficient of correlation of .9990. The secular relationship has been very nearly proportional. During the period covered the average propensity to spend for these nonautomotive outlays has been nearly the same as the marginal propensity, both being about $88\frac{1}{3}$ percent.

The theoretical hypothesis that this evidence suggests raises the possibility that the easy aggregative technique of forecasting other-than-automobile

---

[1] This is not to say, of course, that, once analysts especially concerned with particular commodities or services have adopted a general outlook framework, either by developing it themselves or borrowing it from someone else, they cannot sensibly try to identify the specific sales prospects for processed meats, children's shoes, hospital services, or what have you. They obviously must and do. But we are concerned only with the first step of this process—the formulation of the general outlook—and there the construction of specific forecasts for every commodity segment is more of a task than any single analyst or analytical group should undertake within the time in which a general short-run forecast must be completed to be usable. For a discussion of techniques for making the transition from a general economic forecast to one for a particular company or product, see Richard M. Bailey, "Tailoring the Business Forecast to Company Size," *Business Horizons*, vol. 5, no. 2, pp. 81–88, Summer, 1962.

[2] Note that it is personal outlays—not personal consumption expenditures—less automobiles and parts that we are comparing with DPI. We shall discuss the reasons for this choice in a moment.

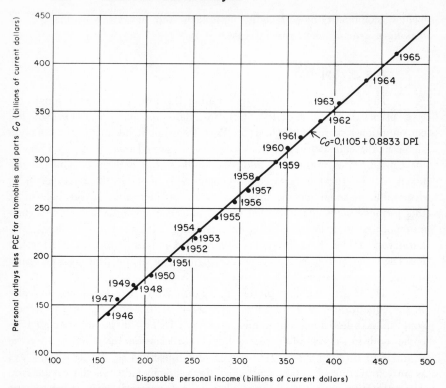

Figure 23–1. The relation between personal outlays less automobiles and parts and disposable personal income in the United States, 1946–1965. Source: U.S. Department of Commerce.

outlays may be intrinsically superior to the best that could be accomplished via the commodity-by-commodity route. That hypothesis is that the most typical characteristic of American consumers' behavior is the tendency of consumers, in the aggregate, to spend a relatively fixed proportion of current-dollar disposable income on total nonautomobile outlays, and that the other factors affecting such spending—population changes, prices, innovations, and the rest—have a significant impact only upon the allocation of this total volume of current spending among particular commodities and services.

Figure 23–1 lends this proposition more powerful support than is directly observable from its data. The period covered is one in which price behavior, the rate of population growth, the age distribution of the population, family size, consumers' long-term economic expectations, and personal income distribution, all have varied significantly. Yet in all years of high and rising income, the sales-income relationship for soft goods and services consumption has been almost uncannily constant. This seems to suggest that nonautomobile outlays as a whole, unlike the particular segments of the category, and probably also unlike automobiles, tend to have a price elasticity of unity; and

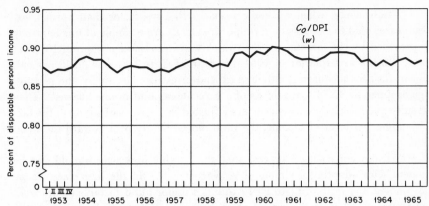

Figure **23–2.**   Personal outlays excluding automobiles as percentage of disposable personal income in the United States, by quarters, 1953–1965.   (Quarterly data at seasonally adjusted annual rates.)   Source: *Survey of Current Business*, U.S. Department of Commerce.

that American consumers, whatever their numbers, ages, and family groupings, keep on spending just about the same fraction of their incomes on non-automotive goods and services of one kind or another.

    This generalization has been put in categorical language for the sake of emphasis. But now we should relax this language a bit and recognize that, although the correlation between consumer expenditures for goods and services excluding autos and DPI is high, it is not perfect. Further, when one examines quarterly, rather than annual, data, it is apparent that small but significant deviations from the $88\frac{1}{3}$ percent rule have occurred and the serious analyst needs to be able to anticipate these small deviations and incorporate them into his model.

    Figure 23–2 illustrates the ratio of personal outlays other than for automobiles to DPI from 1953 to 1965. Both this figure and Figure 23–1 point up one type of situation in which the secular, or trend, relationship should not be expected to yield a good forecast. In years of retarded income growth, such as 1949, 1954, 1958, and 1960, consumers have spent more on goods and services excluding autos than the secular relationship would suggest. This behavior, which recalls the Duesenberry hypothesis noted in Chapter 8, apparently does not require an actual drop in spendable consumer incomes. In each of the postwar recessions, when (on an annual basis) disposable personal income only slowed down relative to the growth in capacity, spending pushed upward faster than income. Thus if a recession is already under way at the beginning of the forecast period and the forecaster accordingly adopts a no-change rather than a normal-growth–initial-income hypothesis, his initial estimates should allow for some strength *relative to income* in the soft goods and services sector.

Conversely, when for some reason DPI rises faster than normal, expenditures tend to rise less than proportionately. An example of this tendency is provided by the tax cut of 1964, which went into effect on March 1 of that year. In the first quarter of 1964, the ratio of C_o to DPI was 88.45 percent. But in the second quarter, although expenditures rose absolutely, the percentage dropped to 87.78—two-thirds of a percentage point in one quarter. Then in subsequent quarters, as consumers adjusted their scales of living to the tax-cut-augmented level of income, the ratio moved slowly back toward the trend line.

These experiences suggest that the careful forecaster should not be content with adopting a simple $88\frac{1}{3}$ percent rule. In the first place, as we have noted, the ratio of C_o to DPI exhibits a minor but detectable contracyclical tendency. And in the second place, unusual events—which may, as in the case of the tax cut, be predictable—sometimes cause the ratio to deviate significantly from its normal trend. And in the third place, we cannot assume that this relationship will continue unchanged for all time. The alert analyst will watch for subtle changes in consumer propensities as revealed by the most recent data.

For operational purposes, we suggest that the forecaster calculate ratios of C_o to DPI for each of the past 30 or 40 quarters, try to provide himself with an adequate explanation of past deviations from the trend line, and then make a reasoned forecast of the C_o/DPI ratio for the quarters under analysis, using his knowledge of the probable general trend of economic activity as postulated in his preliminary income hypothesis or, more importantly, as revealed by the forecasts of the semiautonomous components of GNP that he has already made, plus whatever knowledge he may possess about forthcoming unusual events and predictable changes in consumer attitudes. Experience suggests that the forecaster should be wary of predicting any very significant change in the ratio from the recent past, especially if the recent past has been about on trend, *unless* he has good reasons for expecting a substantial change in consumer behavior. At the same time, the ability to anticipate accurately the direction and magnitude of small but significant changes in the C_o/DPI ratio makes the difference between the mediocre and the good forecaster.

A few paragraphs back, we punctuated the text with a footnote calling attention to the definition of C_o as *personal outlays* less automobiles. Alternatively, it could have been defined as personal consumption expenditures less automobiles. The difference, of course, is the two items of personal expenditure that Commerce treats, in the national income accounts, as transferlike payments: interest paid by consumers and net personal transfers to foreigners. If we are to forecast personal consumption expenditures less automobiles by relating them to DPI, these transfers must be taken into account in one manner or another because they make a claim on DPI. The alternative methods of taking them into account are: (1) to treat them as autonomous variables and deduct them from DPI, and then relate PCE less automobiles to the remainder; or (2) to add them to PCE less automobiles and relate the total (PO less automobiles) to total DPI.

We have chosen the latter method, on the reasoning that these transfer-like expenditures are a function of DPI in much the same sense that the other expenditures included in nonautomobile personal consumption expenditures are a function of DPI. Consumers have an option of incurring installment-payment obligations (part of which is interest), or of using their income for food, clothing, and other goods and services that Commerce does not classify as a transfer. If a larger share of income is spent on interest, less is available for other goods and services, and vice versa. And the array of motivations that determine consumer expenditures for goods and services presumably also determine the expenditures for the time utility obtained by incurring consumer debt.[3] The same argument would seem to apply to personal remittances abroad.[4]

However these transferlike payments are handled, they must be separately forecast. Fortunately, if past experience is a proper guide, this is relatively easy to do. Net personal transfers to foreigners have been small and nearly constant. A projection of last year's figure is not likely to miss the mark by more than $0.1 billion. Interest payments by consumers, for the reason noted in the footnote a paragraph back, change rather slowly and steadily. A simple extrapolation of the recent trend, bent slightly one way or the other depending on the forecaster's evaluation of the prospects for consumer debt, will probably be very close.

THE DPI/GNP RELATIONSHIP

To this point, we have been discussing the *ratio* of C_o to DPI. We still have to derive a method for making an estimate of DPI for the forecast period, to which the ratio can be applied to obtain a dollar figure for C_o.

Here, again, the answer lies in identifying reasonably consistent and predictable relationships between DPI and the totality of GNP. For analytical purposes, because the share of GNP claimed by personal income and the share of personal income taken in personal taxes are determined by quite different sets of influences, it is useful to study the relationship between DPI and GNP

---

[3] The converse argument is that, because interest payments arise from contracts entered into some months back, they are largely fixed *in the short run* and therefore should be treated as an autonomous variable in short-run forecasting. In this sense, however, many other categories of consumer expenditures, notably utility bills and rent (including the rental value of owner-occupied housing), are autonomous in the short run.

[4] In practice, because these two transferlike items are such a small percentage of total personal outlays excluding automobiles, it makes very little difference by which method they are handled; i.e., the ratios are virtually indistinguishable. If the definitions employed in the balance of the forecasting exercise are consistent with the definition of this ratio, essentially the same forecast should result.

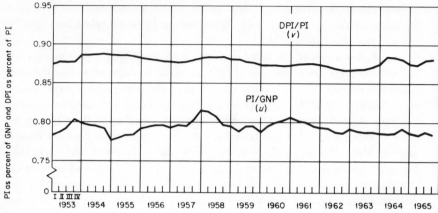

Figure **23–3.**   Personal income as a percent of GNP and disposable personal income as a percent of personal income in the United States, 1953–1965.   (Quarterly data at seasonally adjusted annual rates.)   Source: U.S. Department of Commerce.

in two steps: PI/GNP and DPI/PI (the product of the two ratios, obviously, equals DPI/GNP.) Figure 23–3 illustrates these two ratios over the 1953–1965 period.

The PI/GNP ratio, it will be noted, has exhibited a rough contra-cyclical pattern. It has held fairly close to 79 percent or slightly above in periods of normal expansion, falling below 79 percent only briefly in periods of strong expansion in 1955, 1959, and again in 1962–1965. In periods of declining business activity, the ratio has risen above 80 percent. No secular trend in the ratio is evident.

The explanation of this contracyclical pattern is to be found in varia-tions in the components of GNP that intervene between GNP and PI. Ignor-ing a couple of minor items and the statistical discrepancy, PI is equal to GNP *less* capital-consumption allowances, indirect business taxes, all of corporate profits plus IVA except dividends paid, and contributions to social insur-ance, *plus* subsidies less surpluses of government enterprises, interest paid by government and by persons, and government transfer payments. In principle, each of these should be forecast separately and carefully[5] and a PI/GNP ratio calculated from these separate estimates for the forecast period. In practice, it is usually sufficient to make a rough prediction of the direction and approximate magnitude of the net quarter-to-quarter change in the aggre-gate of these variables and modify the PI/GNP ratio of the most recent quar-ter accordingly.

Given our preliminary income hypothesis—or better yet, given the changes in the quasi-autonomous components in GNP that we have already

[5] In the next chapter, in our consideration of the income side of the NEB, we shall discuss techniques for forecasting these items.

forecast—we do have some clues of probable changes in these intervening factors between GNP and PI. Capital-consumption allowances can be expected to increase steadily, regardless of fluctuations in business activity, except when there is a change in relevant tax law. Corporate profits other than dividends are, we know, quite sensitive to fluctuations in economic activity; indeed, because most corporations prefer to follow stable dividend policies, almost all the variation in total corporate profits is reflected in undistributed profits and corporate profits taxes. Indirect business taxes are positively correlated with the dollar volume of business. Contributions to social insurance can be relied on to reflect variations in the level of employment and income except when there is a change in social security tax rates. Government subsidies less surpluses of government enterprises, unfortunately, reflect such a kaleidoscope of influences that no pattern is readily apparent; fortunately the item is small and a no-change assumption will probably not involve serious error. Government interest payments are steady, except when there is an abrupt change in interest rates, and account for only a small portion of the variations in the PI/GNP ratio. Government transfer payments include two main categories, old age, survivors, and disability insurance payments, and unemployment compensation. The former increase steadily,[6] except when there is a change in the annuity provisions of the law. Unemployment compensation, however, is inversely related to the level of employment and incomes for obvious reasons. Personal interest payments have already been discussed.

On balance, therefore, if our preliminary forecast to this point indicates a strong upward surge in economic activity, we can expect the PI/GNP ratio to fall to 79 percent or less. If a period of moderate expansion is in prospect, the ratio is likely to fall in the 79 to 80 percent range. If a recession is in prospect, however, the ratio is likely to rise toward and perhaps even above 81 percent, the extent of the rise being determined by the level of the ratio at the start and the extent and duration of the decline in business activity.

Before leaving the matter of the PI/GNP ratio, a word of warning is in order. The above generalizations are based on experience at the date of writing. Even though, to this point in time, no secular trend in the PI/GNP ratio is apparent, the competent forecaster will be on the alert for underlying influences that may affect the level and performance of this ratio. The only safe procedure is a careful study of recent data and a careful identification of the forces that have caused or in the future may cause fluctuations in the components that determine PI/GNP.

The DPI/PI ratio, also illustrated in Figure 23–3, is even more stable than the PI/GNP ratio. And two characteristics of the behavior of the ratio are immediately apparent. The first (prior to 1964) is a small but clearly perceptible downward drift. This, indeed, is what we would expect from:

---

[6] See the next chapter for a minor exception to this statement.

(1) the tendency of state and local governments, under pressure to meet mounting needs for education, hospitalization, and streets and highways, to raise tax rates; and (2) the fact that our total tax system is probably slightly progressive—the regressivity of state and local taxes being somewhat more than offset by the progressivity of the Federal tax system. This progressivity of the total system results in a small, gradual rise in the proportion of income taken in personal taxes (i.e., in a decline in the DPI/PI ration) as average per capita incomes rise through time.

The second characteristic of the DPI/PI ratio is a definite contracyclical tendency. This contracyclical tendency is, again, explained by the slightly progressive character of our total personal tax system.

The sharp rise in the ratio in the first two quarters of 1964 reflects, of course, the 1964 tax cut.[7] And this experience provides the clue to the most important event to watch for in predicting the DPI/PI ratio. If a change in tax rates is in prospect, and if the dollar amount of the change—the addition to or subtraction from DPI—can be estimated, it is a matter of simple arithmetic to calculate the effect of the tax rate change on the DPI/PI ratio.

CALCULATING C_o AND GNP

Once these ratios are estimated, the rest of the way is easy sailing. By definition,

$$GNP = G + I + E + C_a + C_o - T \qquad (1)$$

where G = government purchases of goods and services

     I = gross private domestic investment

     E = net exports

     C_a = personal consumption expenditures for automobiles

     C_o = personal outlays less PCE for automobiles

     T = interest paid by consumers plus net personal transfers to foreigners

The first four terms on the right-hand side of this equation have already been estimated, and now, if not earlier, T must be estimated. Only C_o and GNP on the left-hand side are unknown. Let us adopt the following symbols for the three ratios we have been discussing:

     PI/GNP $= u$

     DPI/PI $= v$

     C_o/DPI $= w$

Therefore,

     $C_o = w$ DPI

        $= vw$ PI

        $= uvw$ GNP

---

[7] Also, a part of the small rise in early 1958 reflects the minor adjustment in personal income taxes made that year.

Substituting in equation 1,

$$GNP = G + I + E + C_a + uvw\ GNP - T \qquad (2)$$

Transposing,

$$GNP - uvw\ GNP = G + I + E + C_a - T \qquad (3)$$

Factoring and simplifying,

$$GNP = \frac{G + I + E + C_a - T}{1 - uvw} \qquad (4)$$

Given estimates for u, v, and w, this last equation has only one unknown, and with our previous estimates for the terms on the right-hand side of the equation, the equation can be readily solved for GNP. The value of C_o, of course, is simply GNP times uvw, or, if you prefer subtraction to multiplication, GNP minus $(G + I + E + C_a)$ plus T. And the component we need for our GNP model—personal consumption expenditures for other than automobiles—is GNP minus $(G + I + E + C_a)$, or $C_o - T$.

24

COMPLETING A
SHORT-RUN FORECAST

An outlook analyst who had followed the analytical route suggested in the preceding eight chapters would now have obtained estimates for all the expenditure components of GNP, plus estimates of PI and DPI. In addition, he would have made estimates of the capacity of the economy in the forecast period. These figures, of course, are enough to constitute a forecast, and many practicing forecasters go no further. However, a forecaster who wants to make sure that his figures make economic sense, and who wants to analyze his forecast for its economic significance in an orderly way, will take several additional steps. He will (1) complete a first-approximation array of the Nation's Economic Budget for the forecast period, filling in the receipts and balances as well as the expenditure components; (2) examine this demand pattern for internal consistency; (3) compare the adjusted demand forecast with the capacity forecast, and, if a tendency toward excessive or deficient demand is revealed, appraise the likelihood of secondary reactions in both capacity and demand; and finally (4) arrive at a net qualitative judgment about the outlook, including that for employment, prices, and profits.

FILLING OUT AN INITIAL NATION'S ECONOMIC BUDGET ARRAY

The Nation's Economic Budget (NEB) format, it will be recalled from Part One, arrays the expenditure components of GNP (actually GNE) against the receipts components of GNI by the four major classifications of income receivers and spenders: persons (consumers), business, foreigners, and government (Federal, state, and local). This array permits a comparison of the receipts and expenditures of each of these groups,[1] including a calculation of the (algebraic) excess of receipts over expenditures. We already have made both receipts and expenditure estimates for the consumer sector, and can calculate the excess of receipts—net personal saving—by subtracting the personal consumption expenditures total and interest paid by consumers and net foreign transfers by persons from DPI. We also have, incidentally, a figure for one of the components of government receipts: personal income taxes, which is simply PI less DPI. The other components of the receipts side of the NEB remain to be estimated. Figure 24–1 is a suggested work sheet for arraying these estimates. It should be noted that this work sheet makes a provision for a statistical discrepancy even though, conceptually, there is no discrepancy between GNE and GNI. As will be explained later in the chapter, under certain circumstances it may be better estimating technique to assume a value other than zero.

GROSS RECEIPTS OF BUSINESS

The two main components of gross retained earnings of business are capital-consumption allowances and undistributed profits plus IVA. The third, the excess of wage accruals over disbursements, is nearly always zero, or close to it, when figures are rounded to the nearest tenth of a billion dollars. No significant error is likely to be involved by arbitrarily assuming it to be zero.

Undistributed profits are, of course, a function of total corporate profits. Because corporate profits in business accounting are a residual—the excess of total income over total costs—it makes sense to treat them as a residual in calculating the receipts side of the NEB.[2] Actually, the arithmetic

---

[1] Subject to the qualifications discussed in Chap. 4.

[2] As an independent check on the residual method, various other methods of forecasting corporate profits—given the other components of a general forecast—are available. See Gary Fromm, "Inventories, Business Cycles, and Economic Stabilization," in *Inventory Fluctuations and Economic Stabilization*, Materials Prepared for the Joint Economic Committee, 87th Cong. 2d Sess., 1962, part IV, Supplementary Papers, pp. 84–85. Also Charles Schultze, "Short Run Movements of Income Shares," in Conference on Research in Income and Wealth, *The Behavior of Income Shares: Selected Theoretical and Empirical Issues*, National Bureau of Economic Research, Inc., Studies in Income and Wealth, vol. 27, Princeton University Press, Princeton, N.J., 1964, p. 143; and James Duesenberry, Otto Eckstein, and Gary Fromm, "A Simulation of the United States Economy in Recession," *Econometrica*, vol. 28, pp. 781–786, October, 1960.

Figure 24-1. Forecasting work sheet: NEB. (Current dollars; quarterly data at seasonally adjusted annual rates.)

	Quarter			Quarter			Quarter			Quarter			Year		
	Recs.	Exps.	Bal.	Recs.	Exps.	Bal.	Recs.	Exps.	Bal.	Recs.	Exps.	Bal.	Recs.	Exps.	Bal.

Consumers:
1. DPI
2. Personal transfers*
3. DPI less personal transfers
4. PCE
5. Net personal saving (+)

Business:
6. Gross retained earnings
7. Capital-consumption allowances
8. Undistributed corporate profits + IVA
9. Excess of wage accruals over disbursements
10. GPDI
11. Business fixed investment
12. Residential construction
13. Inventory investment
14. Excess of investment (−)

International:
15. Foreign net transfers by government and persons
16. Net exports goods & services
17. Excess of FNT over NE (+)

Government:
18. Gross receipts
19. Less: Transfers, interest, etc.†
20. Net receipts
21. Purchases goods & services
22. Federal
23. State and local
24. Surplus (+) or deficit (−)
25. Statistical discrepancy‡

26. GNP or GNI

* Interest paid by persons and net transfer payments by persons to foreigners.
† Government transfers to persons, foreign net transfers, net interest paid by government, and subsidies less current surplus of government enterprises.
‡ Statistical discrepancy should be zero unless another figure was deliberately assumed.

is not quite so simple as plugging a number for corporate profits that will make the NEB balance, because the corporate profits figure as such does not appear on the NEB. Profits are split three ways: dividends (a part of personal income); corporate profits taxes (a receipt of government); and undistributed profits plus IVA (a receipt of business). The residual technique, therefore, involves not only estimating the balancing item—corporate profits— but also deciding how it will be split among corporate profits taxes, dividends, and undistributed profits plus IVA. Of these three, the only one we can estimate independently, without knowing the total corporate profits figure, is dividends.

Despite the notorious instability of corporate profits as a whole, dividends paid have shown a remarkably stable growth, reflecting both the gradual increase in the total amount of corporate stock outstanding (which in turn reflects the growth of the aggregate capital of the corporate economy, but not in a 1:1 ratio because of changes in the degree of equity financing) and the practice of many business firms to maintain fairly steady dividend policies, changing dividend rates only in response to significant and presumably lasting changes in earnings. As shown in Figure 24–2, the series is not entirely insensitive to business fluctuations, above-average increases occurring in years of high-level business activity. But in only one year after the Korean War period did dividends paid actually decline, from $11.7 billion in 1957 to $11.6 billion in the recession year of 1958. Unless the analyst has good reason for assuming some change in past tendencies, therefore, a simple

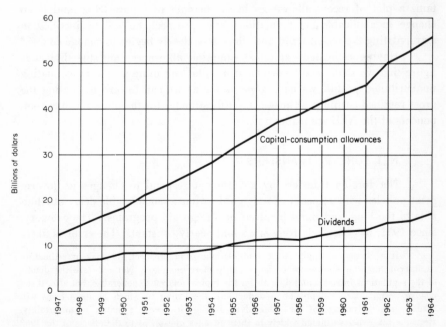

Figure **24–2.** Capital-consumption allowances and dividends paid, 1947–1964. Source: U.S. Department of Commerce.

extrapolation of the trend line, bent slightly one way or the other to reflect the pattern of economic activity that his forecast is apparently revealing, should yield an adequate estimate.

Capital-consumption allowances have been one of the most strongly rising economic series in the United States since World War II. Any really scientific analysis of their prospects in the coming year would require a detailed inquiry into the composition and the age of business' fixed-capital stock and into corporate depreciation practices; it would consume more time than a general forecasting staff typically can afford. In seeking a short cut, the analyst presently finds, as Figure 24-2 indicates, that capital-consumption allowances are also more closely correlated simply with time than with any other readily accessible variable.

Plainly, as the 1954, 1958, and 1960-1961 increases show, the continuing growth in capital-consumption allowances is not directly or sensitively dependent on a steady expansion in total business activity. Instead, as a result of continuing high investment, mounting costs, the growing prominence of relatively short-lived equipment in American industries' plant and equipment mix, and conventional accounting methods, capital-consumption allowances advanced steadily regardless of fluctuations in business activity. (The large increase in 1962—$4.8 billion—is attributable to the change in the regulations on depreciation allowances permissible for tax purposes—"Bulletin F"—made by the Treasury in that year.) It would be foolish to assume that this average rate of absolute growth could continue indefinitely. But if the analyst maintains a plot of recent allowances in the manner of Figure 24-2, and if no change in applicable tax regulations is in prospect, he will be justified in extrapolating the recent trend until the curve clearly begins to change course.[3]

Having estimated capital-consumption allowances and the dividends figure that we shall need to deduct from total corporate profits in estimating undistributed profits, we have gone as far as we can toward estimating the gross retained earnings of business, until estimates for the other receipts components of the NEB are made.

NET FOREIGN TRANSFERS

Net foreign transfers by government respond to changes in government policies with respect to foreign aid—after a considerable delay attributable to the long lead times involved in foreign aid programs. The category, since 1951, has been relatively small and nearly constant. The error is likely

---

[3] If a change in applicable tax regulations *is* in prospect, the task of estimating capital-consumption allowances becomes vastly more complex. Not only are the details of the regulations intricate and difficult for the typical analyst to generalize, but also, if the change permits larger depreciation deductions, the extent to which business firms will actually take advantage of the changed regulations is always a matter of uncertainty. Even the tax experts differed widely in their advance guesses as to the effects of the 1962 revisions in Bulletin F; some business economists went so far as to say that the revision would make virtually no difference in corporate depreciation accounting.

to be small if the analyst simply uses last year's figure, but if a change in foreign aid policy has been made or is in prospect some modification (with due allowance for a lag of a year or so) of this figure will be in order.

GROSS AND NET RECEIPTS OF GOVERNMENT

The gross receipts of Federal, state, and local governments have three categories other than corporate taxes—personal tax and nontax payments, indirect business taxes, and social insurance contributions. The model builder already has a working figure for the first of these as a by-product of his calcuation concerning disposable personal income.

Indirect taxes, as one might expect, bear a close relationship to personal consumption expenditures. Sales, excise, and other indirect levies claimed a gradually increasing share of consumption spending during the eighteen years beginning in 1947. On the average, for the 1947–1964 period as a whole each dollar of *increase* in PCE was accompanied by a 16.6 cent *increase* in indirect taxes, even though, in 1964, total indirect taxes were only 14.5 percent of PCE. Between 1955 and 1964, the marginal increase in indirect taxes was 17.9 percent of the marginal increase in PCE. As Figure 24–3 indicates, the relationship between indirect taxes and PCE is not strictly linear, although from 1955 to 1964 it did not deviate very much from linearity. Unless the analyst foresees a significant change in tax laws (such as a major reduction of Federal excise taxes, as in 1965, not accompanied by a compensating increase in state and local indirect taxes), he cannot go far wrong by assuming that the change from last year's figure will be that indicated by the slope of the regression line between PCE and indirect taxes for the most recent period in which there was no significant change in excise tax rates.

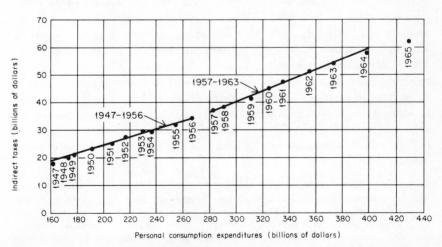

Figure **24–3.**   Personal consumption expenditures and indirect business taxes, 1947–1965.

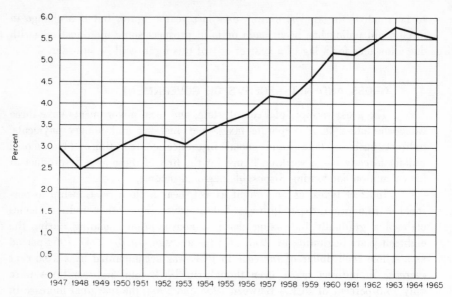

Figure **24–4.**   Contributions to social insurance as a percent of personal income, 1947–1965.   Source: U.S. Department of Commerce.

Social insurance taxes (contributions for social insurance in the national income accounts) are obviously related to income.   The relationship,
however, is not a simple or constant one.   The proportion of personal income
claimed by social insurance taxes is determined by (1) the coverage of the
social insurance program, which has been enlarged from time to time, notably
in 1965 (effective in 1966) when hospital insurance for the elderly was added;
(2) the level of social insurance tax rates, which also has been raised periodically; (3) the maximum level of income (the tax base) against which social
insurance taxes are levied, which has also been raised several times since the
program was initiated; and (4) the average incomes of persons covered.
The last determinant is, however, a tricky one, because the tax applies (as of
1966) only to the first $6,600 of income.   An increase in incomes of persons
receiving less than that amount will raise social insurance tax receipts.   But
an increase in incomes of persons already above the $6,600 level would result
in no increase in social insurance taxes; social insurance taxes as a *percentage*
of income would decline.[4]   The net effect of all these determinants is illustrated
in Figure 24–4, which shows social insurance taxes as a percentage of personal
income.

[4] In addition to changes in the old age, survivors, and disability insurance program
and the addition of hospital insurance, a few changes have been made in the unemployment compensation program.   Prior to 1961, the base rate was 3.1 percent; in 1962 and
1963, however, it was increased to 3.5 percent to cover the cost of temporary extended
unemployment compensation.   Actual tax payments under unemployment compensation are
also determined by the merit rating provisions of the several states.

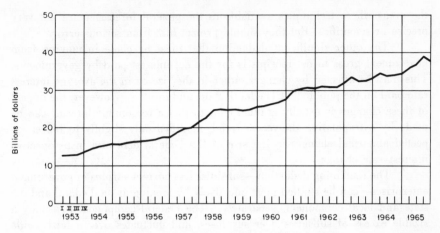

Figure **24–5.** Government transfer payments to persons, 1953–1965. (Billions of dollars, seasonally adjusted annual rates.) Source: U.S. Department of Commerce.

As a forecasting technique, we suggest that the analyst calculate the ratio of social insurance taxes to personal income for several recent years, by quarter, apply his knowledge of pending legislation pertaining to coverage, rates, and the tax base, together with the effects on social insurance taxes of the changes in income implicit in his forecast, and extrapolate the line accordingly. From this percentage estimate, together with the prior estimate of PI, a reasonably dependable forecast of social insurance contributions can be made.

The principal deduction necessary for arriving at an estimate of the *net* receipts of governments is government transfer payments to persons. As Figure 24–5 shows, this category has shown a strong upward trend, reflecting the steady increase in the number of persons eligible for social security benefits, several changes in the law relating to the coverage and amount of benefits, and certain special events. (The sharp increase in the first quarter of 1963, for example, was chiefly the result of a special dividend to National Service Life Insurance policyholders.) It will also be observed from the chart that the curve shows a clear contracyclical tendency. This tendency can be attributed chiefly to unemployment compensation payments which, of course, rise when business activity declines and fall as recovery takes place. In lesser measure, it can also be attributed to the fact that persons reaching the age at which they are eligible for old age and retirement benefits are more likely to retire, and draw their benefits, when employment opportunities are shrinking than when job opportunities are expanding.

In addition to the loose analytical framework just indicated, the Federal budgetary documents and other current indications of relevant new legislation can help to box in the transfer payments forecast. This is another of the areas where techniques available to the general forecaster are not very precise or scientific. But they should protect him from serious error.

The other significant deduction that must be made in moving from government gross to net receipts is for the net interest paid by governments. This may be affected by changes either in the size or in the average interest rate paid on the public debt (Federal, state, and local).[5] However, the impact of these changes is usually gradual enough that a reasonable forecast can be made by extrapolating the recent trend, modified only slightly to reflect expected abnormal changes in the size of the Federal debt and in prospective interest rate changes.

The remaining deduction—subsidies less current surplus of government enterprises—can be studied most effectively by looking at the Federal and the state and local components separately. The Federal component is usually a sizable excess of subsidies over surpluses, and fluctuates over a fairly wide range in response to changing Federal policies with respect to such matters as subsidies to small business, air transportation, the merchant marine, postal users, etc. The state and local component, however, has consistently been a surplus[6] and has risen gradually and steadily. For forecasting purposes, it is suggested that the state and local component be simply extrapolated. The Federal component, however, should be estimated by modifying the figure for the most recent year to reflect known changes in Federal legislation and policies, including, notably, postage rates. Fortunately, the net difference between subsidies and surpluses is almost invariably small, so no significant error is likely to ensue from rather rough forecasting techniques.

ESTIMATING CORPORATE PROFITS

At this point, the analyst has made estimates for the forecast period, in addition to those of GNP (GNI), PI, and DPI made earlier, of capital-consumption allowances, the dividends component of PI, net foreign transfers by government and by persons, personal income taxes (PI minus DPI), indirect taxes, contributions to social insurance, interest paid by persons, and the items that need to be deducted from gross receipts of government to obtain net receipts: government transfers to persons, net interest paid by government, subsidies less surplus of government enterprises, and, again, net foreign transfers. He is now ready to calculate a figure for corporate profits plus IVA that will, in turn, yield the estimates of corporate profits taxes and undistributed

---

[5] Note, however, that changes in interest rates affect interest payments only as debt issues mature and are replaced by new issues. Because such a large proportion of the Federal debt is short term, the effect of interest rate changes on interest costs is fairly prompt. In the case of state and local debt, however, which is of much longer average maturity, the response to interest rate changes is slow.

[6] The national income accounts show only "current surplus of government enterprises," no provision being made for the presumably negligible state and local government subsidies to business.

corporate profits needed to make the NEB balance. The arithmetic is not so complicated as it might seem. Let us use the following symbols, in addition to already familiar ones:

$$GRE = \text{gross retained earnings of business}$$
$$CCA = \text{capital-consumption allowances}$$
$$CP = \text{corporate profits plus IVA}$$
$$UP = \text{undistributed profits}$$
$$DIV = \text{dividends paid}$$
$$(WA - D) = \text{excess of wage accruals over disbursements}$$
$$NFT = \text{net foreign transfers by government}$$
$$NRG = \text{net receipts of government}$$
$$PT = \text{personal tax and nontax payments}$$
$$CPT = \text{corporate profits tax liability}$$
$$IBT = \text{indirect business tax and nontax liability}$$
$$CSI = \text{contributions for social insurance}$$
$$GTP = \text{government transfers to persons}$$
$$NIG = \text{net interest paid by government}$$
$$(S - S) = \text{subsidies less surplus of government enterprises}$$
$$Ti = \text{interest paid by persons}$$
$$Tf = \text{net foreign transfers by persons}$$

By definition,

$$\text{GNI} = \text{DPI} - (Ti + Tf) + GRE + NFT + Tf + NRG$$

Also by definition,

$$GRE = CCA + (WA - D) + UP$$
$$= CCA + (WA - D) + CP - DIV - CPT$$

And,

$$NRG = PT + CPT + IBT + CSI - GTP - NIG - (S - S) - NFT$$

Substituting in the first equation,

$$\text{GNI} = \text{DPI} - (Ti + Tf) + CCA + (WA - D) + CP - DIV - CPT$$
$$+ NFT + Tf + PT + CPT + IBT + CSI - GTP - NIG$$
$$- (S - S) - NFT$$

Consolidating and solving for CP,

$$CP = \text{GNI} - \text{DPI} + Ti + DIV - CCA - (WA - D) - PT - IBT$$
$$- CSI + GTP + NIG + (S - S)$$

Because $\text{DPI} + PT = \text{PI}$, and because conceptually $\text{GNI} = \text{GNP}$, the equation can be rewritten

$$CP = \text{GNP} - \text{PI} + Ti + DIV - CCA - (WA - D) - IBT - CSI$$
$$+ GTP + NIG + (S - S)$$

Translated into words, this equation says, (1) subtract personal income from GNP and add dividends; (2) subtract the nonprofit components of gross retained earnings of business, i.e., capital-consumption allowances and the excess of wage accruals over disbursements; (3) subtract indirect business taxes and contributions to social insurance; (4) add government transfers, interest, and subsidies and interest paid by persons; (5) the result is an estimate of corporate profits plus IVA (assuming the statistical discrepancy to be zero).

A few pages back, we noted that, conceptually, the discrepancy between GNP and GNI (or, in Commerce's terminology, "charges against GNP") is zero, and therefore we should assume it to be zero in our calculations. This means that when we estimate corporate profits by the residual method outlined above, the estimate we get is really corporate profits *plus* (algebraically) the statistical discrepancy. If the best estimate of the statistical discrepancy that we can make is, in fact, zero, there is no problem. But if a study of recent data reveals that the statistical discrepancy has *consistently* been, not zero or close to it, but a significantly positive (or negative) quantity, *and if there is reason to suppose that the statistical estimating procedures are likely to yield about the same statistical discrepancy in the future,* we shall get a more accurate forecast of corporate profits by assuming the statistical discrepancy to be a number that is consistent with recent experience, rather than zero. In this case, the above procedure for estimating corporate profits is followed, but when the estimate is derived, the assumed statistical discrepancy is subtracted from it to obtain the working figure for corporate profits.

The next step is to derive from this estimate a figure for corporate profits taxes, and this involves two preliminary steps: (1) making an estimate of the IVA, because corporate profits tax rates are applied to *stated* corporate profits, not the profits figure after adjustment by the National Income Division for inventory price change; and (2) estimating the percentage of corporate profits that corporate profits taxes can be expected to be.

With respect to the IVA, since one's first-approximation expenditure estimates usually include only limited amounts of price change, it is fairly safe to gloss over this point—i.e., assume that the IVA is zero—or, at most, if one assumes that recent price trends are likely to continue, to plug in a modest figure for the IVA derived from experience in recent years, as was done in estimating inventory investment. (The same figure, obviously, should be employed.)

Determining the corporate profits tax rate—corporate profits tax liability as a percentage of before-tax profits—is a somewhat more difficult matter. Data for the years 1951–1965 are shown in Figure 24–6.

The decreases in the percentage in 1954, 1962, and 1964–1965 reflected significant changes in law—in 1954 and 1964 a cut in rates, and in 1962 enactment of the investment tax credit. Although there were other minor changes in law during the period covered, none was sufficient to explain the

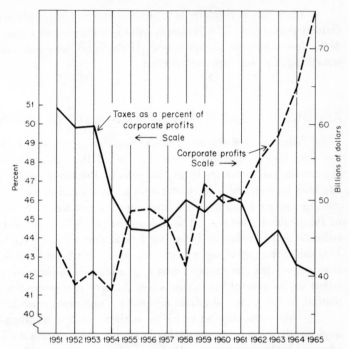

Figure **24–6.** Corporate profits and corporate profits tax liability as a percent of corporate profits, 1951–1965. Source: U.S. Department of Commerce.

other fairly substantial changes in the percentage. The main explanation seems to be the fact that, in high-profit years, corporations with deficits from prior years utilize their loss-carry-over privilege to reduce their tax payment. Thus, taxes as a percentage of profits fell in the high-profit years of 1955 and 1956 (following the low-profit year of 1954) and 1959 (following low profits in 1958). A part of the decline in 1962 may have resulted from loss carry-overs. However, because the previous years of 1960 and 1961 were not especially low-profit years, losses to be carried forward were probably not widely experienced. The lower tax on the first $25,000 also served to reduce the average percentage below the marginal rate, but it does not seem likely that this provision of the law can account for any significant portion of the variation in the percentage from year to year.

Forecasting the percentage, therefore, includes: (1) determining the percentage for the most recent available year; (2) adjusting this figure for any known or anticipated changes in applicable tax laws; (3) modifying this percentage appropriately to allow for the effects of loss carry-over, i.e., raising it slightly if a decline in dollar profits is anticipated, and lowering it if a rise, following a recent low-profit year, is anticipated.

Once this percentage is estimated, the rest is simple arithmetic. Undivided profits plus IVA is simply total corporate profits plus IVA less dividends less corporate profits taxes. If the NEB does not balance perfectly, something is wrong with the arithmetic.

ADJUSTING THE DEMAND AND CAPACITY FORECASTS

Thus far the short-run model-building procedure we have described has been fairly straightforward. Some of the estimating techniques are ponderous, and many are highly imperfect. But the overall sequence of steps has been logical, and a forecaster who follows it can properly have a sense of making orderly inroads on his problem. From here on, however, the nature of the problem changes. The task no longer is to conjure up an array of estimates but to refine and evaluate figures that already have been developed. This calls for a rather more subtle, less systematic kind of analysis. The need is to inspect the collection of first-approximation estimates from new angles, reflect on its general implications, spy out any inconsistencies implicit in the pattern, tinker with and adjust the pattern, and, finally, evaluate its portents.

This is the stage at which an analyst's craft and judgment figure most importantly. Even his mood should change. Up to now he has been somewhat bolder than judicious. He has needed to venture estimates that cautious scholars would avoid. His purpose has been to come up with a set of figures —well-founded figures if possible, but figures in any case. Now, switching to the role of a skeptic, he should become his own severest critic, challenging, cross-examining, and modifying his own handiwork. The purpose of such self-criticism is not to retreat from the responsibility of delivering a reasonably positive, unequivocal statement of the outlook. It is rather to improve the final product on this principle: that the economy is an organic system, not just a random collection of entities and forces; that, therefore, if a group of sector forecasts can be knit into a comprehensive, internally coherent, and sensibly proportioned pattern, the composite will have greater predictive reliability than do the individual pieces that go to make it up.

TESTING THE INTERNAL CONSISTENCY OF
THE NATION'S ECONOMIC BUDGET

When a model builder who is working primarily with arithmetical techniques reaches the adjustment stages of his analysis, the steps to be taken no longer fall into any necessary detailed sequence. They overlap and interact in any case. But for expositional purposes, we shall try to keep the major remaining phases of the analytical procedure distinct. First we shall consider adjustments that become necessary to make the initial estimates that have been inserted into the NEB format consistent among themselves.

Are the Parts and the Whole of the
Expenditure Forecast Consistent?

As good a way as any for the analyst to begin cross-examining his NEB array is to ask himself what changes, if any, should be made in his sector-by-sector first-approximation spending estimates when the initial income hypothesis that underlies most of them is replaced by the sum that they add up to, i.e., by the actual first-approximation forecast of GNP. The needed changes are unlikely to be large, since, under the procedure that has been outlined, the original estimates of nonautomotive goods and services consumption and of net exports already have been based on actual rather than purely hypothetical final-demand prospects. Moreover, government purchases of goods and services are unlikely to be directly or automatically altered by variations in total spending and incomes. And lags in the execution of plant and equipment programs, plus the harnessing of such programs to long-run expectations, are likely to make business fixed-capital formation fairly insensitive to moderate near-term swings in general business activity. Nevertheless, if the total spending and income prospect that has now emerged differs substantially from the initial hypothesis, some adjustment in the plant and equipment forecast and, even more pointedly, in the housing and automobiles forecasts and in the u, v, and w ratios may be in order.

A point should be noted here that will hold for most of the remaining discussion. The making of one adjustment of the kind just suggested tends to generate a need for further adjustments. If, for example, the original estimates of house building and the automobile outlays should be revised downward a couple of billion dollars in the light of a shortfall of the initial GNP forecast below the original working hypothesis that was adopted, this would mean a downward revision in the GNP forecast itself, which in turn would imply less disposable personal income, which in turn would imply less nonautomotive goods and services consumption, which might make the total downward adjustment in spending something on the order of $4 billion instead of $2 billion. And, still further, the latter change would require adjustments in all the receipts components in the original NEB array that had in some measure been based on the original (now revised) GNP forecast. Finally, if it was the lowness of the old GNP forecast that required downward adjustments in the original housing and automobile estimates in the first place, perhaps still further reductions in the latter are indicated now that the GNP estimate has been revised downward. If so, the same analytical cycle must be started all over again.

In theory this kind of adjustment by successive approximation could go on indefinitely. In practice, opportunistic model builders have to learn to short-circuit the process well enough to bring interrelated concepts into a satisfactory balance rather quickly. But with respect to all the adjustments mentioned below, it should be understood that some analytical follow through is necessary; when the forecaster changes one figure in his outlook model he should expect, in consequence, to change others.

Is the Profit Share of Total Income Plausible?

We have suggested that, for purposes of completing a first-approximation NEB array, undistributed after-tax corporate profits be treated as the residual claimant on the gross national income. But if unmodified, such a procedure may well yield an unreasonable result. Suppose, for example, that it pictures retained corporate profits as being squeezed down during the coming year to half the current level while such related variables as sales, wages, and dividends all tend upward. Unless the current rate of profit retentions is extraordinarily high, corporate managers are unlikely to hold still for such a profit squeeze. And they could resist it with some success. They might shave their payout ratios and hold dividends somewhat below the figure that was included in the original personal income estimate. Or employers might resist wage gains more vigorously than the original wage and salary estimate implied. Or firms on the average might raise prices and retain most of the resulting revenue gains as undistributed profit.

If the initial retained-profits residual looks improbable, the analyst may decide to alter his model in some or all of these directions—and if so, of course, to follow through with the further adjustments that these changes require.

Does the Personal Saving Rate Make Sense?

Looking at the horizontal dimensions of the Nation's Economic Budget model, the internal consistency of each of the major domestic sectors deserves examination. In the first place, is the model's personal saving rate (net personal saving as a percentage of disposable personal income) reasonable? If personal outlays less automobiles has been estimated in the manner suggested, this point, in a sense, has already been anticipated. Any abnormality in the personal saving rate should, in this case, be attributable to an expectation of abnormally high or low automobile buying, and presumably the latter estimate already has been well considered. But in the course of the exercise thus far some distortions may have crept into the figures, and it will do the analyst no harm to reconsider whether he really is prepared to defend the saving rate his model implies.

Is the Excess of Business Investment over Retained Earnings Reasonable?

In part the issue here is the consistency of the profit and the plant and equipment expenditure forecast from an incentive point of view. As we saw in Part Two, business' inducement to invest does not appear in the United States to be primarily influenced by the profits that firms happen to realize in the particular years in which the capital outlays are made. On the other hand, plant and equipment spending is not completely insensitive to current profit experience, and if an outlook model shows the two variables moving rather sharply in opposite directions, this aspect of the forecast deserves a second look.

A usually more important internal consistency issue within the business sector of the NEB array is whether the relationship it suggests between gross retained earnings and the business portion (i.e., not including residential structures) of domestic investment is financially feasible. Any excess of business investment over gross retained earnings represents business' requirements for external financing.[7] There are times when such external financial requirements look implausibly heavy and will accordingly prompt the analyst either to shade his plant and equipment forecast downward or to consider the possibility of greater earnings retentions than he first anticipated. On the other hand, his initial estimates may suggest such light demands for external financing that it looks as though, if the present settings on the central bank's general credit controls are not changed, investable funds would be cheaper and more abundant than he originally thought. Accordingly, he may decide that plant and equipment spending, and perhaps also residential structures expenditures, is apt to run a little higher than he first estimated.

How About the Government Budget?

The internal consistency question in the Federal, state, and local government sector of the NEB is basically whether the model shows the consolidated government surplus or deficit behaving in a way that one might expect in the light of the model's GNP estimate. It should be noted that it is easy to overadjust in this respect. Under the restraints we have placed on the particular round of adjustments we are discussing now, this is not the time to anticipate stability-seeking changes in public fiscal policies. Moreover, the analyst's preconceptions about the trend in government budgets are very likely to be nothing but impressions about the Federal budget. Not infrequently the latter are more than offset by opposite movements in state and local budgets.

Nevertheless, it is possible for first-approximation budget pictures to turn up that are so incongruous that they plainly demand double checking. For instance, in a period when total demand is expected to rise sharply and no emergency expansion in defense spending is foreseen, it is very unlikely that the consolidated government budgetary balance would shift strongly in a

---

[7] This statement glosses over the point made earlier, that business investment includes capital expenditures of unincorporated enterprises, but not their income and saving, which are included in personal income and net personal savings.

deficit direction.   Our much-vaunted built-in stabilizers would tend to block such a development, and if a demand model promises it, the model probably is wrong.   It may, for example, not have allowed enough for the progressiveness of the Federal personal income tax.   Possibly, of course, a joint forecast of rising total spending and widening government deficits is correct; maybe abnormally heavy bond-financed construction by state and local government is the explanation.   The point is that the model builder should be prepared specifically to explain and defend any such apparent inconsistency that might appear in his numerical estimates.

The questions that have been noted are not the only counts on which a demand model can be examined for internal consistency.   But they amply illustrate one requirement for competent outlook model building: every relationship that can be detected within the model should make good sense.

COMPARING THE DEMAND AND CAPACITY FORECASTS

By now the forecaster has completed the bulk of his exercise.   But he has not yet diagnosed the business outlook.   To finish the job he must compare the basic demand prospect with his capacity forecast—for two reasons. In the first place, capacity provides the only reasonable yardstick for measuring the degree of economic health that a given level of demand in a given economy in a given period will represent.   In the second place, the analyst must appraise the possibility of secondary reactions in both capacity and demand to any general excess or deficiency of demand that the basic demand-capacity comparison reveals may be in store for the forecast period.

The first thing that must be done in this matter of the capacity and demand comparison is to convert the capacity estimate into prices that are comparable with those reflected in the adjusted GNP estimate.   The capacity forecast, you will remember from Chapter 17, has been made in constant prices of the level in effect at the time of the forecast.   The prices reflected in the demand estimates still are not radically different from this; no inflation- or deflation-induced effects on aggregate demand were injected into the model. But some of the sector estimates have included forecasts of specific price changes in commodity and service areas particularly of the administered price sort.

It is necessary, in order to determine whether the prospective demand for output is likely to undertax, overtax, or match capacity, to value the output capability in the same prices as demand.   This means inflating the original capacity forecast by the price changes included in the expenditure estimates. In principle, this adjustment for price changes should be done by weighting the price change expected in each category of demand by the fraction of GNP that the category represents.   In practice, unless a marked change from recent price behavior by category is expected, it is usually sufficient to hypothesize that the general price level (i.e., the GNP deflator) will change by about the same percentage that it has changed in recent years—somewhat more or less depending on the general economic outlook as revealed by the forecast.

With this limited repricing of the capacity estimate completed, the comparison toward which all the foregoing analysis has been aiming can finally be made, and the size of any primary or basic gap between prospective demand and prospective capacity can be established.   This is the climax of an opportunistic model-building exercise.   For the presence or absence of such a gap, and the size of the gap, indicate what the underlying disposition of the economy is likely to be during the forecast period, and it is the outlook finding that the technique is best designed to yield.   However, a strong word of caution should be sounded against oversignifying any small imbalance between capacity and demand that a model seems to reveal.   A finding of approximate balance between the capacity and demand prospects is quite as significant as is a finding of imbalance.   And if one were to take all the possible capacity-demand comparisons one might encounter, from a radical excess of demand, on the one hand, to a radical deficiency of demand, on the other, there would be a substantial range—not just a knife edge of perfect equality—where the important thing to report was the near balance, not the slight imbalance, of the prospects.   If a short-run forecaster does not take this elementary point to heart he will be forever crying wolf.   For almost never will an honestly constructed outlook model show exactly equal capacity and demand estimates, and it is unrealistic to get excited about minor discrepancies, especially in view of the shakiness of many of the estimates in any short-run model.

The practical question, of course, is, How big can an apparent discrepancy be and still be minor?   There is no accepted forecasting doctrine on this point; analysts must develop their own rules of thumb.   We suggest that, for forecasts of short-run business conditions in the United States, no significance at all should be attached to an apparent demand-capacity gap no larger than $5 billion.   Even one as large as $10 billion may readily be attributable to difficulties in the model rather than in the real world that the model tries to represent.   More significance, perhaps, can be attached to relatively small ($5 billion or $10 billion) *changes* in the size of the gap from the current to the forecast year.   Even though the gap calculation is imperfect in an absolute sense, if the sector forecasts are all based on data for the current year—as they normally are—the sources of error (in the capacity estimate, for example) are likely to be about the same from one year to the next.   If this is true, then an increase or decrease in the calculated gap of $10 billion—say from $30 billion to $20 billion—is a statistic of considerable significance.

Employment

The gap calculation provides a clue to probable changes in the level of unemployment.   Obviously, a narrowing gap would indicate a decline in unemployment and a widening gap a rise in unemployment. At this point, the analyst may wish—despite our warnings about making precise calculations from the absolute size of the gap—to apply "Okun's law" in reverse, i.e., to calculate what the unemployment rate would be if the forecast and the capacity calculation are correct. This is a useful way to quantify the employment consequence of the forecast, in spite of the hazards involved.

Prices

Earlier, we suggested that price developments in the forecast period be estimated by calculating a weighted average of the specific price changes incorporated in the sector forecasts or, if no significant change in recent price experience by sector is expected, that last year's general price change be hypothesized in computing the capacity figure. The gap calculation now provides a basis for testing this calculation or hypothesis. Again, a widening gap probably means somewhat less price pressure than was present in the year before, and a narrowing gap somewhat more. The aggregate-supply path, if it were possible to plot it with precision, would be an ideal analytical tool to use at this point. Lacking such precision, we can nevertheless engage in some rough estimating based on experience. What, for example, has been typical price level behavior when the gap has narrowed to, say, 2 percent of capacity? To 1 percent? To zero percent? What has happened when the gap has widened? Are the circumstances today (or anticipated in the forecast year) such that we would expect similar price behavior this time?

Such reasoning by historical analogy is risky business, because circumstances never are exactly the same. But if it is done by an experienced analyst, who can assess the price effects of changed circumstances, it is a useful approach.

Corporate Profits

With regard to profit behavior, the thing to remember is that profits, by all odds, are the most volatile of the income shares. Almost always they are the fastest gainers in upswings and the fastest losers in downswings. Although there is no satisfactory way to formalize this relationship, some insights into prospective behavior may be gained from inspections of past periods. Figure 24–7, for example, offers this rather interesting finding as to the behavior of United States corporate profits from 1940 through 1965: in years in which the increase in GNP exceeded the preceeding year's gain, corporate profits generally rose; and in almost every year in which GNP declined or, although rising, rose less than in the preceding year, profits suffered an absolute decline. Gary Fromm, in the study cited on page 551, identifies the three principal parameters of a corporate profits forecasting equation as commodity prices, the absolute level of GNP, and the gap between actual GNP

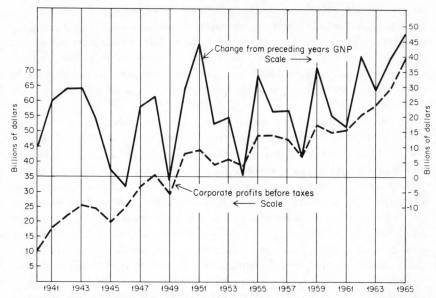

Figure **24–7.**   Corporate profits before taxes and annual changes in GNP in the United States, 1940–1965.   (Billions of dollars.)   Source: U.S. Department of Commerce.

and capacity, and of these, by far the most important is the third.   If an analyst is predicting an excess demand acceleration or a deficient demand deceleration in spending, he should expect a relative change in before-tax corporate profits that is considerably greater than that in total activity.

THE NET APPRAISAL OF THE OUTLOOK

QUALITATIVE EVALUATION OF THE DEMAND AND CAPACITY PROSPECTS

The point we have just reached is the one where, as a practical matter, quantitative forecasting finally runs out of gas.   It may be possible from historical data to calculate functions that will predict some of the secondary reactions to varying degrees of imbalance in demand and capacity.   But certainly we are not yet able to do this for most of the possible effects, nor for the manner in which they will interact with one another.   Too much depends on the foibles of mass psychology and accidents of timing to permit even a moderately precise quantification of the probable net secondary reaction to a sizable gap between demand and capacity.   Quantitative analysis can detect an underlying instability in the outlook and say something about the magnitude of this unstable tendency.   But, beyond this, the available tools of analysis are reliable only for identifying the probable direction, not the sizes, of further adjustments in the demand, capacity, output, employment, and price prospects. The forecaster may still want to go back to his work sheets and make further changes in his numerical models. But if so, this will only be to give sharply drawn, internally consistent expression to conclusions that he must arrive at by the essentially nonquantitative process of judgment, impression, and hunch.

Such intellectual processes must evolve in the analyst's own experience and remain comparatively inarticulate. However, a few insights into the matter of how to make a sensible qualitative evaluation of the probable reaction to an expansionary or contractionary gap can be gleaned from the experience of other forecasters. For one thing, as we have intimated several times already, one of the more common errors among forecasters of contemporary American business conditions is to exaggerate the prospects for cumulative instability. In the abstract, models of spiral processes are such dramatic and persuasive things that they often victimize the imaginations of working analysts. A whole collection of institutional and rather firmly entrenched psychological changes have served during the past generation greatly to increase the collective resistance of American private decision makers to the infections of downward cumulative instability.

A closely related common failing among forecasters is a tendency to exaggerate the speed with which private spending will react to an emerging expansionary or contractionary trend. There are few lags or delays built into the simple spiral models, but such lags often dominate economic developments in the real world.

The same admonition is appropriate in the case of discretionary changes in government policies. Some public stabilization-policy settings can be altered swiftly—notably those in the monetary area—but those requiring legislation usually take a good deal of time to become effective. And time and again business conditions analysts underestimate these lags, just as they underestimate the possibility that other-than-stabilization issues may intervene or delay or curtail the policy changes they expect.

The need to make a final qualitative rendering of one's net short-run outlook appraisal is not limited to those cases where the possibility of secondary reactions to a substantial demand-capacity gap enters importantly into the analysis. Even on the many occasions when the forecast turns out to be one of substantially balanced growth in demand and capacity, it is a verbalization of the outlook that, in the last analysis, the average decision maker wants. To most people an array of numbers, however cogently contrived, refined, and internally consistent, is a highly unanimated thing.

Decision makers want to be told in so many words whether the business outlook is good or bad, better or worse, and to what degree, what its analogies to the past periods may be; what the strategic elements in the outlook appear to be; what items out of the labyrinth of economic indicators should be

watched with special care during the months ahead; and what things promise
to be the principal problems and dangers the economy will encounter during
the forecast period. Even if his clientele did not demand it, it would be
eminently desirable for a general analyst to conclude his short-run forecasting
exercise with such a verbal distillation of the outlook. This forces him to
stand back and look at the overall picture, to identify the crucial factors in it,
and to find some figures of speech that accurately summarize its implications
not only for others but for himself. In effect, this final step requires the
analyst to digest his own work.

SUMMARY

The kind of opportunistic short-run model building that has been
described in this and the preceding eight chapters is a relatively complex
procedure, perhaps better suited to the uses of general forecasting staff than
to those of a single analyst, if the full potentialities of the technique are to be
exploited. Yet the basic design of the procedure is simple enough that,
sometimes in truncated form, it can be adapted to the resource limits of an
individual forecaster who is well grounded in aggregative economics and has
the time and energy seriously to pursue a comprehensive forecasting exercise.
Moreover, one beauty of the technique is that once such an exercise has been
carefully conducted, subsequent ones come much more easily. Indeed, with
a modest amount of current reading and attention to current indicators, it is
feasible for an experienced analyst to keep an opportunistic model of the
coming twelve or fifteen months perennially activated, always in a state of
partial overhaul and, by the same token, of near analytical readiness.

Just to be sure that the broad outlines of the technique are securely
in place it may be well to render a final summary of them.

Opportunistic model building is an effort to build a view of the short-
run business outlook that is comprehensive, that is as quantitatively precise
as the state of our knowledge permits, that is internally consistent, that draws
upon rather than sidesteps all the pertinent insights of modern aggregative
economics but, at the same time, does not make a fetish of theoretical rigor.
Instead, the technique seeks to exploit any and all evidences of business prospects that may come to hand. It is particularly distinguished from pure
econometric model building by its heavy use of data concerning the advance
plans and commitments of certain spending groups, and it retains a sizable
place for judgment and freehand adjustments.

The core of the procedure is to contrive and compare estimates of
the economy's normal full-employment capacity and of its total expenditures
in a forecast period. The technique for predicting the first of these magnitudes is quite simple but, particularly with regard to the decisive factor of
productivity change, is distressingly shaky for year-to-year forecasting pur-

poses. The technique for establishing the basic expenditure prospects for a coming year is quite complex but also a good deal more satisfactory. The particular demand-forecasting procedure favored here has been, first, on the basis of an initial and revisable hypothesis about what total demand and income are going to do during the forecast period, to formulate sector-by-sector estimates of the specific prospects for government spending, plant and equipment investment, consumer investment in housing, outlays for automobiles, and inventory investment; second, on the basis of the indications of actual, not just hypothetical, changes in total activity, to estimate prospects for nonautomotive consumer expenditures and net exports (it being necessary, as an intermediate step, in the first of these two instances, to consider the relationship between gross national income and disposable personal income); third, to estimate the distribution of the resulting gross national product and income among the receipts categories of the Nation's Economic Budget; and fourth, to expend considerable care in adjusting this receipts and expenditures forecast of aggregate demand into as internally consistent a form as possible.

The comparison of the demand and capacity forecasts (after the latter has been adjusted to prices comparable to those included in the expenditure estimate) reveals either a predominantly balanced outlook—and the analyst should not overstrain his efforts to detect imbalance—or symptoms of underlying instability, either in an upward or downward direction. In estimating the implications to prices, profits, and employment of any substantial gap between capacity and demand, the analyst must resort largely to qualitative rather than to quantitative findings. Nevertheless, a number of reasonably reliable rules of thumb are available for retaining some sense of magnitude and proportion even in this phase of the analysis.

In any case, whether or not the forecaster's findings require him to venture into the risky business of predicting dynamic, secondary reactions to incipient imbalances in the economy, including public-policy actions directed toward reversing the trend of events indicated by his forecast, the final and inescapable responsibility of any forecaster worth his salt is to convert his prognostications into language that accurately and succinctly summarizes them for himself and conveys them to others.

PART FIVE

SOME LONG-RUN ISSUES

25

THE COMPLEXITIES OF
LONG-TERM PROGNOSIS

After spending nine chapters on short-run outlook analysis, we shall devote only two to long-run economic prospects—not because the latter are less important than the former but because the ability of the economist *qua* economist to illuminate the more distant future is much more limited.

Even for the short space of a coming year the economic forecaster's work must be hedged with conditioning assumptions. And time and again, to make useful guesses, the economist must venture off the narrow analytical paths of his own discipline into such less familiar terrain as consumer psychology and domestic politics. When the forecast period is only the coming year, however, such extradisciplinary forays can be held to a minimum, and often a sensible enough set of noneconomic working assumptions can be adopted to make the economist's assumption-protected forecast of the coming year a workable operating hypothesis for decision makers.

As a result the short-run outlook problem is the one aggregative context in which a theoretical model composed only of economic variables is a reasonably comprehensive, integrated, approximately sufficient explanation of real-world behavior. It offers the student who is oriented toward the practical side his best chance of understanding the economist's economy as a rigorously coherent, yet not meaninglessly abstract, system.

Long-run prognosis is far less submissive to purely economic analysis. Either the economist must rely on protective noneconomic assumptions that, while plausible in the short run, become more and more unrealistic the further they are extended into the future; or he must admit to his analysis more and more variables of which he has no particular knowledge. Moreover, these extradisciplinary variables are almost sure to include many of the really crucial conditioners of the economy's performance over the decades ahead. In fact, one cannot reliably forecast business conditions in the United States or any other country during the next twenty-five years without reliably forecasting the course of human history during the same period. And that is a task which lies beyond the pretensions of any one discipline. The economist can contribute some valuable insights about certain variables that happen to lie within his professional ken. But his contributions are apt to be no more noteworthy than those of the geneticist, the astrophysicist, the medical researcher, the social psychologist, or the student of international affairs.

This, of course, does not mean that economists should refrain from analyzing long-run problems. In the first place, the problems are too interesting to be bypassed. In the second place, some public and private decision makers require working hypotheses about the shape and character of the economy a quarter of a century or more hence, and it is the duty of the economics profession to make what contribution it can to their formulation. And in the third place, those specializing in short-run analysis badly need the perspective that can be afforded only by occasional reflection on the more persistent trends that may underlie the twists and turns in near-term figures.

Nevertheless, the fact remains that, at best, the economist can make only a rather eclectic set of observations about the economy's long-run future. He can foresee certain developmental possibilities, identify some of the factors that may accelerate or decelerate growth, and spot a few of the challenges with which possible economic changes may, in turn, confront the community. But, by himself, he cannot begin to see the whole picture.

In such a sense is this chapter eclectic. It takes as a point of departure the rather mechanistic type of long-term forecasts of the United States economy's productive capacity that we examined as to technique in Chapter 17, and considers, first, various circumstances that might alter the growth rates that such extrapolations suggest. Then, assuming that the popular growth projections can be taken at least somewhat seriously, we note some of the domestic adjustments within the American economy that growing economic abundance may dictate. Finally, we turn briefly to another set of issues that may overwhelmingly influence United States economic history during the next several decades. These are the profound challenges that confront the nation overseas. They cast a very different light on the long-term future from what appears when one limits one's vision to the domestic scene.

UNKNOWNS IN THE LONG-TERM GROWTH PROCESS

WHAT ABOUT CONVENTIONAL PROJECTIONS?

We have just struck a note of skepticism about economists' long-term predictive powers that may seem at odds with the comparatively confident view expressed in Chapter 17 about economists' ability to forecast the average annual growth in the economy's physical productive capacity for periods extending up to ten or fifteen years into the future. But actually the two positions are not inconsistent.

In the first place, it will be remembered that the five- to fifteen-year normal capacity forecasts discussed in Chapter 17 are conditional predictions. They assume no major war or other violent alteration of any kind in international tensions, as well as no major depression. The assumption of no major depression, if our analysis in Chapter 15 is valid, would seem to be almost as realistic for the next decade or decade and a half as it is for any single coming year; it seems quite plausible in both cases. But the assumption of a relatively static international situation is far less plausible if one is speaking of decades rather than single years. In this particular the growth projections are safely hedged, but the hedging may be highly unrealistic.

In the second place, it was emphasized in Chapter 17 that the growth projections should be interpreted only as (conditional) forecasts of the *average annual* growth in normal capacity over periods *not exceeding about fifteen years*—the fifteen-year cutoff being chosen chiefly because beyond that point the highly unpredictable future birthrate becomes a significant determinant of changes in the labor force. The kind of long-run analysis we now are considering often seeks to peer considerably further than this into the future. Analysts tend to be interested in the next ten or fifteen years partly for the running start that period is thought to give us on still later prospects. It is precisely in this respect that a quite accurate average-annual-growth forecast for the next fifteen years can be highly misleading.

Consider, for example, the extreme case pictured in Figure 25–1. There the dashed line *A* represents a reasonably typical forecast made in 1965 of the average annual growth in capacity during the period of 1965–1980. The net estimate (assuming a capacity of $690 billion in 1965) is for an average annual increment in capacity of $3\frac{1}{2}$ percent and a capacity in 1980 of $1,155 billion in 1965 prices (point 1 on the diagram). Suppose that actually the economy were to follow the path indicated by the portion of curve *B* from 1965 to 1980—a curve that rises at a *decreasing* rate. The fifteen-year forecast would turn out technically to have been perfectly correct: normal full capacity in 1980 would indeed be $1,155 billion in 1965 prices and the average rate of increase would have been $3\frac{1}{2}$ percent.

Nevertheless, it could be highly misleading to extrapolate the 1965–1980 average rate of increase to the year 2000. If the same forces that had

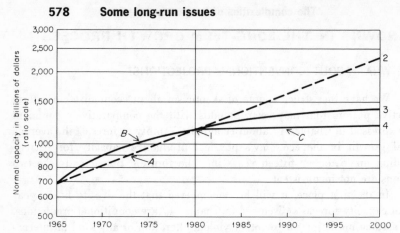

Figure 25–1. The dangers in extrapolating medium-term forecasts of average annual increments of capacity.

made for a diminishing rate of growth from 1965 to 1980 continued to operate, the economy, moving along the extension of curve *B*, might attain a potential GNP of only $1,400 billion (point 3) instead of $2,300 billion (point 2) by the end of the century. Further, if the decline in the birthrate apparent in the first half of the 1960s should continue or accelerate, actual capacity could follow the still lower path *C* when the effect began to register on the labor force in the 1980s and 1990s. In this case, capacity in the year 2000 might be somewhere in the vicinity of point 4 on the diagram. Thus, despite the technical correctness of the 1965–1980 forecast, an extrapolation of it to 2000 could be, for example, over $1,000 billion too high. (The error, of course, could also be on the low side.)

The basic difficulties with extensions of conventional capacity forecasts further than ten or fifteen years in the future stem from the unpredictability of future birthrates and from the danger of extrapolating very far a trend in such a composite variable as labor productivity. If decision makers require a number to represent the size of the economy a generation or so hence, then the crude techniques of conventional capacity forecasting may still be the best way of projecting some sort of tentative quantitative scaffolding out into the unknown. But twenty- or thirty-year growth rate extrapolations should be understood as no more than that. And really, before they are adopted into serious discussion at all, one should be aware of some of the underlying factors that may distort or, conversely, confirm them. By way of illustration, we shall describe briefly but, we hope, foresightedly, factors of seven general sorts that could modify United States growth rates during the next quarter century: population changes and their impacts, attitudes toward work and leisure, the availability of materials and energy resources, the pace of technological change, changes in the disposition to save, shifts in the economy's product mix, and changes in social facilities and policies.[1]

[1] Two very interesting discussions of such uncertainties in the long-run growth

POPULATION PUZZLES

Under the general heading of population, two sorts of uncertainties obscure the long-run prospects for the American economy, There are uncertainties, first, about some of the demographic developments themselves, and second, about what the net business conditions impacts of some of these developments might be. People have both mouths and hands; they are at once consumers and potential producers. But in limited periods population changes may affect demand and capacity unequally. These complexities become particularly evident as one considers the biggest single population enigma that confronts American analysts—that posed by the United States birthrate.

The prospect for the birthrate has thoroughly stumped expert demographers in the past. Without attempting to unravel the complex technical questions that underlie it, a layman can appreciate the difficulty of the projection problem simply by looking at a charted time series of the United States birthrate, like Figure 17–1 in Chapter 17, and covering up everything to the right of 1935. Plainly, the secular trend appeared at that time to be decisively downward. It is easy to see why practically all the experts interpreted the surge of births in the late forties as a transitory war-induced aberration that soon would be reversed. As we have had occasion to observe, the striking thing was that the birthrate held at a relatively high level (as compared with then recent years, not the nineteenth century or even the first quarter of the twentieth century) for more than a decade.

Beginning in 1958, however, a downward trend was again resumed. Part of this decline could be attributed to a change in the age distribution of the population, i.e., a decreasing proportion of the population in the childbearing ages. The latter, of course, was the lagged consequence of the low birthrate of the 1930s. But not only did the birthrate decline, *age-specific fertility* rates in every age bracket declined.[2] The decline in the fertility rate indicates that other influences were at work, including scientific developments in contraceptive techniques, increased knowledge of and gradually changing attitudes toward the use of birth-control methods, and in the latter part of the 1958–1965 period, some decline in the marriage rate.

---

process were presented in *World Economic Growth and Competition, Hearings before a Subcommittee of the Joint Economic Committee*, 84th Cong., 2d Sess., December, 1956, pp. 20–29 (statements by Solomon Fabricant), 39–45 (statements by Martin Gainsbrugh). See also Gerhard Colm, "Economic Projections: Tools of Economic Analysis and Decision Making," *American Economic Review*, vol. 48, no. 2, pp. 178–187, May, 1958.

[2] The term "birthrate" is used to refer to the ratio of the number of babies born to total population (in thousands). The term "fertility rate" or "general fertility rate" refers to the number of babies born per thousand females of childbearing age. The "age-specific fertility rate" refers to the ratio of the number of babies born to females of a given age, e.g., twenty to twenty-four years, to the number of females in that age range, again in thousands.

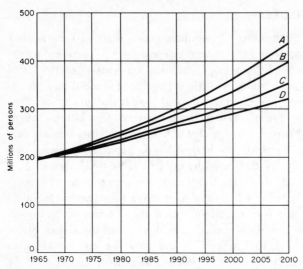

Figure **25–2.** Projections of United States population, 1965–2010. Source: U.S. Department of Commerce, Bureau of the Census, *Current Population Reports*, ser. P-25, no. 286.

In the 1966–1975 decade, the age distribution of the population is again changing, but in the opposite direction, as the bumper crop of babies born in the late 1940s and early 1950s reaches childbearing age. Whether or not the fertility rate will continue to decline, and if it does, whether or not the decline will be enough to offset the age-distribution effect, is a question that no one can answer. Wise demographers are simply suspending their judgment about the outlook.

Figure 25–2 is a chart showing projections of the total population of the United States made by the U.S. Bureau of the Census. The four projections are based on four sets of assumptions as to fertility rates, ranging from essentially no change in age-specific fertility rates (projection A) to substantial declines (projection D). Projection A yields a United States population in the year 2010 of 438 million persons (roughly the 1960 population of India), compared with 194.6 million in 1965. Projection D, however, shows a 2010 population of only 322 million—a 65 percent increase over 1965 but 116 million less than projection A. Even for the year 1985, the projections range from 248 million to 276 million persons, a range of over 11 percent.[3]

---

[3] Even though wise demographers are suspending judgment about the outlook, as we noted a moment ago, it is probably true that most demographers consider the A projection to be unrealistically high, and current guesses are that the best projection for the year 2010 is somewhere between the B projection (399 million) and the C projection (352 million). Corresponding figures for 1985 are 266 million and 254 million. The D projection is not ruled out as a possibility.

If either the A or B projection should prove to be correct, the relatively high birthrates implicit in such a projection would have impacts on both aggregate demand and capacity.   The large increase in the youngest, non-working age groups would mean increased population pressures on soft goods and services consumption and a somewhat heightened need for housing and certain consumer durables.   At the same time, high birthrates would stimulate many types of public outlays, including those for education, and by creating the prospect of more rapid market expansion for many commodities, it might raise business' inducement to invest.

But over a period of several decades the maintenance of a higher birth-rate would not be devoid of impact on the supply of productive resources. There would be at least one and possibly two negative effects: more babies would mean that more women would be excluded from the labor force by their need to mother young children; and if more numerous births stimulated higher personal consumption, they could lower the availability of resources for business capital formation and thereby dampen productivity gains.   On the other hand, by intensifying the need for income, a high birthrate could increase the willingness to work of those not tied down to child raising.   Thus it could mean more second jobs for breadwinners and, on the average, earlier school-leaving ages, and more entry into the labor force by older married women.   Moreover, the greater inducement to invest might mean a stepped-up stimulation of productivity gains if business were able to make good its bid for more resources in the face of sharper consumer demand.

On balance, it is probable that a high birthrate's positive effects on capacity would exceed its negative effects, but that this net increment in capacity would be less than proportional to the increment in population.   In this event, a high birthrate would dampen growth in real income per capita. On the other hand, *expectations* of a rapidly rising population, predictable from birthrate trends, may sustain demand (notably investment demand but also public outlays and housing demand by speculative builders) at a higher level than would otherwise prevail.   In this event, the additional spending thus stimulated could well keep growth in aggregate demand from lagging behind that in capacity, thereby raising incomes.[4]   But these conclusions are almost as controversial as is the outlook for the birthrate itself.   The one fairly sure thing seems to be that a high birthrate would aggravate any tendency toward inflation that might otherwise exist.

Somewhat less conjectural effects of population change can be discerned by examining estimates of the age composition of the United States population extending to 1985.   Table 25–1 shows the Census Bureau B projection, which differs from the A, C, and D projections only for the under-twenty age brackets.   The significant fact revealed by this table is that, during this

[4] See George Stolnitz, "Our Growing Population: Threat or Boon?" *Business Horizons*, vol. 2, no. 2, pp. 37f., Summer, 1959, for an excellent analysis of the economic impact of population trends.

Table 25–1.   Projections of United States Population by Age Bracket, 1965–1980

Age bracket	Thousands of persons			
	1965	1970	1975	1980
Under 20	77,068	82,244	88,625	96,569
20–24	13,623	17,104	19,057	20,624
25–34	22,374	25,220	31,139	36,517
35–44	24,462	22,996	22,458	25,267
45–54	22,068	23,360	23,574	22,194
55–64	16,974	18,500	19,845	21,056
65–74	11,496	12,131	13,227	14,489
75 and over	6,607	7,440	7,945	8,597
All ages	194,672	208,995	225,870	245,313
Age bracket	Percent of total population			
	1965	1970	1975	1980
Under 20	39.6	39.4	39.2	39.4
20–24	7.0	8.2	8.4	8.4
25–34	11.5	12.1	13.8	14.9
35–44	12.6	11.0	9.9	10.3
45–54	11.3	11.2	10.4	9.0
55–64	8.7	8.9	8.8	8.6
65–74	5.9	5.8	5.9	5.9
75 and over	3.4	3.6	3.5	3.5
All ages	100.0	100.0	100.0	100.0

Source: U.S. Department of Commerce, Bureau of the Census, *Current Population Reports*, ser. P-25, no. 279, Feb. 4, 1964. Series *B* projection used. (The *A*, *B*, *C*, and *D* projections differ only in their fertility assumptions. Through 1980, therefore, they are identical for ages twenty and over.)

fifteen-year interval, although the number of persons in the younger and older age ranges will increase, the number in the thirty-five- to fifty-four-year age range will decline absolutely between 1965 and 1975 and rise only slightly between 1975 and 1980. The proportion of the total population in the thirty-five- to fifty-four-year age range will decline from 23.9 percent in 1965 to 19.3 percent in 1980. It is in the younger age brackets that the proportion will rise, the proportion in the fifty-five-years-and-over age ranges showing virtually no change.

The effects of such a population shift on overall labor productivity (and hence on capacity) are hard to assess, because, although younger workers possess more strength and endurance than older workers, they are also less experienced. But the effects on the supply of executive personnel are obvious. In the 1965–1980 period, business firms will find it necessary to move increasingly below the usual age ranges for recruitment of executive personnel, employ more females in executive positions, or raise their executive retirement limits.

One last and far more critical population unknown for the analyst of the long-run outlook is the rate of population growth in the rest of the world, particularly in the economically less developed countries, during the next couple of generations. During the twentieth century so far, population growth in the advanced Western nations has been the joint result of relatively low fertility but still lower mortality. In the less developed economies the typical picture has been much higher mortality but still higher fertility. Since World War II, the introduction of comparatively easily communicated Western public health techniques into Asia, African, and Latin American countries has begun to achieve a radical reduction in death rates that is still far from finished. But fertility remains comparatively unaffected, and there appears to be no quick way to change it. The result has been a world population explosion that may only have just begun. From 1950 to 1960, the estimated world population rose by about $1\frac{3}{4}$ percent a year. If that rate of increase were to prevail until the year 2065—a relatively short span of time in the course of human history—the world population would rise from 1965's $3\frac{1}{4}$ billion to over $18\frac{1}{2}$ billion persons! Even by the year 2000, the world population would double.

Such a crowding of the earth's surface and a taxing of its natural resources would, of course, have many profound effects. Especially in nations that are already overpopulated in relation to their resources, the effects of such population pressures on international political relations could be disastrous. Assuming that these population pressures could be contained, far-reaching economic effects would remain, including some on the performance of the American economy. For one thing, a surging growth in world population in the remaining decades of this century could seriously aggravate the raw materials problems of the United States, perhaps not before 1980 or 1985 but very likely thereafter.[5] And the United States, instead of being a country embarrassed by agricultural surpluses, could be straining its agricultural capacity to help meet the rest of the world's massive food needs.[6]

ATTITUDES TOWARD WORK AND LEISURE

We have just seen that how much American adults in the aggregate choose to work over the decades ahead will depend partly on their desire for

---

[5] See below for a fuller discussion of the resources problem.

[6] Various technological developments other than expanding agricultural production by conventional methods may, of course, help to solve the problem of feeding a rapidly expanding world population. Possibilities are efficient methods of mining fresh-water lakes and ponds and perhaps the oceans for fish and edible plant life, and production of food by synthetic photosynthesis.

income and that this, in turn, will be influenced by how many children they have. In addition, changes in the willingness to work will be influenced by social and psychological factors that, while they may be activated or conditioned by income levels, are significant in their own right.

A fairly concrete example is that of the mores regarding women, especially married women, working. These have been in a state of transition in the United States for at least a century, and the change appears to have accelerated during and since World War II. Many labor force experts are convinced that, partly because of the continuing mechanization of housework, the trend toward increased part-time and full-time job seeking by older married women has by no means run its course. Indeed, they are counting heavily on it to ease the expected shortage of thirty-five- to fifty-year-old men in the 1970s. Attitudes not only to the general appropriateness of women working but to the appropriateness of a much larger role for them in key professional and administrative capacities may bear significantly on the American economy's potential for long-term growth. Already most Americans are women, and women's greater longevity is expected to cause a progressive widening of the numerical discrepancy between the sexes.

Significant changes in United States attitudes toward work and leisure will not be confined to the distaff side of the labor market. The whole course of retirement trends during the next generation is ambiguous. Probably further financial facilitation of retirement will tend to pull down average retirement age. But the success of medicine in lengthening life and in promoting greater physical and mental vigor in older persons has begun to create opposite pulls on retirement preferences. Any shortages of experienced manpower, such as those anticipated for the seventies, will intensify this countertrend.

The more general question that the retirement problem symbolizes is the uncertain attitudes of Americans toward leisure during the decades ahead. Rising labor productivity, if it is properly digested so that it does not simply produce involuntary leisure, i.e., technological unemployment, yields some combination of more output and less work. The latter can take the form of less work per worker year (shorter hours) or less work per worker life (longer schooling and earlier retirement), or more people who are supported throughout their lives without ever being remuneratively employed. And less work per worker year can, of course, take the form of either a shorter workweek or longer vacations and more holidays.

Since choices concerning leisure are, in effect, responses to rising productivity, they are treated later in the chapter when we consider some of the domestic adjustments that continuing economic growth may occasion in the United States. But, clearly, leisure decisions also influence the rate of economic growth itself. It is possible that a rather sharp alteration in Americans' comparative preferences for output and leisure will emerge in the next few decades. If so, a good many extrapolations of historical capacity trends may currently be overestimating the size of the American economy in 1985 or 1990.

THE MATERIALS AND ENERGY REQUIREMENTS FOR ECONOMIC GROWTH

Many long-run projectioneers give little or no thought to whether their extrapolations of historical productivity gains are feasible from a natural resources point of view. Yet, obviously, the availability and real cost of natural resources, except to the extent that shortages can be met by imports, are a limiting factor on any nation's economic growth. During the first century or century and a half of the history of the United States, the resources of the nation, with its vast unexplored or undeveloped areas, could almost be taken for granted. In more recent decades, however, several stark facts have focused attention on resource availability. One was the disappearance of the geographic frontier with its easy access to new lands and new materials. A second was the realization, as improved statistics became available, that the American economy's consumption of natural resources was rising at a rapid rate, considerably higher than the rate of population growth. A third was the rude awakening to the fact that the United States had become a net importer of a number of basic resources. One of these was oil. Another was forest products. Others were iron ore, copper, lead, zinc, tin, bauxite, and a number of the ferroalloys. For minerals as a whole, other than gold and silver, the United States was a net exporter from 1890 to 1940.[7] After 1940, however, the percentage of United States consumption met by imports rose, reaching 15 percent in 1960. Agricultural products, notably cotton, tobacco, fats and oils, and grains, together with chemicals, are about the only major natural resource categories in which the United States was a net exporter in the mid-1960s.

These unpleasant facts led to a number of studies of the adequacy of America's resource base to economic growth. Pioneering studies were made by the National Resources Planning Board in the late 1930s. In 1947, the Twentieth Century Fund published the results of a milestone study of supply and requirements of inanimate and human resources over the upcoming fifteen-year period.[8] In 1952, the President's special Materials Policy Commission (the Paley Commission), appointed by President Truman and composed of a distinguished group of business, government, and educational leaders, rendered its report, projecting needs and requirements to 1975.[9] The findings of this report were alarmingly pessimistic. It found that the Ameri-

[7] Except for a few isolated years when unusual circumstances prevailed.

[8] J. Frederick Dewhurst and Associates, *America's Needs and Resources*, Twentieth Century Fund, New York, 1947, revised 1955.

[9] *Resources for Freedom: A Report to the President*, President's Materials Policy Commission, 1952.

can economy's consumption of natural resources had been rising at a staggering rate and would continue to soar during the next quarter century. It emphasized that the United States, for the first time in history, had become a net
importer of raw materials and that the country's dependence upon foreign
supplies, particularly of petroleum, zinc, and copper, was certain to mount
very rapidly during the next two or three decades. Most ominously of all,
perhaps, it found that, during the decade then just past, a secular downtrend
in the average real costs of the total natural resource inputs into American
production had been reversed.

In the case of exhaustible resources, such as minerals, there is a tendency for the real costs of extraction to rise as progressively less accessible
and lower-grade deposits are used. But there are a number of offsetting factors—improved equipment and techniques, economies of scale, new discov-
eries, and the development of adequate, more readily available substitutes.
For a century these carried the day in the United States so that on the average
it took a declining joint input of capital and labor to yield a given physical
quantity of raw materials and energy. This, of course, provided a direct impetus to total factor productivity. However, the available evidence suggested
that in about 1940 the beneficent trend had come to an end, at least temporarily; the real costs of material and energy had begun to edge upward.

Some of the pessimism of the Paley report clearly was traceable to
very conservative assumptions about the appearance of new bottleneck-
breaking technological innovations. For example, the rather somber
energy outlook that it painted for the United States made no reference at all
to nuclear electric power generation, although it seemed probable in 1952,
and is plain now, that atomic-fission reactors should meet a significant fraction of the nation's energy requirements by 1975. Some students of technology and resources criticize the Commission not only for this oversight but for
its failure to allow at all for technological breakthroughs further in the future,
which, though unpredictable as to their specifics, were highly probable in the
abstract. For instance, there is the possibility that effective civilian exploitation of nuclear fusion—a potentially boundless energy source—may be a
reality before many years are past (though probably not by 1975). This technological breakthrough, we are told, may one day make the generation, although not the transmission, of electric energy virtually costless.[10]

In 1963, Resources for the Future, Inc., a nonprofit corporation created
initially by the Ford Foundation to study resource problems, published its

---

[10] "It is likely that we shall gradually develop procedures more naturally and effectively adjusted to the new source of energy, abandoning the conventional kinks and
detours inherited from chemical-fuel processes. Consequently, a few decades hence, energy
may be free—just like the unmetered air—with coal and oil used mainly as raw materials
for organic chemical synthesis, to which, as experience has shown, their properties are
best suited." John von Neumann, "Can We Survive Technology," *Fortune*, June, 1955,
p. 106.

monumental *Resources in America's Future*.[11] This projection, which extends to the year 2000, is much more of a study of the *economics* of natural resources than its predecessor studies, i.e., of probable supply-demand relationships and the cost of actual resources. The report is based on the assumption of an average annual increase in real GNP from 1960 to 2000 of 3.8 percent. The probable composition of GNP by major categories is also postulated. Although it avoids predictions of specific technological breakthroughs or of specific public policies toward natural resources, the study implicitly assumes, somewhat optimistically perhaps, that which it recommends:[12]

> ". . . maintaining the flow of new and improved resource technology in
>   discovery, production, transportation, and use of natural resources;
> maintaining and expanding a world trading and investing system that
>   can enlarge the opportunities of the United States and other coun-
>   tries for importing raw materials at low cost;
> conserving and using resources in accordance with sound ecological
>   and economic principles."

The report reaches the conclusion that:[13]

> "Neither a long view of the past, nor current trends, nor our most
> careful estimates of future possibilities suggest any general running
> out of resources in this country during the remainder of this century
> (or, if a broad impression may serve in the absence of detailed analy-
> sis, for a long time thereafter). The possibilities of using lower
> grades of raw material, of substituting plentiful materials for scarce
> ones, of getting more use out of given amounts, of importing some
> things from other countries, and of making multiple use of land and
> water resources seem to be sufficient guarantee against across-the-
> board shortage."

The report then proceeds, however, to examine the long-run prospects for the several major resources, and concludes that for a number of them, costs will rise, quality compromises will be necessary, and difficult technological or social adjustments will have to be made. In respect to crop land, the report concludes that no shortage is in sight during the remainder of this century. (In this finding, it should be noted, no allowance is made for a major program of agricultural exports to famine-ridden countries.) Serious shortages of forest land, however, and therefore of forest products, are seen as inevitable. The authors foresee no nationwide water shortages, and given

[11] Hans L. Landsberg, Leonard L. Fischman, and Joseph L. Fisher, *Resources in America's Future*, published for Resources for the Future, Inc., by The Johns Hopkins Press, Baltimore, 1963.
[12] *Ibid.*, p. 5.
[13] *Ibid.*, pp. 4–5.

"sufficient thought and effort" and proper pricing practices, no localized water shortages serious enough to be an impediment to continued national growth during the 1960–2000 period. Energy resources should be available at substantially constant real costs through 1975 or thereabouts. After 1975, supply problems will arise for oil and gas, but these can be offset, though perhaps not at constant costs, by several technological developments, notably the generation of electric power from nuclear sources. They visualize that roughly half of all electricity will come from nuclear reactors by the end of the century.

Generally speaking, the authors conclude, it is the metals that present problems of future adequacy. Increased imports will be required, and for most of them, costs will rise. Significant changes in the pattern of metals use will be necessary, including the substitution of aluminum, one of the relatively more abundant metals, for steel and copper. Domestic supplies of iron ore can be expanded by using taconite ores, though at somewhat higher costs. Copper will be in worldwide shortage, but substitutes are available. Future adequacy of lead and zinc is highly uncertain, but the United States will continue to rely heavily on imports.[14]

> "For the non-communist part of the world a mere continuation for the next forty years of the current level of lead consumption would require more than twice the amount that can now be regarded as reserves of the metal in these countries; in the case of zinc cumulative demand exceeds reserves by nearly 50 percent."

In the case of ferroalloys, probable supply-demand positions range all the way from adequacy plus a surplus for exports (e.g., molybdenum) to nearly complete dependence on foreign sources (e.g., tungsten).

Thus, on balance, the report foresees many difficult problems, but these problems can be solved, the authors feel, at a cost and in a measure that should not seriously interfere with economic growth of a magnitude projected in the study:[15]

> ". . . *provided* technologic advances and economic adaptation of them continue, *provided* foreign sources of raw materials remain open through maintenance of a viable world trading and investing system, and *provided* government resource policies and private management of resource enterprises improve in farsightedness, flexibility, and consistency."

THE PACE AND QUALITY OF INNOVATION

The insights of economics do not illuminate the process of innovation very much. For innovation is a creative, almost artistic, sometimes accidental

[14] *Ibid.*, p. 39.
[15] *Ibid.*, p. 53.

business. It is not the kind of achievement that can be made entirely to order, although certainly its pace is influenced by the volume of resources devoted to it.

The most highly publicized view of the United States prospects for technological innovation during the next generation is that they are unprecedentedly bright because of the swiftly expanding expenditure of effort on research and development activity. The National Science Foundation estimates that private expenditures for research and development rose from $2.4 billion in 1953 to $6.0 billion in 1963, and expenditures by industry (i.e., excluding universities and other nonprofit institutions) rose from $2.2 billion to $5.6 billion. Federal government research and development (R and D) expenditures rose from $2.8 billion in 1953 to $11.3 billion in 1963. Federal R and D expenditures are budgeted at $15.1 billion for fiscal 1967.[16] Further increases in all sectors are anticipated in the following decade. Sober scientists, not given to flights of fancy, contend that, in spite of the heavy investment in research in recent years, we have not begun to scratch the surface of scientific knowledge, and that in the decade or two ahead we shall see dramatic developments in the biological sciences comparable to those in the physical sciences in the past decade or two. At the very least, as was suggested in Chapter 9, the mushrooming of highly organized commercial and government research can be expected to steady the flow of technological changes, and those who are paying for this expanded research also certainly expect it to increase the flow.

But there are some contrary considerations. A very large portion of business' accelerated research outlays goes for what is generally called "new-product development." And a very large part of the activity encompassed by this euphonious heading is concerned, simply, with proliferating and differentiating highly similar products—and, by the same token, with promoting obsolescence in existing products. One has only to examine the grocery shelves of any supermarket, or the counters of any shopping center "drugstore," to be impressed with the thousands of "new" or "improved" products that are put on the market every year in the never-ending search for the consumer's dollar. Each of these additional soups, breakfast cereals, instant coffees, ball-point pens, and electric carving knives presumably claimed research and development funds. So did the displacement of laundry soaps by detergents and the displacement of ordinary detergents by super-detergents. So does the development of every larger-horsepower engine, built-in accessory, and new piece of chromium armor that the automobile industry creates for the purpose of making last year's model a miserable has-been.

Please do not misunderstand. In Chapter 9, when we were discussing

---

[16] Data for 1953 and 1963 from *Reviews of Data on Science Resources*, vol. 1, no. 4, National Science Foundation, Washington, May, 1965. Data for Federal expenditures in fiscal 1967 from *Budget of the United States Government*, Fiscal Year ending June 30, 1967.

stimulants to the inducement to invest, we spoke with high favor of the obsolescence-making effect of innovations. Moreover, endless multiplication of new and usually slightly superior products is presumably a boon for the American consumer. Our point here simply is that—statistically, at least— innovation of this kind does very little for the economy's overall productivity. By itself, the fact that each year the automobile industry puts out a new line of models does not cause the slightest tremor in real gross private product per man-hour. Yet new products have emerged, research and development money has been spent, and a great deal of investment has occurred. Such activity is necessary, firm by firm, to avoid a decline in sales and output. But rather than make for higher output per man-hour, this activity may make for a lower output per unit of capital input than would be the case if the industries in question did a less effective job of displacing old products with new.

Another source of concern about the long-term American innovational outlook is the fear of many people that, in its preoccupation with applied research and development, the United States has been slighting basic, or pure, research, which in the long run must lay the foundations of scientific insights upon which future innovations will be built. This is a very difficult contention to pin down, partly because no one seems to be quite sure of the dividing line between basic and applied research. However, certain points are fairly plain. One is that the tremendous increase in government research contracts with universities during the past decade, although supplying urgently needed revenue to the institutions, has preempted, mostly for fairly specific, defense- and space-oriented purposes, a large part of the total time and creative energy of university scientists. Second, the wave of students hitting the colleges and universities during the sixties is exerting a squeeze on that portion of higher education's resources that can be devoted to noncontract research. And third, only a small fraction of the increasingly large fraction of American scientists who are being bid into industrial and commercial research are provided with the time or facilities for engaging in truly broad, untrammeled inquiry that is not focused on specific-product or -process development. Lest we overstate the case, it should be recorded that some, usually very large, business firms do finance a significant amount of basic research; that, in recognition of this very problem, a rising percentage of the Federal research and development budget, at least since fiscal 1963, has been devoted to basic research;[17] and that the private foundations continue to provide an important financial underpinning to basic research. It still may be true that, for our own long-run good, we are devoting too much of our current effort, in the social as well as the natural sciences, to concrete problem solving.

Further, aside from the basic-research, applied-research problem, the dramatic development since the mid-1950s of strongly mission-oriented organi-

---

[17] *Budget of the United States Government*, Fiscal Year ending June 30, 1966, pp. 443–447, and similar data in earlier budget documents. Comparable data for years before fiscal 1963 are not available.

zation of government-sponsored research has tended to channel funds and research manpower into areas covered by such missions, at the expense of other areas.   Mission-oriented research, be it noted, may, and usually does, encompass both basic and applied research.   But all the research must be relevant to the mission.   The mission of "putting a man on the moon by 1970 and bringing him safely back" benefited from a tremendous concentration of research effort.   So did various defense missions.   Observing the success of the mission-oriented research method, a few nondefense and nonspace agencies of government adopted it in such fields as oceanography and weather control.   But in the main, partly for political reasons, the mission-oriented approach has not been applied on an ambitious scale in the area of civilian technology.   For example, it would have been possible to organize research missions directed toward such objectives as: (1) a new system of mass transportation of people in urban areas that would transport them swiftly, safely, economically, and reasonably comfortably from their homes to their places of work and return; (2) a method of household waste disposal, including both kitchen wastes (e.g., tin cans) and sewage, which would be efficient, economical, independent of sewerage lines, and would purify the water so that it could be recycled and used over again; (3) a new system of low-cost house construction that would make housing units virtually independent of the land on which they sit, and easy to add to or alter to fit changing family needs; (4) a system of electronic communication of written messages that would be virtually instantaneous, low-cost, and private, to supersede a substantial part of the present postal system.   To a significant but minor extent, achievement of such objectives has been advanced by "spin-offs" from existing mission-oriented research programs.   But the failure to apply the mission-oriented approach to such nondefense and nonspace problems is gradually creating a lag of civilian technology behind defense-space technology.

THE DISPOSITION TO SAVE

Even though all investments do not yield equal increments in productive capacity, capital formation is an essential requirement for economic growth.   And over the long run, how much capital the United States forms will depend on how much the economy as a whole abstains from private and public consumption.

Actually the gross national saving and investment rate in the United States in recent years, as we noted in Chapter 15, has not been notably high.[18] During the 1956–1965 decade, United States gross private domestic investment averaged about 15 percent of gross national product, and the addition of pub-

[18] At this point, we are slurring over the conventional United States national income concepts by speaking of saving and investment totals which include public as well as private components, despite the fact that we have no good way of segregating government consumption from government investment in our national income accounting system.

lic capital formation, if we were able to measure it properly, would not raise the total to as much as 19 percent of total production. This figure is significantly lower than comparable figures frequently quoted for European countries, except the United Kingdom. Fortunately, the effects of this disparity seem to have been narrowed by the tendency in the United States to get greater "capacity mileage" out of given quantities of capital formation. But presumably a maintenance of recent United States growth rates will require at least a maintenance of the recent gross investment rate, and the feasibility of this will depend partly on private dispositions to save.

The behavior of the personal saving rate is one of the least predictable unknowns in the long-run economic outlook. Some factors may tend to raise it. For instance, although there is no historical basis for anticipating it, perhaps the economy finally will achieve a degree of opulence wherein consumers begin to become sated with goods and services. Progressive contractualization of the saving process, discussed in Chapter 8, may not only stabilize the saving rate; it may increase it. Or possibly the saving rate will rise because at higher incomes consumers will choose to channel a larger share of their income into housing.

But the possibilities in the opposite direction are perhaps more impressive. Further extensions of old-age and survivors insurance may dampen the individual desire to save, although, as we noted in Chapter 8, there is no clear evidence that they have yet had that effect. A continuing avoidance of major depressions and recessions, gradually building confidence in the maintenance of prosperity, might weaken a significant motive for personal saving. If the size of the labor force should decline relative to that of the total population—whether because of a rise in the birthrate, a relative decline in the working-age population, longer schooling, or longer retirements—there would be a squeeze on personal saving. Also, persisting secular price inflation, which the next chapter will indicate is more likely than not in the United States, might eventually penetrate the consciousness of consumers to the point of creating a bias against liquid saving—the kind of personal saving, i.e., that makes room for a noninflationary use of resources for business investment. Finally, any pronounced shift toward leisure would probably be associated with some decline in the personal saving rate, for Americans typically consume more, especially in the form of recreational services and goods, when they are not at work.

In 1954, when the staff of the congressional Joint Economic Committee was preparing the 1965 projection footnoted in Chapter 17, they had this to say about personal saving: "Equally rational analyses can be constructed which would justify placing the rate as low as 4 or 5 percent or as high as 9 or 10 percent."[19] The authors of the Committee report actually chose to project a rate of 6 percent, a figure that, for the ensuing decade as a whole,

[19] *Potential Economic Growth in the United States during the Next Decade*, Joint Committee on the Economic Report of the President, 83d Cong., 2d Sess., 1954, p. 13.

proved to be an almost perfect forecast. We are not inclined to argue with this choice for another decade, except to underscore the sentence just quoted.

If consumers should be disposed to save less as the next few decades unfold, this would not necessarily prevent the maintenance of as high an investment rate as in the past. But investment could be maintained in this event only by one of three means: by inflation that priced enough consumers out of the market to cause a higher rate of real personal saving than consumers in the aggregate would have chosen under a stable price situation; or by a relatively larger retention of revenue by business; or by a combination of higher taxes and/or lower public consumption outlays that shifted government budgets sufficiently in the direction of a surplus to compensate for the lower personal saving rate. In practice it might be difficult to make any of these adjustments smoothly enough to avoid some inhibition of investment and economic growth if consumers began to lose their taste for saving.

SHIFTS IN THE ECONOMY'S PRODUCT MIX

Often it is harder to foresee what is going to happen in the long run to particular industries and to the composition of the economy's output than it is to get some line on the course of total activity. Yet the progress of overall productivity will be influenced significantly by changes in the composition of output. As was noted in Chapter 5, the historical progress of gross private product per man-hour in the United States has been partly attributable to "economically efficient" shifts of labor from lower-productivity to higher-productivity industries—the outstanding example being the secular exodus of labor from agriculture. It is hard to anticipate what the pattern of such interindustry shifting will be in the future, but some bits of the pattern that do seem visible might, it appears, dampen rather than stimulate aggregate productivity.

For one thing, the exodus from agriculture must abate if the agricultural labor force is not to diminish below zero. In addition, the relative shift of nonagricultural labor out of manufacturing into services and trade may accelerate as more and more manufacturing processes are automated. Typically, this involves a shift of labor from a higher- to a lower-productivity sector of the economy. The dampening effects that these particular changes may exert on total productivity gains may be more than offset by other product-mix developments. Shifts of labor within manufacturing, e.g., from textiles to metal-working industries, or from less to more productive employments within the services and trade sector may occur. Or the future may see revolutionary innovations and radical productivity advances within the service and distribution industries. But these reassuring possibilities are not sure things. The net productivity impact that changes in the nation's product mix will have during coming decades remains obscure.

A special obscurity is created by defense spending, the trend of which, over the long run, of course, cannot be even roughly predicted by economic analysis. Higher national security outlays would mean a heavier commitment to defense-related industries, where value produced per man-hour typically is high. On the other hand, an emphasis on defense production so great that it curtailed the availability of materials, research, and engineering for civilian business investment might inhibit a most important source of productivity gains.

THE PROVISION OF PUBLIC FACILITIES AND SERVICES

Obviously, many kinds of public policy will affect the progress of the United States economy during coming decades. But the point, made originally in Chapter 12, which we want to recall here, is the particularly direct impact that the provision of various civilian facilities and services, especially by local and state governments, will have on private investment and on productivity. The quality and scope of public education may, over the long pull, decisively determine the quality of American science, technology, and business and social management, and may therefore call the tune on the long-term innovational outlook. Special educational programs to raise the earning power of the technologically disemployed and school dropouts will raise national productivity. Public investment will help determine whether our materials and energy resources meet our growth requirements. Public outlays on highways and other aspects of the transport system, especially mass transportation in urban areas, will influence vast areas of private investment. Public provision of the essential community facilities, assistance in urban land development, and leadership in reclaiming blighted central urban areas will influence not only the location but the total volume of new industrial plant building and may largely determine the volume of residential and commercial construction. Many other illustrations of the partial dependence of economic growth upon the provision of social investment and services might be cited, but these will suffice.

For those of us basically confident about the ability of American society to meet and surmount challenges, it would make little sense to highlight this general issue as one of the major uncertainties in the long-term economic outlook if it were not for one thing, and that is the mundane matter of finance. There is no real question about the United States economy's ability to afford whatever expansion-promoting government programs it needs. But there is a very real question about our ability to pay for what we need within the ground rules of our present fiscal structure.

Most of the government outlays needed to facilitate domestic economic growth must be made at local and state levels. However, state and local revenue sources, chiefly property and sales taxes, are notoriously limited, inflexible, and, in the aggregate, laggard in their response to rising incomes. But, says the optimist, hasn't this always been so, and haven't we nevertheless made out all right? Perhaps so, but not, at least until recently, under conditions of persisting inflation, which grossly compound the shortcomings of the state and local tax system. If a continuing updrift in prices should be the pattern of the future, state and local revenues may forever be lagging far behind the need.

From a purely financial viewpoint, the one easy solution to this problem is that of Federal financial grants. The volume of Federal aid to state and local governments has risen from $3 billion in fiscal 1955 to $11 billion in fiscal 1965 and a budgeted $15 billion for fiscal 1967. As a percentage of total state and local revenue, Federal aid accounted for 11 percent in fiscal 1955, 15 percent in fiscal 1965, and probably a slightly higher percentage in fiscal 1967.[20] In spite of this increase, the mounting needs of increasingly urbanized state-local governmental units have constantly tended to outrun revenues. In the past, Federal grants to state and local governments have all been conditional grants, often requiring matching funds by the state or local government concerned, and available for use only for purposes and in accordance with minimum standards established by the Federal government. In 1965, a proposal known as the "Heller Plan" (after Walter W. Heller, former Chairman of the Council of Economic Advisers) was somewhat unofficially advanced to create a new type of "block" grants to state and local governments, not for specific purposes, but simply to add to their general revenues.[21] A principal argument advanced in favor of this plan was the fact we noted in Chapter 12 and again in Chapter 15; i.e., Federal government revenues, in a growing economy with no change in tax rates, tend to rise at a faster pace than GNP. Thus, if economic expansion is sustained, and if total Federal expenditures (including national security expenditures) rise at the same or a lesser rate than GNP, the Federal government is in an advantageous position to pay "fiscal dividends," not only to taxpayers (tax cuts), but also to the hard-pressed states. As of this writing, the plan has not been adopted by the executive branch of the government and has met vigorous opposition in some quarters, partly on political grounds.[22] Unless a continued major expansion of Federal grants of one kind or another to state and local governments occurs, however, the only alternative solution for providing the public investments and programs needed for facilitating vigorous economic growth will be a radical, politically courageous overhaul of state and local tax systems. And seasoned political handicappers, we suspect, would not quote very favorable odds on this eventuality at present. It is common in the analysis of develop-

[20] *Budget of the United States Government, Special Analyses,* Fiscal Year ending June 30, 1967.

[21] One of the early expositions of the plan was by Joseph A. Pechman of The Brookings Institution, in an address before an American Bankers Association symposium. See Joseph A. Pechman, "Financing State and Local Government," *Proceedings* of the Symposium on Federal Taxation, The American Bankers Association, New York, 1965.

[22] See Harvey E. Brazer, "Our Hard-pressed State and Local Governments," *Challenge,* vol. 14, no. 3, pp. 7f., January–February, 1966.

mental prospects in the backward economies of the world to conclude that one of the critical determinants of the feasible pace of economic progress will be the willingness of the populace to pay higher taxes. It is rather ironical that in the most advanced of all economies the same conclusion holds, at least with respect to the lower governmental jurisdictions.

THE DOMESTIC IMPACT OF ECONOMIC PROGRESS

The outlook for growth in a nation's real productive capacity is not the only aspect of its long-run prospects that invites economic comment. Despite all the uncertainties that cloud the physical growth outlook, a strong probability remains that American productive capacity and, more particularly, American productivity, will continue to rise for a very long time to come. Thus one is tempted to go beyond the question of productivity prediction itself and consider what some of the impacts and significance of continuing secular growth may be.

There are two interesting clusters of possibilities along these lines. One concerns the position of the United States in the world around it, a massive subject upon which the final portion of the chapter will touch briefly. The other has to do with some of the internal adjustments within American society that may be necessary for coming to terms with an ever-more-bountiful production mechanism.

AN EMBARRASSMENT OF RICHES?

In citing some of the problems that continuing material progress may generate within the economy, one runs the risk of seeming to carp. By conventional standards, most of the fruits of continuing economic progress in the United States should be eminently desirable. In the words of the Council of Economic Advisers:[23]

> "Technological advance and the rising productivity associated with it have many human payoffs: higher incomes and consumption, longer life, reduced suffering and illness, reduced drudgery, greater leisure, and an improved quality of life that cannot be measured in income statistics. Philosophers may debate whether all this contributes to human happiness or the edification of the soul. Ordinary men— those who have not yet enjoyed the fruits of technological advance, those who have tasted them, and those grown accustomed to the diet —all pursue them with fervor undiminished by the philosophers' doubts."

The persistence of historical productivity gains for another generation should virtually eliminate the age-old specter of poverty from the nation's

[23] *Economic Report of the President,* January, 1964, p. 91.

domestic scene, unless we are singularly unsuccessful as a community in making an income distribution of these gains that will support adequate use of our expanding productive ability.

The percentage of American families with incomes below $3,000 (in 1964 prices) fell from 31 percent in 1947 to 18 percent in 1964, and almost surely, though data are not available at the time of writing, to a lower figure in 1965.[24] The incidence of poverty in the United States today is heavily concentrated in various kinds of special cases—retired persons whose living standards are not so low as their current incomes, married students, widows with young children, physically or mentally handicapped persons, members of minority groups, technologically disemployed persons, persons lacking a basic education, and economically immobile small farmers, especially in the Southeast. During the coming generation, if the typical economic growth projections should be realized, we certainly shall have the national wherewithal, if we also have the legislative and other types of determination it will take, wholly to eliminate such pockets of poverty without any significant leveling of income differentials. This would represent an enormous achievement. For the first time in the world's history a major economic system would have succeeded in supplying virtually all its people with material requirements far above the subsistence level. At the very least, continuing economic progressiveness will solve as many problems as it generates, and much more elemental ones.

But there will be problems generated. One will be that of maintaining, largely through the price-wage-profit mechanism, a distribution of productivity gains that will stimulate not only continuing expansion of productivity and capacity but a matching growth in markets. Of all the needed adjustments to growth, this, perhaps, can be discussed most systematically. It will be dealt with in the next chapter. However, even if we assume nothing happens to the distribution of further productivity gains to interfere with market expansion, this basic question remains: May not the appetite for goods and services consumption of Americans at all levels in the income distribution become progressively jaded as we become more and more opulent?

It has been noted already that no support for the hypothesis of a secularly declining average propensity to consume is to be found in American historical statistics. Estimates of aggregate income and consumption suggest that since the late nineteenth century Americans have increased their consumption just about in proportion to their spendable incomes, not because they have had an insatiable appetite for the consumer products of 1880, but because of the ceaseless appearance of new and improved products. If such product innovation continues unabated—and why not?—will not any subsidence in the secular growth of consumption be quite unlikely?

Perhaps; there is much sense in this view. And yet the century of American experience from which this ever-onward-and-upward view of per

[24] *Economic Report of the President*, January, 1966, p. 228.

capita consumption is drawn may turn out to be a terminable episode in the longer sweep of history. Other societies much less efficient than ours in serving the material wants of their inhabitants nevertheless have shown much less preoccupation with material welfare. Surely it is possible that this pre-occupation will eventually wane in the United States if rising productivity persists. It is possible that the marginal utility of all personal consumption of goods and services, and not just of particular items or categories within the total, will begin to decline.

If we are talking about the very long run in a tranquil America un-troubled by the world outside it, this last would seem to be a sensible hypothesis. Evidently it strikes a great many contemporary business writers the same way. For again and again one encounters the suggestion that our ability to produce threatens to outrun our ability to consume and that during the coming generation, therefore, the key business function will be that of marketing. According to this thesis, business must advertise more intensively, subtly, and effectively than ever; must teach housewives to throw things away faster; must speed up the creation of new status symbols and accelerate the obsolescence of existing consumer durables. In short, to stay economically healthy, Americans must, through the beneficent intervention of Madison Avenue, force themselves to gobble up far more consumer goods and services than they would choose if left more nearly to their own devices.

Although there is really nothing professional that an economist can say about such a line of social policy, we find it rather vulgar. It sounds like solving the farm problem by giving everyone a tapeworm. If the marginal propensity to consume should begin to sag as productivity rises higher and higher, other more sensible social adjustments would be possible. For one thing, even after appetites for additional personal consumption became rela-tively jaded, many unrequited wants for collective consumption in the form, for example, of more elaborate public education and recreation facilities and services would remain. Furthermore, the economy may decide in favor of substantially more leisure. With a little good management, it should be per-fectly possible for this to occur without unstabilizing the results. Whether a large expansion in leisure time would be healthy or demoralizing for the society is another and more difficult question upon which we want to touch in a moment. But first let us consider some of the effects that a continuing productivity advance might have, not only on the propensity to consume, but on the organization and staffing of productive activity. For these, too, will have a bearing on the leisure-time problem.

THE IMPACT OF CONTINUING MECHANIZATION

For hundreds of thousands of years human muscular strain was a major input into most productive processes. This is rapidly coming to an end in the United States, which in another generation may almost literally be a no-sweat economy as far as remunerated activities are concerned. Hard labor in the old physical sense is rapidly disappearing from manufacturing, distribution, and agriculture, and it is diminishing in constructon. Manual labor in general is on the decline; we may move toward a condition in which very few of the labor force, other than certain professional and artistic groups, will earn their livings with hand tools.

Such a minimization of physical toil has been, as has abundant mass consumption, an ageless human goal. And yet it may aggravate certain problems, as does productive abundance. The most obvious of these will be the danger of increasing physical softness and flabbiness in the American people. The psychological effects, however, might be even more disturbing. Every society, to meet its challenges successfully, must have a fair amount of trained discipline. Its members must have well-formed habits of doing difficult and unpleasant things they think they *ought* to do but do not like to do. In this culture, which has attached such overwhelming importance to work and production, the job—the earning of a living—probably has been the principal social context in which such habits have been inculcated. The work role is the one that males of the culture have had to play for keeps and in which they had to come to terms with difficulties and adversities. Work situations, of course, can contain many nonphysical kinds of adversity. But the physical ones have been the most elemental and, in the past, pervasive. As they are subtracted, and as total working time per man declines, one wonders whether the community may not be losing a familiarity with manageable personal hardships which in the past has strengthened its resiliency.

But we should leave such speculation to others more competent. One does not have to range so far beyond the borders of economics to spot some of continuing mechanization's other implications for the organization of production. A perpetuation of the differential rate of productivity growth between manufacturing and nonmanufacturing industries could cause a substantial shift in the structure in the economy and possibly of political power in the United States.

As we have seen, during the past half century, productivity gains in manufacturing appear to have been substantially greater than those elsewhere in the economy. There is no particular reason to believe that this pattern will not persist. If it should, in twenty or thirty years, even more than now, a relatively few highly progressive fabricating and processing industries plus a few networks of energy suppliers will be the wellsprings of economic abundance in the United States. The plants themselves may be more or less numerous and more or less geographically dispersed than now, depending partly on our success in developing low-cost, modest-sized nuclear-energy generation. But in any case, most of them probably will be divisions of a relatively few large corporate establishments.

The need to tap large pools of labor will be a less important factor than now in determining industrial location. For most of these will be very lightly populated plants by current standards. Their labor utilization will be more like that of the electric power and oil refinery industries presently, where labor costs typically claim only a small percentage of total revenues. In many fabricating processes most workers will be replaced by machines, and most foremen by feedback controls and computers. Much the same will apply to office staffs. Only the shop supervisors, some maintenance personnel and technicians, and middle and upper managers will still be human. Most of the rest of us who are not retired or prolonging our education will be employed servicing or distributing goods to each other in response to the opulent wants we all will have, thanks to the twin circumstances of high real incomes and much leisure, both of which, in turn, will be largely due to these mechanized industrial cornucopias.

Specialists on automation quite rightly emphasize that the speed and pervasiveness of the trend toward this kind of thing can easily be exaggerated and romanticized. Nonetheless the trend itself is quite apparent. It suggests the possibility of a long-term decline in the power of organized labor in the United States, inasmuch as labor's stronghold during the past few decades has been the fabricating and processing industries and, within those industries, the manual, nonprofessional, and nonclerical occupations. With the size of the manufacturing labor force declining, in relative if not absolute terms, either there will be an erosion of union power or the unions will have to achieve new effectiveness in organizing technical and professional personnel and workers in distribution and the services. In any case, although the effectiveness of unions in winning traditional wage and working-condition benefits for their shrinking numbers in manufacturing might not be impaired, their long-term effectiveness as an offsetting counterpoise to the discretionary authority of large corporate management would seem to be threatened.

This, as we shall note in the next chapter, may complicate the long-term problem of productivity-gains distribution. Also, if it comes to pass, it will accentuate the exposed position into which management is being thrust in the large-producer-group–dominated economy, which the United States has become. There may be an increasing scope of discretionary managerial authority that is not closely disciplined by the market. At the same time, the countervailing influence of labor to such authority may be weakening. This could lead to mounting public uneasiness about whether the community has sufficiently reliable mechanisms for assuring that private economic power will be exercised in a socially responsible manner. The whole question of whether private institutions and public policies can be adjusted to improve the social accountability of those wielding concentrated economic power without dampening the productiveness and progressiveness of the system may well become the fundamental domestic political-economic problem of the next generation. If so, further mechanization and dehumanization of fabricating, processing, and assembly operations will have helped to pose the problem.

LEISURE AND VALUES

In 1955, George Soule wrote a fascinating book called *Time for Living*, dedicated to the proposition that within a few decades Americans will not need to spend nearly so much of their time earning a living and will have more time for "living" itself.[25] An increasing preference for taking new productivity gains in the form of additional leisure rather than of additional goods and services, Soule reasoned, will permit a vast and varied exfoliation of culture in the United States that qualitatively will be as fine as anything the world has seen and quantitatively will be wholly unprecedented. Our situation will be rather like that of ancient Athens: a superstructure of superb artistic, intellectual, and recreational activity supported by a slave economy— except that this time all the slaves will be machines, and the privilege of leisure will extend to the whole mass of the population.[26] In the last analysis, argued Soule, it will be the brilliance of American society's material achievements that will free it from the charge of excessive materialism.

This is a very pretty picture, and it may be realistic. On the other hand, cynics insist that an accelerated growth of mass leisure and, therefore, of mass-leisure markets can mean only a spreading tyranny of the mediocre and the gross—a further displacement of reading by television, of "worthwhile" TV by adult westerns and medical melodramas, of individual sport by athletic spectacles, of ballet and opera by folk rock, of chamber music by pop concerts, of rigorous academic disciplines by how-to-do-it courses, of family life by "togetherness," travel by tourism, diversity by conformity, and of the Good Society by the Lonely Crowd.

These are some more issues which we cannot pursue here. But this much it is well for any analyst of long-run United States economic prospects to recognize: successful digestion of large increments of leisure in the next few decades will require some reweighting of conventional values in the United States. If this country, wholly untroubled by affairs beyond its borders, could follow its own internal inclinations, the rate of physical economic growth might very well slow down during the next generation. Such a development would not need to indicate any social decadence or stagnation; there would be nothing necessarily sad or regrettable about it, provided the community could find new dimensions in which to strive and achieve. But this would necessitate some reordering of values. For in the culture to date,

---

[25] George H. Soule, *Time for Living*, The Viking Press, Inc., New York, 1955.

[26] A case can be made for the proposition that, in contrast to ancient Athens, the "slaves" of 2050, and perhaps 2000, will be the doctors, lawyers, scientists, social philosophers, and others whose unique and highly developed talents cannot be replaced by machines; that work will be the privilege of the few and the symbol of success. It is significant that average workweeks for highly educated, professional people have apparently declined far less, in recent decades, than have those of the factory workers and the farm hand.

individual success and prestige have been very largely governed by how one has played his occupational role. If occupational roles in the future are to claim a much smaller portion of adult time, Americans, to stay healthy, will have to find greater rewarding challenges in other adult roles they play—as amateur artists, artisans, politicians, churchmen, sportsmen, students, conversationalists, child psychologists, or what have you. And for such challenges to be adequate, greater social prestige will have to be accorded performance in these nonremunerative pursuits.

Slave labor may have been a necessary condition, but it was not a sufficient one, for growing Athenian culture. It was also essential that the community's scale of values attach great importance to nonmaterial achievements. One would no more have cited the Athenian GNP as an adequate index of whether the city-state had had a good or bad year than one would today accept the Harvard football team's cumulative point spread as a fair indication of that university's annual accomplishment.

Economic or occupational achievement in the United States will not have to be deemphasized so much as Harvard football to make a major increase in leisure socially digestible. But economically nonproductive performance may have to be taken much more seriously. It may not be unhealthy for young men who envisage themselves as the steel masters or helicopter magnates of 1990 to ponder the (probably exaggerated) possibility that most bosses of automated commodity production in 1990 will be like the water commissioners of today, and that their fame may depend chiefly on the skill with which they have selected and practice their avocations.

INTERNATIONAL CHALLENGES TO AMERICAN GROWTH AND SECURITY

These are rather bizarre subjects that we have just been discussing. The question whether a populace can become an opulent leisure class without getting soft, bored, and decadent is one with which many aristocracies but few whole societies have had to wrestle in the past. Actually the question may be a little premature even for the United States. At least this is probably so if we extend our appraisal of the American economy's long-term prospects to influences lying beyond the borders of the economy itself. In the turbulent world around us there will be no lack of urgent economic challenges for the next generation of Americans. And while some of these external problems have been generated or aggravated by the very productiveness of the American economy, that same productiveness constitutes our most promising single national resource for meeting them.

The question that holds the key to the American economy's future is far sterner than that of how to become increasingly idle without becoming increasingly lazy. It is the simple question of survival. Or more specifically:

Can the nation marshal its productive potential to facilitate adjustments abroad that can achieve peace and security—security for what is presently the most privileged and envied society in a revolutionary world?

COMMUNIST-WESTERN CONFLICT

There is, first of all, of course, the fact of a dangerous worldwide ideological contest that constantly threatens to erupt into military contest. The contest is one of many dimensions, committed to many arenas. Inevitably it permeates the world's affairs. It casts them in an unusually garish light, because this is one of the few times in history, if not the first, when armed nations have amassed such destructive power that a struggle between them threatens to wipe out civilization.

The most obvious, short-run implication for the American economy is the necessity of maintaining the required degree of military strength—including weapons improvement and underlying scientific development, accommodation of allies, and preparedness to fight small, limited wars if necessary—to keep "the stalemate of mutual terror" a stalemate. Gradual reductions in defense expenditures, as our military posture is improved, as efficiencies can be achieved, and as more immediate tensions ease, can be hoped for. But Soviet technical achievements, and the beginnings of similar achievements in Communist China, have shocked Americans into a realization that the costs of national security will be heavy and long continued.

But this is only the beginning of the strategic problem or of its domestic economic implications. A military stalemate, no matter how assiduously tended, is inherently risky and unstable. If it works, it does not even provide a satisfactory form of competition; the contestants are forestalled by self-interest from joining the issue. In the long run, therefore, other avenues to national survival must be found, and these seem to be of two general sorts.

One possibility is a direct lessening of the tensions between the principal parties—a move in the direction of mutually civil, tolerant, and humane, if not cordial, coexistence. In the long run, some such mutual accommodation through the processes of cultural and commercial intercourse must provide part of the alternative to mutual destruction. If it does, an increasing interpenetration of Western and Communist societies may have important consequences for American business, particularly with respect to overseas operations and trade and the specialization of production within this economy.

A second possibility is that of direct economic rivalry—a rivalry that is already an obvious fact. On the one hand, there is the faster rate of growth that the Soviet Union, at an earlier developmental stage, has apparently achieved by means of exceptionally intensive capital formation made possible by authoritarian belt tightening. On the other hand, there is still the great absolute superiority of United States output, the greater superiority of American output and leisure per capita, and the even greater superiority in consumption per capita. The display significance that such comparisons have and will continue to have, both within the competing economies and in the eyes of onlooking nations, should not be underrated.

All dimensions of Communist-Western rivalry certainly would deserve careful treatment in any extended discussion of the international uncertainties in the long-term American outlook. But in the brief space allocable to the subject here we want to dwell instead on a third, and surely the most crucial, arena of economic competition—the economically less developed countries.

WORLD ECONOMIC REVOLUTION

The insistent, surging demand for material improvement that has burst forth among the economically poorer peoples of this planet during the past couple of decades would inject grave uncertainties into long-term United States prospects even if Americans and Russians were the warmest of allies. For the United States is the supreme "have" in the world of awakening "have-nots." Americans, who constitute some 6 percent of the world's population, probably enjoy about half the world's real income. The security of any person or group who occupies such a favored position relative to his fellows is tentative and dubious.

It is quite true that numerical income comparisons may both exaggerate and oversimplify the problem. For one thing, the available output and income data for many countries still are extremely crude and unreliable. Moreover, even if the figures were technically impeccable, it would be misleading to suppose that the average resident of the United States, where national income per capita in 1965 was $2,850, was more than twenty-eight times "better off" than, say, the average Indian, whose measurable income per capita was less than $100. But this is only a matter of degree, of shading. The essential point remains. However you estimate it, the material welfare differential between the advanced Western economies—particularly the United States—and most of the economies of Asia, Africa, and Latin America is tremendous. And further: the latent unrest that this kind of situation has promised for a century or more is no longer just latent. It has become violently kinetic since World War II. In virtually every Asian, African, and Latin American country a critical, socially controlling leadership minority of the population has been indelibly infected with the demand for development. Almost without exception these countries are irreversibly committed to an adventure in rapid, disruptive, but ambitious social change. Wide mass awareness, where it does not already exist, is only a matter of time. The question is less whether accelerated economic development is in the offing than what form it will take. All of this is a result of a confluence in the mid-twentieth century of some or all of the following forces.

First, there is the drive of nationalism, the demand for political independence, heavily inspired by Western and especially American history and political ideals. And this itself, of course, is a reaction against Western colonialism. Second, thanks to colonialism, increasing trade with the West, and a greatly increased interchange of persons with the advanced Western countries for educational, governmental, military, and business reasons, there is a snowballing awareness of, and appetite for, Western living standards. Related, but distinguishable, there is a spreading knowledge of Western technology and a belief in its transplantability. Third, as we already have noted, in many of the less developed economies an explosive growth in population has been set in motion by the introduction of Western health techniques. Fourth, in many of the Asian countries a redrawing of political boundaries has disrupted established trading and production patterns. In such cases intensified developmental efforts are needed, not just to improve economic welfare, but to recover previous levels. Finally, a number of the Asian countries have decided, partly under Western and particularly American encouragement, to assume considerably larger national defense burdens, mostly to protect themselves against communism. Even with heavy United States military assistance, these undertakings make significant claims on local resources.

This is no place to attempt a comprehensive outline of all the factors that may be needed to achieve the kind of economic expansion for which the forces just indicated create an urgent demand. Three of these requirements, however, are (1) a heavy import and propagation of technological knowledge and skills (adapted to local resource availabilities), (2) population control, and (3) capital formation. The first is vitally important and certainly not easy. Nevertheless, the export of technical assistance from advanced economies is not in itself, as these things go, a highly expensive operation. Moreover, as we should have well learned from the Russians by now, Western technology basically seems to be highly transferable among very different cultures. The second, population control, presents both technological and cultural problems. The latter, though formidable, are not insurmountable over time. The technological problems seem to be well on their way toward solution. Thus it typically is the lack of capital that is the most stubborn, intransigent economic bottleneck impeding the developmental process. It is the more expensive bottleneck to break, and poverty limits the ability of the less developed economies to accomplish this. It is hard for a subsistence economy to channel much of its output into nonconsumption uses. And because available export surpluses in these economies are primarily agricultural raw materials, the demand for which is growing only slowly in the West, it is extremely difficult for them to earn the foreign exchange needed to finance their capital import requirements.

If the West wants to preserve the opportunity for the uncommitted less developed countries to build reasonably liberal institutions not incompatible with our own, it presumably must furnish larger capital exports to the less developed areas than those which the Communists would supply.

This, we must emphasize, is not the whole of the problem. Capital, to be useful, must be packaged together with skills and internal reforms; it must be sensibly combined with local resources into a coherent developmental program. Nor will the adequacy of the West's capital supply to the less developed economies be only a matter of size. Any capital export program can be wrecked by inept diplomacy and administration, by failure to evolve a workable partnership between public and private sources of Western capital, or by incompatible foreign trade policies. But in the present context, where our primary concern is the domestic economic outlook in the United States, it is legitimate to emphasize the capital requirement as that aspect of the economic revolution now in progress overseas which is likely to exert the heaviest demand on American resources.

Obviously, the United States has a most vital selfish interest in facilitating acceptable alternatives to the Communist program of economic development in Asia, Africa, and Latin America. There is self-interest of the most direct commercial sort in maintaining and improving American access to foreign sources of raw materials during a generation in which world material supplies promise to become much tighter relative to demand. Equally important, if American business is to expand and prosper in the years to come, it will need expanding foreign markets. And poor countries make poor markets. Thus, there are sound economic reasons for a continuing program of development assistance to the less developed nations that are willing to help themselves. And there are humanitarian reasons, respected in a nation that believes in the dignity of human beings. But in the words of the Council of Economic Advisers:[27]

> "It is well for us to be frank in admitting, both to ourselves and to others, that our development assistance strategy rests primarily on what are, in the broadest sense, national security grounds. It is well to be realistic about the uncertainties that run through our development assistance strategy—about the fact, for example, that economic development will not necessarily insure democratic governments or peaceful international behavior. But it [is] also wise to rest our policy on the *probabilities*—and these seem to be the following:
>> that free, progressing, open societies typically make better, safer, and friendlier neighbors and members of the international community;
>> that, in nations imbued with surging expectations, vigorous economic development is a necessary, although not a sufficient, condition for the maintenance of orderly political processes; and
>> that for most such nations, substantial external public assistance for a limited period is a necessary, although not a sufficient, condition for economic development.

[27] *Economic Report of the President*, January, 1964, pp. 151–152.

"In short, the premise of our development assistance effort has been—and remains—that, while the risks and uncertainties inherent in making the effort are substantial, the risks of not making it are even greater."

The problems raised in the last few pages have carried us into some strange territory for a book on domestic business conditions. We hope, however, that their relevance is plain enough. The essential points simply are, first, that the United States responses to the international challenges that confront it may heavily determine the pattern of resource use and the intensity of the productive effort within this country during the next few decades; and second, that developments abroad, influenced by American foreign economic policy, among other things, may have a more profound impact on the progress of the American economy during the next generation than any occurrences within the economy itself. It may be quite literally true, for example, that the comparative success of economic development in India and in China during the next twenty years will have a more decisive bearing on the United States standard of living in 1990 or 2000 than will any indigenous influence on American productivity gains.

SUMMARY

This, as advertised, has been a diffuse chapter, essentially because the long-run outlook for the American economy is an exceedingly diffuse subject. Any comprehensive effort at really long-term economic prognosis would have to be a massive interdisciplinary undertaking to which the professional economist is only one among many specialized contributors.

The first major portion of the chapter, with its critique of extrapolations unlimited and its examination of various circumstances that might alter the secular rate of American productivity gains during the next twenty or thirty years, illustrates a kind of contribution to long-run outlook analysis that the general economist is well equipped to make. Our review noted that uncertainties respecting birthrate and other population phenomena, changing preferences for work and leisure, the adequacy of raw materials and energy supplies, the pace and productiveness of innovation, possible alterations in saving habits, the effects of changes in the economy's product mix, and the extent to which the nation succeeds in supplying itself with adequate public services and facilities all tend to obscure the precise pace of American economic growth during the decades ahead.

All the same, the presumption of substantial continuing growth remains, and with it the question of its consequences and implications. In this regard the chapter has pursued two widely separated lines of discussion that differ in their mood as much as their content. On the one hand, if we think only of the domestic economy free to pursue its own fate without foreign distractions, the country's long-term economic challenge would seem essentially to be that of coming gracefully and constructively to terms with a threatening redundancy of output. For all its exotic flavor, this may prove to be a very real problem indeed.

But most such worries are premised upon an exceedingly parochial view of the world's most favored economy. Seen in a world setting, the primary attribute of the United States future appears to be not opulence but insecurity. And the need to meet this challenge—particularly the need to help moderate the relative economic inferiority of underprivileged nations—may maintain the same kind of pressures upon output that have operated to varying degrees ever since the beginning of World War II.

The purpose of the last two portions of the chapter has been to illustrate the pertinence to workaday business conditions analysis of some large and perplexing issues that extend well beyond the narrow boundaries of the craft itself. In the next and final chapter, however, we shall focus on one very vital strain of issues which lies mainly within the territory of conventional applied economic analysis and which, at the same time, threads its way through the vast limbo of the American economy's long-run future. We refer to the long-run outlook for prices in the United States and the wage-price-profit requirements for sustained economic growth. Since these are matters with which the unassisted economist can deal with some coherence and conviction, they will supply a good stopping point for a work addressed more to the capacities than to the incapacities of business conditions analysis.

26

THE LONG-RUN
OUTLOOK FOR PRICES
AND PRICING PRACTICE

In 1950, when *The Economist* ran a series of articles under the general title of "The Age of Inflation," it bestowed a sobriquet on the post-World War II era that many economists throughout the free world continue to find appropriate. Few nations have avoided major upsurges in prices during the postwar decades. A number were ravaged by violent inflations that dislocated production, distorted distribution, and disrupted normal financial and fiscal relationships. Earlier chapters, especially 14 and 15, have traced the course of average prices and, in a general way, of wage rates and profits in the United States in recent decades. They have noted in this country since the

Note: Portions of this chapter are adapted from our papers, "Pricing for Stability and Growth," by John P. Lewis, and "Relationship of Prices to Economic Stability and Growth: A Statement of the Problem," by Robert C. Turner, in *The Relationship of Prices to Economic Stability and Growth*, Compendium of papers submitted by panelists appearing before the Joint Economic Committee, 85th Cong., 2d Sess., 1958, pp. 375–396 and 671–684, respectively. Other portions were adapted from John P. Lewis, "The Problem of Price Stabilization: A Progress Report," *The American Economic Review*, vol. XLIX, no. 2, pp. 309–321, May, 1959. Permission of the Joint Economic Committee and the American Economic Association to use these materials is gratefully acknowledged.

mid-forties the emergence of increasing anxiety over price behavior and price prospects. They also have recorded our doubts, especially in the light of the international challenges touched upon in the preceding chapter, that the price outlook deserves its familiar billing as the greatest problem confronting the American economy during the coming generation.

There is no doubt at all, however, that the inflation issue has thoroughly captured the attention of Americans in the past few years; even in the 1961–1965 period of relative price stability, many sober and influential voices kept insisting that inflation was the American economy's greatest immediate as well as continuing threat. Certainly, moreover, whatever the proper ranking of the economic challenges facing the United States, the price problem is one of them; it is one that threads its way throughout the whole economic fabric; and it is one about which any thoughtful economist is expected to have something to say.

PROBLEMS POSED BY PRICING PRACTICE

"The price problem" is an ambiguous phrase. No economic variable is more ubiquitous than that of price, and most of the uncertainties that infect the long-run economic outlook can be looked at, if one chooses, from a price perspective. If commodity and factor prices were becoming so thoroughly inflexible that relative price changes promised no longer to do much of the job of guiding the allocation of resources in directions that consumer, investor, and government buyers wanted, we could call *that* the price problem. Or if total spending had gotten so into the habit of outstripping our ability to produce that we seemed likely to suffer persistently from the kind of excess demand inflation that afflicted the United States in 1941 to 1945, 1946 to 1948, and during the first eight months after the Korean outbreak, that also might well be dubbed the price problem. Or again, if it looked as though our future were to be riddled with bottlenecks—with stubborn imbalances between demand and supply in particular key commodities and resources—that certainly could be our price problem.

Actually, present American anxieties about the long-run price outlook reflect, in some degree, all the issues just noted. But it is also true that one issue dominates most of the present worrying about the long-run price outlook in the United States, and, although it is related to those listed in the preceding paragraph, it is distinguishable from them. That is the question of whether *pricing practice* in this country—whether the discretionary price making and wage making that are done within the institutional frameworks we have evolved—inadvertently has become antisocial in its economy-wide effects. Have we blundered into a combination of institutional arrangements, including collective wage bargaining, cost-oriented pricing by large industrial corporations, the court-commission system of utility rate regulation, and farm price supports, which, although each of its elements may make good sense in its own sphere, collectively will yield seriously bad consequences for the economy as a whole?

This is the nagging fear that besets many observers, and it is the one to which this chapter will give the bulk of its attention. To evaluate the charges that worriers about the long-run price outlook level against contemporary pricing practice it is necessary to make the indictment more specific. This we shall do shortly. But first it will be well to refresh our understanding of the mechanisms through which pricing practice influences the economy's growth and stability performance.

THE IMPACTS OF PRICING PRACTICE

Taken together, several of the earlier chapters—notably Chapter 6 on prices and price-output relationships, Chapter 12 on the economic impact of government, and Chapter 15 on recent economic history—contain a fairly comprehensive theory of the way in which price and wage decisions affect those aspects of the economy's behavior upon which we have focused in this book. But those chapters were a long way back, and their argument was never explicitly molded into an integrated view of the effects of pricing upon stability and growth. It should be useful, therefore, to render such a summary here.

There are two principal mechanisms through which pricing practice influences the economy's aggregative performance. For one thing, the price system—the relationships among finished, intermediate, and raw commodity prices together with wage rates, rents, interest rates, profit margins, and depreciation rates—is one of the two great devices that determine the distribution of the gross national income among the buyers of the gross national product. The other distributive device is our system of taxes and government transfer payments. The income split that the price and the tax-transfer systems jointly determine heavily influences the abilities and inclinations of purchasing groups to maintain or increase their expenditures.

We have seen that this last is most clearly true in the case of consumers, whose spending plainly is heavily dependent on the volume of disposable personal income. The dependence of business investment expenditures upon the amounts that businesses retain out of their gross receipts, either as depreciation allowances or undistributed after-tax profits, is much less reliable. But there is a relationship, as there is between the net receipts and the expenditures of state and local governments.

Roughly put, the pricing system's function with respect to income distribution is to determine whether the division of private income shares between households and businesses stays within the tolerances required for maintaining a balance between consumption and investment. Stable growth requires a reasonably steady rate of capital formation. Thus current profit rates must be kept high enough to encourage new investment, and current gross retentions by business must be sufficient to facilitate the financing of new capital outlays. At the same time, however, nothing can discourage investment so decisively as a withering of end-user markets. This means that real consumer incomes must be kept growing, mainly through rises in wages relative to product prices, so that consumption growth can parallel and, as it were, make good the growth in productive capacity.

More closely considered, the issue comes down essentially to how we distribute productivity gains. How, under contemporary pricing practice, are the potential savings in unit labor costs accruing to the productive process, from productive improvements that enable us to produce more output per man-hour, divided among the parties in interest? Considering the private economy as a whole, there are three broad channels through which such productivity gains can be parceled out. They can go to property or capital in the forms of higher profits, interest, rents, or depreciation charges per unit of property; they can go to labor in the form of higher earnings, including supplemental benefits, per unit of time worked; or they can go to consumers and other end users in the form of lower product prices. And, of course, they can flow through any combination of these channels. The kind of flow that is needed for steady growth is one that neither impairs the incentives for (or the financing of) investment nor results in a spoilage of markets.

The second of the two mechanisms through which pricing practice affects the economy's production, employment, and price-level performance is more direct. It is that of the aggregate-supply path—the pattern of price and output responses to changes in demand—and was dealt with more extensively in our theory chapters. It should not be necessary to review in any detail the argument that the shape of the aggregate-supply path lies at the very heart of the issue of how well the economy can manage to achieve full employment without inflation; or to review the explanation of how the simplified early Keynesian hypothesis of a beneficently kinked aggregate-supply path seemed to make public stabilization policy exclusively a task for aggregate-demand management; or reiterate the analysis of why this happy hypothesis scarcely fits the facts of the American economy as we know it.

It may be useful, however, to recall our conclusions about the effects that supply bottlenecks and modern price-making and wage-making institutions seem jointly to have the pattern of price-output relations in the United States. In the first place, such bottlenecks and institutions seem to have taken most of the corner or kink out of the old hypothetical short-run aggregate-supply path. They have increased the tendency for average prices to rise in response to rising demand when output is at less than full-capacity levels. Similarly, when the economy is already at full employment, and demand rises faster than capacity, our price- and wage-making procedures yield considerably less violent price-level increases than would result if all our factor and commodity markets were perfectly competitive.

In the second place, the cost-plus orientation of many contemporary pricing arrangements—for example, in the cases of standard-margin business pricing, of cost-of-living wage escalators, and of parity-based farm price supports—has created a vast, lumbering cost-price escalator in the economy that spreads particular cost increases throughout the factor- and commodity-price structure and commits the structure, unless there are adequate offsets, to continuing upward adjustments. This wage-price or price-wage spiral tends to shift upward the short-run pattern of price-output relations associated with any given volume of capacity. This tendency is partially offset by improvements in productivity and expansions in capacity, but the offsets have typically been no more than partial.

In the third place, contemporary pricing practice makes the aggregate-supply path nonreversible when demand declines. There is the ratchet effect. Administered prices and wages are highly resistant to moderate slumps in spending, a characteristic that apparently breaks down substantially only in very severe downturns. It is this circumstance that closely links the magnitude of the secular inflation problem to our success in avoiding episodes of major unemployment and underproduction. It may well be that many of the institutional circumstances that lately have seemed to be giving an inflationary bias to the economy are not inventions of the postwar decades but instead have been with us for a very long time. What indubitably has changed in the post-World War II era, however, is the regularity of the chief counter-deflationary expedients in the old economy—namely, good, robust downturns. To the extent that we have solved the greater problem, we have aggravated the lesser one.

THE PARTICULARS OF THE INDICTMENT

The specific long-run forecast that emerges from the aggregate-supply analysis is, of course, that of secular inflation, and this is the most common concern among those who view the long-term price outlook with alarm. But an inflationary bias is not all that many of the worriers about price prospects are disturbed about. There are distinguishable concerns that in the decades ahead contemporary pricing practice promises, for one thing, to impede the long-term growth process and, for another, to intensify short-run fluctuations in production and employment.

These three anxieties are not unrelated. Indeed, what some of the analysts who forecast and fear secular inflation fear most are not the intrinsic evils of inflation itself but the disruptions of real growth and stability that they believe continuing inflation will cause. However, as we shall argue below, the proposition that the avoidance of gradual inflation is a necessary prerequisite for adequate growth and stability in the real dimensions of the economy—or, what amounts to the same thing, the proposition that creeping inflation cannot be kept creeping—is still a hypothetical inference for the United States. It cannot be readily demonstrated from our history, and it may not be true for the future. There certainly are price, including wage and profit, requirements for sustained growth, and certainly pricing practice can affect the violence of short-run fluctuations in employment and production. But a good pricing performance in these respects is not *necessarily* one that also yields a stable product-price level. Accordingly our best course here will be to separate the charges against contemporary United States pricing practice and consider them one by one, with respect both to the recent record and to future prospects. The following are the counts in the indictment we are to consider:

First, some observers allege that a continuation of recent American pricing practices threatens to produce a distribution of incomes between households and businesses that will impede matching long-run expansions in capacity and capacity utilization.

A second charge is that price and wage decisions characteristically contribute to the onset of temporary slumps in business activity, aggravate such reversals once they are begun, or interfere with recovery-inducing adjustments, and that they bid fair to keep on doing so in the future.

Third, it is charged that the present pattern of pricing practice in the United States probably commits the economy to the prospect of secular inflation.

Finally—and we shall treat this as a subcount of the third allegation—it is asserted that if our long-term outlook does include a persisting inflationary bias, the bias itself will become directly incompatible with sustained physical growth.

Since all the evidence required to substantiate or dismiss these charges is not yet at hand, anyone's judgment about them must be tentative and opinionated. But the verdict we suggest is Not Guilty on the first two counts of the indictment; Guilty on the third. The fourth count is the most difficult of all to assess, and the judgment must therefore be even more tentative, but our preliminary verdict is Probably Not Guilty.

THE PRICE-WAGE-PROFIT REQUIREMENTS FOR LONG-TERM GROWTH

It is said that some years ago, when Walter Reuther was being shown through the new automated Ford engine plant in Cleveland, a company executive pointed to a completely automatic block-boring machine and remarked, "You won't be able to collect any union dues from these things, Walter." Reuther shot back: "And you won't be able to sell many Fords to them either." This, as we have seen, is one core of the problem of productivity-gains distribution—the need to keep real consumer purchasing power growing in line with real productive capacity. The other is the need for sufficient returns to capital to induce adequate capacity expansion.

In trying to specify what pattern of price, wage, profit, and productivity relationships would serve these purposes, and then in trying to judge how closely long-run pricing prospects match up with such requirements, the general business conditions analyst's approach must be essentially pragmatic. Discussions of whether productivity gains are being properly shared frequently get enveloped in moralistic debates over whether this or that group is getting what it "rightfully deserves." Such appeals to equity, ethics, or moral entitlements cannot be scientifically resolved, and furthermore, from the viewpoint of growth and stability maintenance, they are largely beside the point. For anyone interested in the economy's aggregative performance, the key criterion for evaluating the growth effects of pricing practice must be that of workability. There is no sense in debating whether the mass of the public, either in the role of workers or consumers, has any moral claim on gains in output per worker that may have been the result of new equipment, or inspired management, or the brilliant insights of a scientist who sold his rights to a new productive process for a mere $1,000. The point simply is that productivity gains *must*, somehow or other, be widely distributed if the growth process is to keep on functioning smoothly.

Contemporary economics provides no precise formula for productivity-gains distribution that is both widely accepted and readily applicable to real-world problems. The one really elegant doctrine of how incomes should (and, it is argued, in a perfectly competitive economy indeed would) be distributed to the factors of production is the marginal productivity theory: the payment to each factor, per unit of input, should (would) equal the additional output that would result if one unit of that factor, and only of that factor, were added to the total inputs. In principle, if all factors were compensated on this basis, the total compensation would exactly exhaust the total product. But the marginal productivity theory has little direct applicability to actual industrial data or circumstances. In practice, applied economists trying to identify patterns of factor and commodity pricing that will facilitate continuing growth must work in much cruder terms, using average rather than marginal productivity as their reference concept and pointing to desirable ranges and tendencies rather than precise relationships. In such crude, approximate terms, however, a lot can be said about what the needed relationships are.

DESIRABLE PATTERNS OF PRODUCTIVITY-GAINS DISTRIBUTION

Real Wages and Labor Productivity

The first point to be made about the pricing requirements for sustained economic growth is the most fundamental and widely accepted. It is that as a general matter the percentage increase in average real-wage rates in the economy, i.e., in money wages relative to consumer prices, should keep pace with the average percentage growth in national real output per man-hour.

It should be noted that this rule would link the trend in real wages not to actual labor productivity in the particular industry or firm in which a person is employed, but to the national ave.·age. And the standard is not productivity performance in a particular year, which may reflect transitory factors, but in a long enough period of time to establish an average trend—though not so long as to be irrelevant to current circumstances. If we assume that a sustainable growth in total output requires a proportionate growth in personal consumption and that wages will continue to account for the bulk of personal incomes, then the percentage advance in the economy's output per man-hour must be matched by a percentage advance in average real-wage rates to prevent market spoilage. This is not to say that real income *per worker* needs to rise as fast as output *per man-hour;* to the extent that normal working hours decline, the economy takes some of its productivity gains in the form of additional leisure.

A frequently heard objection to this standard for real wages is that it would give to labor *all* the gains of productivity increase, which, as we have seen, come only partly from higher efficiency of labor per se. This reasoning is fallacious. The error lies in failure to recognize that labor costs account for only a portion of the total inputs into the production process. Suppose, for example, that a firm in which labor costs account for 50 percent of total revenue experiences a 5 percent advance in output per man-hour and thereupon continues to employ the same man-hours of work, produces 5 percent more output, maintains its old selling prices, and raises hourly wages 5 percent. After these changes, total revenue is 5 percent higher, labor costs have absorbed half of the increase in revenue and still account for only half of the total, and there has been a parallel 5 percent increase in the other revenue shares viewed as a unit. If the productivity improvement has not been caused by, or at least been associated with, an increase in the quantity of capital, then the return per unit of capital, like wage rates, rises 5 percent. The case that is more typical of American economic development, of course, is one where the rise in labor productivity *has* been accompanied by an increase in the quantity of capital per man-hour worked. In this event, if real wages rise in proportion to labor productivity, the real return per unit of capital cannot rise by the same percentage. But there is nothing intrinsically alarming about this. If the rate of increase in the quantity of capital relative to labor does not exceed the rate of advance in labor productivity, when real wages rise in proportion to labor productivity, the per-unit return to capital can at least be maintained. And if this rate of return has sufficed to call forth an adequate volume of investment in the past, presumably, with expanding markets and assuming no change in the technological and other inducements to invest, it should suffice to call forth an adequately expanding volume of investment in the future.

Just as a failure of real-wage rates to rise as fast as labor productivity threatens market spoilage, so a tendency for them to outstrip productivity (thereby increasing the share of total revenue claimed by labor costs and reducing the revenue share going to property) threatens an attrition of investment incentives and of internal investment finance. However, even if it could be shown that the share of total revenues going to property were decreasing, and the share going to labor increasing, it would not necessarily prove that the stimuli to private capacity expansion were being undermined.[1] For one thing—we shall have other related points to make later—a fall in the property share per unit of product may be offset, so far as the impact of the unit return on investment is concerned, by a rise in output per unit of capital (or property), that is, by a rise in *capital* productivity. To put this point in the language of the preceding paragraph, a rise in capital productivity, by lowering the rate of increase in capital relative to labor that is associated with a given increase in labor productivity, can moderate the encroachment on the returns to capital that otherwise would occur when real-wage rates rise faster than labor productivity.

Despite all this, however, a continuing decline in the share of output going to capital creates at least a presumption of potential difficulties on the investment side of the growth process. So it is reasonable to single out the following as a first fundamental generalization about the pricing requirements for sustained economic growth: real-wages rates ordinarily should advance, not only as fast as, but also not significantly faster than, the gains in real-labor productivity.

Money-wage Increases or Product-price Reductions?

One encounters relatively little dissension from the very general point just established. But the question remains, Should this needed pattern of relationships among the wages, prices, and productivity be built around a falling, a stable, or a rising general product-price level? More specifically, should real wages be raised through the medium of stable money wages and generally declining consumer prices, or stable prices and rising money wages, or (the combination we actually have experienced in the United States in recent decades) rising prices coupled with faster increases in money wages? This is a distinctly secondary issue, as far as the pricing requirements for sustained growth are concerned, but American economists have debated it extensively, and it is here that the consensus about productivity-gains distribution begins to break down.

The principal modern champion of the lower-prices channel of productivity-gains distribution has been Edwin Nourse, first chairman of the Council of Economic Advisers and a specialist in the economics of pricing

---

[1] For evidence that the shares going to property and labor have not changed significantly since the immediate post-World War II period, see the *Economic Report of the President*, 1964, pp. 114–115, and 1965, p. 109.

practice.[2] The case for the price-reductions channel is, in some ways, an appealing one. It can be argued that this is the mode of distribution that most nearly approximates what would happen in a perfectly competitive market, where the inrush of new firms to copy an innovator's cost-saving, profit-raising innovation would quickly drive product prices down and shift productivity gains to the industry's customers. Price reduction is the mode of distribution that spreads the gains most broadly and uniformly throughout the economy. It is the one that would minimize discrimination in favor of the powerfully organized producer groups and against such relatively poor money-income bargainers as pensioners, owners of nonventure assets, government workers, and schoolteachers. It is the one that would be most advantageous to the United States balance of payments.

Presently, however, the great majority of American economists are arrayed—somewhat ruefully, perhaps, in the case of some economists who are also schoolteachers—opposite Nourse. Instead, they are partisans of the rising-money-wages, stable-money-prices mode of productivity-gains distribution. They have many reasons, of which the strongest, or at least a sufficient one, is simply the matter of feasibility. In the group structure that the economy has acquired, with its collective wage bargaining, administered pricing, and lack of consumer organization to match producer organization, it is hard to imagine any forces tending to drive average prices down over the long run that will begin to match the strength of those which will be driving money wages up. In particular it is hard to imagine any union so insensitive to its members' self-interest as to trade a wage increase for a reduction in the prices of its employer's product. Evidently the very best that American lovers of lower prices can hope for is general price stability. There is no sense plumping for the impossible.

Moreover, the majority position is not just an appeal to expediency. If the distribution of productivity gains via rising money wages and profits is somewhat inequitable to the weak bargainers, at least it discriminates in favor of the generally more dynamic groups in the system and avoids discriminating, as a falling price level would, in favor of creditors and hoarders at the expense of debtors. It does not cause the public debt, as a declining price level would, to become an increasing burden on taxpayers. Further, from the point of view of the management of a business firm (or university, or farm organization, or government agency), maintaining morale and motivation among employees is made easier if management is able to recognize normal increases in productivity with the tangible reward of more money.

There are other arguments, some of them equally or more substantial, that could be adduced to support a rising money-wage level and a stable product-price level as the best formula for raising real wages in line with labor

[2] See particularly, E. G. Nourse, *Price-making in a Democracy*, The Brookings Institution, Washington, 1944.

productivity. We want later to note one difficulty that, with the spread of automation, this particular mode of distribution may get us into. But the fact is that the nation seems deeply committed to this mode—if, indeed, we can manage to keep the price level from rising. The alternative—a rising price level with money wages increasing faster than labor productivity—does not deserve to be dignified as an intrinsically desirable form of productivity-gains distribution. But it may well be our fate, and we have yet to find that it would necessarily be incompatible with sustained economic expansion.

Adjusting for Interindustry Differentials

The proposition that preferably over the long run the percentage increase in money-wage rates should match the percentage growth in labor productivity while the product-price level stays put deals only with averages and aggregates. The fact, of course, is that the rates of productivity improvement are never uniform among industries. In any given period the improvement in aggregate output per man-hour is apt to be concentrated in relatively few industries, while in others productivity changes little or none and in some it actually declines. What, to round out our prescription of growth-facilitating patterns of pricing, should be the wage and price responses to such differential rates of progressiveness?

The following are the extreme possibilities. On the one hand, the matching wage-productivity formula could apply in each industry, or even in each firm, individually. The differential changes in productivity would be fully reflected in differential wage movements, and the price-stability principle would apply on an industry-by-industry or firm-by-firm basis. By minimizing relative price flexibility, a full-blown adoption of this ability-to-pay scheme of wage setting would sap the effectiveness of the product-price system as a resource allocator. It would maximize the incentive for labor to shift from less to more progressive industries but, by curtailing differential price changes, would forestall the shifting of end-user demand that would make a reallocation of labor possible. And, by maximizing divergent wage movements, the pattern would create enormous strains on the institutional wage structure.

On the other hand, industry-by-industry or even firm-by-firm wages could be held strictly to uniform increases matching the trend in average national productivity, while all the interindustry variation in productivity changes would be reflected in differential price movements. Such a scheme would interfere with the allocation function of the wage structure just as thoroughly as its opposite would interfere with the price structure.

Obviously both these extreme patterns for distributing differential productivity gains are untenable. What is needed is something in between. In industries experiencing above-average productivity improvements, wage rates should rise somewhat more than average—enough to keep the labor market an effective reallocative device, but not enough to exhaust the productivity gains or prevent some price reductions. The latter, in markets where demand is somewhat elastic, would help shift demand toward the more progressive sectors of production. Conversely, in industries where productivity gains are below average, wages should rise more slowly than the national average, but enough to require some increases in product prices. This, in essence, is the formula adopted by the President and the Council of Economic Advisers in the "price-wage guideposts," first formulated in the 1962 *Economic Report of the President* and reiterated in subsequent *Economic Reports.*[3] Later *Economic Reports,* however, have moved perceptibly in the direction of tying wage increases quite closely to productivity increases and providing for the necessary flexibility in the price area. Thus, the 1966 *Report* concludes:

> "1. The general guidepost for wages is that the *annual rate of increase of total employee compensation (wages and fringe benefits) per man-hour worked should equal the national trend rate of increase in output per man-hour.*
>
> "2. The general guidepost for prices is that *prices should remain stable in those industries where the increase of productivity equals the national trend; that prices can appropriately rise in those industries where the increase of productivity is smaller than the national trend; and that prices should fall in those industries where the increase of productivity exceeds the national trend.*
>
> "Within a given industry, the guideposts allow for individual wage and price adjustments that do not affect the over-all wage or price level of the industry. Increases for some groups of workers or products can be balanced by reductions for others.
>
> "Observance of the guideposts would mean that unit labor costs would decline in the industries where productivity gains are above average, and rise in industries where such gains are below the national average. Average unit labor cost in the economy would remain constant. Similarly, the decrease of prices in industries with above-average increases in productivity would offset the price rises in industries with below-average productivity gains. The average level of prices would remain stable."

UNITED STATES PRODUCTIVITY-GAINS DISTRIBUTION: RECORD AND PROSPECTS

So far, we have been discussing a desirable pattern of pricing practices for sustained economic growth. The obvious next question is, Judging from past experience, are actual pricing practices in the United States likely to

---

[3] See 1962 *Economic Report*, pp. 185–190; 1963 *Report*, pp. 83–88; 1964 *Report*, pp. 116–120; 1965 *Report*, pp. 107–110; 1966 *Report*, pp. 88–93.

conform closely enough to this desired pattern to permit achievement of the sustained growth objective? As will be developed later, the prospects for secular price-level stability are not ideal, but this is a separable issue from that of the manner in which productivity gains are shared. With respect to the latter—to anticipate our conclusion—we find nothing in the recent record of the economy, with the exception of one rather remote problem noted later, that has particularly alarming implications for the future.

The Aggregate Relationships

It was indicated in Chapter 14 that, during the 1920s, failure to make an adequate distribution of productivity gains to the mass of consumers does appear to have caused some degree of market spoilage. And this fact was a major cause of the downturn in 1929–1930, which later, primarily for other reasons, culminated in the Great Depression.

But aggregative American data do not indicate any such tendency in the post-World War II years. Figure 26–1 shows indexes of output per man-hour and total compensation per man-hour in the private economy, both on a base of 1957–1959 = 100. For the 1947 to 1960 period as a whole, compensation per man-hour rose at a substantially more rapid rate than did output per man-hour. There were a few years, notably 1950 and 1955, when the reverse was true. But for the period as a whole, compensation per man-hour rose over 90 percent while output per man-hour was rising only 55 percent. As a result, unit labor costs rose more than unit values added. In the manufacturing sector of the economy alone, there was a generally similar showing for the same period. After 1960, the two curves were nearly parallel; from 1960 to 1964, compensation per man-hour rose 15.3 percent while output per man-hour was rising 14.7 percent. The indexes diverged again, however, in 1965.

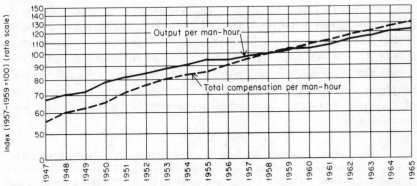

Figure 26–1. Indexes of output per man-hour and total compensation per man-hour in the United States private economy, 1947–1965. Source: U.S. Department of Labor.

Thus the recent pricing pattern in the United States suggests no risk of secular underconsumption. On the contrary, the problem, if any, appears to be that of declining returns to investment. Money wages not only have risen faster than labor productivity, but they have risen sufficiently more than product prices to squeeze the fraction of private income received by property. Superficially, the most striking statistic in this regard is that, on a before-tax basis, the property shares of national income, which received 41 percent of the total in 1929 and 37 percent in 1948, claimed only about 29 percent in 1960–1965 (as the share taken by employee compensation rose from 59 percent to 63 percent to 71 percent). However, this is misleading, for most or all of this apparent shift was attributable to changes in the composition of industrial activity—especially shifts of activity from the unincorporated business sector, where the "wages" of owner-managers are not measured separately from their profits in our national income accounting system, to the corporate sector, where the same type of compensation is treated as wages and salaries. On the other hand, since property incomes have borne a disproportionately large part of the big increase in taxes since 1929, there is no doubt that the after-tax real return to property per unit of output has declined substantially.

Does this represent a growing maladjustment that promises trouble for investment incentives and investment financing over the long run ahead? Probably not. In the first place, while profit-sales ratios (or profit-output ratios) have declined, there has not been anything like a comparable decline in profits relative to net worth. This is because capital-output ratios have fallen very substantially. We are getting much more output mileage out of given quantities of capital; the efficiency of capital utilization has substantially improved.

In the second place, business' internal sources of funds for investment have been augmented by the heavy growth in internal funds. Corporate capital-consumption allowances, which, of course, are not subject to income taxation since they are charged as a business expense, have not only grown in absolute current-dollar terms from $4.2 billion in 1929 and $7.0 billion in 1948 to $36.1 billion in 1965, but have significantly increased their percentage take of the after-tax, after-transfer distribution of the gross national income despite the expansion in government's share of income during the period. Corporate cash flow for the 1955–1964 decade as a whole was 97.8 percent of corporate investment in physical assets and 71 percent of total asset acquisition.[4]

---

[4] Data pertain to nonfarm, nonfinancial corporate business. "Corporate cash flow" includes capital consumption allowances, undistributed profits, and the corporate inventory-valuation adjustment. "Corporate investment in physical assets" includes nonresidential fixed investment, change in inventories, and corporate investment in residential structures. "Total asset acquisition" adds increase in bank deposits, government securities, finance company paper, trade credit, consumer credit, and other financial assets. See *Survey of Current Business*, U.S. Department of Commerce, November, 1965, p. 10.

In the third place, there is the pragmatic test. Certainly the strong rise in investment spending since World War II, and in the 1961–1966 period in particular, does not indicate that a secular decline in the real after-tax returns to property per unit of output has been causing any withering of investment incentives or permanent constriction of investment financing. The appetite for investment has been high, and business has succeeded in financing enormous quantities of capital. (This is not to deny that the volume of investment spending has continued, although in somewhat muted fashion, to fluctuate in the short run, or that the Federal Reserve's tight-money policies have not, on occasion, somewhat restricted the supply of investment finance.) It seems reasonable to conclude (1) that there is no absolute level of real returns to property per unit of output that remains fixed through time as the minimum necessary for calling forth an adequate volume of investment; and (2) that with rising capital productivity a secular decline in profit-sales ratios is a normal and healthy trend. It in no way threatens the economy's growth prospects as long as continuing innovation and continuing rivalry among firms for market shares keep churning up a flow of *relatively* attractive new investment opportunities.

On balance, then, we are brought to the general conclusion that there is nothing obviously wrong, as far as the requirements for continuing growth are concerned, with the average long-run trends in the real distribution of income between capital and labor that contemporary pricing practice has been achieving.

The Matter of Differentials

In recent years in the United States the responses of money-wage rates and of prices to the diversity of productivity changes in different industries have differed notably only in one major particular from the pattern of mixed wage and price flexibility advocated in our prescriptive discussion. Differential movements in both prices and wages have been substantial, but in administered price and wage areas they seldom have been precipitous. In both factor and product markets there has been sufficient price flexibility to protect the markets' allocative functions but not enough to cause sudden, disruptive changes in the administered wage and price structures. Moreover, very roughly speaking, the differentials have corresponded to industries' differing productivity experience. That is, the largest wage increases and the greatest relative price reductions have tended to be concentrated in the most progressive industries, and vice versa. During the post-World War II period, for example, the price of haircuts has gone up far more, and barbers' wages somewhat less, than their counterparts in radio and television manufacturing.

In terms of our prescription, all this sounds very much as it should be. The important difference, of course, is that the whole pattern has been keyed to a rising rather than a stable price level. There have been relatively few absolute price reductions, and wages in the more progressive manufacturing industries, rather than falling short of the above-average productivity gains in their own areas, have, if anything, exceeded them. The sympathetic reaction of wages elsewhere has created heavy cost pressures upon prices in industries with below-average productivity improvements—notably in the services sector.

Thus interindustry wage and price relationships have been a mechanism for spreading inflation. It is for this reason that the strong uptrend in consumer service prices, despite the weakness of labor organization in the services sector, can be partly interpreted as a kind of indirect cost-push inflation that originates in the strongly organized manufacturing industries. However, here again the problem is simply inflation as such, not a maldistribution of productivity gains vis-à-vis the requirements for steady economic growth. As a matter of fact, given the general distaste of administered price makers for absolute price reduction, a generally rising price level can be viewed as a necessary condition for obtaining as satisfactory a pricing response to differential productivity gains as the economy has enjoyed.

A Possible Future Headache

If one is inclined to borrow trouble, it is possible to imagine that our American habit of distributing the fruits of improved productivity chiefly through money-wage rises will eventually get us into trouble. Suppose that future productivity gains continue to be concentrated in selected areas of manufacturing and that these industries eventually achieve highly automated operations and therefore require only relatively small numbers of managerial, technical, and service personnel and few if any production workers. Money-wage increases could become a very ineffective way of making a mass distribution of the income gains accruing in such highly efficient but largely depopulated enterprises.

The obvious solution would be greater reliance on relative price reductions; but if these were to be enough to offset continued price increases in the less progressive industries, price makers in the progressive industries would have to display a greater willingness to engage in absolute price cutting than they have shown in the recent past. A theoretically feasible alternative would be much wider ownership of the stock of highly productive automated manufacturers, so that distribution of productivity gains through the profit (and dividends) channel would have a broad impact on mass consumer purchasing power. But we might encounter a good many disruptive hitches before either of these solutions, or a combination of them, was working smoothly.

However, it may be rightly objected that this last is hypothetical stuff that is scarcely relevant to the near future. With respect at least to the next decade or two, we revert to the judgment that has emerged from the foregoing discussion: the charge that a continuation of contemporary pricing practice in the United States threatens a growth-inhibiting pattern of productivity-gains distribution must be rejected for lack of sufficient evidence. While its record may not be perfect, the present system seems to have been doing pretty well on this score.

WAGE-PRICE ADJUSTMENTS AND SHORT-RUN INSTABILITY

The second of the major complaints commonly leveled against modern American price- and wage-making institutions is that inflexibilities and other imperfections in pricing practice contribute to short-run fluctuations in demand and impede stabilizing adjustments when downturns get under way. It is contended that in boom periods wages lag the surge in sales, causing profits to bulge and thereby both stimulating overinvestment and preventing consumer purchasing power from keeping pace with expansions in productive capacity. It is further contended that in periods of sluggish business, administered price makers do not make sufficiently aggressive use of price cutting as a sales-promoting tool.

There is some appeal in these arguments. In particular, it appears that producers of consumer goods that have a fair degree of price elasticity could often, when an upswing is well advanced, help keep it going and better their own positions by some decisive one-shot price cutting. In this respect some corporate decision makers fail to pursue their own as well as the economy's best interests because of excessively wooden adherence to cost-plus formulas of pricing. In 1961–1966, for example, very few price decreases were made in automobile prices at a time when the profits of automobile manufacturers were soaring.

Nevertheless, the short-run effects of the present pricing practice are far more benign than most of its critics suggest. Especially, we would assert this: the general stickiness of prices and wages is, on balance, a great blessing, not a handicap, for the economy, so far as short-run stability is concerned. The familiar labels of "pure competition" and "perfect competition" are loaded terms, and the loading would be obvious if the extreme sort of price and wage flexibility that one finds in perfectly competitive markets were extended to the whole economy so that prices and wages skyrocketed every time aggregate demand nudged full capacity and then plummeted when it receded a little.

Perfectly flexible prices and wages would be a perfect mess in this regard. They would almost hopelessly disrupt any kind of orderly business planning. Economic rewards would be determined more by the windfall gains and losses handed out by the roulette wheel of violent, unpredictable inflation and deflation, and less by productive contribution. Worst of all, reactions to expectations of price and wage changes would work their maximum effect in aggravating fluctuations in demand. The violent cumulative downward or upward price spiral, when it really fixes its hold on buyers' expectations, is one of the most thoroughly pernicious forces that can afflict the economy. Present pricing practice provides extensive protection against such spirals, and this is a great advantage.

As was first suggested in Chapter 15, our best hope for achieving substantial overall stability in the economy probably lies less in the direction of eliminating fluctuations in particular sectors of demand than in weakening the interdependencies among the sectors. The chief reason that the economy is more stable than it was a generation ago is that the various cumulative mechanisms, which so regularly used to spread the infection of decline from a few sectors to the whole economy and convert limited reversals into general downspirals, have been notably weakened. And the development of contemporary pricing practice has played a significant part in this weakening of the cumulators. For one thing, it checks the vicious expectational downward price spiral in which buyers hang back from buying in anticipation of further price reductions. For another thing, contemporary wage making, by partly disconnecting the course of money wages from short-run fluctuations in business, has contributed to the insulation of disposable personal income from temporary drops in the gross national product.

Thus we view with alarm the suggestions of those who would tinker with the wage-price-profit mechanism in a way meant to make it respond sensitively to each incipient surge and sag in aggregate demand. Such an attempt would strain toward the hope that short-run fluctuations in the various components of demand all can be neutralized and that, year in and year out, the components can be kept in unerring balance. It is doubtful that this is an attainable goal for a dynamic, mostly private economy. In striving for it we could undo some of our good progress toward a less ideal but more feasible alternative, namely, a semicompartmentalized economy in which a sag in plant and equipment or inventory investment does not stampede everything else with it but, instead, has an excellent chance of being more than offset by a spurt in, for example, housing or state and local government outlays.

If this latter approach to stability is our strategy, then we should put aside any thought of major reliance upon price and wage adjustments for short-run stabilizing purposes. Spurts and sags in gross national income should concentrate their impact where they now largely do—upon business profits and on the net receipts of government—and average wage rates should be geared to long-term growth requirements, rising fairly steadily with the trend of productivity increase in both good times and bad. And while it would be nice to see some manufacturers do a little more experimenting with promotional pricing in the advanced stages of booms, any reforms that would greatly increase the volatility of commodity prices should be given a wide berth.

In short, so far as future problems of short-run output and employment stability are concerned, there probably is much more to be gained than lost from a continuation of present pricing practices.

THE THREAT OF SECULAR INFLATION

Nothing is certain in this world, but the evidence and argument supporting the third major count in the indictment against contemporary American price practice—namely, that it has injected a moderate but persistent inflationary bias into our future—seem to be overwhelming, unless present tendencies should be strongly countered by changes in public and private policies. This long-run forecast has been emerging insistently in this chapter and earlier ones. Here at the end we can summarize the case for it and consider briefly some of its implications.

THE CASE FOR THE INFLATIONARY-BIAS FORECAST

It should be emphasized that the belief that, lacking major policy changes, the United States is committed to gradual increases in the price level during the decades ahead is not universally shared by economic analysts. As we have seen, it cannot yet be conclusively inferred from our history. Actually, of the whole postwar period, only the years 1955 through 1958 offer reasonably clear-cut corroboration for the inflationary-bias thesis, and even these were rendered somewhat peculiar by the sluggishness of productivity growth in 1956, 1957, and 1958.[5]   And the period of relative price stability, from 1959 through mid-1965, can be offered as counterevidence. Further, the admitted fact that the price indexes, especially the consumer price index, contain an upward bias means that the statistical evidence of creeping inflation during much of the post-World War II period is less impressive than it appears at first glance.   For these and other reasons, some distinguished economists flatly reject the secular-inflation forecast.   That they are in the minority does not prove them wrong.   Rather, what argues against them is such an accumulation of specific points as the following.

First, during the next quarter century the surging growth of population in the economically less developed regions of the world plus rapid industrialization in some of those areas, plus massive productive expansion in the United States and many other advanced economies, are altogether likely to create extreme demand pressures on many raw materials.   Even with very optimistic allowances for new-materials technology, many temporary supply bottlenecks and resulting increases in raw materials prices are probable.

Second, even if we were to assume no further rises in capital goods prices, further increases in depreciation charges per unit of output would be predictable for some time to come in the United States because of (1) the displacement of old, lower-cost assets with present higher-cost assets, (2) the continuing shift of the composition of business capital from (long-lived) plant

---

[5] As implied in the text earlier, we cannot accept the contention that the 1955–1958 inflation did not have cost-push characteristics because most of the retail price increases were in services.   This argument overlooks the impact of manufacturing wages on wages in the low-productivity services area.

toward (short-lived) equipment, and (3) more rapid obsolescence of given types of capital.

Third, the only safe hypothesis is that, under existing institutional arrangements, average annual increases in money-wage rates will tend to exceed average annual increments in output per man-hour, not in every year, to be sure, but more often than not. In this respect, the wage-price guideposts may play a vital role. If they are accepted by responsible labor and management leadership as reasonable standards that are in their own long-run interest, as well as in the total public interest, the guideposts may exert a strategic moderating effect on inflationary wage and price making. On the other hand, it is seldom literally true that adherence to the guideposts *is* in the long-run interests of the specific union or the specific business firm seeking an increase in its compensation. And the problems of enforcement of the guideposts should not be underestimated. In contrast to some European nations that are willing to accept substantial interventions into private price and wage making, the United States prefers to rely on the exercise of moral suasion. In precedent-setting instances, where major commodities (e.g., steel) are involved or where large numbers of workers (e.g., automobiles) are affected, the power and prestige of the President or of other high administration officials, coupled occasionally with more direct pressures (e.g., sale of stockpiled materials), may be brought to bear. But the supply of such ammunition is limited. Presidential power, if it is to be effective in major cases, must not be squandered on minor ones. It seems reasonable to conclude, therefore, that the effect of the wage-price guideposts and of government efforts to enforce them are more likely to be to constrain inflationary pressures within moderate and generally acceptable proportions, not entirely to eliminate them.[6]

Fourth, the prospect of a continuing relative shift of labor out of higher-productivity manufacturing to lower-productivity service and distribution trades means an expanding prospect for upward pressures on service prices indirectly generated, in the manner we have discussed, by wage patterns established in manufacturing.

Fifth, under existing institutional arrangements, there is no reason to expect a voluntary modification of cost-plus forms of corporate pricing or a voluntary acceptance of lower rates of return on net worth.

Sixth, it seems quite possible, as we have indicated in earlier chapters, that the persisting reduction in capital-output ratios in the United States, which has reconciled declining returns to property per unit of output with the maintenance of adequate returns on net worth, may be in the process of slowing down or reversing. This, if it be so, is because of accelerating obsoles-

---

[6] For an argument to the effect that any serious effort to enforce the wage-price guideposts would be not only impractical but socially harmful, see Arthur F. Burns, "Wages and Prices by Formula?" *Harvard Business Review*, vol. 43, no. 2, pp. 55f., March–April, 1965.

cence in capital goods and the devotion of more and more investment to so-called product development, which mainly entails the proliferation of similar products and the killing off of good older products with slightly improved new ones. While there is nothing intrinsically wrong with such activity, it raises capital costs per unit of output.

Seventh, there is no reason under existing institutional arrangements, particularly if government does not allow any old-style major downspirals in demand to develop during the years ahead, to expect any abatement in the pricing system's ratchet characteristics. We shall, no doubt, experience sudden, emergency-related spurts in demand now and again. When we do, prices will surge upward and never will fully recede to their old levels.

The case for the secular-inflation forecast could be extended. But the foregoing is enough to suggest that, if we continue to avoid a hydrogen war (if we do not, all economic bets not only are off, but inconsequential), few things are more likely than that costs and prices will continue to slip upward as long as existing pricing practice persists. The average rate of slippage is quite unpredictable. At the wholesale level, except for occasional jumps when demand is unusually strong, it is possible that something approaching stability may ensue. But at the retail level, including services, an average annual upward creep in the CPI in the range of 1 to 3 percent would seem the more likely prospect. Such projections, of course, are highly conjectural and could be quickly outdated by events.

THE NATURE OF THE INFLATION

More heat than light has been stirred up in recent years by the debate over whether the kind of price inflation that we have experienced since World War II and that seems likely to extend into the future is of a "cost-push" variety. On one hand, those who refuse to admit that there are any cost-push elements in the inflationary process are in the bizarre position of refusing to accept in the aggregative analysis a view that has been the simplest commonplace of microeconomics ever since Alfred Marshall made his famous point, the better part of a century ago, which we quoted earlier, to the effect that neither blade of a pair of scissors is exclusively responsible for cutting the cloth. Average prices, just as particular prices, are determined by factors both on the supply and the demand sides of the market. We have seen that it took a rather extraordinary hypothesis about the shape of the aggregate-supply path to provide any justification for the conclusion that changes in the price level were exclusively a function of changes in aggregate demand. This was never better than elliptical, rather slipshod thinking, and once the hypothesis of a sharply kinked aggregate-supply path is set aside, it becomes downright specious.

On the other hand, the contention that any inflation is exclusively cost-push in character is, in principle, just as untenable. Any price-level increase is the result of supply-demand interaction, and any that is not associated with an actual (and sufficient) decline in output must involve increases both in aggregate demand and in supply prices. In the context of the 1955–1958 inflation, the cost-push-only contention had certain saving graces. First, those who made it perhaps should be permitted a little exaggeration in their efforts to redress the balance against the extravagant demand-only bias of earlier thinking. Second, the mechanisms of modern American pricing practice are such that the *initial* momentum often comes from the supply side. Third, those who contend that an inflationary process of the sort just described is exclusively cost-push in character have this limited justification: the goodness or badness of demand changes cannot be judged exclusively by their impact on the price level. If demand rises no more than would be necessary to raise output to the near vicinity of normal capacity levels, and the price level nevertheless rises, it makes little sense, to the extent that the economy's real performance is judged as important or more important than its price performance, to call the increase in demand excessive.

The term "cost-push" is nevertheless an unfortunate one, because it focuses attention exclusively on the supply side of the market. It fails to recognize that every cost to one man is income to another. An increase in wages is an increase in costs to the employer, but it is increase in income to the worker. An increase in the price of steel is a cost increase to the automobile manufacturer, but it is income to the steel company. It is sometimes contended that a cost-induced price increase cannot be sustained unless it is matched by a price decrease elsewhere because otherwise the market would not clear. This argument may be valid as applied to the individual firm or industry acting alone. But as applied to an entire economy in which cost-induced price increases are fairly prevalent, if there is no effective monetary restraint on the autonomous creation of money income, and if such increments in income are promptly spent, a cost-push inflation creates its own demand. A better phrase to describe the process, if we may borrow a term from the electronics industry, would be "push-pull" inflation.

Personally, we should prefer to abandon the demand-pull–cost-push terminology entirely and characterize our secular inflationary prospect this way: first, it is our assumption that public policy will seek to promote reasonably full production and employment. But it is also our assumption that public policies, fiscal and monetary, will not be excessively loose. We assume that they will do an adequate job of disciplining aggregate demand, unless a failure fully to anticipate occasional national emergencies or fully to anticipate occasional modest recessions is judged an inadequacy. Given these assumptions, then the difficulties in prospect are primarily ones that inhere in the shape and character of the aggregate-supply path. Some of them are bottleneck problems that are not themselves the creations of American pricing practice. But it is a combination of price-making and wage-making practices —practices which have many good qualities and which, looked at one by one, appear to be anything but predatory—that may cause localized bottlenecks, possibly higher capital costs, and occasional eruptions of aggregate demand, all to actuate a usually slow and lumbering, but usually continuing, one-way inflationary process.

IS SECULAR INFLATION CONSISTENT WITH STEADY GROWTH?

We have arrived at the view that a continuation of existing patterns of pricing practice in the United States may well, at least for some time, yield an income distribution that is conducive to continuing economic growth, and it will be mostly benign in its impact on the problem of short-run instability. But it promises persisting, although usually gradual, price inflation.

This is not an ideal outlook, but just how bad, after all, is it? The inequities of inflation are substantial, but, as a number of commentators have noted, they are not so bad as the inequities of unemployment. If the pace of secular inflation is not too great, perhaps the average hardships it wreaks in any one individual's lifetime will not be excessive—especially if the disadvantaged can be protected with such hedges as variable annuity retirement plans, and especially if creeping inflation is a necessary by-product of a system geared to yield vigorous sustained growth in average real incomes. Some economic historians assert that over the long sweep of history most eras of rapid economic growth also have been eras of inflation. A little upslippage in prices casts a rosy aura over business decision making and saves many marginal investments from failure. When you come right down to it, is a prospect of gradual secular inflation anything to get overwrought about?

Probably not, if we could be sure, in this imperfect world, that continuing gradual inflation could be kept gradual—could be prevented from accelerating into the virulent form that would seriously undermine incentives to work and to save and possibly into the violent, runaway variety of inflation that would bring a crashing interruption in the growth process.

One can never be sure about such matters. On the one hand, it can be argued that the very anticipation of gradual inflation, if it is widespread, invites buying in advance of needs, which itself tends to accelerate the inflation process. Thus far in the postwar period, it appears that consumers have not been so affected. Consumer surveys indicate that households, if pressed, may hypothesize a long-run inflation forecast, but it is not sufficiently firm or central to their thinking to affect their timing of durables buying. However, in the past, inflation has been discontinuous, and the episodes that people remember have been associated with national emergencies. If, in the future, inflation should become a more normal, steadier thing, consumers may begin to take it seriously. A business attempt to beat long-run price rises may become a dominant factor pushing fixed investment up to unsustainable rates. And efforts to ease the inequities of inflation by, in effect, putting more and more groups on cost-of-living escalators may help to accelerate the price spiral to which buyers' self-confirming expectations of inflation will contribute.

On the other hand, efforts to hedge against inflation are not without their costs. For a rational business management to buy capital goods sooner than its forecast of future product demand warrants, it must anticipate an annual rate of inflation in capital goods prices that would exceed the costs of holding the assets in an unproductive state. These would include the cost of money plus warehousing plus any physical deterioration or technological obsolescence in the premature purchases. Consumers would incur similar costs and could not engage in such anticipatory buying very long before bumping into the ceiling of income plus ability to carry debt. While neither investors nor consumers are entirely rational, an expected rate of secular infla- tion of well over 5 percent would probably be required to trigger very much anticipatory buying by either. And even these might be forestalled if the economy continued to produce abundantly, if the monetary authorities did not abdicate, and if higher interest rates accompanied the faster price rises.

A continuing 1, 2, or 3 percent a year inflation would, unquestionably, have unpleasant consequences for certain portions of the financial community, as savings were shifted into equity securities—a shift that does not entail major increases in holding costs. Likewise, it could bid up land prices, strengthen the trend toward owner-occupied housing, and perhaps require new arrangements for placing the public debt. But, while most of these would be unwanted developments, they would not necessarily force an acceleration in the commodity price inflation or disrupt long-term economic growth.

On balance, it seems to the present authors that the dangers of a gradual inflation escalating into a virulent one are much less than they are sometimes depicted. If the achievement of absolute price stability were cost- less, it would no doubt be worth the effort. But such anti-inflation actions are not without their costs in unemployment and income forgone. And these costs become especially painful when we remember that, in part, they are incurred to offset a statistical illusion in the available price indexes. In the words of Albert Rees:[7]

> "We may be paying a high price in terms of restrictive monetary or fiscal policy to keep price indexes from rising when the true level of prices is really stable or declining. It is certainly not inconceivable that the true level of prices is now lower than it was 5 years ago. If there is such a bias, it would be far cheaper to devote resources to improving the indexes than to suffer unnecessary unemployment."

IN CONCLUSION: THE CHALLENGE TO POLICY MAKERS

This book began with an announcement that it was not going to in- clude much prescriptive discussion of public-policy issues, and although our policy preferences often have not been very deeply disguised, we think ensuing

[7] Albert Rees, "Price Level Stability and Economic Policy," in *The Relationship of Prices to Economic Stability and Growth,* Joint Economic Committee, 85th Cong., 2d Sess., 1958, p. 656.

chapters have adhered to that intention about as well as could be expected. But now we want to conclude on an unabashed policy note.

The question of what the United States public-policy responses to the prospect of secular inflation will be is a fascinating one, not only because a lack of adequate response to this particular issue could be costly, but because the issue is, in important senses, representative of many of the difficult business conditions challenges with which the American public and American policy makers are going to be grappling in coming decades. The future inflation problem is rooted in an economic power structure in which crucial decisions of the large producer groups neither are closely disciplined by an impersonal market mechanism nor are formally accountable to the public through the political process. Yet the structure is one in which reasonable private decisions do not always add up to the best course for the economy. Some means of making private decisions more explicitly and effectively responsible to the public interest is needed, and is lacking. This must be accomplished in a context where political as well as economic power is heavily concentrated in the hands of these same producer groups and where there is a strong popular distaste for central government regulation of detailed private decision making.

The secular-inflation issue is typical of the problems ahead in that, in the form we find it, it is peculiarly a problem of a prospering opulent economy. It threatens to become critical only as we solve other more elemental problems. It is also typical in that policy makers cannot afford to attack it single-mindedly without thought to other objectives. They must avoid wrong policies as assiduously as they must seek right ones. Such, we hope, is the lesson we learned from the effort in 1955 to 1960 to bring an inflation that involved no general excess of demand over capacity to a standstill with general monetary and fiscal restraints: it is a costly business to fight a dedicated anti-inflationary battle with self-immolating weapons. And such, we hope, is the lesson we learned from the effort in 1961 to 1965 to use fiscal and monetary policies to stimulate a vigorous rise in demand commensurate with our growing capacity: a dedicated battle to raise the level of income and of employment can, if skillfully done, be waged without serious inflationary consequences.

Above all, the inflation problem may be typical of the challenges ahead because it requires some experimentation and new departures in public policy. There are some useful things that can be done in relatively familiar molds. For example, some feasible and familiar forms of selective demand regulation, such as consumer credit controls, may prove useful. And it is possible that government stockpiles can be used to moderate the domestic price impacts of fluctuations in international raw materials markets. But as for the core of the problem—the inflation-prone characteristics of administered price and wage making—American policy experience offers little in the way of helpful precedent. Peacetime price and wage controls on the wartime model are out of the question on several counts. So, certainly, is any literal extension of the commission-court system of public utility rate regulation. And for reasons that are partly implicit in the foregoing discussion, we doubt that intensified antitrust policy could provide much of the answer.

But none of this means that an answer is unobtainable. It simply means that we need some policy innovations. We have some social inventing to do. We suspect that a workable reform, when it is finally devised, will rely heavily on the social motivations of informed industrial and labor leaders but also will involve a new catalytic, advisory role for government vis-à-vis certain key private price and wage decisions. However, in our present state of ignorance in this area, no one man's initial ideas should be taken very seriously. Instead, the important thing right now is that we avoid complacent fixations on the *status quo* and improve our receptiveness to the idea of reform itself. The United States has shown no lack of imagination in contriving social inventions in the past, but it has done so only when it was willing to experiment, to entertain new ideas, and to view its existing institutions with sufficient candor to see their emerging weaknesses as well as their splendor.

Here, in the last analysis, may be the Achilles' heel of the economic utopia that we seem to be in a fair way of building in the United States. Perhaps we already have become too stable, too prosperous, too expansive to nurture a sufficient continuing dissatisfaction with things as they are. Those of us who grew up in the thirties sometimes, in a mixture of impatience and nostalgia, grumble that the economy needs another dose of such adversity to shed its complacency and regenerate a sufficient appetite for constructive social change. It would be a consummate irony if this should be so.

SELECTED BIBLIOGRAPHY

PART ONE

Alternative Introductory Expositions of National Accounting

Gordon, R. A.: *Business Fluctuations*, 2d ed., Harper & Row, Publishers, Incorporated, New York, 1961.

Hicks, J. R., A. B. Hart, and J. W. Ford: *The Social Framework of the American Economy: An Introduction to Economics*, 2d ed., Oxford University Press, Fair Lawn, N.J., 1955.

McConnell, C. R.: *Economics: Principles, Problems, and Policies*, 2d ed., McGraw-Hill Book Company, New York, 1963.

Rosen, S.: *National Income: Its Measurement, Determination and Relation to Public Policy*, Holt, Rinehart and Winston, Inc., New York, 1963.

Ruggles, R., and N. D. Ruggles: *National Income Accounts and Income Analysis*, 2d ed., McGraw-Hill Book Company, New York, 1956.

Samuelson, P. A.: *Economics: An Introductory Analysis*, 6th ed., McGraw-Hill Book Company, New York, 1964.

Schultze, C. L.: *National Income Analysis*, Prentice-Hall, Inc., Englewood Cliffs, N.J., 1964.

636   Selected bibliography

National Income Accounting Theory

Conference on Research in Income and Wealth: *A Critique of the United States Income and Product Accounts*, National Bureau of Economic Research, Inc., Studies in Income and Wealth, vol. 22, Princeton University Press, Princeton, N.J., 1958.

Income and Wealth: Series 1, International Association for Research in Income and Wealth, Bowes and Bowes, Cambridge, 1951.

Jaszi, G.: "The Statistical Foundations of the Gross National Product," *Review of Economics and Statistics*, vol. 38, pp. 205–214, May, 1956.

Keynes, J. M.: *The General Theory of Employment, Interest, and Money*, Harcourt, Brace & World, Inc., New York, 1936.

Kuznets, S.: *National Income: A Summary of Findings*, National Bureau of Economic Research, Inc., New York, 1946.

—— assisted by L. Epstein and E. Jenks: *National Product since 1869*, National Bureau of Economic Research, Inc., Publication no. 46, New York, 1946.

Margolis, J.: "National Economic Accounting: Reorientation Needed," *Review of Economics and Statistics*, vol. 34, pp. 291–304, November, 1962.

Morgenstern, O.: *On the Accuracy of Economic Observations*, 2d ed., Princeton University Press, Princeton, N.J., 1963.

Ruggles, R.: "The U.S. National Accounts and Their Development," *American Economic Review*, vol. 49, pp. 85–95, March, 1959.

Official National Income and Product Accounting Documents

Gilbert, M., and J. B. Krauts: *An International Comparison of National Products and the Purchasing Power of Currencies*, Organization for European Economic Cooperation, Paris, 1954.

National Income, 1954 Edition: A Supplement to the Survey of Current Business, U.S. Department of Commerce, 1954.

"The National Income and Product Accounts of the United States: Revised Estimates, 1929–64," *Survey of Current Business*, U.S. Department of Commerce, vol. 45, pp. 6–22, August, 1965.

A System of National Accounts and Supporting Tables, rev. ed., United Nations Statistical Office, Studies in Methods ser. F, no. 2, United Nations, New York, 1964.

U.S. Income and Output: A Supplement to the Survey of Current Business, U.S. Department of Commerce, 1958.

The Nation's Economic Budget

Colm, G.: *The American Economy in 1960*, National Planning Association, Washington, D.C., 1952.

—— *Essays in Public Finance and Fiscal Policy*, Oxford University Press, Fair Lawn, N.J., 1955.

U.S. Council of Economic Advisers: "The Nation's Economic Accounts," in the *Economic Report of the President*, pp. 153–163, January, 1953.

Other Forms of Social Accounting

Bhargaua, R. N.: "Social Accounting," *Indian Economic Review*, vol. 4, pp. 16–32, August, 1958.

Bowsher, N. N., J. D. Daane, and R. Einzig: "The Flows of Funds between Regions of the United States," *Papers and Proceedings of the Regional Science Association*, vol. 3, pp. 139–165, December, 1957.

Burton, H.: "Alternative Presentations of Social Accounting," *Journal of the Royal Statistical Society*, vol. 120, pp. 451–456, 1957.

Cameron, B.: "The Future of Inter-industry Analysis," *Economic Record*, vol. 31, pp. 232–241, November, 1955.

Conference on Research in Income and Wealth: *Input-Output Analysis: An Appraisal*, National Bureau of Economic Research, Inc., Studies in Income and Wealth, vol. 18, Princeton University Press, Princeton, N.J., 1955.

————: *The Flow-of-Funds Approach to Social Accounting: Appraisal, Analysis, and Applications*, National Bureau of Economic Research, Inc., Studies in Income and Wealth, vol. 26, Princeton University Press, Princeton, N.J., 1962.

Copeland, M. A.: *A Study of Moneyflows in the United States*, National Bureau of Economic Research, Inc., Publication no. 54, New York, 1952.

Dorfman, R.: "The Nature and Significance of Input-Output," *Review of Economics and Statistics*, vol. 36, pp. 121–133, May, 1954.

Dorrance, G. S.: "Balance Sheets in a System of Economic Accounts," *International Monetary Fund Staff Papers*, vol. 7, pp. 168–209, October, 1959.

Evans, W. D., and M. Hoffenberg: "The Interindustry Relations Study for 1947," *Review of Economics and Statistics*, vol. 34, pp. 97–142, May, 1952.

"A Flow-of-Funds System of National Accounts, Annual Estimates, 1939–54," *Federal Reserve Bulletin*, vol. 41, pp. 1085–1124, October, 1955.

Flow of Funds in the United States, 1939–53, Federal Reserve System, Washington, D.C., 1955.

Goldman, M. R., M. L. Marimont, and B. N. Vaccara: "The Interindustry Structure of the United States: A Report on the 1958 Input-Output Study," *Survey of Current Business*, U.S. Department of Commerce, vol. 44, pp. 10–29, November, 1964.

Goldsmith, R. W.: *The National Wealth of the United States in the Postwar Period*, National Bureau of Economic Research, Inc., Studies in Capital Formation and Financing, no. 10, Princeton University Press, Princeton, N.J., 1962.

———— and R. E. Lipsey: *Studies in the National Balance Sheet of the United States*, vol. I, National Bureau of Economic Research, Inc., Studies in Capital Formation and Financing, no. 11, Princeton University Press, Princeton, N.J., 1963.

————, ————, and M. Mendelson: *Studies in the National Balance Sheet of the United States*, vol. II, *Basic Data on Balance Sheets and Fund Flows*, National Bureau of Economic Research, Inc., Studies in Capital Formation and Financing, no. 11, Princeton University Press, Princeton, N.J., 1963.

———— and C. Saunders (eds.): *The Measurement of National Wealth*, Bowes and Bowes, London, 1959.

Leontief, W. W.: *The Structure of the American Economy, 1919–1939*, 2d ed., Oxford University Press, Fair Lawn, N.J., 1953.

—— (ed.): *Studies in the Structure of the American Economy*, Oxford University Press, Fair Lawn, N.J., 1953.

Leven, C. L.: "A Theory of Regional Social Accounting," *Papers and Proceedings of the Regional Science Association*, vol. 4, pp. 221–237, December, 1958.

Measuring the Nation's Wealth, Hearings before the Subcommittee on Economic Statistics of the Joint Economic Committee, 89th Cong., 1st Sess., June 1, 2, and 3, 1965.

Measuring the Nation's Wealth, Materials Developed by the Wealth Inventory Planning Study of the George Washington University for the Subcommittee on Economic Statistics of the Joint Economic Committee, 88th Cong., 2d Sess., December, 1964.

"Personal Consumption Expenditures in the 1958 Input-Output Study," *Survey of Current Business*, U.S. Department of Commerce, vol. 45, pp. 7–20, October, 1965.

Powelson, J. P.: *National Income and Flow-of-Funds Analysis*, McGraw-Hill Book Company, New York, 1960.

"A Quarterly Presentation of Flow of Funds, Saving, and Investment," *Federal Reserve Bulletin*, vol. 45, pp. 828–859, August, 1959.

Read, L. M.: "The Development of National Transactions Accounts: Canada's Version of or Substitute for Money Flows Accounts," *Canadian Journal of Economics and Political Science*, vol. 23, pp. 42–56, February, 1957.

"Revision of Flow of Funds Accounts," *Federal Reserve Bulletin*, vol. 51, pp. 1533–1538, November, 1965.

Ritter, L. S., et al.: "The Flow of Funds Accounts: A New Approach to Financial Market Analysis," *Journal of Finance*, vol. 18, pp. 219–263, May, 1963.

Stewart, I. G.: "The Practical Uses of Input-Output Analysis," *Scottish Journal of Political Economy*, vol. 5, pp. 50–59, February, 1958.

Stuvel, G.: "A System of National and Domestic Accounts," *Economica*, vol. 22 (new series), pp. 207–217, August, 1955.

Taylor, S.: "An Analytic Summary of the Flow of Funds Accounts," *American Economic Review*, vol. 48, pp. 158–170, May, 1958.

"The Transactions Table of the 1958 Input-Output Study and Revised Direct and Total Requirements Data," *Survey of Current Business*, U.S. Department of Commerce, vol. 45, pp. 33–49, September, 1965.

Young, R. A.: "Federal Reserve Flow-of-Funds Accounts," *American Economic Review*, vol. 48, pp. 158–170, May, 1958.

PART TWO

Aids in Mathematics and Statistics

Allen, R. G. D.: *Mathematical Economics*, 2d ed., St Martin's Press, Inc., New York, 1960.

——: *Mathematical Analysis for Economists*, St Martin's Press, Inc., New York, 1962.

Beach, E. F.: *Economic Models: An Exposition*, John Wiley & Sons, Inc., New York, 1957.

Brennan, M. J.: *Preface to Econometrics: An Introduction to Quantitative Methods in Economics,* 2d ed., South-Western Publishing Company, Cincinnati, 1965.

Cohen, M. R., and E. Nagel: *An Introduction to Logic and Scientific Method,* Harcourt, Brace & World, Inc., New York, 1934.

Crum, W. L., and J. A. Schumpeter: *Rudimentary Mathematics for Economists and Statisticians,* McGraw-Hill Book Company, New York, 1946.

Davis, H. T.: *The Analysis of Economic Time Series,* The Cowles Commission for Research in Economics, Monograph no. 6, Principia Press, Bloomington, Ind., 1941.

Duncan, A. J.: *Quality Control and Industrial Statistics,* 3d ed., Richard D. Irwin, Inc., Homewood, Ill., 1965.

Ficken, F. A.: *The Simplex Method of Linear Programming,* Holt, Rinehart and Winston, Inc., New York, 1961.

Kemeny, J. G., A. Schleifer, Jr., J. L. Snell, and G. L. Thompson: *Finite Mathematics with Business Applications,* Prentice-Hall, Inc, Englewood Cliffs, N.J., 1962.

Klein, L. R.: *An Introduction to Econometrics,* Prentice-Hall, Inc., Englewood Cliffs, N.J., 1962.

Lewis, J. P.: *An Introduction to Mathematics for Students of Economics,* St Martin's Press, Inc., New York, 1963.

Moroney, R. J.: *Facts from Figures,* 3d ed., Penguin Books, Inc., Baltimore, 1956.

Samuelson, P. A.: "Economic Theory and Mathematics: An Appraisal," *American Economic Review,* vol. 42, pp. 56–66, May, 1952.

————: "Introduction: Mathematics in Economics: No, No, or Yes, Yes, Yes?" *Review of Economics and Statistics,* vol. 36, p. 359, November, 1954.

Schelling, T. C.: *National Income Behavior; An Introduction to Algebraic Analysis,* McGraw-Hill Book Company, New York, 1951.

Schlaifer, R.: *Introduction to Statistics for Business Decisions,* McGraw-Hill Book Company, New York, 1961.

Tinbergen, J.: *Econometrics,* McGraw-Hill Book Company, New York, 1951.

Tintner, G.: *Mathematics and Statistics for Economists,* Holt, Rinehart and Winston, Inc., New York, 1953.

Wilks, S. S.: *Elementary Statistical Analysis,* Princeton University Press, Princeton, N.J., 1949.

General Works on Aggregative Economic Theory

Ackley, G.: *Macroeconomic Theory,* The Macmillan Company, New York, 1961.

Allen, R. G. D.: "The Structure of Macro Economic Models," *Economic Journal,* vol. 70, pp. 38–56, March, 1960.

Bach, G. L.: *Economics: An Introduction to Analysis and Policy,* 4th ed., Prentice-Hall, Inc., Englewood Cliffs, N.J., 1963.

Bailey, M. J.: *National Income and the Price Level,* McGraw-Hill Book Company, New York, 1962.

Conference on Research in Income and Wealth: *Models of Income Determination,* National Bureau of Economic Research, Inc., Studies in Income and Wealth, vol. 28, Princeton University Press, Princeton, N.J., 1964.

Dernberg, T. F., and D. M. McDougall: *Macroeconomics: The Measurement, Analysis, and Control of Aggregate Economic Theory*, 2d ed., McGraw-Hill Book Company, New York, 1963.

Dorrance, G.: "A Reexamination of Some Fundamental Keynesian Relations," *Pakistan Economic Journal*, vol. 10, pp. 12–23, December, 1960.

Duesenberry, J. S.: *Business Cycles and Economic Growth*, McGraw-Hill Book Company, New York, 1958.

Fellner, W.: *Trends and Cycles in Economic Activity: An Introduction to Problems of Economic Growth*, Holt, Rinehart and Winston, Inc., New York, 1956.

Fisher, M.: *Macro-economic Models: Nature, Purpose, and Limitations*, Institute for Economic Affairs, Eaton Paper no. 2, London, 1964.

Gordon, R. A.: *Business Fluctuations*, 2d ed., Harper & Row, Publishers, Incorporated, New York, 1961.

Haberler, G.: *Prosperity and Depression*, League of Nations, Geneva, 1939.

Hansen, A. H.: *A Guide to Keynes*, McGraw-Hill Book Company, New York, 1953.

———: *Business Cycles and National Income*, expanded ed., W. W. Norton & Company, Inc., New York, 1964.

Harris, S. E. (ed.): *The New Economics: Keynes' Influence on Theory and Public Policy*, Alfred A. Knopf, Inc., New York, 1947.

Hart, A. G., and P. B. Kenen: *Money, Debt, and Economic Activity*, Prentice-Hall, Inc., Englewood Cliffs, N.J., 1961.

Hazlitt, H. (ed.): *The Critics of Keynesian Economics*, D. Van Nostrand Company, Inc., Princeton, N.J., 1960.

Keiser, N. F.: *Macroeconomics, Fiscal Policy, and Economic Growth*, John Wiley & Sons, Inc., New York, 1964.

Keynes, J. M.: *The General Theory of Employment, Interest, and Money*, Harcourt, Brace & World, Inc., New York., 1936.

Klein, L. R.: *The Keynesian Revolution*, The Macmillan Company, New York, 1947.

Lekachman, R. (ed.): *Keynes' General Theory: Reports of Three Decades*, St Martin's Press, Inc., New York, 1964.

Patinkin, D.: *Money, Interest, and Prices*, 2d ed., Harper & Row, Publishers, Incorporated, New York, 1965.

Ross, M. H.: *Income: Analysis and Policy*, McGraw-Hill Book Company, New York, 1964.

Schumpeter, J. A.: *Business Cycles: A Theoretical, Historical, and Statistical Analysis of the Capitalist Process*, McGraw-Hill Book Company, New York, 1939, vols. I–II.

Sirkin, G.: *Introduction to Macroeconomic Theory*, Richard D. Irwin, Inc., Homewood, Ill., 1961.

Stonier, A. W., and D. C. Hague: *A Textbook of Economic Theory*, 3d ed., John Wiley & Sons., Inc., New York, 1964.

Wiles, P. J. D.: *Price, Cost, and Output*, rev. ed., Frederick A. Praeger, Inc., New York, 1963.

Productivity, Labor Force, and Physical Growth

Abramovitz, M.: "Economics of Growth," in B. F. Haley (ed.), *Survey of Con-*

temporary Economics, Richard D. Irwin, Inc., Homewood, Ill., 1952, vol. II, pp. 132–182.

Adelman, I.: "An Econometric Analysis of Population Growth," *American Economic Review,* vol. 53, pp. 314–339, June, 1963.

Business Cycle Developments, U.S. Department of Commerce.

Colm, G.: *The American Economy in 1960,* National Planning Association, Washington, D.C., 1952.

Current Population Reports, U.S. Department of Commerce, ser. P-25.

Denison, E.: *The Sources of Economic Growth in the United States,* Committee for Economic Development, Supplementary Paper no. 13, New York, 1962.

Dewhurst, J. F., and Associates: *America's Needs and Resources: A New Survey,* The Twentieth Century Fund, New York, 1955.

Dhrymes, P. J.: "Comparison of Productivity Behavior in Manufacturing and Service Industries," *Review of Economics and Statistics,* vol. 45, pp. 64–69, February, 1963.

Eckstein, O.: "Inflation, the Wage-Price Spiral and Economic Growth," in *The Relationship of Prices to Economic Stability and Growth,* Compendium of Papers Submitted by Panelists Appearing before the Joint Economic Committee, 85th Cong., 2d Sess., Mar. 31, 1958, pp. 361–374.

Employment and Earnings and Monthly Report on the Labor Force, U.S. Department of Labor.

Employment and Unemployment, Hearings before the Subcommittee on Economic Statistics of the Joint Economic Committee, 87th Cong., 1st Sess., Dec. 18–20, 1961.

Fellner, W.: *Trends and Cycles in Economic Activity,* Holt, Rinehart and Winston, Inc., New York, 1956.

Hamberg, D.: "Full Capacity versus Full Employment Growth," *Quarterly Journal of Economics,* vol. 66, pp. 444–449, August, 1952.

Harrod, R. F.: *Towards a Dynamic Economics,* The Macmillan Company, New York, 1948.

Hicks, J.: *Capital and Growth,* Oxford University Press, Fair Lawn, N.J., 1965.

Hicks, J. R.: *A Contribution to the Theory of the Trade Cycle,* Oxford University Press, Fair Lawn, N.J., 1950.

Kendrick, J. W.: "National Productivity and Its Long-term Projection," in Conference on Research in Income and Wealth, *Long-range Economic Projection, National Bureau of Economic Research, Inc.,* Studies in Income and Wealth, vol. 16, Princeton University Press, Princeton, N.J., 1954.

————: "Productivity Trends: Capital and Labor," *Review of Economics and Statistics,* vol. 38, pp. 248–257, August, 1956.

————: "Trends in Product Prices, Factor Prices, and Productivity," in *The Relationship of Prices to Economic Stability and Growth,* Compendium of Papers Submitted by Panelists Appearing before the Joint Economic Committee, 85th Cong., 2d Sess., Mar. 31, 1958, pp. 225–236.

———— assisted by M. R. Pech: *Productivity Trends in the United States,* National Bureau of Economic Research, Inc., Publication no. 71, Princeton University Press, Princeton, N.J., 1961.

Lange, O.: *Price Flexibility and Full Employment,* Principia Press, Bloomington, Ind., 1944.

McKinnon, R. I.: "Wages, Capital Costs, and Employment in Manufacturing: A Model Applied to 1947–58 U.S. Data," *Econometrica*, vol. 30, pp. 501–521, July, 1962.

Manpower Report of the President and a Report on Manpower Requirements, Resources, and Training, U.S. Department of Labor, March, 1965.

Massel, B. F.: "Capital Formation and Technological Change," *Review of Economics and Statistics*, vol. 42, pp. 182–188, May, 1960.

Measuring Employment and Unemployment, Hearings before the Subcommittee on Economic Statistics of the Joint Economic Committee, 88th Cong., 1st Sess., June 6–7, 1963.

Morgan, T.: *Income and Employment*, 2d ed., Prentice-Hall, Inc., Englewood Cliffs, N.J., 1952.

Perlman, R.: "A Reformulation of Keynesian Wage Theory," *Southern Economic Journal*, vol. 26, pp. 229–233, January, 1960.

Population Bulletin, Population Reference Bureau, Inc., Washington, D.C.

Salter, W. E. G.: *Productivity and Technical Change*, Cambridge University Press, New York, 1960.

Unemployment: Terminology, Measurement, and Analysis, Study Papers for the Subcommittee on Economic Statistics of the Joint Economic Committee by the Bureau of Labor Statistics, 87th Cong., 1st Sess., November, 1961.

Wool, H.: "Long-term Projections of the Labor Force," in Conference on Research in Income and Wealth, *Long-term Economic Projection*, National Bureau of Economic Research, Inc., Studies in Income and Wealth, vol. 16, Princeton University Press, Princeton, N.J., 1954.

Prices, Price Flexibility, and Price-output Relationships

Balogh, T.: "Productivity and Inflation," *Oxford Economic Papers*, vol. 10 (new series), pp. 220–245, June, 1958.

Beveridge, W. H.: *Full Employment in a Free Society*, W. W. Norton & Company, Inc., New York, 1945.

Bowen, W. G.: " 'Cost Inflation' versus 'Demand Inflation': A Useful Distinction?" *Southern Economic Journal*, vol. 26, pp. 199–206, January, 1960.

———: *The Wage-Price Issue: A Theoretical Analysis*, Princeton University Press, Princeton, N.J., 1960.

——— and S. H. Masters: "Shifts in the Composition of Demand and the Inflation Problem," *American Economic Review*, vol. 54, pp. 975–984, December, 1964.

Bronfenbrenner, M., and F. D. Holzman: "Survey of Inflation Theory," *American Economic Review*, vol. 53, pp. 593–661, September, 1963.

Burns, A. F.: "Wages and Prices by Formula?" *Harvard Business Review*, vol. 43, pp. 55–64, March-April, 1965.

Cartter, A. M.: *Theory of Wages and Employment*, Richard D. Irwin, Inc., Homewood, Ill., 1959.

Cloos, G. W.: "How Good Are the National Bureau's Reference Dates?" *Journal of Business*, vol. 36, pp. 14–32, January, 1963.

Colm, G. (ed.): *The Employment Act, Past and Future: A Tenth Anniversary Symposium*, National Planning Association, Washington, D.C., 1956.

Evans, R.: "Wage Differentials, Excess Demand for Labor, and Inflation," *Review of Economics and Statistics,* vol. 45, pp. 95–100, February, 1963.

Friedman, M.: *Inflation: Causes and Consequences,* Asia Publishing House, New York, 1963.

Gordon, R. A.: "Short Period Price Determination in Theory and Practice," *American Economic Review,* vol. 38, pp. 265–288, June, 1948.

———: "Stabilization Policy and the Study of Business Cycles," *American Economic Review,* vol. 47, pp. 115–126, May, 1957.

Government Price Statistics, Hearings before the Subcommittee on Economic Statistics of the Joint Economic Committee, 87th Cong., 1st Sess., Jan. 25 and May 1–5, 1961, parts 1 and 2.

Haberler, G.: *Prosperity and Depression,* League of Nations, Geneva, 1939.

Hamberg, D.: *Business Cycles,* The Macmillan Company, New York, 1951.

Hansen, A. H.: *Monetary Theory and Fiscal Policy,* McGraw-Hill Book Company, New York, 1949.

———: *The Postwar American Economy: Performance and Problems,* W. W. Norton & Company, Inc., New York, 1964.

Hickman, B. G.: "Postwar Cyclical Experience and Economic Stability," *American Economic Review,* vol. 48, pp. 117–134, May, 1958.

Inflation, Growth, and Employment: A Series of Research Studies Prepared for the Commission on Money and Credit, Prentice-Hall, Inc., Englewood Cliffs, N.J., 1964.

Keynes, J. M.: *The General Theory of Employment, Interest, and Money,* Harcourt, Brace & World, Inc., New York, 1936.

Lewis, J. P.: "The Lull That Came to Stay," *Journal of Political Economy,* vol. 63, pp. 1–19, February, 1955.

———: "The Problem of Price Stability: A Progress Report," *American Economic Review,* vol. 49, pp. 309–321, May, 1959.

Long, C. D.: "Illusion of Wage Rigidity: Long and Short Cycles in Wages and Labor," *Review of Economics and Statistics,* vol. 42, pp. 141–151, May, 1960.

Machlup, F.: "Another View of Cost-push and Demand-pull Inflation," *Review of Economics and Statistics,* vol. 42, pp. 125–139, May, 1960.

Matthews, R. C. O.: *The Business Cycle,* The University of Chicago Press, Chicago, 1959.

Mueller, E.: "Consumer Reactions to Inflation," *Quarterly Journal of Economics,* vol. 73, pp. 246–252, May, 1959.

1966 Supplement to Economic Indicators: Historical and Descriptive Background Prepared for the Subcommittee on Economic Statistics of the Joint Economic Committee by the Committee Staff and the Office of Statistical Standards, U.S. Bureau of the Budget, 89th Cong., 2d Sess., December, 1966.

Nourse, E. G.: *Price Making in a Democracy,* The Brookings Institution, Washington, D.C., 1944.

Ohlin, B.: *The Problem of Employment Stabilization,* Columbia University Press, New York, 1949.

Patinkin, D.: "Price Flexibility and Full Employment," *American Economic Review,* vol. 38, pp. 543–564, September, 1948.

Phillips, A. W.: "The Relation between Unemployment and the Rate of Change of Money Wage Rates in the United Kingdom, 1861–1957," *Economica*, vol. 25 (new series), pp. 283–299, November, 1958.

Pitchford, J. D. A.: *A Study of Cost and Demand Inflation*, Contributions to Economic Analysis, no. 33, North Holland Publishing Company, Amsterdam, 1963.

Rees, A.: "Do Unions Cause Inflation?" *Journal of Law and Economics*, vol. 2, pp. 84–94, October, 1959.

Rothschild, K. W.: *The Theory of Wages*, Oxford University Press, Fair Lawn, N.J., 1956.

Schultz, R. S.: "Profits, Prices, and Excess Capacity," *Harvard Business Review*, vol. 41, pp. 68–81, July, 1963.

Schultze, C. L.: *Recent Inflation in the United States*, Materials Prepared in Connection with the Study of Employment, Growth, and Price Levels for Consideration by the Joint Economic Committee, 86th Cong., 1st Sess., September, 1959, Study Paper no. 1.

Selden, R. T.: "Cost-push versus Demand-pull Inflation," *Journal of Political Economy*, vol. 67, pp. 1–20, February, 1959.

Stigler, G. J.: "Administered Prices and Oligopolistic Behavior," *Journal of Business*, vol. 35, pp. 1–13, January, 1962 (Discussion, vol. 37, pp. 68–86, January, 1964).

Thompson, G. C., and R. W. Taylor: "Inflation, Causes, Trends, and Cures," *Conference Board Record*, vol. 1, pp. 52–65, May, 1964.

Tobin, J.: "Money Wage Rates and Employment," in S. E. Harris (ed.), *The New Economics*, Alfred A. Knopf, Inc., New York, 1947.

Twentieth Anniversary of the Employment Act of 1946, An Economic Symposium, Hearing before the Joint Economic Committee, 89th Cong., 2d Sess., Feb. 23, 1966.

Wilson, T. A., and O. Eckstein: "Short-run Productivity Behavior in U.S. Manufacturing," *Review of Economics and Statistics*, vol. 46, pp. 41–54, February, 1964.

Worswick, G. D. N.: "Prices, Productivity, and Incomes," *Oxford Economic Papers*, vol. 10 (new series), pp. 246–264, June, 1958.

Zarnowitz, V.: "Unfilled Orders, Price Changes, and Business Fluctuations," *Review of Economics and Statistics*, vol. 44, pp. 367–394, November, 1962.

Consumption Determination and Consumer Behavior

Ackley, G.: "The Multiplier Time Period: Money, Income, and Flexibility," *American Economic Review*, vol. 41, pp. 350–368, June, 1951.

Ando, A., and F. Modigliani: "The 'Life Cycle' Hypothesis of Saving: Aggregate Implications and Tests," *American Economic Review*, vol. 53, pp. 55–84, March, 1963.

Bain, A. D.: "The Growth of Demand for New Commodities," *Journal of the Royal Statistical Society*, ser. A, vol. 126 (2), pp. 285–299, 1963.

Beard, T. R.: "Progressive Income Taxation, Income Redistribution, and the Consumption Function," *National Tax Journal*, vol. 13, pp. 168–177, June, 1960.

Brinegar, G. K.: "Short-run Effects of Income Change upon Expenditure," *Journal of Farm Economics*, vol. 35, pp. 99–109, February, 1953.

Cohen, M.: "Postwar Consumption Functions," *Review of Economics and Statistics*, vol. 34, pp. 18–33, February, 1952.

Conference on Research in Income and Wealth: *The Behavior of Income Shares: Selected Theoretical and Empirical Issues*, National Bureau of Economic Research, Inc., Studies in Income and Wealth, vol. 27, Princeton University Press, Princeton, N.J., 1964.

Duesenberry, J. S.: *Income, Saving, and the Theory of Consumer Behavior*, Harvard University Press, Cambridge, Mass., 1949.

Farrell, M. J.: "The New Theories of the Consumption Function," *Economic Journal*, vol. 69, pp. 678–696, December, 1959.

Ferber, R.: *A Study of Aggregate Consumption Functions*, National Bureau of Economic Research, Inc., Technical Paper no. 18, New York, 1953.

———: "Research on Household Behavior," *American Economic Review*, vol. 52, pp. 19–63, March, 1962.

Friedman, M.: *A Theory of the Consumption Function*, Princeton University Press, Princeton, N.J., 1957.

Ghosh, A.: "The Consumption Function in the Light of Recent Controversies," *Indian Economic Journal*, vol. 10, pp. 39–48, July, 1962.

Goldsmith, R. W.: *A Study of Saving in the United States*, vol. I, *Introduction: Tables of Annual Estimates of Saving 1897 to 1949*; vol. II, *Nature and Derivation of Annual Estimates of Saving 1897 to 1949*, Princeton University Press, Princeton, N.J., 1955.

———, D. S. Brady, and H. Mendershausen: *A Study of Saving in the United States*, vol. III, *Special Studies*, Princeton University Press, Princeton, N.J., 1956.

Gordon, R. A.: *Business Fluctuations*, 2d ed., Harper & Row, Publishers, Incorporated, New York, 1961.

——— and L. R. Klein (eds.): *Readings in Business Cycles*, Richard D. Irwin, Inc., Homewood, Ill., 1965.

Griliches, Z., G. S. Madola, R. Lucas, and N. Wallace: "Notes on Estimated Aggregate Quarterly Consumption Functions," *Econometrica*, vol. 30, pp. 491–500, July, 1962.

Haberler, G.: *Prosperity and Depression*, League of Nations, Geneva, 1939.

Hansen, A. H.: *Monetary Theory and Fiscal Policy*, McGraw-Hill Book Company, New York, 1949.

———: *Business Cycles and National Income*, expanded ed., W. W. Norton & Company, Inc., New York, 1964.

Heller, W. W., et al.: *Savings in the Modern Economy*, The University of Minnesota Press, Minneapolis, 1953.

Houthakker, H. S.: "The Present State of Consumption Theory: A Survey Article," *Econometrica*, vol. 29, pp. 704–740, October, 1961.

Katona, G.: "Effects of Income Changes on the Rate of Saving," *Review of Economics and Statistics*, vol. 31, pp. 95–103, May, 1949.

Keynes, J. M.: *The General Theory of Employment, Interest, and Money*, Harcourt, Brace & World, Inc., New York, 1936.

Kuznets, S.: *Uses of National Income in Peace and War*, National Bureau of Economic Research, Inc., Occasional Paper no. 6, New York, 1942.

Lubell, H.: "Effects of Redistribution of Income and Consumers' Expenditures," *American Economic Review*, vol. 37, pp. 150–170, March, 1947.

Mack, R. P.: "Economics of Consumption," in B. F. Haley (ed.), *A Survey of Contemporary Economics*, Richard D. Irwin, Inc., Homewood, Ill., 1952, vol. II.

Mayer, T.: "Permanent Income Theory and Occupational Groups," *Review of Economics and Statistics*, vol. 45, pp. 16–22, February, 1963.

Morgan, T.: *Income and Employment*, 2d ed., Prentice-Hall, Inc., Englewood Cliffs, N.J., 1952.

Paradiso, L. J.: "Consumer and Business Income and Spending Patterns in the Postwar Period," *Survey of Current Business*, U.S. Department of Commerce, vol. 43, pp. 12–17, March, 1963.

Samuelson, P.: "The Simple Mathematics of Income Determination," in *Income, Employment, and Public Policy: Essays in Honor of Alvin H. Hansen*, W. W. Norton & Company, Inc., New York, 1948.

Schultze, C. L.: "Short-run Movements of Income Shares," in Conference on Research in Income and Wealth, *The Behavior of Income Shares: Selected Theoretical and Empirical Issues*, National Bureau of Economic Research, Inc., Studies in Income and Wealth, vol. 27, Princeton University Press, Princeton, N.J., 1964, pp. 143–188.

The Determination of Private Investment

Baumol, W. J.: "Acceleration without Magnification," *American Economic Review*, vol. 46, pp. 409–412, June, 1956.

Bhatt, V. V.: "Aggregate Capital-Output Ratio: Some Conceptual Issues," *Indian Economic Journal*, vol. 9, pp. 397–409, April, 1963.

Brems, H.: "What Induces Induced Investment?" *Kyklos*, vol. 16, pp. 569–582, 1963.

Conference on Research in Income and Wealth: *Problems of Capital Formation: Concepts, Measurement, and Controlling Factors*, National Bureau of Economic Research, Inc., Studies in Income and Wealth, vol. 19, Princeton University Press, Princeton, N.J., 1957.

———: *Output, Input and Productivity Measurement*, National Bureau of Economic Research, Inc., Studies in Income and Wealth, vol. 25, Princeton University Press, Princeton, N.J., 1961.

DeLeeuw, F.: "The Demand for Capital Goods by Manufacturers: A Study of Quarterly Time Series," *Econometrica*, vol. 30, pp. 407–423, July, 1962.

Denison, E. F.: "Saving in the National Economy from the National Income Perspective," *Survey of Current Business*, U.S. Department of Commerce, vol. 35, pp. 8–24, January, 1955.

Duesenberry, J. S.: *Income, Saving, and the Theory of Consumer Behavior*, Harvard University Press, Cambridge, Mass., 1949.

Fellner, W.: *Trends and Cycles in Business Activity*, Holt, Rinehart and Winston, Inc., New York, 1956.

Gehrels, F., and S. Wiggins: "Interest Rates and Manufacturers' Fixed Investment," *American Economic Review*, vol. 47, pp. 79–92, March, 1957.

Goldsmith, R. W.: *A Study of Saving in the United States*, vol. I, *Introduction: Tables of Annual Estimates of Saving 1897 to 1949*; vol. II, *Nature and Derivation of Annual Estimates of Saving 1897 to 1949*, Princeton University Press, Princeton, N.J., 1955.

————, D. S. Brady, and H. Mendershausen: *A Study of Saving in the United States*, vol. III, *Special Studies*, Princeton University Press, Princeton, N.J., 1956.

Haavelmo, T.: *A Study in the Theory of Investment*, The University of Chicago Press, Chicago, 1960.

Haberler, G.: *Prosperity and Depression*, League of Nations, Geneva, 1939.

Hansen, A. H.: *Business Cycles and National Income*, expanded ed., W. W. Norton & Company, Inc., New York, 1964.

Hickman, B. G.: *Investment Demand and U.S. Economic Growth*, The Brookings Institution, Washington, D.C., 1965.

Hicks, J. R.: *A Contribution to the Theory of the Trade Cycle*, Oxford University Press, Fair Lawn, N.J., 1950.

Jaszi, G., R. C. Wasson, and L. Grosse: "Expansion of Fixed Business Capital in the United States," *Survey of Current Business*, U.S. Department of Commerce, vol. 42, pp. 9–18 and 28, November, 1962.

Keezer, D.: *Are We Slaves of Some Defunct Economist?*, Claremont Graduate School and University Center, Claremont, Calif., 1963.

Kendrick, J. W., and R. Sato: "Factor Prices, Productivity and Economic Growth," *American Economic Review*, vol. 53, pp. 974–1003, December, 1963.

Kuh, S.: *Capital Stock Growth: A Micro-economic Approach*, Contributions to Economic Analysis, no. 31, North Holland Publishing Company, Amsterdam, 1963.

Kuznets, S. M., assisted by E. Jenks: *Capital in the American Economy: Its Formation and Financing*, National Bureau of Economic Research, Inc., Studies in Capital Formation and Financing, no. 9, Princeton University Press, Princeton, N.J., 1961.

The Role and Effect of Technology on the Nation's Economy, Hearings before a Subcommittee of the Senate Select Committee on Small Business, 88th Cong., 1st Sess., May 20, 1963.

Roos, C. F.: "The Demand for Investment Goods," *American Economic Review*, vol. 38, pp. 311–320, May, 1948.

A Study of the Antitrust Laws, parts 1–2, *Corporate Mergers*; part 3, *Distributional Practices*; part 4, *Foreign Trade*; part 5, *Northwest Power*; parts 6–8, *General Motors*, *Hearings before the Committee on Antitrust and Monopoly*, 84th Cong., 1st Sess., May-December, 1955.

Stuvel, G.: "The Estimation of Capital Consumption in National Accounting," *Review of Economic Studies*, vol. 23, pp. 181–192, 1956.

Variability of Private Investment in Plant and Equipment, part I, *Investment and Its Financing*; part II, *Some Elements Shaping Investment Decisions*, Report by the U.S. Department of Commerce and Papers, 87th Cong., 2d Sess., February, 1962.

The Role of Money and Finance

Aschheim, J.: "Open-market Operations versus Reserve Requirements Variation," *Economic Journal*, vol. 69, pp. 697–704, December, 1959.

Barger, H.: *Money, Banking, and Public Policy*, Rand McNally & Company, Chicago, 1962.

Bernstein, E. M.: "The Role of Monetary Policy," *American Economic Review,* vol. 48, pp. 88–98, May, 1958.

Chandler, L. V.: *The Economics of Money and Banking,* 4th ed., Harper & Row, Publishers, Incorporated, New York, 1964.

Culbertson, J. M.: "Intermediaries and Monetary Theory: A Criticism of the Gurley-Shaw Theory," *American Economic Review,* vol. 48, pp. 119–131, March, 1958.

———: "Timing Changes in Monetary Policy," *Journal of Finance,* vol. 14, pp. 145–160, May, 1959.

Day, A. C. L.: *Outline of Monetary Economics,* Oxford University Press, Fair Lawn, N.J., 1957.

The Federal Reserve Portfolio: *Statements by Individual Economists,* Materials Submitted to the Subcommittee on Economic Progress of the Joint Economic Committee, 89th Cong., 2d Sess., January, 1966.

The Federal Reserve System: Purposes and Functions, Board of Governors of the Federal Reserve System, Washington, D.C., 1963.

Friend, I., H. P. Minsky, and V. L. Andrews: *Private Capital Markets,* Prepared for the Commission on Money and Credit, Prentice-Hall, Inc., Englewood Cliffs, N.J., 1964.

Goldsmith, R. W.: *The Flow of Capital Funds in the Postwar Economy,* National Bureau of Economic Research, Inc., Studies in Capital Formation and Financing, no. 12, Columbia University Press, New York, 1965.

Gurley, J. G., and E. S. Shaw: "Financial Aspects of Economic Development," *American Economic Review,* vol. 45, pp. 515–538, September, 1955.

——— and ———: "Financial Intermediaries and the Saving-Investment Process," *Journal of Finance,* vol. 11, pp. 257–276, May, 1956.

——— and ———: "The Growth of Debt and Money in the United States, 1800–1950: A Suggested Interpretation," *Review of Economics and Statistics,* vol. 39, pp. 250–262, August, 1957.

——— and ———: *Money in a Theory of Finance,* The Brookings Institution, Washington, D.C., 1960.

Haavelmo, T.: "Multiplier Effects of a Balanced Budget," *Econometrica,* vol. 13, pp. 311–318, October, 1945.

Haberler, G.: *Prosperity and Depression,* League of Nations, Geneva, 1939.

Hansen, A.: *Monetary Theory and Fiscal Policy,* McGraw-Hill Book Company, New York, 1949.

Hansen, B.: *A Study in the Theory of Inflation,* nominal ed., George Allen & Unwin, Ltd., London, 1951.

Hart, A. G.: *Money, Debt, and Economic Activity,* 2d ed., Prentice-Hall, Inc., Englewood Cliffs, N.J., 1954.

Hicks, J. R.: "Mr. Keynes and the 'Classics': A Suggested Interpretation," *Econometrica,* vol. 5, pp. 147–159, April, 1937.

Hoover, E. M.: "Some Institutional Factors in Business Investment Decisions," *American Economic Review,* vol. 44, pp. 201–213, May, 1954.

Horvitz, P. M.: *Monetary Policy and the Financial System,* Prentice-Hall, Inc., Englewood Cliffs, N.J., 1963.

Horwich, G.: *Money, Capital, and Prices,* Richard D. Irwin, Inc., Homewood, Ill., 1964.

————: "Tight Money, Monetary Restraint, and the Price Level," *Journal of Finance*, vol. 21, pp. 15–34, March, 1966.

Impacts of Monetary Policy, A Series of Research Studies Prepared for the Commission on Money and Credit, Prentice-Hall, Inc., Englewood Cliffs, N.J., 1964.

Keynes, J. M.: *The General Theory of Employment, Interest, and Money*, Harcourt, Brace & World, Inc., New York, 1936.

Levin, B. F.: "Monetary Policy and Economic Stability: Speed and Scale of Action," *Journal of Finance*, vol. 14, pp. 161–171, May, 1959.

Lintner, J.: "The Theory of Money and Prices," in S. C. Harris (ed.), *The New Economics*, Alfred A. Knopf, Inc., New York, 1947.

Low, A. R.: "The Varied Role of Central Banks," *Economic Record*, vol. 34, pp. 317–330, December, 1958.

Mayer, T.: "The Inflexibility of Monetary Policy," *Review of Economics and Statistics*, vol. 40, pp. 358–374, November, 1958.

Mints, L. W.: *Monetary Policy for a Competitive Society*, McGraw-Hill Book Company, New York, 1950.

Murad, A.: "The Ineffectiveness of Monetary Policy," *Southern Economic Journal*, vol. 22, pp. 339–351, January, 1956.

Patinkin, D.: *Money, Interest, and Prices*, Harper & Row, Publishers, Incorporated, New York, 1956.

Pesek, B. P., and T. R. Saving: "Monetary Policy, Taxes, and the Rate of Interest," *Journal of Political Economy*, vol. 71, pp. 347–362, August, 1963.

Private Financial Institutions, A Series of Research Studies Prepared for the Commission on Money and Credit, Prentice-Hall, Inc., Englewood Cliffs, N.J., 1964.

Recent Federal Reserve Action and Economic Policy Coordination, Hearings before the Joint Economic Committee, 89th Cong., 1st Sess., Dec. 13–16, 1965, parts 1–2.

Ritter, L. S.: *The Role of Money in Keynesian Theory*, New York University School of Business Reprint, ser. no. 13, New York.

Robertson, R. M.: "The Commercial Banking System and Competing Nonmonetary Intermediaries," *Monthly Review*, Federal Reserve Bank of St. Louis, St. Louis, Mo., vol. 39, pp. 61–69, May, 1957.

Roosa, R. V.: *Federal Reserve Operations in the Money and Government Securities Markets*, Federal Reserve Bank of New York, New York, 1956.

Siegel, B. N.: *Aggregate Economics and Public Policy*, Richard D. Irwin, Inc., Homewood, Ill., 1960.

Tobin, J.: "Liquidity Preference as Behavior Towards Risk," *Review of Economic Studies*, vol. 25, pp. 65–86, February, 1958.

Turner, R. C.: *Member Bank Borrowing*, Ohio State University Press, Columbus, Ohio, 1938.

Turvey, R.: "Some Notes on Multiplier Theory," *American Economic Review*, vol. 43, pp. 275–295, June, 1953.

Wallich, H. C.: "Income Generating Effects of a Balanced Budget," *Quarterly Journal of Economics*, vol. 59, pp. 78–91, November, 1944.

White, W. H.: "Flexibility of Anticyclical Monetary Policy," *Review of Economics and Statistics*, vol. 43, pp. 142–147, May, 1961.

The Economic Impact of Government

Background Material on Economic Impact of Federal Procurement: 1965, Staff Study of the Subcommittee on Federal Procurement and Regulation of the Joint Economic Committee, 89th Cong., 1st Sess., April, 1965.

Baumol, W. J., and M. H. Peston: "More on the Multiplier Effects of a Balanced Budget," *American Economic Review*, vol. 45, pp. 140–148, March, 1955.

Boulding, K. E.: *Principles of Public Policy*, Prentice-Hall, Inc., Englewood Cliffs, N.J., 1958.

Brown, E. C.: "Fiscal Policy in the Thirties: A Reappraisal," *American Economic Review*, vol. 46, pp. 857–879, December, 1956.

Colm, G.: *Essays in Public Finance and Fiscal Policy*, Oxford University Press, Fair Lawn, N.J., 1955.

―――― (ed.): *The Employment Act, Past and Future: A Tenth Anniversary Symposium*, National Planning Association, Washington, D.C., 1956.

―――― and P. Wagner: *Federal Budget Projections*, The Brookings Institution, Washington, D.C., 1966.

Comiez, M. S.: *A Capital Budget Statement for the U.S. Government*, The Brookings Institution, Washington, D.C., 1966.

Dorfman, R. (ed.): *Measuring Benefits of Government Investments*, The Brookings Institution, Washington, D.C., 1965.

Economic Impact of Federal Procurement, Hearings before the Subcommittee on Federal Procurement and Regulation of the Joint Economic Committee, 89th Cong., 1st Sess., April 27–29, 1965.

Economic Report of the President, Hearings before the Joint Economic Committee, annually beginning 1947.

Ezekiel, H.: "The Government Sector in National Income Calculations," *Indian Economic Journal*, vol. 2, pp. 254–262, January, 1955.

The Federal Budget as an Economic Document, Hearings before the Subcommittee on Economic Statistics of the Joint Economic Committee, 89th Cong., 1st Sess., Apr. 23–25 and 30, 1965.

The Federal Tax System: Facts and Problems, 1964, Joint Economic Committee Staff Study, 88th Cong., 2d Sess., September, 1964.

Firestone, J. M.: *Federal Receipts and Expenditures during Business Cycles, 1879–1958*, National Bureau of Economics Research, Inc., Studies in Business Cycles, no. 9, Princeton University Press, Princeton, N.J., 1960.

Fiscal Policy Issues of the Coming Decade, Hearings before the Subcommittee on Fiscal Policy of the Joint Economic Committee, 89th Cong., 1st Sess., July 20–22, 1965.

Groves, H. M.: *Financing Government*, 6th ed., Holt, Rinehart and Winston, Inc., New York, 1964.

Hansen, A. H.: *Business Cycles and National Income*, expanded ed., W. W. Norton & Company, Inc., New York, 1964.

Jaszi, G.: "The Federal Budget on National Income and Product Accounts," *Review of Economics and Statistics*, vol. 44, pp. 335–337, August, 1962.

Lewis, W., Jr.: *Federal Fiscal Policy in the Postwar Recessions*, The Brookings Institution, Washington, D.C., 1962.

Morgan, T.: *Income and Employment*, 2d ed., Prentice-Hall, Inc., Englewood Cliffs, N.J., 1952.

Novick, D., and G. A. Fisher: "The Federal Budget as an Economic Indicator," *Harvard Business Review*, vol. 38, pp. 64–72, May–June, 1960.

Pechman, J. A.: "Financing State and Local Government," *Proceedings of the Symposium on Federal Taxation*, American Bankers Association, New York, 1965.

Poole, K. E.: "Role of Federal Fiscal Policy in the 1957–60 Business Cycle," *Journal of Finance*, vol. 17, pp. 17–37, March, 1962.

Smith, P. E.: "A Note on the Built In Flexibility of the Individual Income Tax," *Econometrica*, vol. 31, pp. 704–711, October, 1963.

Smithies, A.: *The Budgetary Process in the United States*, McGraw-Hill Book Company, New York, 1955.

Spangler, P.: "The Effect of Population Growth upon State and Local Expenditures," *National Tax Journal*, vol. 16, pp. 193–196, June, 1963.

Taxes and the Budget: A Program for Prosperity in a Free Economy, Committee for Economic Development, New York, 1947.

Twentieth Anniversary of the Employment Act of 1946, An Economic Symposium, Hearing before the Joint Economic Committee, 89th Cong., 2d Sess., Feb. 23, 1966.

White, W. H.: "Measuring the Inflationary Significance of a Government Budget," *International Monetary Fund Staff Papers*, vol. 1, pp. 355–378, April, 1951.

Wildavsky, A.: *The Politics of the Budgetary Process*, Little, Brown and Company, Boston, 1964.

PART THREE

Burns, A. F., and W. C. Mitchell: *Measuring Business Cycles*, National Bureau of Economic Research, Inc., Studies in Business Cycles, no. 2, New York, 1946.

Economic Report of the President, annually beginning 1947.

Frickey, E.: *Economic Fluctuations in the United States*, Harvard University Press, Cambridge, Mass., 1942.

Galbraith, J. K.: "The Disequilibrium System," *American Economic Review*, vol. 37, pp. 288–302, June, 1947.

———: *A Theory of Price Control*, Harvard University Press, Cambridge, Mass., 1952.

———: *The Great Crash 1929*, Houghton Mifflin Company, Boston, 1955.

Gordon, R. A.: "Cyclical Experience in the Interwar Period: The Investment Boom of the Twenties," in *Conference on Business Cycles*, National Bureau of Economic Research, Inc., Special Conference ser. 2, New York, 1951.

———: *Business Fluctuations*, 2d ed., Harper & Row, Publishers, Incorporated, New York, 1961.

Hansen, A. H.: *Business Cycles and National Income*, expanded ed., W. W. Norton & Company, Inc., New York, 1951.

Heilbroner, R. L.: *The Making of Economic Society*, Prentice-Hall, Inc., Englewood Cliffs, N.J., 1962.

Hymans, S. H.: "The Cyclical Behavior of Consumers' Income and Spending: 1912–1961," *Southern Economic Journal*, vol. 32, pp. 23–34, July, 1965.

Investigation of the Concentration of Economic Power, Hearings before the Senate Temporary National Economic Committee, 76th Cong., 1st Sess., May 16–26, 1939.

Lewis, W., Jr.: *Fiscal Policy in the Postwar Recessions*, The Brookings Institution, Washington, D.C., 1962.

National Income, 1954 Edition: A Supplement to the Survey of Current Business, U.S. Department of Commerce, 1954.

Robertson, R. M.: *History of the American Economy*, 2d ed., Harcourt, Brace & World, Inc., New York, 1964.

Roose, K.: *The Economics of Recession and Revival*, Yale University Press, New Haven, Conn., 1954.

Schumpeter, J. A.: *Business Cycles: A Theoretical, Historical, and Statistical Analysis of the Capitalist Process*, McGraw-Hill Book Company, New York, 1939, vols. I–II.

———: "The Decade of the Twenties," *American Economic Review*, vol. 36, pp. 1–11, May, 1946.

U.S. Income and Output, 1958: A Supplement to the Survey of Current Business, U.S. Department of Commerce, 1958.

The United States at War: Development and Administration of the War Program by the Federal Government, Historical Reports on War Administration, U.S. Bureau of the Budget, no. 1, 1946.

PART FOUR

General Discussions of Short-run Forecasting

Abramson, A. G., and R. H. Mack (eds.): *Business Forecasting in Practice: Principles and Cases*, John Wiley & Sons, Inc., New York, 1956.

Bassie, V. L.: *Economic Forecasting*, McGraw-Hill Book Company, New York, 1958.

Bates, J., and J. R. Parkinson: *Business Economics*, Blackwell Scientific Publications, Ltd., Oxford, 1963.

Bates, S.: "Government Forecasting in Canada," *Canadian Journal of Economics and Political Science*, vol. 12, pp. 361–378, August, 1946.

Boulden, J. B.: "Fitting of the Sales Forecast to Your Firm," *Business Horizons*, vol. 1, pp. 65–72, Winter, 1958.

Bratt, E. C.: *Business Forecasting*, McGraw-Hill Book Company, New York, 1958.

Brewis, T. N.: "Economic Forecasting," in T. N. Brewis, H. E. English, A. Scott, and P. Jewett, *Canadian Economic Policy*, rev. ed., The Macmillan Co. of Canada, Limited, Toronto, 1965, pp. 214–231.

Burns, A. F., and W. C. Mitchell: *Measuring Business Cycles*, National Bureau of Economic Research, Inc., New York, 1946.

"Business Forecasting," *Business Week*, Sept. 24, 1955, pp. 90–120.

Colm, G.: *The American Economy in 1960*, National Planning Association, Washington, D.C., 1952.

———: "Economic Barometers and Economic Models," *Review of Economics and Statistics*, vol. 37, pp. 55–62, February, 1955.

Conference on Research in Income and Wealth: *Short-term Economic Forecasting*, National Bureau of Economic Research, Inc., Studies in Income and Wealth, vol. 17, Princeton University Press, Princeton, N.J., 1955.

———: *Studies in Income and Wealth*, National Bureau of Economic Research,

Inc., Studies in Income and Wealth, vol. 11, National Bureau of Economic Research, Inc., New York, 1949.

Dewey, E. R., and E. F. Dakin: *Cycles: The Science of Prediction*, Holt, Rinehart and Winston, Inc., New York, 1947.

Eisner, R.: "Interview and Other Survey Techniques of Investment," in Conference on Research in Income and Wealth, *Problems of Capital Formation*, National Bureau of Economic Research, Inc., Studies in Income and Wealth, vol. 19, Princeton University Press, Princeton, N.J., 1957, pp. 513–584.

Friend, I., and J. Bronfenbrenner: "Business Investment Programs and Their Realization," *Survey of Current Business*, U.S. Department of Commerce, vol. 30, pp. 11–22, December, 1950.

——— and ———: "Plant and Equipment Programs and Their Realization," in Conference on Research in Income and Wealth, *Short-term Economic Forecasting*, National Bureau of Economic Research, Inc., Studies in Income and Wealth, vol. 17, Princeton University Press, Princeton, N.J., 1955, pp. 53–98.

——— and P. Taubman: "A Short-term Forecasting Model," *Review of Economics and Statistics*, vol. 46, pp. 229–236, August, 1964.

Geary, R. C., and K. G. Forecast: "The Use of Census of Industrial Production Material for the Estimation of Productivity," *Review of the International Statistical Institute*, vol. 23, pp. 6–19, 1955.

Gehrels, F., and S. Wiggins: "Interest Rates and Manufacturers' Fixed Investment," *American Economic Review*, vol. 47, pp. 79–92, March, 1957.

Hellwig, Z.: *Linear Regression and Its Application to Economics*, H. Infeld (ed.), translated from the Polish by J. Stadler, Pergamon Press, New York, 1963.

Indiana's Economic Resources and Potential: A Projection to 1970, Indiana University Bureau of Business Research, Bloomington, Ind., 1956.

Journal of Business, vol. 27, entire issue, January, 1954.

Kuh, E.: "Econometric Models: Is a New Age Dawning?" *American Economic Review*, vol. 55, pp. 362–369, May, 1965.

Lansberg, H. H., L. L. Fischman, and J. L. Fisher: *Resources in America's Future: Patterns of Requirements and Availabilities, 1960–2000*, The Johns Hopkins Press for Resources for the Future, Inc., Baltimore, 1963.

Lewis, J. P.: "Short-run General Business Conditions Forecasting: Some Comments on Method," *Journal of Business*, vol. 35, pp. 343–356, October, 1962.

Liu, T. C.: "A Simple Forecasting Model for the U.S. Economy," *International Monetary Fund Staff Papers*, vol. 4, pp. 434–466, August, 1955.

McKinley, D. H., M. G. Lee, and H. Duffy: *Forecasting Business Conditions*, American Bankers Association, New York, 1965.

Maisel, S.: "A Theory of Fluctuations in Residential Construction Starts," *American Economic Review*, vol. 53, pp. 359–383, June, 1963.

Maisel, S. J.: *Fluctuations, Growth, and Forecasting: The Principles of Dynamic Business Economics*, John Wiley & Sons, Inc., New York, 1957.

Malanos, G. J., and H. Thomassen: "An Econometric Model of the United States, 1947–1958," *Southern Economic Journal*, vol. 27, pp. 18–27, July, 1960.

Manpower Report of the President, and a Report on Manpower Requirements, Resources, Utilization, and Training, U.S. Department of Labor, 1966.

Mayer, T., and S. Sonenblum: "Lead Times for Fixed Investment," *Review of Economics and Statistics*, vol. 37, pp. 300–304, August, 1955.

Mitchell, G. W.: "Forecasting State and Local Expenditures," *Journal of Business*, vol. 27, pp. 17–21, January, 1954.

Moore, G. H. (ed.): *Business Cycle Indicators*, vol. 1, *Contributions to the Analysis of Current Business Conditions;* vol. 2, *Basic Data on Cyclical Indicators*, National Bureau of Economic Research, Inc., Studies in Business Cycles, no. 10, Princeton University Press, Princeton, N.J., 1961.

Newbury, F. D.: *Business Forecasting: Principles and Practices*, McGraw-Hill Book Company, New York, 1952.

Okun, A. M.: "The Predictive Value of Surveys of Business Intentions," *American Economic Review*, vol. 52, pp. 218–225, May, 1962.

———: "The Gap between Actual and Potential Output," in A. M. Okun (ed.), *The Battle against Unemployment*, W. W. Norton & Company, Inc., New York, 1965.

Okun, A. M., Jr.: "Appraisal of Cyclical Turning-point Predictors," *Journal of Business*, vol. 33, pp. 101–120, April, 1960.

Prochnow, H. V. (ed.): *Determining the Business Outlook*, Harper & Row, Publishers, Incorporated, New York, 1954.

Robinson, C.: "Some Principles of Forecasting in Business," *Journal of Industrial Economics*, vol. 14, pp. 1–13, November, 1965.

Samuelson, P. A.: "Economic Forecasting and National Policy," in G. Colm (ed.), *The Employment Act: Past and Future*, National Planning Association, Washington, D.C., 1956.

Schweiger, I.: "Forecasting Short-term Consumer Demand from Consumer Anticipations," *Journal of Business*, vol. 29, pp. 90–100, April, 1956.

Shiskin, J.: *Signals of Recession and Recovery: An Experiment with Monthly Reporting*, National Bureau of Economic Research, Inc., Occasional Paper no. 77, New York, 1961.

Silk, L. S., with the assistance of M. L. Curley: *Forecasting Business Trends*, McGraw-Hill Book Company, New York, 1963.

Stone, R.: "Models of the National Economy for Planning Purposes," *Operations Research Quarterly*, vol. 14, pp. 51–59, March, 1963.

Suits, D. B.: "Forecasting and Analysis with an Econometric Model," *American Economic Review*, vol. 52, pp. 104–132, March, 1962.

Techniques of Economic Forecasting: An Account of the Methods of Short-term Economic Forecasting Used by the Governments of Canada, France, The Netherlands, Sweden, the United Kingdom, and the United States, Organization for European Cooperation and Development, Paris, 1965.

Tobin, J.: "On the Predictive Value of Consumer Intentions and Attitudes," *Review of Economics and Statistics*, vol. 41, pp. 1–11, February, 1959.

Turner, R. C.: "Problems of Forecasting for Economic Stabilization," *American Economic Review*, vol. 45, pp. 329–340, May, 1955.

———: "The American Economy in 1970," *The Appraisal Journal*, vol. 24, pp. 165–172, April, 1956.

Wilson, G. W.: "Relationship between Output and Employment," *Review of Economics and Statistics*, vol. 42, pp. 37–43, February, 1960.

Wool, H.: "Long Term Projections of the Labor Force," in Conference on Research in Income and Wealth, *Long-term Economic Projection,* National Bureau of Economic Research, Inc., Studies in Income and Wealth, vol. 16, Princeton University Press, Princeton, N.J., 1954.

Particular Short-run Forecasting Techniques

Adams, F. G.: "Consumer Attitudes, Buying Plans, and Purchases of Durable Goods: A Principal Components, Time Series Approach," *Review of Economics and Statistics,* vol. 46, pp. 347–355, November, 1964.

Bailey, R. M.: "Tailoring the Business Forecast to Company Size," *Business Horizons,* vol. 5, pp. 81–88, Summer, 1962.

Bradshaw, M. T., and M. Lechter: "Expansion in Merchandise Exports, Imports, and Trade Surplus in 1963," *Survey of Current Business,* U.S. Department of Commerce, vol. 44, pp. 22–27, January, 1964.

Clones, A. J., and G. C. McKay: "Transportation Transactions in the U.S. Balance of Payments," *Survey of Current Business,* U.S. Department of Commerce, vol. 43, pp. 23–28, August, 1963.

Cutler, F., and S. Pizer: "Foreign Operations of U.S. Industry," *Survey of Current Business,* U.S. Department of Commerce, vol. 43, pp. 13–20, October, 1963.

Demand and Price Situation, U.S. Department of Agriculture (quarterly).

Duesenberry, J. S., O. Eckstein, and G. Fromm: "A Simulation of the United States Economy in Recession," *Econometrica,* vol. 28, pp. 749–809, October, 1960.

Fromm, G., and L. R. Klein: "The Brookings-SSRC Quarterly Econometric Model of the United States: Model Properties," *American Economic Review,* vol. 55, pp. 348–361, May, 1965.

Fujino, S.: "Some Aspects of Inventory Cycles," *Review of Economics and Statistics,* vol. 42, pp. 203–209, May, 1960.

Gordon, R. A.: "Alternative Approaches to Forecasting: The Recent Work of the National Bureau," *Review of Economics and Statistics,* vol. 44, pp. 284–291, August, 1962.

Guttentag, J. M.: "The Short Cycle in Residential Construction," *American Economic Review,* vol. 51, pp. 275–298, June, 1961.

Haberler, G.: "Integration and Growth of the World Economy in Historical Perspective," *American Economic Review,* vol. 54, pp. 1–22, March, 1964.

Hewitt, C. M.: *Automotive Franchise Agreements,* Richard D. Irwin, Inc., Homewood, Ill., 1956.

——: "The Development of Automobile Franchises," *Indiana Business Information Bulletin no. 37,* Bureau of Business Research, Indiana University, Bloomington, Ind., 1960.

Johnson, H. G.: "The International Competitive Position of the United States and the Balance of Payments Prospect for 1968," *Review of Economics and Statistics,* vol. 46, pp. 14–32, March, 1964.

MacDougall, D.: "The Dollar Problem: A Reappraisal," *Essays in International Finance,* no. 35, International Finance Section, Department of Economics, Princeton University, Princeton, N.J., 1960.

Marimont, M. L.: "GNP by Major Industries," *Survey of Current Business,* U.S. Department of Commerce, vol. 42, pp. 6–18, October, 1962.

Marimont, M. L.: "GNP by Major Industries, 1958–62 Revised and Updated," *Survey of Current Business,* U.S. Department of Commerce, vol. 43, pp. 9–10, September, 1963.

Masson, F. G., and J. B. Brodie: "Factors Affecting U.S. Merchandise Exports," *Survey of Current Business,* U.S. Department of Commerce, vol. 43, pp. 20–27, February, 1963.

Metzler, L.: "Nature and Stability of Inventory Cycles," *Review of Economics and Statistics,* vol. 23, pp. 113–129, August, 1941.

————: "Business Cycles and the Modern Theory of Employment," *American Economic Review,* vol. 46, pp. 278–291, June, 1946.

————: "Factors Governing the Length of Inventory Cycles," *Review of Economics and Statistics,* vol. 29, pp. 1–15, February, 1947.

National Income, 1954 Edition: A Supplement to the Survey of Current Business, U.S. Department of Commerce, pp. 135–138, 1954.

Nurske, R.: "The Cyclical Pattern of Inventory Investment," *Quarterly Journal of Economics,* vol. 66, pp. 385–408, August, 1952.

Orcutt, G. H., M. Greenberger, V. Korbel, and A. Rivlin: *Microanalysis of Socioeconomic Systems: A Simulation Study,* Harper & Row, Publishers, Incorporated, New York, 1961.

Paradiso, L. J., and G. B. Wimsatt: "Business Inventories: Recent Trends and Position," *Survey of Current Business,* U.S. Department of Commerce, vol. 35, pp. 9–15, May, 1953.

Reischer, O. R.: *Trade Adjustments in Theory and Practice,* Study Paper Prepared for the Subcommittee on Foreign Economic Policy of the Joint Economic Committee, 87th Cong., 1st Sess., November, 1961.

Salant, W. S., et al.: *The United States Balance of Payments in 1968,* The Brookings Institution, Washington, D.C., 1963.

Theil, H.: *Economic Forecasts and Policy,* North Holland Publishing Company, Amsterdam, 1958.

Wasson, R. C.: "Manufacturing, Investment Since 1929 in Relation to Employment, Output, and Income," *Survey of Current Business,* U.S. Department of Commerce, vol. 36, pp. 8–20, November, 1956.

Capacity Forecasts and Projections

Colm, G.: *The American Economy in 1960,* National Planning Association, Washington, D.C., 1952.

Conference on Research in Income and Wealth: *Long-range Economic Projection,* National Bureau of Economic Research, Inc., Studies in Income and Wealth, vol. 16, Princeton University Press, Princeton, N.J., 1954.

Dewhurst, J. F., and Associates: *America's Needs and Resources: A New Survey,* The Twentieth Century Fund, New York, 1955.

Hickman, B. G.: "On a New Method of Capacity Estimation," *Journal of the American Statistical Association,* vol. 59, pp. 529–549, June, 1964.

Measures of Productive Capacity, Hearings before the Subcommittee on Economic Statistics of the Joint Economic Committee, 87th Cong., 2d Sess., May 14, 22–24, 1962.

Schultze, C. L.: "Use of Capacity Measures for Short-run Economic Analysis," *American Economic Review,* vol. 53, pp. 293–308, May, 1963.

Stolnitz, G.: "Our Growing Population: Threat or Boon?" *Business Horizons*, vol. 2, pp. 37–45, Summer, 1959.

Trends in Output per Man-hour in the Private Economy, 1909–1958, U.S. Department of Labor, Bulletin no. 1249, December, 1959.

Literature Relating to the Behavior of and Prospects for Particular Demand Sectors

Atkinson, L. J.: "Long-term Influences Affecting the Volume of New Housing Units," *Survey of Current Business*, U.S. Department of Commerce, vol. 43, pp. 8–19, November, 1963.

The Balance of Payments Statistics, Hearings before the Subcommittee on Economic Statistics of the Joint Economic Committee, 89th Cong., 1st Sess., May 11, June 8–9, 1965, parts 1–3.

Bell, P. W.: "Private Capital Movements and the U.S. Balance-of-payments Position," in *Factors Affecting the United States Balance of Payments*, Compilation of Studies Prepared for the Subcommittee on International Exchange and Payments of the Joint Economic Committee, 87th Cong., 2d Sess., December, 1962, pp. 395–482, part 6.

Bratt, E. C.: "Availability and Reliability of Inventory Data Needed to Study Economic Change," *Inventory Fluctuations and Economic Stabilization*, part III, *Inventory Fluctuations and Economic Instability*, Materials Prepared for the Joint Economic Committee, 87th Cong., 1st Sess., December, 1961.

Brazer, H. E.: "Our Hard-pressed State and Local Governments," *Challenge*, vol. 14, pp. 7–9 and 41, January-February, 1966.

Brown, M., and P. Taubman: "Forecasting Model of Federal Purchases of Goods and Services," *Journal of the American Statistical Association*, vol. 57, pp. 633–647, September, 1962.

The Budget of the United States Government, Fiscal Year Ending June 30, annually.

Collery, A.: "A Full Employment, Keynesian Theory of International Trade," *Quarterly Journal of Economics*, vol. 77, pp. 438–458, August, 1963.

Colm, G.: "Economic Projections: Tools of Economic Analysis and Decision Making," *American Economic Review*, vol. 48, pp. 178–187, May, 1958.

Conference on Research in Income and Wealth: *Problems in the International Comparison of Economic Accounts*, National Bureau of Economic Research, Inc., Studies in Income and Wealth, vol. 20, Princeton University Press, Princeton, N.J., 1957.

Coppock, D. J.: "The Periodicity and Stability of Inventory Cycles in the U.S.A.," *Manchester School of Economic and Social Studies*, parts I–II, vol. 27, pp. 140–174, 261–299, May and September, 1959.

Current Economic Situation and Short-run Outlook, Hearings before the Joint Economic Committee, 86th Cong., 2d Sess., Dec. 7–8, 1960.

Darling, P. G.: "Inventory Fluctuations and Economic Instability: An Analysis Based on the Postwar Economy," *Inventory Fluctuations and Economic Stabilization*, part III, *Inventory Fluctuations and Economic Instability*, Materials Prepared for the Joint Economic Committee, 87th Cong., 1st Sess., December, 1961.

Dewhurst, J. F., and Associates: *America's Needs and Resources,* The Twentieth Century Fund, New York, 1947.

———— and ————: *America's Needs and Resources: A New Survey,* The Twentieth Century Fund, New York, 1955.

Economic Report of the President, annually beginning January, 1947.

Galbraith, J. K.: *The Affluent Society,* Houghton Mifflin Company, Boston, 1958.

International Payments Imbalances and Need for Strengthening International Financial Arrangements, Hearings before the Subcommittee on International Exchange and Payments of the Joint Economic Committee, 87th Cong., 1st Sess., May 16, June 19–21, 1961, pp. 175–179 and 207–211, statements of Tibor Scitovsky.

Landsberg, H. H., L. L. Fischman, and J. L. Fisher: *Resources in America's Future: Patterns of Requirements and Availabilities, 1960–2000,* The Johns Hopkins Press for Resources for the Future, Inc., Baltimore, 1963.

Lewis, J. P.: "Pricing for Stability and Growth," in *The Relationship of Prices to Economic Stability and Growth,* Compendium of Papers Submitted by Panelists Appearing before the Joint Economic Committee, 85th Cong., 2d Sess., March 31, 1958, pp. 375–396.

————: "The Problem of Price Stabilization: A Progress Report," *American Economic Review,* vol. 49, pp. 309–321, May, 1959.

Lippmann, W.: *An Inquiry into the Principles of the Good Society,* Little, Brown and Co., Boston, 1937.

Long-range Projections for Economic Growth: The American Economy in 1970, National Planning Association, Planning Pamphlet no. 107, Washington, D.C., 1959.

National Economic Projections, 1962–1965, 1970 . . . , Center for Economic Projections, National Planning Association, Washington, D.C., 1959.

National Science Foundation, *Reviews of Data on Science Resources,* vol. 1 (4), pp. 1–11, May, 1965.

Potential Economic Growth of the United States during the Next Decade, Materials Prepared for the Joint Committee on the Economic Report by the Committee Staff, 83d Cong., 2d Sess., October, 1954.

Rees, A. E.: "Price Level Stability and Economic Policy," in *The Relationship of Prices to Economic Stability and Growth,* Compendium of Papers Submitted by Panelists Appearing before the Joint Economic Committee, 85th Cong., 2d Sess., March 31, 1958, pp. 651–663.

Resources for Freedom, A Report to the President by the President's Materials Policy (Paley) Commission, vol. I, *Foundations for Growth and Security;* vol. II, *The Outlook for Key Commodities;* vol. III, *The Outlook for Energy Sources;* vol. IV, *The Promise of Technology;* vol. V, *Selected Reports to the Commission,* 1952.

Saunders, C. T.: "Forecasting and Policy Projection for the Long Term," *Malayan Economic Review,* vol. 8, pp. 19–27, October, 1963.

Soule, G. H.: *Time for Living,* The Viking Press, Inc., New York, 1955.

Turner, R. C.: "Relationship of Prices to Economic Stability and Growth: A Statement of the Problem," in *The Relationship of Prices to Economic Stability and Growth,* Compendium of Papers Submitted by Panelists Appearing before the Joint Economic Committee, 85th Cong., 2d Sess., March 31, 1958, pp. 671–684.

INDEX

INDEX